PERSONNEL ECONOMICS FOR MANAGERS

EDWARD P. LAZEAR

WILEY

JOHN WILEY & SONS, INC.
NEW YORK • CHICHESTER • BRISBANE • TORONTO • SINGAPORE • WEINHEIM

To my wife, Vickie, and my daughter, Julia

Acquisitions Editor	Marissa Ryan
Marketing Manager	Wendy Goldner
Production Editor	Edward Winkleman
Illustration Coordinator	Anna Melhorn

This book was set in 10/12 Jansen Text by Digitype and printed and bound by Donnelley/Crawfordsville. The cover was printed by Phoenix Color.

Library of Congress Cataloging in Publication Data

Lazear, Edward P.
    Personnel economics for managers / Edward P. Lazear.
      p.   cm.
    Includes bibliographical references.
    ISBN 0-471-59466-0 (alk. paper)
     1. Managerial economics.   2. Labor economics.   3. Personnel management.
    4. Human capital.   I. Title.
    HD30.22.L39   1998
    658.3—dc21   97–7933
                                                          CIP

Printed in the United States of America

10 9 8 7 6 5 4 3 2 1

*T*he field of human resources management is in transition. An institutional, and somewhat chatty literature is being replaced by more analytic work, which is based on empirical investigation and rigorous theory. The new material, which is now commonly referred to as *personnel economics*, is being taught in the core curricula at most top business schools. I myself have taught it at Stanford and the University of Chicago. Additionally, much of what forms the essence of the field is creeping into undergraduate courses. As well it should—the modern approach to human resources is directly applicable to business.

My students and I have been frustrated by the absence of a text in the field. In order to expose students to the modern material, it is necessary to assign the original technial papers, which are far too dry and detailed for most readers' purposes. This book is an attempt to fill the current void. The book's format is primarily verbal, with many numerical examples, applications, and graphs. Appendices at the end of chapters present much more technical analyses of some of the material contained in the chapters. The appendices are supplementary; the chapters stand alone without the technical presentations. The reader who is interested in exploring the field further should read the appendices after the chapters and then go on to the original references listed at the end of each chapter.

This book is based on work that I have done over my entire career and that of many other authors as well. Although all the researchers in this field deserve my gratitude, two stand out. Sherwin Rosen, who is my teacher, co-author and colleague, and Gary Becker, a long-time colleague and economic pioneer, influenced my thinking, and therefore this book, enormously. Also important was Melvin

Reder, who helped show me that labor economics could be useful in a business school setting. Robert Topel, Kevin Murphy, Kenneth Judd, and John Roberts provided insights through stimulating discussions that have found their way into the pages that follow. I wish to express my sincere gratitude to my doctoral student assistants, Michael Schwarz and Joseph Guzman, for the writing and rewriting that they did. Also, Eric Stout, Nital Patel, and Ryan Ratcliff assisted in providing material for the applications. Finally, I am grateful to Debbie Wheeler and Patricia Farnsworth for excellent clerical assistance.

CONTENTS

CHAPTER 1   Introduction   1

CHAPTER 2   Setting Hiring Standards   9

CHAPTER 3   Hiring the Right People   45

CHAPTER 4   Learning a Worker's Productivity   73

CHAPTER 5   Variable Pay or Straight Salary?   97

CHAPTER 6   The Theory of Human Capital   133

CHAPTER 7   Turnover, Layoffs and Buyouts   167

CHAPTER 8   Information, Signalling, and Raiding   195

CHAPTER 9   Promotions as Motivators   223

CHAPTER 10   Industrial Politics   259

CHAPTER 11   Seniority-Based Incentive Schemes   281

CHAPTER 12   Teams   303

CHAPTER 13   More on the Employment Relationship: Outsourcing,
               Contracts, Franchising, and More   345

CHAPTER 14   Nonmonetary Compensation   377

CHAPTER 15   Benefits   409

CHAPTER 16   The Job: Tasks and Authority   441

CHAPTER 17   Evaluation   447

CHAPTER 18   Worker Empowerment   505

GLOSSARY   530

INDEX   533

INTRODUCTION

1

Human resources professionals are often treated as if they were the lowest form of managerial life. Personnel people tend to be regarded as obstructive, and frequently receive little respect from their colleagues. They are viewed as company police whose role is to create hassles for others in the firm. Although most managers pay lip service to the notion that human resources issues are important, few outside of the human resources area are willing to act like they believe such platitudes. There is a reason. Until recently, there has been no systematic discipline on which to base human resources decisions. Personnel matters were always regarded as too soft and too human to be dealt with rigorously. Unlike, say, finance, where arbitrage conditions could be modeled, analyzed, and predicted, human resources was a series of important questions begging for clear, unambiguous answers. There is nothing more frustrating to a professional, or a student for that matter, than hearing a question answered, "It all depends," or, "One cannot generalize about emotions." If one cannot generalize or provide answers that can be proven right or wrong, then the field is vacuous and, unsurprisingly, of little value to practitioners. Fortunately, things have changed during the past two decades. Personnel is now a science that provides detailed and unambiguous answers to the issues that trouble managers today. Furthermore, the issues are not confined to the personnel department. Indeed, for the most part, the key human resources issues are those that are dealt with by general managers, not human resources specialists. Significant changes in human resources systems, choice of compensation methods, and hiring and firing decisions, to name a few key areas, are in the realm of the general manager, not the human resources specialists. Personnel people are often consulted when it comes to implementation, but the impetus for any major decision that involves the firm's work force often comes from outside the human resources area. Thus, it is as important for the general manager to understand the strategic aspects of personnel as it is for the human resources specialist.

Personnel Economics for Managers is an economic approach to personnel issues. Some readers might find it incongruous to link personnel with economics. Economics, which focuses on technical and impersonal issues like the allocation of resources, seems to shy away from the more human factors that personnel analysts address. However, the past couple of decades of research prove that appearances are misleading. Economists have overcome their tendency to focus on more easily quantified variables, broadening the scope to ask questions that are of key interest to individuals who manage human resources. This book is the first compilation of the new theory of personnel that is meant for an educated, but not necessarily technically oriented, audience.

To say that economics forms the basis of the analysis does not imply that human factors are ignored. For example, the importance of nonmonetary components of job satisfaction like status, pride, and pleasantness of work are all analyzable in an economic framework. A significant portion of this book is devoted to exactly those kinds of issues. Using economics as the framework merely implies that workers and firms take actions that are in their own best interests. This point requires some elaboration. The statement that individuals and firms act in their own interest is tautological. One can simply imagine tastes that are sufficiently bizarre so that every action caters to the individual's preferences. My statement is not that broad. The economic approach assumes that tastes, while possibly unusual, are stable over time. Thus, behavior is predicted based on the assumption that individuals and firms do what they can to further their well-defined and consistent goals. There is nothing noneconomic about a worker stating that he is willing to trade 10 percent of his salary in order to obtain a corner office. But the economic approach does imply that if he is later offered the corner office for 8 percent of his salary, he will accept.

Since this book is not a traditional personnel text, and since it focuses on an economic approach to personnel, it is likely to stir up some controversy. Although I do not expect it to be embraced by all, I view it as complementary to much of what has gone before. Many topics that are of major significance to personnel practitioners are not addressed by this book. For example, such questions as "how to fire a worker or deliver other bad news," "how to negotiate with unions," "how to improve sinking morale," and "how to counsel employees about career opportunities" are ignored here. For now, economics has little or nothing to say on these issues, and they are better addressed by other specialties.

The allocation of resources and incentives are the central issues in economics. This book extends those topics to the analysis of personnel issues and, I hope, makes a significant contribution in doing so. The book lies somewhere between textbook and treatise. Since the material is new to most readers, this volume introduces a large number of theoretical and empirical concepts into the personnel literature. Much of this material has already appeared in technical academic journals, but very little has made its way into the journals that actual practitioners read. Further, there is no textbook that uses this approach, although there are many that address the same topics. Some of the more novel material requires rigorous derivation, most of which is done in technical appendices. However, the material in the body of the chapters stands alone. It is unnecessary to grasp the technical details in order to understand the logic of the arguments, but some readers may find the technical derivations reassuring.

It is important to point out that adopting a tough, analytic approach does not rob the human resources manager or general manager of compassion. Human resources decisions are often painful because they affect people directly and often in ways that significantly impact their lives. Being analytic accomplishes three things. First, rigorous thought may help employers find a way to make both workers and shareholders better off. Often, a careful analysis can lead to solutions that improve the situations of workers *and* their employers. Second, rigorous analysis may help the worker by preventing some arbitrary and harmful actions from being taken. Serious quantitative thought is just as likely to show that a decision that has adverse impacts on workers is a poor one as it is to reveal that a fuzzy-minded, weak decision is wrong. Third, learning that a particular decision is costly does not preclude compassion. The firm is always better off knowing what its compassion costs. Absent analysis, the firm may overestimate rather than underestimate the cost of being generous to its work force.

TOPICS ADDRESSED IN THIS BOOK ◆ ◆ ◆ ◆ ◆

There are a number of issues that make up standard personnel texts. Many, but not all of them will be addressed by *Personnel Economics for Managers*. To give the reader a flavor of what will come, some of the issues are listed on the following pages.

Recruitment and Hiring

Firms must decide on the type of workers to hire and specifically, on the amount of skill necessary for each job. Should a firm hire the best workers, irrespective of price, or should it hire the lowest cost workers, irrespective of quality? Neither rule seems right, but toward which end of the spectrum should the firm locate itself? What factors influence a firm's willingness to pay for quality workers?

After having made the quality-versus-wage decision, the firm must attract qualified applicants at minimum cost, and in the process, deter those unsuitable applicants who would like the job but are inappropriate for it. Screening applicants is costly. Firms usually set up hiring standards that require that workers possess some level of education or have a given amount of work experience. Are these requirements cost-effective? If not, what other approaches can be used? For example, is it possible to set up a salary structure so that only the right individuals apply for the job? When should credentials like an MBA or a CPA certificate be used to set standards for the job?

Turnover

Workers leave firms at all stages of their careers. As an empirical matter, turnover rates are highest among workers who are very new to the firm or who are nearing retirement age. How should a firm view turnover? When is it profit-increasing for workers to leave, and when is turnover detrimental to profits? Which workers should a firm strive most diligently to retain? What kinds of compensation policies are most likely to lead to optimal turnover patterns?

The starting point for this analysis is the theory of human capital. The section makes clear not only that many actions can affect turnover, but also that there are systematic ways to determine the optimal level and incidence of turnover.

Downsizing

Sometimes economic conditions make it necessary to lay workers off. How should this be done? Buyout schemes can be used to the advantage of both the firm and workers. How are such buyouts to be structured? More fundamentally, when should a firm contract and when should it expand the size of its workforce? How can these decisions be made systematically?

Motivating Workers to High Levels of Productivity

A large part of this book is devoted to incentives. Not only is this a fashionable topic, but it is at the heart of a firm's ability to compete effectively in a world market. There are many ways to provide incentives to workers. Even direct methods that rely on compensation can take a number of different forms. A worker can be paid according to some measure of output or some measure of effort. "Contests" can be run, where a worker receives a bonus for being the best in the group. Stock options can be given so that the worker benefits when the firm does well. Workers can be given bonuses that depend directly on the firm's accounting profits during the quarter or year. The choice among these schemes, and between pecuniary and nonpecuniary motivators, has important implications for the ways in which workers behave.

Once a method is chosen, it is necessary to fill in the details. For example, many salespeople are paid *by the piece*. They receive commission, which means that the amount they earn depends on the number of units or value of the items that they sell. But what formula is best? How much should they receive in commission and how much in fixed salary? What commission rate should be given? How does this vary with the nature of the product and of the relevant labor force?

Teams

Team production provides the major rationale for production that is organized into multiperson firms. In the absence of team production, individuals could simply engage in their own activities in isolation and then trade their products in the market. The fact that a number of individuals are housed under one roof or draw salaries from the same organization suggests that there are links between workers within an organization. One worker's activity affects another worker's output.

The ways in which teams are set up affects the firm's profits. In addition, workers must be motivated to perform appropriately in a team context. Is teamwork overrated? When are teams important, and when can firms allow individuals to act on their own?

Since working in teams requires that individuals cooperate with one another, it is necessary to structure incentives so that workers want to help, rather than compete with one another. How can this be done? Are some organizational structures more conducive to cooperation than others? What monetary and other incentives can be used to produce high levels of teamwork?

Work–Life Considerations

Sometimes it appears that junior workers are more productive than senior ones, but that senior workers are better treated than the junior ones. Other than historical or cultural respect for age, why might firms set up such seemingly counterproductive structures? After all, the existence of such a structure is likely to annoy the younger workers, especially the most productive among them. Does a firm that creates an environment that heavily favors seniority risk its own survival?

Evaluation

Related to the issue of motivation is evaluation. If workers are never evaluated, two obvious problems arise. First, workers who are not well suited to the firm are not sorted out. Second, workers who are well suited may become lazy because their performance is not being monitored.

Although it is easy to say that monitoring is important, it is more difficult to be specific about its nature. In particular, how often should a worker be evaluated? How should standards be set in determining which workers are satisfactory? How long should the probationary period be? How permanent should the decision made after probation be?

The groundwork necessary to provide answers to these questions is laid in the sections on hiring and motivation. But it is necessary to apply the theories and evidence discussed there to the specific issues of performance evaluation, which is important in most organizations.

Benefits

One of the most important areas of personnel analysis involves benefits. Many firms do not recognize explicitly that there is a trade-off between benefits and wages. These firms separate benefits and wage compensation departments so that they operate almost independent of one another. Since compensation is a structure, it is necessary to consider the two components together. The ratio of benefits to wages can be selected in a way that best serves both the firm's and worker's interests.

The provisions that accompany benefits are important and can affect effort and turnover in dramatic ways. Nowhere is this more evident than in pension plans. The conditions attached to pensions, the accrual formulas—indeed, the most basic characteristics of the program (defined benefit versus defined contribution)—have been demonstrated, both in theory and in practice, to greatly affect worker behavior.

Authority

How much authority should each worker be given? How does this vary with the kind of damage that a worker can do? In some situations, workers must obtain approval from their bosses for even the most trivial actions. In others, workers are given a significant amount of free rein. Which method is right, and what conditions cause the choice to vary?

Task Assignments

How many jobs should each worker know? Obviously, flexibility is greater in firms whose workers possess many skills, but there are costs. Even if the old adage, "jack of all trades, master of none," fails to hold, teaching workers many jobs is more costly than teaching them one job. Most of the time, workers will not use many of the skills that they possess. This is wasteful. How can a firm decide on how many skills to provide its workers, or on how many skills it insists workers have before they are hired?

Related is the issue of worker empowerment. Workers who have control over their environments are likely to be happier, and perhaps more productive. The cost is that worker control may shift some of the profit from shareholders to labor. Although workers might find this appealing, few shareholders will. Why might a firm voluntarily empower its work force?

We begin by considering the start of the employment relationship: the hiring decision.

◆ ◆ ◆ ◆ ◆ ADVANCED READING

Baker, George P., Michael C. Jensen, Kevin J. Murphy. "Compensation and Incentives: Practice vs. Theory," *The Journal of Finance*, 43, no. 3 (July 1988), 593–616.

Ehrenberg, Ronald G., ed. *Do Compensation Policies Matter?* Frank W. Pierce Memorial Lectureship and Conference Series, no. 8. Ithaca, N.Y.: ILR Press, 1990.

Freeman, Richard B. *Labor Markets in Action: Essays in Empirical Economics.* Cambridge and London: Harvard University Press, 1989.

Lazear, Edward P. *Personnel Economics*. Cambridge, Mass. and London, Eng., MIT Press, 1996.

Parsons, Donald O. "The Employment Relationship: Job Attachment, Work Effort, and the Nature of Contracts." In Orley Ashenfelter and Richard Layard, eds., *Handbook of Labor Economics*, vol. 2, Handbooks in Economics series, no. 5; Amsterdam; Oxford and Tokyo: North-Holland; distributed in North America by Elsevier Science, New York, 789–848, 1986.

ing configuration, high school graduates are just as good, if not better, than college-trained people. We have to pay the college people more to get 'em, and it just doesn't seem worth it.

MARSHALL: What you say may be right for production and configuration, Mr. Ricardo, but I don't think that it's applicable when we're talking about dealing with the public. I side with Smith. In my view, this is not a place to save money. We ought to go for the best possible people.

KEYNES: I agree that good people are important, but what do you mean by the best possible person? Should we hire someone with a Ph.D. to answer the telephone? A guy like that might cost us $60,000 a year. An able college graduate goes for half that and they're just as good, most of the time. There is surely a limit to how much we want to pay, and what kinds of people we want to put into those sales rep jobs.

RICARDO: Keynes is right, and besides, there are many more college graduates available than there are Ph.D.s. Where would we find a large enough supply of Ph.D.s to take our sales orders, even if we were willing to pay them $60,000 a year?

KEYNES: Yeah, and right now there's plenty of unemployment. So, I think we can pick up the kinds of workers we want pretty cheaply.

SMITH: I go back to what I said at the beginning. Two low-quality sales reps are not as profitable as one high-quality sales rep, even if the high-quality one costs double what each of the low-quality ones cost. I think we need to go for the better people. This is not a job to which we can simply assign lots of marginal people.

MARSHALL: We keep throwing these words like *quality* around. Who are we talking about? Is formal education the only thing relevant here? A lot of the kinds of computer people we want drop out of school, because they can't take the rigid environment. That doesn't mean that they're not knowledgeable computer people.

RICARDO: I'm still worried about going with high-priced people. After all, this company is in big financial trouble right now. I don't see spending a lot of money for high-level workers when we're on the verge of going under. And once we're thinking about the type of person to hire, we need to decide how many. Given our current situation, I'm not sure that we should be expanding employment in a big way, no matter what the potential. Besides, what's the harm in trying some of the lower-skilled workers? If they don't work out, we can go with the higher-cost ones later.

KEYNES: What's clear to me is that we don't know what we're talking about. We have to collect some information before we can make an informed decision. But we don't have much time, so I welcome suggestions on what kind of information we should gather. Any thoughts?

SETTING HIRING STANDARDS

2

*H*iring is the primary role of many personnel departments, but few personnel specialists provide managers of other departments with much guidance on how to set hiring standards. Nor are they often asked. Our first substantive chapter is, therefore, a discussion of hiring. The following scenario raises a number of issues that warrant consideration.

An established, but troubled, New Hampshire–based computer firm has recently produced a new PC. It is to be sold primarily by mail. Orders are to come in by phone and they will be transmitted to the production line, where the computers will be assembled according to the customers' specifications.

The sales representatives, who will answer calls and communicate orders to the configurers, are to be the primary liaisons between customers and the firm. The question is, "Whom should the firm hire for the job?" In particular, what skill standards should be set?

A meeting is held to discuss the issue. Excerpts from that meeting follow:

SMITH: Sales reps are an important part of our firm. They are usually our first contact with the customer, and they're the people who must get the order right. A mistake on their part can cost us a lot of time and effort in shipping and reconfiguration, not to mention lost goodwill that we suffer when customers get angry. I think that we should go with high-quality people. Saving money at this level is likely to be penny-wise and pound-foolish.

RICARDO: Although I think that Smith's comments are on target, I don't buy his conclusion. My experience has been that paying more simply yields us workers with better credentials, but not better workers. I find that when we're do-

9

The previous discussion raised a large number of questions. They include:

- Are highly skilled people better at the job?

- Are highly skilled people worth the additional salary cost?

- How skilled is highly skilled?

- Which levels of skill should be considered for a particular job?

- How should skill be defined? Is formal education the key, or should we use some other criterion?

- What is the trade-off between quality and quantity?

- Are two unskilled workers more or less productive than one skilled worker?

- Do supply conditions matter? Is worker availability an issue?

- Should the financial condition of the firm affect the choice of worker quality?

- How many workers should be hired?

- Once the type is decided, how does the firm decide on the number of workers to be hired?

- What kind of information would help answer these questions?

THE TRADE-OFF BETWEEN HIGHLY SKILLED AND LESS-SKILLED WORKERS

◆ ◆ ◆ ◆ ◆

Some economic thinking can help answer these questions. Initially, let us make our task relatively simple by supposing that we have all the information that we need. We can complicate our lives later by addressing the issues that arise when all the information is not available.

The ultimate question can be put as follows: "Is it better to hire the best people, irrespective of cost, or is it better to hire the cheapest people, irrespective of quality?" Readers may have different views on this question, but the market guarantees that neither rule can be right as a general principle. Consider what would happen if all firms opted for the best worker, irrespective of cost. The demand for high-quality workers would rise, whereas the demand for lower-quality workers would fall. As more and more firms adopted this strategy, the price of high-quality workers would rise relative to the price of low-quality workers. Eventually, some firms would find it worthwhile to switch to low-quality workers. If they did not, low-quality workers would be unable to find jobs and would have to offer their services at an even lower price. In **equilibrium,** the wage spread between high- and low-quality workers would be large enough so that no firms hiring low-quality workers would want to switch to high-quality ones, and no firms hiring high-quality workers would want to switch to low-quality ones. If either side wanted to switch, then demand would change, and wages would adjust until no more switching occurred.

Although this describes what happens at the market level, an *individual firm* has to decide whether to go for the high-quality worker at the high price or to settle for the lower-quality worker whose wage is lower. The example that follows will provide some guidance as to which side of the market any particular firm wants to be on.

An Example: Comparing High School Graduates to College Graduates

The situation just discussed relates to a new product, but past experience might well prove useful. The firm might go to the order histories for its sales representatives to determine relative productivity levels associated with different levels of education. Table 2.1 presents this information.

The ratio of sales by college graduates to those by high school graduates is 1.28; that is, college graduates are, on average, 28 percent more productive than high school graduates. Whether formal education is the best measure of skill remains a question, but these data confirm the suspicion that more educated workers are more productive.

Table 2.2 presents a time-series of data on hourly wages adjusted for inflation for these two types of workers.

TABLE 2.1
1990 SALES AND EDUCATION LEVELS FOR SELECTED WORKERS

Worker I.D. Number	Sales in 1990 (in milllion $)	Education
2531	$1.2	HS
2532	$1.3	College
2533	$1.5	HS
2534	$1.5	HS
2535	$1.6	College
2536	$1.7	HS
2537	$2.0	College
2538	$2.1	College
2539	$2.1	College
2540	$2.2	College
Average sales among high school grads	**$1.475**	
Average sales among college grads	**$1.88333**	

TABLE 2.2
REAL HOURLY WAGES BY EDUCATION LEVEL, 1963–90

| Year | Hourly Wages | | Ratio |
	High School	College	
1963	$6.10	$8.45	1.39
1964	$6.11	$8.97	1.47
1965	$6.23	$9.32	1.50
1966	$6.41	$9.46	1.48
1967	$6.72	$9.86	1.47
1968	$6.90	$10.24	1.48
1969	$7.27	$10.87	1.50
1970	$7.32	$10.82	1.48
1971	$7.24	$10.79	1.49
1972	$7.32	$10.71	1.46
1973	$7.37	$10.43	1.42
1974	$7.10	$10.02	1.41
1975	$7.08	$9.94	1.40
1976	$7.08	$9.76	1.38
1977	$7.06	$9.77	1.38
1978	**$7.05**	**$9.49**	**1.35**
1979	$7.03	$9.55	1.36
1980	$6.92	$9.60	1.39
1981	$6.89	$9.41	1.37
1982	$6.89	$9.51	1.38
1983	$6.78	$9.61	1.42
1984	$6.89	$9.87	1.43
1985	$6.90	$10.04	1.46
1986	$6.93	$10.20	1.47
1987	$6.85	$9.88	1.44
1988	$6.83	$10.13	1.48
1989	$6.81	$10.37	1.52
1990	**$6.82**	**$10.25**	**1.50**

Source: CPS data compiled by Kevin M. Murphy and Karen Lombard,
University of Chicago, 1993.

Wages have gone up and down over time, but the ratio of college wages to high school wages has gone up in recent years.[1] The most recent data are relevant for predicting the cost to the firm of employing different types of workers right now. Thus, in 1990, the ratio of college to high school salaries was 1.50—that is, college grads earned 50 percent more than high school grads.

---

[1]As a factual matter, the rise in the ratio of college grad to high school grad hourly wages has not been smooth. The salaries for college grads dropped in relative terms during the 1970s, but expanded again in the 1980s. See, for example, Murphy and Welch (1992), Katz and Murphy (1992) for documentation of this trend.

Table 2.1 shows that college grads are more productive than high school grads. But Table 2.2 shows that college grads cost more than high school grads. So which way does the firm go? The firm wants to choose the path that is most profitable. Based on the data in Table 2.1, the firm that hires a college grad can expect

$$(\$1.88333 \text{ million per year}) / 12 = \$156,944 \text{ a month in sales}$$

The firm that hires a high school grad can expect

$$(\$1.475 \text{ million per year}) / 12 = \$122,917 \text{ a month}$$

To achieve, say, $1 million in sales a month, the firm would need to employ

$$\$1,000,000 / \$156,944 = 6.372 \text{ college grads}$$

Alternatively, it could employ

$$\$1,000,000 / \$122,917 = 8.136 \text{ high school grads}$$

Which is better? Given that one person-month consists of 176 working hours, the cost of hiring 8.136 high school grads in 1990 would be

$$8.136 \times \$6.82 \times 176 = \$9766$$

The cost of 6.372 college grads would be

$$6.372 \times \$10.25 \times 176 = \$11,495$$

To obtain $1 million in sales, the firm can use high school graduates at a cost of $9,766 or college graduates at a cost of $11,495. Therefore, the better strategy is to hire high school grads. Although college grads are stronger performers, they are not sufficiently stronger to make up for their higher cost.

The General Principle for Selecting Skill Standards

The choice of $1 million in sales was arbitrary. What was true for $1 million is true for any level of sales: Given the differences in wages and productivity just reported, it is cheaper to produce any level of sales with high school labor than with college labor. Of course, if college labor were cheap enough, the reverse would be true. For example, if college labor cost the same as high school labor, it would be cheaper to produce any level of sales with college labor than with high school labor because college labor is more productive and would cost the same as high school labor. This general principle can be written down in a formula.

Suppose that Q_c is the output of the average college grad and Q_b is the output of the typical high school grad during the same time period. Suppose that W_c is the wage of a typical college grad and W_b is the wage of a typical high school grad during a given time period. Then it is more effective to use high school labor if and only if

(2.1)
$$\frac{W_b}{Q_b} < \frac{W_c}{Q_c}$$

In simple terms, the formula says to choose the type of labor that yields the lowest cost per unit of output. In the context of the previous example, the relevant numbers are (from Tables 2.1 and 2.2): $Q_c = \$1.88$ million; $Q_b = \$1.48$ million; $W_c = \$10.25 \times 2112$ hours $= \$21,648$; and $W_b = \$6.82 \times 2112$ hours $= \$14,404$. (The total of 2,112 hours comes from 176 hours a month times 12 months.) Substituting these numbers into Equation 2.1 yields

$$\frac{\$14,404}{\$1,475,000} < \frac{\$21,648}{\$1,883,330}$$
$$.0087 < 0115$$

Thus, it costs .87 cents to generate one dollar of sales if high school labor is used. If college labor is used, the cost per dollar of sales is 1.15 cents. Therefore, it is cheaper in this case to use high school labor.

There are other ways to say the same thing, all of which make straightforward business sense. The firm should hire high school labor if the gain in output from moving to college labor is not as great as the increase in cost from moving to college labor. Rearranging terms in Equation 2.1, we can write that high school grads should be hired over college grads if

(2.2)
$$\frac{Q_c}{Q_b} < \frac{W_c}{W_b}$$

The left side of the expression gives the output gain from hiring college grads. The right side gives the cost increase from hiring college grads. If the cost increase exceeds the productivity increase, then high school grads should be used. Since Equation 2.2 is simply a restatement of Equation 2.1, any set of numbers satisfying (2.1) will also satisfy (2.2).

Thus, the statement, "The cost per dollar of output is lower when high school grads are used," is equivalent to, "The gain in productivity from using college grads does not compensate for the increase in cost from using college grads." Both statements imply that high school grads should be used.

Stated most generally, *the most cost-effective labor is the type that has the lowest ratio of salary to output.*

Whether a firm uses high school or college grads for a particular job depends on the ratios of salary to output. Although it was true that high school grads were the best choice in 1990, college grads may have been more cost-effective in other years. For example, suppose that in 1978, the ratio of sales by college grads to those by high school grads was 1.5. Suppose also that college grads sold $450,000 a year and high school grads sold only $300,000 a year. In such a case, the inequality in Equation 2.2 would not hold. The gain in productivity from hiring college grads would outweigh the increase in cost from hiring them. High school grads, although cheaper, would not be sufficiently productive to make them cost-effective. College grads cost 35 percent more than high school grads in 1978 (they were 1.35 times as expensive), but they were 50 percent more productive. As a result, college grads were the best choice in 1978, and high school grads were more cost-effective in 1990.

Ratios, Not Levels, Are Key

The general principle for identifying the optimal skill level is stated in terms of ratios. A college grad should be hired if the *ratio* of college grad wages to high school grad wages is less than the *ratio* of college grad output to high school grad output. Why are ratios important? Why not levels?

In the previous example for 1990, college grads could produce $400,000 in sales per year more than high school grads ($1.88 million versus $1.48 million). But the difference in costs was far less than $400,000. In 1990, college grads earned $21,648 and high school grads earned $14,403, a difference in cost of only $7,245 for the year. But the gain in sales was $400,000, so why not go with the college graduate? Based on our earlier results using Equation 2.1, the college grad is not worth the cost, but how can this be?

The answer lies in the fact that ratios, rather than **absolute differences,** are relevant. The conditions in Equations 2.1 and 2.2 are conditions on the ratios of wages and outputs, not on the levels of wages and outputs. Ratios are relevant because the firm can do better by hiring more high school grads than fewer college grads. The question is not, "Are college grads worth hiring at all?" The question is whether they are worth hiring over high school grads. To obtain $1.88 million in sales by using college labor requires one worker at a cost of $21,648. To obtain $1.88 million in sales using high school labor requires 1.28 workers ($1.88/$1.48). The cost of 1.28 workers is $18,295.[2] Thus, by using high school labor, the same number of sales are generated at a lower cost. It is more profitable to generate $1.88 million in sales at a cost of $18,295 than it is at a cost of $21,648.

This example points out that ratios of wages and productivity rather than levels of wages and productivity should be the guide. Examining *levels* only tells us whether it pays to have a college grad produce the higher level of sales. The better choice, for any given level of sales, is to hire more high school grads. Because the inequality in Equation 2.1 is satisfied, it is more profitable to hire a larger number of high school grads than it is to hire a smaller number of college grads.

---

[2]Do not be troubled by the fact that this requires hiring a fraction of a worker. First of all, it is not impossible to hire a part of a worker. Workers can be hired for fewer hours per week, or they may be hired full time, but allocated to other jobs for the remainder of their time. More fundamentally, since we are usually not talking about hiring only one worker, the fractions become almost inconsequential. For example, to produce $2.96 million in sales, exactly 2.0 high school grads would be used.

WORKER CHOICE AT DAYS INNS

◆ ◆ ◆ ◆ ◆ ◆ ◆ ◆ ◆

Days Inns of America, a hotel franchiser, traditionally staffed its reservation center with younger employees who were willing to work at the minimum wage. The staff was required to answer phone calls from potential guests and then book reservations. However in 1986, because of a shortage of low-skilled workers, wages began to rise for this age and experience group. Faced with a potentially major increase in compensation cost, Days Inns decided to re-examine their targeted recruiting for these positions.

Young workers were primarily recruited because of their willingness to provide labor at such low wages. Generally, these employees had little business experience or other specific skills. Days Inns management knew that the talent needed for such positions was minimal and that productivity was somewhat independent of the specific employee. However, if the reservation center could hire slightly more productive workers for only a slightly higher wage, the increased expenditure could be justified. Days Inns' executives realized that the sedentary nature of the position seemed to be most suited for elderly workers. In addition, senior citizens were a readily available work force that could be hired at only slightly more than existing young workers, when training and other costs were included.

What happened? With productivity defined as a combination of average call length and number of reservations booked, older workers talked on the phone longer but made more reservations. An empirical analysis revealed that older workers were more productive at only a slightly higher cost. More specifically, although they spoke on the phone longer, the higher proportion of calls that resulted in actual reservations more than offset the additional time used. Essentially, elderly workers had a lower salary to output ratio, making them the most cost-effective labor. The savings were further accentuated by the fact that older employees had a significantly lower turnover rate; thus, when one-time expenditures such as training were amortized over the length of employment, elderly workers actually cost less than young employees.

Source: William McNaught and Michael Barth, "Are Olders Workers Good Buys? A Case Study of Days Inns of America," *Sloan Management Review,* Spring 1992.

The Firm's Financial Condition

Should the firm be more inclined toward low-wage labor when it is in dire financial straits? Intuition here is often misleading, because the correct answer to this question is a clear no. Neither the general principle behind selecting the optimal skill standard for new hires nor Equation 2.1 makes any mention of the financial condition of the firm. Choosing the wrong kind of labor will only make things worse for a financially troubled firm. The only way for the firm to pull itself out of trouble is by making correct—that is, profit-maximizing—decisions, not by trying to save money on necessary business expenses. Being penny-wise may indeed be pound-foolish.

To see this, let us return to the previous examples. Consider a year, say, 1978, when it paid to use college graduates over high school graduates according to (2.1). As already discussed, the wage ratio of college to high school grads in 1978 was 1.35 and the ratio of output by college to high school grads was 1.5. Let us suppose that each college grad produced $30,000 in revenue a year and each high school grad produced $20,000 in revenue a year (which is consistent with the college/high school factor of 1.5). College grads should be hired, because the wage rate ratio of 1.35 is less than the output ratio of 1.5. Now, suppose that the firm is earning profits of $1 million a year. The next college grad hired generates $30,000 in revenue and incurs costs (from wages) of

$$(12 \text{ months})(176 \text{ hours/month})(\$9.49 \text{ / hour}) = \$20,043$$

The firm nets $9,957, increasing profits to $1,009,957.

If a high school grad is hired, output is $20,000 of revenue a year, and cost is $(12)(176)(\$7.05) = \$14,890$ a year. The firm nets $5,110, increasing profits to $1,005,110. Clearly, it pays to hire the college grad since $1,009,957 exceeds $1,005,110.

Now suppose that the firm is currently taking losses of $100,000 a year, say, because it has a large debt to service. If it uses the college grad, the gain is $30,000 while the cost is $20,043 netting $9,957, as just shown. This reduces its losses from $100,000 to $90,043. If it hires the high school grad, losses are reduced by $5,110 to $94,890. Again, it is better to hire the college grad. Since the net contribution remains the same and is independent of whether profits or losses are being taken, the decision should not vary with the firm's current profit level.

The implication is that the choice of labor quality does not depend on the financial condition of the firm. The rule stated in Equation 2.1 is correct, irrespective of the firm's balance sheet. The firm's financial condition affects whether the firm wishes to produce at all, but it has no influence on the determination of the most cost-effective labor, once the firm decides to produce.

Foreign Competition and Labor Markets

The previous analysis is useful for assessing claims about foreign competition. It is often said that foreign competitors are able to drive American companies out of business because foreign firms have access to cheaper labor. The real issue is not whether labor is cheaper, but whether it is more cost-effective. Suppose, for example, that American labor were twice as expensive as Korean labor, but also three times as productive. Americans, not Koreans, would have the cost advantage. A firm that had a

TABLE 2.3
SALARY AND PRODUCTIVITY DATA FOR SELECTED COUNTRIES

Country	GDP Per Worker	Wage*	Cost Per $ of GDP
Germany	$53,254	$23,400	0.439
United States	$45,728	$22,049	0.482
Mexico	$ 5,968	$ 2,884	0.483
Japan	$47,026	$28,374	0.603
Korea	$11,944	$ 8,778	0.735
China	$ 630	$ 468	0.743

Sources: UN Statistical Yearbook, 1992, OECD Labor Force Statistics, 1970–1990, UN Statistical Yearbook, 1989, and The Europa World Yearbook, 1992.

*The wage is the annual salary in manufacturing. Weekly hours were multiplied by 52 to obtain annual hours. Average manufacturing hourly wage was converted to dollars at the 1990 exchange rate.

choice between hiring Americans or Koreans would prefer the more expensive Americans because they would be the most effective, according to Equation 2.1.

Table 2.3 provides productivity and salary data for production and white-collar workers in several countries.

Table 2.3 provides some interesting results. Of the six countries listed, Germany has the lowest labor cost per unit of GDP, despite its high annual wage. The United States is second. Although average wages in U.S. manufacturing are higher than in most countries of the world, productivity is sufficiently high to make American labor costs lower than Mexico, Japan, Korea, and China. China, despite having an annual average salary in manufacturing of only $468 a year, is the highest-cost producer because productivity is so low there. Manufacturing productivity is slightly higher in Japan than it is in the United States, but wages in manufacturing are considerably higher in Japan, implying that the United States is a low-cost producer relative to Japan.

These numbers are meant to be illustrative, rather than definitive.[3] Still, they make clear the point of this chapter. *Cheap labor is not necessarily low-cost labor. High-productivity labor is not necessarily the most profitable labor. The choice of labor inputs is determined by the ratio of cost to output. A firm seeks low cost per unit of output.* Low cost per unit of output is desirable, whether it comes about because wages are low or because productivity is high.

---

[3]The numbers may contain some severe aggregation error. Specifically, wages are from manufacturing, but productivity is for the economy as a whole. So, if Korean manufacturing has much higher productivity than the rest of Korea, whereas U.S. manufacturing productivity is close to that in the rest of the United States, productivity numbers would understate Korean productivity to a greater extent than they understate American productivity. As a result, costs per dollar of manufactured output may be significantly different than they appear in the table.

The Choice of Skill Variables

Our first example focused only on education, and not even all education levels, since we considered only high school graduates and college graduates. Why aren't Ph.D.s relevant for consideration? Why not worry about work experience rather than education? How do we decide which factors are most important?

The question of which factors to consider is a tough one, but one for which there is some empirical evidence. We know, for example, that both education and experience affect earnings.[4] Nothing precludes consideration of other variables, but in practice, there are limitations imposed by the data. As long as a firm can either measure or estimate productivity and wages differences as some factor varies, nothing prevents analysis along these lines.

For example, some may believe that background in video game arcades is important in affecting sales productivity. If we knew how much more those with video game experience were paid, and if we knew how much more productive they were, then it would be straightforward to apply Equation 2.1. The condition in (2.1) could simply be restated, allowing workers to differ only with respect to video game experience. There are two reasons why education and work experience are used for hiring decisions more often than video game experience. First, wage and productivity information based on video game experience is hard to come by. Second, education and work experience have been shown to be the two most important determinants of wages. When assessing a new situation, the best guess is that education and work experience are likely to be more important than other factors.

When more than two levels of skill are under consideration, an elimination approach may be useful. First, any two skill levels, say, high school grads and college grads are chosen arbitrarily. The "winner" of that comparison (say, the high school grad) is then compared to the next candidate (say, Ph.D.s). The winner of that comparison runs against another arbitrarily chosen category. This elimination process is used until all possible categories have been examined. The order in which the analysis is conducted has no effect on the outcome, since the winner must implicitly beat all other categories.[5] Alternatively, wage/output ratios can be computed for every skill type. The type with the lowest wage/output ratio is the type of labor to be used.

Describing the Production Technology

So far, the discussion has proceeded as if production were independent across individuals. In the case discussed so far, sales by one agent are for the most part independent of sales by another agent. In the real world, production is sometimes,

---

[4]See for example, Becker (1975) and Mincer (1974).

[5]That is, suppose there are three categories, A, B, and C. If A and B are compared first, the winner, say B, runs against C. Suppose C beats B. C wins overall. Comparing C to B first would not have changed the result. C would have beaten B. Then C would compete against A, but C beats A, since C beats B and B beats A. Transitivity is preserved in these comparisons.

but not always, independent across workers. To illustrate this point, we will consider three scenarios that represent different types of technologies. In the first scenario, production is independent across workers; in the second, one worker's production depends on the skill of the workers with whom he works; and in the third scenario, production is independent across workers, but workers interact critically with capital. When deciding on the type of worker to hire, the nature of production is key. Let us begin by pursuing the case that we have been discussing throughout.

Scenario 1: Production Independent Across Workers

A manager describes production at his firm as follows:

> My firm is a salesforce and that's it. We do selling for small manufacturers who do not want to have their own sales team. Each salesperson works independently. Most of the time our salespeople are not selling the same product or even working for the same manufacturer as their fellow salespeople.
>
> This is a very small operation. I put the business together myself, and I don't think that anyone else could have done it. Most of the business depends on my personal contacts. The one disadvantage is that I can't expand very much. No one can substitute for me and my time is limited. This firm is very bottom heavy. It consists of all salespeople plus me as manager. What kind of worker should I hire?

The firm described here is one where workers are engaged in activities that are independent of each other. Each worker's sales depend on his own ability and effort, irrespective of the efforts of other salespersons. Since this example fits so closely with the situation described above, the choice between college and high school grads is exactly the one that we have focused on so far. When defining the output of one type of worker, it is not necessary to take into account the effort or skill level of other workers. In this case, we need only count the sales of the typical college and high school grads, and compare these sales levels to their wages in accordance with Equation 2.1. The simplicity of this case is best seen by comparing it to the next example.

Scenario 2: Workers' Productivity Depends on the Skills of Other Workers

A second manager describes her production as follows:

> This firm is engaged in manufacturing small appliances. We find it better to have a combination of worker types. Although the high school grads are cheaper and more cost-effective in the short run, we find that we can't keep their skill levels up without some college grads around. The high school grads forget what they knew. The college grads do too, but since they know more, they keep the high school grads sharp. So we like to use both kinds of workers. No managers other than me are necessary. The problem is that I'm not sure about the appropriate balance.

Here, workers interact strategically with one another. The output of a high school graduate depends on whether there are college graduates at work. College grads affect the output of high school grads, and vice versa: Since college grads are not only producing appliances, but also act as part-time teachers, part of the output of college grads consists of their effect on high school grads, almost as if the firm is producing two specific products. In this case, the second product is not another manufactured good, but instead, is an improvement in the skills of the work force.

Equation 2.1 still holds, but output must be defined carefully. When measuring the output of high school grads, the number of college grads must be specified. Table 2.4 provides an example of the kind of information needed.

Using Table 2.4, it is easy to see that output of a college grad depends on the number of high school grads working. For example, if 100 of each type are employed, then total output is 63.10 units. If the number of college grads is increased from 100 to 110, the gain in output is 3.71 units as total output expands to 66.81 units. However, if 150 high school grads are employed, the gain in total output in going from 100 to 110 college grads would be 4.19, as output jumps from 71.26 to 75.45. The gain from adding 10 college grads is larger when there are more high school grads around. Since college grads train high school grads, their services are more valuable when the firm has more potential "students" for them to teach. The larger the number of high school grads in the work force, the higher the value of adding college grads to the work force.

Similarly, if only 100 college grads are employed, adding 10 high school grads to the initial 100 increases output by 1.83 units from 63.10 to 64.93. But if 150 college grads are employed, then increasing the high school work force from 100 to 110 results in an increase of 2.34 units. High school grads are more valuable the more college grads are on board. Since college grads teach the high school grads, high school grads are more valuable when the "classroom" in which they learn is

TABLE 2.4

RELATION BETWEEN OUTPUT AND THE NUMBER OF COLLEGE AND HIGH SCHOOL GRADS EMPLOYED

		Number of College Grads Employed					
		100	*110*	*120*	*130*	*140*	*150*
		Output					
Number	100	**63.10**	**66.81**	70.39	73.85	77.21	80.47
of	110	64.93	68.75	72.43	75.99	79.45	82.81
High	120	66.64	70.57	74.35	78.00	81.55	85.00
School	130	68.26	72.28	76.15	79.90	83.53	87.06
Grads	140	69.80	73.91	77.87	81.70	85.41	89.02
Employed	150	**71.26**	**75.45**	79.49	83.41	87.20	90.88

less crowded.[6] This example reveals the importance of interaction. This can be generalized as follows.

When workers interact on the job, a worker's contribution to output includes the effect on his co-worker's output. As a result, it pays to hire more and generally better workers when output is interrelated than when it is independent across workers.

This is well illustrated by the common behavior of firms that provide professional services. Consider a typical law firm. There are many jobs that need to be done by the lawyers. Some bring in business, the so-called *rainmakers,* while others do much of the research work. Still others specialize in litigation. The value of lawyers in court depends on the quality of the research behind them, as well as on the cases they get to argue. It pays to have good people behind the court lawyers, because their output is enhanced by the others' efforts. Conversely, the efforts of an energetic rainmaker are wasted if they are not combined with the skills of a highly effective litigator. The litigator's productivity depends on the backup, and the value of the rainmaker and research people depends on the final phase provided by the litigator. Structuring teams of this sort in an optimal manner is one of the more difficult problems encountered by an organization.

Scenario 3: Independent Production Across Workers— Workers Interact with Capital

A third example illustrates the importance of capital considerations. A manager describes one production process as follows:

We are a large department store that has our men's dress shirts produced by a factory in Singapore. Each worker must work on a sewing machine, which costs us $5 per day to rent. We can use skilled labor, which produces an average of 4 shirts per day, or we can use professional labor, which produces an average of 6 shirts per day. Skilled labor costs us $5 per hour and professional labor costs us $8 per hour. The sewing machine company says that it will rent us a machine that will double output per worker, but the better machine costs $11 per day to rent. I have two questions. First, should I rent the new machines? Second, what kind of labor should I hire?

The analysis is easy once the relevant data are compiled, as shown in Table 2.5.

First, consider the old machines. If old machines are used, then it is better to use skilled labor. Professional labor is not cost-effective. Using professional labor, the total cost of producing a shirt is $11.50 ($69 total cost divided by 6). If skilled labor is used, the total cost per shirt is only $11.25 ($45 total cost divided by 4). Note that it is the total cost per shirt that is relevant. The total cost must include the cost of the sewing machine as well.

---

[6]The two statements are not inconsistent. Fewer students per class might mean that each student learns more in the class. But having more students available means that college grads can offer more classes, making them more productive.

TABLE 2.5
OUTPUT AND COSTS FOR DIFFERENT TYPES OF LABOR AND CAPITAL

Wage Rates:	Skilled $5.00	Professional $8.00			
	Output	Labor Cost	Capital Cost	Total Cost	Cost/Output
Old Machines					
Skilled	4	$40.00	$5.00	$45.00	**$11.25**
Professional	6	$64.00	$5.00	$69.00	**$11.50**
New Machines					
Skilled	8	$40.00	$11.00	$51.00	**$6.38**
Professional	12	$64.00	$11.00	$75.00	**$6.25**

Should the firm use the new machines? Without looking at the table, the manager might be tempted to answer no. Since the new machine costs more than twice as much as the current machine, and only doubles output, it appears that it is not cost-effective. But this ignores the fact that the cost of producing a shirt involves using labor combined with machines, not just machines. Although adding the new machine more than doubles the capital cost, it less than doubles total cost. By using the new machines and skilled workers, cost per shirt can be reduced from $11.25 to $6.38 for skilled workers ($51 total costs divided by 8). So there is no doubt that the firm should use the new machines.

Furthermore, given that the firm is using the new machines, it should hire professional rather than skilled workers. When old machines are used, the cost per shirt is higher with professionals than with skilled labor. But when new machines are used, the cost per shirt is lower with professionals than with skilled labor. When expensive capital is being employed, it becomes more cost-effective to use it intensely. Professionals use the machines more efficiently than do skilled workers, which leads us to conclude the following:

A firm should improve the quality of the workers that it employs as it increases the amount or quality of its capital stock. More specifically, the optimal level of skill rises as the capital/labor ratio increases.

This explains why the president of the firm should be very highly skilled. His labor is being combined with the entire capital stock of the firm. It makes no sense to waste this capital by placing it under the stewardship of a low-skilled individual. Thus, it might very well pay to spend a few million more a year to pirate away only a slightly better CEO, if that CEO can affect the output of the firm significantly. A firm with, say, $1 billion in capital stock is implicitly paying around $100 million per year to *rent* its capital. It is likely to be worthwhile to put very highly skilled labor in control of this super-expensive sewing machine.

Availability of Workers

In many communities, more high school graduates than college graduates are available. Does this mean that a firm should have a bias toward hiring high school grads? In almost all cases, the answer is no. Since most employers, even very large ones, employ a relatively small part of the local labor force, the total availability of workers is generally irrelevant. Most employers can assume that they can get as many workers as they want with the basic level of skills at the going market wage. Therefore, the condition stated in Equation 2.1 holds just as it is written, independent of any availability considerations.

Local Labor Markets

There a two exceptions, both of which relate to **monopsony.**[7] The first is the traditional case of monopsony. Suppose that the firm is located in a small town and employs 90 percent of the available work force. When the firm hires more high school grads, it drives up their price. In this case, the relevant wage for Equation 2.1 takes into account the increase in wage that results from hiring the additional worker. For example, if Dow were to try to hire all of its engineers from the pool available in Midland, Michigan, where its headquarters are located, it would have a significant effect on the local market. Of course, it would be impractical for Dow to limit its labor search to such a narrow community. Since the market for engineers is a national one, Dow can avoid rising labor costs by searching more broadly.

Specific Labor

The second exception is more important. When the type of labor being hired is very specific so that the market for it is **thin** (there are few buyers, but also few suppliers of this type of labor), significant search costs may exist. It may take time to find a worker with the relevant skills—for example, video game experience—and it may take the worker some time to find an employer interested in that unusual set of skills. The wage that enters the calculation in Equation 2.1 must build in these amortized search costs. Suppose it costs on average $2,000 to locate a worker with the relevant specialized skills who will be paid $10 an hour. Suppose further that the worker will remain with the firm for an average of five years, or 10,560 hours (i.e., the number of work hours in a year × 5 years). Amortizing the $2,000 over these hours amounts to about $0.19 an hour. So for the purposes of the hiring decision, the wage that should be used is $10.19 rather than $10.00. Except for highly skilled technical people or executives, search costs are sufficiently low or sufficiently similar across worker types so that (2.1) can be applied in its most straightforward way.

---

[7]*Monopsony power* means that the firm employs a sufficiently large part of the relevant market so that it cannot assume that its hiring has no effect on market price.

Determining the Number of Workers to Hire

Once a firm has determined which type of worker is best suited to the organization, there remains the question of how many should be hired. The answer to this is straightforward:

The firm should continue to hire workers so long as the increment to profit brought about by hiring the worker is positive.

This implies that there is a specific number of workers to be hired because of the principle of **diminishing marginal productivity.** As more and more workers are added to an organization, the value of any one worker falls. For example, as more salespeople are added to answer the telephone, the value of the incremental salesperson declines. After hiring a sufficient number of workers, all calls can be handled quite capably. Hiring another worker may take some additional pressure off the other salespeople, but it does not generate many more calls. Table 2.6 makes the point more clearly.

Table 2.6 reveals that as more workers are hired, sales rise. But sales rise by more when the first worker is hired (from 0 to $100,000) than when the second worker is hired (from $100,000 to $141,421). The value of the first worker is $100,000, but the value of the second is only $41,421. Still, each worker only costs $14,404 (per year), so it pays to hire both the first and second worker. The logic

TABLE 2.6
DIMINISHING MARGINAL PRODUCTIVITY

Number of Workers	Total Annual Sales	Marginal Value of Worker	Total Labor Cost	Marginal Cost of Labor
0	$0	$0	$0	$0
1	$100,000	**$100,000**	$14,404	$14,404
2	$141,421	**$41,421**	$28,808	$14,404
3	$173,205	$31,784	$43,212	$14,404
4	$200,000	$26,795	$57,615	$14,404
5	$223,607	$23,607	$72,019	$14,404
6	$244,949	$21,342	$86,423	$14,404
7	$264,575	$19,626	$100,827	$14,404
8	$282,843	$18,268	$115,231	$14,404
9	$300,000	$17,157	$129,635	$14,404
10	$316,228	$16,228	$144,038	$14,404
11	$331,662	$15,435	$158,442	$14,404
12	$346,410	**$14,748**	$172,846	$14,404
13	$360,555	**$14,145**	$187,250	$14,404
14	$374,166	$13,611	$201,654	$14,404
15	$387,298	$13,133	$216,058	$14,404
16	$400,000	$12,702	$230,461	$14,404
17	$412,311	$12,311	$244,865	$14,404

holds until we hit the twelfth worker. While the twelfth worker brings in $14,748 in additional revenue, the thirteenth worker only brings in $14,145 in additional revenue. The twelfth worker has a positive effect on profit because revenues increase by more than worker cost (i.e., $14,748 added sales − $14,404 cost of worker = $344). But the thirteenth worker has a negative effect on profit (i.e., $14,145 added sales − $14,404 cost of worker − $259). The cost of the thirteenth worker exceeds the worker's value and so that worker should not be hired.

MAKING DECISIONS WHEN DATA ARE NOT EASILY OBTAINED

◆ ◆ ◆ ◆ ◆

Throughout this chapter, we have made decisions based on data that either exist or were assumed to exist. Unfortunately, as decision makers we often need data that are unavailable or too expensive to obtain in a short period of time. What is the practitioner to do in these circumstances?

There are three possibilities: (1) Choose a solution independent of any analysis, (2) estimate the relevant numbers, (3) or experiment. Of the three, the first is usually the least attractive.

Choose a Solution Independent of Analysis

A frequent temptation is to conclude that the data are too difficult to obtain. The solution is then to simply guess an answer. Implicit in the guess are a number of calculations that are not made explicit, but are there, nonetheless.

For example, recall the case of hiring video-game-experienced employees. It is difficult to gather data on these kinds of workers, so the firm may just decide not to require video game experience. But this means that the firm is assuming that requiring video game experience does not pay. More specifically, in terms of Equation 2.1, this means that the manager is implicitly assuming that the ratio of wage/output is higher for the video-game-experienced worker than for the one without such experience. In the absence of data, the opposite assumption might be just as valid.

Estimating the Relevant Numbers

Sometimes it is better to estimate the key parameters and then determine whether they seem reasonable. This is the second approach: Rather than guessing at the answer, a manager may estimate the key numbers to determine the appropriate course of action. Guessing each number step by step is a more systematic way to make a decision. The manager can get a better sense for the quality of the decision.

For example, suppose that workers without video game experience earn W per hour. The manager might not know the wage commanded by workers with video game experience, but guesses that the premium cannot be much. Suppose that the manager believes the wage premium for video game experience to be around 2 percent. The premium may be greater or less than 2 percent, but 2 percent is the best guess that the manager can make. It is unlikely that workers with video game experience will command a much higher wage than those without. However, in the particular context of this firm, those workers may be significantly more productive. The manager guesses that workers with video game experience are likely to be, on average, about 5 percent more productive than the base level of Q per hour. He realizes that this is a rough estimate, but it is the best that he can do. He is quite certain that they will not be less productive than those without the experience, and 5 percent is only a modest productivity gain.

The ratio of wage to productivity for workers without the experience is W/Q. The ratio of wage to productivity for workers with the video game experience is $W(1.02) / Q(1.05)$. He should choose the workers with video game experience if

$$\frac{1.02W}{1.05Q} < \frac{W}{Q}$$

$$\frac{1.02}{1.05} < 1$$

which necessarily holds for any W and Q. Rather than saying that this experience characteristic is too difficult to deal with, in this case it would be better to require it. By going through the exercise of estimating wages and output differences, it might become clear that one type of worker is favored over another.

Experiment

The third option is to experiment. Sometimes this is quite easy to do and carries little cost. In the example of the video-game-experienced workers, it is possible to substitute real data for guesses by hiring a few workers. When there is no readily available data on wages and productivity of video game aficionados, it is possible to hire some and track how they do. The results of the experiment may provide important information for future hiring decisions. The cost is that during the trial period (potentially) higher wages must be paid to workers who may not be any more, and are possibly even less, productive. The larger the scale of the experiment, the more reliable the information. But the larger its scale, the greater are the potential short-run costs.

Sometimes experimenting is difficult and potentially costly. Recall the second example, where high school grads learned from college grads. Teamwork is important, but the kind of experimentation necessary to create the data of Table 2.5 could be quite costly and could take a very long time. It is difficult to assess each worker's contribution.

A real-life example comes from the sport of crew in which teams race narrow canoe-like boats. Suppose that a boat has places for six rowers and that ten have gone out for the team. There are 210 ways to create teams of six rowers out of the ten candidates.[8] In theory, the best approach would be to try all of these 210 team combinations and go with the one that is fastest. Of course, this kind of experimentation could take a tremendous amount of time.

It is not always easy to predict the benefits of experimenting. There are five questions that a manager can consider beforehand to determine whether experimenting is a viable option:

1. What are we trying to learn and why do we want to know it?
2. Will obtaining the answer have a large or small effect on profit?
3. What kind of data are necessary to answer the question?
4. How costly is it to obtain these data?
5. Will the data that we are likely to collect provide a reliable answer to the question?

Question 1 must be answered before any experiment can be undertaken. Otherwise, the experimenters may get so caught up in running the experiment that it becomes a purpose in and of itself.

In order to justify a major experiment, the answer to Question 2 must be that the potential effects on profits are large.

Question 3 must have a well-defined answer. If it is difficult to specify in advance the kind of information required, experimentation is likely to result in money spent without useful results. Managers should be able to say in advance that if the results turn out one way, the decision will be to hire one kind of worker. If they turn out the other way, the decision will be to hire another kind of worker. If this statement cannot be made in advance, it makes no sense to gather the data.

Question 4 must be asked to complement Question 2. If the cost of obtaining the data is large, it may not be cost-effective to undertake the experiment, even if the results will have a significant effect on profit.

The data obtained are most valuable if they give an unambiguous answer to the question posed. If the data obtained contain a great deal of error, or if they only roughly approximate the kind of information needed to answer the question, the experiment is less valuable.

HIRING RISKY WORKERS   ◆ ◆ ◆ ◆ ◆

Suppose that a firm is faced with a choice between two workers. Johnson has productivity that is extremely predictable. Say that he can produce $200,000 in sales per year. The other worker, Wilson, is much less predictable. She may turn out to

---

[8]This comes from the theory of permutations and combinations. The number of distinct combinations of n items taken together in groups of k equals $\frac{n!}{(n-k)!k!}$, which in this case, equals $10! / [(4!)(6!)]$.

be a star, in which case, she will produce $500,000 a year, but she may turn out to be a disaster, actually destroying business and costing the firm $100,000 a year. Suppose that each of the two scenarios is equally likely for Wilson. The *expected* (loosely speaking, the *average*) output from Wilson in any given year is $200,000, derived as follows:

Wilson has a 50 percent chance of producing $500,000 and a 50 percent chance of producing − $100,000. The average of these two is:

$$($500,000 − $100,000) / 2 = $200,000$$

The expected output for Johnson is also $200,000 because he is certain to produce $200,000. If the cost of each employee is the same, which one should be hired?

The answer might seem counterintuitive, but usually the firm should go after the riskier employee. Here is why.

Suppose that both Wilson and Johnson are now 30 years old and can be expected to continue working until they are 65. Suppose further that it takes one full year to determine whether Wilson is a $500,000-per-year producer or a −$100,000-per-year producer. The salary that must be paid to both of these individuals is $100,000 a year. If Johnson is hired, the firm nets $100,000 a year on him for 35 years. This means that Johnson yields the firm a net of $3.5 million over his career.[9] The top branch of Figure 2.1, labeled (1), shows this choice.

Alternatively, the firm can hire Wilson. With probability equal to .5, she turns out to produce $500,000 a year, which nets the firm $14 million over the 35-year career, shown as branch (2) in the figure. But with an equal probability of .5, she turns out to be worth −$200,000 because the firm pays $100,000 in salary and then loses another $100,000 on the output that she destroys, which is shown as branch (3) in the figure. If this occurs, the firm will terminate Wilson at the end of a year, losing $200,000 and starting over. But the expected value of this choice is far greater than the value associated with hiring Johnson. Johnson's value was only $3.5 million, but Wilson's expected value is

$$.5 ($14 million) + .5 (-$200,000) = $6.9 million$$

Wilson is therefore worth almost twice as much as Johnson.

Even though the expected value of output in the first year is $200,000 for both Wilson and Johnson, Wilson is worth much more. Since the firm can keep her if she turns out to be a good employee, but dismiss her if she turns out to be a bad one, the long-term value of Wilson, the risky employee, is higher. Because the firm has the option of terminating its bad workers, it pays to take a chance on riskier workers.

This is often the argument made for hiring chancy workers with "potential" over the conservative, proven, ones. With the more proven worker, the firm gets a

---

[9]We ignore issues of present values by assuming that the interest rate is zero.

FIGURE 2.1
HIRING RISKS

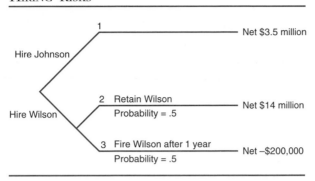

solid performer. With a chancy worker, the firm may find that it made a mistake, which can be remedied only by terminating the worker. But in one of ten cases, it may end up with a star who produces a great deal for the firm. Taking the chance to hire a star is often the best strategy. In general,

> *If two workers have the same expected value and the same wage, then it is better to hire the riskier one. Bad outcomes can be mitigated by* **separation** *and good ones can be magnified through retention of the worker for the worker's entire career.*

The value of taking a chance is so large that it is often the better strategy, even when the safe worker has a higher annual expected value. In the previous example, suppose that Wilson could have been a total disaster, destroying $1,000,000 of output with probability of .5, instead of the mere $100,000, as previously assumed. Then the expected value of her net returns to the firm during the first year would have been

$$.5 \ (-\$1 \ \text{million}) + .5 \ (\$500,000) = -\$250,000$$

Yet it still pays to hire Wilson over Johnson. Since Wilson can be terminated after one year, her value at the time of hire consists of two components. If she turns out to be a star, she nets the firm $14 million. If she turns out to be a slug, she nets the firm −$1.1 million during the first year, which consists of $100,000 in salary and $1 million in destroyed output. If the undesirable outcome is obtained, she is fired after the first year. Thus, her expected value at the time of hire is

$$.5 \ (\$14 \ \text{million}) + .5 \ (-\$1.1 \ \text{million}) = \$6.45 \ \text{million}$$

It remains true that Wilson dominates Johnson, even though her expected output, in this case a negative $250,000, is lower.

Wilson was preferred to Johnson because the cost of one bad year was far outweighed by the chance to receive benefits associated with many very good years. Correspondingly, the value of hiring a risky worker decreases with the age of the worker. If, for example, Johnson and Wilson were 64 instead of 30, and Wilson could cost the firm $1 million, Johnson would be the better choice. When there is no time to reap the benefits of a star worker, the value of taking the risk declines. In the case where Wilson can destroy $1 million of output if she turns out to be a bad worker, her expected value during the first year is −$250,000. But that is her expected net lifetime value as well. Since she will only work until 65, the option to fire her has no value. Johnson, whose expected value was the certain $200,000 is the better choice in this case. The younger the worker, the greater is the value of the option. Therefore, arguments about the value of the risky strategy are particularly relevant when discussing the hiring of young workers.

The claim that risky workers are always better than less risky ones is quite general, but not universal. Necessary to reverse this conclusion is that risky workers may have lower expected value than safe workers. Not only might Wilson be riskier than Johnson, but she might also be worth sufficiently less on average to make the gamble unprofitable. Suppose that instead of being worth $500,000 with probability .5, she is worth only $201,000 with probability .5. Suppose further that she destroys −$100,000 of output with probability .5. Now it does not pay to take the chance on Wilson. If she turns out to be good, the firm nets $101,000 for 35 years, or $3,535,000. If she turns out to be bad, the firm loses $200,000 ($100,000 of which is salary) during the first year and then fires her. The expected value of hiring Wilson is then

$$.5 \ (\$3.535 \ \text{million}) + .5 \ (-\$200,000) = \$1.6675 \ \text{million}$$

But Johnson yields a net benefit of $3.5 million, so Johnson dominates Wilson.[10] The risky worker's expected annual output is sufficiently below that of the safe worker to offset the advantage of the option to fire.

This example shows that when the risky worker's annual expected output is below that of the safe worker, it may pay to hire the safe worker. Although lower expected annual output is a necessary condition for choosing the safe worker, it is not sufficient. Even when Wilson's disaster scenario cost the firm $1 million (so that her expected annual output was −$250,000), it still paid to hire her over Johnson. The option to fire bad workers is so valuable to a firm that it makes it very difficult to prefer the safe worker over the risky one at similar wages.

Futhermore, *the shorter the time required to learn the employee's productivity, the more valuable is the risky worker.*

If it required 34 out of the 35 years to determine Wilson's productivity, her value would be greatly lessened. Then, the firm would have to retain her until age 64 to learn her productivity. If the firm chooses to hire her at all, it might as well keep her for 34 years. Since nothing is revealed before that time, if it was a good idea to hire her in the first place, it is a good idea to retain her for each year until her information is revealed. But it is neither a good idea to hire her nor to retain

---

[10]In order to favor the safe choice over the risky one, it is necessary (but not sufficient) that the expected value of the safe worker in any given year exceed the expected value of the risky one. Otherwise, the risky worker is the more valuable hire because of the option of termination.

her under these circumstances. Given the numbers, her lifetime expected value would be

$$.5 \times 34 \times -\$1.1 \text{ million} + .5 \times 35 \times \$400,000 = -\$11.7 \text{ million}$$

Because she works for the firm for 34 years, during which she may be costing the firm $1.1 million per year, she is potentially a very costly hire. The value to hire her and then fire her early if she turns out to be a dud is small, because she is not fired until after she has done a tremendous amount of damage. This leads to a related point.

In most countries, firms are prevented from terminating workers at will. Legal (or social) restrictions can make the option of termination after one year more costly, or can remove this option altogether.[11] Even with large firing costs, the firm is better off hiring the riskier worker unless the expected annual value of the risky worker is actually below that of the safe worker. To see this, consider an extreme case. Suppose that the firm could never fire a worker. If it hires Wilson, it is stuck with her for her entire lifetime. But if her expected output in each year of work is $200,000, then she has an average value that exactly equals that of Johnson. There is no advantage to hiring Johnson over her, even when she cannot be fired. Since she is just as likely to yield the firm a surplus of $500,000 as she is to cost the firm $100,000 per year, her expected output is $200,000 per year, the same as Johnson's. Only if her expected annual output were below that of Johnson would there be any case for hiring the safe worker over the risky one.

The point that risky workers are to be preferred over safe ones is so strong that it often holds even when the firm has a strong distaste for risk. Since the value of hiring the risky worker is so much greater than that of hiring the safe worker, it may pay almost all firms to hire risky workers. Firms with a deep dislike of risk are likely to find the risk-taking strategy sufficiently profitable to overcome their distaste.

It follows from this discussion above that:

1. The younger the worker, the greater the value of a risky worker.
2. It is often better to hire the risky worker even when the expected value is less than that of the worker's less risky counterpart.
3. Even if termination costs are high, in order to prefer the safe worker over the risky one, the risky one must have lower expected annual output than the safe one.

---

[11]The reader might assume that workers are unambiguously better off when employment is more secure. However, a risky worker may have a difficult time finding a job in a country where layoffs are costly. If an employer does not have the option to fire a worker, he may be reluctant to hire the worker in the first place. I have found that as a general rule, layoff penalties reduce overall levels of employment, using data from 23 of the world's largest economies. See Lazear (1990).

◆ ◆ ◆ ◆ ◆   COORDINATION ISSUES

This chapter has focused on the question of which workers to hire, not on what to do with them once hired. The allocation of labor to jobs or task assignments within firms is a more difficult problem than deciding whom to hire, although deciding whom to hire implicitly allocates those hired to various assignments. Job assignment will be discussed in later chapters, but to provide a sense of the problem's complexity, consider the following.

In the example of choosing a 6-person crew from 10 applicants, there were 210 possibilities. The selection ignored job assignment. That is, we were unconcerned about which rower was assigned to which position in the boat. But position assignment matters. It may be best to have the strongest rower in the back, in the front, or somewhere in the middle. In baseball, the batting lineup usually puts a strong home-run hitter in the "clean-up" position to drive in baserunners who preceded him. Once position and task assignment is a concern, the problem gets much more difficult. In the rowing problem, the 210 possibilities expand[12] to 151,210 when seating position matters. Since each of the 10 applicants must be tried in each of the six seats, while all the remaining applicants vary their seats as well, the possibilities in this case are enormous. And this involves only the selection of 6 from 10.

Even if the six team members were already chosen, there would be 720 different arrangements of those six members into the six seats on the boat. As the size of the firm expands, it is obvious that some method other than raw experimentation must be used to assign workers to tasks. This adds rationale for understanding the theory behind hiring personnel.

◆ ◆ ◆ ◆ ◆   RECAP

Recall the introductory scenario at the beginning of the chapter in which managers were trying to determine whether to hire more skilled workers or less skilled ones. The discussion raised a number of questions.

1. Managers were uncertain whether to hire expensive, highly skilled workers, or cheaper, less skilled workers. The answer hinges on the ratio of productivity to cost of the various types of workers. Using data from 1990, it appeared that in this firm, college grads were too expensive relative to the gain in productivity to justify hiring them. Although the data showed that with little doubt, college grads were more productive than high school grads, the data also revealed an unambiguous necessity to pay the college grads about 50 percent

---

[12]There are 10 candidates to choose from for the athlete who is the first rower, the second rower is selected from 9 candidates etc. $151,200 = 10 \times 9 \times 8 \times 7 \times 6 \times 5$.

more. Since they were less than 50 percent more productive in this firm's context, they were not worth the cost. Remember that the conclusion can differ across firms and over time. For example, in earlier years, college grads were not so expensive relative to high school grads, and they would have been the appropriate choice, even for this firm. This means that reevaluation must be done often enough to capture significant changes in relative wages or relative productivity.

2. How should skill be defined? In theory, any characteristics that may be relevant can be examined using Equation 2.1. An elimination approach was suggested to compare all possible categories of characteristics. The problem, of course, is that the number of possible comparisons can be very large, and the data may be difficult to obtain. As a result of past empirical evidence, the primary focus is usually on education and work experience as the two key variables.

3. When should a few highly skilled workers be used instead of a larger number of low quality workers? The principles articulated in the chapter answer this question. But defining the output of a given worker is sometimes tricky. Particularly when capital is involved, the cost of using more workers is not just the additional wage rate, but also the machines that are tied up. As a result, it will usually be profitable to move toward higher-skilled workers when the amount of capital with which labor must be combined is great.

4. Does worker availability matter? Under most circumstances, this is not an issue. Most firms hire a small enough portion of the total labor force so that they can employ as many workers of a given skill class as desired at the market wage. In rare circumstances, especially those that relate to very highly skilled technical workers, availability may be an issue, and the costs of search must be taken into account.

5. One manager points to the difficult financial conditions of the firm and argues that lower-cost labor should be used as a result. His argument is defective. Low-cost labor may be more cost-effective, but the financial condition of the firm has no bearing on the matter. If expensive, highly skilled workers are the appropriate choice, choosing low-cost labor to conserve on costs during a financial crisis will only worsen the crisis.

6. The number of workers to be hired is determined by comparing the marginal value of a worker to the cost of the worker. Additional workers should be hired as long as the marginal value exceeds cost. This rule, coupled with the principle of diminishing marginal productivity, leads to a specific number of workers to be hired.

7. Information is not always available to answer all questions. When information is lacking, the managers can guess the solution, guess at the missing information, or experiment. The choice among these three methods depends on the costs and benefits. Five criteria were discussed on which the data-gathering decision can be made.

8. It generally pays to hire risky workers over safe ones. As long as there is some probability that the risky worker will turn out to be worth more than the safe worker, the firm should have a bias toward the risky one. The firm can always keep and encourage the unexpected stars and terminate unexpected failures.

◆ ◆ ◆ ◆ ◆ REFERENCES

Becker, Gary S. *Human Capital: A Theoretical and Empirical Analysis, with Special Reference to Education,* 2d ed. New York: Columbia University Press for National Bureau of Economic Research, 1975.

Katz, Lawrence F., and Kevin M. Murphy. "Changes in Relative Wages, 1963–87: Supply and Demand Factors," *Quarterly Journal of Economics* 107 (February 1992): 35–78.

Lazear, Edward P. "Job Security Provisions and Employment," *Quarterly Journal of Economics* 105, no. 3 (August 1990): 699–726.

Mincer, Jacob. *Schooling, Experience, and Earnings.* New York: Columbia University Press for NBER, 1974.

Murphy, Kevin M., and Finis Welch. "The Structure of Wages," *Quarterly Journal of Economics* 107 (February 1992): 285–326.

◆ ◆ ◆ ◆ ◆ APPENDIX

The formal theory behind our conclusions in this chapter is little more than the standard economic theory of production, reinterpreted slightly. Let us write that firm output, Q, depends on labor (including sales) used in production, and in management, denoted P and M, respectively. Consider two types of labor, high school, denoted by H, and college, denoted by C. Thus, C_P refers to college grads who are assigned to production or sales, H_M refers to high school grads who are assigned to management, and C_M and H_P are defined analogously. In addition to labor, capital, K, is generally required. Thus, output, Q, is given by

$$(A2.1) \qquad Q = f(C_P, H_P, C_M, H_M, K)$$

The firm wants to maximize profits. To do this, the firm must decide how much of each type of labor to hire. This decision can be broken into two subsidiary decisions. First the firm must decide how to produce any given amount of output. Then it must decide how much output to produce.

The first problem requires solving the Lograngean:

$$(A2.2) \qquad W_C(C_P + C_M) + W_H(H_P + H_M) + \lambda[Q - f(C_P, C_M, H_P, H_M, K)]$$
$$\text{for } C_P, C_M, H_P, H_M$$

where W_C and W_H are the wage rates of college grads and high school grads, respectively. Let K be given at K_0.

The first-order conditions are:

(A2.3)

a. $W_C - \lambda\dfrac{\partial f}{\partial C_P} = 0$

b. $W_C - \lambda\dfrac{\partial f}{\partial C_M} = 0$

c. $W_H - \lambda\dfrac{\partial f}{\partial H_P} = 0$

d. $W_H - \lambda\dfrac{\partial f}{\partial H_M} = 0$

e. $Q - f(C_P, C_M, H_P, H_M, K_0) = 0$

The multiplier, λ, reflects the marginal cost of output for a given Q. Once λ has been determined, the firm sets marginal cost equal to price to determine the amount that it wants to sell.

We are more interested in the first problem here—how to produce a given amount of output—so let us consider some scenarios. They relate to various technologies. The goal of this section is to translate verbal statements about the way production works at the firm into a more rigorous formulation. We repeat the discussions presented in the previous section here.

Scenario 1: Production Independent Across Workers

My firm is a salesforce and that's it. We do selling for small manufacturers who do not want to have their own sales team. Each salesperson works independently of every other one. Most of the time, they are not even selling the same product nor working for the same manufacturer as their fellow salesperson.

This is a very small operation. I put the business together myself, and I don't think that anyone else could have done it. Most of the business depends on my personal contacts. The one disadvantage is that I can't expand very much. No one can substitute for me and my time is limited. This firm is very bottom heavy. It consists of all salespeople plus me as manager. What kind of worker should I hire?

This manager is describing a situation in which workers operate independent of one another. The lack of interaction is best captured by an **additive production** function, but there is one additional feature: The manager's time cannot be expanded, if we take his story literally. The following production function captures the essential features:

(A.24)
$$Q = [aC_P + bH_P]^z$$

where $0 < z < 1$

The z parameter reflects the fact that the manager's time is limited. Additional units of input increase total output, but at a decreasing rate because the manager gets stretched more thinly. Of course, the values of a, b, and z are not necessarily known to the manager, but they can be estimated. For now, ignore the issues of estimation and let us simply consider the effects of various parameters on the firm's choice.

Because individuals work independently, the firm should hire either college grads or high school grads, but not both. This can be seen using mathematics as well. In this case,

$$\frac{\partial f}{\partial C_P} = aZ[aC_P + bH_P]^{z-1}$$

$$\frac{\partial f}{\partial b_p} = bZ[aC_P + bH_P]^{z-1}$$

(A2.3a) and (A2.3c) taken together imply that

$$\frac{a}{b} = \frac{W_C}{W_H}$$

but a, b, W_C, and W_H are all given exogenously. This means that the first-order conditions cannot be met. Instead, a corner solution is implied. Either $C_P > 0$ and $H_P = 0$, or $H_P > 0$ and $C_P = 0$, or both $C_P = 0$ and $H_P = 0$.

If $\frac{a}{b} > \frac{W_C}{W_H}$, then college grad labor should be used. If not, then high school grads should be used.

In the discussion in the text, we were told that in 1990, $W_C = \$21,648$ and $W_H = \$14,404$. We also know that the output of the average college grad was $\$1.88$ million and the output of the average high school grad was $\$1.48$ million. Suppose we also knew that the data on college grads came from the first half of 1990, when only college grads were employed in sales, and the data for high school grads came from the second half of 1990, when only high school grads were employed in sales. Suppose further that there were 100 college grads working and 150 high school grads working.

Then we know that

$$aC_P{}^z = (\$1.88 \text{ million}) \, C_P$$

which is equivalent to

$$a(100)^z = (1,880,000) \, (100)$$

We also know that

$$bH_P{}^z = (\$1.48 \text{ million}) \, H_P$$

which is equivalent to

$$b(150)^z = (1,480,000) \, (150)$$

We are trying to determine a and b, but do not have enough information yet to obtain them. In addition, we know that when 50 college grads are used along with 50 high school grads, total sales were $\$180$ million.

Then
$$(50a + 50b)^z = \$180,000,000$$
From this, we now have three equations and three unknowns. The solution to these equations is

$$a = 2.009 \text{ million}$$
$$b = 1.591 \text{ million}$$
$$z = .986 \text{ million}$$

The ratio of productivity among college grads relative to high school grads is

$$\frac{2.009}{1.591} = 1.26$$

The ratio of wages, $W_C/W_H = 1.50$ in 1990. Thus, in this case, college grads are too expensive relative to their output to be used in sales.

Scenario 2: Workers' Productivity Depends on the Skills of Other Workers

This firm is engaged in manufacturing small appliances. We find it better to have a combination of worker types. Although the high school grads are cheaper and more cost effective in the short run, we find that we can't keep their skill levels up without some college grads around. . . . So we like to use both kinds of workers. No managers other than me are necessary. The problem is that I'm not sure about the appropriate balance.

This firm's production might be modeled as

(A2.5) $$Q = zC_P^a H_P^b$$

The data are provided in Table A2.1.

If production is given by (A2.5), then by taking logs of both sides, the equation can be written as

(A2.6) $$\ln Q = \ln z + + a\ln C_P + b\ln H_P$$

This is a standard linear equation where the dependent variable is $\ln Q$, and the independent variables are $\ln C_p$ and $\ln H_p$. Any personal computer spreadsheet program can perform the appropriate analysis. Table A2.2 contains a printout of one such program.

The data are fed in and they form the first four columns of Table A2.2. The logs of columns 2–4 are taken and appear as columns 5–7. A regression of column 7 ($\ln Q$) on columns 5 and 6 ($\ln C_p$, $\ln H_p$, respectively) is run and the results are reported at the bottom of the table.

The coefficients obtained in Table A2.2 imply

(A2.7) $$Q = 2.51 \, C_P^{.59} \, H_P^{.27}$$

(Remember that $z = 2.51$, since $\ln z = .92$.)

TABLE A2.1
EXAMPLE 2 FOR CHAPTER 2

		Data	
Year	C_P	H_P	Q
1975	90	189	143.3884
1976	93	187	145.7714
1977	96	185	148.0994
1978	99	183	150.3739
1979	102	181	152.5964
1980	105	179	154.7681
1981	108	177	156.8902
1982	111	175	158.9637
1983	114	173	160.9897
1984	117	171	162.9691
1985	120	169	164.9027
1986	123	167	166.7912
1987	126	165	168.6354
1988	129	163	170.4360
1989	132	161	172.1934
1990	135	159	173.9082

From this, it is straightforward to answer the manager's question.

The cost minimization algebra given (A2.3a and A2.3c) implies that

$$\frac{H_P}{C_P} = \frac{bW_C}{aW_H}$$

using the estimates of *a, b* from Table A2.2, and the 1990 wages, this implies that

$$\frac{H_P}{C_P} = \frac{(.27)(10.25)}{(.59)(6.82)} = .69$$

Thus, the desired ratio of high school labor to college labor is .69. There should be about 70 percent as many high school grads as college grads. But in 1990, this firm had more high school grads working than college grads. Although college grads are more expensive, their higher productivity, coupled with the positive spillovers that they provide for high school grads, makes them more valuable, so the firm is underutilizing their talents. Profits would rise if more college labor were used.

Note that nothing fancy was required to perform this analysis. Data on output and employment, coupled with wage data, are sufficient to determine whether college or high school labor should be used.

TABLE A2.2
SPREADSHEET ANALYSIS

1 Year	2 C_P	3 H_P	4 Q	5 $\ln C_P$	6 $\ln H_P$	7 $\ln Q$
1975	90	189	143.3884	4.49981	5.241747	4.965557
1976	93	187	145.7714	4.532599	5.231109	4.98204
1977	96	185	148.0994	4.564348	5.220356	4.997884
1978	99	183	150.3739	4.59512	5.209486	5.013125
1979	102	181	152.5964	4.624973	5.198497	5.027797
1980	105	179	154.7681	4.65396	5.187386	5.041928
1981	108	177	156.8902	4.682131	5.17615	5.055546
1982	111	175	158.9637	4.70953	5.164786	5.068676
1983	114	173	160.9897	4.736198	5.153292	5.08134
1984	117	171	162.9691	4.762174	5.141664	5.093561
1985	120	169	164.9027	4.787492	5.129899	5.105356
1986	123	167	166.7912	4.812184	5.117994	5.116743
1987	126	165	168.6354	4.836282	5.105945	5.127739
1988	129	163	170.4360	4.859812	5.09375	5.13836
1989	132	161	172.1934	4.882802	5.081404	5.148618
1990	135	159	173.9082	4.905275	5.068904	5.158528

Regression Output:

Constant	0.919139
Std Error of the Est	9.19E−06
R Squared	.9999999
No. of Observations	16
Degrees of Freedom	13
Coefficients for $\ln C_P, \ln H_P$:	0.589387 0.265994
	0.000235 0.000550
Std Err of Coef	

Scenario 3: Independent Production Across Workers— Workers Interact with Capital

The third example comes from a firm that has recently changed the amount of machinery that it is using. This is a modification of the simpler example used earlier in the text.

The firm has installed expensive new equipment and has thereby changed its technology. It must decide which quality of worker is most cost-effective to run the new machinery. The manager's discussion follows:

> We produce automobile parts. Each machine must be tended by one worker. We recently upgraded our machinery and the new equipment produces output at exactly twice the rate as the previous machines using high school grads. Of course, they cost

us much more as well. We rent our machines from another company. The old machines cost us $100 per day rental, whereas the new machines cost us $160 per day rental. The college labor is more productive on both kinds of machine than the high school labor, but college grads cost us more. We found that in the past, we were indifferent between using college and high school labor. The cost per unit of output was the same, because the 150 percent higher wages of college grads offset their cost savings through higher productivity. Should we go for college grads now?

Since output is independent across workers, we want to choose the worker/machine combination that minimizes cost. We can use fewer machines if we hire college labor for any given level of output.

We know that with the old machines, the firm was indifferent between college and high school grads. This means that cost per unit of output is given by

$$\frac{100 + 8W_C}{Q_C} = \frac{100 + 8W_H}{Q_H}$$

where Q_C, Q_H are the daily output levels of the typical college and high school grads, respectively and each individual works eight hours a day. Cost per unit of output is the same whether college or high school grads are used.

Since $W_C = 10.25$ and $W_H = 6.82$, this means that with the old equipment

$$\frac{Q_C}{Q_H} = 1.18$$

After the new equipment is installed, cost per unit of output using high school labor is:

$$\frac{160 + 8W_H}{2Q_H}$$

Cost per unit using college labor is:

$$\frac{160 + 8W_C}{2Q_H(1.18)}$$

since $Q_C = 1.18Q_H$.

College grads should be used *iff*

$$\frac{160 + 8W_C}{2Q_H(1.18)} < \frac{160 + 8W_H}{2Q_H}$$

or *iff*

$$\frac{160 + 8W_C}{160 + 8W_H} < 1.18$$

Substituting $W_C = 10.25$ and $W_H = 6.82$ into $\dfrac{160 + 8W_C}{160 + 8W_H}$ yields 1.13, which is less than 1.18, so only college grads should be used.

College grads are only 18 percent more productive and cost 50 percent more than the high school grads, yet the calculation says that college grads should be used. Why? The answer is that the productivity of each worker is not independent of the machine. When we use high school labor to produce a single given level of output, we must combine them with more machines than when we use college labor. To obtain one additional unit using high school labor requires that $1/Q_H$ more machines be used. To obtain one additional unit using college labor requires that $1/Q_c$ more machines be used. Since $Q_C > Q_H$ and since machines are expensive, it pays to use the higher-quality labor and conserve on machines. Put differently, in order to produce any level of output, it is better to use college grads and fewer machines than to use more machines and high school grads. As capital becomes relatively more expensive, it becomes more profitable to use higher-skilled labor. It makes no sense to waste an expensive machine on someone who cannot operate it efficiently.

One final point: Note that the conditions in (A2.3) do not depend in any way on the overall profitability of the firm. The firm should not go with lower-cost labor simply because it is encountering bad times. The only factors that affect the choice between high-skilled and less-skilled labor are wage rates and productivity levels. Choosing the wrong kind of labor only makes the situation worse, whether times are good or bad.

HIRING THE RIGHT PEOPLE

3

$\mathcal{T}$he computer firm introduced at the beginning of chapter 2 has performed an analysis and has determined that it would like to hire skilled workers because they are more cost-effective. Now the firm must figure out how to attract applicants and which ones to hire. The firm is small relative to the total pool of applicants, so it must select a strategy that will induce the best people to come to the firm at the minimum possible cost. Excerpts from a meeting held to discuss the issue follow:

BENTHAM: I think we need to advertise a high wage. That way we get a large group of skilled workers applying and we can choose the best ones.

JEVONS: Great idea, but that will cost a lot. I prefer to offer low wages and then pay more to those who work out for us.

FISHER: Both points make sense. How about if we just require some skill level in our ad, and then pay what's required to hire the people?

JEVONS: Not a bad idea, but the advantage to using my approach is that by paying more only to those who work out, we don't have to pay much to those we end up firing.

BENTHAM: But who will work for such a low starting wage? Only the dregs who can't get hired elsewhere. If we want top-quality people, we need to pay them well right from the start.

FISHER: Perhaps, but if we offer a high wage, we'll get everyone in the world applying for a job. That will clog our personnel office and waste too much of their time. Beyond that, how will we know which ones to hire from such a large group?

JEVONS: I see your point Irving, but if we insist on some credential like a college degree we may be eliminating good applicants.

BENTHAM: Not only that. College people cost more than other well-qualified workers without college. I think that we can do just as well if we are careful in our hiring procedure.

JEVONS: That's a big if. If we knew who we wanted to hire, we wouldn't have to advertise. What makes you think our personnel office will be able to pick out the right ones? That's why my approach is better. I still think we need to start by paying low and then give raises only to those we like.

FISHER: What about paying some kind of piece rate? Then if they don't perform for us, they don't earn much.

BENTHAM: Well, there is something to that. I recently saw a study that showed that workers paid piece rates are more productive than those paid a straight salary. I think the piece rate idea is great, especially if it can turn bad workers into good ones.

JEVONS: I'm not convinced that paying a piece rate is a better approach than the one that I suggested. We are still going to want to get rid of the bad workers, no matter what we pay them.

A number of questions were raised in the preceding discussion. They include:

- How can a firm cut down on undesirable applicants, and how can it reduce interview costs?

- What can be done to discourage inappropriate workers from applying for the job?

- Should a high or low salary be offered when recruiting workers?

- Should the focus be on starting pay or some other variable?

- Should credentials be required when hiring?

- Are there advantages to paying piece rates? Why do firms that pay piece rates have higher levels of productivity?

- Should a probationary period be used?

- If so, how much should workers receive during probation?

- How large a raise should workers receive if they make it through the probationary period?

- Who should be retained after probation?

SELF-SELECTION

◆ ◆ ◆ ◆ ◆

The managers at the computer firm were worried about being stuck with the wrong kind of employees. Their entire discussion centered around ways to weed out undesirable workers and select only the most desirable. Also of concern was how to induce only the appropriate applicants to come to the personnel office in the first place.

One strategy suggested was to offer a high wage, thereby generating a large pool of applicants, and select only those best suited for the job. Although this idea has some merit, it also has its drawbacks. At a minimum, simply offering a high wage without any stipulations will encourage too many low-quality applicants to apply for the job. Thus, the personnel office will indeed be flooded by a large number of applicants, only a small proportion of whom are suited to the firm's needs. An even worse consequence is that some of the undesirable workers will slip through the screening process and actually get hired. During the time they work for the firm, they can cause major problems, disrupting output and costing the firm wages not justified by their productivity. Some may even manage to disguise their ineptitude, remaining with the firm for a very long time. These problems, sometimes severe, are faced by every firm that does a significant amount of hiring.

The computer firm is plagued by the problem of self-selection, and in particular, **adverse selection.** It is often said, "People are our most important asset." If true, having the right workers is an important ingredient to the success of an organization—it can entirely change the face of an organization. Adverse selection results when the *wrong* kinds of workers are attracted to the firm because of a particular policy that the firm uses. But a number of approaches can help to mitigate the effects of adverse selection. Although none is perfect, every firm must use some combination of these methods to ensure that it ends up with the proper work force for its needs. Let us consider a few possibilities in detail.

Screening

The manager Fisher suggested that credentials be used to weed out the unqualified workers. Implicit in this suggestion are a couple of assumptions. First and foremost is that one's ability to obtain a credential is highly correlated with one's performance on the job. Indeed, this was one of the concerns raised by another manager. Obtaining a college degree may signal a high underlying level of ability. The question, however, is whether it correlates well with the ability to do the particular job. In chapter 8, we will discuss the signaling or screening hypothesis in greater detail. For our purposes here, it is sufficient to point out that education may be used as a proxy for productivity on the job, but in some situations it is a poor one.

A second assumption is that the additional cost of the educated person is justified by the additional productivity. This is the essence of the discussion in chapter

2. One of the concerns there, also relevant here, is that highly educated people may not have the most relevant skills for a particular job. Still, education or some other credential process may be useful in sorting out low-quality workers. When are these assumptions likely to hold? The following list offers conditions under which it makes sense to require credentials of applicants:

1. The ability to perform well in school and to perform well on the job are highly correlated. This is more likely to be true in white-collar jobs than in blue-collar jobs.
2. If the difference in wages between educated workers and less educated workers is not very great, small differences in educational attainment will signal large differences in ability.
3. Obtaining the relevant credential is relatively easy for well-qualified workers, but very difficult for poorly qualified workers.

The first condition, that obtaining a credential and job performance be closely related, holds for some jobs and not for others. For example, it would make no sense to require a college degree for a job whose primary requirement is physical strength. Other "credentials" are much more highly correlated with physical strength than are college degrees. For example, physical size and weight per inch of height might correlate well with strength. It is not necessary that the *credential* involve formal schooling. The objective is to select the credential that best signals a worker's ability in a particular job.

The second condition, that when jobs do not pay more for credentials, the credentialed workers tend to be significantly more capable, can be explained as follows. Suppose that the credential in question is a college degree. If the wage that college graduates receive in a particular job is only slightly more than the wage high school graduates receive, then only those who find it easy to obtain college degrees will get them. Those who find it easy will also tend to be the most capable in the group. Thus, when wage differentials between highly educated and less educated are small, then small differences in education will signal large differences in underlying ability. It is under these circumstances that credentials are the most accurate signal of differences in raw ability. When the pay premium for a degree is large, even some not-so-able people can be induced to get the degree.

The third condition is that a credential be cheap to obtain for qualified workers but expensive to obtain for unqualified workers. When this conclusion is satisfied, a credential is very likely to signal relevant differences in ability. For example, suppose that a firm wants to hire an accountant. It is not very difficult for a qualified accountant to pass the CPA exam, but it is virtually impossible for someone with no training in accounting to pass. The CPA exam, while onerous, does not impose huge cost on individuals who have already obtained the relevant training. Thus, using the CPA exam as a screen will effectively sort between qualified and unqualified applicants.

On the other hand, a credential that is extremely expensive for all workers to obtain will not do well in sorting workers by their characteristics. For example, suppose that a firm is interested in hiring a public relations manager. The firm believes that important qualifications for the job are the ability to speak to people in a friendly, but coherent way, and the ability to think quickly on one's feet. It is likely to be true that talk-show hosts possess both skills. Thus requiring all applicants to have talk-show host experience might seem likely to produce a well-qualified applicant pool. This is not a good screen, because it is so expensive and difficult a credential to obtain that very few of the qualified applicants will have it. In order for a credential to be effective, it must be the case that most of the qualified applicants possess the credential and that most of the unqualified applicants do not. If a very small subset of the qualified applicants possesses the credential, or if the vast majority of unqualified individuals possess the credential, then that credential will not be an effective hiring screen.

Contingent Contracts

One of the most effective ways to induce the appropriate people to apply for a job is to structure compensation in a way that is attractive to highly skilled workers, but less attractive to unskilled workers. Piece-rate pay is the most basic form of contingent contract. Workers who are paid a piece rate are compensated on the basis of output. Compensation is strictly contingent on the amount of output produced. If a worker does not produce any output in a given pay period, it is reflected in the worker's compensation. If the worker produces a great deal in that period, then compensation reflects the positive performance.

Piece rate pay induces the appropriate workers to come to the firm under a variety of circumstances. Consider the case of a firm producing kloycks (a very useful contraption made from violin bows and Swiss Army knives). Suppose that, as illustrated by Table 3.1, unskilled workers can produce four kloycks per hour, while skilled workers produce six. Suppose further that both unskilled and skilled workers have outside employment options available to them that pay $16 and $20 per hour, respectively. These options can be associated with another job in an established firm or with self-employment. Conceptually, it is perhaps easier to think of the alternatives as self-employment.

TABLE 3.1
OPTIONS FOR SKILLED AND UNSKILLED KLOYCK MAKERS

	Hourly Output of Kloycks	*Hourly Wage—Other Option*
Skilled	6	$20.00
Unskilled	4	$16.00

A piece rate of $3.35 per kloyck will induce skilled workers to apply for the job and unskilled workers to stay away. Since skilled workers earn $6 \times \$3.35$ or $20.10 an hour and unskilled workers would earn $4 \times \$3.35$ or $13.40 an hour, skilled workers are better off working for the kloyck firm than elsewhere. Conversely, unskilled workers are worse off working for the kloyck firm than elsewhere.

Key to this contingent contract is that workers have an accurate assessment of their own output before they start the job. If they do not, then the unskilled might not stay away from the kloyck firm and the skilled might not bother applying. For example, suppose both skilled and unskilled workers believe they can produce six kloycks per hour. There is no piece rate that will induce skilled workers to apply and unskilled workers to stay away. Any piece rate that will induce skilled workers to apply would have to pay them more than $20 an hour. At this level of compensation, the unskilled workers, operating under the mistaken belief about their productivity, will also expect to earn more than $20 an hour. Under these beliefs, both types apply for the job.

Conversely, any piece rate low enough to keep out unskilled workers must necessarily keep out skilled workers. To keep out unskilled workers, the firm would have to offer an effective hourly compensation of less than $16 for six units of output. Since skilled and unskilled erroneously believe that they have the same output per hour—namely six units, skilled workers would also earn less than $16 an hour at the firm, and would therefore opt for their $20 an hour alternative.

The essence of the adverse selection problem, which the managers discussed at the beginning of the chapter, is that workers know more about their own ability levels than firms do. It is under these circumstances that workers will attempt to come to the firm when they know that they simply do not have sufficient talent to do better elsewhere.

A More Sophisticated Contingent Contract

Piece rates compensate a worker on the basis of each period's output, but it is sometimes very costly to attempt to measure a worker's output in any given period. For example, most middle managers at large corporations produce output that does not lend itself well to measurement and is sometimes difficult to even define. It would be virtually impossible to offer piece rate pay to the assistant manager of a personnel department. Although there are obviously measurable aspects to the job, compensating on the basis of those measurable aspects would produce the wrong behavior. For example, if a personnel manager were paid on the number of applicants she screened or the number of individuals she hired, she would have direct incentive to waste the time of many people in the organization. Attracting unqualified applicants and hiring them would serve her well, but it would clearly hurt the company. It is better to evaluate these kinds of workers sporadically, and then perhaps qualitatively rather than quantitatively. If the worker's output exceeds some standard, then the worker is given a particular reward. If the worker's output falls short of the standard, then the worker is denied the reward.

Probation

A concrete application of this kind of reward scheme is the initial probationary period that most organizations impose on new employees. Workers are hired in for a probationary period, say six months. At the end of the probation, successful workers are given permanent assignments and unsuccessful workers are dismissed. Thus, successful workers receive a reward for having completed the job appropriately and unsuccessful workers are denied the reward.

Probationary periods and properly designed compensation schemes can generate the appropriate pool of applicants for a firm. Recall the previous example in which skilled workers produce six units and unskilled workers produce only four units. Given the wages that were available to workers on the outside, the firm's decision to hire the skilled workers was correct, since

$$\text{Skilled} = \frac{\$20/\text{hr}}{6 \text{ Kloycks/hr}} = \$3.33/\text{Kloyck}$$

$$\text{Unskilled} = \frac{\$16/\text{hr}}{4 \text{ Kloycks/hr}} = \$4.00/\text{Kloyck}$$

making it cheaper to use skilled workers than unskilled workers. Thus, the firm's decision to hire skilled workers was appropriate and a probationary period could be used to induce only skilled workers to apply.

The probationary period can be set up as follows: Suppose that a worker is going to be in the labor force for the next 20 years. She can either work at the kloyck firm or she can work at her alternative occupation, which pays $16 or $20, depending on her skill level. Suppose that she plans to work for 2,000 hours per year.

Let us set up a one-year probationary period. After that probation, the worker can either be granted "tenure" so that she continues to be employed throughout the next 19 years or she can be dismissed. If she is dismissed, she goes to her alternative job, where she earns the wage corresponding to her skill level. The goal is to set up a probationary period wage and a post-probation wage such that skilled workers will apply for the job and unskilled workers will not.

The problem, of course, is that detection of unskilled workers is not perfect. To make things simple, let's suppose that skilled workers are always sufficiently able to reveal their quality during the probation period that they never get dismissed inappropriately. Thus, a skilled worker is certain to retain the job, but unskilled workers may or may not be found out. Suppose that P is the probability that an unskilled worker makes it past the probationary period; then $(1 - P)$ is the probability that the unskilled worker is fired at the end of the probationary period. The conditions that must be met are given by

(3.1) $$2000\, W_1 + (2000)(19)W_2 \geq (20)(2000)W_s$$

and

(3.2) $$2000\, W_1 + (P)(2000)(19)W_2 + (1 - P)(19)(2000)W_u < (20)(2000)W_u$$

where W_1 is the wage during the probationary period, W_2 is the wage after probation, W_s is the wage the skilled worker can receive outside, and W_u is the wage that an unskilled worker can receive outside.

Condition 3.1 says that in order to be able to attract skilled workers, they must make more over their 20-year career with the kloyck firm than they do outside. Since they work 2,000 hours per year, their wages during the probationary period are 2,000 times W_1. Over the next 19 years of their career, they earn 2,000 times W_2 for each of the 19 years. Thus, the left side of (3.1) yields earnings in the kloyck firm over the 20-year career. On the right side of (3.1) is the amount that a skilled worker can earn outside over a 20-year career. This is simply 20 years times 2,000 hours per year times the hourly wage rate. The greater-than-or-equal sign simply says that the worker will not come to work making kloycks unless what he receives at the kloyck firm is at least as large as what he receives elsewhere.

Condition 3.2 keeps unskilled workers away from the kloyck firm. It is somewhat more complicated, but the interpretation is still straightforward. The first term reflects the amount that the unskilled worker will make during the probationary period. Once hired, the worker is certain to be given a full year's worth of wages, receiving $2,000 \times W_1$ with certainty. Then the worker can either be given a permanent job or be dismissed. With some probability P, the worker is given a permanent job (P is a number between 0 and 1) and with the probability $(1 - P)$, the worker is terminated at the end of the probationary period. Note that each one of these workers should be terminated for lack of skill. Thus, the wage that workers expect to receive if they are unskilled and come to work for the kloyck firm is given by the left-hand side of (3.2). After the first year, there is a probability P that a worker will be able to continue for 19 years at a wage of W_2. But there is a probability of $(1 - P)$ that the worker will end up spending the next 19 years in the alternative job after being terminated by the kloyck maker. The right-hand side of the expression is simply what an unskilled worker could make by going to the alternative job right from the start. The inequality says that wages should be set such that unskilled workers find that they are better off going elsewhere than coming to work for the kloyck firm.

The goal, then, is to find a probationary wage W_1 and a post-probationary wage W_2 so that Conditions 3.1 and 3.2 are both satisfied. If that is done, then the skilled workers will want to work for the kloyck producer and the unskilled will not apply.

Let us solve this system of two conditions to find some wages that work. First, let us suppose that (3.1) holds with equality. Then we can rewrite (3.1) by rearranging terms as shown

(3.3)
$$W_2 = \frac{20}{19} W_s - \frac{W_1}{19}$$

We obtain W_1 from (3.4)

(3.4)
$$W_1 + (P)(19)\left(\frac{20}{19} W_s - \frac{W_1}{19}\right) + (1 - P)(19)W_u < 20W_u$$

TABLE 3.2
PRE- AND POST-PROBATIONARY WAGES

Given $W_u = 16$; $W_s = 20$

P	W_1	W_2
0	15.99000	20.21105
.01	15.18190	20.25360
.05	11.77947	21.26368
.20	−4.01000	21.26368
1	−∞	∞

Given $W_u = 19$; $W_s = 20$

P	W_1	W_2
0	18.99000	20.05316
.01	18.78798	20.06379
.05	17.93737	20.10856
.20	13.99000	20.31632
1	−∞	∞

After obtaining W_1, we substitute it back into Equation 3.3 to obtain W_2. Although the analysis may seem a bit complicated, the algebra is actually quite straightforward. Some numerical examples are instructive. Examine the data in Table 3.2. In the upper panel of Table 3.2, the wages of unskilled and skilled workers are assumed to be $16 and $20 per hour, respectively. In the lower panel of the table, the unskilled workers are assumed to earn $19 per hour.

Recall that W_1 is the wage during the probationary period and W_2 is the wage that the worker receives in the 19 years after probation. Consider first the line corresponding to $P = .01$. This means that 99 percent of the time unskilled workers are found out during the probationary period and do not get the opportunity to work for the subsequent 19 years. Under these circumstances, paying a wage of $15.18 per hour during the probationary period and $20.25 after probation will succeed in keeping out unskilled workers while still attracting skilled workers. The reason is that unskilled workers are sufficiently certain that they will be fired.

During the first year, unskilled workers give up about $.82 per hour because they could have received $16 at their alternative job, but instead make only $15.18 while on probation at the kloyck firm. If the unskilled worker is not found out, which happens only 1 in 100 times, she will make $20.25 for the next 19 years, an increase of $4.25 per hour for every year that she continues to work at the kloyck firm. Since the probability of detection is extremely high, the chances of ever earning the $20.25 are very slim for an unskilled worker. To see that this will keep the unskilled workers out, simply plug $15.18 and $20.25 into (3.2). The left-hand side of that expression is equal to $639,994, while the right-hand side equals $640,000. Unskilled workers expect to make $639,994 by working at the kloyck producer, but they can receive $640,000 at their alternative job. Thus, unskilled workers will choose to work at the alternative job. The reverse is true for skilled workers. This can be seen by plugging in the relevant numbers into Condition 3.1. When the wage during the probationary period is $15.18 and the wage after probation is $20.25, the skilled worker receives a total of $800,014 by working at the kloyck firm. He receives exactly $800,000 by working outside as well, so he prefers to work at the kloyck firm.

The same calculation can be done for every row in the top panel of Table 3.2. It will reveal the same thing. When the probability of succeeding is .05, an unskilled worker has a 95 percent chance of being detected during the probationary period and fired. A wage of $11.77 before probation, coupled with $20.43 after probation, will induce unskilled workers to stay away from the firm, but skilled workers will apply. If the probability of detection becomes 100 percent, so that $P = 0$ (i.e., there is no chance that an unskilled worker will succeed in the firm), a wage in period 1 of anything under $16 per hour will do the trick. Since the unskilled workers know that they will not be retained past the first period, paying less than the outside wage is sufficient to discourage them from applying. At a probationary wage of $15.99, a post-probation wage of $20.21 over 19 years will be sufficient to make up for the $4.01 that the skilled worker loses during the probationary period. Therefore, the skilled worker will be willing to apply. When $P = 1$, it is impossible to discourage unskilled workers from applying while still encouraging skilled workers to apply. Since the probability of being detected is zero, unskilled workers and skilled workers are in every respect identical. Any wage sufficiently high to attract a skilled worker will also attract an unskilled worker, and any wage sufficiently low to discourage an unskilled worker will also discourage skilled workers.

The principle illustrated by the first panel of Table 3.2 is that the difference between the probationary wage and the post-probationary wage increases as the probability that unskilled workers will retain their jobs increases. As detection of unskilled workers becomes more difficult, it is necessary to spread out the wages more and more so that unskilled workers are less attracted to the kloyck-producing firm.

Another principle is illustrated by comparing the bottom panel of Table 3.2 with the top panel. The difference between the bottom panel and top panel is that the wage of the unskilled worker in the bottom panel is $19, whereas in the top panel it is $16. Thus, unskilled and skilled workers have more similar outside opportunities in the bottom panel than they do in the top. When this is true, it is easier to separate unskilled workers from skilled workers. Unskilled workers have less to gain by passing themselves off as skilled workers because their outside opportunities are relatively better. When detection is certain, so that $P = 0$, a probationary wage of $18.99 will certainly keep unskilled workers out. They can earn $19 outside and they know that there is no chance that they will succeed past the probationary period. Any wage less than $19 prevents the unskilled from applying to the firm. By paying skilled workers slightly more than $20.05 an hour in the post-probationary period, they can be induced to apply because the extra $.05-

plus per hour in the post-probationary period covers the $1 per hour during the probationary period relative to what they can earn outside. It is still true within this panel that as the probability of surviving the probationary period rises for unskilled workers, the wage spread between unskilled workers and skilled workers must go up. But at any given probability, the spread is always greater between probationary wage and nonprobationary wage in the upper panel than it is in the lower panel.

The probationary scheme is likely to be most successful when the probability of detecting an unskilled worker is high and when unskilled workers earn wages that are close to those of skilled workers. When those conditions are not met, the spread between the probationary wage and post-probationary wage may be too high. For example, consider the top panel of Table 3.2. Suppose unskilled workers have a 20 percent chance of making it past the probationary period. In order to discourage them from applying, the wage during the probationary period must be −$4.01 per hour. All workers would actually have to *pay* the firm $4.01 per hour during the entire year of the probationary period. This would amount to a payment of about $8,000 during the first year of employment. Of course, no positive earnings would be received during that period. Workers would not only have to finance their own consumption out of savings or borrowing, they would also have to pay the equivalent of an $8,000 tuition fee to the firm. Although this would discourage unskilled workers, it might also discourage skilled workers unable to borrow the funds during the probationary year. Were they able to support themselves, the post-probationary wage of $21.26 would be high enough to make up for the lost earnings during the first year. But again, this would require skilled workers to borrow against future earnings, which, for a variety of reasons, is unlikely.

Because a probationary system induces unskilled workers to go elsewhere, firms that do not insist on probationary periods will tend to attract more unskilled workers. But unskilled workers receive lower wages, so firms that hire these workers can earn profits as well. Some firms are well suited to using unskilled workers at low wages, while other firms are better suited to using skilled workers at higher wages.

The above discussion leads us to the following conclusions:

- When a firm wants to induce skilled workers to apply and unskilled workers to stay away, and the firm cannot identify the skill level of the worker before employment, a probationary period can be an effective tool for discouraging unskilled applicants. The wage during the probationary period can be set low enough to keep unskilled workers out; the wage in the post-probationary period is high enough to induce skilled workers to come to the firm.

- The difference between the probationary and the post-probationary wage decreases as the probability that an unskilled worker will be found out increases. When it is easier for the firm to determine that a worker is inappropriately matched, a smaller difference in wages between the probation-

©Jim Unger. HERMAN is printed with permission from Laughingstock Licensing Inc., Ottawa, Canada.

ary period and post-probationary period is necessary. When detection is very likely, even a small wage differential will keep unskilled workers from applying.

- As the difference between the skilled and unskilled workers' outside opportunities declines, it becomes easier to discourage unskilled workers from applying. When unskilled workers have almost the same wage as skilled workers outside, the difference between the probationary wage and post-probationary wage can be small.

◆ ◆ ◆ ◆ ◆ MONITORING COSTS AND WORKERS SORTING IN MORE DETAIL

Instead of making an explicit choice about the kind of worker a firm would like to hire, the firm can simply offer to pay a piece rate, paying workers strictly on the basis of their output. The disadvantage of using a piece rate is that output must be closely measured and the measurement of output is sometimes costly.

Who bears the cost of measuring output? This depends on whether or not the information obtained about the worker's output is useful elsewhere. Let us assume that the information is completely general, so that a worker who is revealed to be highly skilled can use that "certification" elsewhere to obtain a job as a skilled worker. Under these circumstances, the worker will be required to pay for the costs of certification. The reason is that another kloyck producer, with the same technology, can take advantage of the producer who bears the cost of measurement. If the first kloyck producer pays to ascertain the workers' skill level, then the second kloyck firm will have an advantage. The second firm can merely wait for the results and hire away the skilled workers. Since the first firm pays for evaluating the raw recruits, the second firm, which does not bear this cost, has higher profits. Of course, then every firm would want to be like the second firm and no measurement would ever take place.

Measurement can occur, however, if the worker bears the cost of measurement, say by accepting a lower wage. Skilled workers are willing to bear the cost because they know that their total compensation, which is based on output, will be higher as a result.

To see this, let us consider an example. The activity that I have in mind comes directly from a job that I held as a young lad. During each summer, apricot farmers in the San Francisco suburb of Los Altos needed to pick and cut their apricots, which were dried and sold to local fruit packers. The farmers hired neighborhood kids and paid 50 cents for each tray of apricots that they cut. My friends and I often worked for a couple of weeks during the summer, helping the local economy and boosting our meager budgets for the coming school year. Of course, dexterity varied from kid to kid. Some could cut as many as ten trays per day, while others could cut no more than four. The best cutters would take home $5 per day, whereas the worst cutters would take home only $2 per day.[1] After a while, the farmer would decide that the slower cutters were not worth the bother of counting trays and issuing payment, so he'd only keep the faster kids.

An alternative scheme would have worked as well or better. There were a number of farms in the neighborhood, but two will suffice for this illustration. Suppose that Jones offers piecework. He pays 50 cents per tray, but subtracts a fixed amount of $1 per day from every worker to cover the cost of counting trays. Smith simply pays $3 per day to each of his cutters, irrespective of the amount produced. Thus, Smith pays a straight salary, whereas Jones pays a piece rate. Who will choose to work at each firm?

Consider Tommy Tops, who can cut ten trays per day. If he works for Jones, he earns $5 minus the $1 fee and takes home $4 per day. This is clearly preferable to the $3 that he would make from Smith. Thus, Tommy works for Jones.

Clumsy Carl, on the other hand, can cut only four trays per day. If he works for Jones he'll earn $2 minus the $1 per day fee, which comes out to just $1 per day. Carl can do better by working for Smith. Smith offers each worker a fixed salary of $3 per day, which is $2 more than Clumsy can earn at the Jones farm. Mediocre Mike can cut eight trays per day. If he works for Jones, he earns $4 − $1, or $3 for the day. If he works for Smith he earns $3. Mike earns the same at either farm.

Figure 3.1 illustrates the choices. The horizontal axis lists the number of trays cut per day and the vertical axis lists the pay that each worker receives at either the Smith or Jones farm. The Smith farm pays $3 per day irrespective of output, so the pay line is horizontal at $3. The Jones farm pays $1 per day to Carl, $3 per day to Mike, and $4 per day to Tom. The Jones line is upward sloping, reflecting higher pay to more productive workers—that is, piece rate pay. Mike is indifferent between the farms because the two pay lines intersect when trays = 8, which happens to be his

[1]Although these numbers seem very low, they were paid in 1960 when prices and wages were much lower than they are today.

FIGURE 3.1
PIECE RATE VERSUS SALARY

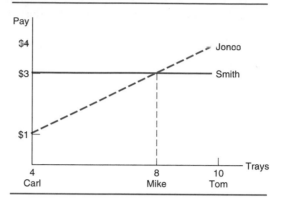

output level. Anyone with output greater than Mike's eight trays prefers Jones, because the Jones pay line lies above the Smith pay line for trays greater than eight, but anyone with output less than Mike's eight trays prefers Smith because the Smith pay line lies above the Jones pay line for trays fewer than eight.

How does each farm make money? Jones gets the best workers, but he pays them more. The additional pay is made up for by the additional output. Furthermore, Jones must monitor his workers' output, which is costly. He reduces their pay just enough to cover the cost of monitoring and loses no money by measuring his workers.

Smith doesn't bother to measure output. He knows that he will be getting the poorer workers, but low wages, coupled with the absence of measurement costs, counterbalance their low productivity. Rather than hire a supervisor to count trays, Smith merely instructs the cutters to place their filled trays in the drying area. He attracts workers whose output varies between four and eight trays, yielding an average of six trays per worker. His payment of $3 per day is equivalent to paying an average of 50 cents per tray, exactly what Jones pays after being compensated for his costs of measurement. Thus, Smith and Jones pay the same amount per tray. Both farms presumably would have remained in business until the early 1980s, when their land became so valuable for housing that they could no longer afford to use it to grow apricots.

This example leads us to the following conclusion:

Firms that pay piece rates generally attract higher quality workers than those that pay straight salaries, but the firms that pay piece rates pay higher average wages and may bear greater monitoring costs.

In the previous example, the piece rate attracted the better-quality worker because the workers with the most output had the most to gain from pay based on output. Lower-quality workers preferred not to be measured, especially when it meant that they had to give up $1 per day to do it. A worker having low output

TABLE 3.3
AGGREGATE OUTPUT

	Piecework Firms	Salary Firms	Economy
Before Law	.5 (50)	.5 (25)	37.5/worker
After Burnt Law	(1) (25)	0	25/worker
After Bridges Law	0	(1) (50)	50/worker

would just as soon leave that fact undiscovered. Firms that pay straight salaries attract lower-quality workers, but they can earn a profit just as easily as firms that pay piece rates to attract high-quality workers.

Indeed, the measurement of worker output, at least in this example, was actually wasteful. When effort is not affected by measurement, then spending $1 per worker to measure output is simply a waste of society's resources.

The following apocryphal story makes the point. The numbers are merely illustrative, and should not be given much weight. Two senators, Bob Burnt and Bill Bridges, are presented with data from the Bureau of Labor Statistics (BLS). See Table 3.3.

The table is read as follows. Before any law is passed, .5 of the firms[2] in the economy are piecework firms, each producing an average output of $50 per hour per worker. Thus, the entry in the "Before Law" row, "Piecework Firms" column is .5 (50), signifying that in half of the economy, workers have an average output of $50. The other half are firms that pay salaries and whose average worker output is $25. Thus, the entry in the "Before Law" row, "Salary Firms" column is .5 (25), signifying that in half of the economy, workers have an average output of $25. The average output for the economy as a whole is

$$.5(\$50) + .5(\$25) = \$37.50$$

as shown in the "Before Law" row, "Economy" column.

Senator Burnt notices that piecework firms are more productive than salary firms and infers that incentives generated by piece rate pay are important. His reaction is to put forward a bill that requires all firms to pay piece rates.

Senator Bridges, on the other hand, has his staffers do some further investigation. Bridges finds out that the highest-paid worker in the piecework firm earns three times as much as the lowest-paid worker there. He also learns that all workers in the salary firm are paid exactly the same amount. Favoring equality, Bridges proposes a law requiring all firms to pay straight salaries.

Burnt's staffers then discover that, while Bridges's data are correct, they failed to notice that the lowest paid worker in the piecework firm earns $25, and the highest paid worker in the piecework firm earns $75. So, while it is true that the highest paid worker in the piecework firm earns three times as much as the lowest paid worker, and it is also true that every worker in the salary firm earns the same

_____

[2]Assume, for simplicity, that all firms are of equal size.

amount, there is no worker in the piecework firm who earns less than any worker in the salary firm. Equality in the salary firm, Burnt concludes, is achieved only by reducing everyone to the lowest possible level.

Senator Bridges's bill seems absurd, since everyone in the salary firm earns the same amount, but everyone in the piecework firm, except for the lowest paid worker, earns more than every worker in the salary firm. Yet there is an interpretation of the data under which his bill would increase output, albeit for a reason that was not in the thoughts of the senator. In a nutshell, if the reason that salary firms have lower output workers is that they attract poorer quality workers, and not that piece rates motivate workers to produce more, then elimination of piecework firms would make the economy better off. To see this, consider the following scenario.

Suppose that measurement costs are $25 per worker per hour and that workers have different ability levels. The lowest-quality worker produces zero, while the highest quality worker produces $100 per hour.

Applying the earlier discussion, suppose that salary firms offer $25 per hour. Suppose further that it costs $25 per hour to measure the output of workers in the piecework firm. Then workers who had the ability to produce more than $50 per hour would go to piecework firms. They would earn their output minus $25 per hour measurement cost, resulting in pay greater than $25 per hour. Since the salary firm pays only $25 per hour, these high-output workers do better by going to the piecework firm. Those workers with ability levels that result in output less than $50 would choose the salary firms. At the salary firm, their compensation is $25 per hour. At the piecework firm, they earn their output minus $25 per hour for measurement cost. For workers with output less than $50, this results in an hourly wage of less than $25. The marginal worker who produces $50 per hour would be indifferent between the piecework firm and the salary firm. At the piecework firm, that worker can earn $50 minus the $25 cost of measurement, or $25 per hour. At the salary firm, the worker can earn $25 per hour. All workers with higher ability prefer the piecework firm. All workers with lower ability prefer the salary firm.[3]

Before the law, 50 percent of the work force was employed at the piecework firm. The average output of workers in the piecework firm was $50, consisting of $75 average output minus $25 for measurement cost per hour. At the salary firm, which employed 50 percent of the work force, the average output was $25. Therefore, over the whole economy, the average output per worker was $37.50.

After the law, every worker is required to work at the piecework firm. The average output for the economy is $50 (since worker output is distributed evenly between 0 and $100). From that $50 average, $25 must be subtracted for measurement costs. The average net output is $25 per worker in the piece rate sector, where 100 percent of the work force now works. No one works in the salary sector, so the average for the economy is then $25 per worker. The law has reduced output from $37.50 per worker to $25 per worker. The reason is that before the law only 50 percent of the work force was being measured, at a cost of $25 per

[3]If the distribution of worker ability is uniform between 0 and 100, the average output in the salary firm will be $25, which is equal to the wage paid.

hour. Now 100 percent of the work force is being measured. Under this scenario, ability is given, so paying a piece rate in no way changes output. Again under this scenario, output per worker does not change when moving to an all-piece rate economy, so total output for the entire economy does not change. Therefore, average output per worker remains at $50 per worker. Moving half the workers from salaries to piece rate pay means that more resources are now wasted to measure output. Measurement under this scenario does nothing to improve productivity and is merely a social waste.[4] Under the all-piece-rates scenario, individuals have an incentive to identify themselves as high ability, since this increases their compensation, but the verification that is done in no way affects their actual output. In this sense, it is a social cost.

The piecework firm merely serves to redistribute high wages to more able workers from less able workers. Given our original scenario, if all firms were required to pay a straight salary, as is shown in the final row of the table, then society would actually be better off. As before, average output for the economy is $50 per worker, but since no measurement occurs net output is also $50. The law proposed by Senator Bridges would actually improve output, in addition to assisting wage equality.

Few economists believe that the conditions of this example hold. Specifically, it is difficult to accept that paying a piece rate, which is based on output, will not generate incentives to put forth more effort.

The point of this exercise, rather, is to show that even in the absence of any incentive effects, piecework firms will tend to have more able workers because the most able workers choose to work at piecework firms. Ignoring this point can lead to serious misinterpretations of data, and can even result in a firm making the wrong personnel decisions.

The senatorial example generalizes to the industrial environment. Rather than comparing piecework firms to salary firms in the overall economy, we could just as well have compared two divisions in a particular corporation, one paying piece rates and the other salaries. After looking at the output numbers, a vice-president at the head office might infer that the piece rate compensation scheme actually causes workers in the first division to produce at higher levels of productivity when, in fact, the observed differences in productivity reflect nothing more than a sorting of the most able workers to the piece rate division and least able workers to the salary division. If this is the case, then switching the firm to straight piece rates from a mixture of piece rate and salaried compensation would actually lower profits as additional measurement costs were imposed.

Of course, this ignores any beneficial incentive effects derived from piece rate compensation schemes. This assumption that effort is not affected by compensation structure is erroneous in almost all work environments. Modifying the assumption could very well imply that moving to piece rates would increase profit and the firm's productivity. If paying a piece rate actually increased workers' pro-

---

[4]This result is akin to the signaling results that will be discussed in chapter 6. There, individuals have incentives to invest in education to distinguish themselves from other individuals, even if the education is not, in and of itself, productive.

VALUEJET

◆ ◆ ◆ ◆ ◆ ◆ ◆ ◆ ◆

When ValueJet began operation in 1993, one of the most important decisions the company faced was how to hire, motivate and compensate employees. As a low-cost carrier with an uncertain future it was natural for ValueJet to use a probation system. New hires at ValueJet were employed through a temporary service for the first 90 days. After the trial period was up, employees who made the grade were asked to become "team members" for ValueJet, which meant they were hired by the company. In the airline industry this practice was unique according to Joe Moody, a ValueJet manager and a ten-year airline industry veteran. Wages largely determined by seniority are a typical feature of compensation system of airlines. At ValueJet, the company took advantage of its compact size and monitored the performance of individual employees instead. Performance-based bonuses were given out instead of raises. The compensation system based primarily on current performance has a piece rate flavor to it.

At first glance, it may appear strange that ValueJet deviates so drastically in its personnel policies from the industry norms. However, there are substantial differences between the low-cost carrier and major airlines in size, target market and mode of operation. As a result the optimal personnel policy of ValueJet should be expected to be different from the industry average.

ValueJet has had its problems. A question that remains is whether the difficulties can be attributed to selecting the wrong quality work force, to a motivation system that emphasizes the short-term, or simply to bad luck.

Source: Kerissa Hollis, "Plane smart: Nofrills approach working for ValueJet." *Memphis Business Journal*, Vol. 16, No 50, p 42.

---

ductivity sufficiently, then moving to a piece rate compensation scheme could make the economy, or any particular firm, more profitable.

Again, there is no way to tell simply from the data presented whether sorting or incentives are generating the differences between salary and piecework firms. In order to ascertain the effect of the compensation scheme, one would have to look at the same workers under two different compensation schemes. If a given worker produced higher levels of output under a well-designed piece rate scheme than under a salary system, there would indeed be evidence to support Senator Burnt's conjecture. Even if piece rate compensation does increase productivity, it must be traded off against the costs associated with monitoring worker performance. In later sections we will say a bit more about monitoring costs and their implications for compensation and incentives.

Sorting

Sorting theories can be used to explain the pattern of male–female wage differentials. Most of the differences between men and women in the labor market are reflected in the distribution of jobs, rather than in the distribution of wages within jobs. Although there may be some residual wage differential within a job, for the most part women get paid less than men because they hold jobs that have lower earnings on average.[5] Even the men in female-dominated jobs receive much less than males with similar skills holding male-dominated jobs. This means that the sorting of males and females into different kinds of jobs is an important part of labor market behavior. The analysis that we have already presented can assist in understanding the data. The following stylized example illustrates, once again, the importance of sorting in the labor market (see Figure 3.2).

Suppose that men and women have exactly the same underlying distribution of ability. Suppose further that there are only two jobs in the economy: a good job, labeled a, and the bad job, labeled b. The following fact is presented: The average ability of women in every job is higher than the average ability of men in

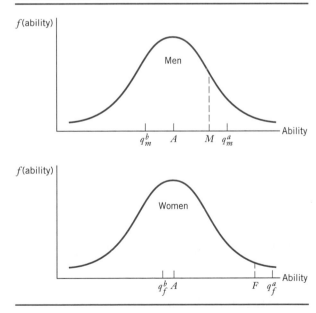

FIGURE 3.2
HYPOTHETICAL DISTRIBUTION OF ABILITY
IN MALE AND FEMALE POPULATIONS

[5]See, for example, Blau (1984) and Groshen (1991).

both jobs a and b, but the average abilities of women and men in the economy as a whole are equal. How can this happen? The answer is quite straightforward. As long as the cutoff ability level to obtain the high-paying job is higher for females than it is for males, it will be the case that women are better in both jobs than men. To see this, consider Figure 3.2. The distributions of ability for both men and women are shown in the top and bottom panels, respectively.

The two distributions are identical. Suppose that a male must have ability level greater than M in order to be selected for the good job and a female must have ability level greater than F in order to be selected for the good job. At this point it is unimportant why the selection criteria are different for males and females. Simply take as given that the cutoffs are different.

All men whose ability exceeds M are in job a. All men whose ability falls short of M are in job b. The average level of ability among men in job a is then given by q_M^a in Figure 3.2. The average level of ability for men in job b is shown as q_M^b in Figure 3.2. For women, the average ability in the high level job a, is q_F^a. Note first that because the cutoff criterion is higher for females than males, the average level of ability among females in job a is higher than the average level of ability for males in job a. Some relatively low-ability males are able to get into job a because they exceed a standard that is set below the female minimum cutoff. But what is also true is that the average level of ability of females in job b exceeds the average level of ability of males in job b. The reason is quite simple. High-ability females are excluded from job a and are thereby forced into job b, bringing up the average quality of females in the b job. Moving a woman whose ability level is just below F to job a drags down the average ability of females in job a. This also lowers the average ability of females in job b, since the woman who was promoted to job a was the highest-ability female previously holding job b. Now, instead of being the highest-ability female in job b, she is the lowest-ability female in job a.

No matter which job women finds themselves in, the average ability of women in the economy remains the same. The same is true for men, so it is quite possible for men and women to have the same average ability in the economy as a whole, in this case equal to A^* in Figure 3.2, but to have different ability levels in each job. Given the cutoff rules, women have the same average ability as men, but are of higher ability in each of the two jobs in the economy!

This example is simply a graphic illustration of the old joke told by Harvard students, where a Harvard undergraduate moves from Harvard to Yale and brings the average up in both places. Incidentally, Yale students tell the identical joke, but reverse the schools. As in the case of the Burnt–Bridges story, worker sorting into different jobs can lead to surprising results. In this case, sorting alone is sufficient to make women better in every job in the economy, even though they have the same ability distribution as men.

An Additional Example of Adverse Selection

The problem that was introduced at the beginning of this chapter was adverse selection, where firms had to weed out the undesirable workers from a large pool of applicants. Sometimes adverse selection takes other forms in the labor market. A real-world example is presented here.

In 1979, the Age Discrimination in Employment Act was modified. The modifications resulted in temporarily raising the mandatory retirement age for tenured professors from 65 to 70, culminating in the elimination of mandatory retirement altogether, starting in 1993. Most universities were concerned that their classrooms would come to be filled by senile, lethargic professors rather than the erudite and energetic ones to which the students had grown accustomed.

In order to induce older professors to leave voluntarily, a number of universities offered buyout plans where professors beyond 55 years of age were offered a sweetened pension if they would retire immediately. A number of professors accepted the offers. Unfortunately, in many cases, the professors who departed were the ones that the universities wanted to keep, while too often those who declined were the ones that the universities had hoped would leave.

The problem was adverse selection. The best professors left because they were able to obtain employment easily at other universities. So, for example, a Nobel Laureate from Stanford could accept the buyout offer, retire from Stanford, and quickly obtain a position at University of California, Berkeley. But the Stanford professor who had stopped producing years ago did not have the same option. He could not afford to accept Stanford's offer because he would be unable to obtain employment elsewhere for anywhere near his current earnings.

Adverse selection of this type was a predictable, but unnecessary consequence of the buyout plan. There are a number of ways that it could have been avoided. Most obvious is to make the buyout offers inversely contingent on current performance. The star professors could have been offered less than the poor performers, which would make the poor performers more likely and the stars less likely to leave. In fact, targeted buyouts, negotiated individually with professors and not based on any explicit formula, is what most universities ended up using to deal with the early retirement problem.

The underlying problem, however, was not the buyout provision, but the wage structure itself. If Stanford found itself losing the good professors and keeping the bad ones, this was because the good ones were relatively underpaid and the bad ones were relatively overpaid. The bad professors were reluctant to leave because they were receiving more at their current jobs than they were worth. When they tried to obtain another job at or near their current wage, they were unable to do so because they were already overpaid. Thus, they could not afford to accept the buyout offer. Conversely, the high-quality professors were underpaid relative to their productivity and were able to obtain new positions at or near their current salary quite easily. Another remedy to the adverse selection problem would have been to adjust Stanford's internal salary structure, spreading it out more so that good professors received much more than bad professors. If the bad professor's salary at Stanford were low enough, they would find the buyout attractive, even if it meant retiring completely.

Salary compression, where the best workers' salaries move closer to the worst workers' salaries, is a common phenomenon. It results in adverse selection in general, because other firms can pick off the underpaid high-quality workers and leave the current firm with the overpaid, low-quality workers. In subsequent chapters, we will discuss salary compression and provide some rationale for its existence. We will point out when salary compression is most likely to hurt profits and when it is most likely to increase profits.

◆ ◆ ◆ ◆ ◆ RECAP

The problem for the firm is to attract the desired workers and weed out those who will not be cost-effective. When a high salary is offered, workers will apply for the job if there is a significant chance that they can survive. This is true even if the workers are unqualified.

There are a number of ways to cut down the number of undesirable applicants. One way to get the right workers is to screen applicants on the basis of some credential that is correlated with job performance. This works well when the credential is easy to obtain for qualified people but difficult to obtain for unqualified ones.

Workers can be induced to join the firm when they are given a contingent contract. Paying a piece rate, where pay depends directly on output, is the most straightforward kind of contingent contract.

Alternatively, workers can be placed on probation. During the probationary period, they receive sufficiently low wages so that only those who believe that they will be successful are willing to apply for the job. A well-crafted probation and post-probation salary schedule can keep undesirable applicants from applying while attracting the desirable ones. This is easiest to achieve when it is difficult for unqualified workers to sneak past the probationary period and when qualified and unqualified workers have similar outside opportunities.

Firms that use probationary periods or pay piece rates attract higher-quality workers than firms that pay straight salaries independent of performance. To attract higher-quality workers, firms must pay correspondingly higher wages.

An understanding of the way that workers sort themselves across firms or jobs is essential for constructing profitable hiring policies. Firms that pay piece rates may have better workers not because the piece rates motivate workers to put forth more effort, but because the better workers choose to work at the piecework firm.

◆ ◆ ◆ ◆ ◆ REFERENCES

Blau, Francine D. "Occupational Segregation and Labor Market Discrimination: A Critical Review." In Barbara Reskin, ed., *Sex Segregation in the Workplace: Trends, Explanations, Remedies*, Washington, DC: National Academy Press, 1984, pp. 117–43.

Groshen, Erica. "The Structure of the Female/Male Wage Differential: Is It Who You Are, What You Do, or Where You Work?" *Journal of Human Resources* 26 (Summer 1991): 457–72.

ADDITIONAL ADVANCED READING   ◆ ◆ ◆ ◆ ◆

O'Flaherty, Brendan, and Aloysius Siow, "Up-or-Out Rules in the Market for Lawyers," *Journal of Labor Economics* 13 (October 1996): 709–35.

APPENDIX   ◆ ◆ ◆ ◆ ◆

In the text, it was claimed that increasing the probability that an unskilled worker could pass the probationary period undetected necessitates a larger spread between the probationary and post-probationary wage. It was also claimed that increasing the difference between skilled and unskilled workers' outside opportunities would necessitate a larger spread between probationary and post-probationary wage. These claims are derived formally here.

W_S = skilled worker's alternative wage

W_u = unskilled worker's alternative wage

W_1 = probationary wage

W_2 = post-probationary wage

P = probability that an unskilled worker passes probation

Suppose, for simplicity of notation, that the probationary period is equal in length to the post-probationary period. Then, in order to attract skilled workers, it is necessary that

(A3.1) $$W_1 + W_2 \geq 2W_s$$

To keep the unskilled worker out, it is necessary that

(A3.2) $$W_1 + PW_2 + (1 - P)W_u < 2W_u$$

There is a unique set of wages W_1 and W_2 that make (A3.1) and (A3.2) hold with equality. If (A 3.1) holds with equality, then

(A3.3) $$W_1 = 2W_S - W_2$$

For (A 3.2) to hold, it is necessary to set the post-probationary wage larger than W_2 that makes (A 3.2) hold with equality, or that wage must exceed the solution to

(A3.4) $$W_2 > \frac{2W_s - W_u - PW_u}{1 - P}$$

To obtain (A3.4), substitute (A3.3) into (A3.2).

Define X as the difference between W_1 and W_2. Thus,

(A3.5) $$X \equiv W_2 - W_1$$

(A.3.6) $$X > 2\frac{(1 + P)(W_s - W_u)}{(1 - P)}$$

which is obtained by substituting (A3.3) and (A3.4) into (A3.5).

Differentiating the *r.h.s.* of (A 3.6) with respect to P, W_s, and W_u, respectively, yields

(A3.7)

a. $\dfrac{\partial}{\partial p} = \dfrac{2\,(W_s - W_u)}{(1 - P)} + \dfrac{2\,(1 + P)(W_s - W_u)}{(1 - P)^2} > 0$

b. $\dfrac{\partial}{\partial W_s} = \dfrac{2(1 + P)}{(1 - P)} > 0$

c. $\dfrac{\partial}{\partial W_u} = \dfrac{-\,2(1 + P)}{(1 - P)} < 0$

As P rises, it is harder to detect unskilled workers. A larger spread is needed to keep unskilled workers out.

The same is true as $W_s - W_u$ rises. For a given W_u, an increase in W_s means that unskilled and skilled are more different. Thus, the unskilled have more to gain by passing themselves off as skilled. This means that the spread between the pre-probation and post-probation wage rises when W_s rises or W_u falls.

It is unnecessary to assume that the probability that a skilled worker makes it through the probationary period is 1. Indeed, we could assume that the probability is P_s for skilled workers and P_u for unskilled workers. As long as P_s is greater than P_u, there will be some probationary wage scheme that attracts the skilled, but deters the unskilled. To do that, it is necessary to satisfy:

$$W_1 + P_s\,W_2 + (1-P_s)\,W_s \geq 2W_s$$

$$W_1 + P_u\,W_2 + (1-P_u)\,W_u < 2W_u$$

For example, if $W_u = 16$, $W_s = 20$, $P_s = .8$, and $P_u = .2$, then a wage slightly below \$13.60 during probation and slightly above \$28.00 after probation will deter the unskilled but attract the skilled. As P_u approaches P_s, the probationary and post-probationary wages must get farther apart.

Salaries and Piece Rates

In this section, a formal treatment of piece rates and salaries is presented. Suppose that there are (at least) two firms. One pays a piece rate and the other pays a salary. The piecework firm must measure output in order to pay by output. It costs θ to measure output in the piecework firm. Because there is competition for workers, the piecework firm is forced to pay a worker who produces q a wage of $q - \theta$. At any amount of pay less than $q - \theta$, another firm can offer the worker more and still make a profit. This is true until the wage is bid up to $q - \theta$, which is productivity, net of measurement costs.

Analogously, the salary firm must pay the average productivity of its workers. If it were to pay any less than the average productivity of the workers, another salary firm could pick off the workers by paying more than the current salary, but less than average productivity.

FIGURE A3.1
HYPOTHETICAL DISTRIBUTION OF OUTPUT LEVELS

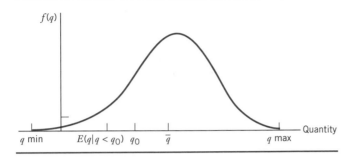

   The salary firm does not pay the average of productivity in the work force, but only the average of productivity at the firm. Since the salary firm may not get a random sample of the population, this must be taken into account.

   Suppose that the density of ability, q, is given by $f(q)$, with cumulative distribution function $f(q)$. A typical distribution is shown in Figure A3.1.

   The mean for the entire population is given by $\bar{q}$. But suppose that the highest-ability workers go to the piecework firm and the lowest-ability workers go to the salary firm. Specifically, suppose that all workers with $q > q_0$ go to the piecework firm and those with $q < q_0$ go to the salary firm. Then the average output among those at the salary firm is not, $\bar{q}$ out instead, $E(q \mid q < q_0)$, which is lower than $\bar{q}$.

   There will be a worker who is indifferent between working at the salary firm and working at the piecework firm. Denote this worker's ability type as q^*. If this worker is just indifferent, then all workers with $q < q^*$ prefer the salary firm, and all with $q > q^*$ prefer the piecework firm. The salary firm must pay the average of output from their workers, which equals $E(q \mid q < q^*)$. The worker with ability level q^* will receive $q^* - \theta$ to work at the piecework firm. In order for workers to be indifferent between two firms, it must be that

Pay at Piecework Firm = Pay at Salary Firm

or

$$q^* - \theta = E(q \mid q < q^*)$$

or

(A3.8)
$$q^* - \theta = \frac{1}{F(q^*)} \int_{q_{min}}^{q^*} q f(q) dq$$

   Equation A3.8 defines the ability level q^* such that the individual having that ability is just indifferent between the two types of firms.

   An example is instructive. Suppose that θ is $\frac{1}{4}$ and that q is distributed uniformly between 0 and 1. Then

FIGURE A3.2
UNIFORM OUTPUT DISTRIBUTION

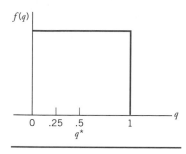

$$f(q) = 1 \text{ and } F(q) = q \text{ for } 0 \leq q \leq 1$$
$$f(q) = 0 \text{ and } F(q) = 0 \text{ for } q < 1$$
$$f(q) = 0 \text{ and } F(q) = 1 \text{ for } q < 1$$

The density function is shown in Figure A3.2.

Substituting the density function into (A3.2), the solution for q^* is given by

$$q^* - \theta = \frac{1}{q^*} \int_0^{q^*} qdd$$

or

$$\frac{q^*}{2} = q^* - \theta$$

so that $q^* = 2\theta$.

In this case, since $\theta = \frac{1}{4}$, $q^* = \frac{1}{2}$. This checks out. If $q^* = \frac{1}{2}$, then all those with

$$\frac{1}{q^*} \int_0^{q^*} qf(q)dq = q^* - \theta$$

or

$$\left(\frac{1}{q^*}\right)\left(\frac{q^{*2}}{2}\right) = q^* - \theta$$

output less than $\frac{1}{2}$ go to the salary firm, which pays average productivity, equal to $\frac{1}{4}$. Individuals whose level of utility, q_1, exceeds $\frac{1}{2}$ choose the piecework firm. For example, a person with a $q = 1$ earns $1 - \frac{1}{4} = \frac{3}{4}$ at the piecework firm, but only $\frac{1}{4}$

at the salary firm. The individual who has output equal to ½ is just indifferent. He earns ¼ at the salary firm and ½ − ¼ or ¼ at the piecework firm.

Were $\theta = 0$, the equilibrium would be $q^* = (2)(0) = 0$. Anyone with q greater than the mean for the salary firm would leave to go to the piecework firm. In this case, only the workers with $q = 0$ remain with the firm.

At the other extreme, let θ exceed ½, say, let $\theta = .6$. Then $q^* = 1.2$. But no one has q greater than 1, so all work at the salary firm. The salary firm pays ½. Even the most able individual with $q = 1$ would want to leave, because that person would earn only $1 − .6 = .4$ at a piecework firm. Measurement is too costly to make it worthwhile, even for the most able.

Learning a Worker's Productivity

4

$\mathcal{T}$he previous chapter was concerned with problems of adverse selection—problems that arise when workers have better knowledge about their productivity than firms do. Although it is true that the worker often has better information than the employer, there are also circumstances where the reverse is true. Sometimes an employer may even have a better assessment of a worker's value than the worker himself. After all, employers have many workers on which to base their evaluations. A worker can only base his opinion on his own limited observations. Limited observation, coupled with delusions of grandeur, can lead a worker to less accurate assessments of her own ability than that held by her employer.

Perhaps the most realistic assumption is that neither worker nor employer has a very good idea of what workers will be worth before hiring them. This creates a dilemma for the employer, which may create an environment where learning about worker productivity will occur. Alternatively, the firm may simply concede its inability to learn about a given worker's productivity and hope that the law of averages will treat it kindly, allowing the good ones to balance out the bad ones. The following discussion illustrates the problem.

GIFFEN: Every worker who comes in the door claims to be the greatest thing since Adam Smith. I don't necessarily think the applicants are lying—they really believe it. The problem is that it just can't be true for everybody. I don't know what to do with these guys.

HOTELLING: Why not just treat them all the same? Some will turn out better than others, but so what? It will all average out.

HUME: No, it won't. The good ones will be picked off, and we will be left with the dregs.

HOTELLING: How will they get picked off? Who's going to tell our rivals who the good ones are?

HUME: The workers will tell them themselves. I see very few applicants who are modest about their own abilities.

HOTELLING: Exactly the point. As I said, they all claim to be the greatest. Which ones will our rivals believe? They are just as likely to get the bad ones as they are to get the good ones. It all averages out.

HUME: That sounds right, but somehow something is missing. Won't we be able to get better workers if we try to figure out who the good ones are?

HOTELLING: I don't think so. The workers themselves do not know how good they are.

HUME: Something still seems wrong. If one guy is terrible at our firm, can't we do better by getting rid of him?

HOTELLING: Sure, if we can figure out who he is, but that costs money.

HUME: Well, maybe it's worth the money. Once we find out about the worker in the interview process, we also have a better basis on which to make an assignment decision. We can think of our screening process as being like the army's. When I got drafted during the Vietnam War, the army made me take an ability test as part of the physical. To prevent people from failing it intentionally, they made your assignment contingent on your test performance. Low scores went straight to infantry. Maybe we could use our interview information in the same way.

HOTELLING: I knew you'd get another army story in before this discussion ended. How are you going to use the screening information? We have no infantry in this firm!

A number of issues are raised by this discussion.

- Who is better at predicting the worker's performance? The worker or the interviewer?

- When is it worth the bother and cost to determine an individual worker's productivity?

- If workers are treated the same, under which circumstances will the best ones be hired away by a firm's competitors?

- When is it useful to find out who the worst workers are and get rid of them?

- Should information extracted during the interview be used to determine work assignments within the firm?

Who Knows What? Asymmetric Information or Symmetric Ignorance

◆ ◆ ◆ ◆ ◆

Workers frequently come to an interview having relevant **private information** about themselves. Workers may have undocumented expertise that is likely to increase their productivity in the job. Alternatively, workers may know about hidden problems that would prevent them from performing at peak level in particular positions (i.e., a bad back or an F in statistics). These are examples of **asymmetric information**. The workers know more about their likelihood of succeeding than does the recruiter.

In other cases the situation may be reversed. Workers might have very good information about their general skills and physical abilities, but not have a good sense of how these underlying skills match up with the task to be performed. The recruiter, on the other hand, may have a large sample of individuals (from past experience) on which to base an assessment of the applicants. The recruiter has seen individuals with varying amounts and types of work experience and education, and she knows how they performed on the job. Although the past may not be a perfect predictor of the future, her assessment of a given individual's prospects may very well be better than the applicant's own assessment. For example, business school professors study and analyze business throughout their careers. Some even leave academia and move into business (with varied success). It is not easy for a particular professor to predict the likelihood that he will succeed in business. Those who have already worked in a given industry may be better at knowing which professors are likely to succeed and which are likely to fail. Incidentally, it goes the other way as well. Many businesspeople think that academic life is a breeze, and that any good businessperson can succeed as a business professor, but few businesspeople are actually able to convey their experiences in a coherent fashion, especially in a classroom setting. A dean is likely to be better at predicting success in the classroom than the businessperson is.

In the previous chapter, the focus was on situations like those just described, where one party (usually the worker) had better information about his ability or drive than the other. However, in many cases, neither side has a very good sense about whether or not an applicant will succeed. This situation can be termed **symmetric ignorance**, because each side is equally uninformed about the worker's prospects.

Many cases fit the situation of symmetric ignorance. Complete ignorance is not required. It is only necessary that both parties be equally uninformed of the relevant details. Both applicant and recruiter may have a great deal of information relevant to the decision: type of college, degree, grades, and so on. This information is normally common knowledge, but even within the category of people who earned bachelor's degrees with a 3.7 GPA from Caltech, there are variations in abilities to perform any particular job. Even with such a select group of applicants, no one can be sure to pick the best applicant.

◆ ◆ ◆ ◆ ◆ DETERMINING A WORKER'S PRODUCTIVITY

Finding out how much a worker is worth has obvious value to a firm. It enables management to hire the best workers and to avoid being stuck with individuals who are not particularly useful to the firm. Determining productivity also implies certain costs, though. The first is that it may be expensive to determine a worker's ability.

When is attempting to determine productivity sufficiently useful to justify the expense of doing it? Part of the answer seems to depend on whether the information gained can be kept confidential. If certifying a worker as having ability simply means that a firm informs all of its competitors about the worker's value, then the wage that the firm is forced to pay will be bid up by market pressure. The firm may be no better off than it was before it learned the worker's ability. In fact, even if the information becomes public, the firm might still have a strong incentive to determine the worker's ability. Given that the worker captures the returns from a certification of ability, the worker should be willing to pay the firm to supply it. This type of payment often takes the form of lower wages during the certification period.

A worker's willingness to pay for this information and the firm's ability to make a profit by selling it depends on the cost of obtaining the information.

Example 1: Productivity Easy to Determine

Suppose a firm can hire a worker into a particular job, such as investment banking. Individuals differ dramatically in their abilities to put together deals and perform the other unique functions that are part of the investment banker's job. Past experience has shown that individuals can be categorized into productivity levels. Table 4.1 gives the proportion of people in each type and their annual outputs.

Suppose a particular worker is currently employed for $40,000 per year. If the firm were simply to hire the worker by matching his salary, the firm would expect to net the difference between the $40,000 and what the worker is worth at the investment banking firm. According to Table 4.1, the average worker in the population is worth

$$[.1 \times (-100)] + [.2 \times (0)] + [.3 \times (50)] + [.3 \times (100)] + [.1 \times 200] = \$55K$$

TABLE 4.1

SAMPLE BREAKDOWN BY PRODUCTIVITY TYPE AT AN INVESTMENT BANK

Type	A	B	C	D	E
Proportion of population of that type	.1	.2	.3	.3	.1
Average output for people of that type	−$100K	0	$50K	$100K	$200K

or the average workers nets $55,000 for the firm. Put differently, for every ten randomly chosen workers hired, the firm receives

$$1 \times -100,000 + 3 \times 50,000 + 3 \times 100,000 + 1 \times 200,000$$
$$= \$550,000 \text{ in input}$$

If the firm hired all ten workers, it would net $150,000 ($550,000 output − $400,000 salary). On average, hiring the worker for $40,000 still results in a profit of $15,000 to the firm, but there is a clear opportunity to do better. The firm is losing money on all the Type A workers. They cost $40,000 annually in salary and end up losing the firm $100,000 a year in bad deals. The net value of the Type A workers is −$140,000. Similarly, the net value of the Type B workers is also negative. They cost $40,000 in salary and end up producing zero output for the firm. Thus, the firm nets −$40,000 from Type Bs. It would be better if the firm were able to weed out these workers.

Screening provides an additional option for the firm. Suppose that the firm can put workers through a series of tests before hiring them. The battery of exams costs $1,000 to administer, but it gives definitive information on whether the worker is Type A or B before being hired.

For every ten workers that the firm hires, we expect one A, two Bs, three Cs, three Ds and one E. If the firm could identify the As and Bs, it would not hire them. The firm makes money on the C, D, and E types because their output levels exceed the requisite salary of $40,000.

After screening, the firm would expect to hire three Cs, three Ds, and one E for every ten persons interviewed. Their combined output would be

$$(3 \times 50,000) + (3 \times 100,000) + (1 \times 200,000) = \$650,000$$

or

$$\$650,000/7 = \$92,857 \text{ per worker}$$

In order to obtain this much higher average output ($92,857 per worker instead of the earlier $55,000 per worker) it was necessary to test ten workers. The cost of testing the ten workers was $10 \times \$1,000 = \$10,000$. Thus, the net output per worker after taking screening costs into account is

$$(\$650,000 - \$10,000)/7 = \$91,429$$

Each worker costs $40,000 in salary, so the screening approach results in a profit of $51,429 per worker. This is much more than the $15,000 per worker that was earned in the absence of screening. Given the numbers in this example, it pays for the firm to screen its applicants. Weeding out the poor performance is worth doing in this context.

When the firm pays for screening to hire only the seven remaining workers, total output is $650,000. The firm pays out $280,000 in salary and nets $370,000 in profit. This compares very favorably with the expected $150,000 profit without screening. In fact, it means that the firm could spend up to $220,000, or $22,000 per worker, screening ten applicants and still come out no worse off than if it simply hired everyone who applied. Whenever screening costs less than $22,000 per worker, the firm increases its profits by screening all applicants.

Example 2: Productivity Harder to Determine

Let's consider another example. Instead of an investment bank, suppose that the firm faced with the screening decision is a commercial bank. Commercial banks are similar to investment banks, but worker productivity in a commercial bank setting does not vary as much as it does at in an investment bank. Thus, Table 4.2 replaces 4.1.

Now suppose that the firm does not screen its workers. For every ten workers that it hires, it receives an expected output of

$$-5,000 + (2 \times \$50,000) + (3 \times \$60,000) + (3 \times \$70,000) + \$90,000 = \$615,000$$

Suppose that the type of worker who is employed in a commerical bank can be hired on the competitive labor market for $40,000, as before. If the firm were to hire ten workers without screening them, the cost would be $400,000 and the firm would net $215,000 profit on those ten workers.

Suppose that for a fee of $1,000 per applicant, the firm can know the identify of the Type A applicants. Since hiring As is unprofitable (they produce $35,000 but cost $40,000), whereas Bs, Cs, Ds, and Es all generate profits, the firm might be expected to hire all types other than As. Out of a group of ten workers, it would receive an expected output of

$$(2 \times \$50,000) + (3 \times \$60,000) + (3 \times \$70,000) + \$90,000 = \$580,000$$

Now, the output of the ten applicants, nine of whom were hired, is $580,000. Their combined salaries amount to $9 \times \$40,000 = \$360,000$. The difference is $220,000, which exceeds the $215,000 netted above. But the cost of screening the ten applicants is $10,000. After the $10,000 is subtracted, the resulting profit is $210,000, which is less than the amount that would have been earned in the ab-

TABLE 4.2

SAMPLE BREAKDOWN BY PRODUCTIVITY TYPE AT COMMERCIAL BANK

Type	A	B	C	D	E
Proportion of population of that type	.1	.2	.3	.3	.1
Average output for people of that type	$35K	$50K	$60K	$70K	$90K

sence of screening. Screening the applicants does not pay. The return to screening the applicants is that one Type A worker is weeded out. That worker reduces profits by $5,000. But the cost of weeding the Type A out is $10,000, since ten applicants must be screened for every one A that is spotted. Thus, screening is a net loser to the tune of $5,000. What is the difference between this example and the one in Table 4.1? There are two differences. First, screening at the investment bank resulted in the refusal to hire three of the workers. At the commercial bank, screening resulted in the refusal to hire only one. Thus, more workers were weeded out as a result of screening in the first case. Screening can be viewed as a means of cutting a loss. If there are fewer of the type targeted for screening, then there is less of a loss to cut.

Second, it was more important to weed out workers at the investment bank than at the commercial bank. At the investment bank, Type As reduced output by $100,000 which, after accounting for salary, resulted in a net loss of $140,000. Since Bs produce zero, they net the firm −$40,000, after paying $40,000 in salary. In the second example, Type As produce $35,000 at a cost of $40,000. The net loss of Type As in Example 2 is only $5,000, far less than the $140,000 or $40,000 losses of the first example.

These examples lead to three conclusions about screening of applicants:

1. *Screening applicants is more profitable when the screening costs are small.* Other things being equal, the less it costs to screen, the greater the net value of screening. Net value is defined as output in dollars after all variable costs, including wages, are subtracted. Variable costs include the costs of materials and services necessary to produce additional units of output. Variable costs exclude sunken costs, such as payment on a lease that has already been signed.

2. *Screening of applicants is more profitable when a larger proportion of applicants are refused employment as a result of the screening.* The firm hires workers when their net value is positive. This means that screening is most profitable when there exists a significant fraction of applicants who yield negative net value to the firm. It rarely pays to screen 1,000 applicants to weed out one bad one. Since the costs of screening are borne on every applicant, it is better to spend very little on screening when a very small proportion are to be refused employment.

3. *Screening applicants is more profitable when employing those targeted by the screening would be costly to the firm.* If the expected gain from weeding out workers of a particular type is less than the cost of discovering their identity, then it does not pay to engage in screening. When worker output is relatively homogeneous—that is, bad workers are not very bad—then screening is less valuable and it may not pay to bear the costs of finding them out. So in cases where fewer workers are likely to be weeded out or those targeted to be weeded out won't cost the firm much even if they are hired, screening will not be as profitable.

SCREENING, TRIAL PERIODS, AND TEMPORARY SERVICE AGENCIES
◆ ◆ ◆ ◆ ◆ ◆ ◆ ◆ ◆ ◆

Temp agencies are becoming increasingly popular. It suffices to say that the country's largest employer is Manpower Inc., a nationwide temporary service agency. In the business climate where many companies are reconsidering their staffing needs, flexibility appeals to many companies. A rapidly growing segment of the temporary help industry is so called temp-to-hire—that is, a hybrid of a full-time placement service and a temp agency. In the era of outsourcing when companies increasingly focus on their core business, it is natural that many businesses turn to staffing firms that have expertise in recruiting, screening, and training to help recruit individuals in full-time positions. For example, Danhill Temporary Systems in Creve Coeur offers tem-to-perm as one of their services. According to Eric Anderson, a manager of Danhill, 60 percent of the company's business is in temp-to-hire business. Danhill is not an isolated example; a recent survey by the National Association of Temporary Services (NATS) reveals that 38 percent of temporaries found permanent work through their assignments. The president of Impact Solutions, Inc., Aleta Mitchell, also noticed the trend. Aleta says, "Approximately 10 percent of our temporary placements within the last six months have resulted in a permanent hire. We are receiving calls from clients indicating that they have a permanent opening within their organization. However, they would like an individual to work temporarily for at least three months." Aleta believes that the trial period is a valuable opportunity for employers to review the individual's work quality as well as attitude, attendance habits, and the "compatibility" with the job environment.

The hiring practices described above provide a natural trial period. When is it a good idea to screen workers on the job by means of a trial period and when is it better to do all screening before the start of employment? Offering a trial period is a good strategy if the following conditions are satisfied.

- The quality of the worker and her productivity are observed on the job at a lower cost than during a job interview.

- The cost of hiring a "wrong person" is not very high. For instance, hiring a poorly trained diamond cutter may be an immensely costly mistake, while hiring a poor typist normally does not result in large damages.

Lower-level jobs are usually characterized by the above features. That is why temporary employees tend to occupy the lowest rungs in a company. In light of this, Dinte Resources Inc., which specializes in short-term placement of top executives, runs a very peculiar business. Yet, Dinte is a successful placement agency, with 12 employees and over $3 million in annual revenues. The value proposition of this "Rent-a-Boss" business is threefold. It lets a company "test drive an executive" and at the same time allows it to fill a position quickly, which may be very important for a small, rapidly growing company. Finally, it lets a small company obtain specialized expertise that it needs only temporarily. For example, Bill Gregory, former CFO at Fairfax-based Globalink, a software company, has used Dinte's service to find several specialized executive-level employees he needed temporarily. Now he finds himself on the other side of the hiring table. When he chose to leave Globalink, he used Dente's services to land a job of VP of sales at Prosoft, a high-tech startup with $2 million in annual revenues.

The method and the amount of screening of new employees is an important and difficult choice for a company to make. There is no one-size-fits-all solution. The above examples illustrate how companies use temporary service agencies and trial periods in order to screen employees and when and why it may be a good strategy.

Source: Kirstin Downey, "Recruiter Pioneers 'Rent-a-Boss' Idea; To Ensure a Good Corporate Fit, Try Executives on For Size" *The Washington Post*, November 20, 1995, Pg. F09, and "It is Only Temporary—or is It?" *St. Louis Commerce*, March 1995, Sec 1; pg 30.

DIFFERENT DIVISIONS: THE ASSIGNMENT PROBLEM

◆ ◆ ◆ ◆ ◆

The lessons of the last section can be applied to a somewhat different problem, namely the decision on where to assign a particular worker. Firms have a stock of workers who must be assigned to various positions within the firm. Every worker has a comparative advantage. The firm can gain the most by assigning workers to the tasks at which they are comparatively better, but it is not always easy to discover a worker's talents. Doing so requires a period of observation and monitoring and thus an expenditure by the firm. Most costly, perhaps, is that the worker must be tried out in both tasks. This may mean teaching a worker two jobs instead of just one. Duplication of teaching is wasteful if the worker will eventually perform only one task. Thus, we're led to ask whether an expenditure of this sort is worthwhile and, if so, how should workers be assigned?

To understand the issues, let us consider the data presented in Table 4.3.

There are 30 workers in a given labor pool, all of whom are employed at General Woods. They can be employed in the hardwood division or they can be put in the plywood division. Their productivity in each division is given in Table

TABLE 4.3
MONTHLY OUTPUT AT GENERAL WOODS INC.

Worker I.D. No.	Hardwood	Plywood	Mac(H,P)	Diff
1001	$15,873	$9,572	$15,873	$6301
1002	$3,674	$4,689	$4,689	$−1015
1003	$14,126	$6,826	$14,126	$7300
1004	$13,675	$6,470	$13,675	$7205
1005	$10,954	$4,578	$10,954	$6376
1006	$9,282	$3,827	$9,282	$5455
1007	$19,168	$9,860	$19,168	$9308
1008	$10,806	$2,541	$10,806	$8265
1009	$6,581	$7,201	$7,201	$−620
1010	$13,562	$5,893	$13,562	$7669
1011	$16,006	$8,635	$16,006	$7371
1012	$7,860	$4,666	$7,860	$3194
1013	$5,256	$3,692	$5,256	$1564
1014	$19,013	$7,139	$19,013	$11874
1015	$7,141	$9,403	$9,403	$−2262
1016	$7,335	$9,096	$9,096	$−1761
1017	$9,477	$300	$9,477	$9177
1018	$8,137	$3,816	$8,137	$4321
1019	$15,073	$8,413	$15,073	$6660
1020	$11,732	$2,080	$11,732	$9652
1021	$1,745	$3,274	$3,274	$−1529
1022	$3,432	$2,171	$3,432	$1261
1023	$2,303	$1,915	$2,303	$388
1024	$3,551	$9,869	$9,869	$−6318
1025	$4,560	$8,866	$8,866	$−4306
1026	$7,399	$8,457	$8,457	$−1058
1027	$11,329	$6,160	$11,329	$5169
1028	$5,292	$8,714	$8,714	$−3422
1029	$421	$3,326	$3,326	$−2905
1030	$2,539	$8,922	$8,922	$−6383
Average	$8,910	$6,012	$9,963	

4.3. General can screen each worker carefully before assigning him or her to a division, or it can simply assign workers without any screening whatsoever. If the firm screens its workers carefully, the cost is $700 per worker.

What is gained by screening? That depends on the technology. To make things simple, we first consider the easiest case. Suppose that the number of workers in each division is completely variable. The firm can put all 30 workers in plywood or in hardwood, or it can assign them in any way it chooses without affecting any individual worker's productivity.

The second and third columns of Table 4.3 report each worker's estimated monthly productivity in hardwood and plywood, respectively. The fourth column, labeled Max(H,P), simply reports the maximum productivity in either of the two divisions.

If workers are screened, they can be assigned to the divisions in which they are most productive. For example, worker 1001 would be assigned to hardwood and 1002 would be assigned to plywood. If workers are not screened, then the firm has no information on them. Under these circumstances, it is better to assign every worker to the hardwood division. The average worker produces more in hardwood than in plywood, and the firm has no information on which to base an assignment. Therefore, putting everyone in hardwood maximizes expected productivity.

Were every worker assigned to hardwood, output would be

$$30 \times \$8,910 = \$267,300$$

The firm has an alternative. It can screen every worker at a cost of $700 per worker and assign each worker to his or her most productive activity. If it embarks on this route, the firm receives Max(H,P) from each worker, minus $700 per worker. Under these circumstances, workers 1002,9,15,16,21,24,25,26,28,29 and 30 would be assigned to plywood. The rest would be assigned to hardwood. All workers for whom the difference between hardwood and plywood is positive, as reported in the last column of Table 4.3, would be assigned to hardwood because they are worth more there than in plywood.

If screening were done, total output would be the sum of each worker's output in the relevant division minus $700 per worker in screening costs. This is equivalent to 30 times the average output minus 30 times $700, or

$$30 \times (\$9963) - 700 = \$277,890$$

The choice is clear—screening workers pays off. Even though it costs $700 per worker to assess productivity, the gains from an optimal assignment more than cover the costs. Screening workers would increase the firm's output by about $10,500, or by about 4 percent, which is a significant gain.

What if there were only a certain number of slots available in each division? Suppose, for example, that for the near future it is impossible to have more than 20 people work in hardwood or more than 10 people in plywood. Which should be assigned to hardwood and which to plywood?

Without screening, all workers appear to be identical, so the firm simply assigns workers randomly. The expected output when workers are assigned randomly is

$$(20 \times \$8,910) + (10 \times \$6,012) = \$238,320$$

Alternatively, the firm can screen. If it does so, it has all the data from Table 4.3. How should it make the assignments? It can be shown (see the appendix) that the optimal assignment rule uses the difference between output in hardwood and output in plywood for each individual. The difference between output in hardwood and output in plywood is called the worker's absolute advantage in hardwood. The individuals with the 20 highest differences or the 20 greatest absolute advantages in hardwood should be assigned to hardwood; the rest should be assigned to plywood.

The logic is that the firm wants to put the people who are best at hardwood and worst at plywood in hardwood. Conversely, those who are best at plywood and worst at hardwood should go to plywood. Ranking people by the difference between their output in the two sectors and assigning them accordingly accomplishes this. Table 4.3 lists each worker's absolute advantage in hardwood. Worker 1014 has the largest advantage and would therefore be the first assigned to hardwood. Worker 1030, with the smallest (most negative) difference, would be the first assigned to plywood. The assignments must result in 10 workers to plywood and 20 to hardwood. The total output is then $297,246. From this, screening costs of 30 × $700, or $21,000, must be subtracted. The net output is then $276,246, which exceeds $238,320 by a margin of 16 percent. The difference between this case and the previous one is that worker 1009 would be assigned to plywood if the number of workers in each division were variable. His output is higher in plywood than in hardwood. But when only ten slots are available for plywood, he is assigned to hardwood because he is the worker on whom the least is lost by moving him from plywood to hardwood.

When workers' tasks are assigned randomly, output is much lower than when they are assigned strategically. Random assignment ignores the fact that some workers who are good at one thing may be very bad at another. The gains from sorting on the basis of skill are greatest when ability is not too highly correlated across divisions. It is most valuable when ability is negatively correlated across divisions. Negative correlation means that a worker who is good at hardwood is bad at plywood, and vice versa. If the worker who is best in hardwood is also best in plywood, then it does not make a great deal of difference where the worker is assigned. But if the worker who is best in hardwood is very bad in plywood, screening and strategic sorting become very valuable.

The following conclusion can be drawn from these examples:

1. When the number of slots is variable, workers should be assigned to the task where their output is highest in absolute terms.

2. When the number of slots is fixed because of technological constraints, workers should be ranked on the basis of absolute advantage and then assigned to the appropriate task until all slots are used up.

Thus, the workers with the largest difference between hardwood and plywood go to hardwood first. When all 20 slots have been used in hardwood, the rest of the workers are assigned to plywood. Absolute advantage in the previous example was defined as the difference between output in hardwood and output in plywood.

Independent of the technology, some general points can be made:

1. Sorting into jobs is most important when workers have very different skills. Investing resources in discovering worker types is most valuable when workers who are good at job A are bad at job B, and vice versa.

2. Screening is less valuable when workers are homogeneous so that their skills are similar in every job.

Screening is not always easy to do. In order to determine whether workers differ greatly in their relative abilities, some form of skills measurement must be used. Of course, measuring all workers for the purposes of screening can be costly. How does a firm make a reasoned decision on whether or not to engage in screening without first actually bearing the costs of screening? One possibility is to do a *pilot* study. By selecting a small sample of workers and measuring their abilities in the various jobs, it is possible to determine the amount of variability in the work force. Then the firm can make a more informed decision about whether to screen.

Public or Private Information?

The screening of applicants that takes place at the time of hire produces information for the firm that does the screening, but this information is private for the most part. It remains with the firm that has invested in it. Sometimes, however, it is more difficult to keep the acquired information private. For example, when workers are assigned to various divisions, their assignments become part of their resumes. Workers can and do report on their prior experiences when applying to a new firm.[1]

Does this give outside firms the opportunity to pick off the best workers? The answer depends on the wage that a worker receives. Workers who are paid less than they can receive outside are likely to take another job. As a result, the firm must pay workers as much as they can receive elsewhere. Thus, perhaps the facts given in the General Woods example were unrealistic.

Recall that in the General Woods example, it was optimal (when the number of slots was variable) to assign 11 workers to plywood and 19 workers to hardwood. The assignments and outputs are shown in Table 4.4.

Those workers who General Woods sorted into hardwood each produce an average of $11,424. Those who were sorted into plywood each produce an average of $7,438.

Another firm, hiring a random collection of 30 workers without any sorting, would find that the average worker hired would produce only $8,910 in hardwood and only $6,012 in plywood. Thus, General Woods's rival, United Woods, can do better by hiring General Woods employees who have already been sorted into a division by General Woods. United could simply mimic General's sorting and save the screening costs that General had incurred. Indeed, United would be willing to pay more for sorted employees than they would for employees about whom nothing was known.

What can General Woods do about this situation? General bears the costs of screening, but United gets to reap the benefits. There is little doubt that General

---

[1]Waldman (1984) has examined the effects of assignment to a particular job on wages and worker mobility.

TABLE 4.4
MONTHLY OUTPUT OF SORTED WORKERS, BY DIVISION

I.D.	Hardwood	Plywood
Workers in Hardwood		
1001	$15,873	$9572
1003	14,216	6,826
1004	13,675	6,470
1005	10,954	4,578
1006	9,282	3,827
1007	19,168	9,860
1008	10,806	2,541
1010	13,562	5,893
1011	16,006	8,635
1012	7,860	4,666
1013	5,256	3,692
1014	19,013	7,139
1017	9,477	300
1018	8,137	3,816
1019	15,073	8,413
1020	11,732	2,080
Average among hardwood workers	$11,424	$5,287
Workers in Plywood		
1022	$3,432	$2,171
1023	2,303	1,915
1027	11,329	6,160
1002	3,674	4,689
1009	6,581	7,201
1015	7,141	9,403
1016	7,335	9,096
1021	1,745	3,274
1024	3,551	9,869
1025	4,560	8,866
1026	7,399	8,457
1028	5,292	8,714
1029	421	3,326
1030	2,539	8,922
Average among plywood workers	$4,567	$7,438
Average over all 30 workers (from Table 4.3)	$8,910	$6,012

will be forced to pay higher wages to its screen employees, as long as United knows that workers at General are assigned to divisions on the basis of productivity, and not just randomly. Any refusal by General to pay the higher wages will result in employees being picked off, just as the executives in the opening scenario feared.

The remedy is for General to pay higher wages and retain the workers. General can reap benefits, not by trying to keep the wages of designated workers low, but by reducing the wages of workers when they are hired initially. If workers can earn $40,000 elsewhere, General can get away with paying somewhat less than the $40,000. The information that General will produce will end up raising the wages of its workers. Workers at General like this and are willing to pay for it in the form of lower initial wages. Thus, General should offer an initial wage of, say $38,000, for the first two years. Then, after workers are assigned to their divisions permanently, General will have to raise wages, say, to $41,000, to meet the competition from United, which is willing to pay more to screened workers. Workers are better off because for an implicit investment of $2,000 per year during the first two years of employment, they get to receive an extra $1,000 per year thereafter. (If wages would have risen anyway, then the $1,000 increment must be added to the normal wage growth.) General is also better off than it would be had it made the investment, paid for it, and then been forced to raise wages or lose workers. By this strategy, General "sells" certification to the worker as either a hardwood or plywood specialist. This sale results in additional profit to General.

General must decide whether to offer this certification or not, based on the cost of doing the screening and the benefits derived from it. One possibility is for General to behave as United does, and merely pick off workers at $41,000 from other producers. If it does this, it does not get to enjoy the profits from paying workers $38,000 during their first two years of employment, but it does not have to bear the screening costs either. It will choose to screen, rather than be the buyer of already screened workers, when the costs of screening are smaller than the profits that it earns from screening. In this example, General comes out ahead by screening if it can classify workers at a cost of less than $2,000 \times 2$, which is what it gains by paying $38,000 rather than $40,000 for unscreened labor.[2]

These points are not mere abstractions. Firms frequently use prior experience as a guide to determine current job assignment, as well they should. These examples showed that large gains can be had by using the information inherent in prior job assignments.

DOES SCREENING AFFECT A FIRM'S ABILITY TO ATTRACT APPLICANTS? ◆ ◆ ◆ ◆ ◆

Why would an applicant come to a firm that engages in screening? An applicant that goes to a firm that does not screen will almost certainly be hired. But at a firm that screens like the one that hires workers corresponding to the Table 4.1 example, the applicant has only a 70 percent chance of being hired. Why not apply to firms that guarantee employment to all reasonable candidates?

The answer must lie in the increased compensation that a worker receives from a firm that screens. Recall that without screening, the average worker pro-

---

[2]Screened labor must be paid $41,000 per year, but is more productive than unscreened labor. The alternative on new workers who are unscreened is $40,000, not $41,000, since no firm is willing to pay inexperienced workers the higher fee of $41,000 per year.

duced $55,000 of output. With screening, after netting out the screening costs, a worker was worth $91,429 because the low productivity workers were not hired. The firm that screened could afford to pay as much as 91,429/55,000, or 1.66 times as much as the firm that did not screen. Although one might expect the screening firm to keep some of the profit from screening to itself, it must pass some of it along to its workers. If the screening firm did not offer some gains, then workers would have no incentive to subject themselves to screening, and no one would apply.

The reason a worker applies to a firm that screens is that the screening firm hires more productive workers and is able to pay more as a result. Since workers do not know for certain whether they will be hired, they must get something for investing the time in applying to the firm where a job offer is less likely. What they get is a sufficient wage increase to compensate them for the chance that they will not be hired. Since the effort associated with the application process is not too great, the wage differential between the screening firm and the nonscreening firm may well be quite small.[3]

There may be a cost, other than the wasted time of going through an application process, which does not result in a job offer. A worker who has been turned down for a job now has negative information about his ability. If this information becomes public, then the worker will be unable to get a job even at a firm that does not screen. If the firm that does not screen knows that the worker was turned down by a screening firm, then it can infer that the worker is from a rejectable category. In the example of Table 4.1, the firm would know that the worker was either in category A or category B. Since there are twice as many Bs as there are As, the firm would infer that the worker's productivity would be

$$(\frac{1}{3} \times -100,000) + (\frac{2}{3} \times 0) = -\$33,000$$

The firm would estimate the rejected worker's productivity to be $-\$33,000$ and would not be interested in hiring that person at any salary. This worker would then be forced to go back to some other, presumably less attractive job. For example, the worker might be able to earn $40,000 if self-employed.

Firms that do not screen can hire unscreened applicants off the street. Using the number from Table 4.1, the random worker produces $55,000, on average, so a firm could pay up to that amount. Suppose that competition forces firms that do not screen their workers to pay $55,000.

Firms that do screen receive $91,429 from their workers. If they split the difference, their workers are paid

$$(\$55,000 + 91,429)/2 = \$73,215$$

---

[3]There may be considerable surplus to be split between the screening firm and the workers who are hired by it. The shares depend on the amount of competition on each side. If many firms can engage in screening and applicants are scarce, the workers get a larger share. If applicants are abundant and only one or two firms can screen, most of the surplus goes to the firms.

(Workers at the screening firm may receive different wages, but the average must be $73,215).

A worker who applies to the screening firm knows that there is a 70 percent chance of being hired and paid $73,215, but a 30 percent chance of being rejected. If the rejection spoils the chances of being employed elsewhere, the worker might have to choose self-employment, earning $40,000. Thus, expected compensation from applying to the screening firm is

$$(.7 \times \$73,215) + (.3 \times 40,000) = \$63,251$$

The firm that does not screen would pay $55,000. Since the expected wage, $63,251, is higher than the $55,000 that would be received at the nonscreening firm, workers prefer to go to the screening firm even though there is a chance that they will not be hired.[4]

In the business environment, some firms are known as high-wage firms. These firms often position themselves to be wage leaders intentionally, knowing that they will have their pick of the labor force. In order to use the large pool of applicants effectively, these firms must screen. Otherwise, they will be flooded by a large number of applicants, many of whom are not worth the premium salaries.

RECAP ◆ ◆ ◆ ◆ ◆

Five questions were posed at the beginning of this chapter. We will review them here.

1. Who can better estimate a worker's performance, the worker or the firm? Often, a firm is in as good a position to estimate a worker's performance as the worker. The view that one party can take advantage of another is probably the exception, rather than the rule.

2. Firms are most likely to screen their applicants when three conditions hold: costs of screening are low; there is a substantial number of workers who will not be hired as a result of the screening; the difference in output between acceptable and unacceptable workers is large.

3. Competition from rival firms pushes up the wage that a screening firm must pay its workers. Screening firms can get back the cost of screening (and sometimes more) by reducing the wages that it pays to new workers. New workers are willing to accept reduced wages because they know that this will result in higher expected wages later on.

---

[4]In this simplest case, where all workers are ex ante identical, only one kind of firm could survive. Since workers prefer to go to the screening firm, no nonscreening firms will exist in equilibrium. If instead the nonscreening firm generated higher income than that expected at the screening firm, only nonscreening firms would exist.

4. It can suit the interests of both parties to undertake screening at the time of hire. Even though some workers may lose as a result of screening, both firms and workers may prefer screening. When neither party has much information about a worker's productivity and the wrong type of worker can drag down the average, it pays to screen. Engaging in this kind of screening makes the worker better off because, on average, the worker will end up making a higher salary as a result. Some workers may lose, but if more gain than lose, workers who do not know their own abilities will prefer the firm that does screening to the one that does not.

5. Screening can be used not only to decide whether or not to hire a worker, but also to decide to which job a worker should be assigned. Sorting into jobs is most important when workers have very different skills. Investing resources in discovering worker types is most valuable when workers who are good at one job are bad at another, and vice versa. Screening is less valuable when workers are homogeneous so that their skills are similar in every job. Big absolute advantages make screening more valuable.

Assigning workers to jobs in the appropriate manner can have very large effects on productivity. When the number of slots for each job is variable, workers should be assigned to the job at which their absolute advantage is highest. When the number of slots is fixed, workers should be ranked according to absolute advantage and should be assigned in descending order until all slots are exhausted

---

◆ ◆ ◆ ◆ ◆ REFERENCES

Hölmstrom, Bengt. "Moral Hazard and Observability," *Bell Journal of Economics* 10 (Spring 1979): 74–91.

Lazear, Edward P. "Salaries and Piece Rates," *Journal of Business* 59 (July 1986): 405–31.

Stiglitz, Joseph E. "Incentives, Risk and Information: Notes Toward a Theory of Hierarchy," *Bell Journal of Economics and Management Science* 6 (August 1975): 552–79.

Waldman, Michael. "Job Assignments, Signalling, and Efficiency," *Rand Journal of Economics* 15 (Summer 1984): 255–67.

◆ ◆ ◆ ◆ ◆ ADDITIONAL ADVANCED READING

Baker, George, Michael Gibbs, and Bengt Hölmstrom. "The Internal Economics of the Firm: Evidence from Personnel Data," *Quarterly Journal of Economics* 109 (November 1994): 881–919.

Baker, George, Michael Gibbs, and Bengt Hölmstrom. "The Wage Policy of a Firm," *Quarterly Journal of Economics* 109 (November 1994): 921–55.

Demougin, Dominique, and Aloysius Siow. "Careers in Ongoing Hierarchies," *American Economic Review* 84 (December 1994): 1261–77.

Farber, Henry S. "The Analysis of Inter-Firm Worker Mobility," *National Bureau of Economic Research Working Paper: 4262,42* (January 1993).

Gibbons, Robert. "Piece-Rate Incentive Schemes," *Journal of Labor Economics* 5 (October 1987): 413–429.

Hart, Oliver D. "Optimal Labour Contracts under Asymmetric Information: An Introduction," *Review of Economic Studies* 50 (January 1983):3–35.

Lazear, Edward P. "The Job as a Concept," in William J. Bruns Jr., ed., *Performance Measurement, Evaluation, and Incentives*. Boston: Harvard Business School Press, 1992, 183–215.

APPENDIX   ◆ ◆ ◆ ◆ ◆

This section is divided into two parts. The first sets up the general model for worker sorting when workers and firms have symmetric information (or lack thereof). The second part considers the specific example of allocating workers to slots and shows that when there are a specific number of slots, ranking workers by absolute advantage and assigning on the basis of absolute advantage maximizes output.

Suppose that workers can work at some alternative job that has a guaranteed wage level of w. The choice that a worker faces is between going to a firm that screens and going to one that does not. At firms that screen, workers take a chance on being hired at a salary that exceeds what they could receive elsewhere, or being offered a wage that falls short of their alternatives. If the workers are unfortunate, they can always return to the alternative job, which pays wage w.

A worker may prefer, however, not to be screened and simply to accept the wage that equals the average output of all workers. When workers are not screened, the bad workers hired will drag down the average for all. Since those workers could be earning w instead of some lower amount that they contribute to the firm, having them work with the others is detrimental. The advantage is that no screening costs need be borne to weed out the bad workers. In the work environment, this appears as a firm that simply hires workers randomly and pays them for showing up at the job. Payment of this kind does not distinguish among workers, since talents are never measured. Instead, at the nonscreening firm, each worker is paid the competitive wage, which is equal to a worker's expected output or

$$(A4.1) \qquad\qquad \text{Salary} = \int_{q_{min}}^{q_{max}} q f(q)\, dq$$

where we define q as the worker's output and $f(q)$ as the density of that output.

Alternatively, a firm can put workers on probation for a proportion λ of their work life ($0 \le \lambda \le 1$). Suppose that during the probationary period, a worker's output is measured at cost τ and, since his ability is unknown, he is paid his expected output. After the probationary period, the worker's output is known. If it is known to other firms as well, the worker must be paid the level of his output, after subtracting other costs of production. Otherwise, the worker will be stolen away by competitors.

The advantage of undertaking measurement and paying the corresponding piece rate is that low-quality workers are sorted out to a higher-valued use. Doing so maximizes total output when τ is sufficiently low. Risk-neutral workers, and even those who are not too risk-averse, prefer this as long as measurement costs are not too high. Of course, if measurement costs are too high, what is gained by sorting is more than offset by the costs of measurement.

Risk-neutral workers will prefer to apply to firms that screen when the worker's expected pay is higher with screening than without. What is gained is that poorly matched workers are screened out and moved to jobs where they are more productive. What is lost is the measurement costs that must be borne on all applicants, whether they are hired or not. Screening of applicants is done when the expected wage at the screening firm exceeds that at the nonscreening firm.

Before measurement, workers do not know whether they are high- or low-quality workers. All they know is that their ability to produce output is described by the density function $f(q)$. As a result, if one worker in this category prefers to be screened, they all prefer it. Similarly, if one worker prefers no screening, they all prefer no screening. Workers prefer to be screened when their expected wage is higher by being screened than by not being screened, or when

$$(A4.2) \quad \lambda \int_{q_{min}}^{q_{max}} qf(q)\, dq + (1 - \lambda) \left[\int_{q_{min}}^{q_{max}} qf(q)\, dq + wF(w) \right] - \tau > \int_{q_{min}}^{q_{max}} qf(q)\, dq$$

The first term on the left-hand side gives the worker's expected output during the proportion λ of his life. During this period, he has not yet been screened. Thus, a random sample of the population is employed at the firm during this period.

After screening—during the latter $(1 - \lambda)$ proportion of his life—the worker will either end up working for the firm or taking his alternative. He takes his alternative when his wage offer, which equals his actual q, falls below w, the alternative. This happens $F(w)$ of the time since $F(w)$ is the probability that q is less than w. When it does occur, the worker earns w instead of the very low q. This is the saving that screening brings. It raises the output (and implicit wage) of every worker who is below w up to w. All workers who are hired (consisting of $1 - F(w)$ of the population) receive their actual q for $(1 - \lambda)$ of their lives. This comes at a cost of τ to each worker, which is subtracted off as the last term. The right-hand side of the expression is what a worker earns for a whole lifetime at the nonscreening firm.

After some algebraic manipulation, (A4.2) can be rewritten as

$$(A4.3) \qquad wF(w) - \int_{q_{min}}^{w} qf(q)dq > \frac{\tau}{1 - \lambda}$$

If this inequality holds, every worker prefers the screening firm to the salary firm. As a result, the market will have only firms that screen. If this inequality does not hold, every worker prefers the nonscreening firm. As a result, the market will consist only of firms that do not screen.

Contrast this with the results of earlier chapters. Since workers do not possess information that firms do not have, there is no sorting by workers. In the previous chapter, we consider what would occur when workers knew their own abilities but firms did not have this information. Under these circumstances, two types of firms exist. Some firms screen their workers and pay on the basis of productivity. Others do not. But the nonscreening firms know that their workers are not a random sample of the population. Instead, these firms recognize that they get workers who cannot make the grade at the screening firms. As such, wages at the nonscreening firms are adjusted (downward) accordingly.

The expression in (A4.3) has the following implications.

1. Firms do not screen when the cost of measurement is high. The inequality favoring piece rates is less likely to hold as τ gets large.

2. Firms do not screen when measurement requires a long time. It makes no sense to spend valuable resources measuring worker productivity if workers are close to the end of their careers by the time the information has been gathered. In the limit, when $\lambda = 1$, the right-hand side is infinite so a piece rate is never used.

3. The higher the value of the alternative use of time, w, the more likely firms are to screen. Under these circumstances, it pays to weed out bad workers because their alternatives are good. Further, the higher the alternative wage, the larger the proportion of workers who are better suited to the alternative activity.[5]

4. As a corollary, workers who do not have a great deal of firm-specific human capital are the best candidates for measurement. If worker productivity at the current firm is much greater than it is elsewhere, worker sorting, which costs τ per worker, is less likely to be worthwhile. Thus, young workers with less specific human capital are better candidates for screening. It makes no sense to measure the output of senior partners in law firms because they are much less likely to have an alternative at which they are more productive than they are in their current activity.

5. The more heterogeneous the work force, the more valuable screening can be. It does not pay to measure the entire work force to weed out workers who are only slightly worse than the average. Sorting is most valuable when there are some workers who are so poorly suited to the firm that they dramatically lower average output. Formally, this is captured by the second term on the left-hand side of (A4.3). This is the non-normalized expected output among

---

[5]Differentiate the left-hand side of (A4.3) with respect to w: $F(w) + wf(w) - wf(w) = F(w) > 0$.

those workers who would leave the firm when screening occurs. When this term is very low, the left-hand side, and thus screening becomes more attractive. The term is low when the distribution has fat tails, reflecting heterogeneity.

Before leaving this topic, it is useful to consider the role of risk aversion. In the previous example, sufficiently risk-averse workers might always prefer the straight salary without screening. Although average income might be sacrificed slightly, the straight salary without measurement provides complete income insurance to the worker. The cost is that the lifetime expected wage is higher when firms screen than when they do not, but with screening the worker is uncertain about income. A sufficiently risk-averse worker would be willing to give up the higher expected salary for the lower certain one that no screening offers.[6]

The Assignment Problem

In the text of this chapter, an example was presented where there was a specified number of slots to be filled. The rule used was to rank workers by their absolute advantages and place workers in job assignments according to their absolute advantages. In this section, we show formally that this is the appropriate rule to use.

Suppose that there are z workers and z jobs. There are m hardwood machines and $z - m$ plywood machines so that m of the z workers must be assigned to hardwood and $m - z$ workers must be assigned to plywood. Denote by H_i and P_i worker I's output in hardwood and plywood, respectively. The optimal assignment maximizes the sum of output of all workers. Let us give workers subscript names such that the optimal assignment has workers 1 through m assigned to hardwood and $m + 1$ to z assigned to plywood (i.e., if it were optimal to assign worker 2 to plywood and worker s to hardwood, simply rename worker 2 s and rename worker s, 2). Since we have defined names such that it is optimal to assign 1 through m to

---

[6]Others, most notably Stiglitz (1975) and Hölmstrom (1979), have focused on the trade-off between risk and incentives. The same kind of argument applies. Making workers full residual claimants provides the best incentives when workers are risk neutral. But risk-averse workers object to this kind of compensation scheme, especially when the luck and measurement error account for a large part of the variation in measured output.

Not only does a compensation scheme that caters to risk aversion induce moral hazard, it also causes adverse selection. Moral hazard means that workers who are insured against reductions in their incomes will not work as hard as those who are not insured. Adverse selection means that lower-quality workers prefer to work at the firms that pay an average wage to all workers. The best workers opt for firms that pay on the basis of individual output, leaving the lower-quality workers to go to the nonscreening firm. Low-quality workers prefer these firms, independent of risk considerations. Because moral hazard and adverse selection problems are so pronounced, it is difficult to believe that insurance motives have much of an effect on optimal compensation schemes. Most of the variation in wages is across individuals, not over time, and it is this residual corss-sectional variation that is most difficult to ensure without causing other problems.

hardwood and $m + 1$ through z to plywood, it must be true that maximum output is given by

(A4.4) $$\text{Maximum output} = H_1 + \ldots + H_m + P_{m+1} \ldots P_z$$

But if this is maximum output, then it must be true that switching jobs between any two workers results in lower output; that is,

(A4.5) $$H_1 + \ldots + H_m + P_{m+1} \ldots + P_z > H_r \sum_{\substack{j=1 \\ j \neq k}}^{m} H_j + P_k \sum_{\substack{q=m+1 \\ q \neq r}}^{z} P_q$$

$$\forall \ (1 \leq k \leq m, \ m + 1 \leq r \leq z)$$

which can be written as

(A4.6) $$H_k - P_k > H_r - P_r \quad \forall \quad (1 \leq k \leq m, \ m + 1 \leq r \leq z)$$

The expression in (A4.6) says that the absolute difference between k's productivity in hardwood and her productivity in plywood must exceed the difference between r's productivity in hardwood and r's productivity in plywood. This must be true for all k and r where k is defined as a worker whose name is between 1 and m and r is defined as a worker whose name is between $m + 1$ and z. In other words, every worker assigned to hardwood has a higher difference between hardwood and plywood production than any worker assigned to plywood. This is exactly the rule discussed in the text of this chapter: Rank workers by their absolute productivity differences between hardwood and plywood and assign them to the open slots in hardwood on the basis of the ranking (highest to lowest difference) until all hardwood slots are used up.

VARIABLE PAY OR STRAIGHT SALARY

5

*W*orkers can be screened at the time of hire, but that is not the only time a worker's output can be measured. Should workers be paid on the basis of their output, or should they merely be given a fixed salary? Some of these issues depend on what is known to a competitor about a given worker's productivity. If a rival knows particular workers are underpaid relative to their peers, then the rival can profitably steal these workers away by offering them more than they currently earn but less than their full worth. Outside competition is not the only reason to pay workers on the basis of their output. Incentives, risk, and quality production also enter into the picture. The following discussion illustrates some of these issues:

JOHNSON: I've been thinking about our compensation practices. I think we need to change them. We have too many workers who are being paid just for showing up every morning. I think at least one-third of our work force is just coasting.

KNIGHT: Well, everyone is talking about variable pay these days. Maybe we should move in that direction.

STIGLER: My understanding is that variable pay attempts to tie pay to some measure of output. That sounds good, but I don't see how we can make that work here. This is a consulting firm. It's hard enough to define what workers are producing without having to measure and pay on the basis of it.

REID: Right. You guys think that pay is everything. Once we start trying to pay for everything that gets done around here, we'll find that the things we don't pay for directly won't get done at all. This reminds me of those schemes that try to pay football players for performance. Tampa Bay cut their quarterback's salary every time he threw an interception. You know what happened? He threw no interceptions because he wasn't willing to throw any passes. That's what will happen to us.

STIGLER: In our case it's even worse. This isn't football, and we can't easily measure the things our guys are doing.

JOHNSON: True, but there are lots of things we can measure. Billed hours, for example. That relates pretty closely to what we care about.

REID: In the short run, yes. But then we'll get all our people generating billable hours and none working on bringing in big clients who benefit the entire firm.

KNIGHT: Well, we can pay for bringing in big clients, too.

STIGLER: Sure, but eventually we'll forget to pay for something, and we'll end up getting too little of it. This variable pay stuff is trendy, but it's fundamentally a bad idea.

JOHNSON: Well, I think that we should try it. If it doesn't work, we can go back to our current scheme.

A number of points were raised in the previous discussion. Among them:

- Should pay be based on some measure of output, or should it just be a fixed amount for coming to work?

- How should output be defined?

- Does payment for output cause workers to seek the wrong goals?

- How can compensation schemes be altered to ensure that workers do the right thing?

- Does output-based compensation induce people to focus on the short run at the expense of the long run?

- If output-based compensation is used, should it be tied to individual output or to some measure of group output?

◆ ◆ ◆ ◆ ◆ PAYMENT BY INPUT VERSUS PAYMENT BY OUTPUT

What does it mean to pay on the basis of output? Output is not always easy to measure. The key feature of output-based pay is that compensation depends on some measure of what comes out, not on a measure of the time or effort that goes in. When a worker is paid on output, the amount of time spent on a project does not affect the firm's willingness to pay the worker. Some examples are useful:

1. Agricultural workers often earn a straight piece rate. For example, a worker who is hired to pick apricots may be paid a certain amount for each tray of fruit picked. The amount of time spent picking does not enter the compensation formula. A worker who picks twice as fast earns twice as much, even if the person spends no more total time working than the slower worker.

2. A salesperson who is on straight commission receives output-based pay. Suppose the salesperson is selling cosmetics on a commission basis.[1] The amount the salesperson takes home depends only on the amount of product sold. The amount of time that it takes to sell the product is irrelevant. The size of the salesperson's check is independent of the amount of time spent selling. It depends only on the value of goods sold. Any complaints about having put forth too much effort will fall on deaf ears.

3. Top executives often receive a large part of their compensation in the form of stock or stock options. The value of a firm's stock relates, at least in part, to the executive's performance. If, say, the CEO is resourceful, makes good decisions, and implements them effectively, a firm's stock price will rise. When the CEO holds a significant portion of wealth in the stock of the firm, the CEO's performance is rewarded. The amount a CEO receives does not depend directly on the amount of time spent at work. Members of the compensation committee are unlikely to be sympathetic to a CEO who worked 80 hours a week, but ran the company into the ground. Instead, CEO bonuses and stock value are more closely tied to performance than they are to effort. Thus, CEOs tend to receive output-based pay.

Input-based pay is compensation that depends on *the amount of time or effort spent on an activity*. It is independent of output considerations. Input is not easy to measure, but firms use proxies in order to assess effort. The most commonly used measure is time at work. For example, an hourly wage rate compensates workers for being at the job and presumably putting forth some effort. The assumption implicit in hourly pay is that the more hours spent at work, the higher the effort that goes into the job. On average, this assumption is almost certainly accurate. Individuals who work 40 hours per week get more work done on average than individuals who work only 10 hours per week. This is not to say that they burn more calories per hour, but only that the total amount of effort exerted is positively related to the total time worked.

Even workers on a monthly or annual salary are paid for time worked. But just as an hourly wage does not consider the exact number of seconds per hour that are actually worked, a salary does not take into account the exact number of hours per month or year that are actually worked.

---

[1] The Mary Kay company is famous for having an army of salespeople who receive commission and bonuses depending on the amount of cosmetic products that they sell.

◆ ◆ ◆ ◆ ◆ OUTPUT-BASED PAY

Paying on the basis of output has advantages. We focus on two. First, output-based pay induces the good workers to stay and the bad workers to leave the firm. Second, output-based pay motivates workers to put forth effort instead of merely showing up to work. Let us consider each in turn.

Screening Workers

Payment by output induces workers who are inefficient to leave the firm. If workers are paid exactly their output, they will leave whenever their payments fall short of the wage at their next best alternative job. Conversely, all workers whose payments exceed the alternative wage stay on the job. Since a firm that pays a piece rate cannot pay its workers more per piece than they produce, those who stay are also those for whom output exceeds product in the alternative job. They are the workers whom efficiency dictates should stay at their current firm.

To see this, consider paying salespersons according to two schedules, as shown in Figure 5.1.

The line marked A starts workers out at zero and pays them $100 per set of encyclopedias sold. A salesperson who sells five sets earns $500 per week. The line marked B pays a straight salary of $500 per week. Workers who sell two sets earn $500, as do those who sell ten sets.

Which scheme does the company prefer? It depends on who comes to work under each scheme. Suppose there are two encyclopedia companies. World Book offers scheme A, while Britannica offers scheme B. Britannica does better on all workers who sell more than five sets of encyclopedias. A worker at Britannica who sold, say, ten sets would cost the firm only $500, which is equivalent to $50 per set. The same worker at World Book would cost the firm $1,000, which is equivalent to $100 per set.

FIGURE 5.1
COMPENSATION OF ENCYCLOPEDIA
SALESPEOPLE

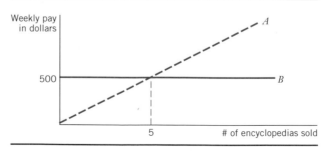

Unfortunately for Britannica, it will not be able to retain workers who sell more than five sets. Workers who can sell more than five sets per week prefer to work at World Book, where they can earn more money. This means that Britannica will be able to keep only workers who sell five units or less. Given this, which firm does better? The answer is World Book. At Britannica, the best worker sells five per week, while the worst may sell none at all. The average number of sets sold per worker might be three. This results in an average salary payment per set sold of $500/3, or $166.67 per set. All high-productivity workers go to World Book and sell more than five sets per week. But the number sold does not affect World Book's average salary per set. It is fixed at $100. It does not matter whether one worker sells 20 sets or four workers sell 5 sets each. The total salary cost to World Book is $2,000 in either case, which is equivalent to $100 per set. This must be true, of course, since World Book's salary scheme is fixed at $100 per set sold.

World Book's average salary payment of $100 per set is lower than Britannica's $166.67 per set because Britannica gets stuck with the lower-productivity workers. This is one reason in favor of paying piece rates: It induces the more-profitable, higher-productivity workers to come to work for your firm and leaves the less-productive, lower-productivity workers to be employed by your salary-paying rivals.

Using Incentives

The second reason for using output-based pay relates to incentives. Paying on this basis provides workers direct incentives to produce more. We can determine the appropriate output-based formula for offering incentives.

Example 1: Taxidriver's Compensation

To get a sense of how to think about compensation formulas, consider the example of a taxicab driver. There are a number of possible ways to compensate cab drivers. One of the most common is to allow the driver to rent the cab and medallion for a fee, pay for his or her own gas, and then keep all revenues. In other words, the cab driver is paid a commission rate of 100 percent, after variable costs—in this case, gasoline—have been covered. But before the drivers can receive any commission, they must pay the rental fee. If commissions fall short of the rental fee, drivers cover the shortfall out of their own pockets.

Let us consider a specific example. In most cities, the meter rate for cabs is regulated by a Transportation Authority. Suppose the Transportation Authority in a particular city sets the amount that cabs can charge at $2.00 per mile. A cab company like Yellow Cab might set the following daily compensation scheme for its drivers:

$$\text{Compensation} = -\$100 + \$2 \times (\text{miles driven}) - \text{gasoline expense}$$

This scheme says that the driver rents the cab and medallion for $100 per day and then allows the driver to take home everything on the meter after paying for gasoline.

PERFORMANCE PAY AT SAFELITE GLASS
◆ ◆ ◆ ◆ ◆ ◆ ◆ ◆ ◆ ◆

Safelite Glass Corporation installs automobile glass in about 600 small repair centers across the country. In January 1994 CEO Garen Staglin and President John Barlow decided to alter their compensation system for auto-glass installers. Over the course of two years, installers would be switched from hourly wages to a performance pay system based on amount of glass installed, while still guaranteed a base salary of $11 per hour. The next year Safelite earned net profits of $16 million on $358 million in revenues.

Safelite was able to implement this system without a great cost because it already used a very sophisticated computerized information system that tracked, as part of inventory control, the number of units installed by each worker in a given week. Since output was easy to measure, a compensation scheme based on this measure apparently seemed most logical to Safelite's management.

The sophisticated computer system also allowed for a detailed analysis of the effect of the new piece rates. Safelite's overall productivity rose by an astonishing 36 percent as measured by units of glass installed per worker per day. Further examination revealed that almost two-thirds of this increase was the result of increased productivity by existing workers. The remaining increase can be accounted for by the selection of workers who choose to join and stay in such an environment. With an overall annual turnover rate of about 50 percent before the pay system was changed, those high-productivity workers who were previously more likely to leave under the hourly wage system would now fare much better under piece rates (and thus stay). In addition, new hires (adjusting for experience) were more productive than those employees hired under the hourly system. In summation, the average worker, whose output was 2.6 installations per day before the new compensation plan, increased to an output of 3.1 units.

This increase in productivity would serve no purpose if compensation costs rose at the same rate. However, the data show that the pay for the average employee increased by only 9 percent, but productivity increased by 36 percent. Both the worker and the company are better off under this new pay system. One must recall that the system for measuring output for workers already existed at Safelite; had it not, measurement costs might have eliminated any gain from a changed compensation system. But the gain in productivity is so large that the costs of implementing a measurement scheme may have been justified.

Although productivity increased dramatically, quality must also remain high for the business to be successful. The standard practice at companies using piece rate systems where quality is easy to detect has been to force the employee who installed the defective component to replace it without pay. Initially, Safelite required the installer's co-workers to reinstall any defective glass. A peer pressure system was implemented. Those installers who could not perform had to improve or resign. Now, installers must redo their own defective installations without pay. Apparently, in an environment where output is easy to measure and monitor, a piece rate compensation plan is effective, since profits rose.

Source: Edward Lazear, "Performance Pay and Productivity," NBER working paper #5672 (August 1996). "The 500 Largest Private Companies in the U.S.," *Forbes*, December 5, 1994.

There are, of course, many other possible schemes. For example, the company can simply give the driver the cab and split the revenues received according to some predetermined proportion, say 50 percent to each.

The revenue-splitting scheme has a couple of problems. Among the most obvious is that, since the company cannot monitor the amount of driving done, the cabby and passenger can make a deal that makes each better off, but hurts the company. The ride is given with the meter off and the customer agrees to pay 75 percent of what the meter would have shown. The cabby is better off because 75 percent of the full fare beats the 50 percent that he would have received with the meter on, and the customer is better off because she pays 75 percent of the full fare—all at the expense of the company, which receives nothing from the transaction.

Monitoring workers, though possible, is often impractical. In this case, when the meter is off, the cab's "for hire" sign is on. The company can detect cheaters, but it is very costly for supervisors to patrol the streets looking for a full cab with a lighted "for hire" sign. It is better to use a compensation scheme that aligns the incentives of the cabby with those of the company. The scheme where the cab is rented to the driver provides those incentives, especially when it is recognized that the amount the driver is willing to pay to rent the cab increases when he can make more in revenues.

Another rationale for giving the driver all revenues after a rental fee is paid relates to effort. A 50 percent commission rate induces insufficient effort on the part of the driver. Consider a taxi driver who has been working for 11 hours on a particular day and is trying to decide whether to drive the cab for a twelfth hour. He reasons that if he drives the cab, he expects to pick up $10 in cab fare that hour. Let's suppose that he values the leisure associated with that hour of work at $8. That is, at any price greater than $8, the taxicab driver would be willing to put forth the effort and drive the cab. It is clear that the cab should be driven during that twelfth hour. If there were a way to give the driver, say, $9 for driving that hour, both the cabby and the company would be better off. Since $9 exceeds $8, the driver prefers the money to the leisure. The company is clearly better off because if the driver does not drive, the company earns nothing on hour 12. If the cabby drives, the company gets the $1 difference between revenues of $10 and payment of $9.

Suppose the cab driver takes home 50 percent of his compensation and does not pay any rental on the cab. In this case, the driver will not supply the twelfth hour of effort. Since he takes home only half of the $10 fare, and since he requires at least $8 to drive, he prefers the leisure to the $5 of revenue. If instead, the worker rents the cab and receives all revenue, he will opt to drive during that hour. Since he receives the full $10 for that hour, and since $10 exceeds the $8 necessary to induce him to drive, he opts to work. The company can extract a higher rental fee from the driver who works 12 hours than it can from one who works only 11 hours. The additional hour provides more revenue to the driver, which increases the value of renting the cab.

Sorting

There is another reason to make the worker receive the full marginal output, which has nothing to do with effort. If workers differ in their characteristics, then paying a worker less than the full amount will cause **adverse selection** problems in the hiring process—the wrong workers will want to work at the firm. This is the point made in the earlier encyclopedia example. Because of its importance, we repeat it in a somewhat different context here.

Suppose that one cab company, Black and White (B&W), pays 50 percent commission, but no rental fee and another, Red Cab, pays 100 percent commission after a $100 rental fee. The situation is shown in Figure 5.2.

Any worker who plans to produce more than Q^* units prefers to work at Red Cab. Hard-working drivers make more money by renting the cab and keeping all

FIGURE 5.2
COMPENSATION OF CAB DRIVERS

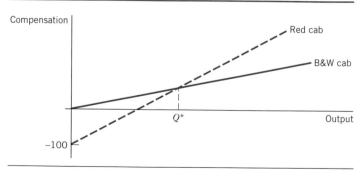

of the proceeds. This can be seen in the diagram because Red Cab's compensation line is above B&W's when output exceeds Q^*.

Those who are not as hard working prefer B&W. They do not produce enough output (rides, in this case) to justify the $100 rental fee. Workers whose output falls below Q^* make more money at B&W because the B&W compensation line lies above the Red Cab's compensation line for $Q < Q^*$.

Sorting is produced by the two rival cab companies who vie for workers with different compensation schemes. Red Cab gets the high productivity workers; B&W gets the low productivity ones. A cab is capital. As long as Red Cab chooses its initial rental fee appropriately, Red Cab can earn more per cab than does B&W. B&W suffers from adverse selection.

Example 2: Salesperson's Commission

In some occupations output can be easily observed. For example, a salesperson's output is easily observed because most, if not all, of what a salesperson produces is reflected in the revenue generated.

Consider the example of a salesperson who sells personal computers by phone. The cost of producing computers is given by Table 5.1.

The numbers in Table 5.1 reflect a fixed cost of $1 million. Before any output is even produced, the firm must bear a set-up cost of $1 million. Beyond that, every additional computer costs the firm $900 to produce. This cost relation holds at least up through the production of 100 million computers, which is well beyond the range that need be considered by this company.

Suppose the company sells each computer for $1,000. The net revenue generated by the sale of one computer is $100. The firm can make money on the sale of a computer by paying the salesperson anything up to $100 per computer. Note, by the way, that giving the salesperson a 10 percent commission on the sale of a $1,000 computer would result in a payment to the salesperson of exactly $100, which would mean that the firm would exactly break even on the production and sale of each computer.

Of course, if the full $100 were paid to the salesperson, the firm would be left with no profit. Seeing this, management may be tempted to offer a commission less than 10 percent to the salesperson. For example, they might offer 5 percent. A

TABLE 5.1

COST OF COMPUTERS EXCLUDING
SALESPERSON'S COMPENSATION

Number of Computers Produced	Cost
0	$1,000,000
100	$1,090,000
200	$1,180,000
10,000	$10,000,000
100,000	$91,000,000
100,000,000	$90,001,000,000

policy of this sort brings about the wrong result and reduces profits for the firm. The lower commission rate causes salespersons to slack off and induces the most productive salespeople to go elsewhere. Each of these points will be discussed in greater detail.

The appropriate scheme induces workers to put forth efficient levels of effort and causes the most cost-effective workers to stay with the firm. Rather than reducing the commission rate to 5 percent, a better idea is to "charge" the salesperson for his desk and pay the full 10 percent commission rate.

The compensation scheme would then have the following formula:

(5.1) $$\text{Compensation} = \lambda + ((.1)(\text{Sales revenue}))$$

The parameter λ is chosen by the firm to maximize its profits. Below, we will describe how best to choose λ. For concreteness, suppose that $\lambda = -\$10,000$ per week. Then the salesperson does not take home anything unless he or she can sell at least 100 computers per week. When the salesperson sells 100 computers, sales revenue is exactly $100,000 and commission equals $10,000, just offsetting the $10,000 that the worker must "pay" in order to "rent" a desk. Figure 5.3 shows this graphically, represented by the dashed line.

When sales equal 100, the worker receives zero. When sales equal 200, the worker receives $10,000. If a typical salesperson sells an average of 110 computers per month, then over a year that person will earn

$$52 \times (-\$10,000 + .1(110)(\$1,000)) = \$52,000$$

How much does the firm earn? Every time the firm hires a new employee, it can expect to receive an annual revenue on the new salesperson of $52 \times 110 \times \$1,000$, which equals $5,720,000. It costs $900 to produce each computer, so the additional cost of production is then $52 \times 110 \times \$900$, or $5,148,000. But the firm pays the salesperson $52,000 in annual compensation. Thus, the total cost of adding one more salesperson and producing the computers that he or she sells is $5,148,000 + \$52,000 = \$5,200,000$. The profit on this employee is therefore

$$\$5,720,000 - \$5,200,000 = \$520,000$$

FIGURE 5.3
COMPENSATION OF COMPUTER SALESPEOPLE

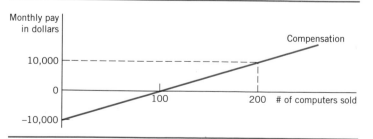

Note that the firm is paying out a 10 percent commission rate, so the amount that it makes per sale is zero. How, then, is the firm earning profit? It does so by "charging" $10,000 per month for every desk. The change takes the form of deducting from total commissions an amount equal to $10,000 before the paycheck is written. This is equivalent to renting the worker the job for $10,000 a month. As a result, the firm earns $520,000 a year on each worker.

Is the worker willing to work for $52,000 a year? This depends on the amount she can earn at an alternative job. If the worker's best comparable effort alternative pays $1,000 per week, then she will be indifferent between accepting this job and taking the other one. If, on the other hand, the worker's best alternative job paid only $26,000 per year, then the firm would not have to offer anything more than $26,000 to keep her. Since the commission at 10 percent amounts to

$$52 \times 110 \times .1 \times \$1,000 = \$572,000$$

the firm must charge a total of $546,000 per year in "rental" fees in order to leave the worker with $26,000 per year. Now, $546,000/52 = $10,500 so a rental fee of $10,500 per month instead of $10,000 per month would leave the worker indifferent between this job and the best alternative. Under these circumstances, the compensation scheme would look like

$$\text{Compensation} = -\$10,500 + (.1 \, (\text{Sales revenue}))$$

instead of

$$\text{Compensation} = -\$10,000 + (.1 \, (\text{Sales revenue}))$$

The firm would be better off because it would collect another $26,000 in revenue per year, but the firm's ability to do this depends on the alternative wage that the worker can receive.

Why not simply lower the commission rate, rather than charging a higher job rental rate? For example, the worker could be given some smaller percentage commission, while leaving the rental rate at $1,000. The reason is the effect on effort.

A commission rate of 9.55 percent (instead of the earlier 10%) would result in commission of $52 \times 110 \times \$1000 \times (.0955) = \$546,000$.

If, from total commissions, $10,000 were deducted as rental every week, the year's deduction would be $520,000, leaving the worker with $26,000 for the year. But at a commission rate of 9.55 percent, the worker's incentives to put forth effort are lower than at 10 percent. Recall the taxicab logic. At lower meter rates, the cab driver goes home earlier. Here, at a commission rate of 9.55 percent, the salesperson puts forth the effort to sell an additional computer only if the value of her leisure is less than $95.50. Were the commission rate 10 percent, the salesperson would put forth the effort to sell an additional computer if the value of her leisure were less than $100. Therefore, more effort is expended when the commission rate is higher.

Table 5.2 presents some hypothetical leisure values as they correspond to computer sales. For now, we leave our assumption of the $10,000-a-week desk charge and look at a slightly less lucrative example.

TABLE 5.2
REQUIRED COMPENSATION FOR A
GIVEN LEVEL OF COMPUTER SALES

Computers Sold	Value of Effort
1	$2
2	$6
3	$10
4	$14
5	$18
6	$22
7	$26
8	$30
9	$34
10	$38
11	$42
12	$46
13	$50
14	$54
15	$58
16	$62
17	$66
18	$70
19	$74
20	$78
21	$82
22	$86
23	$90
24	$94
25	$98
26	$102
27	$106
28	$110
29	$114
30	$118

Table 5.2 should be interpreted as follows. Workers must be paid at least $2 to sell the first computer. Having sold one computer, workers must be paid another $6 to be willing to work hard enough to sell the second computer. Similarly, if 22 computers are sold, salespeople must be paid an additional $90 to induce them to put forth the effort to sell the twenty-third computer, and so forth.

A commission rate of 9.5 percent would induce salespeople to sell only 24 computers. The next computer requires compensation of at least $98, which exceeds the $95.50 paid when the 9.5 percent rate is used. If 10 percent were paid, the twenty-fifth computer would be sold. Furthermore, workers would be better off because they would each receive $100 for a task that only cost $98 of effort. The firm is no worse off, because its total cost on the twenty-fifth computer is

$900 in costs + $100 in commission, which exactly equals the sale price. In fact, the firm could be made better off. Since a salesperson would have accepted as little as $98 to sell this unit, an additional charge of $2 can be added to the rental fee.

If a 10 percent commission rate is good, isn't an 11 percent rate even better? The answer is a definite no. At 11 percent, the salesperson earns $110 per machine. Under these circumstances, using Table 5.2, we see that the salesperson is willing to sell 28 computers. The value of the effort that goes into selling the 28th unit is exactly $110. But in order to want to sell computers, the salesperson must net at least $102 on unit 26, $106 on unit 27, and $110 on unit 28. The firm, however, only has $100 of revenue left on each computer after covering its other costs. Thus, paying above 10 percent results in a loss on each of these units.

Another way to see this is to consider the total amount that must be paid in order to induce the salesperson to work the job. Table 5.3 reports the total compensation necessary to induce the individual in question to work, given that she puts forth the effort required to sell the number of computers listed on the left.

In order to hire a worker who will sell only one computer, $2 must be paid to cover the effort. To hire a worker who will sell two computers, the total pay must be at least $8, in order to cover the effort value of $2 on the first computer and $6 on the second. To hire a worker who will sell three computers, the total pay must be at least $18, in order to cover the effort value of $2 on the first computer, $6 on the second, and $10 on the third.

As already argued, the commission rate determines the number of computers sold. At a commission rate of 10 percent, the salesperson stops selling at 25 computers because the revenue received from selling the the next one is $100, whereas the effort value is $102. The salesperson will not sell only 24 computers, because the revenue from the next one is $100, whereas the effort value is $98.

If the salesperson sells 25 computers, Table 5.3 shows that total compensation required is $1,250. But 10 percent commission on 25 sales results in revenues of $2,500. As a result, the firm can "charge" the salesperson $1,250 per day for the job. In other words, the compensation scheme would be

$$\text{Compensation} = -\$1,250 + (.1 \, (\text{Sales revenue}))$$
$$= -\$1,250 + \$2,500 = \$1,250$$

The firm would earn $25 \times (\$1000 - 900) = \$2,500$ in net revenue on sales before paying the compensation. Since the firm ends up paying the salesperson $1,250, the true net to the firm on those sales is $2,500 − $1,250, or $1,250.

Suppose instead that the firm chooses a commission rate of 9 percent. Then, because the salesperson's revenue on each computer is only $90, she will choose to sell only 23 units. The effort cost of selling the twenty-fourth computer is $94 and the revenue received is only $90 so the salesperson will not work hard enough to sell unit 24.

The commission on 23 computers is $23 \times \$90$, or $2,070. Table 5.3 shows that the salesperson must earn at least $1,058 to be willing to take a job where she will sell 23 computers. Thus, if the firm charged $1,012 for the job, she would be willing to work.

TABLE 5.3
TOTAL COMPENSATION REQUIRED FOR SALESPERSON

Computers Sold	Value of Effort	Total Required Compensation
0		
1	$2	$2
2	$6	$8
3	$10	$18
4	$14	$32
5	$18	$50
6	$22	$72
7	$26	$98
8	$30	$128
9	$34	$162
10	$38	$200
11	$42	$242
12	$46	$288
13	$50	$338
14	$54	$392
15	$58	$450
16	$62	$512
17	$66	$578
18	$70	$648
19	$74	$722
20	$78	$800
21	$82	$882
22	$86	$968
23	$90	$1,058
24	$94	$1,152
25	$98	$1,250
26	$102	$1,352
27	$106	$1,458
28	$110	$1,568
29	$114	$1,682
30	$118	$1,800

The compensation scheme would be

$$\text{Compensation} = -\$1,012 + (.09(\text{Sales revenue}))$$
$$= -\$1,012 + \$2,070 = \$1,058$$

and the firm would earn $23 \times (\$1,000 - 900)$, or $2,300 in net revenue on her sales before paying her compensation. Since the firm ends up paying the salesperson $1058, the true net to the firm is $2,300 − $1,058, or $1,242. With a 10 percent commission rate, the firm nets $1,250 so the amount the firm nets with the 9 percent commission rate is lower than the amount it nets with the 10 percent commission rate. Thus, it is clear that the firm makes more profit by offering a 10 percent commission rate with a charge of $1,250 than it does by offering a 9 percent commission rate with a charge of $1,012.

Similarly, the firm makes more with a 10 percent commission rate than it does with an 11 percent commission rate. If the firm pays 11 percent, the salesperson makes $110 per computer and sells 28 computers. Selling unit 29 would result in a commission of $110, but an effort cost of $114.

Commission on the 28 computers is $28 \times \$110$, or $3,080. Table 5.3 shows that the salesperson must earn at least $1,568 to be willing to take a job selling 28 computers. Thus, the firm can charge $1,512 for the job.

The compensation scheme would be

$$\text{Compensation} = -\$1,512 + (.11(\text{Sales revenue}))$$
$$= -\$1,512 + \$3,080 = \$1,568$$

The firm would earn $28 \times (\$1000 - 900)$, or $2,800 in net revenue on sales before paying her compensation. Since the firm ends up paying $1,568, the true net to the firm is $2,800 − $1,568, or $1,232. The amount that the firm nets with the 11 percent commission rate is lower than the $1,250 it nets with the 10 percent commission rate. The firm clearly makes more profit by offering a 10 percent commission rate with a charge of $1,250 than it does by offering 11 percent commission and imposing a charge for the job of $1,512.

It is not mere coincidence that the firm does best by setting the commission rate to exhaust total revenue. Doing this and then charging the worker a fee to extract some profit is always more lucrative than trying to extract profit by lowering the commission rate. When the commission rate is lowered, incentives are reduced. As a result, the worker does not work hard enough and the job is not worth as much to the person. Therefore, the amount that the firm can extract from the worker is smaller. Analogously, too high a commission rate results in too much work. The amount that the worker must be compensated in order to be willing to put forth this level of effort exceeds the value of that effort. The effort cost is higher than the value of what is produced. This is another application of the taxicab logic. The general proof of this proposition is contained in the appendix to this chapter.

Reality versus Theory

One rarely sees workers paying firms for jobs, especially for $10,000 a week. Although it is common in the case of taxicabs, this explicit payment from workers to firms is the exception rather than the rule. Does this mean that the theory of optimal salesperson compensation is nothing more than a theory? As the reader might have guessed, the answer is a resounding no. Although explicit payment is not common, implicit payment is pervasive. Recall Figure 5.3.

The compensation scheme reflects what is often termed a *draw*. Workers are guaranteed a salary of $10,000 per month even if sales fall short of the 200 computer mark. But workers receive no commission until they have sold at least 200 computers. After 200, a salesperson begins to earn $100 per unit, as before. Thus, the compensation line is horizontal up to 200 units and then rises at a slope of 100.

Is this substantively different from the scheme shown by the dotted line, which starts out at −$10,000? It is different for sales of less than 200 units, but it is identical for sales of 200 units or more. If the salesperson sells 200 computers, she earns $10,000 whether she receives the draw or is forced to pay $10,000 for the job. If she sells 300 units a month, she receives

$$\$10,000 + 100 \times (300 - 200) = \$20,000$$

with the draw scheme. With the initial buy-in scheme, she earns

$$-\$10,000 + 100 \times 300 = \$20,000$$

The amounts are equal, irrespective of scheme.

The commonly used draw scheme differs only when sales fall short of 200 units, but workers whose sales fall short of 200 units and who dip into their draw as a result will find themselves out of a job in short order. Firms do not tolerate workers who repeatedly produce below the break-even point. Therefore, as a practical matter, virtually all workers will be producing in the range where both schemes are identical. This also means that the commonly used compensation schemes implicitly charge workers for their jobs by preventing them from receiving commission until they have hit some target level—in this case, 200 units. The job-purchase scheme discussed in the previous section is the scheme commonly used for salespersons, even though explicit payments by workers to firms are rare.

One Hundred Percent Commission Rates

The taxicab example argues for the efficiency of a 100 percent commission rate. After the cab is rented, the driver takes all revenue and pays for his own gasoline. But 100 percent commission rates are extremely rare. Taxi drivers and peanut vendors at the ballpark are among the few in the economy who are on 100 percent commission schemes.

Once again, appearance is not reality. Recall that the taxi driver receives 100 percent of revenue, but must pay for his own gasoline. This means that the driver takes home something less than 100 percent of revenue, the difference being the costs of operation. The same may well be true of the typical salesperson. In the computer example given earlier, the salesperson's $100 commission was thought to reflect the difference between revenue on the computer and the variable costs associated with building the machine. Thus, the commission on *net* revenue was 100 percent, but the commission rate on *gross* revenue was much smaller. Since the selling price of the computer was $1,000, and commission was $100, the commission rate on sales equaled 10 percent.

This is typical of most salesperson compensation. Rather than stating commission as 100 percent of net revenue, commission is stated as some percentage of sales. Why? The answer is straightforward and is best illustrated by a real-life example.

A few years ago, an actor sued the producer of a movie in which he appeared. The actor's contract stated that he would receive some percentage of profit on the movie as part of his compensation. In response, the movie company allegedly loaded up much of its overhead costs, like those for space and equipment use on other films, on this one movie. This was an accounting trick to reduce the measured profit on the movie for which it had to pay commission to the actor. The court ordered the studio to pay the actor some royalties, based on what it deemed a more appropriate measure of cost.

The problem with tying commission to profit is that the measure of profit is too easily manipulated by management. Workers do not like these kinds of contracts and demand too much from the firm in order to accept them. A more efficient and equitable contract states commission as a function of sales—the figures are much more difficult to manipulate. As a result, commission rates are stated as 10 percent of sales, rather than 100 percent of net revenue. The two are equivalent, but tying commissions to sales is cleaner.[2]

Capital Distortions

Most people who take taxis on a frequent basis can generally tell whether a cab is owner-driven as soon as they enter. Owner-driven cabs tend to be cleaner and in better condition than those that are leased from a large company. Why? Drivers who own their cabs care about their upkeep because they bear the cost of repairs. Drivers who simply rent cabs on a daily basis from a large company have almost no concern about the long-run condition of the cabs. Not only will they not bear the costs of repair, but might not drive the same cabs for days.

Making the driver a 100 percent commission recipient does not solve all incentive problems. Since the drivers do not own the capital, in this case the cabs, they do not take proper care of it. There are two solutions to the problem. One is simply to sell the cabs to the drivers. This assumes that the driver has the funds necessary to buy the cab. Yellow Cab stays in business precisely because there are individuals who want to drive cabs, but for any number of reasons, do not want to purchase their own cabs. The second solution is to charge drivers for actual depreciation and damage to the cabs. If it were easy to assess damage, this would be a perfect approach. The difficulty arises because it is complicated and costly to measure damage to a cab on a sufficiently frequent basis. As a result, the rental fee to the driver reflects only average damage and depreciation, but does not penalize drivers for any incremental damage. Charging a fixed rental fee removes any incentive to care for the cab.

---

[2]Incidentally, the situation was repeated in the case of *Forest Gump*. Writer Howard Groom sued the studio for claiming that the wildly successful movie was a money loser. Groom had been promised a share of the profits.

The problem of neglecting capital stock comes up in virtually all contexts. For example, in agriculture, one problem with renting land to a farmer is that the farmer does not take appropriate care of the land. Specifically, rotating crops and fertilizing the soil cost the farmer money, but do not yield any long-term benefits to a farmer who may rent another plot of land in the future. One way around this is to have a very-long-term lease agreement. In this way, farmer and owner incentives become more closely aligned. Another way to deal with this is to have the owner bear the cost of care for the land directly. The owner could pay to have the soil fertilized and could even hire a third party to perform the work.

Professional football provides another example where incentives are not properly aligned. Before players had the ability to become free agents, they were essentially owned by their teams. Before a player could play for another team, his current team would have to agree to let him go. These trades usually involved fees paid to the current team by the acquiring team. As a result, teams viewed their players as property. A player who was injured would neither perform for the current team nor bring a very high price in trade. Free agency significantly reduced the power that a team has over its players. Now, most of the gains from moving from one team to another are captured by the player. Teams are now renters of a player's talents, rather than owners. As renters, they do not have the appropriate incentives to care for the player's human capital. When a free agent player has a small injury, the team is more likely to insist that he play with free agency than it would have been under the previous regime. The long-run damage to the player that may result is reflected in the player's future salary, rather than in the profit that the team receives. The player may prefer to stay out, but team management has no incentive to consider the player's future viability.

Hybrid Schemes

Workers who are paid on the basis of input may in fact have their compensation adjusted to some measure of output. This is generally done after the fact and for the future, rather than for the past. For example, an individual who receives an annual salary might find that next year's annual salary reflects output this year. This is not the same as basing this year's compensation on this year's performance. One difference is that the worker must stay with the firm for another year in order to capture the return to good performance. Conversely, a worker may be able to avoid being punished for poor performance by quitting the job and taking employment elsewhere.

Analogously, workers who are paid on the basis of output may find that their piece rates are adjusted as a function of last period's time input. This sometimes manifests itself in the *ratchet effect*.[3] A firm might reduce a worker's piece rate if it finds that the worker was able to produce a very high level of output in a short period of time. In this way, the firm tries to "ratchet up" the amount of work done by the worker for a given amount of pay.

---

[3] See Martin Weitzman (1980).

The firm's ability to reduce the piece rate when time spent is too low depends on a worker's alternative opportunities. Unless the worker is somehow locked into the firm, she may leave to go elsewhere as a result of a reduction in piece rate. Thus, ratchet effects depend on there being some loss associated with moving. This necessitates that the relationship between the worker and his firm be special. There are a number of factors that can make it special. The worker may be unhappy about moving because of friendships in the current firm. The worker may be more valuable at the current firm than elsewhere because of acquired skills, or it may simply be that a job search would be too costly and unpleasant. Any of these factors can give the firm leverage over the worker and allow the ratchet effect to operate. One way to offset the ratchet effect is by using a carefully constructed compensation scheme that requires piece rates to fall over time in a particular way. The details of this scheme are derived and presented in the appendix to this chapter.

INPUT: TIME-BASED PAY   ◆ ◆ ◆ ◆ ◆

Most workers are paid salaries or hourly wages that are based on input rather than on output. Recall that input-based pay is compensation that depends on the amount of time or effort spent on an activity and is independent of output considerations. Given the value of output-based pay in providing incentives and in sorting out the best workers, why is such a large proportion of the work force paid on the basis of a time unit?

Cost Advantage in Measurement

There are a number of factors that push a firm away from paying piece rates and toward paying salaries. The first and most obvious is that it is costly to measure output, even imperfectly. Consider, for example, the vice-president of finance of a large corporation. Tasks are highly varied, nonrepetitive, and affect a large number of individuals in the organization. Measuring the VP's output, even on the most mundane of tasks, is extremely difficult. It may well pay simply to ignore differences in output across individuals and pay a fixed salary. Conditions under which measurement does not pay are discussed in chapter 4.

Quantity versus Quality

It is often argued that paying a piece rate induces workers to focus on producing a high number of low-quality units. The quality, of course, must be sufficiently high so that the output "counts," but the worker, it is alleged, is unconcerned with the unit's quality beyond that.

Piece rates do not necessarily overweight quantity. The exact compensation formula determines the balance on quality versus the quantity. For example, the typist who is paid on the basis of the number of the pages might type too quickly and make too many errors. On the other hand, the typist who is penalized significantly for each error may actually end up with only a couple of error-free pages.

There is always an appropriate compensation formula that will induce workers to put the correct emphasis on quantity versus quality. Ideally, that formula should approximate the trade-off between quantity and quality that consumers make in their demand for the final product. By doing this, workers can be induced to produce quality when consumers are willing to pay for it.

To see this, consider the example of a self-employed typist who makes her living by typing student dissertations. The better her accuracy, the higher the price she can charge per page. Suppose the price that she can charge per page is given by Table 5.4.

Perfect copies command a price of $8 per page, whereas those with four or more errors cannot be sold at all. It takes longer to produce a perfect page than it does an imperfect one. The time per page is shown in the third column of Table 5.4. Given the required time per page and price that pages of various qualities command, revenue per hour of time spent typing can be computed. The fourth column shows that $24 can be earned by typing perfect pages because only three per hour can be produced. By typing pages with three typos each, the typist can earn $18 per hour because she can produce six pages, each of which carries a price of $3. The typist will choose to type four pages per hour with an average of one typo per page. Doing so yields her revenue of $28 per hour, which exceeds the amount earned by choosing any other option.

A self-employed worker does the right thing: She chooses the trade-off between quality and quantity that maximizes her compensation. Now suppose the typist is employed by a firm that provides dissertation services. Students bring their untyped dissertations to a central desk. Dissertations are typed by one of the hired typists. What compensation scheme should the firm offer its typists?

It is obvious that if the firm simply pays a certain amount per page to its workers and ignores the number of typos, it will go out of business. Typists will produce a large number of pages having on average four or more typos and the revenue that the company receives will equal zero. If the company pays the typists, say, $10 per page, but subtracts $5 for every typo, it will get perfect pages, but it will lose money. Since a typist can produce three perfect pages per hour, a typist

TABLE 5.4
TYPIST'S TIME AND REVENUES PER PAGE

Typographical errors per page	Price per page	Minutes per page	Revenue per hour
0	$8	20	$24
1	$7	15	$28
2	$5	12	$25
3	$3	10	$18
4	0	9	0
5	0	8	0

who produces perfect pages earns $30 per hour. A typist who makes one error per page produces four pages per hour, but receives only $5 per page, yielding $20 per hour. This scheme does not produce the most profit for the firm. Indeed, the firm would like to induce the typists to do exactly what the self-employed typist would do. The easiest way to do this is to offer the schedule of Table 5.4, after charging the typist for the job. The typist essentially rents the brokerage services of the firm by paying some up-front fee, α, and then receives all the revenue generated by his services. The firm simply states that after paying α per day, the typist receives $8 for each perfect page, $7 for each page with one typo, $5 for each with two typos, $3 for each with three typos and nothing for any page with four or more typos. Given this schedule, the typist makes the highest hourly income by typing four pages per hour, with an average of one typo each. This is exactly the same choice the self-employed typist made. It also maximizes the profit of the firm. Just as in the taxicab example, the typists are willing to pay the largest α for the job that allows them to make the most money per hour.

Is there any tendency, then, for pieceworkers to emphasize quantity over quality? The answer is yes, and it is a result of measurement costs. The compensation scheme offered by the dissertation typing services requires that each page be proofed to count typos, since the payment per page depends on the number of typos. In the case of the brokerage firm, a supervisor must read every page to determine how much to pay the typist. It would be much easier simply to look at the typed page without reading it and to pay a fixed amount per page, irrespective of typos. Quality is usually more costly to measure than quantity. This fact induces firms to ignore quality considerations and pay on the basis of quantity, thereby causing workers to overemphasize quantity.

One way to reduce the cost of measuring quality is to sample randomly and pay on the basis of the sample. Rather than reading every page, a supervisor could read only one-twentieth of the pages and base the total compensation on that figure. As long as the number of total pages typed is large enough, this sampling approach will induce workers to behave almost exactly as if every page were being checked. Of course, monitoring must be done randomly, or the typist will put extra effort only into those pages that are being read.

When even sampling is impractical, the worker may be paid on the basis of input. A worker who is paid on the basis of his level of effort has no incentive to err in one direction or another with respect to quality versus quantity. Under these circumstances, workers can simply be given an instruction as to how much time to devote to each particular unit. Workers who are paid on the basis of time are, to a first approximation, indifferent between spending a great deal of time producing one unit and spending much less time per unit, but producing many more units.[4]

---

[4]This problem has been modeled explicitly by George Baker (1992), who has analyzed the optimal compensation scheme when output is measured imperfectly. The general result is that the optimal piece rate, β, moves towards zero as the index of output becomes a poor measure of the true output. As the measure becomes more accurate, the optimal piece rate coefficient moves toward one.

Cost-Plus versus Fixed Payments for Projects

The quantity–quality analysis can be applied to consider the issue of whether a contractor should be paid on a cost-plus or a fixed payment basis. Cost-plus pay is payment by input. Fixed payment pay is payment by output. The disadvantage of fixed payment is that when quality is difficult to observe, those who are given a fixed payment—that is, a piece rate—will have an incentive to skimp on quality. Conversely, when individuals are paid on a cost-plus basis, they may not have the right incentives to finish the job in a timely and cost-effective manner. More will be said on this in chapter 13.

The Appropriate Time Unit

We have defined a salary as compensation that is based on input rather than output, but have not, as yet, distinguished between a monthly or annual salary and an hourly wage. Most production and clerical workers are paid an hourly wage, whereas most managerial workers are paid a monthly or annual salary. Why the difference?[5]

The easiest way to think of the distinction is that salaries are payment for input and that the unit of time is selected so as to obtain the best proxy for effort. In the case of an assembly line worker, hours worked are not a perfect proxy for effort but are a pretty good indicator of the amount of effort expended. Since the line is moving along at a fixed rate, the speed of line and the number of minutes spent working on the line are the main ingredients to measuring effort.

For managers, hours worked may provide some index of effort, but the relation is much rougher. Managers' tasks are less routinized and are not as easily prescribed. Once managers are free to choose their tasks, hours worked becomes a poor measure of effort. If all that mattered in managerial compensation were hours of work, managers would choose easy tasks or those that furthered their own interests, and would ignore the interests of the firm.

Instead, managers are given much looser contracts that specify a general sum of money for an understood, albeit largely undefined, set of tasks. They generally have some discretion over their hours of work and are motivated to work long hours and spend them engaged in the right tasks by other compensation rewards. Specifically, the raise they receive at the end of the year depends on an overall, somewhat subjective evaluation of their performance. Perhaps more important are the incentives provided by the quest for promotion. These are discussed in chapter 9.

The general principle is that the more difficult it is to state the tasks ex ante, the longer the time period for compensation.

---

[5]This is the subject of Fama (1991).

RISK AVERSION

◆ ◆ ◆ ◆ ◆

Despite all the advantages of a piece rate, piecework has one major disadvantage. Sometimes, variations in output are beyond the worker's control. For example, a salesperson may put in a 60-hour week, may do everything right, and may still find it difficult to move the product simply because of an economic downturn. The salesperson has no control over macroeconomic events, but can benefit or suffer from them nonetheless. When economic conditions are good, the commissioned salesperson does better than expected, given certain effort. When economic conditions are bad, the commissioned salesperson does worse than expected for the same amount of effort. Most salespersons do not like this volatile aspect of their earnings. A firm that can smooth out those earnings will find it easier to attract labor while paying somewhat less.

A salesperson who is paid on an hourly basis is "insured" against the vagaries of the business cycle. As long as the hourly wage is independent of business cycle conditions, the salesperson who is paid an hourly wage has smooth earnings. Although incentives may be reduced so that total pay is lower, some workers may prefer this situation to that of commissions. Under commissions, the salesperson expects to receive a larger, but more variable, paycheck. Paying a salary is a lower-earning, lower-risk form of compensation.

Of course, when a salary is paid to the worker, the firm provides the insurance, which means that the firm now bears the risk. When times are good, the firm does well because sales are high and salaries remain constant. When times are bad, the firm does poorly because sales are low and salaries are not reduced. Paying on the basis of time does not eliminate risk; it merely shifts it from worker to firm.

Who should bear the risk? Other things being equal, it is usually better to have the firm bear the risk. The firm is generally in a better position to diversify the risk by pooling it with other projects or by selling it to a third party through the capital market. Workers find it more difficult to deal with the risk. Their liabilities—which consist of food, housing, clothing, and other expenses—are relatively fixed; variations in their income may cause significant difficulties for them. This is particularly true for low-wage workers. Highly paid executives are more likely to have substantial savings to cushion any decrease in earnings. As a result, it is generally better to have the firm bear risk.

The problem, however, is that when the firm bears the risk and the worker is insured, the worker's incentives are reduced. This has already been shown. As the commission rate goes to zero, the amount of effort expended falls. Thus, there is a trade-off: More risk taking by the worker means more effort and higher average compensation. However, more risk taking also means more variable pay. The general rule is that high-productivity workers, whose average compensation is high, should bear a greater proportion of the risk than low-productivity workers. Risk considerations push toward a fixed wage for the lowest-level workers and toward incentive pay for higher-level workers. However, other factors push in the other direction. These include the increased difficulty in observing output among those with more complex tasks.

◆ ◆ ◆ ◆ ◆ INTERMEDIATION

The method of compensating workers for their effort generally differs from the method of compensating the firm for the products that it produces. For example, few workers at GM are paid a piece rate, but GM receives a "piece rate" for its output. Customers pay GM for each car they purchase. An alternative would be for customers to enter into a contract with GM that required GM to provide an automobile in working condition with various specifications to a customer for a given amount of time. This would be closer to a time rate, but products are generally sold on a piece rate basis. Why the difference?

For many products, the answer is straightforward. Output is easily measured at the firm level, but much less easily measured at the worker level. When GM produces a car, it can be observed and recognized as a distinct unit, having certain amenities and characteristics.[6] It is much more difficult to attribute the car or any of its various components to a specific worker. Thus, GM is paid on the basis of output and its workers are paid on the basis of input. GM is an *intermediary*. The firm intercedes to ensure that the workers who produce the car do what needs to be done and that they are paid for their services. The consumer implicitly "hires" GM to put together a group of workers who will build a car for the consumer. This happens indirectly so that the consumer need not monitor the performance of each worker. In this case, the output of the firm is more easily measured than the output of each worker.

Another example is instructive because it is less straightforward. When an individual needs a lawyer to represent him in a particular situation, he sometimes approaches a partner at a large law firm. The particular partner may end up passing the assignment off to another lawyer in her firm, or she may work on the case along with other lawyers in a team setting.

Consider, for example, the case where an inventor sues a large firm alleging that the firm made use of an idea on which the inventor owned the patent without proper compensation. The law firm may take the case on a contingency basis. The firm collects some portion of total award given to the inventor if successful. The associate lawyers in the firm are paid an annual salary. The salary compensates them for the effort they put into the case. There may also be some bonus associated with having won the case, but bonuses for associates tend to be quite small relative to their salary.

The law firm is receiving a piece rate (in this case, the commission rate is less

---

[6]Of course, it is more difficult to observe quality ex ante, which is one reason for providing a warranty.

than 100%) because it receives some proportion of the total award, but the lawyers in the firm receive a salary. Why?

The inventor plaintiff cares about the size of the award and pays the law firm based on it. The inventor could instead have paid the individual lawyers for their inputs, but the inventor is in no position to know how much input and what combination of inputs should be used to win the case. Thus, that decision is delegated to the intermediary, namely the law firm. The firm could pay the lawyers a piece rate as well, but this would induce the lawyers to maximize the award on that particular case and would place the young lawyers at great risk. If the case is lost, an associate could be in serious financial trouble. Also, the firm might want the lawyer to focus some attention on learning new skills and building future business contacts, none of which would be encouraged by the payment of a piece rate. Finally, as in the case of GM, since the case may require team effort, it is difficult to attribute the rewards to any given lawyer on this case. Thus, the associates are paid salaries and instructed to perform in a particular way. They are motivated by the promise of promotion to partner for a job well done.

It is also interesting that law firms are organized as partnerships, rather than as corporations with outside investors. The partners are in positions to bear more risk than the associates, since they are generally richer, older, and as a result, have accumulated assets. A partnership makes the lawyers residual claimants, essentially paying them piece rates for performance. Lawyers' shares in company profits are determined in part by their performance during the year.[7] Later, (in chapter 12) we shall examine the effects of basing rewards on group performance rather than individual performance.

SHORT-RUN AND LONG-RUN INCENTIVES   ◆ ◆ ◆ ◆ ◆

Managers are often accused of focusing on the short run and ignoring the long run. The view is that managers' time horizon differs from that of shareholders. The evidence on this point is shaky, but if true, it reflects a failure to structure incentives appropriately for the manager.

Why do owners have a long-run view of the firm? The idea comes directly from the financial theory of efficient markets, which says that the stock price of the firm reflects the capitalized value of future profits. An action that increases future profits makes the firm more valuable to owners, who can enjoy the higher profits through future dividends, or unanticipated, through capital gains. (A firm that is privately held pays the profits directly to its owners.) It is for this reason that owners want a firm to take actions that increase the long-term value of the firm.

Managers may not share owners' views. A manager may care more about retaining a job than about maximizing the long-run value of the firm. Particularly when actions cannot be observed easily by owners, managers may do something to

---

[7]See Gilson and Mnookin (1985).

make themselves look good in the short run that may have adverse long-term consequences. By the time the negative results come in, the manager may be working at another firm or enjoying a well-paid retirement.

The issue here is not much different from the question of quality versus quantity. Long-term profits are to short-run profits as quality is to quantity. If observability were not an issue, it would be easy to motivate the manager to think of the long term, simply by paying for long-run results. Just as a typist who makes many mistakes can be penalized sufficiently to induce the desired accuracy, a manager can be paid to take actions that benefit the long run. The problem is that those actions are not easily observed. What can be done?

There are a number of possible solutions, none of which is perfect. Let us list the possibilities and then discuss their advantages and disadvantages.

1. Make managerial compensation a function of stock appreciation.
2. Pay managers for actions that promote long-run performance.
3. Pay for input and instruct managers to put appropriate emphasis on the long run.

Compensating Through Stock Appreciation

If the stock market reflects the long-term value of the firm, then tying managerial compensation to stock price will reward the manager for activities that improve long-term performance. Indeed, paying on the basis of stock price appreciation may be good, even if information does not permeate the market perfectly. Owners care about the value of their stock. Any actions that managers can take to improve the value of the firm's stock will benefit the owners, whether or not such actions actually improve long-term performance of the firm. Since it is precisely stock price appreciation that owners care about, paying managers on the basis of stock price appreciation aligns incentives of managers and owners.

The primary problem with using stock price as a motivator is that stock price is often affected by factors beyond any particular manager's control. Risk-averse managers do not like having so much of their compensation tied to factors over which they have no control and which vary significantly over time. In order to accept such risk, their average salaries must be higher to compensate. This is the major cost of tying compensation to stock price variation.

Promoting Long-run Performance

Risk can be shifted back to the firm if managerial pay is based on input, rather than output. Paying a manager for taking the appropriate actions irrespective of outcome shifts the risk away from the manager to the shareholders. This shift may be desirable, but it has the major problem that the appropriate actions need to be observable. Those who decide on a manager's compensation must be able to determine whether the actions taken were appropriate. This is sometimes difficult.

Consider the case of the compensation of a CEO, which is determined by the compensation committee of the board of directors. Directors are generally part-timers, who meet perhaps once per month and whose primary responsibility is to another employer. They earn a fee for being directors, but only devote a limited amount of time to monitoring the company that they direct. The CEO, on the other hand, is a full-timer who should have a much better sense of the appropriate actions than the board. Because of this asymmetry in information, it is unlikely that the directors can assess accurately whether actions taken are appropriate or not. If they cannot, then the same concerns about risk apply. A CEO might do the right thing and still be penalized by an errant compensation committee. Alternatively, CEOs who emphasize short-run performance may persuade a naive compensation committee that appropriate actions were taken and that the fine short-run performance may persist into the long run.

An additional problem is that the board may not behave independently. It could be captured by the CEO. Paying on the basis of actions instead of output may give a CEO-loyal board a way to justify a high salary to the CEO, even when the high salary is unwarranted. Payment on the basis of objectively measured output variables, like stock price, does not suffer from this problem, but payment by stock valuation has other difficulties, just mentioned.

Paying for Input and Instructing Managers to Put Appropriate Emphasis on the Long Run

A manager who is paid an annual salary that is independent of specific outcomes can be told to maximize the value of the firm, taking into account long-run and short-run considerations. Since the salary is independent of the specific actions or outcomes, a manager has no incentive to ignore this instruction.

As discussed before, the problem is that the manager's effort must be monitored. A fixed salary does not provide any direct motivation to the manager. Thus, the salary must be made contingent on putting forth a specific level of effort, and enforcement of that agreement may be difficult. Another disadvantage is that there may be implicit incentives to emphasize the short run, even when a fixed salary is paid. To the extent that promotion is based on observable performance and short-run performance is more readily observed than long-run performance, salaried managers may focus too heavily on the near term.

Overall, a combination of some straight salary with bonus pay that is contingent on growth in stock price may be the best way to move managers away from the short run and toward the long run.

Recap ◆ ◆ ◆ ◆ ◆

Output-based pay compensates individuals for work that is in some way related to a measure of output. Sometimes that measure is imperfect. Output-based pay is used when ready measures are inexpensive.

The best incentives are provided when the worker is the full residual claimant. If a taxi driver receives the full net revenue from his efforts, then adverse selection is avoided and the driver puts forth the efficient amount of effort. The taxi company can charge a higher rental price for the cab under these circumstances and can make more money than by attempting to extract payment through low commission rates.

A salesperson may receive a commission rate that is well below 100 percent. The commission is generally on sales, not net revenue, because sales figures are more difficult for the firm to manipulate through accounting tricks. A 10 percent commission on sales might be equivalent to a 100 percent commission on net revenue.

Rental fees are often implicit in many salesperson compensation schemes, because the salesperson receives a draw and does not start to earn commission until after selling more than some target amount.

Paying workers the full net revenue does not solve all incentive problems. Unless workers own the capital, they will not take appropriate care of it. Sale of the capital to the worker solves this problem, but may not be feasible or desirable for other reasons.

Time-based pay is payment on the basis of input, not output. It is used when measurement is costly, when quality is difficult to measure, or when workers are risk averse and output varies greatly as a result of extraneous factors. The appropriate time unit for pay varies with the difficulty of stating the task in advance. When tasks are complicated and uncertain, workers are paid an annual salary. Intermediation often occurs when the firm's output can be measured, but an individual worker's output cannot be measured.

Although group compensation has not yet been discussed, it can be said that paying on the basis of individual output may cause workers to promote their own interests at the expense of the firm's overall profitability.

◆ ◆ ◆ ◆ ◆ PUTTING THE ANALYSIS TO WORK

Paying lawyers on a contingency basis, where the lawyer receives say, one-third of the settlement, causes some adverse incentives. What are they, and how might they be remedied? Does the solution to this problem create other difficulties?

A contingency payment makes the lawyer want to win the case. It does not induce the lawyer to be impartial. But that is not a major problem, since lawyers are assumed, indeed expected, to be advocates. The problem is that he or she will not advocate hard enough. Just as taxi drivers do not use cabs efficiently when they receive only half of the commission, attorneys who receive only a fraction of the total award will not want to work hard enough on the case. They may ignore the value to the other side, namely the plaintiff (or defendant), of working a few extra hours.

It is easy to solve this problem, but other difficulties are created. A plaintiff could "sell" the case to the attorney, making the attorney the residual claimant. The plaintiff would receive a fixed amount based on the expected value of the case. The attorney would bear the risk. If things turned out well, the attorney would earn more than he or she paid for the case. If things turned out poorly, the attorney would earn less. On average, the attorney would pay the correct amount, earning a normal return on her investment in cases. Analogously, defendants could buy out of their obligation. They could pay the attorney to take over the case. The amount of payment would reflect the expected loss associated with the trial. Once again, the attorney would bear the risk. If the attorney did well, the award paid would be less than the amount collected from the defendant. If things went badly, the attorney would end up paying the plaintiff more.

When the attorney owns the case, every additional dollar that is generated by the attorney's effort goes to the attorney. Under these circumstances, the attorney will work enough.

What are the difficulties with such a scheme? Besides the likelihood that juries will not be as kind to attorneys as they would to the actual litigant, at least two problems can be identified. First, plaintiffs (or defendants) have no incentive to cooperate once they sell their case to the attorney. Just as the attorney would not work hard enough when the attorney only received a fraction of the returns, so the plaintiff will not want to participate enough when there is nothing at risk. Winning the case without the victim's help might prove difficult.

Second, since the plaintiff and defendant have the most information about what actually transpired, they can take advantage of the attorney. (Most would consider this a switch for the better.) The litigants may portray their case as better than it is in order to maximize the price that the attorney will pay, or, in the case of the defendant, minimize the price that the attorney will accept. When most of the benefits or costs are borne by the litigants, they have more incentive to reveal the truth to the attorney so that the attorney can be most useful in winning the case.

Thus, if the attorney receives too much of the returns, the litigants will not cooperate enough. If the litigants receive too much of the returns (or bear too much of the cost), then the attorney, who has little at risk may not work hard enough. The solution is generally to give attorneys a minority share in returns and hope that concern for professional reputation is sufficient motivation. Even if the attorney received none of the direct returns, or bore none of the direct costs, the attorney prefers to do well in a case because future business depends on current performance. If the reputation effect is strong enough, then even an attorney who was paid a lump sum for the case might still put forth a great deal, and perhaps the optimal amount, of effort.[8]

---

[8]This is the mechanism that Fama (1980) discusses. He calls this "ex post settling up" because the ex post market price of the attorney adjusts to reflect performance in this case.

◆ ◆ ◆ ◆ ◆ REFERENCES

Baker, George. "Incentive Contracts and Performance Measurement," *Journal of Political Economy* 100 (June 1992): 598–614.

Fama, Eugene F. "Agency Problems and the Theory of the Firm," *Journal of Political Economy*, 88 (April 1980), 288–307.

Fama, Eugene F. "Time, Salary, and Incentive Payoffs in Labor Contracts," *Journal of Labor Economics*, 9,1 (January 1991): 25–44.

Gibbons, Robert. "Piece-Rate Incentive Schemes," *Journal of Labor Economics*, 4, 4, Part 1 (October 1987): 413–429.

Gilson, Ronald J., and Robert H. Mnookin. "Sharing among the Human Capitalists: An Economic Inquiry into the Corporate Law Firm and How Partners Split Profits," *Stanford Law Review* 37 (January 1985): 313–92.

Lazear, Edward P. "Salaries and Piece Rates," *Journal of Business* 59 (July 1986): 405–31.

Weitzman, Martin. "The 'Ratchet Principle' and Performance Incentives," *Bell Journal of Economics* (Spring 1980): 302–8.

◆ ◆ ◆ ◆ ◆ ADDITIONAL ADVANCED READING

Brown, Charles. "Wage Levels and Method of Pay," *Rand Journal of Economics* 23 (Autumn 1992): 366–75.

Fama, Eugene F. "Time, Salary, and Incentive Payoffs in Labor Contracts," *Journal of Labor Economics* 9 (January 1991): 25–44.

Flanagan, Robert J. "Implicit Contracts, Explicit Contracts, and Wages," *American Economic Review* 2 (May 1984): 345–49.

Ickes, Barry W., and Larry Samuelson. "Job Transfers and Incentives in Complex Organizations: Thwarting the Ratchet Effect," *Rand Journal of Economics* 18 (Summer 1987): 275–86.

Jensen, Michael C., and Kevin J. Murphy. "Performance Pay and Top-Management Incentives," *Journal of Political Economy* 98 (April 1990): 225–64.

Leonard, Jonathan S. "Executive Pay and Firm Performance," *Industrial and Labor Relations Review* 43 (Special Issue, February 1990): S13–29.

Ribitzer, James B. "Is There a Trade-Off Between Supervision and Wages? An Empirical Test of Efficiency Wage Theory," *Journal of Economic Behavior and Organization* 28 (September 1995): 107–29.

Seiler, Eric. "Piece Rate vs. Time Rate: The Effect of Incentives on Earnings," *Review of Economics and Statistics* 66 (August 1984): 363–76.

APPENDIX

◆ ◆ ◆ ◆ ◆

In the following, it is shown that a firm maximizes profit by paying a piece rate equal to 100 percent of net revenue.

The problem is broken into two parts. First, the worker's behavior as a function of piece rate is analyzed. Then the firm chooses the piece rate to maximize its profits, given worker behavior.

Workers like money, but dislike putting forth effort. The pain associated with a given amount of effort, E, is given by $C(E)$. This has the interpretation that a worker would not work for a firm that required E_o level effort without being paid at least $C(E_o)$. So, for example, if

$$C(E) = E^2$$

a worker would not be willing to work at a firm that required 3 units of effort unless he were paid at least 9. If the firm required 10 units of effort, he would have to be paid 100.

Define E such that one unit of E produces \$1 of net revenue for the firm. $C(E)$ is then the dollar value of worker pain associated with producing \$$E$ of net revenue to the firm.

How does the worker choose effort, once he decides to work for a given firm? The worker wants to maximize utility, given by the difference between income and the dollar value of the pain of effort or

(A5.1)
$$\underset{E}{Max}\ \alpha + \beta E - C(E)$$

where $\alpha + \beta E$ is the worker's total compensation; β is the piece rate and α is the intercept.

The first order condition is

(A5.2)
$$\frac{\partial}{\partial E} = \beta - C'(E) = 0 \text{ or}$$
$$C'(E) = \beta$$

Equation A5.2 is the worker's labor supply. It tells how responsive a worker's effort is to a change in the piece rate. It simply states that the worker sets the marginal cost of effort equal to β, which is the marginal return to effort.

Now, the firm can choose α and β, but it has two constraints. First, the choice of β will affect the worker's choice of E according to (A5.2). Second, whatever the worker's choice of E turns out to be, denoted E^*, the firm must ensure that the total compensation to the worker exceeds $C(E^*)$ or the worker will not accept the job at all. This means that

(A5.3)
$$\alpha + \beta C^* = C(E^*)$$

The firm wants to maximize net revenue minus wages paid to the worker. Net revenue as defined is simply E, so that the firm chooses α and β to maximize

(A5.4) $$E - \alpha + \beta E$$

subject to the behavior given in (A5.2) and to the constraint (A5.3). Substituting (A5.3) into (A5.4) yields

(A5.6) $$\underset{\beta}{Max}\ E - C(E)$$

subject to $C'(E) = \beta$. (Note that α does not affect the choice of E in (A5.2) so it is not part of (A5.6).)

The first order condition is

(A5.7) $$(1 - C'(E)) \frac{\partial E}{\partial \beta} = 0$$

or β must be chosen such that $C'(E) = 1$. But (A5.2) says that $C'(E) = \beta$ so

$$1 = C'(E) = \beta$$

or $\beta = 1$ is the solution. The optimum is to pay the worker 100 percent of net revenue.

Once β is set equal to 1, an E^* is determined from (A5.2). Given this E^*, the firm selects α so as to satisfy

$$\alpha + E^* = C(E^*)$$

that is, to make the worker just indifferent between taking and not taking the job.

A numerical example is instructive. Suppose that $C(E) = \dfrac{E^2}{10}$. The worker maximizes his utility by choosing

$$\frac{2E}{10} = \beta$$

$$\text{or} \quad E = 5\beta$$

If the commission rate were 20 percent, the worker would set $E = 1$. If it rose to 60 percent, he would increase his level of effort to 3. This is like the taxi driver altering the number of hours worked, depending on how much of the fare he keeps for himself. If commission is 100 percent, he puts forth 5 units of effort.

The firm's profit is then

$$E - \frac{E^2}{10}$$

To maximize profits, it is necessary to choose β such that

$$1 - \frac{2E}{10} = 0$$

i.e., such that $E = 5$. The only way to get $E = 5$ is to pay a 100 percent commission rate because $E = 5$ only when $\beta = 1$.

Now, if $\beta = 1$, the worker takes home

$$\alpha + E$$

which, given $\beta = 1$, is

$$\alpha + 5$$

To induce him to accept the job,

$$\alpha + 5 = \frac{E^2}{10}$$
$$= \frac{25}{10}$$
$$= 2.5$$

Thus, $\alpha = -2.5$. The optimal compensation formula is

$$\text{pay} = -2.5 + E$$

Since the commission rate is 100 percent, the worker chooses $E = 5$. Since $E = 5$, the pain of effort is $\frac{5^2}{10} = 2.5$. Also, since $E = 5$ and $\alpha = -2.5$, pay equals 2.5, which just covers his pain.

Ratchet Effects

We now show formally that the *ratchet effect*, where firms make next year's targets a function of this year's performance, can be offset by the appropriate multiperiod piece rate.

The problem can be analyzed in the context of two periods.[9] The firm can commit to paying a worker a particular piece rate formula in period 1, but the worker knows that despite promises, the firm will take advantage of her to the extent possible next period. The firm can take advantage of the worker only to the extent that the worker is locked in—that is, only to the extent that the worker can earn more at this firm than elsewhere. Let output in period 1 be q_1 defined to be equal to E_1 where E_1 is effort in period 1. Define output in period 2 as q_2, defined to be equal to E_2. The cost of effort is given by $\tilde{C}(E_1)$ in period 1 and by $\tilde{C}(E_2)$ in period 2. Costs are unknown to the firm in advance, but the worker's choice of effort in period 1 will give the firm information on which to base the compensation decision in period 2.

---

[9]The analysis comes from Lazear (1986), pp. 422–25. Gibbons (1987) has also analyzed this problem.

Since period 2 is the last period, the piece rate problem that the firm solves for period 2 is identical to that for the one-period problem, solved in the first part of the appendix. There it was shown that the firm will pay a piece rate that has two parts to it: The payment in period 2 will be of the form

(A5.8) $$\text{Pay in period 2} = \alpha + \beta_2 q_2$$

where $\beta_2 = 1$ and α_2 is chosen such that

(A5.9) $$\alpha + q_2 - \tilde{c}(E_2 = 0)$$

so that the worker is just indifferent between coming to work and not working in the second period. Even though the firm cannot commit to any compensation scheme for period 2, it will pay according to (A5.9) with $\beta_2 = 1$.

Now, the firm does not know the worker's cost of effort, $\tilde{c}(E_2)$ and so must form an estimate of it based on performance in period 1. It is this effect that induces the worker to slack off in period 1. Hard work during period 1 brings higher wages during that period, but also reduces α_2 in period 2.

How does the worker behave in period 1? The worker knows that the firm will form an estimate of $\tilde{c}(E_2)$, denoted $\hat{c}(E_2)$, based on output in period 1. The worker also knows that

$$\frac{\partial \hat{c}(E_2)}{\partial q_1} < 0$$

that is, more output in period 1 makes the firm believe that the job was easy. Thus, in period 2, since the firm cannot observe $\tilde{c}(E_2)$, it will choose α_2 such that

$$\alpha_2 = \hat{c}(E_2) - q_2$$
$$= \hat{c}(q_2) - q_2$$

because $q_2 = E_2$. Also, $\dfrac{\partial \alpha_2}{\partial q_1} < 0$ because $\dfrac{\partial \hat{c}}{\partial q_1} < 0$.

The worker's formal maximization problem in period 2 is simply

(A5.10) $$\underset{q_2}{\text{Max}} \; \alpha_2 + q_2 - \tilde{c}(q_2)$$

so the worker sets

(A5.11) $$\tilde{c}'(q_2) = 1$$

This is what the firm wants, since doing so maximizes period 2's profits. The problem arises in period 1. The worker reduces effort because she knows that working hard will cut her compensation in period 2. Her period 1 maximization problem is

(A5.12) $$\underset{q_1}{\text{Max}} \; \alpha_1 = \beta_1 q_1 - \tilde{c}(q_1)$$

subject to (A5.11). The first order condition is

(A5.13)
$$\tilde{c}'(q_1) = \beta_1 + \frac{\partial \alpha_2}{\partial q_1}$$

The second term on the right-hand side of (A5.13) picks up the effect of reduced compensation in period 2 associated with more effort in period 1.

Now, $\frac{\partial \alpha_2}{\partial q_1}$ is simply $\frac{\partial \hat{c}\,(E_2)}{\partial q_1}$.

This is the amount by which the firm reduces its estimate of the effort cost associated with one more unit of effort in period 1.

To maximize profits, the firm must induce the worker to behave efficiently, that is, it must induce the worker to set

$$\tilde{c}'(E_1) = 1 \text{ and } \tilde{c}'(E_2) = 1$$

The second follows from (A5.11). To get the worker to set $\tilde{c}(E_1) = 1$, it is necessary that

$$\beta_1 + \frac{\partial \alpha_2}{\partial q_1} = 1$$

from (A5.13), so

$$\beta_1 = 1 - \frac{\partial \alpha_2}{\partial q_1}$$

Thus $\beta_1 > 1$ (since $\frac{\partial \alpha_2}{\partial q_1} < 0$). The firm overpays effort in period 1 to offset the ratchet effect. Thus, the piece rate falls over time. Also, since

$$\alpha_1 = \hat{c}(q_2) - q_2$$

it is necessary that α_1 be set sufficiently high to attract workers. Specifically, it is necessary that

$$\alpha_1 + \beta_1 q_1 + \alpha_2 + \beta_2 q_2 - \tilde{c}(E_1) - \tilde{c}(E_2) = 0$$

given $\alpha_2 = \hat{c}(q_2) - q_2$. The higher is α_1, the more workers that are attracted to the firm.

The Theory of Human Capital

6

O ne of the best ways to understand training and turnover is to apply the theory of human capital to personnel issues. The theory is rich in implications. An understanding of the theory will allow managers to make a variety of better reasoned personnel decisions. We start with a discussion that illustrates some of the questions involved.

A durable goods manufacturer has many new machines that use the most modern robotic technology. Few workers in the current work force have the requisite skill to operate the new equipment. The firm is considering a new training program to bring its workers up to speed. The issue is whether the program should be instituted, and, if so, how it should be financed. A meeting is held to discuss the issue. Excerpts from that meeting follow:

CLARK: There is no doubt that we need to train these people. Without training, we are wasting a valuable resource. We have to make our people effective at operating these machines or we might as well write off the investment in robotics right now.

EDGEWORTH: You're right about that. The problem as I see it is that our competitors will benefit from our training expenditures. They'll steal our guys once we get them trained, and then where will we be? We train the workers and our rivals get to enjoy the benefits of their training without bearing the costs. I've seen this happen before in other industries. The innovator comes in, trains its people, and then the new kid on the block picks off the best people.

MARX: Well, we could pay our guys more. That will keep them with us. After all, if they are more productive, why not share some of the gains with them? I think that is the best way to have a productive organization anyway.

HAYEK: Karl is always worried about the workers' welfare. That's fine, but we've got to protect our shareholders. Why should we pay the workers more if we put out for the cost of the training? How are we going to make any money on the deal?

MARX: I am worried about the workers' welfare because if we ignore these issues, they will end up costing us in the long run. It is short-sighted to train workers and then let them be picked off by the competition just because our pride gets in the way of paying them what they deserve.

ROBBINS: How do we know that our competitors are going to want our trained workers? We're making a lot of assumptions about the kind of technology that they are going to have. Who says that they will follow our lead into robotics? If they don't, they're not going to want workers trained in robotics.

EDGEWORTH: Maybe. But I don't want to count on that possibility. Is there some way that we can tie them to the firm? We've got to be clever about this. They aren't our slaves, so we need to get them to stay because they want to stay.

CLARK: I don't want to muddy the waters, but an issue that we've ignored is that we may actually want to lose some of our workers. First of all, the new robotics mean less labor is required to do a given amount of work. Second, some of the current work force may be poorly suited to the new technology. Others may not want to undergo the training. After all, this is going to be like going back to school for some of them. A lot of them weren't particularly enamored with school when they started here; chances are, they're even less likely to want to spend time doing homework now.

HAYEK: That's a good point. We might come out better if we just let some of our workers go. In fact, from what I've seen, we might even want to pay some of them to leave.

The previous discussion raised a number of questions. They include

- When does it pay to train a worker?

- How can the training costs and rewards be structured so as to make both the shareholders and workers better off?

- Does a firm have to pay its trained workers more?

- What kind of training should be given? Should it be as general as possible, or should it be idiosyncratic to the current firm?

- What can be done about retention of trained workers? How can they be tied to the firm?

- What kinds of workers are the best candidates for the training program?

- Who should be laid off if downsizing is necessary?

- How do age and seniority figure into the training and layoff calculations?

- How do we know when it is better to lay off a worker?

HUMAN CAPITAL: SOME BASIC THEORY

◆ ◆ ◆ ◆ ◆

These questions are important and are issues that businesses must frequently address. Fortunately, there is a well-developed theory that yields clear and concise answers to these questions. The appropriate theory is called the theory of **human capital.** It is such an important part of modern economics that two Nobel prizes in economics were given out at least in part in recognition of the theory's contribution.[1]

Human capital theory applies to the acquisition of skills. Skill acquisition can be done in a number of ways. Right now, you, as the reader of this book, are probably investing in human capital by going to school. Formal education is perhaps the primary way to acquire human capital. More is spent on investment in human capital through formal schooling than on investment in human capital through any other vehicle.

The second most important method of investing in human capital is on-the-job training (OJT). Although second to formal education in terms of magnitude of dollars spent, on-the-job training is the most important kind of human capital in its impact on business practice. The entire discussion at the beginning of this chapter revolved around on-the-job training. As a topic, explicit or implicit training programs are paramount on a firm's agenda. The issues involved in on-the-job training are considerably more complicated than those associated with formal schooling. Other examples of investment in human capital include exercise, personal beautification expenditures, enrichment courses, and health care. We limit our discussion to formal education and on-the-job training because these topics are most important for a human resources manager. Health care will be discussed in a later chapter in the context of **benefits.**

---

[1]Theodore Schultz and Gary Becker were awarded the Nobel Memorial Prize in Economic Sciences in 1979 and 1992, respectively. Both scholars were pioneers in human capital analysis.

Although on-the-job training is the most important kind of investment from a personnel standpoint, we begin with formal schooling because it is the most straightforward and yields many interesting implications.

◆ ◆ ◆ ◆ ◆ FORMAL SCHOOLING

What made you decide to go to college? There were probably a number of factors, but most people base their decisions on career considerations. It is clear to even the most naive high school student that individuals who progress further in school, on average, get better jobs. Cardiologists have many years of graduate training, whereas individuals who work at the car wash rarely have gone past high school. It is also quite clear that on average, cardiologists earn more than car wash attendants. Empirical observations like this form the basis of the theory of human capital.

The theory of human capital, most clearly articulated by Gary Becker (1975), is identical to the theory of physical capital, except that the terms are changed. The reference in human capital is to people and skills, rather than plants and equipment. In the theory of investment in physical capital, a manager decides to buy a machine if the **present value** of the flow of additional revenues generated by the machine exceeds the operating and purchasing cost of the machine. A standard cost–benefit calculation is done. The only complicating factor in standard capital theory is that the cost of the machine is borne now, while the returns accrue over a period of time into the future. A machine that is purchased today will yield higher productivity to the firm in the future, so it is necessary to compare future revenues to current costs. The additional profit from incremental productivity must be measured against the cost of the machine to decide whether the investment is worthwhile.

In the theory of human capital, a similar calculation occurs. The individual must bear a cost now to pay for schooling or other training in hopes that it will bring higher earnings in the future. If the higher earnings are sufficient, it makes the cost of going to school worth bearing.

The cost of going to school has two components. The first, called direct costs, includes tuition, books, additional expenses in living away from home, and other incidentals. An equally important component of cost is the opportunity cost, defined as earnings associated with going to school. For example, when an individual gets an MBA by going to business school full time, he gives up the opportunity to work that would have earned him a substantial salary. The forgone salary is one of the costs of going to school because the individual could have had it had he not opted for the MBA.

An Example: Choosing Whether to Stay in School

Consider an individual who is making a rational choice about whether to drop out or to finish the last year in high school. High school graduates generally earn more than those who drop out after eleventh grade. The additional earnings will be received in every year of the individual's work life. The earnings differential between high school grads and high school dropouts need not be the same in every year that work occurs, but it is likely to be some positive amount in every year of work. It is helpful to be a bit more formal. Consider a decision being made in 1997. If the individual gets a high school diploma, he or she will earn K_1 in 1998, but if the student drops out now, he or she will earn J_1 dollars in 1998. We expect that K_1 exceeds J_1.

Of course, the worker does not receive the difference until 1998, and it is now only 1997. Thus, we must discount the difference to bring it back to present value. This means that the amount that the individual gains in 1998 from having finished high school has a present value of

$$\frac{K_1 - J_1}{(1 + r)} \equiv D_1$$

where r is the rate of interest that the individual could have received. In other words, if the individual had D_1 dollars today, he or she could put it in the bank, earn D_1 on it, and have $K_1 - J_1$ one year from now, since

$$D_1 + rD_1 = D_1(1 + r)$$

and

$$D_1(1 + r) = K_1 - J_1$$

That is not all. In 1997, a high school graduate is expected to earn K_2 whereas a high school dropout earns only J_2. In present value terms, that difference is worth

$$\frac{K_2 - J_2}{(1 + r)^2} = D_2$$

The discount factor is squared because difference D_2 is not received for two years. As is now clear, there is a differential to be earned in each year of the individual's work life. Thus, the total return to be earned is

(6.1)
$$Return = \sum_{t=1}^{T} \frac{K_t - J_t}{(1 + r)^t}$$

where T is the year of retirement. (If a worker were currently 18 and planning to work until 65, then $T = 47$.) There are some costs as well. First, there are direct costs such as tuition, books, and other incidentals. Denote those costs C_0. The zero subscript calls attention to the fact that those direct costs are borne up front and so are not discounted. The second component of cost consists of earnings that would be received if the individual were to drop out after the eleventh grade. In other words, it is J_0, the earnings of high school dropouts during 1995. The individual invests in the final year of high school if the following condition holds:

(6.2)
$$C_0 + J_0 < \sum_{t=1}^{T} \frac{K_t - J_t}{(1 + r)^t}$$

When (6.2) is satisfied, the returns that the individual receives in higher wages exceed the costs of the schooling. This is an investment that pays. If the costs exceed the returns, then the individual is better off dropping out. Why? While more schooling may mean higher wages, it does not raise wages sufficiently to overcome the higher costs that must be borne to finish high school. Put another way, an individual who wants to invest $C_0 + J_0$ would be better off working during 1997 and putting the money in the bank. The interest earned on it would exceed what he or she could get in higher earnings by finishing high school.

For early years of schooling, the returns to schooling exceed the costs. There are two reasons. First, there is much to be learned when an individual knows very little. A little bit of school can affect productivity dramatically—say, by teaching an individual how to read simple directions. The diminishing-returns effect can be summed up in the phrase, "All I need to know, I learned in kindergarten." College professors, whose incomes depend on continued demand for education, hope that this is an exaggeration. It is not a stretch, though, to say that the most important year of school is first grade, where individuals learn reading and writing, the most important cognitive skills.

Second, the costs of going to school are very low during the early years of schooling. With public subsidies to education, direct costs are virtually zero up through high school. Further, forgone earnings are low. A seven-year-old has very few market opportunities for labor. It is almost certain that the returns to second grade exceed the costs that consist of forgone earnings at a lemonade stand.

Eventually, however, the reverse must be true. Consider an individual who already has six Ph.D.s and is working on the seventh. Severe cases of labor market phobia are unlikely to be reversed by additional investment in schooling. This 53-year-old student would be better off working for the next few years, or the person will reach retirement age before beginning employment. The point is that the seventh Ph.D. will not alter productivity by much, and is unlikely to result in significant wage gains.

The logic implies that it pays for everyone to invest in some formal education, and there is also an optimal stopping date for each individual as well. The simple formula in Equation 6.2 defines the stopping date. The stopping date is the year when the inequality in Equation 6.2 switches from having returns greater than the cost to one where costs are greater than returns. If returns exceed costs for year 12, but not for year 13, the student should leave school after high school graduation. In addition to defining the stopping date, the expression in (6.2) has some interesting implications that are borne out in the real world. We begin with the most straightforward and progress to more interesting and controversial ones.

Effects of Costs and Benefits of Education on the Optimal Amount of Schooling

First, increases in tuition rates decrease school enrollment. If annual tuition in an MBA program were doubled, fewer students would choose to complete the MBA. The reason is that individuals who were close to the margin on the decision of whether or not to attend business school will now find that the costs exceed the expected benefits.

Related is the point that those individuals who already have high-paying jobs will be reluctant to go back to school to acquire an MBA. The earnings given while in school are a major component of the cost associated with obtaining the MBA. Those people who must give up a great deal to attend school are less likely to do so. Successful stock traders who have nothing more than an undergraduate degree will be reluctant to give up their high-paying jobs to acquire an MBA.

Second, increases in the interest rate mean less schooling. This is true of all investments. For example, "housing starts," a measure of the number of new house construction projects being initiated, generally vary with the rate of interest. Building a house is an investment. It yields a flow of services into the future in the same way that a year of education yields a flow of higher earnings into the future. The higher is the interest rate, the lower is the value of future earnings. Alternatively, the higher is the interest rate, the better it is to work and put your money in the bank. Schooling is a better investment when the alternative investments are poor choices.

Interest rates do not have dramatic effects on school attendance rates. Why not? First, since schooling is an investment with a long payout period, long-term rates are relevant rather than short-term ones. Long-term rates are generally less volatile than short-term rates. Second, the rate that is often relevant is the implicit borrowing rate that parents charge their children to finance schooling. What parents extract in kind or through direct transfer from their children later may not be closely tied to the interest rates that were in effect when the child was in school.[2]

A more direct implication of varying interest rates relates to who goes to school and who does not. Children may find it very difficult to borrow against their future earnings. Banks are generally reluctant to lend to students whose only collateral is their future earning power. Only mobsters and shifty uncles are willing to float such risky loans, and the rates charged might be exorbitant. This means that children whose parents are poor might face much higher borrowing costs and consequently, would drop out of school to work at an earlier age. Financial aid programs that target the poor could offset this tendency.

The third set of implications involves the T term in (6.2). The longer the work life, the more investment in schooling. Since T is interpreted as the number of years after the investment during which the individual will work, this implies that people are more likely to attend school when they are young than when they are old. The numbers of years left in the labor market declines with age, so the chances that returns exceed costs are greater for young workers than for older ones. Stated differently, if a year of schooling is worth undertaking when the

---

[2]They are not completely divorced from market rates of interest. Since parents have the opportunity to borrow and lend in capital markets, rather than to lend to their children, the lending rate to the child will be connected to the market rates of interest. The problem is somewhat complicated by altruism between parent and child.

worker is old, it is most certainly worth undertaking when the worker is young. Going to school when young allows the returns to be enjoyed over a longer period of time.

The same logic predicts that women will obtain less schooling than men. Why? Women actually have longer life expectancies than men, so one might guess that women would be more inclined to invest in their human capital. But the average woman spends less time in the labor market than the average man, and the time that is relevant for optimal schooling decisions is labor market time (T), not life time. This point requires some elaboration.

First, the women who are reading this book are not likely to be very different from the men reading it, at least in terms of labor force behavior. Women who are specializing in advanced fields have already made clear by their investment behavior that they plan to participate in the labor market. Further, the fact that their wages will be high, in part as a result of the training that they now undertake, will help fuse those women to the labor market.

Second, even if women are less likely to spend time in the labor market, their training may be valuable in increasing their productivity at home. More educated people may be better at raising children, cooking, shopping, and a variety of other tasks. But then the K term in (6.2) should be thought of as the value of the different productivity at home attributable to a year of education. Once that is done, it becomes reasonable to expect that the kinds of courses taken by individuals planning to be out of the labor market will differ from those taken by those committed to the labor market. Housewives are less likely to concentrate in electrical engineering or nuclear physics than are their female counterparts who end up in the labor market. Instead, future housewives may take more humanities and education courses, which have more general applicability.

The final set of applications revolves around differences in K. When $K - J$ increases, school attendance should rise. What interpretation can we give to changes in $K - J$? Recall that $K - J$ is the difference in earnings between educated and less educated workers. As such, it is likely to reflect differences in productivity between educated and less educated workers. Improvements in school quality would be expected to have a positive effect on K. If teachers and teaching techniques get better, then the hope is that students learn more, which would be reflected later in their productivity at work. Thus, technological innovation in education would be expected to increase education. But this is unlikely to be tremendously important in explaining trends over time.

We observe that average levels of education are much higher in the United States today than they were at the turn of the century. Also, the average level of education in the United States exceeds by a significant margin the average for Bangladesh. The common feature that distinguishes turn-of-the-century America and Bangladesh from the United States today is the level of technology associated with the average job. Although a college education may be helpful to farmers, it is not likely to have as much value to a farmer as it is to an accountant. Education is complementary with a technologically advanced society. Being uneducated, being unable to read, or being unable to do simple mathematical calculations is more inhibiting in a society that has a majority of white collar jobs than in a society of farmers. Thus, K is higher in 1997 America than in 1900 America.

Bridging the Theory and the Real World

Many readers are probably thinking that this model, although logically sound, is not the one that students use when deciding whether to drop out of school. After all, how many students sit down and perform a calculation like the one in (6.2)? Even economists don't do this.

In fact, students implicitly go through exactly the kind of calculation reflected in (6.2). When a potential business student is deciding whether to come back to get an MBA, she is considering primarily the effect of that degree on her career path. She knows that the MBA will help somewhat with her career, and must make some guess as to the amount by which it will improve her opportunities. Against that she weighs the costs of returning to get an MBA. Those costs include tuition, hours of homework, and current earnings and opportunities lost by going back to school to get the MBA. The question, "Is it worth it?" is one that every person who returns to get an MBA asks, even if the inequality in (6.2) is not firmly in the individual's mind.

Of course, many might claim that MBAs are a money-conscious lot. It is little wonder that a rational model that assumes maximization of economic goals applies well to MBAs. But what about high school dropouts? The model applies to them as well. When a student is deciding whether to complete high school, one of his main concerns is, "What do I get out of it?" Will my life change substantially by getting the diploma? Somewhat cynically, he might ask himself, "What difference does this make to what I will be doing, say, two years from now?" His answer may well be "very little." Against this, he considers the costs. School is difficult, and, perhaps in his view, irrelevant. Further, attending prevents him from participating in other activities that may be more enjoyable and perhaps even more lucrative. He is mentally tallying up the returns, that is, the $K - J$, and weighing them against the costs. If he concludes that dropping out is the right decision, he has estimated that the right-hand side of (6.2) exceeds the left-hand side. No calculator is needed to perform this calculation, but his thought processes and all the arguments that he provides on the advantages of leaving school can be expressed as part of (6.2).

Non-Pecuniary Benefits of Schooling

There is one final point, to which we will return again and again. The discussion here has been a financial one, with the emphasis on earnings and dollars spent as the benefits and costs of schooling. Yet we know that individuals attend school for other reasons. Nothing precludes thinking of K as reflecting nonmonetary rewards to schooling. We have already discussed this point in the context of housewives who view the return as the effect of schooling on their productivity as a homemaker. But we can do the same thing in the labor market. Even the money-conscious MBA discussed previously might have returned to school, not because it would increase her earnings, but because it would put her in position for a more rewarding job. The rewards can take the form of higher status, more flexibility, more interesting assignments, but the details do not matter. We need only think of K as the value of the improvement in well-being at work that results from the additional schooling. That value can derive from improved working conditions, rather than improved salary. Although it may be difficult to translate nonmonetary rewards into dollar values, it is quite possible to do, both conceptually and empirically. We ask the reader to accept this point on faith for now. Chapter 14 will discuss the conversion of non-pecuniary rewards into monetary values in depth.

◆ ◆ ◆ ◆ ◆ ON-THE-JOB TRAINING

Human capital that takes the form of on-the-job training is the most important type of human capital investment for personnel analysts. This is true, not only because the firm provides the training, but also because the type and timing of the training must be coordinated with compensation.

Two types of on-the-job training must be distinguished, because the two types have very different implications for earnings. They are **general on-the-job training** and **firm-specific on-the-job training.**

General on-the-job training is an investment in human capital that is effective in raising productivity at the firm providing the training and at some other firms by an identical amount. Firm-specific on-the-job training is at the other extreme. Firm-specific on-the-job training makes a worker more productive at the current firm, but has no effect on productivity elsewhere. Obviously, most training is a hybrid, but it is important to consider the polar cases to understand the importance of the distinction between the two.

A plumber's apprentice receives primarily general training. Suppose that Sue goes to work right out of high school at Patinkin Plumbing as a plumber's apprentice. Having had no background in this field, she must learn everything fresh. She spends time learning how to unstop bathtubs, how to adjust the water level in toilets, and how to repair leaky faucets. As a result, her productivity during the second year on the job will be higher than her productivity during the first year. But the improvement in productivity is not limited to work at Patinkin. Suppose that Sue moves to Williams Water Works after one year at Patinkin. All the skills that she picked up are transferable to Williams. She is sent out to fix the same tubs, toilets, and sinks, so her training is completely general. (If Patinkin specialized in servicing different brands than Williams, then the training would not be completely general.)

Contrast the plumbing case with that of an attorney. Attorneys acquire general human capital in learning how to try cases and prepare briefs, but some of their human capital is firm-specific. Consider Heaton Adams, who works for a major New York law firm, Fox and Williams, nicknamed FoBill. FoBill has responsibility for the Greenwich Village Earth Shoe (GVES) account. Now, in the process of representing GVES, Heaton learns a great deal about earth shoes. Furthermore, he learns some of the idiosyncrasies of Ms. Gemini Freedom, the CEO of GVES. Gemini likes her sprouts marinated in Vodka, and Heaton has become an expert at making the dish to her liking. All of these seemingly useless pieces of information are valuable to Heaton in dealing with this account. The account is lucrative, and the specific training that he has been given in learning how to deal with GVES and Ms. Freedom increases his productivity while at FoBill.

Unfortunately, disaster hits the earth shoe industry. Balding flower children do not buy earth shoes, and GVES folds. At the same time, Heaton accepts another job at Glickstein, Gomez and Giovani, where he handles the United Pipe Company account. All the time spent learning about earth shoes and Gemini Freedom is for naught. Although Heaton's productivity was enhanced by these skills while he was at FoBill, the information is useless for his new account and his new law firm, 3G.

The reason that it is important to distinguish between general and specific on-the-job training is that the earnings and turnover behavior differs in the two cases. We begin by examining the case of general human capital.

General On-the-Job Training

Suppose that the firm has the opportunity to provide a 25-year-old worker with one year of on-the-job training. Suppose further that the training, which costs $500 during the first year, raises the worker's productivity by $1,000 per year thereafter. At any normal interest rate and work life expectancy, this is an investment that is extremely worthwhile. The condition in (6.2) is surely satisfied. The cost side of the equation amounts to $500 and $K - J$ is $1,000 for every year that work occurs. This relation seems to imply that the firm should invest in this individual's human capital by providing on-the-job training. But that is not quite true.

Suppose that the firm makes the investment in general on-the-job training that raises productivity by $1,000 per year. What wage should the firm pay the worker? Since the firm bore the full costs of the training, it may feel that it should recoup the full return to the investment. The only way to accomplish this is to leave the worker's wages unaltered. But that is not a viable strategy. Since the OJT is completely general, the worker's productivity has risen by $1,000 not only at this firm, but at other firms as well. Rival firms will be happy to offer the worker, say, a $500 per year raise. By doing so, the new firm obtains someone who is worth $1,000 more and pays only half that additional amount to get the worker. Now the original firm is forced to match the $500 raise. But that will not be sufficient. New firms can give the worker a raise up to the full $1,000 of increased productivity and still make a profit on the hire. To keep the worker, the original firm will be forced to raise wages up to the new level of worker productivity. (Recall that this was exactly Edgeworth's concern in the introductory scenario.)

The original firm is unlikely to make the same mistake twice. The firm is unwilling to bear a $500 cost to make the worker more productive when it can capture none of the gain to that productivity. As a result, it seems that a valuable investment opportunity is lost. But this is not the case. Although the firm will be unwilling to pay for the investment, the worker will be happy to do so. By paying $500 at the outset, he buys himself a raise of $1,000, which persists for each year that he works thereafter. Thus, the worker should offer to pay the firm for the on-the-job training and the firm should be happy to oblige.

This sounds fine in theory, but workers rarely pay firms for training. During the days of formal apprenticeships, the practice was quite common, but it is almost unheard of now. However, workers do pay for their training by accepting lower wages than they would otherwise receive.

Examples abound. Young attorneys take jobs with the district attorney's office at lower pay than they could receive in private practice to acquire valuable trial experience. This human capital is general. After a few years, a lawyer can return to the private sector and receive wages many times the level of the wages available in the D.A.'s office.

Young cooks work in established restaurants at low wages, learning the trade so that they can open their own establishments later. The skills acquired are general, which is one reason why their wages are so low as trainees, even in very profitable restaurants.

The idea can be made more rigorous. Consider a machinist who produces widgets (our generic commodity). A widget generates $.10 in profit after all expenses are subtracted (including management time) and 60 per hour can be produced by a novice. Thus, the worker is worth $6 per hour to the firm, and competition will drive his wage up to that level. Alternatively, the worker can take 15 minutes per hour and watch the master widgeteer at work. By doing this, the novice acquires information that increases his productivity, so that after a year of watching, the novice can produce 75 widgets per hour. The cost of watching is that during the first year, he produces only $4.50 per hour rather than $6.00 per hour of profit on widgets. The firm is only willing to pay $4.50 per hour, because a "student" worker is only producing 45 widgets per hour.

As a result of having watched the master widgeteer, the worker is now able to produce 75 widgets per hour. But he may decide that some additional widget watching is profitable. Suppose that the worker spends six minutes, or one-tenth of an hour watching the master. Productivity falls to 67.5 widgets, so his wage rate is $6.75 per hour rather than the $7.50 that full-time widget production would yield. But as a result of having watched the master during the second year of employment, skills are acquired that enable the worker to produce 80 widgets per hour. Suppose that instead of producing the 80, the worker opts to spend three minutes per hour watching the master. This reduces productivity by one-twentieth, or by two widgets. Instead of earning $8.00 per hour during the third year, the worker earns only $7.80 per hour. But now, his maximum production during the fourth year is 81 widgets. The worker, in turn, concludes that it is no longer profitable to engage in additional widget watching and produces full time, yielding a wage of $8.10 per hour. Unless something else changes, the wage of $8.10 will persist. Figure 6.1 shows the age-earnings profile that results from this type of investment pattern. The diagram assumes that the worker begins employment

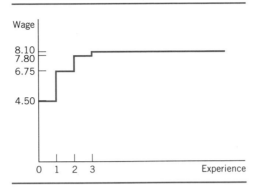

FIGURE 6.1
WAGE-EXPERIENCE PROFILE

with the firm at age 25. The stepped pattern of wage growth is typical in the real world, where raises are granted on a periodic basis. But the pattern shown might be somewhat extreme, since we are allowing the wage to adjust only once per year. On many jobs, wages adjust more frequently, especially during the first few years on the job. If wages adjusted instantaneously, then the age-earnings profile would be smooth, as shown in Figure 6.2.

There are three noteworthy features of the **age–earnings profiles.** They reflect the ways that a firm and its workers think of on-the-job training.

First, if the worker did no investment in human capital, then the profile would have been flat at $6.00, as shown by the dotted line in Figure 6.2. This means that the investor's profile starts below, but rises above the profile of the noninvestor. Human capital investors forgo wages early in their lifetimes and are rewarded by higher wages later on.

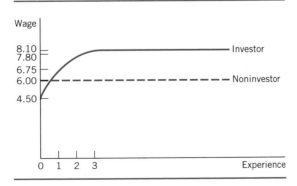

FIGURE 6.2
WAGE-EXPERIENCE PROFILE, SMOOTHED

In the real world, individuals who are out on the road selling often make more than those in the home office who are engaged in management. It is common for salespersons to take cuts in pay when they take a management job. One reason for taking the lower-paying job is that it puts the worker on a different job track. The skills acquired as a junior manager will make the person more productive later. Often, the trade-off of lower wages now for higher wages later is worth making, so the worker moves in from the field.

Second, the profile is positively sloped. Workers earn less when they are young than when they are old. This reflects two forces. The first, and most obvious, is that workers are more productive as they acquire experience on the job. It is reasonable to expect that workers' wages will rise as productivity rises. The second is that the amount of the workers' productivity devoted to investment decreases. Thus, observed wages rise. Even if a worker's productivity remained constant at $6.00, the fact that he spends 15 minutes watching during the first year and only 6 minutes watching during the second year means that his observed wage would rise from $4.50 during the first year to $5.40 per hour during the second. So wages rise over the life cycle because productivity rises and because the investment rate falls.

The third point is that the profile is concave—that is, it becomes flatter with age. It rises more steeply at the beginning of the worker's career than it does later on. This, too, is a phenomenon that is observed in the real world. Raises tend to be larger during the early stages of a worker's career than during the later stages. Again, there are two reasons. First, the payoff to investment declines after more of it has been done. The most important skills are learned first, then less important polishing of those skills occurs. Children learn more about language from ages 2 to 5 than they do from ages 17 to 20. The same is true on the job. The most information is transmitted early. The second reason for the concave shape is that the amount of time devoted to investment declines as the worker ages and acquires experience. This means that earnings do not jump by as much later as they do initially.

The theory of general OJT does well at explaining what is observed in the real world. Age-earnings profiles are positively sloped, and they are concave. Further, those who invest in training find that they give up something. They must accept lower earnings initially in order to receive higher earnings later on.

An Application of General On-the-Job Training

The scenario at the beginning of this chapter focused on providing training that would have value at other firms. Some of the managers were worried that the training would make the workers more productive, but that their additional productivity would be enjoyed by competitors who would steal the workers away. In this application, we consider general training and ask which workers should get it and how their pay should be structured before and after the training period.

Suppose that the durable goods manufacturer, which we will call General Durables, has two job categories for its production workers: machinist and technical artisan, labeled M and A, respectively. A worker can be assigned to either job.

The machinist's job provides only minimal on-the-job training, whereas the apprentice position is geared toward training workers to operate the new robotics equipment. Table 6.1a provides productivity data on workers in both jobs. Workers are categorized as either able or less able.

"Earning Difference I" is the discounted difference of earnings between A and M for able workers up to the year of experience in that row. For example, the entry in row 3 is

$$(10000 - 20000)/(1+r)^0 + (14159 - 20693)/(1+r)^1 + \\ (16591 - 21099)/(1+r)^2 + (18318 - 21386)/(1+r)^3 = -24110.$$

In this case, $r = 0$.

The interpretation of the third row entry of column I is that an able worker who worked in years 0 through 3 would lose \$24,110 by choosing the technical artisan's job over the machinist's job.

Similarly, the column labeled "Earning Differences II" does for less able workers what the previous column does for able workers. Thus, the entry in row 2 is

$$(8000 - 18000)/(1+r)^0 + (11466 - 18624)/(1+r)^1 + (13493 - 18989)/ \\ (1+r)^2 = -22654.$$

The interpretation of the third row entry of column II is that a worker who worked in years 0 through 2 would lose \$22,654 by choosing the technical artisan's job over the machinist's job.

Table 6.1b is identical to Table 6.1a, except that a 5 percent rate of interest was used to compute present values rather than the 0 percent used in Table 6.1a.

A large amount of information is contained in Table 6.1a, b. In Table 6.1a, the interest rate is assumed to be zero. The first column lists years of experience with the firm. The second column lists the annual production of an able individual who holds the machinist position in each of 35 years. The third column lists the annual production of an able individual who holds the technical artisan position. Notice that the A worker's productivity starts out below that of M because the technical artisan is spending time on training. After the sixth year, production of A exceeds that of M.

The same information is contained in columns 4 and 5, but for less able workers. Their productivity in every job and every year is lower than that for their more able counterparts. The same pattern, where A starts below but ends above M holds, even for the less able, but there is a difference. The able get more out of training than the less able. For example, in the thirty-fifth year of work, an able A produces about \$8,000 more than an able M, whereas a less able A produces only about \$4,700 more than a less able M. Columns 6 and 7, labeled I and II, report information derived from the other columns. They are sufficient to determine which job to assign to a given worker. Column 6, labeled I, contains the information on the discounted difference of earnings between A and M for able workers up to the year of experience in that row. For example, the entry in row 3 of column 6 is computed as follows: From row 1, we learn that technical artisans produce \$10,000 and machinists produce \$20,000 during their first year on the job.

TABLE 6.1a
ANNUAL PRODUCTION

			(Interest Rate = 0)			
1	2	3	4	5	6	7
	Able Workers		Less Able Workers		Earnings Difference	
Exp.	Machinist	Tech. Ar.	Machinist	Tech. Ar.	I Able	II Less Able
0	**$20,000**	**$10,000**	**$18,000**	**$8,000**	($10,000)	($10,000)
1	**$20,693**	**$14,159**	**$18,624**	**$11,466**	($16,534)	($17,158)
2	**$21,099**	**$16,591**	**$18,989**	**$13,493**	($21,041)	**($22,654)**
3	**$21,386**	**$18,318**	$19,248	$14,931	**($24,110)**	($26,970)
4	$21,609	$19,657	$19,448	$16,047	($26,063)	($30,371)
5	$21,792	$20,751	$19,613	$16,959	($27,104)	($33,025)
6	$21,946	$21,675	$19,751	$17,730	($27,374)	($35,047)
7	$22,079	$22,477	$19,871	$18,397	($26,977)	($36,521)
8	$22,197	$23,183	$19,978	$18,986	($25,991)	($37,513)
9	$22,303	$23,816	$20,072	$19,513	($24,478)	($38,072)
10	$22,398	$24,387	$20,158	$19,989	($22,488)	($38,241)
11	$22,485	$24,909	$20,236	$20,425	($20,064)	($38,052)
12	$22,565	$25,390	$20,308	$20,825	($17,239)	($37,536)
13	$22,639	$25,834	$20,375	$21,195	($14,044)	($36,716)
14	$22,708	$26,248	$20,437	$21,540	($10,504)	($35,613)
15	$22,773	$26,636	$20,495	$21,863	($6,641)	($34,245)
16	$22,833	$26,999	$20,550	$22,166	($2,475)	($32,629)
17	$22,890	$27,342	$20,601	$22,452	$1,977	($30,779)
18	$22,944	$27,667	$20,650	$22,722	$6,699	($28,706)
19	$22,996	$27,974	$20,696	$22,979	$11,678	($26,424)
20	$23,045	$28,267	$20,740	$23,223	$16,901	($23,941)
21	$23,091	$28,546	$20,782	$23,455	$22,356	($21,268)
22	$23,135	$28,813	$20,822	$23,677	$28,033	($18,413)
23	$23,178	$29,068	$20,860	$23,890	$33,924	($15,383)
24	$23,219	$29,313	$20,897	$24,094	$40,018	($12,185)
25	$23,258	$29,549	$20,932	$24,290	$46,309	($8,827)
26	$23,296	$29,775	$20,966	$24,479	$52,788	($5,314)
27	$23,332	$29,993	$20,999	$24,661	$59,449	($1,652)
28	$23,367	$30,204	$21,031	$24,836	$66,285	$2,154
29	$23,401	$30,407	$21,061	$25,006	$73,291	$6,099
30	$23,434	$30,604	$21,091	$25,170	$80,461	$10,178
31	$23,466	$30,794	$21,119	$25,329	$87,790	$14,388
32	$23,497	$30,979	$21,147	$25,483	$95,272	$18,723
33	$23,526	$31,158	$21,174	$25,632	$102,904	$23,181
34	$23,555	$31,332	$21,200	$25,777	$110,681	$27,758
35	**$23,584**	**$31,501**	**$21,225**	**$25,918**	$118,598	$32,451

TABLE 6.1b
ANNUAL PRODUCTION

1	2	3	4	5	6	7
	Able Workers		Less Able Workers		Earnings Difference	
Exp.	Machinist	Tech. Ar.	Machinist	Tech. Ar.	I Able	II Less Able
0	$20,000	$10,000	$18,000	$8,000	($10,000)	($10,000)
1	$20,693	$14,159	$18,624	$11,466	($16,223)	($16,817)
2	$21,099	$16,591	$18,989	$13,493	($20,311)	($21,802)
3	$21,386	$18,318	$19,248	$14,931	($22,962)	($25,530)
4	$21,609	$19,657	$19,448	$16,047	($24,568)	($28,329)
5	$21,792	$20,751	$19,613	$16,959	($25,384)	($30,408)
6	$21,946	$21,675	$19,751	$17,730	($25,586)	($31,917)
7	$22,079	$22,477	$19,871	$18,397	($25,304)	($32,964)
8	$22,197	$23,183	$19,978	$18,986	($24,636)	($33,635)
9	$22,303	$23,816	$20,072	$19,513	($23,661)	($33,996)
10	$22,398	$24,387	$20,158	$19,989	($22,440)	($34,100)
11	$22,485	$24,909	$20,236	$20,425	($21,022)	($33,990)
12	$22,565	$25,390	$20,308	$20,825	($19,449)	($33,702)
13	$22,639	$25,834	$20,375	$21,195	($17,755)	($33,267)
14	$22,708	$26,248	$20,437	$21,540	($15,967)	($32,710)
15	$22,773	$26,636	$20,495	$21,863	($14,108)	($32,052)
16	$22,833	$26,999	$20,550	$22,166	($12,200)	($31,312)
17	$22,890	$27,342	$20,601	$22,452	($10,258)	($30,504)
18	$22,944	$27,667	$20,650	$22,722	($8,295)	($29,643)
19	$22,996	$27,974	$20,696	$22,979	($6,325)	($28,740)
20	$23,045	$28,267	$20,740	$23,223	($4,357)	($27,805)
21	$23,091	$28,546	$20,782	$23,455	($2,399)	($26,845)
22	$23,135	$28,813	$20,822	$23,677	($458)	($25,869)
23	$23,178	$29,068	$20,860	$23,890	$1,460	($24,882)
24	$23,219	$29,313	$20,897	$24,094	$3,350	($23,891)
25	$23,258	$29,549	$20,932	$24,290	$5,207	($22,899)
26	$23,296	$29,775	$20,966	$24,479	$7,029	($21,911)
27	$23,332	$29,993	$20,999	$24,661	$8,814	($20,930)
28	$23,367	$30,204	$21,031	$24,836	$10,557	($19,960)
29	$23,401	$30,407	$21,061	$25,006	$12,260	($19,001)
30	$23,434	$30,604	$21,091	$25,170	$13,918	($18,057)
31	$23,466	$30,794	$21,119	$25,329	$15,533	($17,130)
32	$23,497	$30,979	$21,147	$25,483	$17,104	($16,220)
33	$23,526	$31,158	$21,174	$25,632	$18,629	($15,329)
34	$23,555	$31,332	$21,200	$25,777	$20,109	($14,457)
35	$23,584	$31,501	$21,225	$25,918	$21,545	($13,607)

(Interest Rate = 0.05)

The difference is −$10,000, which is incurred right now. During the second year of work (after the worker has 1 year of experience), A produces $14,159 and M produces $20,693, for a net difference of −$6,534. During the third year of work (after experience equals 2), the net is $16,591 − $21,099, which equals −$4,508. During the fourth year, the difference is $18,318 − $21,386 which equals −$3,068. When the interest rate is zero, the sum of these four years' differences is

$$(10000 − 20000)/(1+ r)^0 + (14159 − 20693)/(1+ r)^1 + (16591 − 21099)/(1+ r)^2$$
$$+ (18318 − 21386)/(1+ r)^3$$

or

$$− 10000 − 6534 − 4507 − 3068 = − 24110$$

A worker who worked only four years would be $24,110 less productive in job A than in job M. Column 6 shows that as the number of years of work grows, the difference between the total productivity of the A job and M job rises toward zero, and eventually becomes positive. For an able worker who stays with the firm 17 years, the value of the A job minus the value of the M job is $1,977. If the worker were to stay for 35 years, the difference would grow to $118,598.

Column 7 is identical in structure to column 6, but it uses the information in the fourth and fifth columns rather than that in the second and third columns. Thus, column 7 computes for the less able what column 6 computes for the able.

Table 6.1 provides enough information to decide who should be assigned to each job, which, in this case, is tantamount to determining who should receive training. First, let us suppose that the interest rate is zero, so that the data in Table 6.1a are relevant. An able worker who plans to stay with the firm at least through year 17 should be assigned to the A job. For workers who stay at least 17 years, the net difference in value to the firm of the two jobs tips in favor of A. Although job A is worth more than job M by year 7, the worker must work another ten years to make up for the reduced production associated with job A during the first six years.

The productivity of any able worker who plans to stay in the labor market for more than 16 years benefits from being a technical artisan instead of a machinist. Similarly, the productivity of any less able worker who plans to stay in the labor market for more than 27 years benefits from being a technical artisan instead of a machinist. While the productivity may benefit, the question is whether the firm or worker benefit from it. The answer to that question depends on the compensation associated with each job.

Since the training is general, the answer must be that workers are paid the value of their actual productivity. If they are paid less than that, a competitor will induce the worker to leave by offering something in between current wage and productivity. Again, since the skills are general, a rival's threat to steal away workers is indeed credible. Thus, suppose that able machinists are paid exactly what they produce—that is, in each year of work, they are paid in accordance with the numbers in column 2. Similarly, suppose that able technical assistants in each year are paid in accordance with the numbers in column 3.

The firm need not even make the decision on which workers to train. The workers will do it themselves and do it appropriately! No able worker who planned to work fewer than 17 years would want to be a technical artisan. Every able worker who planned to work more than 17 years would choose to be a technical artisan. It would not matter whether the worker remained with the firm that trained him or not. Since skills are general, he would receive the same wage at every firm.

Furthermore, the firm would be indifferent. As long as a firm pays no more than the worker's productivity (and it cannot get away with paying any less), the firm does not care whether it has productive workers, whom it pays a high salary, or less productive workers, whom it pays a low salary.[3]

Thus, the question of who gets training when the training is general is answered quite simply: Anyone who wants general training and is willing to pay for it can and will receive it.

Which kind of workers choose the high-training job? The answer is clear from the tables. Those workers who plan to stay in the labor force for the longest amount of time benefit the most from the training. Thus, the young and committed workers are most likely to take the A job over the M job. Also, the able get a bigger boost out of the training than the less able. So, at least in this case, more able workers are more likely to take the job.

What about women versus men? There is no reason to expect that a woman who plans to stay in the labor market will make any different decision than her male counterpart. Therefore, an able woman planning to work 20 years should take the A job, whereas an able man who plans to retire in 15 years should take the M job.

What happens if the interest rate is higher? Table 6.1b tells the story. A higher interest rate makes investment less worthwhile. When the interest rate is zero, an able worker who planned to stay for more than 17 years would choose the investment job. When the interest rate is 5 percent, an able worker must be planning to work more than 23 years to make the investment worthwhile. Furthermore, no less able worker should ever choose the technical artisan job at an interest rate of 5 percent. But at an interest rate of zero, a less able worker who planned to work more than 28 years would still prefer the high investment job. This application leads to the following conclusions:

1. *When on-the-job training is general, workers must pay for it themselves through reduced wages. This means that any worker who would like to undertake the training program should be given the opportunity to do so.*
2. *The workers most likely to select jobs that offer training at the cost of low initial wages are young workers and others who plan to remain in the labor market for a long period of time.*

---

[3]This ignores capital considerations discussed in chapter 2.

152 • The Theory of Human Capital

As long as workers pay for training themselves, there is no reason to steer the most able workers into the training program. In most, but not all cases, the most able workers will get the most out of training and will be more inclined to choose the high investment jobs.

Firm-Specific On-the-Job Training

So far, attention has been confined to general on-the-job training, which affects a worker's productivity at many firms in the same way. Since Sue has general plumbing skills, there is competition among firms for her services. The firm that provides the training cannot get away with paying her less than she is worth. This means that the firm cannot recoup the costs of its investment. Workers' firm-specific OJT cannot be pirated by other firms. Heaton's vodka-sprouts recipe is of use only at FoBill, where the GVES account is lodged. Since the skills are firm specific, the compensation that the training firm can offer always exceeds that which any other firm can offer. This suggests that the firm, in this case FoBill, should be willing to pay for firm-specific on-the-job training. But such is not the case.

To see FoBill's predicament, suppose that the firm agreed to finance all the training, in return for which the firm would expect to receive the entire difference between productivity and the outside wage that the worker could receive. Now Heaton knows that he has the firm over a barrel. If Heaton quits, the firm loses its investment. Further, Heaton is indifferent between working here and working elsewhere because the wage is the same.

The alternative of letting the worker bear the full cost of training has no better effects. Since the worker has borne the full cost of the investment, he expects to get the full return. But that would make the firm indifferent between hiring the skilled, but highly paid worker and hiring the unskilled, less well-paid worker. Now the worker is at a disadvantage. The firm can threaten to fire the worker unless the worker takes a lower wage. And the threat is taken seriously because the firm has nothing to lose under the circumstances by firing the worker and replacing her with another.

There is a solution. Since the firm needs to give up some of the profit from investing in the worker, it can ask the worker to bear some of the costs. Put differently, since the worker knows that the firm will be able to force Heaton to accept a wage less than his productivity when he is skilled, Heaton can ask the firm to bear some of the cost. The solution is to split the costs and benefits. See Figure 6.3 for a graphical depiction of the solution.

Consider the widget scenario again, but now imagine that the widget is made only by the worker's current firm. Thus, learning to make widgets has much more value in the current firm than elsewhere, where it has no value. An untrained widget maker can earn $6.00 outside. A trained widget maker can earn $6.00 outside because widget skills have no value in another firm. Thus, the outside value curve is completely flat at $6.00. But inside, the investor is worth only $4.50 when being trained, but $8.10 when fully trained. Thus, the inside value starts at $4.50 and rises to $8.10.

FIGURE 6.3
WAGE-EXPERIENCE PROFILE:
SPECIFIC HUMAN CAPITAL

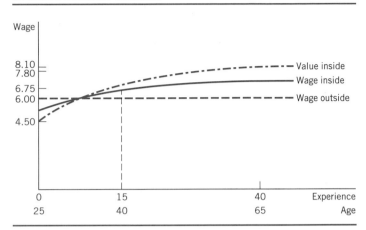

The wage function splits the difference. Since the initial wage exceeds $4.50, which is what the worker is worth, the firm is paying more than it gets back from the worker initially. This means that the firm bears some of the cost. Since the wage falls short of the $6.00 that the worker could receive outside, the worker is bearing some of the cost in forgone earnings.

Compare that to the situation at age 40. Since the wage exceeds the outside value, which is what the worker could receive if she were to quit, the worker is reaping some of the benefit. But since the firm pays the worker less than the inside value, the firm is making money on the worker. The size of the firm's "quasi-rent," or *profit*, ignoring the cost of investment, is measured by the difference between the inside value and the wage.

The worker and firm share the costs and share the benefits. The shared benefits mean that both worker and firm have incentives to remain together. This is a marriage that is meant to last. The worker is worth more to this firm than to any other. It would be wasteful for a separation to occur. The scheme that shares the costs and benefits makes separation much less likely to occur.

Once the bulk of the investment has been completed, the worker earns more at the current firm than she does at any other firm. This makes her reluctant to leave the job. In addition, the firm makes money on the worker. Even though the worker is being paid more than she could earn elsewhere, she is also being paid less than she is worth to the firm. The firm wants to keep her employed because replacing her with a new worker means less profit. The investment costs have already been borne and the firm is now reaping the benefits to that investment. This is perhaps the most important implication of the theory of specific human capital. When workers have specific human capital, turnover rates are likely to be low. Thus, jobs with firm-specific human capital should have lower turnover rates

TRAINING INTERNATIONAL MANAGERS AT GILLETTE
◆ ◆ ◆ ◆ ◆ ◆ ◆ ◆ ◆ ◆

Gillette Corporation (Boston, Massachusetts) is a large consumer product business that focuses on grooming products, stationery, and small electrical appliances. More than 70 percent of the company's total sales and operating profit come from international operations. While the company already has a strong presence in Western Europe and Central America, currently Gillette is expanding into the emerging market countries. In order to fill the growing number of entry-level management positions created in these areas, in the mid-'80s management decided to train and develop nationals instead of relying upon expensive expatriates. Gillette created an international trainee program that brings bright, young, career-oriented university graduates already working for Gillette in their home countries to their international headquarters for 18 months of training.

The company pays the employees $1,000 (net) per month and provides free housing. Paired with a senior executive mentor, the trainees perform existing jobs at headquarters in one or two of five major business areas: marketing, finance, manufacturing, personnel, and market research. As a result, the trainees learn not only about these general functional areas, but also how to work effectively within Gillette. According to company executives, the productivity (and thus, success) of these employees increases dramatically as a result of this program.

Gillette is essentially offering these trainees a chance to develop both specific and general job skills. Consequently, wages are abnormally low based on productivity in order to compensate the company for training costs. However, the benefits and the costs of the training are shared to an extent (that is, trainee wage differentials do not reflect all training expense) because of the specific nature of some of the skills acquired. Apparently, this incentive structure seems to be working: of the 113 graduate trainees, 53 percent are still with Gillette. In addition, the positions held by these nationals would otherwise have to be filled by expatriates, who can cost up to ten times as much.

Source: Jennifer Laabs, "How Gillette Grooms Global Talent," *Personnel Journal* (August 1993).

and flatter age-earnings profiles than jobs with the same amount of general human capital. The age-earnings profiles are flatter because the costs and benefits are shared. The worker's initial wage is not as low as the $4.50 per hour that productivity would dictate. Correspondingly, the worker's wage after training is not as high as the $8.10 per hour that productivity would dictate.

Workers who have general human capital have no necessary attachment to the firm that provides the training. Workers who have firm-specific human capital have a definite attachment to the firm that provided the training because they are not worth as much outside.

A corollary is that workers with specific training are less attached to the firm when young. Since specific human capital tends to grow over time, workers and firms have more to lose by a senior separation than by a junior one. Senior employees who have been with the same firm for many years often complain about losing their jobs. It is very difficult for them to find new jobs at wages comparable to those that they were receiving at their long-term job. This is consistent with investment in specific human capital. Since the worker is worth more to the current firm than to any other firm, an unexpected job loss usually means a wage decline.

Similarly, firms are often upset when "key" senior workers leave. While those workers were often among the most highly paid in the firm, they were also among the workers on which the firm made the highest profit. It is the difference between productivity and wage that determines profit. It is the difference between wage at the current firm and wage elsewhere that determines a worker's desire to leave. Both sides are generally made better off when investment in specific human capital occurs. When external events induce separation of the worker and the firm, at least one of the parties will be unhappy.

The Choice Between Job-Specific and General Training

The application in the section on general on-the-job training examined the question raised in the opening scenario: "Which workers should we train, and how do we prevent them from being stolen away by our competitors?"

When OJT is general, workers can be allowed to choose investment strategies themselves. As long as wage profiles are set up appropriately, only workers who derive a positive net benefit from the training will opt to work in high investment jobs. When OJT is firm specific, the situation is somewhat more complicated.

Using Table 6.2, let us reconsider General Durables. Suppose that now the comparison is not between two jobs within GD, but, rather, between a job in GD that requires investment in firm-specific OJT and one at another firm with no firm-specific investment. (There may be some general OJT at the outside firm.) Suppose for simplicity that the interest rate is zero.

Column 4 is the difference of earnings between the inside and the outside for able workers up to the year of experience in that row. For example, the entry in row 3 is

$$(10000 - 20000)/(1+r)^0 + (14159 - 20693)/(1+r)^1 + (16591 - 21099)/(1+r)^2$$
$$+ (18318 - 21386)/(1+r)^3 = -24110$$

In this case, $r = 0$.

The interpretation of the third row entry of column I is that a worker who worked in years 0 through 3 would reduce his productivity by \$24,110 if he worked at the inside job over the outside job. Since investment in firm-specific OJT involves costs that are borne during the first years on the job, a worker who

TABLE 6.2
ANNUAL PRODUCTION

				(Interest Rate = 0)			
1	*2*	*3*	*4*	*5*	*6*	*7*	*8*
				Wage	Wage	Sum Wage	Sum Wage
Exp.	Outside	Inside	Difference	Inside	Outside	Inside	Outside
0	**$20,000**	**$10,000**	($10,000)	$15,000	$20,000	$15,000	$20,000
1	**$20,693**	**$14,159**	($16,534)	$17,426	$20,693	**$32,426**	**$40,693**
2	**$21,099**	**$16,591**	($21,041)	$18,845	$21,099	$51,271	$61,792
3	**$21,386**	**$18,318**	**($24,110)**	$19,852	$21,386	$71,123	$83,178
4	$21,609	$19,657	($26,063)	$20,633	$21,609	$91,756	$104,787
5	$21,792	$20,751	($27,104)	$21,271	$21,792	$113,027	$126,579
6	$21,946	$21,675	($27,374)	$21,811	$21,946	$134,838	$148,525
7	$22,079	$22,477	($26,977)	$22,278	$22,079	$157,116	$170,605
8	$22,197	$23,183	($25,991)	$22,690	$22,197	$179,806	$192,802
9	$22,303	$23,816	($24,478)	$23,059	$22,303	$202,865	$215,104
10	$22,398	$24,387	($22,488)	$23,393	$22,398	$226,258	$237,502
11	$22,485	$24,909	($20,064)	$23,697	$22,485	$249,955	$259,987
12	$22,565	$25,390	($17,239)	$23,977	$22,565	$273,933	$282,552
13	$22,639	$25,834	($14,044)	$24,237	$22,639	$298,169	$305,191
14	$22,708	$26,248	($10,504)	$24,478	$22,708	$322,647	$327,899
15	$22,773	$26,636	($6,641)	$24,704	$22,773	$347,352	$350,672
16	$22,833	$26,999	($2,475)	$24,916	$22,833	$372,268	$373,505
17	$22,890	$27,342	$1,977	$25,116	$22,890	$397,384	$396,395
18	$22,944	$27,667	$6,699	$25,306	$22,944	$422,690	$419,340
19	$22,996	$27,974	$11,678	$25,485	$22,996	$448,175	$442,336
20	$23,045	$28,267	$16,901	$25,656	$23,045	$473,830	$465,380
21	$23,091	$28,546	$22,356	$25,819	$23,091	$499,649	$488,471
22	$23,135	$28,813	$28,033	$25,974	$23,135	$525,623	$511,607
23	$23,178	$29,068	$33,924	$26,123	$23,178	$551,747	$534,785
24	$23,219	$29,313	$40,018	$26,266	$23,219	$578,013	$558,004
25	$23,258	$29,549	$46,309	$26,403	$23,258	$604,416	$581,262
26	$23,296	$29,775	$52,788	$26,535	$23,296	$630,951	$604,558
27	$23,332	$29,993	$59,449	$26,663	$23,332	$657,614	$627,890
28	$23,367	$30,204	$66,285	$26,786	$23,367	$684,400	$651,257
29	$23,401	$30,407	$73,291	$26,904	$23,401	$711,304	$674,658
30	$23,434	$30,604	$80,461	$27,019	$23,434	$738,323	$698,092
31	$23,466	$30,794	$87,790	$27,130	$23,466	$765,453	$721,558
32	$23,497	$30,979	$95,272	$27,238	$23,497	$792,691	$745,054
33	$23,526	$31,158	$102,904	$27,342	$23,526	$820,033	$768,581
34	$23,555	$31,332	$110,681	$27,444	$23,555	$847,477	$792,136
35	$23,584	$31,501	$118,598	$27,542	$23,584	$875,019	$815,720

works only for three years will have lower overall productivity than if he did not invest at all. This is almost identical to the situation above with general OJT. The difference here is in interpretation. Before, we interpreted column 2 as the productivity in the noninvestor's job and column 3 as productivity in the investor's job. Here, we interpret column 2 as productivity in the outside job, where no, or only general, OJT is acquired, and column 3 as productivity in the inside job, where firm-specific OJT occurs.

The numbers in Table 6.2 imply that there should be investment in firm-specific OJT when workers expect to remain with the firm for more than 17 years. A key to predicting whether a worker will remain with the firm for more than 17 years is a knowledge of the wage rate. If the wage is too low, the worker will be inclined to quit. If the wage is too high, the worker will be happy to stay, but the firm will not be anxious to keep him.

In column 6, the worker's wage in the outside job is reported. Since skills in this job are completely general, the worker is assumed to receive as his wage exactly the value of his productivity. This is the outcome in a competitive labor market. In column 5, one possible schedule of inside wages is reported. The inside wage is a "split-the-difference" schedule. A worker is paid the average of his productivity inside and what he could receive outside. During the first few years, the worker receives less than he could earn outside. After seven years of experience, the worker's inside wage finally rises above what he could earn outside and remains above for the rest of his work life.

The worker shares the costs and benefits of firm-specific OJT. During the first year, the worker's productivity is only $10,000, but he is paid a wage of $15,000. Since this wage exceeds his productivity, the firm is paying for some training. In this case, the firm is putting out $5,000 during the first year of work. But the worker also bears some of the cost of the training. Since the worker could have earned $20,000 on the outside, the worker forgoes $5,000 in order to take the job with firm-specific OJT.

Benefits are shared as well. Once the worker has been with the firm for seven years, his productivity lies above that in the outside job. The firm pays the worker more in every subsequent year than the worker would receive in the outside job. But the amount paid falls short of his inside productivity. As a result, both sides gain. If the worker stays with the firm for a long enough period, then the worker gains from choosing specific OJT over the outside.

In column 7, the present value of the flow of inside wages up through the year of experience in that row is listed. Since the interest rate is zero, this amounts to simply adding up wages paid up through that year. Thus, the interpretation of row 2 of column 7 is that by the end of the second year, the worker will have been paid $32,426 in the inside job. Similarly, column 8 adds up wages for the outside job, so in row 2, column 8, the worker would have earned $40,693 in the outside job during years 0 and 1.

A worker who plans to stay with the firm for at least 17 years will find that the total earnings at the firm that offers firm-specific OJT exceeds the total earnings at the outside firm without OJT. A worker of this sort would choose the firm-specific OJT profile over the outside firm voluntarily. The key to making this choice viable is to share the gains from investment in firm-specific OJT between the worker and firm.

Furthermore, once a worker has made the choice to work in this kind of firm and to invest in firm-specific OJT, he will be reluctant to leave. The worker suffers a loss on his investment if he leaves and takes a job at another firm. Personal reasons and other factors may induce even a worker who has invested in firm-specific OJT to take another job, but the existence of firm-specific OJT and the corresponding wage profile reduce the likelihood of a departure.

Let us return then to the original question: Who should be given the training? Now the firm cares a great deal about which workers get trained, because an investment in a worker who leaves costs the firm money. When OJT is general, the worker bears the full cost of the training so the firm does not care whether the worker leaves or not. When OJT is firm-specific, a departure imposes costs on the firm.

The answer to the question, "Who do we train?" remains almost the same as the answer in the case of general OJT. The firm need not select workers to train as long as workers know the true likelihood that they will leave. Then, simply offering a "split the difference" wage profile (or one like it) causes workers to choose the right firm and the right training program. No workers who know they will work less than 17 years would choose to invest in firm-specific OJT. No workers who know that they will work more than 17 years would pass up the opportunity to invest in OJT.

The reason the answer is almost, but not exactly the same as the answer for general OJT is that the workers are not certain about their chances of working for 17 years or more. In the case of general human capital, the firm did not care. If a worker was wrong and worked only ten years, the worker lost, but the firm was unaffected. Since the worker bore the full cost of the training in every year of work life, the firm breaks even on every worker, independent of the amount of time spent at the firm. But when OJT is firm specific, a mistake by the worker also harms the firm. Suppose, for example, that the worker expected to work 20 years, but ended up leaving after a year. The firm that invested in the worker's OJT would have paid $15,000 for a year that yielded only $10,000 in output. The firm was willing to do this because it expected that it would receive benefits starting seven years after the worker began work. But if the worker leaves after one year, the firm is hurt. The worker loses on the investment as well, by receiving only $15,000 instead of the $20,000 that could have been earned outside, but the misery-loves-company view will not make the firm feel any better about the loss.

Sometimes a firm has better information about the likelihood that a worker will stay than the worker does. The firm has seen many workers and knows which type of worker is most likely to succeed in that particular firm's environment. As a result, the firm's choice of worker may serve both firm and worker better than the worker's own choice. The above discussion leads to the following conclusions:

1. *When on-the-job training is firm-specific, workers and firms share the cost and benefits of the training. This reduces turnover and provides incentives for both parties to make appropriate investment decisions.*

2. *As with general on-the-job training, the workers most likely to invest in firm-specific OJT at the cost of low initial wages are young workers and those who plan to remain in the labor market for a long period of time.*

3. *Since workers may not always have the best information about their departure proba-*
    bilities and since firms bear costs when workers with firm specific human capital
    leave, a firm takes a more active role in selecting workers to offer firm-specific OJT
    than it does for general OJT. The workers that the firm wants to train are those
    with low turnover probabilities whose productivity will be greatly enhanced by the
    training.

SOME LEGAL ISSUES OF HIRING   ◆ ◆ ◆ ◆ ◆

Finally, management should be aware of the legal issues related to hiring. It is outside the scope of this book to cover specific employment laws. The laws vary
widely among countries and even among the states within the United States.
Some U.S. laws require employers to give advanced notice of major layoffs. European employment laws tend to make laying off workers very difficult and expensive. The minimal required length of the notice may depend on the number of
employees who are being laid off, as well as on many other factors. Firms may be
tempted to bind workers with contracts that prohibit future employment by competitors. In general, such contracts are unenforceable—that is, illegal—in the
United States. However, a contract that prohibits future employment by competitors in order to protect trade secrets may be legitimate. In the United States, the
law provides a certain degree of layoff protection to older workers. Race, gender,
and age discrimination are also illegal.

ADDITIONAL POINTS   ◆ ◆ ◆ ◆ ◆

Determining Specificity of Human Capital

How can we determine whether a group of workers has primarily general or specific human capital? An examination of the age-earnings profile is insufficient because both specific and general human capital models predict upward sloping,
concave, profiles. A flatter profile may mean that a greater proportion of the human capital is firm specific, or it may mean that an individual with only general
human capital simply has not invested too much in it.

There is one approach, however, that is useful. It relies on the distinction between *experience*, defined as total time in the labor market, and *tenure*, which is defined as experience in a particular firm. The following example illustrates the
approach.

Suppose that there is a group of 35-year-old workers at ABC Electronics. Half of
them have been with the firm for all of their ten years in the labor market. The other
half worked at ABC during their first seven years, but then moved on to other
firms—say, because they had to change locations to accommodate a spouse's job.
Wages have risen over their work careers at a substantial rate. If there is no system-

atic difference in wages between the groups, then it can be inferred that the human capital obtained at the first firm must be general. Otherwise, a job switch would imply lower productivity for workers at the new firms than at the old, which would be coupled with a decline in earnings. Alternatively, if wages are lower for the group that leaves the firm than for the group that stays, it can be inferred that some of the human capital was probably firm specific. The specificity of the capital would account for the decrease in earnings associated with a job switch.

One quick way to determine the importance of specific human capital is to examine turnover rates. If quit rates are low, it can be inferred that wages at ABC are higher than those obtainable elsewhere. This may be interpreted as signifying the existence of specific human capital. But there are other explanations. As the application section will illustrate, quit rates may be low simply because the firm is erring in its compensation policy.

Within the firm, the approach can be reversed. The extent to which skills are general or specific may not be known in advance. A firm may be trying to decide, for example, whether it will lose much by hiring from the outside rather than training its own workers. If most of the skills required are general, there is no loss in going to the outside. If, on the other hand, skills are firm specific, workers brought in from outside will not produce at the same level as those from the inside.

It is possible to determine the level of specificity by examining the productivity of existing workers. While productivity is never easily measured, virtually all firms attempt to assess individual worker performance, if only for annual salary evaluation. ABC Electronics can compare the productivity of workers with ten years of experience at ABC to that of workers with ten years of total experience, but who began their careers elsewhere and now work at ABC. If there is a systematic advantage in productivity to those whose entire careers were spent at ABC, the firm can reasonably conclude that there is a valuable specific training component.

Using the Marriage Metaphor

The metaphor *marriage* was used earlier to discuss the worker's attachment to the firm. Others, most notably Gary Becker, Elizabeth Landes, and Robert Michael (1977), have built a theory of marriage that has many labor market analogs.

The attachment of the worker to firm is furthered by the importance of specific human capital. Similarly, the attachment of an individual to his or her spouse depends on specific capital. Becker argues that children are the most important form of marriage-specific capital. The prediction is that marriages are less likely to dissolve when children are present. Analogously, recall that senior workers have more firm-specific capital than junior ones and are therefore less likely to separate. Similarly, older marriages should be more stable than newer ones.

Both predictions are borne out in the data.[4] It is found that young marriages

---

[4]See Becker, Landes, and Michael, (1977).

are less likely to survive than older marriages and that the presence of children is a good predictor of the continued viability of a marriage.

RECAP   ◆ ◆ ◆ ◆ ◆

Armed with the analytical tools that were developed in this chapter, we are prepared to answer the questions that managers raised in the introductory discussion.

Managers were uncertain about the amount of OJT that the workers should be given. It is worthwhile to train workers up to the point at which returns on investment in human capital is equal to the interest rate. This is a general principle that applies to all investments—that is, those in physical capital, formal schooling, or OJT.

It is important to understand how the training costs should be divided between workers and employers. If training is general, the worker will be able to capture 100% of the training benefits, because outsiders will be willing to pay what he or she is worth. Thus, the firm must charge for the training when it is provided. Workers who receive job specific training share the costs and benefits with the firm that provides the training. Turnover is an important issue for all firms. Firm-specific training creates an incentive for worker and firm to remain together. General OJT provides no such incentive. Finally management should be aware of legal issues involved in hiring and training. The laws vary widely among countries and even among the states within the United States.

Consider Oldies-But-Goodies Inc., a record company that distributes older records. OBG has been in operation for more than 30 years and now has a work force that includes a large group of older workers, many of whom started with the firm at its outset. The current problem is that the firm is concerned that its wage bill is too high. The large number of senior employees earn more than the younger workers and their turnover rates are very low. A meeting is called to discuss the situation. The following dialogue ensues.

PRESLEY: I think that we need to induce some of our older workers to retire. Perhaps we can buy them out.

HOLLY: Do you think that is wise? Some of them are very productive.

PRESLEY: We can do it selectively—keep the good ones and get rid of the bad ones.

HOLLY: Sure, but my sense is that all of the older guys are better than the young guys that replace them.

PRESLEY: I agree, but they are costing us a fortune, and they never quit. We would be better off with the younger ones.

HOLLY: I don't think so.

PRESLEY: Can we get any of the analysts to provide data on this issue? How about asking those new hot shots from Southern California to look at it?

HOLLY: Fine with me.

The problem is given to Brian and Dennis Wilson. Brian looks at the records division and Dennis analyzes the CD division. Because the record division was started so much earlier, the data available from it are much sketchier. The CD division has detailed information on wages and productivity per worker. Dennis reports first.

DENNIS: Let me start with the bottom line. Keep the old guys. This looks like the textbook case of firm-specific human capital. The young workers make more than they are worth. The old workers make less than they are worth to the firm, but more than they are worth outside. This means we make money on them when they are old, not when they are young. It also means that the old guys aren't about to quit, since they will take a large salary cut if they do. It is true that the old guys cost us more, but they are well worth it.

BRIAN: Look at a couple of examples. I put the data up in Table 6.3, which you now see on the computer screen.

Let me pick some specific workers. Take worker 1008. She is 22 and only costs us $39,580 per year. But we only are making $27,780 per year on her before paying her salary, so we lose money. Contrast her with employee 1004. He is 66. He costs us $64,220 per year, but yields over $78,000 before paying

TABLE 6.3
DATA FROM THE CD DIVISION

Worker ID Number	Age	Salary	Profit from Sales	Typical Outside Salary
1001	37	50,155	47,355	49,055
1002	55	59,875	67,875	53,375
1003	45	54,875	56,875	51,375
1004	**66**	**64,220**	**78,820**	**54,420**
1005	24	41,120	30,520	43,920
1006	59	61,595	71,995	53,895
1007	57	60,755	69,955	53,655
1008	**22**	**39,580**	**27,780**	**42,980**
1009	31	46,195	39,795	46,895
1010	46	55,420	58,020	51,620
1011	53	58,955	65,755	53,055
1012	51	57,995	63,595	52,695
1013	29	44,795	37,195	46,095
1014	38	50,780	48,580	49,380
1015	44	54,320	55,720	51,120
1016	20	38,000	25,000	42,000
1017	22	39,580	27,780	42,980

Regression results:
Salary = 20000 + 1000 (AGE) − 5 (AGE × AGE)
Profit = 5000 + 1600 (AGE) − 5 (AGE × AGE)

Note: Profit from sales is reported before taking account of the worker's salary. Net profit is then the difference between profit and salary.

FIGURE 6.4
OLDIES BUT GOODIES PROFILES

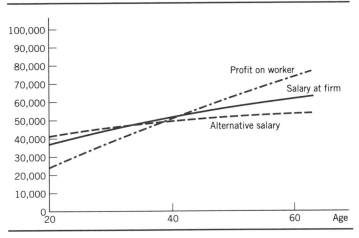

out his salary. The only reason to have 1008 is that we hope she'll turn out to be like 1004. The last thing we want to do is encourage 1004 to leave when we are finally making money on him.

In fact, the pattern persists throughout the entire work force. I did some regressions to determine the relation between age, salary, profitability, and outside salary. That sounds fancy, but all it does is fit curves to our data points, which consist of information on our workers. The regression results are reported at the bottom of the table, and I have graphed them for ease of inspection in Figure 6.4.

You can see what I mean. We start by paying our young workers more than they are worth to us, but less than they can get outside. At some point mid-career, things switch. They earn more here than elsewhere, and they earn less here than they are worth. That's why they want to stay, and it is also why we want to keep them.

PRESLEY: Sounds convincing. Good work, Boys.

REFERENCES ◆ ◆ ◆ ◆ ◆

Becker, Gary S., *Human Capital: A Theoretical and Empirical Analysis, with Special Reference to Education*, 2d ed. New York: Columbia University Press for National Bureau of Economic Research, 1975.

Becker, Gary S., Elisabeth Landes, and Robert Michael, "An Economic Analysis of Martial Instability," *Journal of Political Economy* 85, 6 (1977) 1141–87.

Mincer, Jacob, *Schooling, Experience, and Earnings*. New York: Columbia University Press for NBER, 1974.

◆ ◆ ◆ ◆ ◆ ADDITIONAL ADVANCED READING

Altonji, Joseph G., and James R. Spletzer, "Worker Characteristics, Job Characteristics, and the Receipt of On-the-Job Training," *Industrial and Labor Relations Review* 45, 1, (Oct. 1991), 58–79.

Ashenfelter, Orley, and Alan B. Krueger, "Estimates of the Economic Returns to Schooling from a New Sample of Twins," *American Economic Review* 84, 5, (December 1994), 1157–73.

Card, David, and Alan B. Krueger, "Does Schooling Quality Matter? Returns to Education and the Characteristics of Public Schools in the United States," *Journal of Political Economy* 100, (February, 1992), 1–40.

Cameron, Stephen V., and James Heckman, "Determinants of Young Male Schooling and Training Choices," April 1993, National Bureau of Economic Research Working Paper: 4327, 19.

Hashimoto, Masanori, "Firm-Specific Human Capital as a Shared Investment," *American Economic Review* 71, (June 1981), 475–82.

Parsons, Donald, "Specific Human Capital: Layoffs and Quits," *Journal of Political Economy* 80 (November 1972): 1120–43.

◆ ◆ ◆ ◆ ◆ APPENDIX

The human capital model has been the main engine behind empirical analyses of wage determination. Most of the work derives from Jacob Mincer's early papers on earning profiles. The logic behind the empirical models is summarized below.[5]

Schooling is one of the major investments that individuals make in human capital. In order to make the investment, it must be profitable. Indeed, an individual will choose to complete s years of schooling such that the value of going to the s year just equals (or slightly exceeds) the costs. The present value of earnings for an individual who acquires s years of school is

$$(A6.1) \qquad\qquad V_s = Y_s \int_s^{n+s} e^{-rt}\, dt$$

where V_s is the present value of earning, Y_s is the amount that an individual earns in each year, given s years of schooling, and n is the number of years the person works after school completion until retirement.

---

[5]Much of this analysis was laid out in Mincer (1974).

Now consider another identical individual who chooses no schooling (obviously, only hypothetically). The present value of earnings equals

(A6.2)
$$V_0 = Y_0 \int_0^{n+s} e^{-rt}\, dt$$

where Y are the annual earnings of an individual with no schooling. Equations A6.1 and A6.2 can be rewritten as

(A6.3) (a)
$$V_s = \frac{Y_s}{r} e^{-rs}(1 - e^{-rn})$$

(b)
$$V_0 = \frac{Y_0}{r}(1 - e^{-rn})$$

Now, if two identical individuals make different choices, it must be because the choices have equal value, so $V_s = V_0$.
Using this fact, we can use (A6.3 a, b) to obtain

$$Y_s e^{-rs} = Y_0$$

or

$$Y_s = Y_0 e^{rs}$$

Taking logs,

(A6.4)
$$ln\, Y_s = ln\, Y_0 + rs$$

This is the basic human capital estimating equation. By collecting data on wages of individuals and then levels of schooling, a regression is run that has the form

$$ln\ (\text{annual income}) = a + b\ (\text{years of schooling})$$

This is identical to (A6.4), with $a = ln\, Y_0$ and $b = r$. The constant term is the estimate of how much an individual would earn without any schooling. The coefficient b is interpreted as the rate of return to schooling. This varies over time and across groups, but is in the neighborhood of 5 to 10 percent (real). Investments in human capital seem to yield somewhat more than investments in physical capital.

TURNOVER, LAYOFFS AND BUYOUTS

7

*H*iring and firing are common features of the modern firm. In manufacturing, many firms see 20 to 25 percent of their workers turn over each year, even in periods of stable overall performance. Firms are not indifferent to the identity of the individuals who leave, nor are they indifferent to the timing and terms of those departures. In this chapter, we examine issues of turnover. Specifically, we ask whether and under which conditions turnover is to be encouraged or avoided. When turnover is desired, which workers should be targeted for termination and how should the reduction be handled? The following discussion introduces some of the issues.

MISES: I asked Ms. Robinson to look at the composition of our labor force and she has some alarming results to report to us. Joan?

ROBINSON: Well, it's not good. Things are getting pretty tough. Our labor costs are extremely high and as a result, our net profitability is negative. Unless we cut our labor costs, we are not going to be a viable firm for much longer. We've got to downsize.

NEF: The easiest way to fix the problem is to get rid of the worst of the senior workers. Then we not only cut our costs among the older employees, we also raise the average productivity of those who remain.

SLICHTER: That sounds good, but we could run into some real legal trouble by doing that. These workers are protected by the Age Discrimination in Employment Act, and if we fire them, we could end up with a huge lawsuit on our hands. Remember what happened to Continental Can?

NEF: No, what happened?

167

SLICHTER: They lost an age discrimination suit for systematically terminating older workers. They were bought out, but the company that owned the liability ended up having to pay the former workers a huge settlement, running into the hundreds of millions of dollars. This stuff can't be taken lightly, especially by a large and visible company like us.

NEF: Isn't there any way that we can get the older workers to leave voluntarily? What about some of these window plans that offer a special payment to workers who take early retirement within some specified period, after which the buyout offer explodes?

SLICHTER: Sure, there are buyout schemes that lots of companies use to induce older workers to leave, but these schemes sometimes result in losing the wrong workers and they can be very expensive. We'd have to tailor our buyout very carefully.

NEF: Granted. Let's call someone in who knows how to set up these things. There must be a dozen consulting firms that have experience with these buyout schemes. After all, very large companies like IBM and Bank of America have recently gone through dramatic downsizing. As I recall, IBM changed its offer midway, deciding that the initial buyout plan was too generous. Maybe we can avoid making the same mistakes.

SLICHTER: Good idea. We've got to figure out to whom we should offer these buyouts. We don't want our most valuable workers leaving while the deadwood stays on.

MISES: I can't believe this discussion. You are taking for granted that we want to get rid of our older workers without even questioning the wisdom of the policy. Let's assume that Joan's numbers are correct. That still doesn't imply that we want to terminate our older workers, does it?

Don't you remember reading the case about the record company that went through the exact same thought process that we are going through now? They were worried about losing the skills that older workers had, which were paying back a handsome return to the firm. Maybe we are in the same situation. There are skills that the older workers have that are absent in younger cohorts. Can we afford to do without these? Shouldn't we be thinking about these issues first, before we figure out the best way to fire these guys?

How do we know it is the older and not the younger workers that should go? After all, if we just followed strict reverse seniority, layoffs would be concentrated among the young, not the old. So let's assume that we need to cut the size of the work force. Why not start with the most junior workers?

ROBINSON: (After a long silence) Well, I guess I'm to blame. The tone of my comments got everyone talking about the cost side without examining the benefits side. Maybe the next step should be to get some additional data that bears on the other side of the question. Anyone have any suggestions before I put my department to work on it?

NEF: I suppose what we want to know is which workers are the most valuable, but productivity is difficult to measure. This is going to be a real chore, and I'm not confident that the results of our study will tell us much.

SLICHTER: I have an idea. We can measure average productivity for the firm just by dividing total output by the size of our work force. Once we know that, we can estimate productivity by age group as long as we know one group's output relative to another's. We don't have to measure older workers' productivity. We just need to know whether they are twice, three times, or half as productive as the younger workers. That ought to be much easier to do.

MISES: That won't help us distinguish good young workers from bad young workers, but at least it will give us a handle on whether we should follow strict reverse seniority on layoff order. I'm going to leave this one to Joan. Let's meet again two weeks from now and discuss the results.

This discussion raises many questions. Among them:

* Which groups should be targeted for layoffs?

* How can layoffs be accomplished in the lowest cost fashion that is compatible with the law and consistent with business interests?

* Sometimes high turnover is viewed as a problem and companies try to devise ways to reduce it. Sometimes turnover is viewed as desirable. How can a firm determine which situation it is in?

* If turnover is deemed desirable, how can adverse selection be avoided so that the high-profit workers stay and the low-profit ones leave?

TURNOVER: IS IT DESIRABLE? ◆ ◆ ◆ ◆ ◆

It seems apparent that in a stable environment, where demand for the firm's product is consistent, turnover involves costs. New workers must be found, trained, and integrated into the production process. If new workers and old workers were perfect substitutes for one another, there would be little reason to cycle workers into and out of the firm. However, under certain circumstances, the productivity of younger workers is enhanced by the presence of older workers, and vice versa. When these factors operate, there is value to moving senior workers out and junior workers in. The following section discusses this idea.

COMBINING SENIOR AND JUNIOR WORKERS ◆ ◆ ◆ ◆ ◆

Young workers bring new skills and new ideas with them into the firm. This is likely to be most important to industries that are undergoing rapid technological change. In these industries, new entrants have often learned the latest techniques through formal schooling. More senior workers who received their formal training many years prior may have well-honed job skills, but are unlikely to know as much about the most recent research as their younger counterparts.

Offsetting this effect is that senior workers may have a much better handle on the information that is most relevant to this particular firm. Although the new entrant may have command at a general level of the latest methods, the senior worker is likely to know the details of those new and old processes that are most directly related to his or her sphere of production. Also, the older worker has an advantage in knowing those general skills and facts that are best learned on the job. Finally, since firms tend to be somewhat idiosyncratic, older workers have an advantage in understanding those attributes of the industry and of production that are specific to the firm. In short, older workers are almost certain to have an advantage over younger ones in firm-specific human capital and in the general human capital that is best learned on the job. Younger workers are more likely to have the edge in the general human capital that is best acquired through formal schooling.

These arguments suggest that some mixture of young and old is likely to produce the most productive work environment. Younger workers can introduce new techniques to older workers. Older workers can impart the knowledge that they have obtained through years of experience about the idiosyncrasies of the industry and especially of the firm in which they work.

The point about combining young and old can hold even in the absence of any firm-specific human capital. Even if older workers were perfectly substitutable across firms, it may still be true that their skills complement those of their younger counterparts. Table 7.1 provides data for a hypothetical numerical example that illustrates the point.

Table 7.1 lists various combinations of old and young workers. Old workers earn $200 per day and young workers earn $120 per day. Human capital is general, so the workers can earn these wages at any other firm as well. Output and costs vary, depending on the number of workers used. Costs depend directly on the number of workers in each category and are shown in the third through fifth columns of Table 7.1.

For any given number of old workers, there is an optimal number of younger workers. If the firm chooses to hire only one senior worker, profit is maximized by combining the senior worker with three junior workers. If the firm hires two senior workers, profit is maximized by combining them with four junior workers. Indeed, the choice of two senior and four junior workers maximizes profit over all possible choices of numbers of workers.

The numbers in Table 7.1 reflect complementarities between old and young workers. The firm makes more money by hiring two senior and four junior workers than it does by hiring either six senior and no junior or six junior and no senior workers. But the importance of complementarities between types of workers diminishes after a point. Although the output of two senior and five junior workers exceeds that of two senior and four junior workers, the difference is not sufficiently great to cover the cost of the additional worker. This may reflect the fact that a senior worker can supervise two junior workers productively, but the ability

TABLE 7.1
PRODUCTION COMPLEMENTARITY BETWEEN OLD AND YOUNG WORKERS

Wage old $200   Wage young $120
(Units are all per day)

# Old	# Young	Cost Old	Cost Young	Total Cost	Output	Profit
1	0	$200	$0	$200	$200	$0
1	1	$200	$120	$320	$600	$280
1	2	$200	$240	$440	$766	$326
1	3	$200	$360	$560	$893	$333
1	4	$200	$480	$680	$1,000	$320
2	1	$400	$120	$520	$766	$246
2	2	$400	$240	$640	$966	$326
2	3	$400	$360	$760	$1,119	$359
2	4	$400	$480	$880	$1,249	$369
2	5	$400	$600	$1,000	$1,363	$363
2	6	$400	$720	$1,120	$1,466	$346
2	7	$400	$840	$1,240	$1,560	$320
2	8	$400	$960	$1,360	$1,649	$289
3	2	$600	$240	$840	$1,119	$279
3	3	$600	$360	$960	$1,293	$333
3	4	$600	$480	$1,080	$1,439	$359
3	5	$600	$600	$1,200	$1,568	$368
3	6	$600	$720	$1,320	$1,685	$365
3	7	$600	$840	$1,440	$1,792	$352
3	8	$600	$960	$1,560	$1,892	$332
4	3	$800	$360	$1,160	$1,439	$279
4	4	$800	$480	$1,280	$1,600	$320
4	5	$800	$600	$1,400	$1,742	$342
4	6	$800	$720	$1,520	$1,870	$350
4	7	$800	$840	$1,640	$1,987	$347
4	8	$800	$960	$1,760	$2,097	$337
7	5	$1,400	$600	$2,000	$2,160	$160
7	6	$1,400	$720	$2,120	$2,315	$195
7	7	$1,400	$840	$2,240	$2,458	$218
7	8	$1,400	$960	$2,360	$2,591	$231
7	9	$1,400	$1,080	$2,480	$2,717	$237
7	10	$1,400	$1,200	$2,600	$2,835	$235
8	7	$1,600	$840	$2,440	$2,591	$151
8	8	$1,600	$960	$2,560	$2,731	$171
8	9	$1,600	$1,080	$2,680	$2,863	$183
8	10	$1,600	$1,200	$2,800	$2,987	$187
8	11	$1,600	$1,320	$2,920	$3,105	$185
8	12	$1,600	$1,440	$3,040	$3,218	$178
9	8	$1,800	$960	$2,760	$2,863	$103
9	9	$1,800	$1,080	$2,880	$3,000	$120
9	10	$1,800	$1,200	$3,000	$3,130	$130
9	11	$1,800	$1,320	$3,120	$3,253	$133

Continued

TABLE 7.1 *(Continued)*

Wage old $200   Wage young $120
(Units are all per day)

# Old	# Young	Cost Old	Cost Young	Total Cost	Output	Profit
9	12	$1,800	$1,440	$3,240	$3,371	$131
9	13	$1,800	$1,560	$3,360	$3,484	$124
10	9	$2,000	$1,080	$3,080	$3,130	$50
10	10	$2,000	$1,200	$3,200	$3,265	$65
10	11	$2,000	$1,320	$3,320	$3,393	$73
10	12	$2,000	$1,440	$3,440	$3,516	$76
10	13	$2,000	$1,560	$3,560	$3,634	$74

to maintain supervision diminishes as the number of junior workers increases. Alternatively, it may be that four junior workers can communicate most of their knowledge of new techniques effectively to two senior workers. Adding another junior worker does not enhance the flow of information sufficiently to cover the cost of the additional junior worker.

The conclusion is that removing a senior worker can enhance or lower profits, depending on the number of senior workers and the number of junior workers. There is no unambiguous statement that can be made, but the following factors influence the optimal ratio of younger to older workers:

1. *Technological change is very rapid in an industry.* Technology is often embodied in the new entrants.

2. *The amount of skills learned on the job is low relative to the amount learned in formal programs before entering the labor force.* When on-the-job training is important, there is a greater need for "teachers," and senior workers are well suited to be teachers.

3. *The firm's experiences are not idiosyncratic.* When the experiences of the firm are special, it is unlikely that they can be learned elsewhere, either in formal training or from experience at other organizations. Senior workers are more likely to have particular knowledge of the firm's idiosyncratic details. Thus, all else being equal, their value relative to junior workers will be higher.

◆ ◆ ◆ ◆ ◆   SPECIFIC HUMAN CAPITAL

In the last chapter, much was made of the distinction between specific and general human capital. It was pointed out that when senior workers have more firm-specific human capital, the firm is less likely to want to fire them. Since there is a wedge between the amount that the workers are worth at the current firm and the amount that they are worth elsewhere, there is likely to be some deal that can be

FIGURE 7.1
WAGES, PRODUCTIVITY,
AND ALTERNATIVES

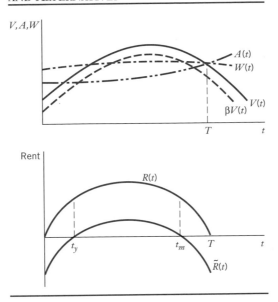

struck that can make both workers and firm better off. That is, the firm can offer a worker more than he can receive elsewhere and still pay less than what he is worth at his current firm.

It is quite straightforward to determine which groups should be laid off when downsizing is necessary. The conclusion can be stated as follows:

> When firm-specific human capital is important, the firm maximizes its profits by laying off from both ends of the age distribution first. That is, workers who have just started with the firm and those who are about to retire make the best targets.

The analysis is somewhat lengthy, but worth presenting. Then the intuition behind the conclusion above will be clear.

The top panel of Figure 7.1 is a familiar diagram, which portrays age-earnings and age-productivity profiles for an individual who invests in firm-specific human capital.[1] Productivity at the firm is given by V(t). The individual is paid wage $W(t)$ and has an alternative use of time given by $A(t)$. The $A(t)$ schedule can be thought of as the amount that the worker would earn at another firm.

Under normal circumstances, the worker would be employed from time 0 to time T, at which point the worker would retire. The present value of the $W(t)$ profile must equal the present value of the $V(t)$ profile. If the present value of

---

[1]Additional details can be found in Lazear and Freeman (1997).

wages exceeded the present value of productivity, the firm would lose money. If the present value of productivity exceeded wages, then the firm would face competition by other similar firms for the worker, driving up wages until all the profits were taken. Thus, as in chapter 6, the present values of the two streams are the same in equilibrium. The present value of wages at the firm generally exceeds the present value of $A(t)$, which is the amount that the worker could receive if she moved to another firm at time t, given that she had been at the initial firm until t.[2]

The present values of wages, $W(t)$, and productivity, $V(t)$, are equal at the time that the worker is hired, but not thereafter. Since the worker is investing in firm specific human capital, both worker and firm must bear some of the initial cost. Once that cost is borne, there is value to both parties from continuing employment. Specifically, at any time after zero, the present value of $V(t)$ exceeds the present value of $W(t)$. Since $W(0)$ exceeds $V(0)$, the firm has made an investment and enjoys the returns to that investment during the remaining period.[3]

The amount of *rent*, or surplus, going to the firm is shown in the bottom panel of Figure 7.1 by $R(t)$, which is defined as the difference between the present value of $V(t)$ and $W(t)$ from t until T. Once the firm has invested something in the worker, it makes its money back only by keeping the worker for a significant amount of time.

A worker who leaves one day before T costs the firm almost nothing because, at most, there is one day's worth of surplus to capture, if any at all. Thus $R(0)$ and $R(T)$ are both zero. The firm loses nothing on a worker who quits on the day she begins. At that point, the amount that the firm must pay out over the remaining work life exactly equals the amount that the firm receives in productivity over the remaining work life. Analogously, the firm loses nothing on a worker who resigns on the day of retirement, because there is no remaining work life.

It is this point that provides the intuition behind this discussion. When productivity falls, the firm loses the least by laying off the oldest workers and the youngest workers. The oldest workers are going to retire soon, so little gain remains. The youngest workers have not yet seen much investment in firm-specific human capital. Since little or no investment has yet been made, little or no returns are there to be lost.

Suppose, for example, that demand for the firm's product decreases. The price of the goods being sold must be lowered, which reduces the dollar value of worker productivity. This is shown as a drop in productivity from $V(t)$ to $\beta V(t)$ in the top

[2]If the worker had started at another firm at time zero, she might have invested in specific capital there. But since she has been at the initial firm until t, her productivity elsewhere differs from that here. Initially, her productivity elsewhere is actually higher because investment in firm specific human capital is costly. This pushes $V(t)$ below $A(t)$ at time zero. But later, $V(t)$ rises above $A(t)$ because the value of firm specific human capital raises productivity at the initial firm enough to cover the costs of investing.

[3]This must be true because present values were equal at zero, but $W(0)$ exceeds $V(0)$. Thus, what remains in productivity from any t to T must exceed what remains in wage payments over the same period to make things add up.

panel of Figure 7.1. This changes the amount of rent available to the firm. It no longer pays to make an investment on young workers, since the firm is laying off workers in order to downsize.[4] Similarly, it would like to lay off older workers, on whom the rent is negative. The bottom panel of Figure 7.1 shows the new situation after the price of the product has fallen. Now, rent is given by $\tilde{R}(t)$, which lies below $R(t)$. For all workers older than t_m, rent is negative. For all those younger than t_y, rent is negative. It is the middle-aged workers who are worth keeping. The investment in specific human capital has already been made on them, so their productivity is relatively high and there are many years over which to recoup the return to the same investment. Under the new situation, the firm would be unwilling to make the investment in firm-specific human capital because it is a losing proposition, given the decline in demand. But sunk costs are sunk. Since the investment has already been made, the firm does better by keeping these workers and enjoying the period during which there are returns.

The firm is unwilling to keep any workers who are older than t_m, however, because t_m is the time at which $\beta V(t)$ falls below $W(t)$. Beyond t_m, each day the worker stays with the firm costs the firm money. Thus, the firm wants to lay off workers from both ends of the age distribution. In other words, the decline in demand means that older workers, on whom little rent was earned previously, should be separated from the firm. Similarly, a firm that is in the process of cutting its workforce does not make money by hiring new workers and making the same investment mistake as it made on the previous generation. Not only will it not hire, it will also fire some of its youngest workers on whom the firm's investment in specific human capital is not yet too great.

Buyout or Layoff?

Since the firm would like some of its older workers to leave, it cannot simply use reverse seniority layoffs to accomplish the task. It will either have to lay older workers off directly or it will have to induce them to retire voluntarily.

How might the courts view a layoff of older workers? Probably not very well. While a firm is free to lay off workers when business conditions demand it, the Age Discrimination in Employment Act prohibits firms from laying off workers based on age.[5] A firm that engaged in layoffs of its oldest and youngest workers would probably be subjected to lawsuits by older workers, charging that they were discriminated against relative to the middle aged workers over whom older workers have seniority.

Legal constraints are one reason why buying out older workers in some fashion may be necessary. Even in the absence of legal restrictions, the firm might want to buy out its older workers. When workers have invested in firm-specific human capital, they are counting on the firm to comply with an implicit contract.

---

[4]For now, we are ignoring any imperfect substitutability between the old and the young, which might make the firm want to hire some young even as it was laying off some old.

[5]All workers who are forty and older are protected by ADEA.

Once an investment has been made, workers receive returns only insofar as the firm honors its commitment to pay workers more than they can receive elsewhere. By terminating workers before the expected retirement date, the firm is defaulting on its promise to pay the full amount for the investment undertaken. When defaults occur frequently, the firm develops a reputation for being dishonest and cannot induce other individuals to invest in firm-specific human capital. Severance pay may be awarded to older workers when the firm wishes to preserve its reputation as an honest employer whose commitments are reliable.

Reputation is not as important in a declining industry. In the absence of legal considerations, a firm that is relatively confident that it is on its last leg may opt to ignore reputational considerations and terminate its older workers without offering severance pay. Additionally, terminating workers who are close to retirement should not adversely affect a firm's reputation, as long as the firm makes good on its pension commitment. Workers who are close to retirement have little to lose from early termination. The breach of the implicit contract is only a minor one for these workers, and reputation should not suffer much.

It is generally unnecessary to buy out younger workers. They are neither legally protected, nor is their termination likely to result in significant harm to a firm's reputation. Until workers have invested a significant amount in firm-specific human capital, they lose little by being terminated.

Thus, termination of the oldest and youngest workers should not have a significant adverse effect on reputation. The difference between the old and young is that only the old are protected against age discrimination.

Buyout Formulas

If a firm does opt to award severance pay, how much should it be, and who should be eligible to receive it?

First, recall that the workers who produce the least rent for the firm are the very oldest and the very youngest. Firms generally do not worry about buyouts for new employees. They have little to lose from termination and are not entitled to much, even if reputation is a concern. The most senior workers do have some claim to be treated properly, but just as the rent to the firm is smallest on older workers, the rents that older workers receive from continuing to work at the firm are also quite small. Workers who are one day from retirement receive a premium over the value of their leisure (or wage at the next best job) for only one more day. Terminating them one day early has little impact on their wealth. Furthermore, it is easy to buy them out. Since they were only planning to work for one more day, the cost of getting them to retire early is at most one day's pay and is likely to be much less than that. As we consider workers who are further from retirement age, the buyout premium is higher.

Table 7.2 presents a hypothetical example from Los Cabos Graphics that is consistent with the age–earnings, age–productivity, and alternative wage profiles in Figure 7.1.

TABLE 7.2
BUYOUT PROBLEM AT LOS CABOS GRAPHICS

Age	Wage	Alt.	V	βV	PV(W)	PV(A)	PV(V)	PV(βV)
25	30000	20000	20000	14000	145462	99306	145462	101823
26	30000	20125	23175	16222	145459	99909	158056	110640
27	30000	20250	26200	18340	145456	100512	169924	118947
28	30000	20375	29075	20353	145451	101115	181063	126744
29	30000	20500	31800	22260	145445	101716	191475	134032
30	30000	20625	34375	24063	145438	102316	201158	140811
31	30000	20750	36800	25760	145429	102914	210113	147079
32	30000	20875	39075	27353	145417	103510	218340	152838
33	30000	21000	41200	28840	145402	104104	225838	158087
34	30000	21125	43175	30222	145384	104694	232607	162825
35	30000	21250	45000	31500	145360	105280	238646	167052
36	30000	21375	46675	32672	145331	105861	243956	170769
37	30000	21500	48200	33740	145294	106436	248534	173974
38	30000	21625	49575	34703	145247	107002	252381	176667
39	30000	21750	50800	35560	145189	107558	255495	178847
40	30000	21875	51875	36313	145115	108101	257875	180512
41	30000	22000	52800	36960	145021	108628	259519	181663
42	30000	22125	53575	37503	144904	109134	260424	182297
43	30000	22250	54200	37940	144756	109613	260588	182412
44	30000	22375	54675	38273	144569	110060	260008	182006
45	30000	22500	55000	38500	144335	110466	258679	181075
46	30000	22625	55175	38623	144039	110820	256594	179616
47	30000	22750	55200	38640	143666	111108	253748	177624
48	30000	22875	55075	38553	143196	111313	250131	175092
49	30000	23000	54800	38360	142605	111414	245732	172012
50	30000	23125	54375	38063	141860	111384	240536	168375
51	30000	23250	53800	37660	140921	111189	234525	164168
52	30000	23375	53075	37153	139738	110786	227677	159374
53	30000	23500	52200	36540	138248	110120	219964	153975
54	30000	23625	51175	35823	136371	109124	211349	147944
55	30000	23750	50000	35000	134006	107712	201788	141251
56	30000	23875	48675	34073	131027	105775	191222	133855
57	30000	24000	47200	33040	127274	103178	179581	125706
58	30000	24125	45575	31902	122545	99748	166773	116741
59	30000	24250	43800	30660	116588	95270	152685	106880
60	30000	24375	41875	29312	109084	89471	137174	96022
61	30000	24500	39800	27860	99630	82007	120057	84040
62	30000	24625	37575	26303	87720	72448	101108	70776
63	30000	24750	35200	24640	72716	60247	80039	56027
64	30000	24875	32675	22873	53813	44719	56488	39542
65	30000	25000	30000	21000	30000	25000	30000	21000

The interest rate used in Table 7.2 was about .25. Columns are defined such that:

Wage is the wage at the given age.

Alt. is the value of leisure (or the wage on the next best job) at each age.

V is the dollar value of initial productivity at Los Cabos at each age.[6]

βV is the dollar value of productivity after the decline in demand at Los Cabos at each age.

PV(W) is the present value in dollars at the time of the given age of the wage stream from that age until retirement at 65.

PV(A) is the present value in dollars at the time of the given age of the alternate (Alt.) stream from that age until retirement at 65.

PV(V) is the present value in dollars at the time of the given age of the V stream from that age until retirement at 65.

PV(βV) is the present value in dollars at the time of the given age of the βV stream from that age until retirement at 65.

Age is reported in the first column. The second column reports the wage received at the corresponding age. In this example, the worker is always paid $30,000 per year. Alt. gives the value of his best alternative use of time. This may be the wage on the next best job at any age, given that the worker has been with Los Cabos until that age, or it may be the value of leisure. V is the worker's initial productivity by age at Los Cabos, given that he has worked at Los Cabos from 25 until that age. βV is the worker's productivity at any given age after the decline in demand that reduces the price of the product to 70 percent of its initial value.

The last four columns are of primary interest for the buyout problem. They give the present value of wages remaining to be earned at Los Cabos, alternative use of time, and productivity at Los Cabos from that age until retirement the day before the worker turned 66. For example, at exactly age 64, the worker would earn $30,000 for two more years. The present value of that amount is

$$\$30,000 + \$30,000/(1 + .2598) = \$30000 + \$23,813 = \$53,813$$

which is the value shown in the PV(W) column in the row corresponding to age 64.

Similarly, at age 64, before the decline in demand the worker would have produced $32,675 that year and $30,000 in the last year, as can be seen from column V. The present value of this sum at age 64 is

$$\$32,675 + \$30,000/(1 + .2598) = \$32,675 + \$23,813 = \$56,488$$

which is the value shown in the PV(V) column in the row corresponding to age 64.

---

[6]The interest .2598 is generally high for the real world. Still the principles illustrated by this table are valid, irrespective of the interest rate used.

Note that at age 25, when the worker begins, PV(W) equals PV(V). The firm pays over the worker's lifetime an amount equal in present value to the worker's productivity. Competition forces this result.

After the decline in demand, the present value of output is reduced to one-half its prior value. Thus, after the decline in demand, PV(βV) at age 64 is only $39,542 because the value of output has fallen. This comes from taking the present value of the two years of productivity, or

$$\$22,873 + \$21,000/(1.2598) = \$39,542$$

Now consider the 64-year-old. If she leaves, she receives a present value of $44,719 in either leisure or the alternative wage (see column PV(A)). If she stays, she receives a present value of $53,813. What is she worth to the firm? Had demand remained unchanged, she would have been worth a present value of $56,488 over the two years. But because of the decline in demand, she is now only worth a present value of $39,542 over the two years. There is room for a bargain.

If she stays, the firm will pay her a present value of $53,813, which is (53813 − 39542), or $14,271 above what she is worth. The firm loses $14,271 if she works for the last two years. Alternatively, the firm can offer to buy her out for, say, $10,000. The worker would be better off, because the $10,000 plus the value of the alternative, $44,719, equals $54,719, and $54,719 is better than the $53,813 to be earned at Los Cabos. Thus, a buyout offer of $10,000 would be accepted by the employee. Furthermore, the firm would save $4,271, because her continued employment implies a net loss of $14,271 instead of just the buyout payment of $10,000.

The firm can afford to buy out everyone who is 62 or older. At age 62, the present value of βV falls below the present value of A, which means that a deal can always be struck. But 61-year-olds cannot be bought out profitably, because PV(A) is less than PV(βV) for 61-year-olds.

Consider the 62-year-old. If she does not retire, the firm will pay her a present value of $87,720 and will receive $70,776 in productivity. This implies a loss of $16,944 from keeping her. If the firm can buy her out for anything less than $16,944 it is better off. The worker, on other hand, earns $87,720 from staying, but only $72,448 if she leaves. To leave, she must be paid at least ($87,720 − $72,448) = $15,272, but since $15,272 is less than $16,944, the worker will accept less than the firm is willing to offer. Since the amount the firm is willing to offer for her to leave exceeds the minimum that the worker will accept, then both can be made better off by striking an agreement. A buyout of, say, $16,000 will be accepted by the worker and will save the firm $944. Thus, the buyout is feasible.

Now consider the 61-year-old. If he does not retire, the firm will pay a present value of $99,630 and will receive $84,040 in output. This implies a loss of $15,590. If the firm can buy him out for anything less than $15,590 it is better off. The worker, on the other hand, earns $99,630 from staying, but only $82,007 for leaving. He must be paid at least ($99,630 − $82,007) = $17,623 to leave. Since $17,623 exceeds $15,590, the minimum acceptable buyout to the worker exceeds the maximum buyout offer that the firm is willing to make. Thus, no profitable buyout is feasible.

This discussion leads to the following conclusion:

Profitable buyouts are possible whenever the present value of the worker's alternatives exceeds the present value of the worker's productivity at the firm.

This is shown formally in the appendix. The logic is that the better the worker's alternatives, the easier it is to buy the worker out. The lower is the worker's output in the current firm, the more anxious is the firm to buy the worker out. Thus, low output and good alternatives make buyouts feasible. Specifically, as was seen in the numerical example, whenever the present value of output is below the present value of alternatives, the firm's desire to buy the worker out is sufficiently strong to cover the amount that a worker would demand to be bought out. A deal can always be struck under these conditions.

Now, the firm would like to lay off all workers for whom the present value of wage payments exceeds the present value of output. If the present value of the worker's wage exceeds the present value of output, then the firm loses money. Any worker whose present value of output falls short of the present value of wages represents a net cost to the firm.

It is very important to recognize that the individuals the firm would like to lay off are not necessarily the ones for whom a buyout offer is possible. In the example in Table 7.2, the firm would like to lay off all those workers who are 57 and older and those who are 30 and younger. For these workers, the present value of wages, PV(W) exceeds the present value of output (after the decline in demand), PV(βV), but not all of these workers will accept a buyout offer that the firm is willing to make. Specifically, as already discussed, only workers 62 and older have alternatives sufficiently attractive to make a feasible firm offer acceptable to them. The firm loses money on workers between 57 and 61, inclusive, but the amount the firm loses on these workers is not sufficiently large to permit an acceptable buyout offer to be made. For these workers, the alternatives are worse than output in this firm, so no deal can be struck. In this situation, the firm's best choice is simply to offer buyouts to workers older than, say 55, of perhaps $15,400. All workers 62 and older will accept, and the rest will decline. A higher offer can induce those between 57 and 61 to resign, but the higher offer is not profitable.

Additionally, the firm wants to lay off all workers who are 30 and younger, because the present value of wages exceeds the present value of output, but none of these workers can be bought out. Since the present value of their alternatives is below the present value of their outputs, there is no offer that the young are willing to take that the firm is willing to make. The young workers' alternatives in this example are so poor that it is too expensive to induce them to leave.

For the young, the solution is simply to lay the workers off. None of those who are 30 or younger are protected against age discrimination. Also, since the layoff would conform to the reverse seniority standard, it poses little reputational risk.

Table 7.2 is reproduced here as Table 7.3. It is identical, except that the data for individuals whom the firm would like to lay off are underlined. The data for individuals whom the firm can successfully buy out are in bold.

How does a firm realistically go about getting the kind of numbers that are

TABLE 7.3
THE BUYOUT PROBLEM AT LOS CABOS GRAPHICS

Age	Wage	Alt.	V	βV	PV(W)	PV(A)	PV(V)	PV(βV)
25	30000	20000	20000	14000	145462	99306	145462	101823
26	30000	20125	23175	16222	145459	99909	158056	110640
27	30000	20250	26200	18340	145456	100512	169924	118947
28	30000	20375	29075	20353	145451	101115	181063	126744
29	30000	20500	31800	22260	145445	101716	191475	134032
30	30000	20625	34375	24063	145438	102316	201158	140811
31	30000	20750	36800	25760	145429	102914	210113	147079
32	30000	20875	39075	27353	145417	103510	218340	152838
33	30000	21000	41200	28840	145402	104104	225838	158087
34	30000	21125	43175	30222	145384	104694	232607	162825
35	30000	21250	45000	31500	145360	105280	238646	167052
36	30000	21375	46675	32672	145331	105861	243956	170769
37	30000	21500	48200	33740	145294	106436	248534	173974
38	30000	21625	49575	34703	145247	107002	252381	176667
39	30000	21750	50800	35560	145189	107558	255495	178847
40	30000	21875	51875	36313	145115	108101	257875	180512
41	30000	22000	52800	36960	145021	108628	259519	181663
42	30000	22125	53575	37503	144904	109134	260424	182297
43	30000	22250	54200	37940	144756	109613	260588	182412
44	30000	22375	54675	38273	144569	110060	260008	182006
45	30000	22500	55000	38500	144335	110466	258679	181075
46	30000	22625	55175	38623	144039	110820	256594	179616
47	30000	22750	55200	38640	143666	111108	253748	177624
48	30000	22875	55075	38553	143196	111313	250131	175092
49	30000	23000	54800	38360	142605	111414	245732	172012
50	30000	23125	54375	38063	141860	111384	240536	168375
51	30000	23250	53800	37660	140921	111189	234525	164168
52	30000	23375	53075	37153	139738	110786	227677	159374
53	30000	23500	52200	36540	138248	110120	219964	153975
54	30000	23625	51175	35823	136371	109124	211349	147944
55	30000	23750	50000	35000	134006	107712	201788	141251
56	30000	23875	48675	34073	131027	105775	191222	133855
57	30000	24000	47200	33040	127274	103178	179581	125706
58	30000	24125	45575	31902	122545	99748	166773	116741
59	30000	24250	43800	30660	116588	95270	152685	106880
60	30000	24375	41875	29312	109084	89471	137174	96022
61	30000	24500	39800	27860	99630	82007	120057	84040
62	30000	24625	37575	26303	87720	72448	101108	70776
63	30000	24750	35200	24640	72716	60247	80039	56027
64	30000	24875	32675	22873	53813	44719	56488	39542
65	30000	25000	30000	21000	30000	25000	30000	21000

necessary to do the calculations performed in Table 7.3? (Only economists believe that firms have the kind of data presented in the table.) Although it is not easy to obtain these data, firms make implicit computations of this sort all the time. In fact, anytime a buyout is being considered, it is being done because the firm believes that there are gains to be had. The gains take the form of reduced wages, which exceed the lost productivity plus the buyout.

There are some steps that a firm might go through to try to estimate the numbers needed for such a table. An outline of the approach is given here:

I. **First, to do the calculation, the firm needs to obtain estimates of the promised wage stream, W, of the alternative, A, and of output, βV.**

Once these numbers are obtained, a spreadsheet program will produce a table of the sort given by Table 7.2.

Table 7.2 ignored all differences across workers. We will discuss differences in greater detail shortly, but for the purposes at hand, we define a job narrowly and create a data matrix for each job.

II. **Estimate wages.**

To obtain the wage numbers, take the average wage for workers by age and job category. It is necessary to define the job and age range broadly enough so that there are reasonable numbers in each category. If there are too few workers who are exactly 59, 62, or whatever age, take the average for a block, like 55 to 60, assume that the wage reflects the wage at the midpoint (age 57.5), and interpolate between blocks to fill in the wage. Use current wages,[7] then create column 1 of Table 7.4.[8]

III. **Estimate alternatives.**

This task is somewhat more difficult. It requires that the firm estimate either the value of leisure or what the worker could receive elsewhere. One possibility is to use data on the amount that workers who left the firm received when they went elsewhere. There are two problems with this approach. First, it is difficult to obtain information on wages from severed employees. Second, those who quit often do so to take a higher-paying job. Thus, the sample would have to be drawn from those laid off, which creates biases in the other direction, since they may be poorer than average quality workers.

Another approach is needed. It is possible to estimate the alternative value of retiring workers by using the wage at retirement of those who retire voluntarily. When a worker retires voluntarily, the alternative must be worth at least as much as the current wage. Conversely, during the worker's last year on the job, the wage must exceed the value of the alternative, or the individual will not continue to work. Thus, an estimate of the alternative wage at retire-

---

[7] Ignore inflation because inflation affects wages and prices similarly, at least on average.

[8] A more sophisticated approach is to fit a regression through the wage data to get a smooth earnings function. Then wages at any desired age can be computed by plugging the value into the earnings function. This approach is shown in the technical appendix.

TABLE 7.4
ESTIMATED WAGE, ALTERNATIVES, AND OUTPUT

Age	Wage	Alternative	Output
25	70383	70383	55512
26	72066	71142	59128
27	73702	71901	62598
28	75290	72660	65922
29	76831	73419	69099
30	78325	74178	72129
31	79771	74937	75013
32	81170	75696	77750
33	82522	76455	80341
34	83826	77214	82785
35	85083	77973	85083
36	86292	78732	87234
37	87454	79491	89238
38	88568	80250	91097
39	89635	81009	92808
40	90655	81768	94373
41	91627	82527	95791
42	92552	83286	97063
43	93430	84045	98189
44	94260	84804	99167
45	95043	85563	100000
46	95778	86322	100685
47	96466	87081	101225
48	97106	87840	101617
49	97699	88599	101863
50	98245	89358	101963
51	98743	90117	101916
52	99194	90876	101723
53	99598	91635	101382
54	99954	92394	100896
55	100263	93153	100263
56	100524	93912	99483
57	100738	94671	98557
58	100904	95430	97484
59	101023	96189	96265
60	101095	96948	94899
61	101119	97707	93387
62	101096	98466	91728
63	101026	99225	89922
64	100908	99984	87970
65	100743	100743	85872

ment is the actual wage paid to workers who retire voluntarily. Similarly, when workers are hired, they are paid approximately what they could earn elsewhere. Thus, an estimate of the alternative for those who are just starting out is also the current wage.[9]

Given the shape of age–earnings profiles, it is reasonable to conclude that workers have the largest amount of firm-specific human capital when they are in their forties. When jobs have no firm-specific human capital, the alternative equals the current wage, even for 40-year-olds. Jobs that have a great deal of specific human capital may pay the worker as much as double the amount that could be received elsewhere. Thus, assess the job for its firm-specific human capital component. If it is low, estimate the alternative as being close to the current wage. If it is high, then estimate the alternative at age 40 as being significantly below the current wage, perhaps by as much as half. Now, three points are available (starting wage, retaining wage for those who leave voluntarily, and some fraction of wage at age 40) and interpolation provides a way to estimate the alternative at every age.

This is an inexact approach, but no worse and likely better than what firms currently do. Firms implicitly estimate the alternatives every time they offer a buyout. Although they generally do not sit down and calculate output, wages, and worker alternatives, they make subjective decisions that rely on some notion of what output is relative to earnings. Further, in structuring a buyout offer, they ask or should ask themselves, "How much do we have to offer to induce the worker to leave voluntarily?" If they overestimate the alternatives, the buyout will be too low and will not be accepted by many. If they underestimate the alternatives, the buyout offer will be too high. Then too many may accept, and the firm overpays the departing workers. Our approach, albeit inexact, provides a more scientific way to reason through the firm's problem, and it is likely to provide a better guide to the size of the buyout.

IV. Estimate output.

To estimate output, the firm must ask itself, "How much net revenue will we lose when we lay off Charlie?" The answer is Charlie's contribution. A firm must have some sense of the answer. Without having a sense of what a worker is worth, it cannot possibly hope to know whether it should be hiring or firing.[10] Since this number is speculative and is of central importance to the layoff decision, it is probably wise to generate independent estimates. Multiple estimates reduce the amount of "noise" and improve accuracy.

---

[9]This must be adjusted for investment in human capital. If the worker is investing in human capital, the observed wage is actually lower than the "true" wage, the latter of which includes the value of the human capital investment.

[10]A firm should add more workers when the value of the incremental worker's output exceeds worker cost and should cut when the value of the incremental worker's output falls short of the worker's cost.

AMOS PRESS INC.

◆ ◆ ◆ ◆ ◆ ◆ ◆ ◆ ◆

Amos Press Inc., a family-owned $25-million publishing company, realized that some of its older workers were becoming less productive than the newer employees. Physical difficulties, as well as increased absences, reduced productivity (relative to wages) to such a level that the elderly employees could no longer be kept without severe financial consequence. The Age Discrimination in Employment Act made it difficult for Amos to lay off its older workers because it places the burden of proof on the employer. In order to lay off a protected worker, it is necessary to show that the worker is less productive than others. In order to overcome this problem at Amos Press, early retirement packages were offered a select group of employees.

The early retirement was offered only to those workers who were aged 60 and older. The plan consisted of a one-time payment based on years with the company. It provided continued health benefits, a full pension, and a monthly check based on anticipated Social Security benefits. In addition, the company sponsored seminars to aid the transition to retirement or another career. Most of these older workers presumably were paid wages that exceeded their productivity. As a result, through the use of a carefully calculated payment, Amos Press could (and did) induce these workers to leave the company.

The plan was largely successful. A savings of $175,000 resulted through the retirement of about half the targeted workers, mostly by job consolidation and promoting younger personnel with lower salaries into the vacant positions. Given legal constraints, Amos Press adeptly changed the composition of its work force to improve productivity and reduce costs.

Source: Ellen Kolton, "An Offer They Couldn't Refuse," *INC.*, April 1985.

Although there is no obvious way to estimate the output of a worker, the thought experiment that the firm conducts is to ask itself (or a number of its employees), "What is the greatest amount per month (or year) that we would be willing to pay to keep Charlie working at the firm?" The answer to this question is an estimate of Charlie's net revenue production.

Once output estimates have been obtained for each worker, there are two possibilities. First, workers can be laid off or offered buyouts on an individual basis. Second, the data can be used to estimate a typical output schedule as a function of experience. The first approach will be discussed later. For now, we focus on the second.

Using the data that are obtained for a sample of (randomly) selected individuals, it is possible to estimate output for all ages or experience levels through a method of interpolation. The method described above in section B or the more sophisticated one, using regression techniques as described in the appendix, can be used to perform the task. Then Table 7.4 can be constructed.

V. Target the groups to lay off.

After the numbers are obtained for Table 7.2, target the groups that should be laid off by finding those groups for whom the present value of wage exceeds the present value of output. The firm would like to lay off all of these workers. In Table 7.4, this means that the firm would like to lay off all workers who are outside of mid-career age range.

VI. Determine seniority.

The younger workers can be laid off on grounds of least seniority. The older workers may have to be bought out.

A. The amount of the buyout must just exceed the minimum value that the worker is willing to accept. The worker is willing to accept any value B such that

$$B + \text{Present value of Alternatives} > \text{Present value of Wages}$$

or

$$B > \text{Present value of Wages} - \text{Present value of Alternatives}$$

Thus, the buyout should just exceed the difference between the present value of remaining wages and the present value of alternatives. This is the least the firm can pay that will be acceptable to the worker.

B. Table 7.5 calculates these using the following method based on the data given in Table 7.4.

In Table 7.5, present values of the remaining wages, alternatives, and outputs are calculated. The firm is willing to pay up to the difference between its wage liability and the amount of output. This is labeled *bid*. Bid is positive for workers 30 and younger and for those 48 and older. These are the workers the firm would like to lay off.

Ask is defined as the difference between the present value of the remaining wage stream and the present value of alternatives. This is the amount of *rent* that the worker earns by remaining at the firm. Any severance payment greater than this amount will be accepted by the worker since, when coupled with the alternative wage, the worker makes more by leaving than by staying. Only workers who are 55 and older can be bought out, because only those workers have asks that are lower than the bids. Workers younger than 30 can be laid off with little fear of other repercussions. Those between 48 and 54 are more problematic. The firm would like to lay them off because the present value of their remaining wages exceeds the present value of their output. But the offer that the firm is willing to make is small because of the small difference between $\text{PV}(W)$ and $\text{PV}(V)$. The offer that the firm will make is not acceptable to the workers, whose asks exceed

TABLE 7.5
BUYOUT AMOUNTS

Age	PV(W)	PV(A)	PV(V)	BID	ASK
25	886641	833599	837298	49343	53042
26	897884	839538	859965	37919	58346
27	908400	845235	880921	27479	63165
28	918168	850668	900155	18013	67500
29	927165	855809	917656	9509	71356
30	935368	860629	933413	1955	74739
31	942747	865096	947413	−4666	77651
32	949273	869175	959640	−10367	80098
33	954913	872826	970079	−15166	82087
34	959631	876009	978712	−19081	83622
35	963385	878674	985519	−22134	84711
36	966133	880771	990480	−24347	85362
37	967825	882243	993571	−25746	85582
38	968409	883027	994766	−26357	85382
39	967825	883055	994036	−26211	84770
40	966008	882250	991351	−25343	83758
41	962889	880531	986676	−23787	82358
42	958388	877804	979973	−21585	80584
43	952419	873970	971200	−18781	78449
44	944888	868917	960313	−15425	75971
45	935691	862525	947260	−11569	73166
46	924714	854658	931986	−7272	70056
47	911829	845169	914431	−2602	66660
48	896900	833897	894527	2373	63003
49	879773	820663	872200	7573	59110
50	860281	805270	847370	12911	55011
51	838240	787504	819948	18292	50736
52	813446	767125	789835	23611	46321
53	785677	743874	756924	28753	41803
54	754688	717463	721096	33592	37225
55	720207	687576	682220	37987	32631
56	681939	653865	640153	41786	28074
57	639557	615949	594737	44820	23608
58	592701	573406	545798	46903	19295
59	540977	525773	493145	47832	15204
60	483949	472543	436568	47381	11406
61	421139	413154	375836	45303	7985
62	352022	346992	310695	41327	5030
63	276018	273378	240864	35154	2640
64	192492	191569	166036	26456	923
65	100743	100743	85872	14871	0

their bids. These workers cannot be laid off without fear of legal and reputational problems. As a result, the firm is likely to tolerate them, regarding the losses on them as a cost of doing business.[11]

◆ ◆ ◆ ◆ ◆ ◆ SELECTIVE LAYOFFS, BUYOUTS, AND SPECIFIC POLICIES

The discussion to this point has focused on layoffs and buyouts as they relate to age. But there are other obvious factors that a firm wants to consider. The most obvious is that workers in a given job and age category do not all have the same productivity. Some workers are more able, ambitious, or more energetic than others, and are therefore more desirable to the firm. The tables of the last example made no allowance for these differences, but they are surely important business considerations. How do they weigh in?

Firm-Specific Human Capital

The first factor to consider is the amount of firm-specific human capital that an individual possesses. Even within a given job and age group, some workers may have more firm-specific skills than others. Workers with the most firm-specific human capital are the ones for whom the alternatives are likely to be lowest relative to their output at the firm. They are the ones least susceptible to buyouts, since their ask price tends to be high and the bid price tends to be low. Who has the most firm-specific human capital? Workers who have idiosyncratic duties are among the best candidates. This includes those who work directly with long-term customers, those who have designed or operated systems that are unique to the firm, and those whose duties necessitate relationships with large blocks of the firm's employees.

Productivity Differences

Is ability a factor? Should the more able or harder working individuals be retained over others? The answer is not as obvious as it may appear. Although the better workers produce more, they may cost more. Also, the better workers have better alternatives. Recall that the desire to lay off workers depends on the difference between the present value of their wages and the present value of their output. When this is positive, the firm wants to lay the workers off. The ability to buy out a worker depends on the difference between the present value of output and the present value of alternatives. When and only when this is negative, is it profitable to buy out a worker.

---

[11]Once again, the theorem, proved in the appendix, that buyouts are feasible only when $PV(A) > PV(V)$ is borne out in the numbers of Table 7.5.

In earlier chapters we pointed out that the most productive workers are not necessarily the most profitable. A firm should go for workers who are the best value—that is, the workers who produce the most relative to their wages. In a firm where wage scale is compressed, the most productive workers tend to be underpaid relative to their less productive counterparts. In such a firm, the most productive workers are the best value.

As mentioned, workers with a great deal of firm specific human capital tend to generate more rents for the firm than their counterparts with general human capital. Consequently, a downsizing firm would prefer to retain the workers with firm-specific human capital relative to those with more general skills. An across-the-board buyout offer may accomplish this goal. Since the value of alternatives for workers with firm-specific human capital is low relative to their output and wages within the firm, they will reject buyout offers that workers with smaller differences between inside and outside wages will accept.

A potential danger of buyout offers is adverse selection.[12] In any wage category there are some workers who are more productive than others. The firm may not be able to determine who is more productive between two workers who have similar background and identical wages. However, it is not unlikely that the more productive of the two has a higher value alternative than his less able counterpart. In this case, the more productive workers in each wage category may be induced by the buyout offer to leave, while the least productive and least profitable workers may choose to stay with the firm.

Implementation

Window Plans

Often, the time during which a buyout is offered is limited and its announcement is unanticipated. Such buyouts are sometimes called *window plans* because there is a small window period during which the buyout is available.

There is a very good reason for both limiting the amount of time during which the plan can be used and making it unanticipated. Recall that the "bid" price that a firm is willing to offer to buy out a worker depends on the difference between her wage and her productivity. The lower her productivity, the more anxious a firm is to be rid of her and the higher the buyout offer that the firm is willing to make. Were the plan anticipated, a worker would have incentives to reduce her productivity and thereby increase the price that the firm would be willing to pay to buy her out.[13] Productivity reductions are costly to the firm, especially if they go on for a significant amount of time. A short fuse on the window plan prevents a worker from strategically reducing productivity for any significant time period to gain a higher buyout price. Making a window plan unanticipated reduces the likelihood that a worker will reduce her productivity before the plan period begins.

---

[12]See Michael Schwarz (1997).
[13]This is a problem primarily when buyout offers are tailored to the individual.

DILBERT reprinted by permission of United Feature Syndicate, Inc.

Retirement Bridges

There is little value in buying out a worker who is close to voluntary retirement. Indeed, the buyout prices in Table 7.5 fall for the worker's last few years on the job. But a buyout formula that offers 65-year-olds less than it offers 56-year-olds might run into legal difficulties. A provision that is less likely to encounter legal challenges, but that has the effect of paying a larger premium to those still a few years from voluntary retirement is a *retirement bridge*. A retirement bridge gives a worker seniority credit for the purpose of pension calculation as if he had stayed on until the normal retirement date. For example, if the normal retirement age is 65 and a worker leaves at 55 with 18 years of service, he is treated as if he had 28 years of service for the purpose of calculating retirement benefits. A worker who leaves at 64 with 29 years of service would be treated as if he had 30 years of service. Since pensions generally increase with prior service, the retirement bridge can be a substantial inducement to retire early. But since the number of years awarded by the bridge declines with age, older workers are in effect given a smaller buyout award than their juniors. Thus, retirement bridges generally work in the right direction. They automatically reduce the size of the buyout for the oldest workers.

Job Placement Services

Firms sometimes elect to set up job placement services for their workers. Is this rational, or does it merely reflect the employer's guilt about laying off workers?

The practice is not only rational, it can result in cost savings. Since the "ask" price that a worker demands depends on the difference between the present value of wages and the present value of alternatives, raising the value of alternatives also reduces the worker's ask price. To the extent that a firm can help severed workers find new jobs, the alternatives rise and the firm may get the worker to leave at a lower buyout price.

Whether the firm decides to set up a placement service, however, depends on the firm's efficiency in securing new employment for its workers. Setting up such services is quite costly. The job placement service should be offered only if the firm can provide the service more cheaply than the worker can buy job placement services from outside agencies. Otherwise, the firm would find it cheaper to simply pay for the outside services that a worker purchases. In most cases, this is probably the best route. Since placement firms specialize in relocating workers, they are likely to be more efficient at relocation than the firm doing the layoffs. It is usually less expensive to pay an outside placement firm to run a relocation program than it would be to set up an internal placement service.

In either case, however, the point remains.

> By offering job placement services to severed employees, the price that the firm must pay to buy the worker out can be reduced. A firm should provide placement services only when doing so increases the value of the targeted workers' alternatives by more than the cost of the service. Otherwise, the firm is better off simply paying a higher buyout premium and allowing workers to find employment on their own.

RECAP ◆ ◆ ◆ ◆ ◆

This chapter focused on layoffs and buyouts. It has answered the initial questions in considerable detail.

1. The groups to be targeted for layoffs are the oldest and youngest workers in the firm when there is a decline in demand for the firm's product. The youngest can be laid off directly, without much difficulty or need for apology. Older workers must be handled more carefully, both for legal and reputational reasons. It is frequently better to buy older workers out than to have them leave involuntarily.

2. The firm wants to lay off all workers whose present value of remaining wages exceeds the present value of remaining productivity. It is possible to buy out only those workers whose present value of alternatives exceeds the present value of their productivity. These two groups are not the same, the feasible group usually being a (proper) subset of the desired layoff group. The firm must offer severance pay of at least the difference between the present value of remaining wages and the present value of alternatives. This is the minimum amount that the worker will accept to leave voluntarily. The firm is willing to pay up to the difference between the present value of wages and the present value of productivity. When the amount that the firm is willing to pay (the bid) exceeds the amount that the worker is willing to accept (the ask), a profitable buyout can occur. A necessary and sufficient condition for the bid to exceed the ask is that the present value of alternatives exceeds the present value of productivity.

3. Whether turnover is desirable or not depends on the worker's productivity relative to wages. Firms may want to retain a worker whose current wages exceed current productivity as long as the present value of remaining productivity exceeds the present value of remaining wages. It is conceptually straightforward to make this calculation. In practice, obtaining the data necessary to make the decision can be difficult. Still, implicit in every layoff decision is the

notion that the present value of future output falls short of the present value of the wage obligation. It is better to attempt to gather the data and to perform the analysis demonstrated in this chapter than it is to simply make a decision based on instinct. Performing the analysis forces management to think clearly about all the costs and benefits of the layoff decision.

4. There are steps that can be taken to mitigate adverse consequences of layoffs and buyouts. These include using unanticipated, narrow-window buyout plans so that workers cannot diminish output to increase the buyout offer. Additionally, retirement bridges, which tend to provide larger payments to workers further away from retirement, can decrease the tendency to provide too much severance pay to the oldest workers who would retire voluntarily without much additional motivation.

♦ ♦ ♦ ♦ ♦ REFERENCES

Lazear, Edward P,. and Richard Freeman, "Relational Investing: The Worker's Perspective" (August 1994), forthcoming in *Meaningful Relationships: Institutional Investors, Relational Investing and the Future of Corporate Governance*, ed. Ronald Gilson, John C. Coffee and Louis Lowenstein (New York: Oxford University Press), expected 1997.

Schwarz, Michael, "Downsizing and Layoff Mechanisms," Stanford Graduate School of Business doctoral dissertation, unpub., 1997.

♦ ♦ ♦ ♦ ♦ ADDITIONAL ADVANCED READING

Burdett, Kenneth, "A Theory of Employee Job Search and Quit Rates," *American Economic Review* (March 1978): 212–220.

Hall, Robert E., and Edward P. Lazear, "The Excess Sensitivity of Layoffs and Quits to Demand," *Journal of Labor Economics* (April 1984): 233–57.

Jovanovic, Boyan, "Firm-Specific Capital and Turnover," *Journal of Political Economy* (December 1979): 1246–60.

Kiefer, Nicholas M., and George R. Neumann, "Layoffs and Duration Dependence in a Model of Turnover," in *Search Models and Applied Labor Economics*. Cambridge: Cambridge University Press, 1985, pp. 139–59.

Leonard, Jonathan S., and Louis Jacobson, "Earnings Inequality and Job Turnover," *American Economic Review* (May 1990): 298–302.

Leonard, Jonathan S., "Carrots and Sticks: Pay, Supervision, and Turnover," *Journal of Labor Economics* (Part 2, October 1987): S136–52 .

Mincer, Jacob, and Yoshio Higuchi, "Wage Structures and Labor Turnover in the United States and Japan," *Journal of the Japanese and International Economy* (June 1988): 97–133.

Sicherman, Nachum and Oded Galor, "A Theory of Career Mobility," *Journal of Political Economy* (February 1990): 169–92.

APPENDIX   ◆ ◆ ◆ ◆ ◆

It is shown that a profitable buyout opportunity exists if and only if the present value of alternatives exceeds the present value of productivity.

First, we show that a necessary and sufficient condition for there to exist a profitable buyout possibility is that the present value of future alternatives exceeds the present value of future productivity at the firm.

Let w_i, a_i, and v_i correspond to wage, alternative and output at age i. Define $PV(W_t)$ as the present value of wages from t to T in year t dollars, or

$$\sum_{i=t}^{T} \frac{w_i}{(1 + r)^{i-t}}$$

where w_t is the wage at age t and T is the age of retirement.

Analogously, define $PV(A_t)$ as the present value of alternatives from t to T in year t dollars, or

$$\sum_{i=t}^{T} \frac{a_i}{(1 + r)^{i-t}}$$

Finally, define $PV(V_t)$ as the present value of output from t to T in year T dollars, or

$$\sum_{i=t}^{T} \frac{v_i}{(1 + r)^{i-t}}$$

A worker will accept a buyout B if the present value of the alternative plus the buyout exceeds the present value of wages at the current firm, or if

$$B + PV(A_t) > PV(W_t)$$

so that

$$B > PV(W_t) - PV(A_t)$$

A firm will offer a buyout B if the present value of the buyout is less than what is lost from keeping the worker, or if and only if

$$B < PV(W_t) - PV(V_t)$$

When both conditions hold, the buyout B will be offered and accepted. Both conditions hold when

$$PV(W_t) - PV(V_t) > PV(W_t) - PV(A_t)$$

or when

$$PV(A_t) > PV(V_t)$$

Thus, a necessary and sufficient condition for a profitable buyout to be offered is that the present value of alternatives exceeds the present value of output.

INFORMATION, SIGNALLING, AND RAIDING

8

oes the training make the worker or does the worker justify the training? As you read this text, you are aware that neither you nor your classmates are simply the "average" individual. Your choice to go to school and to acquire knowledge sets you apart from other individuals. Those who choose to undertake higher education tend to be more able than those who do not. Do employers seek educated workers because education has made them more productive, or do employers seek them because those who will be most productive are also the individuals who choose to go to school? Does the answer have any impact on a firm's decision to hire? The following conversation illustrates several important principles regarding these questions.

JEVONS: I think we ought to stop hiring MBAs. We are better off getting those who could make it in an MBA program right out of undergraduate school. They cost less and are just as good.

WEBB: I've heard this before. I learned a lot in business school that is directly or indirectly applicable to what I do now. I learned how to think about problems, I learned to distinguish real issues from buzzwords, and I learned some analytic techniques that I use frequently as a vice president. I know how to think through problems, and can get my people moving in the right direction. I wasn't born with this knowledge and knew none of this stuff before going to business school.

JEVONS: Granted, we all picked up some information in school. The question is whether spending two years of listening to boring lectures does much to increase productivity. That's a lot of time and a lot of wasted money. There needs to be a great deal learned to offset it. I don't think that the output is there.

195

WEBB: If that's true, why do other firms spend all that money to hire an MBA?

JEVONS: Because dummies like us are willing to pay them huge salaries after they get out of school.

WEBB: I think that you are being myopic. Even if they didn't learn it in school, does it matter? If those who go to school are worth the additional money, who cares where they learned it?

JEVONS: If we can get them before they get the MBA, then maybe we can get the same productivity without paying the high salary.

WEBB: Good luck on finding talented managers who don't want to go on to get the MBA.

JEVONS: I agree that it may be difficult. But why don't we let our competitors do the work? They hire workers without MBAs. We can just pick off their best ones. Then we don't have to take chances on unproven workers, but we can still get the advantage of paying a low wage.

WEBB: How are we going to hire them if we pay them a low wage?

JEVONS: We'll pay them more than they're making at our competitor's place, but less than we pay for MBAs.

This exchange raises a number of issues that are summarized in the following questions:

- Does schooling affect worker productivity, or does it merely certify those who are highly productive?

- If schooling is just certification, should this affect the firm's hiring and pay decisions?

- For which workers is education and training most likely to actually enhance productivity?

- Is there an opportunity to steal undervalued workers away from rivals?

◆ ◆ ◆ ◆ ◆   SIGNALLING PRODUCTIVITY

The idea behind this discussion was first analyzed by Michael Spence.[1] He showed that it might be rational for individuals to acquire education and for firms to pay higher wages to educated individuals even if education had no effect on productivity. He argued that individuals might go to school *not* to learn skills that will be

_____

[1]See Spence (1973).

useful on the job, but rather to **signal** to employers that the student was capable of performing well on the job.

The basic idea can be illustrated quite easily. There are two key ingredients. First, asymmetric information is necessary: The worker must know his productivity, and the firm cannot know it. Second, there must be a correlation between the ability to perform well in school and the ability to perform on the job. If individuals who are likely to be productive in the labor force are also those who will do well at school, then the attained level of schooling can serve as a signal of underlying potential.

Consider the following stylized example. There are two types of individuals in the world: quicks and slows. Quicks produce $20 per hour of output, while slows produce only $18. These values are given and determined by factors beyond an individual's control and have nothing to do with schooling. Consistent with the point of the last paragraph is the idea that the quicks can complete the work associated with a year of schooling in less time than the slows. Thus, quicks could conceivably work more hours while going to school than could slows. Specifically, assume that it takes quicks only .76 as long to complete a year of school as it does to slows.

Now suppose that firms announce that they will pay according to the following schedule:

$$\text{Hourly Wage} = \$12 + (\$0.50) \times (S)$$

where S is the number of years of schooling completed. Thus, a worker with 10 years of schooling earns $17 per hour ($12 + 0.50×10), whereas one with 11 years of schooling earns $17.50 per hour ($12 + 0.50×11). If a worker works 2,000 hours per year, each year of additional schooling will yield revenues of 0.50×2000, or $1,000 for every year worked. Suppose that a worker plans to work for 40 years. To make things simple, let us ignore discounting by pretending that the interest rate is zero. In that case the present value of one additional year of schooling is

$$\$1000 \times 40 = \$40,000$$

Schooling also has its costs, which we must consider. For higher levels of schooling, tuition and other direct costs are important. For all higher levels of schooling, a student forgoes wages. Recall that employers do not know a worker's underlying ability, but they can observe the number of years of schooling undertaken. It costs quicks less to complete a year of schooling than it costs slows because quicks can complete a year of schooling with only .76 the amount of time that it takes slows. Thus, the quicks have lower forgone earnings for a given year. All individuals, quicks or slows, with the same number of years of schooling completed, receive the same wage because employers cannot assess worker ability without knowing about schooling differences. The amount of forgone earnings increases as the number of years of schooling increases, because those with more schooling earn higher wages. See Table 8.1, which summarizes this information.

TABLE 8.1
SUMMARY OF DATA FOR SIGNALLING MODEL

Variable	Quicks	Slows
Output	$20/hr	$18/hr
Wage	$12 + $0.50 S	$12 + $0.50 S
Costs of schooling	Direct costs + .76 (forgone earnings of slows)	Direct costs + Forgone earnings
Hours worked per year	1800	1800
Years worked over lifetime	40	40
Interest rate	0	0
Lifetime benefit of a year of schooling	$40,000	$40,000

The costs of schooling depend on the number of hours in a given year of schooling and also the wages forgone per hour spent in school. Table 8.2 shows the costs and benefits from undertaking each additional year of schooling for quicks and slows. We only consider grades 12 and higher, because we assume, for the purpose of this example, that schooling up to year 12 is compulsory.

These numbers are presented by way of example. They are based on underlying assumptions about the number of hours used in each year of schooling (2,000 hours per year) and on hypothetical tuition numbers.

Every year of schooling yields the same benefit of $40,000, as noted in the second column of Table 8.2. But costs go up as workers acquire more schooling. Individuals can earn higher wages with each additional year of schooling completed, which increases the costs of going to school. The direct costs of schooling are zero until workers reach the thirteenth year of their education. Quicks'

TABLE 8.2
COSTS AND BENEFITS OF EACH YEAR OF SCHOOLING

Years of School	Benefit	Direct Cost	Forgone Earnings Quick	Forgone Earnings Slow	Cost Quick	Cost Slow
11						
12	$40,000	$0	$26,600	$35,000	$26,600	$35,000
13	$40,000	$10,000	$27,360	$36,000	$37,360	$46,000
14	$40,000	$10,000	$28,120	$37,000	$38,120	$47,000
15	$40,000	$10,000	$28,880	$38,000	$38,880	$48,000
16	$40,000	$10,000	$29,640	$39,000	$39,640	$49,000
17	$40,000	$10,000	$30,400	$40,000	$40,400	$50,000
18	$40,000	$10,000	$31,160	$41,000	$41,160	$51,000

FIGURE 8.1
COSTS AND BENEFITS OF SCHOOLING BY YEAR

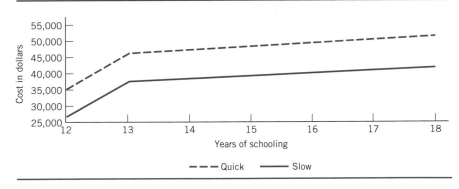

forgone earnings costs are lower than slows' because they can complete school assignments more quickly.[2]

For slows, the thirteenth year costs $46,000 and yields only $40,000 in return, so slows stop at 12 years of schooling. For quicks, benefits are above costs through 16 years of schooling. The seventeenth year costs $40,400 and yields only $40,000 in return, so quicks stop at 16 years of schooling.

Given the promise by firms to offer a wage of $12 + $0.50 S, it pays for every rational individual to undertake schooling up to the point where the marginal benefits are swamped by the marginal costs of additional years of schooling. This means 16 years of schooling for quicks and 12 years of schooling for slows.

We can translate Table 8.2 into the chart shown in Figure 8.1, which plots the marginal cost of a year of schooling for quicks and for slows.

The marginal costs for slows intersects the $40,000 line, which is the marginal benefit of a year of schooling, before the thirteenth year. Thus, it does not pay for slows to acquire the thirteenth year of schooling, so they obtain 12 years of schooling. The marginal cost of schooling for quicks intersects the $40,000 line after 16 years, but before 17 years of schooling. Thus, it does not pay for quicks to acquire schooling beyond the 16th year.

Once slows choose 12 years of schooling, their wage rate is $18 per hour. Similarly, quicks, with 16 years of schooling, earn $20 per hour. Recall from Table 8.1 that quicks produce $20 per hour and that slows produce $18 per hour. Thus, in equilibrium, quicks choose to obtain 16 years of schooling, which yields a wage of $20 per hour that equals the quicks' productivity. Slows choose to obtain 12

---

[2]For example, a quick may find time to work part time while in school or alternatively, it may take slow more than a year to complete "one year of schooling".

years of schooling, which yields a wage of $18 per hour that equals the slows' productivity.[3]

While this is an equilibrium, it results because firms announced a wage of

$$\$12 + \$0.50\ S$$

per hour. But it appears that this was pulled from the sky, simply to make the example work. In fact the numbers used are consistent with a competitive labor market. Here is why:

Suppose that firms called out a different wage schedule, say,

$$\$12 + \$0.51\ S$$

Because an additional year of education brings $0.51 per hour instead of $0.50, the value of a marginal year of education is now

$$\$0.51 \times 2000 \times 40 = \$40{,}800$$

instead of $40,000. Now an individual will undertake an additional year of schooling as long as its cost is less than 40,800. Table 8.1 reveals that slows will continue to leave school after 12 years, but quicks will find it worthwhile to acquire 17 years of schooling.

If the wage, $12 + $0.51 S, were paid so that the benefit to a year of schooling is $40,800, then quicks find that it pays to undertake 17 years of schooling. Slows still find that $40,800 does not cover the marginal cost of the thirteenth year and stop going to school after 12 years. The cost of the seventeenth year of schooling is $40,400 for quicks, which is less than the return of $40,800. They undertake year 17, but not year 18, which costs $41,160 and therefore exceeds $40,800. The cost of the twelfth year of schooling for the slows is $35,000. But the thirteenth year costs $46,000 (see Table 8.2), which exceeds $40,800, so the slows stop at 12 years of schooling.

Given the wage formula, quicks earn $20.67 per hour and slows earn $18.12 per hour. This creates two problems. First, both types of workers are being paid more than their productivity. Slows earn $18.12 (12 + 12(.51)), but are only worth $18.00. Quicks earn $20.67 (12 + 17(.51)), but are only worth $20.00. Second, quicks are overpaid relative to slows. Quicks earn $2.55 more than slows, but quicks are only $2.00 more productive than slows.

Firms could reduce the constant term in the wage equation (i.e., reduce the $12 to something like $11) to take care of the problem of general overpayment. But that will still leave the second problem. Even if all types of workers were not

---

[3]There are some additional technical details to consider. One is whether the slows would simply choose to undertake zero years of schooling, causing the equilibrium to break down. We have eliminated consideration of this possibility by assuming that students cannot choose to attend fewer than 12 years of schooling. Early works by Wilson (1979) and Riley (1979) discuss these points in rigorous detail.

paid more than they are worth, the quicks would still be too expensive relative to slows. For example, if the wage scheme were

$$\$11 + \$0.51\,S$$

slows would earn $17.12 and quicks would earn $19.67. Both types of workers would have output that exceeded their productivity, but the slows would be the better value in the market. Quicks would be more productive, but not enough more productive to justify the additional $2.55 in hourly wage. Statements like, "The college grads are better, but not enough better to justify the higher wage," would be applicable in this case. Employers would try to snap up the high school grads and there would be excess supply of those with 17 years of education. Under these conditions, market forces would depress the premium for additional schooling. Equilibrium would be reached when the premium was back at $0.50 per hour rather than $0.51 per hour.

A formula of $12 + $0.50 S meets all market constraints. Both types of workers are paid exactly what they are worth, and the spread in hourly wage between quicks and slows would just match their spread in productivity. In this situation, the firms would be indifferent between hiring quicks and slows. The quicks are more productive, but the additional productivity is exactly matched by the wage premium.

The opposite problem would result if workers were paid some amount less than $0.50 per hour for each additional year of schooling. Suppose, for example, that the formula were

$$\$12 + \$0.49\,S$$

Then, an additional year of schooling would be worth

$$\$0.49 \times 2000 \times 40 = \$39{,}200$$

At this lower benefit of $39,200, quicks would choose 15 years of schooling, whereas slows choose 12. This creates two problems as well, but they are the opposite of those created before. Now, both quicks and slows are underpaid. Further, quicks are underpaid relative to slows.

First, both types of workers are being paid less than their productivity. Slows earn $17.88 (12 + 12(.49)), but are worth $18.00. Quicks earn $19.35 (12 + 15(.49)), but are worth $20.00. Second, quicks are underpaid relative to slows. Quicks earn $1.47 more than slows, but quicks are $2.00 more productive than slows.

The underpayment of quicks and slows means that there will be an excess demand for labor. Workers are cheap relative to what they produce, and all firms will want to hire more of them. To cope with this situation, firms could raise the constant term in the wage equation. This will alleviate the problem of general underpayment, but will still leave the second problem. The slows are too expensive relative to quicks. For example, if the wage scheme were

$$\$12.75 + \$0.49\,S$$

slows would earn $18.63 and quicks would earn $20.10. Workers, on average, might not be paid more than they are worth, but the quicks would be the better value in the market. Quicks who are $2 more productive only cost $1.47 per hour more than slows. The following statements would be applicable: "The workers with some college are far better. They are well worth the additional cost. We get more in additional output than we pay to hire the more educated workers." Employers would try to snap up those with college and there would be excess demand of those with 15 years of education. Under these conditions, the premium for additional schooling would be forced up. Equilibrium would be reached when the premium was back at $0.50 per hour rather than $0.49 per hour.

Once again, the wage formula that prevails on the market is

$$\$12 + \$0.50\,S$$

which meets all market constraints: Both types of workers are paid exactly what they are worth, and the spread in hourly wage between quicks and slows would just match their spread in productivity. Firms would be indifferent between hiring quicks and slows. The quicks are more productive, but the additional productivity is exactly matched by the wage premium.

Schools—A Social Evil

The scenario just described illustrates the signalling model. Workers are endowed with a given level of productivity. Schooling does not affect their productivity, but is correlated with it because the more productive individuals find it easier, and therefore cheaper, to get through school. Indeed, schooling is socially wasteful in this view. It does nothing to affect productivity, but society's resources are wasted as individuals spend resources to acquire schooling. The $20,000 to over $40,000 per year spent to pay teachers and other school personnel does nothing to raise society's output. Worse, it creates needless wage inequality between quicks and slows, who are in their respective bodies strictly by genetic luck.

If this extreme version of signalling were correct, then schools would be a social evil that should be discouraged or outlawed. One way to induce individuals to eschew schooling is to prevent discrimination on the basis of education. If employers were not permitted to pay different wages to more educated workers, the return to a year of schooling would fall to zero. No one would go to school, and there would be no waste of society's resources.

Under this view, firms and quicks are implicit co-conspirators. Firms hire educated workers because they are hoping to hire a more able individual. The firm might know full well that the schooling itself has no effect on the worker's productivity, but the firm cannot find out who is quick and who is slow without resorting to the education game. Everyone whom the firm asks will claim to be quick in order to receive the high wage. Thus, schooling allows workers to credibly reveal their type, without affecting their productivity.

Schools—A True Benefit

This view of the world is too extreme, even for the most skeptical reader. Surely schooling must be productive in some contexts. There are a number of counterarguments to the signalling view of schooling.

Signalling Is Not Applicable

Some vocations are learned in school, which are clearly not part of an individual's stock of knowledge before entering the program.

Consider, for example, the training obtained by a surgeon. One could argue that there are some people who are born knowing how to remove an appendix and others who are born without such knowledge. Medical training, it could be claimed, merely certifies the ones who are the best appendix removers, without teaching them anything. But this stretches the imagination of even the strongest supporter of the signalling view of education.

At best, then, the issue is one of when schooling is least likely to produce actual skills and when it is most likely to certify ability. One reasonable possibility is that schooling is likely to be most important when the program is technical and highly specific. More general programs seem to fit the signalling story somewhat better.

Education: A Very Expensive Signal

An MBA is relatively general, and some might argue that obtaining the MBA is merely a signal of productivity. But acquiring an MBA is an extremely expensive proposition. The forgone earnings amount to close to $100,000 for two years, plus an additional $50,000 in direct costs. One would think that accurate information about an individual's ability and drive could be acquired by subjecting prospective employees to a battery of tests at a cost far less than $150,000. The fact that individuals undertake the MBA instead of merely presenting information about performance on GREs or other entrance exams suggests that there is something substantive in the MBA program itself.

Contingent Contracts

Contingent contracts might be a cheaper alternative. Although an employer might not know a worker's productivity before the job starts, if a two-year MBA program can determine productivity, then it probably takes significantly less than two years on the actual job in question to obtain information about a worker's productivity. Employers could make the following offer: During the probationary period it is assumed that the worker is a slow, and he is paid $18 per hour. After his productivity becomes known, he receives his actual productivity, equal to either $18 or $20. In addition, quicks receive back pay of $2 per hour for every hour that they worked during the probationary period. This avoids the cost of schooling, but still allows quicks to distinguish themselves from slows.

Schools—A Less Extreme View

It seems difficult, therefore, to accept the most extreme version of the signalling view of education. Even though the pure signalling view seems unreasonable, the signal from schooling may be valuable, much in the way that Spence suggested.

Suppose that schooling is productive, but at the same time provides a joint product, namely, information about an individual's ability and suitability for various jobs. Then employers would care about an applicant's educational background and performance in the program. Information on an individual's ability or specific skills might help the firm sort new hires into their most productive job. It might provide information on which workers are likely to be the best learners. It might also allow employees to get a sense of which workers are not well suited to a particular firm. All of these provide social as well as private reasons why schooling might be worthwhile and seem more consistent with the facts.

Some Evidence

There is some empirical evidence on the distinction between the two views of education, which we label *signalling* and *productivity augmentation*. Work by Kenneth Wolpin (1977) examines attained levels of schooling for self-employed and wage and salary workers. If schooling were only a signal, then individuals who planned to become self-employed would not invest in this signal. After all, there is no point in signalling something that is already known. (Recall that for signalling to work, it is necessary that individuals obtaining the signal know whether they are quick or slow.) It turns out that if one examines attained levels of schooling across individuals, then one finds that wage and salary workers get trivially more education than self-employed workers. The fact that levels of attained schooling are so similar across groups suggests that schooling must be productivity augmenting. Otherwise, the self-employed would have significantly lower levels of schooling.

Of course it is possible that self-employed individuals are signalling to their customers rather than to their employers. For example, doctors and lawyers display their diplomas and various certificates, sometimes including Boy Scout Merit Badges. Wolpin, therefore, throws out the data on professionals. He still obtains the same results—namely that self-employed and wage and salary workers have about the same levels of attained schooling.

Another possible drawback is that individuals do not know whether they will be self-employed when choosing schooling levels. As a result, they hedge. The previous fix speaks to this issue as well. When professionals are deleted, most of Wolpin's revised sample consists of farmers. Farmers have pretty good knowledge of whether they will be self-employed when they choose schooling. Individuals whose parents do not own farms are very unlikely to own farms themselves. Thus, growing up on a family-owned farm increases the likelihood that an individual will be self-employed.

Although Wolpin's evidence supports the productivity augmentation view, work by Andrew Weiss (1984) supports signalling. Weiss looks at data from a manufacturing plant and finds that high school graduates are no more productive than high school dropouts for any given day of work, but that high school graduates tend to have better attendance levels and quit less often. He argues that this reflects persistence or "stick-to-it-ness." It is difficult to argue, he claims, that persistence is learned during the twelfth year of high school. A much more plausible explanation is that those individuals who are willing to finish high school are the same individuals who will stay at work and go to a boring job on a Friday or Monday, when they would rather call in sick. If so, then education is merely signalling underlying characteristics, rather than actually affecting worker productivity.

The CPA: An Application of the Theory

Accounting firms often require their new accountants to be CPAs (certified public accountants). Much of the reason behind the practice is to comply with legal constraints, which mandate the use of CPAs in a variety of circumstances. But there are also many jobs that CPAs are assigned that do not have external legal requirements associated with them.

It is costly to study for the CPA exam. Studying takes a great deal of time and few find exam taking a pleasant experience. In order to induce accountants to acquire the CPA certification, a premium must be paid to CPAs that makes it worthwhile for individuals to bother with certification.

Suppose that accountants without the CPA can average $30 per hour and that those who have passed the CPA average $35 per hour. People have different abilities. The best can pass the exam with little study; the least able may never be able to pass the exam. Table 8.3 gives the distribution of accountants by ability to pass the exam.

Ten percent of the population of accountants falls into each category. The highest-ability individuals are in group 1, and the lowest ability individuals are in group 10. Suppose, consistent with signalling, that studying for the CPA exam does nothing to improve an individual's skills.

TABLE 8.3
CPA EXAMPLE

Ability Group Number	Hours Spent Studying	Cost
1	100	$4,000
2	101	$4,030
3	116	$4,480
4	181	$6,430
5	356	$11,680
6	725	$22,750
7	1396	$42,880
8	2501	$76,030
9	4196	$126,880
10	6661	$200,830

We pose three questions and answer them in the context of this example.

1. Are older or younger individuals more likely to take the exam?
2. Do firms benefit by hiring the CPAs?
3. What alternative strategies can a firm use to avoid requiring CPA certification?

First, since it is assumed that studying for the CPA exam does nothing to increase productivity, this fits the pure signalling framework. Who will take the exam?

The answer is the standard one. An accountant will study for and take the exam if the return to doing so exceeds the cost. Table 8.3 gives the cost for different parts of the population. What is the return? The answer depends on the interest rate and the number of years left in an individual's career. The following expression gives the return to passing the CPA exam:

$$(8.1) \qquad Return = \sum_{i=1}^{T} \frac{(hours\ worked\ per\ year)\ (wage\ differential\ per\ hour)}{(1\ +\ r)^i}$$

As usual, r is the interest rate that permits a conversion to present value.

This equation looks much like the human capital investment equation of the last chapter. Indeed it is. The individual accountant does not really care whether passing the exam actually makes him more productive or whether it simply gives the perception that he is more productive. The individual merely cares about the amount by which passing the exam will raise earnings and the number of years over which returns can accrue. Whether earnings increase because study makes the individual more productive or because passing the exam lets prospective employers know that the individual is productive is irrelevant to the accountant. It is also irrelevant to the prospective employer. Unless there is another way to identify the able workers, using the CPA certification as a source of information is profit increasing for the employer.

The decision to take the exam boils down to whether the present value of benefits exceeds the present value of earnings. Table 8.4 shows the present value of benefits for each of the ten ability groups for various age categories. It is assumed that an individual works 2,000 hours per year and retires at age 65. It is also assumed that the relevant interest rate is 10 percent. The benefit from passing the exam is simply the value that Equation 8.1 yields at the various ages.

Table 8.4 illustrates several points. First, the benefit to passing the exam is independent of ability group. This is because the value of passing the exam is that it increases wages by $5 per hour (from $30 to $35), irrespective of ability level. Ability affects the costs of passing the exam, but not the return to it.

Second, as age increases, the present value of passing the exam declines. For example, individuals who are 64 have only one year left of work. They will work for 2,000 hours and earn a $5 premium as a result of passing the exam. Thus, the return to passing the exam is $5 × 2000 = $10,000. At age 25, the return to passing the exam is $107,791, which is the present value of $10,000 × 41 = $410,000

TABLE 8.4

PRESENT VALUE OF RETURNS TO PASSING THE CPA EXAM IN
DOLLARS AT TIME OF EXAM

	Age at Time of Exam				
Ability Group	24	34	44	54	64
1	107791	104269	95136	71446	10000
2	107791	104269	95136	71446	10000
3	107791	104269	95136	71446	10000
4	107791	104269	95136	71446	10000
5	107791	104269	95136	71446	10000
6	107791	104269	95136	71446	10000
7	107791	104269	95136	71446	10000
8	107791	104269	95136	71446	10000
9	107791	104269	95136	71446	10000
10	107791	104269	95136	71446	10000

of total dollar return, discounted back to the time when the individual is taking
the exam, namely age 24.

Whether an individual opts to take the exam depends on the difference between benefits and costs, not just on benefits. The costs are independent of age
because individuals are assumed to earn $30 per hour, irrespective of age, without
the CPA certification. But the costs are not independent of ability. More able individuals can pass the exam with fewer hours of study, as illustrated by the numbers
in Table 8.3.

Table 8.5 reports the net value of passing the exam for different age and ability categories. It is the same as Table 8.4, except that the appropriate costs are subtracted from benefits for each group.

The last column of Table 8.5 is identical to the last column of Table 8.3; it
shows the cost of taking the exam by ability group. Again, costs are the same for
every age category within an ability group, just as benefits are the same for every
ability category within any age group.

Table 8.5 shows the net benefits, with all positive net values in bold print. Individuals in those groups will become CPAs. For example, individuals who are in
ability group 1 and are 64 years old receive benefits of $10,000 from taking the
exam (from Table 8.4). They also bear exam-passing costs of $4,000, leaving a net
benefit of $6,000, as shown in row 1, column 6, of Table 8.5. Similarly, a 64-year-
old in the lowest ability group has a negative net benefit from taking the exam.
The cost of passing the exam, given more limited ability, is $200,830, while the
benefit from passing is only $10,000, leaving a net benefit of

$$\$10,000 - \$200,830 = -\$190,830$$

Table 8.5 illustrates two facts. First, at any given age, the least able individuals
are less likely to take the exam. This is why the CPA has value as a signal;

TABLE 8.5

PRESENT VALUE OF NET BENEFITS FROM PASSING THE CPA EXAM
IN DOLLARS AT TIME OF EXAM

Ability Group	Age at Time of Exam					
	24	34	44	54	64	Cost
1	103791	100269	91136	67446	6000	4000
2	103761	100239	91106	67416	5970	4030
3	103311	99789	90656	66966	5520	4480
4	101361	97839	88706	65016	3570	6430
5	96111	92589	83456	59766	−1680	11680
6	85041	81519	72386	48696	−12750	22750
7	64911	61389	52256	28566	−32880	42880
8	31761	28239	19106	−4584	−66030	76030
9	−19089	−22611	−31744	−55434	−116880	126880
10	−93039	−96561	−105694	−129384	−190830	200830

high-ability individuals are more likely to have the certificate than low-ability individuals.

Second, in any given ability category, older individuals are less likely to invest in certification. Since they have fewer years left in their work life, older workers have a shorter period over which to reap the benefits of CPA certification. This is the standard result that comes from the theory of human capital. It makes little difference whether the exam is productive or merely a signal of productivity. Workers behave the same way in either case.

The tables allow us to answer some of the questions posed earlier. First, younger individuals are more likely to take the exam than older individuals because the returns to doing so are lower to older individuals. Second, since high-ability individuals are more likely to become CPAs, firms who pay a premium for CPAs are hiring more able workers. The market wage premium for CPAs will adjust so that the premium paid to CPAs does not exceed the productivity advantage of CPAs over other accountants. This implies that it can be profitable for firms to hire CPAs, even when studying for the exam in no way affects worker productivity.

Another important question is whether there are more profitable alternatives to paying a premium for CPAs, when studying for the CPA exam does nothing for productivity, in and of itself. One possibility is to use contingent contracts that make both workers and the firm better off. If all workers in categories shown in bold in Table 8.5 become CPAs, then the productivity of the most able individuals in that set of workers must exceed $35. The reason is that the wage equals $35, which means that average productivity among CPAs must be at least $35 (or firms would lose money). But if average productivity is $35, then surely the productivity of the most able is greater than $35.

There is an opportunity for firms to steal away the most able workers from other firms. As long as a firm can observe productivity after some period on the job, the firm can offer to pay $30 to all workers, with the provision that those who are found to be in the top ability category will earn $35 after the probationary period, and will be given back-pay or a bonus to make up for all compensation at the $30 figure during the probationary period. The most able prefer this to obtaining CPA certification. The wage that they receive is the same, but this alternative would imply that they need not bear the costs of taking the exam.

The firm also prefers this scheme to paying $35 to every CPA. If $35 is paid only to the most able, then the surplus will be greater than it will be when $35 is paid to every CPA. It is clear from Table 8.5 that individuals who may be in ability groups as low as category 8 are willing to become CPAs. By restricting the premium only to individuals in the highest ability group (or groups), the firm can do better. The relatively low-ability CPAs go elsewhere.

RAIDING OTHER FIRMS: BENEFITS AND PITFALLS

◆ ◆ ◆ ◆ ◆

Sometimes an individual who is working at another firm is a particularly attractive hire. This is generally the case when the individual has some idiosyncratic set of skills. It is the unusual nature of the skills that make raiding another firm, rather than hiring from the pool of self-announced applicants, attractive.

If an individual has skills that are commonly found throughout a large fraction of the work force, the disadvantages of hiring from another firm may outweigh the advantages of hiring from the pool of applicants. The major disadvantage of hiring from another firm is that the worker's current employer usually knows more about a worker than does an outsider. Outsiders are usually in a weaker position to judge the quality of a worker.

This is sometimes called the problem of **winner's curse.** More often than not, the workers who are easy to steal are the ones not worth stealing. After all, a worker's current firm always has the option of raising the worker's salary to keep the employee. If the outside firm can outbid the worker's current employer, then maybe the outsider is bidding too much. This is much like the old Groucho Marx line that goes, "I wouldn't join any club that would have me."[4]

When a worker's skills are sufficiently rare, and when those skills are a particularly good match with an employer other than the current one, it may pay for an outside firm to launch a raid. Figure 8.2 illustrates all the decision possibilities related to raiding an employee by an outside firm.

Workers generally have specific skills that make them more valuable to the current employer than to an outsider. But such is not always the case. There are

---

[4]The analysis of this section is based on Lazear (1986).

situations in which a worker has skills that are so special and so well-suited to another firm's current situation that the outsider is willing to pay more for the worker than is the current employer.

Consider, for example, the case of Lee Iacocca, who was hired away from Ford by Chrysler. Chrysler was on the verge of closing, and Iacocca was judged by Chrysler's board as one of the few people with the skills to steer the company back to prosperity. As such, he was worth more to Chrysler than he was to Ford. Ford either underestimated his talents or believed that he was not as valuable to Ford because of Ford's stronger economic position.

The Iacocca situation is illustrated by box II.A.2 in Figure 8.2. Branch II shows the situation where the worker is more valuable to the outsider than to a current employer. There are two possibilities in this situation—the outsider can raid (shown on branch II.A), attempting to acquire the worker, or the outsider can fail to raid (shown on branch II.B), either because the outsider does not recognize the worth of the other firm's employee or because it is deemed too costly to go through the process of trying to acquire the worker. Even if the outsider raids, there are two possibilities. The current employer can let the

FIGURE 8.2
TO RAID OR NOT TO RAID—THE DECISION DIAGRAM

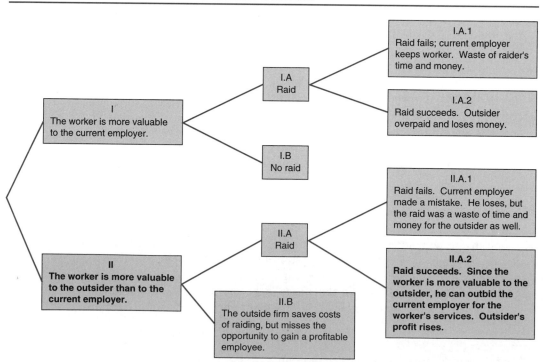

worker go to the outsider, as was the case with Ford and Iacocca, or the worker can mistakenly be kept at the current firm. It is a mistake to keep the worker at the current firm because, as already given in this case, the worker is worth more to the outsider than to the insider. Consequently, the outsider can always pay more than the worker is worth at the current employer and still earn a profit. If this does not happen, either the current employer paid too much, or the outsider offered too little.

The more common situation is found in the illustration branch I. Because of investment in specific human capital, a worker is more likely to be worth more to the current employer than to the outsider. Under these circumstances, the outsider should not raid; rather, the firm should end up at I.B. But if an outsider goes after the worker (on branch I.A.) and succeeds in acquiring this person, a mistake was made. Since the worker is worth more to the current employer than to the outsider, the current employer can always pay the worker more than the raider and still make money. If this does not happen, either the current employer did not pay enough to keep the worker, or the outsider overpaid. Given the current employer's natural informational advantage, the latter is more likely to be the case. This, again, is winner's curse. The raider acquires the worker, but at too high a price.

When should a firm raid another firm for workers? The first criterion is that the raider must be very certain that the target worker's value is higher to the raider than to the worker's current firm. The second criterion is that the worker's current firm not overvalue and, therefore, overpay the worker.

If the worker is more valuable to the current firm than to the raider, then branch I.A of Figure 8.2 is relevant. Either the raider acquires the worker, but pays too much, or, more likely, the raider simply fails to attract the worker away and wastes time and money in the process.

Raiding is most likely to yield profitable outcomes when the target worker is worth more to the raider than to the current firm and when the current firm is aware of that fact. If the worker is worth more to the raider than to the current firm, branch II. A. is relevant. If the worker's current employer is aware of the target worker's value, the raider will succeed in outbidding the current employer. This yields a profitable worker to the raider. If the current employer is unaware of the worker's value, the firm may try to keep the worker by paying too much for his services. This hurts the current employer, but also results in a waste of time and money for the raider. For this reason, a raider hopes that the raided firm does not overvalue the target worker.

In which situations are the conditions for a profitable raid most likely to be met? The main condition, that a worker is worth more to another firm than to the current firm, is most likely to hold when recent changes have occurred, either with respect to the worker's skills or in the industry in question. Some examples come to mind.

First, workers who have recently completed a schooling program are ripe for the picking. Chances are that a new degree recipient can be more productive in a job other than the one the worker currently holds. The current firm may be able

RAIDING AND RISK

◆ ◆ ◆ ◆ ◆ ◆ ◆ ◆ ◆ ◆

In March 1994, Brounoff Claire & Co., an inter-dealer bond brokerage firm, suspended operations after a staffing raid by Patriot Securities. Although founded in 1993, Patriot has expanded rapidly in the corporate bond trading arena to about 175 brokers. Conversely, Brounoff Claire has only about 20 full-time brokers. Since the company that owns 65 percent of Patriot, Liberty Brokerage, was founded by the large Wall Street bond re-brokers and McGraw Hill, the above action was viewed as a large corporation taking advantage of a smaller firm. But did the disparity in size affect the raiding of employees?

Patriot hired Brounoff's entire long-term utility bond department, as well as two other brokers, for a total of six employees. Usually, it pays for a firm to raid employees only if the worker is more valuable to the outside employer than to the current one. Based upon this rationale, Patriot must have believed that Brounoff's brokers could be more productive at their firm; and consequently, offered prospective employees higher salaries. However, in reality, Patriot relied heavily upon long-term contracts and guarantees to lure workers. The CEO of Brounoff, Frank Claire, claimed that as a small firm, he could match the incentive system offered by Patriot but could not guarantee minimum salaries.

Because Patriot Securities was a larger firm, the six raided workers would hardly be noticed at their new firm, but their departure represented 30 percent of the staff at Brounoff. The risk involved with Patriot paying a guaranteed wage is much less than at Brounoff, where salary costs could ruin the company in a bad year. With a net loss of $560K on only $4.6 million in revenues for 1993, if Brounoff also had to pay out fixed salaries for at least the six employees, the losses would exceed one-fourth of revenue; Brounoff may not have been able to continue to do business. Patriot, having a large number of employees who cannot singlehandedly significantly affect profits, could offer a guaranteed salary that would appeal to risk-averse employees. Because of the risk factor, the value of the compensation package would be lower at Brounoff, even though the expected value of wages was the same in both. Because Patriot was large enough to be less concerned about risk, it could bear the risk instead of the employee. Even in the worst case scenario, Patriot would still be able to meet its financial obligations because of its deep pockets and risk pooling; Brounoff did not have this luxury. By offering risk-averse employees a guaranteed wage, Patriot used its relative size to its advantage.

The raid was successful in this case, not so much because the worker was worth more to Patriot than to Brounoff. It was successful because Patriot could make the worker better off for a given level of productivity. Since workers care about income risk, and since Patriot was in a better position to ensure its workers against such risk, Patriot could offer a more attractive package to a prospective worker.

Source: Jack Willoughby, "Brounoff Claire was pummeled by Patriot Securities raid," *Investment Dealers' Digest* (March 28, 1994).

to offer the better job, but it is just as likely that the current firm does not have an opening in a higher-level position. A raiding firm will probably succeed in attracting the new graduate from the current firm. Indeed, the statistics on this are impressive. Schools that have part-time MBA programs report that the vast majority of their graduates leave the firm that they were with during graduate school within a short time of graduation.

Second, workers who are employed by firms in rapidly changing industries, especially those that are declining, are good targets. Since the firm in which the worker is currently employed is changing, the expectations that brought the worker to the firm in the first place are probably not being met. As a result, the worker's value at the current firm is probably below what it could be elsewhere. This is exactly the situation in which the worker is more valuable elsewhere than at the current firm.

Third, workers who are employed in industries that are undergoing rapid technical change are likely to be good targets. When change is rapid, it is not neutral, so that some firms experience significantly more rapid increases than others. Workers who are capable, but are located in a firm that is behind the leader, are good candidates for a raid. This explains why there is so much turnover among software and hardware employees. A worker who starts out with an innovative firm may find that firm to be trailing the industry within a period of six months. The worker is probably worth more elsewhere, and will seek out a new job or will be pirated away by a leading firm.

Is it always better to be a raider? If that were the case, all the firms would raid the best employees from each other and nobody would hire unproven talent.

Firms that hire directly from the pool of applicants get a random sample of the population. Some of the workers are very able, and some are less able. As long as the firm does not pay more than commensurate with the average quality of worker, it can survive quite well. But firms must recognize that the average quality of the workers who are employed by the firm that hires all applicants is not as high as the average for the population as a whole. Raiders are going to steal away a nonrandom sample of the population. Specifically, raiders tend to steal away the most able. Thus, the wage that a primary employer pays to its workers must be low enough so that it can avoid losses even after the secondary raiding firms have picked off some of the better employees. So, for example, if the average worker is worth $30 per hour, a wage of $30 per hour will cause a firm to lose money. Since the better workers tend to be picked off, those who are left do not provide an average productivity of $30 per hour. The wage that will prevail in the market among the various types of employers is derived in the appendix.

In the Brounoff Claire versus Patriot example, turnover was easily accomplished because the workers in question had general skills that were about equally valuable at both firms. Furthermore, a nonmonetary aspect of compensation, namely income security, was an important factor. In the next section, we examine how firm specificity and nonmonetary components affect the firm's strategy when faced with a raid by another firm

◆◆◆◆◆ OFFER MATCHING

We now realize that bidding for a worker is a common part of labor market competition. But sometimes, current employers refuse to match offers of outsiders. An announced policy of "no offer matching" is thought to discourage disloyal attempts by employees to raise their salaries by obtaining outsider offers at higher wages.

When is it reasonable to match outside offers and when not? First, it is important to determine what affects worker search behavior. Let's take a stylized example. Suppose that a worker is currently earning $20 per hour. Suppose further that there is one (and only one job) in his labor market that will pay him more than $20 per hour. That job pays $20.50 per hour. There are 50 firms other than his own where he believes that he has some prospect of finding the high-paying job. The problem is that he doesn't know which firm of the 50 is the high payer.

The worker can take time to fill out applications for some of the 50 firms. Each application takes time and effort, which the worker values at some amount, say X. The question is, When does it pay to search?

Suppose that the worker's current firm agrees to match any outside offer. Then he will search whenever the expected present value of the increased earnings exceeds the costs. The expected present value of searching at the first firm is

$$(8.2) \qquad \text{Returns} = \frac{1}{50} \sum_{t=0}^{T} \frac{(2000)(.50)}{(1 + r)^t}$$

This is like a human capital return formula, because searching for a job is like investing in human capital. The 1/50 that precedes the summation sign shows that, on the first inquiry, the worker has a 1/50 chance of finding the high-paying job. If he does, because his firm matches the offer, he gets to enjoy an increase in hourly wage for 2,000 hours per year for every year that he works from time zero to time T. If returns are greater than cost, he searches. Thus, he searches if

(8.3)
$$\frac{1}{50} \sum_{t=0}^{T} \frac{(2000)(.50)}{(1+r)^t} > X$$

Low values of X and long work lives are conducive to making (8.3) hold. For example, if $r = .1$, and if $T = 40$, the returns would be

$$\text{Returns} = \frac{1}{50} \sum_{t=0}^{40} \frac{(2000)(.50)}{(1+.1)^t} = \$215.58$$

Thus, whenever the cost of search is less than \$215.58, it pays the worker to search.[5]

The firm is unhappy that the worker is searching for a high-paying job. Under offer matching, the search may result in the firm having to pay higher wages for any given worker. How will a policy of "no offer matching" affect the worker's behavior?

This depends on whether the worker will actually leave to take another job. If he is willing to leave for the new job, then there is no effect on search behavior of announcing no offer matching. The returns to the worker are the same. The only difference is that in order to reap the returns, it is necessary that the worker actually take the job offer at the new firm. With offer matching, the worker need only threaten to leave.

Which situation does the firm prefer? With no offer matching, the worker leaves. With offer matching, the worker stays. Although the firm might not always want to match offers, one would think that the firm would always prefer having the option to match offers. If the wage that the firm must pay exceeds the worker's worth, then the firm can always let the worker go. If not, the firm can keep the worker.

Since the policy of "no offer matching" does not seem to discourage search, why announce it? The answer is that it might discourage certain kinds of search under special circumstances.

Suppose, for example, that the worker has a strong preference for his current firm, perhaps because he likes his co-workers, the plant's location, or its general work environment. The worker might be unwilling to move to another firm, even at a wage of \$20.50 per hour. If the firm matches alternative offers that are below the worker's value to the firm, it will raise wages to \$20.50. This provides the worker with an incentive to search for an offer that he has no intention of accepting. If the firm had a policy of "no offer matching," the worker would not search, because he would actually have to accept the job in order to reap the benefits of

---

[5] If the worker applies to the first firm and fails, he will surely apply to a second. The returns to applying to the second are greater than applying to the first, because the odds of finding the high paying firm have risen to 1/49 from 1/50. Of course, if subsequent searches are more costly than the first, say, because he starts to dip into more valuable time, then the worker might stop searching before finding a new job and before exhausting the total set.

his search. Since the worker is unwilling to accept the job at the higher wage, the policy of no offer matching discourages search and saves the firm money.

Now, were the firm to know that the worker was unwilling to accept the $20.50 to work for a competitor, it could simply refuse to match that offer. In essence, the firm could declare that the offer was not a genuine threat, because the worker had no intention of accepting it. The problem is that it is sometimes difficult for a firm to distinguish between genuine threats and offers that the worker would decline. When this is the case, firms can benefit from a policy of no offer matching.

This situation is most likely to arise when the following conditions apply.

1. There is a large nonpecuniary component to compensation.
2. The worker is being paid less than he or she is worth to the firm.

Compensation with Nonpecuniary Component

Wages can be compared easily, but compensation packages that include a nonpecuniary component may be difficult to compare. If jobs were identical, except for their monetary compensation, the firm could quickly determine whether a worker was likely to accept an outside offer. If the dollar wage offered by the competitor exceeded that being paid by the current employer, the worker would accept the offer and leave. Under these conditions, the outside offer is a credible threat to the current employer.

Unfortunately, evaluating offers is not so easy. Much of what a worker receives on the job is psychic. Working conditions, status, flexibility, and value of a particular location may be quite important, but may have different values to different individuals. When the nonpecuniary aspects of a job are important, it will be difficult for an employer to evaluate the significance of an outside offer. Workers are then more likely to search for outside offers that have high monetary rewards, that compensate for psychic disadvantages unobservable by the current employer.

As such, the gains to a worker from engaging in a strategic search for offers that are high, but which the worker has no intention of accepting, are largest when the nonpecuniary component of compensation is significant. Under these circumstances, an employer benefits from discouraging search for nonserious offers by announcing a policy of no offer matching.

When workers are in the job "for the money," the nonmonetary components of the job are less important. This is a situation where little is gained by announcing a policy of no-offer-matching. Workers will simply move if the firm does not match, and the firm cannot discourage needless search by refusing to match. Investment banks rarely adopt no offer matching policies, because money is the driving factor in these industries. Public utilities, on the other hand, are more likely to have such policies. At public utilities, nonmonetary components of the job, including job security, short hours, and perhaps easier workdays, are of significant concern to workers. At these firms, it is more difficult for management to know whether an outside offer at a slightly higher wage is indeed a credible threat. To prevent workers from searching for such offers merely to raise their salaries, public utilities can refuse to match outside offers.

Undervalued Workers

A firm that matches offers is most susceptible to disingenuous search by workers when the firm has much to gain from keeping the worker. If the firm were paying the worker exactly what she was worth, then an offer from an outsider that exceeds her current wage, credible or not, would elicit no response from the current employer. It would be better to lose the worker than to increase the wage.

The worker is most likely to succeed in getting her wage raised by an outside offer when the firm makes a fat profit on her. This happens when the worker is paid less than she is worth. If there is surplus to be had, the worker can capture some of that surplus by threatening the employer with a departure. It is under these circumstances that a policy of no offer matching is most likely to be profitable.

To summarize, retaining that flexibility is generally better than being locked into a rigid policy. As such, a policy that prevents a firm from matching offers is usually a bad idea. To every rule, however, there is an exception. When a worker's current employer is uninformed about a worker's willingness to accept outside offers, a no-offer-matching policy may be a good idea. This is particularly relevant when the firm is paying its workers less than the value of their output.

RECAP ◆ ◆ ◆ ◆ ◆

Four questions were posed at the outset. First, we wanted to ascertain whether schooling was productive or merely a certification of the most able. If schooling is only certification, why do individuals spend time and money to obtain education? An answer, based on Spence's signalling theory, was provided. Even if schooling is not productive, firms may pay higher wages to those who have more schooling. When the ability to acquire education is positively related to the ability to perform on the job, and when firms cannot observe worker ability directly, incentives are created for individuals to obtain certification.

Even if schooling merely certifies, it may still be rational for firms to base pay on schooling level. Unless the firm has an alternative way to determine worker productivity, it is profitable to pay more to more educated workers since they will also be the more productive. Whether they acquired that additional productivity in school or had the skill all along is almost irrelevant to the employer. If the employer cannot assess ability in any other way, allowing schools to do it, and paying for it, makes sense. Thus, we answer the second question posed: Neither the firm's hiring nor pay decision is likely to be affected by whether schooling is actually productive or not. Workers have every incentive to acquire schooling and firms have every incentive to pay for it, even when education is merely certifying.

Still, there are many situations in which it is difficult to believe that education is mere certification. Vocational training clearly impart skills on workers. Also, the ability to make contingent contracts suggests that in a number of situations, schooling must be productive or firms would offer alternative compensation schemes that make both workers and their employers better off. This is particularly true since education seems to be such an expensive certification device in many fields. The third question relates to this discussion: Education is likely to be productive in fields that are vocational. When the field is technical and very specific, it is unlikely that the skills were possessed by the individual before the worker entered the educational program.

Finally, workers can be stolen away from rivals, but a raiding firm must be careful. If the raider is uncertain about the worker's ability, it is likely to succeed in picking off workers that it does not want to have. Winner's curse can be an important force in labor markets, particularly when workers' productivity is difficult to observe. On the other side, workers have incentives to make their employers believe that their alternatives are better than they are. This is particularly the case when bringing in outside offers will raise a worker's compensation. In this situation, discouraging a worker's strategic behavior, say, by committing to a policy of *no offer matching* may be profitable.

◆ ◆ ◆ ◆ ◆ REFERENCES

Lazear, Edward P., "Raids and Offer Matching," in *Research in Labor Economics*, vol. 8, pp. 141–65, ed. Ronald Ehrenberg. Greenwich, CT: JAI Press, 1986.

Riley, John G., "Testing the Educational Screening Hypothesis," Part 2, *Journal of Political Economy* 87 (October 1979): S227–52.

Spence, A. Michael, "Job Market Signalling," *Quarterly Journal of Economics* 87 (August 1973): 355–74.

Weiss, Andrew, "Determinants of Quit Behavior," *Journal of Labor Economics*, 2,3 (July 1984): 371–87.

Wilson, Charles A., "Equilibrium and Adverse Selection," *American Economic Review* (May 1979): 313–317.

Wolpin, Kenneth, "Education and Screening, *American Economic Review* 67, 5 (December 1977): 949–58.

◆ ◆ ◆ ◆ ◆ ADDITIONAL ADVANCED READING

Dye, Ronald A., and Rick Antle, "Self-Selection Via Fringe Benefits," *Journal of Labor Economics* (July 1984): 388–411.

Greenwald, Bruce C., "Adverse Selection in the Labour Market," *Review of Economic Studies* (July 1986): 325–47.

Heckman, James J., and Guilherme L. Sedlacek, "Self-Selection and their Distribution of Hourly Wages," *Journal of Labor Economics* (Part 2, January 1990): S329–63.

Willis, Robert J., and Sherwin Rosen, "Education and Self-Selection," *Journal of Political Economy* (Part 2, October 1979): S7–36.

APPENDIX

◆ ◆ ◆ ◆ ◆

The Derivation of Equilibrium Wages[6]

Suppose that there are only two firms; the current employer, j, and a potential raider, k. The worker's output at firm j is given by

$$Q_j = M + S$$

and at firm k, by

$$Q_k = M$$

where M and S are both random variables. M represents general ability of the worker and, so, is j-specific ability. If $S < 0$, the worker is worth more at k than at j.

To make things simple, suppose that j knows Q_j and k knows Q_k, but j does not know how much of output reflects the worker's general ability and how much is firm-specific.

When j hires a worker, j must announce some wage W. Let the density of M in the population be given by $f(M)$ and the density of S in the population be given by $g(S)$ with distribution functions, $F(M)$ and $G(S)$. Assume M and S are independent.[7]

Firm k cannot tell whether a raid will succeed until k tries because raids succeed if and only if $Q_j < Q_k$, but k only knows Q_k.

If the cost of attempting a raid is zero, then k will attempt to raid whenever $Q_k > W$, that is, whenever worker's output at firm k exceeds what he is being paid at firm j.

The raid succeeds whenever $S < 0$. Then, firm k can always outbid j because the worker is worth more at k than at j. The outcomes for different parameter values are shown in Figure 8.A.1.

On branch 1, no raid occurs because $M < W$, so k would lose by offering a wage greater than what the worker is being paid at his current firm. The worker stays with firm j, and his wage remains unchanged.

---

[6]This is a simplified version of the model presented in Lazear (1986), referenced in the text of chapter 8.

[7]A positive correlation between M and S does not affect the results.

FIGURE A8.1
POSSIBLE OUTCOMES OF RAIDING

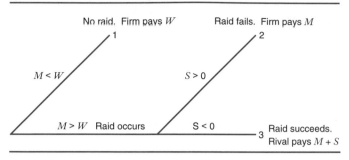

On branch 2, a raid is attempted because $M > W$, but it fails. Since $S > 0$,

$$Q_j > Q_k$$

so j can always match any offer that k makes. Firm j pays the worker M, because k stops bidding at wage $= M$.

On branch 3, the raid succeeds. Firm k raids because $M > W$ and can outbid j because $S < 0$. Firm k pays the worker $M + S$ because j stops bidding when the wage reaches $M + S$.

Let us calculate expected profit for firm j. Firm j keeps the worker on branches 1 and 2. Thus, expected profit is

(A8.1)   Expected profit = prob (on branch 1) $[E(M + S \,|\, \text{branch 1}) - W]$
$\qquad\qquad\qquad\qquad + \text{prob (on branch 2)} \, [E(M + S \,|\, \text{branch 2}) - M]$

because W is paid on branch 1 and M is paid on branch 2. Output is $M + S$. Given the assumptions of independence, (A8.1) can be rewritten as

(A8.2)   Expected Profit = $F(W) \, [E(M + S \,|\, \text{branch 1}) - W]$
$\qquad\qquad\qquad\qquad + [1 - F(W)] \, [1 - G(0)] \, E(S \,|\, \text{branch 2})$

To make things concrete, consider a specific example. Let $M \sim U[0,1]$ and $S \sim U\left[-\dfrac{\alpha}{2}, \dfrac{\alpha}{2}\right]$ where α is a parameter. Given the uniform densities, (A8.2) becomes

(A8.3)
$$\text{Expected Profit} = W\left[\left(\frac{W}{2}\right) - W\right] + \left(\frac{1 - W}{2}\right)\left(\frac{\alpha}{4}\right)$$
$$= \frac{-W^2}{2} + \frac{\alpha(1 - W)}{8}$$

In competitive equilibrium, wages are pushed up until expected profit is zero (otherwise other firms could enter and earn a profit). Solving

$$O = \frac{-W^2}{2} + \frac{\alpha(1-W)}{8}$$

yields

(A8.4) $$W = \frac{1}{8}[-\alpha + \sqrt{x^2 + 16}]$$

Here are some values of α and the resulting wage:

α	W
.25	.22
1	.39
2	.5
5	.66

As α rises, the average wage rises because there are two effects of being raided: (1) Firm j loses its high M workers, which pushes W below ½ (the average of $M + S$), and (2) Firm j loses its low S workers, which helps output and thereby raises the wage that j can pay. As the variance in S gets larger, the second effect becomes more important and raises the equilibrium wage offer. For $\alpha > 2$, the second effect is so strong that it raises the average wage paid to entering workers above ½, which is their mean productivity. Since the low S workers get stolen, the initial hirer, j, is ridded of its low productivity workers.

What wage does k pay on average?

Raids only succeed on branch 3. The raider must pay the amount that j bids last, which is equal to $M + S$. The raider, therefore, pays on average

(A8.5) $$E(M + S \mid M > W, S < 0)$$

where W is derived by setting expected profit in (A8.3) equal to zero.

Given independence, (A8.5) becomes[8]

(A8.6) $$E(M \mid M > W) + E(S \mid S < 0)$$

What is average productivity at k? The worker is worth M, so average output is

(A8.7) $$\begin{aligned} E(Q_k) &= E(M \mid M > W, S < 0) \\ &= E(M \mid M > W) \end{aligned}$$

---

[8]Actually, the point at which j drops out of bidding is when the wage that j offers is above $M + S$, or W, whichever is greater. Thus, the expected wage is $E[\max[M + S, W \mid M > W, S > 0]$.

It is clear from comparing (A8.7) to (A8.6) that output exceeds the expected wage paid by k. This follows, since $E(S \mid S < 0) < 0$. Thus, k makes a profit by raiding.

This analysis shows that raiders make profits, but initial hires do not. Competition drives the wage paid by initial employers up to the point where they earn zero profit. But raiders seem to come out with some surplus. This suggests that every firm should prefer to let someone else do the hiring and simply raid their workers.

Indeed, if information about another firm's workers were free, this would be a good strategy.[9] Unfortunately for raiders, it is very difficult to acquire information about another firm's workers. When such information becomes available, a raid may be in order. But, as a general proposition, the costs of gathering the information about another firm's workers exceeds the benefit to be had by stealing them away at a bargain price.

---

[9] If information were free, firm j would simply hire those that it knew it could keep.

PROMOTIONS AS MOTIVATORS

9

Climbing the corporate ladder is a very strong motivator for young managers. The size of the steps in that ladder will affect the manager's performance in the firm. Consider the following discussion.

PAASCHE: Everyone in this firm wants to have some glorified title. My secretary wants to be called "administrative assistant." The parking attendant wants to be promoted to "garage manager." Where am I going to get all the money to pay for these promotions? Besides, I don't have enough high-level positions to go around.

LASPEYRES: They only want the titles. They probably don't even care about the money.

PAASCHE: That may or may not be true, but I care about the money. If I promote them, I must pay them.

LASPEYRES: I have an idea. You can give them the promotion without the raise. That will satisfy them.

PAASCHE: Your idea sounds disastrous. Can you imagine what the workers will say when I tell them that they are getting promoted, but that I don't want to pay them for the higher-level job? Some workers may even sue us under the Equal Pay Act.

LASPEYRES: How about creating another title and paying that title the same amount as you paid for their previous job? Financially, the move is lateral, but in the worker's minds, it will be viewed as a promotion.

PAASCHE: That sounds like cheating. Do you think they will fall for it?

LASPEYRES: Well, what's the purpose behind a promotion anyway? You want them to feel good about the job. You can make them feel good by giving them recognition and status rather than money. You don't even have to change the tasks that the workers perform; just change their titles and they'll be happy.

PAASCHE: The recognition point is a good one. But that means that I can't promote too many of the workers to the new job or it will lose its meaning.

LASPEYRES: Meaning in what sense?

PAASCHE: If everyone gets a promotion, the promotion has less value. Also, if everyone gets one, why should workers bother doing anything to distinguish themselves? They get the promotions anyway.

LASPEYRES: True. I think we need to think this through carefully. This could explode if we handle it wrong, especially in light of yesterday's announcement about the $6.8 million that Smith is getting this year.

PAASCHE: What do you mean?

LASPEYRES: Everyone is going to think we are swimming in money if we can pay the CEO that much, especially given our dismal performance this year. Between you and me, I don't think he's worth a tenth of what he's paid.

PAASCHE: True. I wouldn't mind having his job at that kind of money. When is some of this trickle-down stuff going to take effect, anyway?

LASPEYRES: Oh, come on Herm. Work hard, and the board will pick you over me to replace Smith when he retires. But back to more mundane issues, let's think about restructuring our job titles and filling them in the most productive way.

This discussion raises a number of issues. Among them:

- What does a promotion do for worker morale and effort?

- How many promotions should be given?

- What criteria should be used to determine promotions?

- How large a salary increase should a promotion carry?

- Are CEOs overpaid, and how can this be determined?

- What is the effect of promoting workers from within the firm, versus hiring outsiders into senior positions?

Underlying this discussion is the notion that there is some appropriate salary structure in the firm and that salary is somehow tied to the worker's level in the firm's hierarchy. How does a firm decide to choose that structure? Market competition must place some constraints on salary setting, but that can't be all of it. Workers will not necessarily leave a firm when their current wage is low. Career considerations are also important. Even a poorly paid worker may stay if a promotion implies a big raise and seems likely in the near future. This gives the firm some operating space. What should the firm do with it?

THE TOURNAMENT MODEL ◆ ◆ ◆ ◆ ◆

In order to think about raises and promotions, we introduce a framework that has come to be known as *tournament theory*.[1] The theory is easily described using the metaphor of a tennis match. Consider a tennis match between Agassi and Sampras. There are a few features of a tennis match that are relevant for thinking about the corporate hierarchical structure.

First, prizes are fixed in advance and are independent of absolute performance. Suppose that Sampras wins the match. He receives a predetermined prize and that prize does not depend on the amount by which he beats Agassi. Furthermore, both players may do exceedingly well and play an extremely tight contest. The total prize money will not be affected, nor will the distribution of prizes between contestants.

This description fits the operation of the typical firm. In many firms, slots are fixed in advance. Associated with each slot is a salary or salary range. For example, there may be one vice president slot and four assistant vice president slots. The person who becomes vice president receives the salary associated with the vice president's job. The tournament model, taken literally, implies that the pay that goes to the vice president is predetermined. It does not depend on how good the vice president is, reflected perhaps in the amount by which that person beat others competing for the job.

Second, a tennis player receives the winner's prize not by being good, but by being better than the other player. Relative performance, rather than absolute performance, is key. Sampras wins the top prize because he is better than Agassi, not because he is good, and it is the comparison between the two that is essential. Indeed, in top tennis tournaments, all players are inherently excellent. But of the group, one must be better than the others, at least on any given day.

The tennis tournament analogy also fits the modern corporation. Most of a typical firm's promotion activity is internal, being restricted to the incumbents in the level just below the job that is open. A worker is promoted not because he is good, but because he is better than everybody else at his current level. It is relative performance, not absolute performance, that matters.

Third, the level of effort with which the worker pursues the promotion depends on the size of the potential increase in his wage. Again, consider the tennis match. Suppose that the prize money totals $500,000. The prizes could be split evenly so that the winner gets $250,000 and the loser gets $250,000. Although nothing financially is gained by winning, players might still put forth a reasonable amount of effort because people like to win simply for pride, if nothing else. But if

---

[1]The theory was introduced in Lazear and Rosen (1981).

the prize money were distributed in a winner-take-all fashion, winning would become even more attractive. Not only would a player's pride be enhanced by winning, but he would find himself $500,000 richer than the loser as a reward for his effort. This suggests that the larger the spread between the winner's and loser's prizes, the higher the effort exerted by both players.

Turn now to the corporation. The winner receives the higher position. Along with the higher position comes a bigger salary. The spread is the difference between the higher salary and the lower salary that corresponds to the two positions. The larger the spread, the higher the effort that workers exert to get the job.

This is the key point of tournament theory. The larger the raise associated with a given promotion, the greater the incentive to be promoted. As a result, workers strive hard to obtain promotions that carry large raises. This means that the salary of the vice president acts not so much as motivation for the vice president as it does as motivation for the assistant vice presidents. Put somewhat differently, the vice president's salary is high not because it makes someone work as vice president, but because it induced someone to work hard as an *assistant* vice president. The vice president's salary is a reward to those who make it to the position for working hard when they were assistant vice presidents.

Further, the reward that takes the form of a high salary for vice presidents is not given because the corporation is altruistic. Far from it. The salary structure, with its implicit rewards from promotion, induces individuals to put forth more effort and thereby increases profits.

The final point that comes from the tournament model is that there is a limit to spread. Taken literally, the tournament model implies that contestants will exert more effort in a winner-take-all tournament than they will in one with a more equal split of the prize money. But corporations do not pay their assistant vice presidents nothing so that they can give all of labor's compensation to the vice president, or to the president. Even the most well-paid CEOs at large corporations still earn only a small percentage of the total wages paid in the firm. What limits the spread?

Firms use smaller spreads because the optimal amount of effort is not infinite. Recall from chapter 5 that when setting piece rates the goal was not to get workers to put forth the maximum amount of effort. More effort requires more pay. At some point, the amount of output produced by the additional effort does not cover the additional wages that must be paid in order to induce the effort. The same reason implied that optimal commission rates do not rise above 100 percent, and this applies to the tournament structure as well. Additional spread induces more effort, but the firm must pay higher average wages in order to get people to work in environments that have high effort requirements. At some point, it simply does not pay to induce people to work harder. The firm must pay too much for the additional effort to make it worthwhile. If increasing the spread increases the work effort, then at some point it pays to stop increasing the spread.

To illustrate the point, think back to ancient Rome, where the difference between the prize going to the winning gladiator and the prize going to losing gladiator was about as large as one could imagine. The problem was that people did not voluntarily sign up for the job. Gladiators had to be drafted into service. Although the spread was large, the average salary was not sufficiently large to induce people to risk their lives for the compensation. Given the amount of effort associated with the activity, and the size of the average prize, in this case life to the winner and death to the loser, gladiators had to be drafted into service.

Of course, it would be quite possible with the appropriate level of compensation to induce some people to volunteer. For example, a sufficiently large payment to one's heirs might induce some to be willing to compete for their lives. After all, that is exactly what happens when individuals volunteer for military campaigns. Although the level of effort is high, and the loser's prize is extremely negative, the gains from winning are sufficiently large to induce people to enlist. The primary conpensation received is the satisfaction derived from protection of one's homeland and citizens.

This is important because in the context of the firm, individuals must be induced to join the organization voluntarily. Not only must the spread be large enough to induce effort, but the average prize money must be sufficiently high to attract workers to come to the firm in the first place. Otherwise, workers will opt for some other activity.

Salary Structure and Effort

We begin by stating a principle

> The larger the spread between the winner's and loser's prizes, the greater the effort
> that contestants exert. In the context of the firm, the larger the raise associated with a
> promotion, the higher the effort that individuals exert to obtain the promotion.

A numerical example will help illustrate the mechanism. Consider the development department at a large aircraft manufacturer. Suppose that the firm wants to motivate their development group to produce plans for a new plane, the Mallard. The ten-year plan for the firm is to produce the Mallard within five years of start date. After that, work will begin on a smaller version of the same plane, called the Pigeon, also expected to take five years to completion.

To make things simple, suppose that the group assigned to this project consists of two engineers only, Katy and Joe. Both currently hold the title of research engineer and both are 55 years old. Assume that they have equal ability, energy and ambition. The engineer who does the best job on the Mallard will be named project head for the Pigeon. Consider the three wage structures given in Table 9.1.

The engineer eventually promoted to project head will have five years of earnings at the engineer level and five years of earnings at the project head level. Table 9.2 gives the total (remaining) lifetime salaries for engineers under the three wage structures. The interest rate is assumed to be zero for simplicity so that present value and sum of earnings are the same.

How do the firm and workers feel about the wage structures in Table 9.1? The firm and worker both care about two factors: average pay and the amount of effort

TABLE 9.1
ANNUAL SALARIES OF THE ENGINEERS

Structure	Salary of Research Engineer	Salary of Project Head
Structure A	$50,000	$200,000
Structure B	$50,000	$100,000
Structure C	$100,000	$250,000

induced by a particular wage structure. All else being equal, workers prefer higher average pay and the firm prefers lower average pay. The firm wants a wage structure that induces high effort from workers, and workers prefer that the wage structure does the opposite. That is, a worker would prefer to work less for any given wage, while the firm would prefer that the worker work more for any given wage.

First consider wage structures A and C. Wage structure C is higher than wage structure A. In C, engineers earn $100,000, whereas in A, they only earn $50,000. In C, project heads earn $250,000, whereas in A, they only earn $200,000. It is clear that worker would prefer C to A if the effort required were the same in both situations. The (remaining) lifetime earnings of an engineer is 10 × $50,000, or $500,000, in structure A, but 10 × $100,000, or $1,000,000, in structure C. This is shown in Table 9.2. So the "loser" does better in C than in A. Thus, lifetime earnings of the winner are:

Structure A   5 × $50,000 + 5 × $200,000 = $1,250,000
Structure C   5 × $100,000 + 5 × $250,000 = $1,750,000

Thus, winners receive more in C than A as well. Since each worker has a 50 percent chance of being the winner and a 50 percent chance of being the loser, the expected or average lifetime earnings are $875,000 in A and $1,375,000 in C. The spread between what the winner gets and what the loser gets is the same in both cases. In A, the winner earns $750,000 more over a lifetime than the loser. In C, the winner earns $750,000 more over a lifetime than the loser. This is shown in Table 9.2.

TABLE 9.2
TOTAL EARNINGS FOR WINNER AND LOSER

Structure	Total Earnings of Loser	Total Earnings of Winner	Difference between Winner and Loser Earnings	Average Remaining Lifetime Earnings
Structure A	$500,000	$1,250,000	$750,000	$875,000
Structure B	$500,000	$750,000	$250,000	$625,500
Structure C	$1,000,000	$1,750,000	$750,000	$1,375,000

How much effort would be put forth? The tournament story says that the effort level should be the same in both cases. The gain to winning is $750,000 in each case, so an engineer who gets promoted to project head increases his or her earnings power by the same amount in structure A as in structure C. Thus, engineers who are thinking about the value of working late should come up with the same answer whether the structure is A or C. Working late increases the chances that a given individual will get the promotion. The value of the promotion is directly related to the size of the raise. The size of the raise is the same in structure A as it is in structure C. If it pays to work late when the wage structure is A, then it pays to work late when the wage structure is C, and vice versa. Of course, the worker prefers C to A because effort is the same, but average salaries are higher in C. For the same reasons, firms prefer A to C. Effort levels are the same, and the amount that the firm pays is lower.

Bigger spreads create higher effort levels because each worker knows that the value of a promotion is greater. If Katy knows that Joe has gone home at 5 p.m., she can improve her chances of promotion by working late. She is more likely to work late when the promotion has higher value—that is, when the promotion yields a bigger raise. Suppose that Katy does stay late. The next day, Joe arrives at work to find that Katy has already shown the results of her evening's endeavors to the associate vice president. The next night, Joe also stays late. Because the promotion has high value, he decides to put forth the extra effort, knowing that the promotion is likely to be lost unless he matches Katy's effort. Now that Joe is working extra hours, Katy cannot slack off. Doing so would result in a lower probability of promotion, and promotions carry big raises. Thus, Katy and Joe get into a *rat race*, working long hours as they compete with one another for the same prize.[2]

Of course, both Katy and Joe would like to agree to work only until 5 p.m. The problem is that if Katy goes home, Joe has every incentive to stay, perhaps hiding his extra effort from Katy, but making it visible to the associate vice president. The agreement to slack off is difficult to enforce. This difficulty rises as the number of individuals competing for the same job rises. In any reasonably sized group, there is likely to be one person who will deviate from the collusive strategy.

Returning to our example, note that structure C induces the same effort as structure A, but costs the firm more. Why would a firm ever offer structure C over structure A? The answer is simple. A worker's willingness to take a job depends on how much he or she gets paid and how much work is required. Since both A and C induce the same amount of work, they differ only on the amount of pay offered. If a firm can attract the relevant quality workers with wage structure A, then this is what the firm will and should pay. Offering C would be unprofitable, because the firm would be overpaying its workers. Conversely, if the firm cannot attract the workers with A, but can with C, then the firm has to make a decision. It can pay

---

[2]Rebitzer, Landers and Taylor (1996) argue that this occurs in law firms as workers rush to obtain promotions.

the higher wages or it can do without the workers. As long as the workers' output exceeds the wage, it pays for the firm to offer the higher salaries. Otherwise, the answer is clear. The firm does without the workers.

Structure *B* does make choice more difficult. Of the three salary structures, *B* pays the lowest amount. But the spread between the winner's salary and loser's salary is also the smallest in *B*. This means that effort is less with salary structure *B* than it is with either *A* or *C*. When a worker is trying to decide whether to work late, structures *A* and *C* offer a $750,000 lifetime premium to the winner. Structure *B* offers only a $250,000 premium to the winner, as is shown in Table 9.2. Consequently, workers are more enthusiastic about getting the project head position when either structure *A* or *C* prevails than when *B* is in effect. Structure *B* also pays a lower average wage than either *A* or *C*. Engineers get $50,000, which is the same as in structure *A*, but project heads receive only $100,000, which is considerably less than that received in either *A* or *C*. Do workers prefer *A* or *B*? Structure *A* pays more, but structure *A* induces and thereby requires higher levels of effort. When *A* is paid, the job is harder than it is when *B* is paid. Both workers put forth more effort in their quest for the winner's prize when *A* is paid than when *B* is paid. But workers expect to earn more with structure *A* than with structure *B*. Is it worth it? This depends on workers' views about effort. If workers find effort especially painful, they would prefer the lower paying job that induces less effort than the higher paying, higher effort job. If the reverse is true, then they prefer *A* to *B*. Since workers prefer *C* to *A*, any worker who prefers *A* to *B* also prefers *C* to *B*. The reverse is not true. Workers might prefer *B* to *A*, but *C* is always preferred to *B*. Structure *C* is preferred to *B* because under *C*, even if the worker puts forth no effort and loses, he will be paid more than under *B*. The loser's prize in *C* equals the winner's prize in *B*.

The employer views the situation differently, but not exactly the reverse. Whether the employer prefers *B* over *A* depends on the amount of additional output that the employer receives when structure *A* is used. If *A* induces sufficiently more effort, then it may pay to offer *A* over *B*. The higher average level of compensation could be more than offset by the higher average level of output. If this is not true, then the employer will prefer the lower effort level induced by *B* and pay the correspondingly lower wages. If the employer prefers *B* to A, then it surely prefers *B* to *C* since *C* induces the same effort as A, but at a higher cost. However, even if the employer prefers *A* to *B* because the additional effort justifies the cost, it does not necessarily imply that the employer prefers *C* to *B*. Structure *C* may cost so much more than *A* that the output gain relative to *B* does not cover the cost increase, even though it does for *A*.

In summary, a salary structure has two features. The first is its level. Some salary structures are higher than other salary structures. Other things being equal, firms prefer lower salary structures, and workers prefer higher salary structures. Thus, other things being equal, the firm prefers salary structure *A* to salary structure *C*, whereas the workers prefer salary structure *C* to salary structure *A*. Of course, other things are not equal. Firms must attract workers in a competitive labor market. Although the firm may prefer to pay structure A, structure *A* may not attract any qualified workers. The firm may be forced, therefore, to offer compensation structure C.

The second feature of the salary structure is the spread. The spread refers to the difference between the salaries that high and low level employees receive. The higher the spread, the more anxious is any given employee to obtain a promotion to the higher level job. When the high-level job pays very little more than the low-level job, promotions have less value. When the high-level job pays a great deal more than the low-level job, promotions have more value. Then each worker puts forth more effort in an attempt to secure the higher-level job. This results in a higher overall level of effort as workers are forced into a rat race to attempt to win the higher position. The benefit of the rat race is that it produces higher levels of effort and therefore higher levels of output for the firm as a whole. The cost is that since workers are putting forth more additional effort, they must be compensated accordingly. It is unreasonable to expect that workers will put forth high levels of effort when the *level* of the compensation structure is low. Thus, structure A and structure C both induce workers to put forth the same level of effort because they each imply a spread of $150,000 per year in salary. But at the high level of effort, engineers may simply be unwilling to work for the firm when the wage structure is A. On the other hand, since structure C offers considerably more compensation (to both the winner and loser) it is quite possible that the high level of effort is compatible with structure C and not with structure A. Structure B induces a lower level of effort and pays lower overall wages. It may be possible to attract workers by offering structure B, because they know that the wages are low, but the level of effort is also low.

Luck

The amount of luck or **noise** inherent in the promotion process affects the appropriate salary structure. Noise can result from a number of factors, the most common of which are production uncertainty and measurement error.

Production uncertainty occurs when workers who put forth high effort levels still produce low output. In such a case, the noise (or luck) is negative. An example would be a manager whose work force comes down with the flu on the day that an important project is due. The manager might have organized the work force appropriately and put forth all the appropriate effort. The flu was simply a negative random factor that was both unanticipated and uncontrollable. Sometimes noise can be positive. A project manager may be in the fortunate situation of having the government release a contract for the goods that the firm produces at exactly the right moment. The letting of the government contract has nothing to do with the manager's effort, but simply reflects good luck.

An alternative source of noise is measurement error. Some workers may put forth a great deal of effort, but may be perceived, inappropriately, by their superior to be only mediocre performers. It is also possible that the boss mistakenly ascribes high performance to a worker who is not performing well at all.

How does noise affect worker effort? The answer is the higher the noise, the lower the level of effort. The reason is that noise reduces the value of effort by reducing the probability of winning a promotion. We can reformulate this point as a general principle.

> Worker effort declines as the probability of promotion depends less on effort and more on other factors. When promotions are heavily influenced by luck, the tendency toward reduced effort can be offset by increasing wage spreads between high level and low level jobs.

To elaborate, let us return to the metaphor of the tennis match. Suppose that Agassi and Sampras were playing their tournament in a hurricane. There would be a great deal of noise associated with the outcome of the contest. Whether Agassi or Sampras won a particular point would depend largely on how the wind happened to be blowing. Effort would have almost no effect on outcome. As a result, Sampras and Agassi might as well give up and let luck determine the outcome of the match. Neither Agassi nor Sampras could do much about affecting their probability of winning and would reduce their levels of effort.

This happens in corporations as well. When supervisors are capricious and award promotions to individuals on the basis of factors that are beyond their control, workers tend to give up. Similarly, if one particular manager's effort has very little effect on the actual output on which a promotion is based, then the incentive to put forth effort is diminished. Tournaments motivate people when the participants feel that the outcome is a direct consequence of their effort. When the link between output and reward is broken, worker effort declines.

When luck is important, it is necessary to offset the decline in effort by using a larger spread. Thus, in the previous example, if structure B would have been appropriate in an environment without measurement noise, then structure A may be required when measurement noise is present. Noisier or more random production environments are associated with larger salary differences between highly placed individuals and those holding lower-level jobs. The larger salary differences help offset the downward effect of noise on effort. Thus, some firms may have a more widely varying wage structure simply as a reflection of underlying uncertainty in the production process. A numerical example illustrates the point.

Suppose that Joe and Katy, the research engineers in the previous example, each decide to become independent contractors. Their former employer declares bankruptcy. But the U.S. government offers a prize of $2 million to the engineer who comes up with the best design for the Mallard. Joe and Katy are the only two engineers in the running to win the prize. Table 9.3 provides some information on work effort and the likelihood of winning.

The number of hours worked by a given individual are listed in the first column. In the second column is the probability that the given researcher, either Katy or Joe, wins as a function of the number of hours that he or she works. That is, if Katy does not change the number of hours that she works and Joe increases his hours worked from 2,500 to 3,000, he increases his probability of winning from .06 to .09. This means an increase in the probability of winning of .03, which is shown in the third column of Table 9.3.

TABLE 9.3
HOURS OF WORK AND PROBABILITY OF
WINNING THE GOVERNMENT PRIZE

Hours Worked	Prob	Δ prob
1500	0.00	
2000	0.03	0.03
2500	0.06	0.03
3000	0.09	0.03
3500	0.11	0.02
4000	0.14	0.03
4500	0.16	0.02
5000	0.18	0.02
5500	0.20	0.02
6000	0.22	0.02
6500	0.24	0.02
7000	0.26	0.02
7500	0.28	0.02
8000	0.30	0.02
8500	0.32	0.02
9000	0.34	0.02
9500	0.36	0.02
10000	0.38	0.02
10500	0.40	0.02
11000	0.42	0.02
11500	0.44	0.02
12000	0.46	0.02
12500	0.48	0.02
13000	0.50	0.02
13500	0.51	0.01
14000	0.52	0.01
14500	0.53	0.01

What is the return to winning? The winner of the competition receives a government prize of $2 million. Thus, the expected return from increasing hours from 2,500 to 3,000 is

$$(.09 - .06) \times \$2 \text{ million} = \$60,000$$

Anyone who is risk-neutral (i.e., would accept a **fair bet**) would judge the value of the increase in probability this way. This is equivalent to a lottery. If there were 100 tickets, then the value of all 100 tickets would be $2 million, since the owner of all the tickets would be certain to win the lottery. The value of zero tickets is $0 because anyone with no tickets is certain to lose the lottery. The value of 50 tickets is $1 million, because a holder of 50 tickets would win the lottery half of the time. If someone played the lottery over and over again, buying 50 tickets each time, the average win would be $1 million per lottery—$2 million half of the time and nothing half of the time. By extension, owning 9 of the 100 tickets would be worth $180,000, because over the long haul, the owner of 9 tickets per lottery would win an average of $180,000 per lottery. Also, owning 6 of the 100 tickets would be worth $120,000 because the owner would expect to win $120,000 per lottery. Thus, increasing one's tickets from 6 to 9 would be worth $60,000. So increasing the probability of winning the government contract from .06 to .09 has a value of $60,000.

Katy and Joe can each earn $75 per hour working as consultants for other aircraft manufacturers. Thus, when Joe spends 500 hours chasing the prize, he forgoes

$$500 \times \$75 = \$37,500$$

It pays, therefore, for Joe to increase hours from 2,000 to 2,500, because the expected return is $60,000 and the cost is only $37,500. In fact, it pays for Joe to increase his hours worked on the project up to 13,000 hours. Every block of 500 hours raises Joe's chance of winning the prize by at least .02 up through 13,000 hours. This means that the expected return is at least $40,000 for each block of 500 hours up to 13,000 hours, but the cost in terms of forgone earnings is only $37,500. It is worthwhile to continue working to win the government prize up to 13,000 hours. But it does not pay to go beyond 13,000 hours. The next block of 500 hours only raises the probability of winning by .01, which has an expected return of (.01)($2 million)=$20,000. Since Joe can sell these 500 hours as consulting time for $37,500, he is better off spending hours beyond 13,000 working for others. Joe therefore stops when his probability of winning the prize is just 50 percent. Note that the probability of winning need not be 50 percent for every contestant. The 50 percent result is a function of the numbers chosen for this example and the fact that there are two identical contestants competing for the prize.

Katy goes through a similar thought process. If Katy and Joe have identical ability and identical outside opportunities, then the decision that Katy makes will mimic Joe's. She, too, will spend 13,000 hours chasing the prize. Each will end up with a 50 percent chance of winning after having spent 6.5 years (13,000 hours) on the Mallard project.

What would happen if the government award were actually determined by a pure lottery? That is, what if Katy and Joe's name were simply put on two slips of paper, tossed into a fishbowl, and then drawn by a blindfolded government bureaucrat? How many hours would Katy and Joe devote to the project? The answer is none. Since hours of work would have absolutely no effect on the probability of winning, it would be pointless to put forth any effort. Katy and Joe would simply spend their time consulting for other firms and hoping for the best on the government drawing. When the outcome of the contest is independent of effort, no effort is exerted.

When noise is infinite (as in a lottery), effort goes to zero, but the situation need not be so extreme. To understand the significance of noise, simply imagine that each contestant is given one ticket per hour worked. In the case where Katy and Joe were each to work 13,000 hours, each would hold 13,000 out of 26,000 tickets, corresponding to a 50 percent chance of winning. Now suppose that in addition to one ticket per hour worked, each contestant is given 5 million tickets.

There are a total of 10 million tickets, plus the tickets reflecting hours worked by both Katy and Joe, but now each hour worked has only a trivial effect on the probability of winning. Most of the probability is wrapped up in the 10 million tickets that are given independent of effort. This is analogous to adding noise to the environment. When the probability of winning depends primarily on factors other than effort, the incentive to put forth effort declines dramatically. Since each hour has only a trivial effect on the probability of winning, the expected return to each hour worked is very close to zero. It would be impossible to work, say, a million hours, but anything less than a million hours has only a small impact on the probability of winning. As a result, contestants will be induced to spend their time consulting rather than working toward winning the prize.

What can be done to offset the tendency of excess luck or noise to kill off effort? The immediate answer is to increase the spread in order to mitigate the effort-reducing effects of luck. For example, if the government prize were $10 million, instead of $2 million, then the expected return to every hour worked would go up by a factor of five. The spread between the winner's prize at $10 million and the loser's prize at zero would serve as a motivator, even in the presence of significant luck. Of course, this would require that the government put out considerably more money for a given prize.

A firm would prefer to induce high levels of effort without putting out much more money, but this, too, is possible. Recall that it is the spread that affects the amount of effort that an individual is willing to put into an activity. The average level of the prize determines whether people are willing to work at all. A spread of $10 million could be created, even with only $2 million in prize money. This would necessitate that each contestant put up $4 million in order to enter the contest. The winner of the contest would take home the $2 million prize money plus the other individual's ante of $4 million and would receive his own ante back in return. The loser would get back nothing and would have lost the ante of $4 million. Thus, the loser comes out with $-$4 million, and the winner comes out with $6 million, creating a spread of $10 million.

While there are companies that could, and might be willing to, put up $4 million as an ante, few individuals could do so. Antes are not unheard of in business propositions. When venture capitalists fund new start-ups, they often require that the inventors put up almost all of their wealth as collateral. Even though the wealth of the inventors is a very small amount relative to the total cost of the project, the loss of that wealth to the inventors would impose significant costs on them and thereby provides substantial incentive effects.

In the context of the firm, the spread can be increased by lowering the loser's salary relative to the winner's salary. Thus, for example, one wage structure could pay a vice president $300,000 and an assistant vice president $100,000. Another structure could pay the vice president $250,000 and the assistant vice president $150,000. If there were one of each position, the average compensation would be the same. But the spread would be larger in the first case than in the second. It would cost the firm no more to use the first compensation scheme than the second one, but the first one would produce more effort. Of course, the higher level of effort is disliked by the workers and generally must be compensated for in the form of higher average salary.

Comparisons

The point that luck matters and affects the optimal salary structure has implications for the way that compensation structures vary by industry or country. Consider, for example, the difference between the United States and Japan. The Japanese wage structure is more compressed than the American wage structure. Top executives in Japan get paid less relative to production workers than do their counterparts in the United States. Some have interpreted this as extravagance on the part of American firms or, worse yet, as a subtle form of graft, where CEOs are able to convince their boards that they are entitled to higher salaries than they indeed deserve. Although we may not be able to completely rule out these explanations, there is an alternative. It may simply be that the American environment is riskier than the Japanese environment. Promotions in the United States may depend more on random factors than they do in Japan. This is likely for a number of reasons. First, promotions in Japan come later in life than they do in the United States. Although there are many American CEOs in their forties and even some in their thirties, the Japanese firm tends to wait much longer before choosing an individual to be its CEO. By the time a Japanese manager has made CEO, the firm has very clear signals on productivity. It is unlikely that measurement error or factors such as luck will play an important role in determining the choice of CEO. On the other hand, in the United States decisions are made earlier and workers are more mobile. It is possible that noise plays a larger role in American promotions. If promotions in the United States are more heavily influenced by luck, then American firms optimally offset the effort-reducing effects of luck by choosing larger salary spreads. This could show up as less wage compression in the United States than in Japan.

It could be perfectly rational for Japanese firms to use more compressed salary structures than American firms. Neither extreme is necessarily inappropriate. Rather, each set of salary structures might be the best response by firms in that country, given the noise levels that their workers encounter.

A similar point could be made with respect to new versus old industries. If extraneous luck factors are more important in affecting an individual's performance in new industries than in old industries, then new industries would tend to have higher variance in their salary structures. Thus, start-up companies and firms in high-tech, as a result of "newness" and the implied randomness, would have a more variable salary structure than older, more established industries.

More important, firms setting up salary structures should take into account that the wage spread affects worker incentives differently, depending on the amount of luck involved. If the environment is one where luck is extremely important, then a firm should select a higher wage spread.

ARCHITECTS AND NEW PRODUCT DEVELOPMENT
◆ ◆ ◆ ◆ ◆ ◆ ◆ ◆ ◆ ◆

All or nothing tournaments, where the work of losing teams is discarded and only the work of the winning team is utilized, may appear wasteful and unrealistic. Yet, in practice one encounters numerous examples of such tournaments. For instance, it is common practice to announce a competition in order to select the best design for a landmark building. The San Francisco Museum of Modern Art and Vietnam War Memorial in Washington are a few high-profile examples of successful tournament use. Typically, each architect who participates in a competition of this type has to develop an original design and construct a model that illustrates his or her vision for the project. Of course, only the work of the winner of the contest ends up being utilized, and only the winner gets the prize. This seemingly wasteful practice prevails because such tournaments are the most efficient way to encourage outstanding design. The cost of developing a design and constructing a model of a building is negligible compared to the cost of constructing the building itself. If a tournament of this type results in even a slightly better building, the tournament is well worth the extra expense because the cost of designing and constructing a model is very small as compared with the construction cost. In some instances, the difference between the top design and the second design is immense—it may be a difference between a masterpiece and a solid piece of work.

Architecture is not the only field where tournaments are used. Less explicit use of tournaments is not uncommon in product development. A firm that wants to develop a new product sometimes has a few teams of engineers independently designing the same product. Again, only one design will be used. Although both teams are on the firm's payroll, the engineers of the winning team are likely to receive a bonus and/or a promotion.

Today, most high-tech companies face fierce competition, which allows firms to assess the quality of the work of their development teams by comparing their products to the products of their competitors. In the days when IBM had a near monopoly position in the computer industry, Big Blue found it difficult to evaluate the work of its development teams. In order to deal with this problem, IBM occasionally put two teams to work on exactly the same project simultaneously. Each of the two competing teams was trying to win by making a superior product in the shortest possible time.

One such example involves the development of the 4300 series of main-frames by IBM. Two competing teams with identical objectives were located at the different corners of the world. One was based in Boeblingen and the other in Endicott. The competition was dead even, and eventually the design from Endicott was used to build the 4341 (the high-end machine), whereas the design from Boeblingen was used to build the 4331 (the low-end version). Both teams were building machines according to the same specifications; consequently, the benefit from having two designs was probably minimal. The real value of the tournament was in creating an incentive to develop the machine as quickly as possible.

◆◆◆◆◆ TOURNAMENTS AND THE ORGANIZATIONAL CHART

The basic principles illustrated by tournament theory are quite straightforward. The larger the wage spread, the bigger the premium to winning and, therefore, the more effort workers exert. Also, the more important luck and measurement error are in determining a winner, the less effective the tournament in motivating a worker. While these principles are quite appealing, how can they be put into practice? Specifically, how might one determine whether a firm had an appropriate or an inappropriate salary structure? Some intuition can be gleaned from a firm's organizational chart. Consider Figure 9.1.

The figure shows the top three levels of the firm's hierarchy. The president earns $350,000 a year. There are 6 executive vice presidents, each of whom earns $300,000 a year, and 12 vice presidents, each earning $150,000 a year. If each of the executive vice presidents is identical in ability and ambition, then each would have a 1/6th chance of making it to president. The raise associated with getting the promotion to president is $50,000 a year, so each individual would have a 1/6th shot at a $50,000 a year raise.

Consider the next level. There are 12 vice president and 6 executive vice president slots. This means that each vice president eventually has a 50 percent chance of making it to executive vice president. Furthermore, the salary goes from $150,000 a year to $300,000 a year when an individual is promoted to executive vice president. Thus, each vice president has a 50 percent chance at getting a $150,000 raise. Of course, what is relevant is not so much the chance of receiving a promotion, but rather the effect of effort on *changing* the chances of receiving a promotion. Still, with a structure like the one shown in Figure 9.1, it is unlikely that the executive vice presidents are going to feel particularly motivated, and our expectation is that the vice presidents have greater incentives to put forth effort than the executive vice presidents. A consultant could take a quick look at this hi-

FIGURE 9.1

AN EXAMPLE OF A SALARY
STRUCTURE

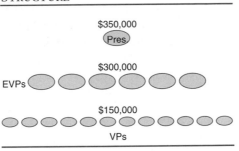

erarchical structure and determine that something is wrong at one of the three levels. The most likely scenario is that the president is underpaid, or that the executive vice presidents are overpaid.

There are other aspects of the firm's incentive structure that can be gleaned from looking at simple diagrams of the firm's hierarchy. Consider Figure 9.2.

The two panels represent two salary structures that might be observed in a typical firm. There are two things to notice. First, salary structure 2 has a larger spread than salary structure 1. Salary structure 2 has a bottom wage that is lower than the bottom wage of salary structure 1, and a top wage that is higher than the top wage of salary structure 1. Thus, the spread is larger. Furthermore, the jumps are more or less uniform in salary structure 1, but they are very different in salary structure 2. In salary structure 1, the absolute level of the raise in going from job level 1 to job level 2 is about the same as the absolute level of the raise in going

FIGURE 9.2

TWO COMPENSATION STRUCTURES

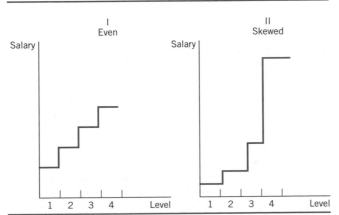

from 2 to 3, which is the same as the absolute level of the raise in going from 3 to 4. In salary structure 2, however, the raise that workers receive when they are promoted from 3 to 4 is much greater in absolute terms than the raise that they receive when being promoted from level 1 to 2.

Salary structure 2 is much more typical than salary structure 1. The big jumps at the end are there for a purpose. There are a couple of ways to rationalize very large wage increases at the top of the hierarchy. We leave until later chapters arguments that are based on high-level jobs being riskier or more demanding than lower-level jobs. Here, we consider incentive reasons for this asymmetric structure. Again, consider the metaphor of the tennis match. When an individual wins the quarter-finals, he accomplishes two things. First, he guarantees himself the prize associated with winning the quarter-finals and second, he gives himself the opportunity to play in the next round of the tournament. If he goes on to win the semifinals, he not only guarantees himself the prize associated with the semifinals, but also gets the opportunity to play in the finals. These additional opportunities are valuable, since they carry with them some probability that the individual may, in fact, win the championship prize. Indeed, it is possible that individuals would put forth effort in the quarter-finals, even if the winner and loser of the quarter-finals received exactly the same prize. Since the winner has the right to compete in the next round, and the next round might have some additional value, winning the quarter-finals has value. It is this "option" value of competing in the subsequent rounds that provides additional motivation to individuals at lower levels of the tournament. But when the individual reaches the final round, there is no longer any option value. Winning the championship of the tournament is the end of the story. All the winner can hope to receive at that point is the championship prize. It does not provide an option to play a super-championship round.

In the corporation, being promoted from file clerk to clerical supervisor not only provides the worker with a higher salary, but it also allows him to compete for subsequent jobs. Thus, the promotion has value even if file clerks and clerical supervisors earn exactly the same amount. As the individual moves toward the top of the hierarchy, the option value diminishes. In the very last round, the winner gets the CEO's salary and only the CEO's salary. Becoming CEO does not carry with it any additional option value. As such, it is necessary to put all the prize money into the CEO's salary. Individuals will not work hard to win the CEO's prize on the basis of the additional opportunities it affords. As a practical matter, becoming CEO is the end of the story. There are few further opportunities that will be presented after that.[3] Firms that have symmetric structures, like those shown in panel 1 of Figure 9.2, are likely to be using some

---

[3]The argument here is based on Rosen (1986). It is possible, of course, that becoming CEO does provide some additional opportunities that would not otherwise be there. But since most promotions to this level are internal, the major reward comes from higher salary, with very little based on prospects of jumping to other higher paying jobs.

other form of worker motivation such as piecerate pay or compensation on the basis of effort. Firms that reward workers on relative performance rather than absolute performance are more likely to have structures like the one shown in panel 2.

EMPIRICAL EVIDENCE ◆ ◆ ◆ ◆ ◆

It is difficult to observe the effects of tournament-like pay structures on effort because in cases where tournaments are used, neither effort nor output is easily observed. If effort or output could be observed easily, then the case for using a relative performance-based incentive scheme would be diminished. There is, however, one arena in which output is easily measured and in which the tournament pay structure is explicit—professional sports. Some economists have examined the effect of compensation in sports tournaments on performance of the players. Ehrenberg and Bognanno (1990) look at data from the Professional Golfers' Association and relate the quality of play to the structure of compensation. Their results are strongly supportive of tournament theory, and indeed somewhat surprising. One would think that golfers would put forth maximum effort in every tournament, but Ehrenberg and Bognanno find that the same golfer achieves better average scores on the same course when the difference between the winner's prize and the loser's prize is great. Apparently, knowing that much is at stake helps focus a golfer's concentration to the point that a pattern of better scores in high-spread contests can actually be observed.

In another series of studies, Knoeber (1989) has looked at chicken farming and found that compensation of chicken farmers fits the tournament model. Because a major factor in raising chickens is weather, and because weather affects farmers in the same region in a similar way, individuals compete against one another and take compensation that is based on relative performance. They are compensated in this way because the relative compensation incentives motivate the farmers without making them subject to the kind of risk that variations in weather can produce.

Drago and Garvey (1997) use data from Australian firms. They find the effort increases and absenteeism is reduced when firms give larger raises upon promotion. Workers recognize the value of large raises and are more likely to come to work.

Finally, a number of experiments have been run using university students as subjects. Experimenters set up situations that resemble tournaments. By varying the prizes, they can induce the subjects to behave in ways that are completely consistent with the tournament model. In particular, when the spread between the winner's prize and the loser's prize is increased, students put forth more "effort." Further, the amount of effort put forth by each student converges quickly to the precise amount predicted by tournament theory.[4]

---

[4] See Bull, Schotter, and Weigelt (1987).

THE EVOLVING TOURNAMENT OF LAWYERS
♦ ♦ ♦ ♦ ♦ ♦ ♦ ♦ ♦ ♦

The "up or out" promotion scheme of most law firms is a good example of the tournament model in action. The jump from associate to partner (the most significant rung in the legal corporate ladder) yields many rewards: more than double an associate's annual income, as well as a bigger office, better secretary, etc. Of course, the firm announces only a set number of promotions to partner, which is generally less than the number of eligible associates. Of this pool of potential partners, those who are not promoted are asked to leave: those who do not move up move out. The set number of promotions, the large reward for success, and the high price of failure create a competitive scenario which is designed to motivate associates to give their all for the firm.

However, the Chicago firm of Winston and Strawn inserted another rung into the ladder: the income partner. The income partner earns between $100,000 and $200,000 annually—about halfway between the associate's salary and the junior partners. These partners can sign opinion letters, negotiate business, and do many of the other activities normally reserved for full partners. The only difference is that they are salaried employees, and do not earn a share of net profits. Those income partners who distinguish themselves at this new level by bringing in a significant amount of new business—the "rainmakers"—will then be promoted to full partner. Those who do not are permitted to stay on as income partners . . .

What are the incentive effects of this new scheme? Promotions to non-equity partner are still limited and specified beforehand, and the promotion still carries a sizable raise, an increase in responsibilities and prestige, and a significant "option value" associated with the possibility of promotion to full partner. However, the price of losing has decreased somewhat: talented lawyers who can't create business are no longer pushed out of the firm. While the incentive structure has been weakened by limiting the downside in this way, the need to keep both rainmakers and lawyers with technical expertise on board in a more competitive business environment limits the extent to which up or out policies could be continued—the income partner represents an effective compromise.

Source: S. Torry, "Economics Pushes Some Firms to Tiers," *Washington Post* (March 4, 1996), pF7.

ABSOLUTE PERFORMANCE AND
RELATIVE PERFORMANCE

◆ ◆ ◆ ◆ ◆

Piece rate pay is based on absolute performance. An individual salesperson gets commissions that are a function of only his or her own sales and are independent of what other people sell. Relative compensation, which comes about as individuals are promoted over their peers, provides incentives by creating competition (either explicit or implicit) within an organization. Both methods provide incentives. Each has its advantages and disadvantages.

When should relative compensation be used over absolute compensation as a motivator? Incentives based on promotion and relative comparisons have two advantages over incentives that are generated by paying on the basis of absolute performance. First, it is sometimes easier to observe relative performance than it is to observe absolute performance. Consider the example of coal miners who must go into a shaft in the morning and mine coal. The miners could be paid on the amount of coal that they bring out at the end of the day. One possibility is to have a scale at the site to weigh the coal. Miners would be paid on the basis of the coal's weight. An alternative is simply to compare the piles of coal produced by each of the miners. The one with the largest pile of coal gets the top prize. The one with the smallest pile of coal gets the booby prize. It might be cheaper simply to examine the piles of coal than it is to weigh each one carefully. Saving on measurement costs can be an important reason to use relative compensation as a motivator. In this example, the cost differences seem small. There are other cases, however, where the cost differences may not be small, particularly for measurement of managerial employees.

Sometimes output is difficult to define, let alone measure. Consider, for example, two managers in the information systems department of a large corporation. It is clear that their output has something to do with providing information in an efficient and timely manner to other members of the firm. Because the nature of information requests or programming demands may vary over time, it would be difficult to specify in advance an objective measure of output. In these circumstances, promotions serve as the best motivator. It may be difficult to know what it is that any individual produces, but it may be relatively easy to know that whatever it is they produce, Chris does a better job at it than Shannon. When relative comparisons are easy to make, promotions should be used as the primary motivator.

Another reason to use promotions and relative compensation as the major motivator is that relative compensation eliminates the effect of luck on reward, when luck is common to the individuals being judged. This was already discussed in the context of chicken farmers. Since weather is a component that has a large effect on output, and since weather is beyond the control of any of the individual farmers, its effect would be to diminish incentives. However, since weather affects all farmers in the same region in a similar way, relative comparisons are unaffected by variations in weather over time. If the weather is very hot, then all farmers in the region suffer similarly. Basing a promotion on relative comparisons does not add noise or luck to outcomes and thereby serves to improve incentives.

Other examples abound. When business conditions are highly variable and beyond the control of individual workers, luck is important and diminishes incentives. To offset these effects, promotions can be based on relative performance. If conditions are bad for one worker, then they tend to be bad for another worker as well. Since the firm must choose one worker to promote, being in a bad economy will not adversely affect the rewards given to any given worker. As such, the firm bears the risk and removes this common component of luck from the individual reward structure. This improves the incentives for the workers involved.

Another reason to prefer tournaments involves measurement risk that can be introduced by relying on subjective supervisory evaluation. Suppose that workers are compensated on the basis of annual evaluations, which are the responsibility of their supervisors. A worker who happens to draw a supervisor with a positive attitude may receive high praise and enjoy large raises each year. The same worker assigned to a supervisor with a much more negative outlook would receive poorer ratings and therefore lower raises. The individual's performance could be identical in both cases, and yet compensation would vary based on the subjective evaluation of the supervisor. Workers who are risk averse do not like having their compensation vary as a result of chance. Being lucky or unlucky in the draw of a supervisor would have a negative effect on incentives.

An easy way around this problem is to give each supervisor the right to promote a fixed number of workers. Then, even supervisors who are tougher graders must choose some workers to promote over others. While a supervisor may think all of the workers are terrible, the requirement that they be ranked removes the variation in pay that results from drawing supervisors with negative or positive outlooks.

This example points out that the way in which the tournaments are organized can have an important effect on incentives. In the previous scenario, if supervisors were not constrained to select a given number of workers for promotion, relative compensation would not remove this common source of luck. Some supervisors would simply recommend very few individuals for promotion and others would recommend a large number for promotion. This would introduce the same elements of luck that we were trying to eliminate in the first place. In the previous scenario, it was important to require that each supervisor promote a given number of workers. Although the number need not have been the same across supervisors, the supervisor could not be given discretion over the number to be promoted. Once the number is specified, most luck is removed from the outcome.

The same point applies to other forms of compensation that are based on relative positions. Consider, for example, annual bonuses that are handed out to workers. Suppose a firm sets up a pool of bonus money to be given only to those workers who are deemed exceptional. As before, those supervisors who are positive about life might tend to recommend many of their workers for bonuses, while those who are negative might recommend very few. One possible solution could be to assign a pool of bonus money to each supervisor. This would eliminate some of the problem, but not all. Although positive and negative outlooks on life would not affect whether or not a worker received a bonus, another tendency could creep into the system. Supervisors might want to smooth the bonuses, so as to cause the least amount of unhappiness among the work force. At the extreme, the supervisor, whether positive or negative in outlook, could simply take the entire pool of bonus money and divide it evenly among all the workers. This would then eliminate any incentive effects of the bonus pool itself.

In order to prevent the supervisor from taking this action, the firm must constrain the way in which bonuses are handed out. Rather than giving the supervisors a pool of money to be allocated as they see fit, management must attach conditions to the bonus money. For example, management could give each supervisor a $100,000 pool of bonus money, but insist that one individual receive $50,000, one individual receive $25,000, two receive $10,000, one receive $5,000 and the rest receive nothing. Again, this would force the supervisor to make choices, thereby providing incentives and removing any sources of common luck from the structure.

We have enumerated two major advantages to using promotions or other forms of relative compensation. Two disadvantages of using relative pay are collusion and the opposite problem, competition.

When pay is based on relative performance, both workers would prefer to put forth less effort and simply split the winner's prize. If workers can collude to shirk, both will be better off. Collusion is less likely to occur in situations where there is a large number of potential winners and when the parties do not know all of the contestants. This is one reason for hiring from the outside on occasion. Reserving the right to hire an outsider gives notice that collusion will not be tolerated. If all internal candidates are deemed to have put up a sufficiently poor showing, then the firm hires an outsider. Since the identity of the outsider is not known in advance, collusion is prevented among the insiders, who know that all parties cannot be included.

Similarly, as the number of individuals in the competition increases, it becomes more difficult for workers to collude with one another. When there are a large number of potential candidates, it is more difficult to get all of them to reduce their effort and split the proceeds. Since workers always have an incentive to say that they will abide by the agreement, but then to deviate from it, enforcement of collusion is difficult in large groups.

The second problem is the opposite one. Workers who are paid on the basis of relative performance have incentives to be too competitive with one another. One worker my fail to cooperate with another because he does not want the other worker to gain recognition. If workers are paid on the basis of absolute performance, there is no incentive to be uncooperative. Cooperation is good for the firm, even if not for an individual worker. The next chapter will discuss the industrial politics that result from competition.

Sorting

The competition that takes place in an organization serves a sorting function as well as an incentive function. Sometimes it is important to find out who should be assigned to which job. Some individuals have skills that make them better suited to some positions than to others. A tournament is one of the best ways to perform this sorting function. By having individuals compete with one another, and then having winners compete with other winners, eventually the comparisons end up sorting individuals to their best use. Obviously, mistakes are made by this process, but the relative comparison aspect is extremely useful in determining who should hold which job. There are two principles that are important to remember when using intra-firm competition as a sorting technique.

> The longer the period before the promotion decision is made, the higher the likelihood that the most able individual wins the promotion. The tradeoff is that waiting to promote causes the firm's most capable workers to spend more of their time in jobs better left to less able workers.

A formal statement of this principle is given in the appendix. This point is much like the one made about the comparison between Japanese and American CEOs. Japanese managers do not become CEOs until a great deal of information is available, and so mistakes are less likely to be made. The cost of waiting is that the manager who eventually becomes CEO is misplaced, working in a lower level position than the one for which he is best suited for too long. This cost is traded off against the advantage of waiting long enough to ensure that the right choice is made.

Sometimes sorting is not particularly important. For example, senior consultants and consultants may do exactly the same kind of work on exactly the same kind of accounts. The title *senior* may simply designate that the individual in question has more seniority and receives a higher wage. In this case, promotion to senior consultant serves an incentive function, but is probably less important for sorting. In such a case, there may be good reasons to postpone promotion until later in the career. Doing so reduces the amount of noise and thereby increases incentives for any given spread, which helps when workers are risk averse. Also, putting the promotion off until later in the career provides incentives for the individual over a longer period of time. Once a worker receives his last promotion, other incentive devices must be used to motivate workers. To the extent that the last promotion can be delayed, the promotion incentive continues to operate.

The second point is stated as the following principle:

> The more layers there are in a firm that promotes on the basis of relative comparison, the larger is the difference between the ability of the people in the top job and the ability of the people in the bottom job.

At some level, this principle is obvious. If a firm having 100 employees is divided into ten jobs, then the person who holds the top job is likely to be more able than the person in the bottom job because the person at the top had to win nine contests to obtain that job and because the person at the bottom had to lose the only contest in which he or she competed. If there were only two jobs in the firm, those in the top job would only have won one promotion contest to get the job. Therefore, the criterion for obtaining a promotion in a two job firm is less selective than the criterion for obtaining the top job in a ten layer firm.

Firms that have flat hierarchical structures are likely to have individuals of similar abilities at all levels. The ability distribution among junior lawyers in the typical law firm may not be much different from the ability distribution of senior lawyers in the firm. But the average ability of CEOs in larger corporations is likely to be much higher than that of management trainees. Many more levels of sorting exist in large corporations than in law firms, or for that matter, than in universities.

Heterogeneous Work Forces

Effort suffers when heterogeneous workers compete with one another. Effort has the largest effect on changing the probability of winning when contestants have similar ability. If ability differs among contestants, then both the less able and more able tend to slack off. Suppose that Tom is more able than Sarah. Sarah knows that putting forth effort may increase the probability that she wins the promotion, but not by a great deal because Tom almost has the promotion locked up. Tom sees that Sarah is not trying very hard and realizes that he can win even without exerting much effort. Thus, the effort levels of both individuals decline when contestants are heterogeneous.[5]

To maintain high levels of effort, it is important to group workers so that, at least at the outset, workers feel that they are evenly matched with those against whom they will directly compete for a particular promotion. This may require creating additional levels in the firm's hierarchy. It is not necessary that individuals with different job titles or at different levels of the hierarchy perform different tasks. Indeed, the tasks of associate professor and of full professor are almost identical, even if the salaries are not. As will be discussed in a later chapter, job titles can serve many roles. Job titles may describe tasks that are assigned to a particular individual. Alternatively, or additionally, job titles may refer to salary and to level in the hierarchy. The level designates the persons with whom an individual competes for the next promotion.

Skewed Salary Structures

It was argued above that a good salary structure is likely to have bigger absolute raises at the top than at the bottom of the hierarchy. Is there a limit to this? Why not give all managers the same salary except for the CEO, who has compensation ten times that of the other managers?

When workers are heterogeneous, a highly skewed salary structure, with extremely large raises at the top and very low raises at the bottom will not motivate well. The reason is that many workers may give up.

In the story earlier, it was pointed out that a file clerk might hope to become clerical supervisor even if the clerical supervisor earned no more than the file

---

[5]The formal derivation of this argument is contained in Lazear and Rosen (1981).

clerk. The reason is that being clerical supervisor allows a worker to compete for other, higher-level jobs that might offer more pay. Implicit in this argument is that all individuals have a chance at obtaining the higher-level jobs.

An alternative possibility is that some workers are inherently more able than others and that the workers all have a good sense of their relative positions. Sarah may believe that she can compete with Tom, but she may feel that she is unable to do much against Molly. If Sarah and Molly are both promoted to clerical supervisor and if Sarah knows that she is very unlikely to get the next promotion because she competes against Molly, then Sarah will not work to become clerical supervisor. Since, by assumption, clerical supervisor and file clerks all earn the same amount, the value of being promoted to clerical supervisor is only the option value of being able to compete for the next job up the ladder. Now if Sarah knows she will lose that competition, then being promoted to clerical supervisor has no value at all. Thus, Sarah gives up, and Tom, her competitor at the file clerk level, also relaxes. To avoid this situation, the salary structure cannot be too skewed. There must be some direct value of going from file clerk to clerical supervisor to keep individuals who think that they are unlikely to go beyond that level from giving up.

The lessons, then, are twofold. First, it is best to keep as much similarity at each level as possible so that individuals are not induced to give up. More will be said on this later. Second, it is necessary to provide some reward at every level of promotion so that workers who believe that they can move to the next level, but not beyond, have some incentive to obtain the promotion. Additionally, the more heterogeneous is the underlying work force, the more intermediate rewards must be given and the less skewed should be the salary structure.

Firms that do a great deal of initial screening are better at separating their workers and sorting their work force to produce more homogeneity at each level. Thus, pre-employment or early employment screening is a substitute for using a smooth wage structure. Firms that do more screening are more likely to fit the skewed structure of panel 2 in Figure 9.2. Those that do little screening and therefore tolerate significant heterogeneity at each level may have to settle for an even salary structure like that in panel 1 of Figure 9.2. The skewed structure provides better incentives than the even structure when workers are homogeneous, but may be deficient when the work force has diverse ability levels that are known to those competing for the jobs.

♦ ♦ ♦ ♦ ♦ INTERNAL PROMOTION VERSUS HIRING OUTSIDERS

Why do firms seem to favor insiders over outsiders? There are a number of obvious reasons, some having to do with firm-specific human capital. Insiders know the routine and need not be trained in the specific happenings of the particular firm. But sometimes when firm-specific aspects are unimportant, outsiders who dominate insiders by a significant margin are passed by to promote an internal candidate.

Tournament theory provides an explanation of this practice and suggests that in most circumstances, some favoring of insiders over outsiders is appropriate.[6] When outsiders are included in the set of contestants for a particular position, the number of contestants expands. This reduces the probability that any particular individual will win the promotion. More precisely, it reduces the effect of effort on the probability of getting promoted. As a result, individuals who know that they compete with a large number of outsiders tend not to work as hard as those whose competitor pool is limited to those currently at the firm. Increasing the spread between the winner's and loser's prizes can offset the effects of enlarging the set of contestants, but increasing the spread has its disadvantages. All else being equal, risk-averse workers prefer that the difference in prizes between winners and losers be small. If it is possible to increase effort by excluding outsiders, then workers are better off except in rare cases. Firms can pay lower salaries, and effort is increased.

This logic implies that promotion from within is a good strategy. The other side of this argument is that introducing outsiders breaks collusion that might occur within the firm. That give us this principle:

> Internal promotion produces better incentives than outside hiring. Outside hiring should only be used when the outside candidate is significantly better than all internal candidates, or when insiders have colluded to put forth too little effort in the past.

RECAP
◆ ◆ ◆ ◆ ◆

In this chapter, we have argued that tournament theory is a guide to determining the internal salary structure of a firm. In particular, the size of the raise associated with any given promotion affects the effort of workers below that level.

Tournament theory works whether firms are conscious of it or not. Management may not think explicitly about the contests that they inadvertently structure within their firms. This does not imply that tournaments can be ignored. As long as workers are pitted against one another and relative comparisons affect worker compensation, workers will behave according to tournament theory. Whether this was the intent of the firm or not is almost irrelevant. Ignoring the lessons of tournament theory can lead to wasted resources and unexploited opportunities.

We summarize some of the key points and rules that come from the theory:

1. A firm's compensation system should be viewed as an entire structure. An individual's compensation not only affects his or her own behavior, but more important, the behavior of those below who aspire to be promoted into the job.
2. Salary structures have two features—spread and level. The spread, given by the difference between the salaries of high-level and low-level jobs, affects the

---

[6]See Chan (1996).

amount of effort that individuals put forth. Higher spread means more effort. The salary level refers to the expected or average salary that a typical worker can expect to receive. This level affects a worker's willingness to work for the firm. Workers prefer higher levels and firms prefer lower levels. The firm is constrained to offer a high enough level to attract workers to the firm, given the effort implied by the spread. The larger the spread, the higher the effort, and the higher the necessary salary level. This implies that firms tend to pay high average wages when promotions carry large raises.

3. Increasing salary spread does not imply increasing salary levels. The spread can be increased by lowering the bottom salaries and by raising the top salaries. In order for workers to accept this, however, the overall level must be high enough to justify the implied effort.

4. Noise, or luck, has adverse effects on effort. When the outcome of a promotion race is affected by extraneous factors, workers reduce their effort because effort is less likely to affect the outcome. To offset the effects of luck, it is necessary to increase the spread. Thus, salary spreads are greater in work environments where measurement error or production uncertainty are large. New firms and new industries are most likely to have large luck components and should therefore use larger spreads.

5. It is possible to get a sense of whether a structure is out of line by drawing the firm's organizational chart. When too many workers compete for a promotion that carries with it a small raise, effort will suffer.

6. Raises tend to be larger for high-level promotions than for low-level promotions because the "option" value of winning subsequent rounds vanishes for the final promotion. The greater the remaining option value is, the smaller the raise from one level to the next can be.

7. Incentives can be produced either by relative comparisons or by absolute measurements. Piecework provides absolute incentives while promotions, based on relative performance, provide relative incentives. The advantages of relative incentives are twofold. First, relative comparisons are often easier and cheaper to make than absolute judgments. Second, relative comparisons reduce the effects of common noise, like business conditions or supervisor attitude, that would affect pay based on absolute standards. The disadvantage of relative incentives is that they may foster either collusion, or induce negative competition between workers which could be harmful to the firm.

8. The likelihood of collusion between workers can be reduced by increasing the number of contestants for each job. When this is done, the raise associated with a promotion must be increased to make the promotion, which is now less likely, worthwhile. Alternatively, the number of slots into which promotions occur can be increased. Instead of having two persons competing for one job, the firm can have ten persons competing for twenty jobs. Collusion is more difficult in the latter case.

9. Internal promotion produces favorable incentive effects, but lends itself to worker collusion. One way to reduce the likelihood of collusion is to hire

from the outside. Therefore, internal promotion should be favored over external hiring unless the outside candidate is significantly superior to the best insider or the insiders have colluded to put forth low effort.

10. The longer the firm waits to decide on a promotion, the greater the likelihood that the better candidate will be chosen for the job. However, waiting imposes a cost in that able workers spend more of their time in jobs that are better suited to less able workers. When sorting is unimportant relative to incentives, later promotions will provide incentives over a longer period of time.

11. When the pool of contestants for a particular promotion is heterogeneous, effort suffers. There are two solutions. First, the firm can create more job titles so that within each job title, workers are ex ante homogeneous. That is, at the time that they are hired (or promoted) into the job, they are all deemed to have similar abilities and similar chances for the next promotion. Failing that, the salary structure should not be too skewed. If only the very high-level managers are well paid, those who do not think that they can make it to the top will give up. This will encourage their more able competition to relax as well. A less skewed salary structure offsets this tendency.

A number of issues were raised at the beginning of the chapter. The first question related to the effect of promotions on worker morale and effort. The tournament model was introduced to answer this question. We argued that the hope of promotion was a key determinant of effort in an organization. When a worker's probability of promotion can be enhanced by additional effort, workers have an incentive to work harder. The larger the raise associated with the promotion, the greater the incentive.

The structure of promotions within the firm was also discussed. It was pointed out that the addition of layers to the hierarchy need not require a refinement of tasks. Levels can relate to salaries rather than to task assignments.

Promotions are based on relative comparisons. Relative comparisons are sometimes easier to make and eliminate most common noise associated with measurement error and with production uncertainties.

The size of the raise associated with a promotion is determined primarily by the amount of luck in the promotion process and the amount of underlying heterogeneity. When luck is important, raises need to be large. When there is a great deal of heterogeneity, there should be more layers of salary categories in the organization, meaning that any one promotion carries a smaller increase.

It is impossible to know whether top executives are overpaid without understanding the entire structure of the firm. The CEO's salary motivated her to put forth effort before becoming CEO, and it provides motivation to others in the firm to work hard in hopes of achieving the valuable top position.

Promotion from within has favorable incentive features. When workers are promoted from within, the overall effort level in the firm is higher for a given wage spread. External hiring into high-level jobs should be used only when there is a substantial drop between the ability of the best internal candidate and the outside candidate.

◆ ◆ ◆ ◆ ◆ REFERENCES

Bull, Clive, Andrew Schotter, and Keith Weigelt, "Tournaments and Piece Rates: An Experimental Study," *Journal of Political Economy* 95 (February 1987): 1–33.

Chan, William, "External Recruitment versus Internal Promotion," *Journal of Labor Economics* 14 (October 1996): 555–70.

Drago, Robert, and Gerald Garvey, "Incentives for Helping on the Job: Theory and Evidence," forthcoming, *Journal of Labor Economics* (1997).

Ehrenberg, Ronald G., and Michael L. Bognanno, "Do Tournaments Have Incentive Effects?" *Journal of Political Economy* 98(6) (December 1990): 1307–24.

Knoeber, Charles R., "A Real Game of Chicken: Contracts, Tournaments, and the Production of Broilers," *Journal of Law, Economics & Organization* 5 (Fall 1989): 271–92.

Lazear, Edward P., and Sherwin Rosen, "Rank-Order Tournaments as Optimum Labor Contracts," *Journal of Political Economy* 89 (October 1981): 841–64.

Rebitzer, James, Renee M. Landers and Lowell J. Taylor, "Rat Race Redux," *American Economic Review* 86 (June 1996): 329–48.

Rosen, Sherwin, "Prizes and Incentives in Elimination Tournaments," *American Economic Review* 76 (September 1986): 701–15.

◆ ◆ ◆ ◆ ◆ ADDITIONAL ADVANCED READING

Gibbons, Robert, and Kevin J. Murphy, "Relative Performance Evaluation for Chief Executive Officers," *Industrial and Labor Relations Review* (Special Issue, February 1990): S30–51.

Green, Jerry R., and Nancy L. Stokey, "A Comparison of Tournaments and Contracts," *Journal of Political Economy* (June 1983): 349–64.

Kahn, Charles, and Gur Huberman, "Two-Sided Uncertainty and 'Up-or-Out' Contracts," *Journal of Labor Economics* (October 1988): 841–64.

◆ ◆ ◆ ◆ ◆ APPENDIX

The appendix is divided into two sections. The first presents a formal presentation of the tournament model. The second presents a formal treatment of sorting.

The Tournament Model

Consider a firm that has only two workers and sets up two jobs: boss and operator. Workers compete against one another with the winner being designated boss and the loser being designated operator. The winner receives wage W_1 and the loser receives wage W_2. No wages are paid until after the contest is completed. The probability of winning the contest depends on the amount of effort that each individual exerts. Let the two individuals be denoted j (for Joe) and k (for Katy) and let j's output be given by equation (A9.1a) and k's output by (A9.1b).

(A9.1a)
$$q_j = \mu_j + \epsilon_j$$
(A9.1b)
$$q_k = \mu_k + \epsilon_k$$

where μ_j and μ_k are the effort levels of j and k, respectively, ϵ_j and ϵ_k are random luck components, and q_j and q_k are output.

The problem can be split up into two parts. It is first necessary to model worker behavior. After worker behavior is understood, we model the firm, which maximizes profits, taking worker behavior into account by setting up the optimal compensation scheme.

Equation A9.2 is j's optimization problem.

(A9.2)
$$\underset{\mu_j}{\text{Max}}\ W_1 P + W_2 (1 - P) - C(\mu_j)$$

where W_1 is the boss's wage, W_2 is the worker's wage, and P is the probability of winning the contest, conditional on the level of effort chosen. Also, $C(\mu_j)$ is the monetary value of the pay associated with any given level of effort μ_j. The first-order condition is

(A9.3)
$$(W_1 - W_2) \frac{\partial P}{\partial \mu_j} = C'(\mu_j)$$

This first-order condition has a straightforward interpretation. The left-hand side is the spread times the change in the probability associated with an additional unit of effort. This is the marginal return to effort because it gives the value of winning, $(W_1 - W_2)$, times the amount by which the probability of winning changes as effort changes. The right-hand side is just the marginal cost of effort. So the first-order condition says that the worker will exert effort up to the point where the marginal value of effort just equals its marginal cost.

The probability that j defeats k is given by

$$P = \text{Prob}\ (\mu_j + \epsilon_j > \mu_k + \epsilon_k) = \text{Prob}\ (\mu_j - \mu_k > \epsilon_k - \epsilon_j)$$
$$= G(\mu_j - \mu_k)$$

where G is the distribution function on the random variable $\epsilon_k - \epsilon_j$ and g is the density function.

Now, $G(\mu_j - \mu_k)$ is the probability that $\epsilon_k - \epsilon_j$ is less than $\mu_j - \mu_k$. But we are interested in $\partial P / \partial \mu_j$, not P itself. Thus, it is necessary to differentiate P with respect to μ_j, which yields $g(\mu_j - \mu_k)$.

There is a corresponding problem for worker k. Since j and k are ex ante identical, we suppose the existence of a symmetric equilibrium where j and k choose the same level of effort. Thus, at the optimum $\mu_j = \mu_k$, so (A9.3) becomes

(A9.4)
$$(W_1 - W_2)g(0) = C'(\mu_j)$$

Equation A9.4 has two implications that are consistent with the tennis match story. First, the increase in $W_1 - W_2$ implies a higher equilibrium level of effort, since $C'(\mu_j)$ is monotonically increasing in μ. A bigger raise induces workers to compete harder for the promotion.

In Figure A9.1, the marginal cost of μ is plotted as $C'(\mu)$. The solution to the first-order condition is where $C'(\mu) = (W_1 - W_2)g(0)$. This implies the solution $\mu = \mu^*$. If the spread were raised to $(W_1 - W_2)'$ the optimum would be at μ' rather than at μ^*. Note that $\mu' > \mu^*$ since $C'(\mu)$ is necessarily increasing in μ.

A second implication is that the lower is $g(0)$, the lower is the level of effort exerted in equilibrium, since $g(0)$ is the measure of the importance of luck in this production environment. When luck is completely unimportant so that $\epsilon_k - \epsilon_j$ is degenerate, $g(0)$ goes to infinity. When luck is very important—that is, when the distribution of $\epsilon_k - \epsilon$ has fat tails—$g(0)$ becomes very small. Thus, as the importance of luck increases, the amount of effort exerted for any given wage spread declines. Again, with reference to Figure A9.1, if the spread were $W_1 - W_2$, but the density function were $\tilde{g}(0)$ instead of $g(0)$ (and $\tilde{g}(0) < g(0)$), then the optimum level of μ would be only $\tilde{\mu}$. Luck is shown as being more important when the distribution is $\tilde{g}$ than when the distribution is g in Figure A9.2. When luck is less important, $g(0)$ is higher.

The logic behind this result is also straightforward and was discussed extensively in the text of this chapter. If luck is the dominant factor in determining the outcome of the promotion decision workers will not try very hard to win the promotion. In production environments where measurements of effort are noisy, large raises must be given in order to offset the tendency by workers to reduce effort. In fact, as will be shown momentarily, it is optimal to offset *any* reduction in effort induced by an increase in the importance of luck. Let us now turn to the firm's problem. Given the workers' labor supply behavior, characterized by Equa-

FIGURE A9.1
OPTIMAL EFFORT

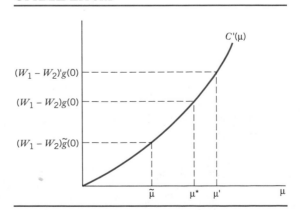

FIGURE A9.2
DISTRIBUTION OF LUCK

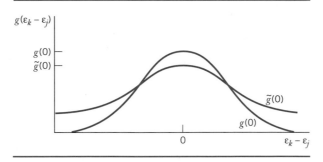

tion A9.4, the firm now wants to maximize expected profit, or equivalently, profit per worker, since the number of workers hired is exogenous to this problem. The firm's problem then is

(A9.5)
$$\underset{W_1, W_2}{\text{Max}}\, \mu - (W_1 - W_2)/2$$

subject to

(A9.6)
$$(W_1 + W_2)/2 = C(\mu)$$

Equation A9.6 is merely the condition that says that workers must be paid enough, on average, to induce them to apply for the job: $C(\mu)$ is the dollar value of the pain associated with the activity, whereas $(W_1 + W_2)/2$ is the expected wage that each risk-neutral contestant can expect to receive. Thus, (A9.6) merely says that the expected wage level must be high enough to induce workers to apply. Substituting (A9.6) into (A9.5), the maximization problem becomes

(A9.7)
$$\underset{W_1, W_2}{\text{Max}}\, \mu - C(\mu)$$

with first-order conditions

(A9.8)
$$\frac{\partial}{\partial W_1} = (1 - C'(\mu))\, \frac{\partial \mu}{\partial W_1} = 0$$

$$\frac{\partial}{\partial W_2} = (1 - C'(\mu))\, \frac{\partial \mu}{\partial W_2} = 0$$

The solution to Equation A9.8 implies $C'(\mu) = 1$. In other words, firms should set up a compensation scheme that induces workers to exert effort up to the point where its marginal cost is equal to its marginal benefit to the firm, namely, $1. Thus, tournaments are efficient and induce the first-best level of effort. In other words, there is no better arrangement that can profitably be made with the worker. From this relation, an optimal level of effort is determined, which after substituting into (A9.6) gives the average wage necessary to attract workers to the firm. The wage spread is found by substituting the fact that $C'(\mu) = 1$ into Equation A9.4 to obtain

(A.9.9)
$$(W_1 - W_2) = \frac{1}{g(0)}$$

Equations A9.6 and A9.9 are systems of two equations in two unknowns that solve for wage level and wage spread. As promised, the optimal wage spread varies inversely with $g(0)$, so that the size of one's wage is increased to offset any increase in luck as reflected by a fall in $g(0)$. The average wage does not change at all as a function of $g(0)$.

Sorting: Date of Promotion

The following shows that promotion mistakes are less likely to be made, the longer is the decision period.

Suppose that there are two workers vying for the same job. The one who is more able has a probability P of winning the promotion each round with $P > 1/2$. If there is only one round, the more able person wins p of the time, but the less able wins $(1 - p)$ of the time. If three rounds are played, the person selected for promotion is the one who wins at least two out of the three rounds. The probability that the more able player wins exactly two out of three rounds is given by the binomial distribution. It is

$$\binom{3}{2} p^2 (1 - p)$$

or

$$\frac{3!}{2! \, 1!} p^2 (1 - p)$$

or

$$3p^2 (1 - p)$$

It is also possible that the most able gets promoted by winning all three rounds. This happens with probability

$$\binom{3}{3} p^3$$

or

$$p^3$$

Thus, the probability that the more able person wins a three-round contest is

$$p^3 + 3p^2 (1 - p)$$

In one round, the probability that the more able person wins is exactly p. But

$$p^3 + 3p^2 (1 - p) > p \text{ for } \frac{1}{2} < p < 1$$

So, the probability[7] that the more able person wins is greater in three rounds than it is in one round.

In general, if there are N rounds (N an odd number), the probability that the most able person wins is

$$\text{Prob (more able wins in } N \text{ rounds)} = \sum_{X=\frac{N+1}{2}}^{N} \frac{N!}{X! \, (N-X)!} p^X (1-p)^{(N-X)}$$

which is increasing in N for any $p > \frac{1}{2}$.

For example, if $p = .7$ so that the more able person wins a round 70 percent of the time, the more able wins a 1-round contest with probability of .7, a 5-round contest with probability of .84, and a 15-round contest with probability .95. If each round were a year, waiting 15 years to make a promotion decision would result in the right choice 19 out of 20 times.

---

[7]The roots of

$$p^3 + 3p^2(1-p) - p = 0$$

are

$$p = \frac{1}{2}, 1$$

For

$$\frac{1}{2} < p < 1$$

the l.h.s. is positive since the expression can be written as

$$p^2 + 3p(1-p) - 1 = 0$$

and

$$\frac{\partial}{\partial p} = -4p + 3 > 0 \text{ when } p = \frac{1}{2}$$

INDUSTRIAL POLITICS

10

*W*orker morale is a central focus of much business discussion today. Management conversations about personnel matters rarely fail to mention cooperation, morale, and corporate culture. These words have important connotations, but move the discussion toward ideas that are fuzzier and less quantitative than most concepts analyzed in preceding chapters. In this chapter, we discuss some ways in which these important factors can be made more concrete. As usual, we start with a hypothetical discussion among managers.

FISHER: I'm concerned that our younger managers are a bunch of back-stabbers. I don't know whether this is the "me-generation" thing, or what, but this group is about as selfish and ruthless as they get.

SHAW: You've heard the joke about new MBAs, haven't you?

FISHER: No. Let's hear it.

SHAW: How many MBAs does it take to change a light bulb? Two. One to change the bulb and the other to knock the ladder out from under him.

FISHER: Very funny. This is a serious problem. I can't get my people to cooperate with one another.

WEBER: That's true. Forget about teamwork with these guys. They won't even give one another directions to the restroom, let alone work together on a project. The selfishness is undermining corporate morale. Why can't they be more like we were when we were their age?

SHAW: Maybe we are hiring the wrong type of person. We could put some more effort into screening at the time of hire. Many other firms spend much more time and effort on hiring activity than we do.

WEBER: Do you think that this has to do with our hiring practices? I have a hunch that these guys are just good at hiding their true character at the job interview. Then we are surprised when their sweet interview personality melts away.

FISHER: There is another possibility. Maybe we are taking in perfectly reasonable people, but creating an environment that turns them into sharks. Some of the incentives to compete they encounter during their first few years on the job can't be good for cooperation.

WEBER: Maybe. But we can't simply have a love-in here. We've got to get some work out of our people, and the best way to do it is to have them compete against one another. Competition is what made our company great.

FISHER: Competition may have made us great in the past, but I think it may be killing us now. We need to think about this more seriously. Maybe there is some way to reorganize the company to provide good incentives without inducing workers to hate each other.

SHAW: I still think that the problem is the basic personalities of the people we hire. If we fix that, we fix the problem. Even if we can't hire the right people, maybe we can move them around after they get here so as to make the most use of them.

FISHER: People are people. No matter what we do, they are always going to try to find ways to waste my time and toot their own horns.

The discussion focuses on industrial politics. The managers in this group are concerned that the attitude that prevails in the firm among junior employees is not conducive to high levels of productivity. As a result the managers face the following challenges:

- Motivating workers to cooperate with one another to produce a team environment in the workplace.

- Hiring individuals whose personalities are compatible with the culture of the organization.

- Organizing the firm so as to minimize backbiting behavior without eliminating incentives to put forth effort.

- Motivating the employees to work rather than spend time lobbying.

- Observing and rewarding cooperation while punishing selfish behavior.

- Assigning individuals to parts of the organization where they are most productive.

TOURNAMENTS AND COMPETITION ◆ ◆ ◆ ◆ ◆

The last chapter points out that in the workplace, tournaments provide incentives to put forth effort. But tournaments also may have some adverse consequences. As we discussed earlier, a collusion among workers may be a costly consequence of tournament-like incentive schemes. Namely, workers could make a pact to put forth too little effort, and simply divide the prize in some way deemed fair before the outcome of the promotion race were known. But collusion is difficult when the group is of any significant size. Another problem, however, is more important and can affect the entire atmosphere of an organization. This problem is the opposite of collusion. Rather than workers getting together to reduce effort, workers end up competing with one another in unproductive ways.[1]

There are incentives for uncooperative behavior in any firm that awards pay, benefits, or other perquisites on the basis of some relative comparison between employees. Like it or not, the fact that workers see themselves competing with one another for a limited resource will elicit a certain kind of behavior. This is a direct result of using relative rather than absolute compensation. For example, workers who are paid commissions based on the amount that they sell, independent of what other workers do, have no reason to sabotage the work of their co-workers. The incentives change if an organization alters the reward structure, so that the commission rate goes down as average level of sales of two workers in the same area goes up. Then, each worker would want the other to do badly so that the commission rate will be high. Workers will not only fail to help their colleagues, but they may even try to undermine others' activity.

DILBERT reprinted by permission of United Feature Syndicate, Inc.

---

[1]This chapter is based on Lazear (1989).

It is possible that the negative effects of relative pay on cooperation are offset by its positive effects on effort. A story may be helpful here.

Consider tuna fishing, where tuna are caught in nets, dumped into a holding tank, and then brought back to shore live. If the tuna continue to swim and remain active in the tank, their meat stays fresher and the product is improved. If, instead, the tuna become lethargic, or, at the extreme, die on their way back to shore, the meat is of poor quality. One way to encourage tuna activity in the tank might be to introduce a shark into the tuna tank. Because the shark is aggressive and a back-biter (literally), it has an adverse affect on output because, every so often, the shark eats some of the tuna. But the presence of the shark in the tank may produce another effect. It may cause each surviving tuna to swim around more rapidly, causing the meat to remain fresher.

This suggests that it might pay to hire aggressive workers to liven up a somewhat sleepy organization. In the previous discussion, Shaw might have had it exactly backward. Rather than hiring cooperative types, it might actually be better to hire individuals who are aggressive. Bringing competitive people into an organization might make it perform better.

Rewards Structure and Worker Cooperation

While this story works well for sharks and tuna, it does not apply to workers. This is not because people are different from fish but, rather, because firms have an alternative way to affect worker behavior. Instead of employing highly aggressive individuals, the firm can change the structure of reward in the organization. There are a few strategies available to help the firm do this. First, the firm can choose the wage spread. Second, it can structure competition in a variety of ways. Third, it can segregate workers by personalities, putting the most aggressive types of individuals together and the most cooperative types together. Alternatively, it can integrate the personality types, depending on which is best. It is shown formally in the appendix that the following statements hold:

- In the circumstances where cooperation among workers is important, the wage spread should be lower for aggressive workers than for less aggressive ones.

- To the extent possible, workers should be segregated by personality type.

- Workers should directly compete only against those with whom cooperation is unimportant. Individuals who must cooperate in order to make a project succeed should not compete with one another for the same job or reward.

The following example illustrates the idea. Consider four workers, two of whom are *hawks* and two of whom are *doves*. Hawks are aggressive, while doves are passive and completely cooperative. Let their names be H1, H2, D1, and D2, to reflect their respective types (hawks or doves) and their names (1 and 2). There are a number of ways to arrange the workers into production teams. Table 10.1 lists some possibilities.

TABLE 10.1
WORKER CONFIGURATION BY PERSONALITY TYPE

Configuration	Group 1	Group 2	Group 3	Group 4
A	H1,H2,D1,D2			
B	H1,D1,D2	H2		
C	H1,H2	D1,D2		
D	H1,D1	H2,D2		
E	H1	H2	D1	D2

The two polar cases are A and E. In configuration A, all workers work to-gether, irrespective of personality type. In configuration E, all workers work separately. Configuration E loses all advantages of worker interaction. Configuration A maximizes group interaction, but combines personality types.

In organizing a work force, there are two factors to take into account. The first is the magnitude of potential synergy from teamwork. For example, imagine having to move a large object by hand. The task might be impossible for any fewer than three people working together; a group of six might be able to handle the task easily. Or, consider the example of a consulting firm that has to complete a project for a client within a certain time frame. In order to get the work done on schedule, the project requires more than one consultant. But using multiple consultants on one project requires that they be able to work together effectively, which may be difficult to achieve. For example, it is difficult to imagine that shark and tuna could join forces to set a trap for some smaller fish.

More is not always better. Sometimes there can be too many people working together. Consider, for example, an open office area that is crammed full of people and desks. It is possible that the levels of noise and chaos are so high that almost no work gets done. Some kinds of work are best accomplished alone in the quiet of one's own office. (Writing this textbook is an example of such an activity.) Thus, working together can be helpful in some circumstances and less helpful in others.

The discussion just completed relates to the efficient size of a team, rather than to industrial politics, which is the central focus of this chapter. Let us move, therefore, to consider the second factor, which relates directly to industrial politics. We do this by assuming that the activity in question requires exactly two individuals. A somewhat colorful (and real) example comes to mind.[2]

Professional gamblers in Las Vegas often use a technique called *card counting*.[3] In the game blackjack, a player can increase the odds of winning by betting heavily when there are many aces and picture cards remaining in the deck. Casinos do

---

[2]This example relates the practices of a friend, who in earlier days was a card counter in Las Vegas.

[3]Card counting has become less popular over time as casinos have figured out ways to make card counting more difficult and less profitable.

not like card counters and generally deny them the right to play in the casino. In order to avoid being detected, card counters often wear disguises and use other methods to confuse the casino. Despite disguises, card counters can be detected if they always increase their bets when the deck is rich in aces and pictures cards. Then the dealer will notice that the player is counting cards and will have the person thrown out of the casino. To frustrate the casino, a system that involves two players is used. The card counter signals another person when the deck is rich in the relevant cards. The second person then joins the table as a fresh player, betting heavily. The dealer cannot tell whether the new player is betting heavily because the deck is rich or merely because the person is a heavy bettor. This system is quite effective, but requires two players.

Mix or Match?

Suppose that the situation in Table 10.1 refers to card counting. The firm consists of a manager and four players, who can be organized into teams of two.

The firm finances the bets, takes the winnings, and pays players. It is the manager's job to make sure that the teams are structured in a way that maximizes profits and that players are putting forth the appropriate amount of effort. This brings us to the second factor, which involves the sorting of workers by personality type. Combining workers to take advantage of team economies requires that workers be able to work together effectively. If workers have different personality types or subscribe to different corporate cultures, then it may be impossible to combine them effectively. To get at this factor, consider configurations C and D. Configuration C is a match configuration, whereas configuration D is a mix configuration because it combines a hawk and a dove into a team.

The card-counting firm can either mix or match personality types. If it mixes types, perhaps the more aggressive player will motivate the less aggressive player. This depends on the compensation structure. Assume that the manager tells each team that at the end of the month, a prize will be given to the best player in *each* team. By having players switch positions (sometimes a player is the counter and sometimes the bettor), the manager makes a judgment about which of the two players on each team is contributing the most to firm profits. Now players compete with one another, which creates incentive problems.

Recall that doves are cooperative and that hawks are aggressive and are willing to engage in activities that will make the team member, who is now also a competitor for the monthly prize, look bad. Suppose that configuration D is adopted, so that a hawk is paired with a dove. Now, in each team, there is a hawk who is trying to make his partner look bad. What can the manager do about this? The obvious solution is to reduce the size of the monthly prize that is being offered. At the extreme, if the prize were zero, the hawk would have no reason at all to make his partner look bad. It is the existence of the prize, which is based on a relative comparison between the two players, that is causing all of the problems. Were there no prize, or were the awarding of the prize based on some other allocation method, there would be no reason for negative interaction between the hawk and dove.

Reducing the size of the prize eliminates the incentive to behave badly, but it also reduces incentives to put forth effort. When hawks are paired with doves, however, this trade-off must be made, because the prize that would induce the appropriate level of effort would also lead to too little cooperation. At the other extreme, the prize that induces maximum cooperation—that is, a prize of zero—would induce too little effort. Thus, the manager must compromise. By choosing a prize or bonus somewhere between the one that optimizes effort and the one that optimizes cooperation, the manager maximizes profits given the constraint that the hawk must be kept from sabotaging the dove.

Now suppose that two doves are paired and two hawks are paired. The doves can be told that the most productive player will receive a large prize at the end of the month. They will both put forth effort because they want to win the prize. Neither will undermine the other because the personalities preclude this type of behavior.

The hawks must be treated differently. Because they have a tendency to sabotage one another, the monthly prize that is offered to them must be below that offered the doves. Just as before, the manager will choose a prize that trades off the benefits of higher effort against the costs of less cooperation and will not go to either extreme. A prize of zero is too low because it induces too little effort. A prize as large as the doves' prize is too high because it induces too much adverse competition.

The advantage of segregating workers by type is that the doves' output need not be reduced simply because low prizes must be used to prevent hawks from behaving badly. In fact, it is possible to set up two distinct organizations. One firm would consist exclusively of cooperative types, while the other would consist of uncooperative types. The cooperative firm would use larger prizes or spreads, and the uncooperative firm would use smaller prizes or spreads. Output at the cooperative firm would be higher, and wages would also be higher as a result.

Hawks and doves are different looking birds. Unfortunately, personalities are not so easily observed in people. Firms devote resources to trying to determine an individual's personality at the time of hire. Many readers have probably already been through this process, where seemingly odd questions are asked at job interviews. Often, these questions are attempts to get at underlying personality traits to ascertain whether an applicant is a good fit in an organization. But even those who specialize in preparing personality tests will confess that the results are inexact, probably to an even greater degree than in economics! The problem of separating workers by personality types would be solved if workers were to sort themselves by personality type voluntarily. If hawks preferred to work with hawks, while doves preferred to work with doves, a firm would need only to advertise its type and applicants would choose the appropriate firm voluntarily. The system would work much like restrooms. Signs are posted that announce either "Men" or "Women" and individuals voluntarily segregate by gender. No policing is necessary. But in other situations, self-sorting does not occur to a sufficient degree. The fact that certain universities have high rejection rates implies that if they were simply to admit any individual who wanted to attend, universities would not achieve the sorting by academic achievement that they desire. One question that we could ask here is, "Are firms more like restrooms or more like universities?" The next section deals with this issue.

Self-Sorting

In situations resembling the card-counting example, it is better to match than to mix, or alternatively, to set up two independent firms, one employing hawks and the other employing doves. But we also know that there is a problem if doves and hawks do not have incentives to identify themselves. Will individuals sort according to their personality type, even if they know their own type? Unfortunately, the answer is no. Although cooperative workers will always want to identify themselves as cooperative, uncooperative types will be inclined to misrepresent their personalities to make themselves appear more cooperative than they really are.

Suppose that there were two firms, initially having only one type of worker. A dovish applicant would always prefer to work at the doves' firm. Doves cooperate with one another, creating the environment where output, and therefore wages, are higher. Furthermore, since the other workers are doves, the new applicant has a fair shot at winning a promotion or the monthly prize, as illustrated by the card-counting example.

If a dove were to work at a firm with hawks, his income would be lower for two reasons. First, average salaries at the hawkish firm are lower because the failure of hawks to cooperate lowers output and, therefore, wages. Second, a dove in a firm of hawks is at a definite disadvantage. The cooperative person raises everyone else's output and refuses to engage in backstabbing. But the uncooperative individuals who populate the hawkish firm are perfectly happy to take advantage of the dove's kind personality. They may be undermining the dove's efforts, making the dove look bad. Because the dove does not strike back, the hawk comes out the relative winner. For these reasons, a cooperative applicant will not want to work at a firm that is dominated by uncooperative types.

The reverse is not true. For the same reasons that the cooperative individual shuns the uncooperative firm, the uncooperative individual prefers the cooperative firm. Because the dovish firm is comprised of individuals who cooperate with one another, output and average income is higher than it is at the hawkish firm. In addition, the hawk has an advantage at the dovish firm. Workers are cooperative at the dovish firm and do not engage in adversely competitive behavior. But the hawk has no qualms about backstabbing the doves. This gives the hawk an advantage. While all other workers are making the hawk look good, the hawk is going around undermining the dovish competition. Doves are easy targets for the aggressive-behaving hawk.

This story is somewhat extreme, but it illustrates a number of points:

- Whenever rewards of any kind are based on relative performance, workers have little incentive to cooperate and every incentive to compete. The competition induces workers to put forth effort, but it also may induce some individuals to undermine their fellow workers, whom they view as rivals.

- It is better to segregate workers by personality types and then to use different compensation schedules for each type. The incentive structure that is best for one type is not best for the other type.

- Workers will not self-sort. Aggressive individuals like to work with cooperative ones; the reverse is not true.

PERSONALITY SORTING AT HAMBRECHT & QUIST
♦ ♦ ♦ ♦ ♦ ♦ ♦ ♦ ♦

Sandy Robertson, cofounder of the investment bank Robertson Stephens and Company, once said, "you can't be effective in our business unless you go flat out. Investment banking is an immersing business. It's not just a job; it's a way of life." Many investment banks are organized according to the "up or out" principle: Employees at any level compete for a small number of promotions, and the losers of this tournament end up moving on (or being moved out). This highly competitive atmosphere gives investment banking a reputation for intensity bordering on extremism: Employees can expect to work a hundred hours a week, including weekends, in hopes of distinguishing themselves from their peers.

As these employees move up within the bank, even the most energetic will begin to burn out. This is partially by design: the up or out principle seeks, in part, to ensure that upper management is populated by the most aggressive and dedicated of the bank's personnel. But some have begun to question the wisdom of this policy. In 1994, Dan Case, the president of the San Francisco-based investment bank Hambrecht and Quist, asked whether it was wise to demand so much from senior management: "The people with wisdom don't necessarily want to keep pushing hard forever."

With this in mind, he began a program designed to provide separate career tracks. Those who had the intensity and ambition to spend twelve hours a day at work could still follow the path from analyst to associate to managing director and on to increasingly management-oriented positions, while those who preferred to work at a less feverish pace could take positions that blended high-level analyst work with a small amount of management.

For example, the vice chairman in charge of syndication at H&Q still chooses to work from 5:30 a.m. to 5:30 p.m. every day, even as he approaches 60. On the other hand, the director of life sciences research came to H&Q from heading up Smith Barney's Research Department precisely because of the opportunity to slow down a bit. His position at H&Q allows him to follow specific companies like other lower-level financial analysts, while also serving as a mentor to the younger employees. "Instead of directing the orchestra [at Smith Barney], I'm directing with one hand and playing an instrument with the other. That gives me more psychic satisfaction." Thus, the management function is split. The largest supervisory responsibilities still lie with the more aggressive employees who have stuck with the highly demanding fast track, while other senior employees bring their own expertise to bear on many of the more important day-to-day issues, as well as passing on some of their accumulated wisdom to the next generation.

This personality sorting has several advantages. First, Case believes that the new policy has lessened the backbiting atmosphere that prevailed when all personality types worked in the same jobs with the same expectations. This, he claims, has given H&Q a competitive edge in recruiting both younger and older employees. Several of the firm's managers also claim that this new organizational system has decreased turnover within the firm, which allows H&Q to differentiate itself from the competition in this relationship-based industry. The CEO of Executone, one of H&Q's biggest clients, said: "I want my banker to know my business inside and out, and that means I don't want to work with teams that change often. . . . What's happening at H&Q makes me comfortable that we'll stick with the firm for a long time."

Source: Steve Kaufman, "Cutthroat Workload is Easier to Swallow at Uncommon Firm," *The Orlando Sentinel* (November 27, 1994), p. H1.

Other Solutions

There are three other methods that may be used to form the best teams and to encourage workers to cooperate and put forth effort.

Introducing Competition Among Workers of Different Teams

When workers on different teams compete with one another, effort increases without discouraging valuable cooperation. Recall the card-counting example. The manager promised to give one prize to a member on *each* team. The manager set up the prize structure such that one player from each team would be selected for the prize. A problem arose when individuals who needed to cooperate with one another were given incentives to compete with one another. An alternative scheme that has superior incentives is to have individuals on opposite teams compete with one another. If team I consists of D1 and D2, and team II consists of H1 and H2, then the manager can have D1 compete against H1 and D2 compete against H2. Since the Ds and Hs are on different teams, there is no way that H1 can undermine D1's performance. Given the chance, H1 would try to reduce D1's output, but H1 and D1 do not work together. The manager could even place the teams at separate casinos so that they had virtually nothing to do with one another.

Under these circumstances, putting the hawks together has no adverse consequence. Although H1 would be willing to inflict punishment on his teammate, H2, doing so would produce no benefit to H1 since his competition is with D1, not H1. The same is true for H2 who would be happy to harm either H1 or D2. But harming H1 has no benefit and may have a cost because it reduces the output of H2's team. Harming D2 has a benefit because doing so improves H2's chances of winning the prize, but harming D2 is technically infeasible because H2 does not work with D2.

The lesson to remember here is that individuals who must cooperate with one another should not compete for the same prize. It is much better to set up competition among those for whom cooperation is unimportant.

For example, consider a firm that owns 20 new car dealerships in a particular area. At each dealership, it is important that the salesperson and automobile loan person cooperate with one another. Otherwise, deals cannot be closed. Therefore, it would be unwise to have the head of sales at the San Francisco Jeep dealership compete with the head of loans at the San Francisco Jeep dealership for the job of general manager of that dealership. Instead, the head of sales at San Francisco Jeep should compete with the head of sales at Oakland Ford for the job of general manager at San Jose Chevrolet. Similarly, the head of loans at San Francisco Jeep could compete with the head of loans at Oakland Ford for the general manager's job at Marin Honda. Then, each head of loans department wants to help each head of sales. Both look good if many deals are closed at their dealership, which bolsters their chances for promotion relative to those at other dealerships.

Pay on the Basis of Team Output

Rewarding the members of the team on the basis of the team output can be a good policy. Indeed, the emphasis on cooperation can be made even greater by making compensation depend on group output. There are a number of ways to tie an individual's well being to group performance. In the example of card counters, the solution is obvious. Each player can receive some proportion of the group winnings and nothing else. In the example of auto dealerships, each employee can receive a bonus that depends on dealership profits. This would induce individuals to strive to make dealership profits higher.

Unfortunately, group-based compensation is a relatively weak incentive. Because any one individual reaps only a small part of the reward for his or her effort, a worker has little incentive to put forth effort. This is the free-rider effect in action. In the car dealer example, a dealership might have 100 employees in its profit-sharing plan. Thus, a deal closed by a given salesperson produces, say, $3,000 in profit for the dealership. But even if profits are divided equally among the 100 employees in the profit-sharing plan, the salesperson who closed the deal only receives $3,000/100, or a $30 bonus. This is a small fraction of the total, and provides only a small incentive to the salesperson who actually makes the deal happen.

Rewards for Cooperation

The final, and most obvious way, to bring about cooperation between employees who might otherwise compete with one another is to pay for cooperation or to punish uncooperative behavior. Thus, a hawk who fails to cooperate with a co-worker or who undermines the other workers' activity may find her salary or promotion chances adversely affected by the activity. This strategy requires that the manager observe cooperative activity. This is easier said than done. A clever employee is not about to make uncooperative actions readily observable to managers. Thus, punishing uncooperative behavior or rewarding cooperative activity requires that the manager have the ability to look into the production process at a micro level.

Perhaps profit sharing creates an incentive for mutual monitoring. Since each worker knows that his or her compensation is reduced when other workers shirk, workers get angry at individuals who do not take their work responsibilities seriously. But the free-rider effect is a problem in terms of mutual monitoring as well. A worker who catches a colleague shirking is unhappy about it. But if he reprimands the co-worker, he bears the full cost of having to deal with the shirking worker. The worker reaps only a small part of the benefit since, again, he gets only a very small share of the profits created by inducing his co-worker to put forth more effort. Thus, the worker bears all of the pain of confrontation and receives little benefit. Some have argued that a desire for revenge may provide sufficient motive to discipline a deviant co-worker.[4]

Who Succeeds?

Two factors contribute to winning a job tournament, which, by design, depends on relative performance. An individual may receive a promotion either because he or she was the best person for the job, or because he or she was effective in playing the politics of the situation well. By playing politics, we mean that the person was able to convince decision makers that his or her ability or performance dominated that of other candidates. As we already have discussed, playing politics may involve some ruthless behavior. Individuals who are particularly good at this behavior have an advantage over equally able individuals who find the politics, and particularly the negative activity associated with it, very distasteful. This means that those who win promotions will be disproportionately represented by the able, but also by the aggressive, and perhaps even ruthless, individuals. To the extent that ruthless behavior can be spotted, it can be punished. As stated earlier, promotions can be denied to the uncooperative. But the nature of politics means that sometimes the best and even most ruthless individuals may be able to disguise their behavior. When this is the case, too many individuals at the top of an organization will be excessively aggressive and ruthless people. Since these individuals are particularly good at political behavior, their reward structure should be set up to avoid inducing them to behave even worse.

[4]See Posner (1981), Hirshleifer (1987), Frank (1988), Carmichael and MacLeod (1996) and Romer (1996), who provide reasons why certain personality characteristics may have evolved because of their survival value. Revenge might be one of them.

Because the top level of the firm is likely to be populated by competitive individuals, it may be better to use absolute rather than relative standards for rewarding individuals who are near the top of an organization. Doing so will prevent the type of negative interaction between managers among whom cooperation may be especially important. The last thing that a firm needs is for its top executives to be working against one another, trying to make the others fail. Refraining from making too large a raise contingent on a promotion that is based on a relative comparison may be a good policy for the top executives. Instead, top executives maybe give individual bonuses that are tied to individual performances rather than relative comparisions.

Evidence: The Case of Tool Sharing

It is difficult to find evidence on the amount of cooperation that occurs in a firm, in large part because if cooperation were observable, it could be rewarded directly. But some evidence on the issue of cooperation comes from a study by Drago and Garvey (1997). Using data from 23 Australian firms, Drago and Garvey obtained robust results showing that workers are less likely to let other workers use their equipment, tools, or machinery when there are large raises associated with promotions, which are based on relative comparisons.

Note that these findings are consistent with this chapter's view of industrial politics and inconsistent with other, more psychological views. Some have argued[5] that when wage dispersion is great, workers will reduce effort because they will feel that the structure is unfair. The tournament story, on the other hand, says that higher wage inequality increases a worker's own effort, but reduces the amount of cooperation that a worker engages in with co-workers. Drago and Garvey find that the larger the prize associated with promotion, the greater is a worker's own effort and the lower is the amount of cooperation. They use absenteeism as a measure of individual shirking and find that absenteeism is significantly reduced by increasing the size of the prize associated with promotions, even as sharing and cooperation decline. But tool sharing declines as the size of the raise increases. This is exactly the trade-off on which this chapter focused.

OTHER ASPECTS OF INDUSTRIAL POLITICS ◆ ◆ ◆ ◆ ◆

Fairness

We have already argued that one response to aggressive, anticooperative behavior is to compress the pay structure. Reducing the prize or narrowing the spread between highly paid jobs and less well-paid jobs increases the amount of cooperation in the firm. The cost of doing so is that such an action also results in reduction of effort put forth by workers.

---

[5] See Akerlof (1982), for example.

There is another reason for compressing salary structures that has little to do with incentives. Sometimes workers believe that a particular structure is "fair," and that another structure is unfair. Bosses frequently use "fairness" as a reason for refusing to match offers or to raise the wages of workers who feel that they are underpaid. But fairness is likely to mean different things to different workers. The able worker who produces twice the amount of output of a less able worker may believe that it is unfair to receive anything less than twice the wage of the less able worker. The less able worker is likely to believe that the difference in output reflects luck (if nothing else, genetic luck) and that both workers should receive the same compensation if they put in the same number of hours.

Although there may be some socially accepted notions of fairness, they are likely to have little impact on wage determination. In the end, market forces severely constrain the amount of latitude that a firm has to indulge its taste for fairness. A worker who is twice as productive as a less able worker is likely to be able to command an outside offer that is about double the amount that the less able worker can command. In the end, the firm will be forced to choose: Either it comes close to matching the outside spreads, or it loses its most valuable workers. There is a significant body of empirical evidence showing that workers who are underpaid are more likely to leave and find new employment.[6]

Guaranteed Tenure

When workers receive compensation or other benefits based on their relative performance, their judgments may be affected. A good example involves hiring choice. Suppose that workers have say over whom is hired. When will workers want to hire the best person? One way to make workers reluctant to hire the best person is to make their compensation depend on relative comparisons where the new hire is part of the comparison set. Then, by hiring a very able applicant, members of the current staff impair their own relative positions and adversely affect their expected compensation. Under these circumstances, it is likely that workers will behave strategically, and will prefer hiring someone who is easy competition. The less able applicant may be a poorer choice for the firm, but is an easier target in the relative game that incumbents will have to play with the new hire.

The problem is caused by the relative nature of compensation. There are two solutions to this problem. The most obvious is to remove the hiring decision from the workers with whom the new employee will compete. This works as long as the supervisor can make as good a decision as the workers can. In highly technical fields, it is often necessary to consult workers when making hiring decisions because only the workers have sufficient knowledge to evaluate the applicants. Under these circumstances, another solution must be found. Some suggest[7] that pro-

---

[6] See Topel and Ward (1992), Bartel and Borjas (1981).
[7] See Carmichael (1988).

tecting incumbents by giving them guaranteed tenure, which guarantees them a position and wage, solves the problem. Because workers know that they are protected from competition with the new employee, they have no incentives to behave strategically.

Another possibility is to allow incumbents to share in the profit, providing them with some desire to see the firm do well. But, as we already have argued, the profit-sharing incentive is likely to be quite weak, because each worker would receive only a small share of the profit. On the other hand, the incentive to hire a less-qualified worker as a strategic move may be quite strong, since the worker who helps to make a hiring decision may be most concerned about prospects for promotion and direct compensation.

Politics in the Absence of Relative Performance

Rewards that are based on relative performance create tension between employees and may result in lack of cooperation. But even when rewards are not relative, industrial politics can play a role. Whenever managers have some discretion over the treatment of their subordinates, the subordinates have incentives to lobby the managers for better treatment. The lobbying effort is time-consuming, both for the workers and for their supervisors. But it is difficult to eliminate it as a factor.[8] What can be done?

There are a few steps that a firm may take in order to curtail lobbying by the employees. One is to compress pay, in much the same way that a relative-reward firm deals with hawkish workers who will backstab if the rewards of winning are too great. In the firm that pays based on absolute performance, compressing pay reduces the gains to lobbying. Since gains are smaller, the incentives to lobby are weakened.

Another strategy is to refuse to listen to lobbying. The problem with this option is that sometimes subordinates have important information to convey to their superiors. Managers who close the channels of communication with subordinates may not only reduce lobbying, but also may impede the flow of valuable data. While there is no complete solution to this problem, having a good gatekeeper may be the best policy here. A secretary who acts as a filter can be a very valuable asset. The gatekeeper screens out individuals who want to engage in irrelevant chit-chat, but permits those with crucial information to get through.

There is a key difference between the political activity that occurs in a firm that rewards on relative performance and one that rewards on absolute performance. When pay is absolute, it is only necessary to have two parties for there to be lobbying activity. Whenever there is a worker and a compensator, conditions are present for lobbying to take place. Lobbying occurs between a worker and his

---

[8]Milgrom (1988) refers to this as influence activity.

AT&T PRESIDENT SELECTION POLICY
♦ ♦ ♦ ♦ ♦ ♦ ♦ ♦ ♦ ♦

Before the break-up of AT&T, the Bell operating companies (those associated with regions, such as Pacific Telephone, New England Telephone, New York Telephone, and Illinois Bell) had their own presidents who were subordinate to the president of AT&T. The head office of AT&T was in New York and had a full staff of managers who worked for AT&T directly, with no direct responsibility to any specific operating company. Managers at the head office were involved in those activities that spanned all of the operating companies.

When the president of AT&T retired, he was often replaced by a president of one of the operating companies, rather than by one of the next-in-line at the AT&T headquarters. Was there any reason to select operating company presidents over senior executives at headquarters? One advantage to selecting the president from outside the head office is that doing so avoids conflict among executives at the head office. Necessary cooperation at headquarters might suffer if top executives were competing for the president's job. Taking these managers out of the running reduces their incentives to undermine the activities of each other. Of course, this means that the presidents of the operating companies might not cooperate with one another. While true, cooperation at this level was probably less important. Illinois Bell operated in an entirely different market than did Pacific Telephone. Although it is true that managers at Illinois Bell could have learned from managers at Pacific Telephone, and vice versa, a failure to have significant cooperation between the operating companies was probably not of great significance. On the other hand, it would be very harmful if the executive vice president of finance were working against the executive vice president of human resources because each was vying for the presidency.

---

boss, and does not relate to inter-worker activity. The kind of politics that occurs in an environment where relative compensation is used requires at least three parties—two workers and a compensator. Reward cannot be relative unless there is a measurement system that allows comparison of performance among workers. Obviously, comparisons are impossible unless there are at least two workers whose outputs are assessed relative to each other. Thus, the kind of political activity that occurs when relative performance is used may be of two sorts. Workers may lobby their bosses, but, in addition, workers also may have interaction with each other, much of which is negative.

RECAP

Paying on the basis of relative comparisons has adverse effects on cooperation within a firm. Knowing that an uncooperative act may improve his chances for a bonus or promotion, a worker may attempt to undermine his colleagues. Although these actions further his own career, they do not help the firm's overall productivity. To improve cooperation in this type of team setting, some alternative methods can be used. For example, firms can pay workers on the basis of team or firm output, or they can implement a profit-sharing scheme or bonus that depends on group output. Unfortunately, these schemes provide only weak incentives, because no one individual reaps a large proportion of the benefits associated with his or her efforts. Alternatively, managers can attempt to observe cooperation directly and to pay for it. This requires effort by supervisors, however, and may be more costly than it is worth. Finally, the promotion paths can be restructured so that individuals who must cooperate with one another do not compete for the same jobs. This last approach may be the easiest and most effective solution to many of the political problems that inevitably arise in a firm.

When worker personality types are identifiable, segregation by personality type is usually a good management strategy. Compensation and reward structures can then be tailored to each type of worker so as to use each worker most effectively. When personalities are mixed, neither type can be accommodated well.

A further problem arises because not all types of workers want to identify their personalities at the time of hire. A firm might be anxious to hire only inherently cooperative individuals. But, other things being equal, cooperative individuals are more productive. As a result, firms with cooperative workers have higher output and higher wages. They also have workers who do not undermine their coworkers. Both of these factors make the firm attractive not only to cooperative types, but also to more ruthless, excessively aggressive individuals. Thus, those individuals whose personalities do not match the culture of the firm may, nevertheless, attempt to sneak in. As a result, screening at the time of hire is important, particularly in firms that have a very high need for cooperative workers. Pay compression is another way to reduce unhealthy rivalry among employees.

Even when workers are compensated on the basis of absolute performance, they have a tendency to spend too much time lobbying their supervisors. One solution to this problem is to limit access to supervisors strategically to allow the relevant information to get through and to screen out the lobby noise. Another strategy is to compress wages so that lobbying has only limited payoff. Of course, compressing wages reduces effort, but also reduces the negative political activity that occurs in the firm.

REFERENCES

Akerlof, George A., "Labor Contracts as Partial Gift Exchange," *Quarterly Journal of Economics* 97 (November 1982): 543–69.

Bartel, Ann P., and George J. Borjas, "Wage Growth and Job Turnover: An Empirical Analysis," in S. Rosen, ed., *Studies in Labor Markets*. Chicago: University of Chicago Press for National Bureau of Economic Research, 1981.

Carmichael, H. Lorne, and Bentley MacLeod, "Territorial Bargaining," unpub. manuscript, Queens University, 1996.

Carmichael, H. Lorne, "Incentives in Academics: Why Is There Tenure?" *Journal of Political Economy* 96 (June 1988): 453–72.

Drago, Robert, and Gerald T. Garvey, "Incentives for Helping on the Job: Theory and Evidence," forthcoming, *Journal of Labor Economics*, 1997.

Frank, Robert, *Passions within Reason: The Strategic Role of the Emotions*. New York, Norton: 1988.

Hirshleifer, Jack, "On the Emotions as Guarantors of Threats and Promises," in John Dupre, ed., *The Latest on the Best: Essays on Evolution and Optimality*. Cambridge: MIT Press, 1987.

Lazear, Edward P., "Pay Equality and Industrial Politics," *Journal of Political Economy* 97 (June 1989): 561–80.

Milgrom, Paul R., "Employment Contracts, Influence Activities, and Efficient Organization Design," *Journal of Political Economy* 96 (February 1988): 42–60.

Posner, Richard A., *The Economics of Justice*. Cambridge: Harvard University Press, 1981.

Romer, Paul, "Preferences, Promises, and the Politics of Entitlement," in Victor Fuchs, ed., *Individual and Social Responsibility*. Chicago, University of Chicago Press, 1996.

Topel, Robert, and Michael Ward, "Job Mobility and the Careers of Young Men," *Quarterly Jornal of Economics* 107 (May 1992), 441–79.

◆ ◆ ◆ ◆ ◆ ADDITIONAL ADVANCED READING

Rebitzer, James B., William E. Encinosa III, and Martin Gaynor. "The Sociology of Groups and the Economics of Incentives: Theory and Evidence on Compensation Structures," for Universities-NBER Research Conference, *What do employers do?* December 1996.

Rotemberg, Julio J., "Human Relations in the Workplace," *Journal of Political Economy* (August 1994) 684–714.

Williamson, Oliver E., "Calculativeness, Trust, and Economic Organization," *Journal of Law and Economics* (Part 2, April 1993): 453–86.

◆ ◆ ◆ ◆ ◆ APPENDIX

This appendix is devoted to deriving three propositions stated in the chapter. To do this, we reintroduce the tournament model, but add a twist. Now, workers can behave strategically against their rivals. This captures the essence of industrial politics, the topic that formed the theme of this chapter.

As before, there are two individuals, j and k. Output for each is given below:

(A10.1)
    a. $q_j = \mu_j - \theta_k + \epsilon_j$
    b. $q_k = \mu_k - \theta_j + \epsilon_k$

As before, it is painful to put forth effort. Also, it requires effort (or guilt) to sabotage one's rival, and the pain is given by

(A10.2) $$\text{Cost} = C(\mu_j, \theta_j)$$

with C_1 and C_2 both positive.

The winner's wage is W_1, and the loser's wage is W_2. The probability of winning, which depends on effort μ and sabotage θ, is given by P. The worker's maximization problem is then

(A10.3) $$\underset{\mu_j, \theta_j}{Max}\; W_1 P + W_2(1 - P) - C(\mu_j,\, \theta_j)$$

with first-order conditions

(A10.4)
    a. $(W_1 - W_2)\dfrac{\partial P}{\partial \mu_j} = C_1(\mu_j, \theta_j)$

    b. $(W_1 - W_2)\dfrac{\partial P}{\partial \theta_j} = C_2(\mu_j, \theta_j)$

There is a symmetric problem for player k.

For any given wage spread, the ability to sabotage one's rival affects effort only insofar as $C_{12} \neq 0$. If C_{12} were equal to zero, then effort would be independent of sabotage. Since sabotage is simply another form of effort, it is likely that $C_{12} > 0$, which means that, for any given wage spread, effort tends to be lower for players who can sabotage. Rather than working, these players can spend some of their time and energy undermining their partners.

Which wage spread is appropriate for workers? First, assume segregation by type. Define a *hawk* as an individual who is capable of committing sabotage (at a cost). Thus, a hawk is an individual who has costs described by (A10.2). A *dove* is defined as an individual who is incapable of sabotage. A dove has an infinite cost of sabotage. Thus, θ_j is equal to zero for all doves. They have cost functions given by $C(\mu)$, as given in the appendix to chapter 9.

The firm's problem is to maximize profits per player. In the case of hawks, this problem can be written

$$\underset{w_1, w_2}{Max}\; q_j - (W_1 + W_2)$$

or

(A10.5) $$\underset{w_1, w_2}{Max}\; \mu_j - \theta_j - C(\mu_j, \theta_j)$$

subject to

$$\frac{W_1 + W_2}{2} = C(\mu_j, \theta_j)$$

with first-order conditions. Since j and k are symmetric, the first-order conditions become

(A10.6)

a. $(1 - C_1)\dfrac{\partial\mu}{\partial W_1} - (1 + C_2)\dfrac{\partial\theta}{\partial W_1} = 0$

b. $(1 - C_1)\dfrac{\partial\mu}{\partial W_2} - (1 + C_2)\dfrac{\partial\theta}{\partial W_2} = 0$

In the absence of sabotage, the first-order conditions are

(A10.7)

a. $(1 - C_1)\dfrac{\partial\mu}{\partial W_1} = 0$

b. $(1 - C_1)\dfrac{\partial\mu}{\partial W_2} = 0$

Because $C_2 > 0$, the equilibrium level of μ for hawks is lower than it is for doves. But in order to induce a lower level of effort, the spread must be lower for hawks. Thus, pay compression is an appropriate response when individuals have the ability to harm one another or when cooperation is important. This is one of the statements postulated in the text of the chapter.

It is also straightforward to show that workers should be segregated by type. When workers are integrated, the firm must satisfy more constraints than when workers are segregated. This means that segregation (weakly) dominates integration. To see this, note that in the case of integration, the firm must deal with one hawk and one dove. Let superscripts denote type. Then a generalization of (A10.7) shows that the first-order conditions in an integrated firm are

(A10.8)

a. $(W_1 - W_2)\, g(\mu^D - \mu^H + \theta^D - \theta^H) = C_1^D$

b. $(W_1 - W_2)\, g(\mu^D - \mu^H + \theta^D - \theta^H) = C_2^D$

c. $(W_1 - W_2)\, g(\mu^H - \mu^D + \theta^H - \theta^D) = C_1^H$

d. $(W_1 - W_2)\, g(\mu^H - \mu^D + \theta^H - \theta^D) = C_2^H$

where g is the symmetric density of the random variable, $\epsilon_j - \epsilon_k$.
If the firm segregates by worker types, then the first-order conditions are

(A10.9)

a. $(W_1^D - W_2^D)\, g(0) = C_1^D$

b. $(W_1^D - W_2^D)\, g(0) = C_2^D$

c. $(W_1^H - W_2^H)\, g(0) = C_1^H$

d. $(W_1^H - W_2^H)\, g(0) = C_2^H$

The wage structure in the dove's firm can differ from that in the hawk's firm when worker types are segregated. When they are integrated, both firms are identical, so only one wage structure will prevail.

Now, since function g is symmetric around zero, this means that the left-hand sides of (A10.8) all equal the same value for any μ,θ. That fact, along with the independence of $W_1^D - W_2^D$ from $W_1^H - W_2^H$ implies that the system in (A10.9) weakly dominates that in (A10.8). Any value of μ and θ that can be implemented by (A10.8) also can be implemented by (A10.9). The reverse is not true.

This proof lies behind the logic that by segregating types, a firm can cater directly to the characteristics of those workers specifically. When types are integrated, there must be a compromise. The wage spread that is right for doves is not right for hawks; the one that is right for hawks is not right for doves. Thus, segregation of worker types improves the situation. This proves the statement in the text that segregation of worker types is preferred.

It follows directly from the previous analysis that workers should compete only with individuals with whom cooperation is unimportant. Formally, when cooperation is unimportant, the ability to enhance productivity by cooperating or to detract from it by sabotaging is removed. If individuals cannot sabotage, they become like the doves. There is no ability to reduce output of other workers through sabotage (θ). This means that total output is higher for two reasons. First, the direct effect that $\theta = 0$ means that output is higher. Second, there is an indirect effect. The level of effort, μ, is higher because the firm can use a larger wage spread. Larger wage spreads are optimal when the firm need not worry about sabotage. This completes the derivation of the three statements postulated in the chapter.

SENIORITY-BASED INCENTIVE SCHEMES

11

*W*hat can a firm do to motivate workers who stand little chance of future promotions? Many such workers are still productive. Potentially, they can be even more productive if their incentives are structured properly. Workers in dead-end positions may be difficult to motivate. If they realize that they are unlikely to move up, but also very unlikely to be fired, there is little to keep them interested in their jobs. The following discussion during annual job evaluations illustrates some of the problems.

SCHULTZ: How would you rate Sarah's performance this year?

PALGRAVE: Well, she is a fine manager, but nothing special. She's been in that job forever, so she really knows the work, but there is rarely any spark of creativity, or even extra effort. I'd call her "satisfactory."

MORGENSTERN: She sounds like almost every middle manager that I have. The exceptions are the ones that go through those jobs very quickly on their way to the top. They are fine, sometimes stellar employees. But the long-time incumbents are dull as dishwater.

SCHULTZ: True, but everyone can't be president. This company runs because we have a hundred or so managers who carry the burden of the day-to-day operations. We have to treat them pretty well or we risk losing the entire thing.

MORGENSTERN: Why can't everyone be president? I don't mean literally, but we could change our structure a bit, creating a few more slots higher up. After all, banks get away with making every successful manager a vice president. We don't have to go to that extreme, but we can move in that direction.

PALGRAVE: Laspeyres' group already considered that and decided against it. Aren't there other things we can do?

MORGENSTERN: Well, I think the main problem is pay compression. We treat our middle managers like they were government workers. Everyone gets the same raise. Salaries depend only on experience and grade level.

PALGRAVE: What's wrong with that? It creates equity in the organization and makes deciding who gets what much easier.

MORGENSTERN: Any system that mimics the federal pay structure must be bad.

SCHULTZ: Seriously, it doesn't seem so bad to me to give everyone about the same raise as long as they are making the cut. We still have the option of firing those who fall below some minimum acceptable level. That provides some incentive to work hard.

PALGRAVE: True. Besides, the big problem in deviating from uniformity is that we will be giving standard raises to some, but large raises to others. This has got to cost us money over the long haul.

MORGENSTERN: Fair enough, but I think that defines our problem. The standard must be too low and the raises too small. Our system encourages mediocrity among our employees. We need to think of some way to inspire excellence.

SCHULTZ: I think you suffer from delusions of grandeur, but I'm willing to believe that we can do better. Now, back to the problem at hand. How big a raise do I give Sarah?

PALGRAVE: Well, she's getting on in years. If we give her too big a raise, she'll never want to retire. Now that mandatory retirement is illegal, we have to worry about making our jobs too attractive.

SCHULTZ: True, but she's still going to be with us for awhile. If we want to keep her producing, we'd better keep her happy.

The issues raised by this discussion include the following:

- Promotions fail to be motivators for some workers. What can be substituted for promotions as a motivator?

- Raises within grade may motivate workers. How can these be given, while controlling costs?

- Do uniform raises cause problems, or are they consistent with providing incentives?

- If large raises are given in order to motivate workers, will this induce them to stay with the firm too long, extending their careers well beyond the optimal length?

To approach these issues, the following model is presented.

SENIORITY AND INCENTIVES: A MODEL ◆ ◆ ◆ ◆ ◆

Consider a firm that has only one position. All workers do essentially the same thing. The company is owned by its founder and there are no promotions foreseen. (The firm will be turned over to the owner's only daughter at the time of his death.) The problem is to keep workers motivated throughout their careers.

The easiest way to provide motivation is to pay workers a straight piece rate. Since each worker earns what he or she produces, they have appropriate incentives to put forth effort. But suppose that the output is difficult to observe (or define) at the individual level. Although a monitor can get a sense of what and how much is being produced, it is too costly to make these assessments on a frequent basis. As a result, some scheme other than a piece-rate system must be used.

In the end, what must be involved is some kind of sampling scheme, somewhat like the system of probation discussed in earlier chapters (see especially chapters 3 and 4). Without any monitoring at all, workers cannot be expected to do too much. Pride in one's own work might provide some incentive, but pride cannot be counted on to be a primary motivator. As a result, the owner will have to check on individual performance occasionally, and may want to hand out large rewards for good performance or large penalties for poor performance.

The point can best be understood in the context of Figure 11.1.[1]

To make things simple, suppose that workers in the firm can either choose to work at a high level of effort or at a low level of effort. A worker who works at a high level of effort will produce output given by the curve labeled V in Figure 11.1. As the worker gains experience in the firm, output is expected to rise up to some point, after which it declines. Alternatively, the worker can choose to work at a low level of output, in which case the worker produces V'. Like V, V' also rises and then falls, but does so at a lower level than does V. A lower level of effort results in a lower level of output over the entire career.

There is another path, labeled Alt, which reflects the worker's alternative use of time. As the worker nears retirement, the best alternative is likely to be leisure. Thus, T is the date that a worker should retire. Put in other terms, a self-employed worker producing V would voluntarily retire at T because this is the date at which the value of leisure goes from being less than the value of what is produced to more than the value of what is produced. A self-employed worker taking home V would determine that it is not worth continuing work beyond T.

Still another path, labeled W, is a possible wage profile. It is drawn such that the present value of W from time zero to time T is exactly equal to the present value of V from time zero to time T. A worker who is paid according to V would always receive exactly the value of his or her output. A worker who is paid according to W would almost never receive exactly the value of the output. Until time t_0, the worker would be paid less than he is worth. After time t_0, he would be paid more than he is worth. But over his entire lifetime, his wage payments would add

---

[1]This is based on Lazear (1979).

FIGURE 11.1
LONG-TERM INCENTIVES

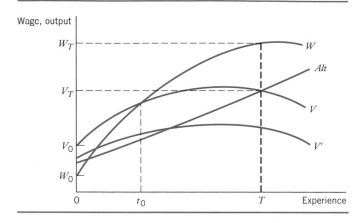

up to the value of his output. Why bother distorting the wage profile in this fashion? The reason is that incentives are not the same along each profile. The work incentives generated when the worker is paid along W are superior to those generated when the worker is paid V. In fact, a worker paid exactly V would end up producing less than V.

The reasoning goes as follows. Suppose that a worker is going to retire at time T. On the day before retirement, the worker goes through the following thought calculation.

> "I'm going to retire tomorrow. I can either work hard today, or I can loaf. If I loaf, the worst thing that can happen to me is that I will be fired. If I am fired, I cannot work tomorrow and I forgo V_T dollars. But if I am fired, I get to take the day off tomorrow. The value of my leisure tomorrow is V_T, because on the day of retirement, the value of my alternatives exactly equals the value of my output on the job. Therefore, I have nothing to lose by loafing. Even if I am fired, I gain in leisure what I lose in wages. I'll choose to shirk."

If the reader thinks about this intuitively, it makes perfect sense. One does not expect to get a great deal out of workers right before the retirement date unless there is some large pot of money that will be lost if the worker is caught loafing.

Now consider the alternative. If workers are paid W, then as long as they work up to retirement date T, they will have earned in present value exactly the same amount as they would have had they been paid V. As before, abstracting from capital market considerations, which are already implicit in the present value calculation, workers should be indifferent between path V and path W.[2] But incentives to work are different when W is paid than when V is paid, even though the two paths

---

[2]Lowenstein and Sicherman (1991) have argued that workers have a preference for steeper profiles because steep profiles provide individuals with favorable anticipation rather than dread of steady or falling wages.

offer the same total compensation. Let us repeat the thought process of the retiring worker, but now it is assumed that the worker is paid W rather than V.

> "I'm going to retire tomorrow. I can either work hard today, or I can loaf. If I loaf, the worst thing that can happen to me is that I will be fired. If I am fired, I cannot work tomorrow and I forego W_T dollars. But if I am fired, I get to take the day off tomorrow. The value of my leisure tomorrow is V_T, because on the day of retirement, the value of my alternatives exactly equals the value of my output on the job. Now I have something to lose. Since W_T exceeds V_T, the amount that I earn from working tomorrow exceeds the amount that I lose from not working. By not working, I take a chance of losing wages that are greater than the amount that I gain in leisure. My incentives to work are improved. I think that I will work today. I can consume leisure the day after retirement."

This worker recognizes that shirking risks the loss of very high wages. Since the high wages exceed the value of his leisure, the incentives to shirk are reduced. In fact, the steeper the profile, the smaller the incentives to shirk. By making the profile steep enough, shirking can be deterred.

Profiles are made steep by paying young workers less than they are worth and by paying old workers more than they are worth. Steepening profiles have no cost as long as capital markets can be used by workers to finance consumption early in life and as long as the firm can be trusted to pay the workers back when they are old.

WORK OR SHIRK? CREATING INCENTIVES TO WORK

◆ ◆ ◆ ◆ ◆

Why do workers accept the steeper profile? Wouldn't workers prefer an alternative firm that simply paid V throughout the workers' career? The answer is no, for two reasons. First, since the present value of W is the same as the present value of V, there is no reason to prefer the flatter profile to the steeper one.[3] The more important point is that a firm that offers the flatter V profile cannot actually pay V. Since the V profile induces workers to loaf, the entire productivity profile is lower when a worker is paid V than when a worker is paid W. In fact, a worker who was paid V would choose to work at the low effort level and would produce only V'. But this means that the firm must assume that the worker will produce only V' and must pay accordingly. Thus, the choice that workers face is not between W and V, but rather, between W and high effort and V' and low effort. The flat profile pays less over the lifetime and induces lower levels of effort than the steep profile. Under a variety of circumstances, workers prefer the steep profile.

This is like the apocryphal story of the Chinese merchant boat with a cruel

---

[3]There may be some reason to prefer the flatter profile. The steeper profile puts more money at risk. Firm bankruptcy or intentional default on the firm's obligation is more harmful to a worker who is paid W than to one who is paid V.

taskmaster. In earlier times, boats were powered by men with oars. The faster they rowed, the faster the boat traveled and the more money they made. The story goes that an observer was remarking to an oarsman about the cruelty of the taskmaster, who whipped the rowers when they slacked off. The observer says, "It must be terrible to have to work for such a cruel master." The oarsman replied, "He works for us. We do not work for him. The oarsmen own the boat and hire him to make sure that we do not shirk on the job."

A steep age–earnings profile is like a tough taskmaster. Because the profile is steep, workers are induced to put forth more effort. As a result, they make more money. Just as the rowers hired a taskmaster to make them put forth effort, so workers might also choose a firm with a steep age–earning profile to motivate effort. Whether they do or not depends on the value of the additional output produced relative to the pain associated with the additional level of effort. If the pain is not too great, then it is efficient to induce workers to work at the high effort level. Paying W rather than V' is then preferred.

The Worker as Lender

Workers who are paid less than they are worth when young are lenders. Implicitly, these workers are lending to the firm because they are accepting less than they are producing. This is equivalent to being paid what they are worth and then giving back some money to the firm, which acts like a bank. In Figure 11.1, the worker produces V_0 at time 0, but receives only W_0. The difference, $V_0 - W_0$, is an implicit loan that the worker makes to the firm. That money is the principal, which is repaid with interest when the worker is old. The worker is a "bond holder." He "buys" a bond from the firm, which promises to pay back the principal and interest when the worker is older.

Whether we think of the loan from the worker to the firm as a bond or as equity depends on the payback arrangement. In the case of a bond, the interest payment is fixed in advance. In our context, this means that the payback the worker receives on the loan is invariant to market conditions and other factors. By contrast, when a firm issues equity, equity holders understand that the value of their shares depends on market conditions and, in particular, on how well the firm does. If the firm does well, stock price rises. If the firm does poorly, stock price falls. Thus, the return on assets depends on company performance. In a similar vein, workers could be equity holders rather than bond holders. In Figure 11.1, the worker could "buy shares" with $V_0 - W_0$ instead of buying a bond. No explicit shares are issued, but the firm implicitly promises to pay the worker back when old. The size of the payback depends on the performance of the firm. If the firm does well, then the payback is large. This means that older workers' wages would be higher than expected. But if the firm does poorly, then the payback is small, which results in workers' wages that are lower than expected.

Either method, implicit bonds or implicit equity, provides workers with incentives. Independent of whether the repayment amount is fixed in advance or varies with the conditions in the market, it remains true that workers expect to receive more than they are worth when old. It is this premium wage that keeps them motivated. The choice between a bond-like wage structure and an equity-like wage structure depends on the risk-sharing decision. When workers are bond holders, they bear no risk on the nominal interest rate that they receive. When workers are equity holders, they share some of the nominal interest rate risk with the firm. If times are good, the rate they receive is high, but if times are bad, the rate they receive is low.

One interpretation of the much-discussed Japanese wage structure is that Japanese workers are major financiers of the firm. Japanese age-earnings profiles are steeper than American age–earnings profiles.[4] One interpretation is that Japanese workers lend more to their firms than do American workers. This is consistent with another fact. Japanese workers receive a larger part of the total compensation in the form of profit sharing than do American workers. But profit sharing is essentially an equity arrangement. When workers are involved in profit sharing, they receive an amount that depends on the performance of the firm. A profit sharer is an equity holder in the firm. Furthermore, Japanese firms tend to hold stock in other firms as well. This means that the portfolio of an individual firm is somewhat diversified, because it is made up of a cross-section of stocks. When the value of the portfolio rises, so does the wealth of the particular firm in which a given worker is employed. The worker receives some of that return through higher wages. Rather than taking the money in wages and then investing it privately through independent stock brokers, Japanese workers accept lower wages when young. The firm takes the difference between what the worker is worth and what he or she is paid and invests it. Some goes into the worker's own firm; some goes into a portfolio of stocks in other firms. Earnings at old age depend on how the firm does, which, in turn, depends on the performance of that firm and on the performance of other firms' stock held in the employer's portfolio. Large Japanese firms act as employers and also stock brokers for their workers.

American firms use less profit sharing and have flatter age–earnings profiles. This means that a smaller proportion of the workers' wealth is invested directly by the employer. Instead, some of it is paid out to the workers, and the workers can then consume it or invest it, as they see fit. It is still true, however, that some earnings are retained, placed in a "bond" for workers, and repaid when they are older. This provides incentives that prevent them from producing at level V' rather than V.

Bankruptcy and Default Risk

One problem that workers face when they accept profile W is that a significant fraction of money is tied up in the firm. In Figure 11.2, at time t_0, the worker has loaned the firm an amount equal to the line-shaded triangle. The dotted triangle is owed as repayment. From time t_0 on, the firm is paying the worker more than

---

[4]See Hashimoto and Raisian (1985).

FIGURE 11.2
IMPLICIT LOANS AND HONESTY

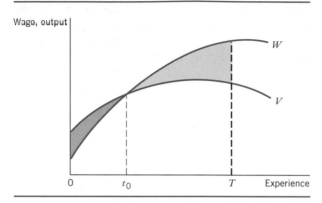

he is worth. As a result, the firm would like to terminate the worker at time t_0.

What keeps the firm from firing a worker who has been promised future payback? Reputation is probably the main factor. A firm that obtains a reputation for terminating its workers before the implicitly promised pay is received is likely to find it difficult hiring workers in the future. Reputation may carry so far, but if the profile is sufficiently steep, there will be a great deal of worker money that is being held by the firm. At some point, it might pay even a reputable firm to fire their work force and pocket the dotted triangles in Figure 11.2 that would otherwise have to be paid back. Thus, the steeper the profile, the more likely that the firm will default on its obligations.

Even firms that are concerned with their reputations may default on a payment obligations. If business conditions turn sour, a firm may end up going bankrupt, defaulting on its promises to workers. The steeper is the profile, the more that is owed to the work force. This is another force that pushes toward flatter age–earnings profiles.

Since there is some chance that any firm might default on its implicit wage obligation to workers, either intentionally or otherwise, workers will be wary of promises to pay W when the worker produces V in Figure 11.2. As a result, steep age–earnings profiles are usually best used by older firms with established reputations, operating in growing or stable industries. New firms that have not yet built a reputation for honesty will have to settle for flatter profiles and lower productivity, or they will have to find some other way to motivate workers. Firms that do not have established track records will find it difficult to attract workers by promising them high wages in the future in return for low wages today. Similarly, firms in declining industries will find that workers are not so willing to accept the promise of high future wages in lieu of wages today. Even established firms with good reputations cannot control the external forces that might cause their bankruptcy, thereby forcing them to renege on promises made to workers. Firms in declining industries must offer flatter profiles and reduce the size of the labor force until the marginal worker's product is sufficiently high to pay the market wage. Failure to do so will result in difficulty attracting workers.

Inappropriate Work Decisions and Mandatory Retirement

One problem with steeping the age–earnings profile is that a steep profile distorts the work–leisure decision. In particular, older workers want to work too much. This can be seen in Figure 11.1. The most obvious way to make the point is to examine time T, the date at which a self-employed worker would voluntarily retire. At time T, a worker earns W_T, which exceeds V_T. But at time T, the value of the alternative (shown by the height of the *Alt* curve) also equals V_T. This means that the wage exceeds the value of leisure, so the worker is anxious to work at time T. Indeed, this was exactly the point of steepening the age–earnings profile. In other words, because a large part of compensation is deferred, a worker is less willing to loaf and risk early termination. Unfortunately, steepening the profile eliminates the effort-per-hour problem, but it creates a problem in total hours worked. Workers now want to work at T and beyond. Because the wage exceeds the value of their leisure, it is beneficial to continue working. But it is not desirable to have these workers continue. This point can be made in a number of ways.

Note that beyond time T, the value of leisure exceeds the value of output. That is, *Alt* is higher than V. A worker gives up higher valued leisure for lower valued output. He is willing to do this because wages exceed the value of his leisure (and also the value of his output). At that point, he does not care about the value of output. He only cares about his wage relative to the value of his alternatives, and his wage is high relative to the value of his alternatives. But the money to pay these wages must come from somewhere.

Over the lifetime, the present value of wages paid out cannot exceed the present value of output. Any firm that paid more in wages than it received in output would be taking a loss on that worker and would do better by not hiring the worker in the first place. Thus, if the worker works longer, the rest of the earnings profile must be altered to take this into account.

It is always true that when a worker works past the point where the value of alternatives equals the value of output, the necessary adjustment in wages always makes the worker worse off. It would be better to force workers to retire at T than to permit them to work beyond and to adjust wages as necessary. This means that mandatory retirement is an efficient complement to an age–earnings profile that starts below and ends above the value of output.

To see this point, consider the following numerical example. In Table 11.1, a typical worker's V profile is reported. The individual begins work at time zero, and should retire at the end of year 40. As already stated, it is appropriate for the worker to retire at that point because the next year of work contributes \$38,667 to output, but robs \$43,713 of leisure. Since the leisure is worth more than the output, it is efficient to retire. Put differently, if the worker were self-employed, this

TABLE 11.1
STEEP AGE–EARNINGS PROFILES AND THE RETIREMENT DECISION

Year	V	Alt	Wage A	Wage B	Sum V	Sum Wage A	Sum Wage B
0	$20,000	$20,000	$10,000	$10,000	$20,000	$10,000	$10,000
1	$23,462	$20,000	$11,195	$11,171	$43,462	$21,195	$21,171
2	$25,487	$20,001	$12,389	$12,342	$68,949	$33,584	$33,513
3	$26,924	$20,001	$13,584	$13,513	$95,872	$47,167	$47,026
4	$28,038	$20,002	$14,778	$14,684	$123,911	$61,946	$61,710
5	$28,949	$20,002	$15,973	$15,855	$152,859	$77,918	$77,564
6	$29,719	$20,003	$17,167	$17,026	$182,578	$95,086	$94,590
7	$30,386	$20,005	$18,362	$18,197	$212,963	$113,447	$112,787
8	$30,974	$20,006	$19,556	$19,368	$243,937	$133,004	$132,155
9	$31,500	$20,008	$20,751	$20,539	$275,437	$153,755	$152,693
10	$31,976	$20,011	$21,946	$21,710	$307,413	$175,700	$174,403
11	$32,411	$20,014	$23,140	$22,881	$339,824	$198,840	$197,283
12	$32,810	$20,018	$24,335	$24,052	$372,634	$223,175	$221,335
13	$33,180	$20,023	$25,529	$25,223	$405,815	$248,704	$246,558
14	$33,525	$20,030	$26,724	$26,393	$439,340	$275,428	$272,951
15	$33,847	$20,039	$27,918	$27,564	$473,187	$303,346	$300,515
16	$34,150	$20,050	$29,113	$28,735	$507,337	$332,459	$329,251
17	$34,436	$20,064	$30,307	$29,906	$541,773	$362,766	$359,157
18	$34,706	$20,082	$31,502	$31,077	$576,479	$394,268	$390,234
19	$34,962	$20,106	$32,696	$32,248	$611,440	$426,965	$422,483
20	$35,206	$20,135	$33,891	$33,419	$646,646	$460,856	$455,902
21	$35,438	$20,173	$35,086	$34,590	$682,084	$495,941	$490,492
22	$35,660	$20,222	$36,280	$35,761	$717,744	$532,221	$526,253
23	$35,872	$20,284	$37,475	$36,932	$753,616	$569,696	$563,185
24	$36,076	$20,363	$38,669	$38,103	$789,692	$608,365	$601,289
25	$36,272	$20,464	$39,864	$39,274	$825,965	$648,229	$640,563
26	$36,461	$20,594	$41,058	$40,445	$862,425	$689,287	$681,008
27	$36,642	$20,760	$42,253	$41,616	$899,068	$731,540	$722,624
28	$36,818	$20,971	$43,447	$42,787	$935,885	$774,987	$765,410
29	$36,987	$21,242	$44,642	$43,958	$972,872	$819,629	$809,368
30	$37,151	$21,588	$45,837	$45,129	$1,010,023	$865,466	$854,497
31	$37,309	$22,031	$47,031	$46,300	$1,047,332	$912,497	$900,797
32	$37,463	$22,597	$48,226	$47,471	$1,084,795	$960,722	$948,268
33	$37,612	$23,321	$49,420	$48,642	$1,122,407	$1,010,143	$996,909
34	$37,757	$24,246	$50,615	$49,813	$1,160,164	$1,060,757	$1,046,722
35	$37,897	$25,429	$51,809	$50,984	$1,198,061	$1,112,567	$1,097,706
36	$38,034	$26,941	$53,004	$52,155	$1,236,095	$1,165,570	$1,149,860
37	$38,168	$28,874	$54,198	$53,326	$1,274,263	$1,219,769	$1,203,186
38	$38,297	$31,346	$55,393	$54,497	$1,312,560	$1,275,162	$1,257,683
39	$38,424	$34,506	$56,587	$55,668	$1,350,984	$1,331,749	$1,313,350
40	$38,547	$38,547	$57,782	$56,838	$1,389,531	$1,389,531	$1,370,189
41	$38,667	$43,713	$0	$58,009	$1,428,198	$1,389,531	$1,428,198

is when he or she would choose to retire.

It is also true that even if the person works for another firm, he or she prefers a profile that forces retirement at the end of year 40 to one that allows work until the end of year 41, *given that wages must be adjusted so that workers are not paid more than they are worth over their lifetime*. Let us examine the specifics.

The Wage *A* profile is designed to be steeper than the *V* profile, but also to ensure that the firm breaks even when the worker retires at the efficient date of retirement. The last year of work should be 40, because in the next year (and beyond), the value of the alternative (*Alt*) exceeds the value of output (*V*). The column labeled sum *V* keeps track of the present value of *V* up through the relevant year. All numbers in this table are calculated on the assumption that the interest rate equals zero. Thus, a worker who works only during year 0 produces $20,000 in output. The $20,000 shows up in the *V* column and also in the Sum *V* column. A worker who works through year 1 produces $20,000 + $23,462 from the *V* column, which equals $43,462, as reported in the sum *V* column. A worker who works through year 40 produces a total of $1,389,531, as reported in the sum *V* column in the row for year 40.

Since the worker produces a total of $1,389,531 over his career, he cannot be paid more than that. The Sum Wage *A* column does for Wage *A* what the Sum *V* column does for *V*. That is, it reports the sum of wages paid up through the relevant year. A worker who works only during the first year receives $10,000. A worker who works through year 40 will, over the course of his career, earn a total of $1,389,531, as reported in the Sum Wage *A* column. Note that the wage profile has been constructed such that wage starts below *V*, ends above *V*, but such that the present value (in this case just the sum) of wages over the work life exactly equals the sum of output over the work life. This way, the firm can afford to pay the worker, but there are no excess profits left on the table. If there were profits available, other firms could come in and offer the worker a better deal, thereby stealing away the worker.

The problem is this: In year 40, the worker's wage is $57,782, but the value of the alternative during the next year is only $43,713. Even without a raise, the worker would still prefer to continue working beyond year 40. At the previous year's wage, he would be happy to stay. Indeed, given the choice, the worker would not retire voluntarily.

After year 40, the firm has already paid the full value of his output. If he were to work another year, the firm would only be willing to pay $38,667 because that is the value of *V* in year 41. He would be unwilling to work for this amount, because the value of his alternative is $43,713, which exceeds $38,667. There is another upward sloping age–earnings profile that could keep the person working beyond year 40, but he will not prefer it. The reason is that in the end, the firm cannot pay over his lifetime more than he is worth. No matter how it is spread out, if he works during year 41, the firm will offer no more than an additional $38,667. Since this is less than the value of the alternatives, the worker prefers the Wage *A* schedule.

To see this, consider the Wage *B* schedule. It pays less than the worker is worth when young and more than the worker is worth when old. It is also constructed such that the total value of wage payments up through year 41 exactly equals the total value of output up through year 41. To see this, note that Sum V is $1,428,198 in year 41, as is Sum Wage B. Which profile does the worker prefer—Wage A through 40 years or Wage B through 41 years? The answer is Wage A through 40 years. The difference between the Wage B amount and the Wage A amount is $1,428,198 − $1,389,531, or $38,667.

The value of the alternatives in year 41 is $43,713. By selecting Wage B and working through year 41, the worker earns $38,667 more than if he were to select Wage A and work through year 40. But the worker forgoes alternatives during the year 41, which are worth $43,713. Thus, the profile that couples mandatory retirement at the efficient date (i.e., the date at which V equals Alt), is always preferred by the worker to profiles that induce him to work longer, while allowing the firm to break even.

This is not merely a fluke of this example. It is always true. When a worker is induced to work past the efficient retirement date, it either costs the firm more than the worker is worth, or the worker is implicitly being paid less than the value of alternatives during the extra years. The formal proof of this proposition is given in the appendix to this chapter.

A worker who was offered a choice between the Wage A profile with mandatory retirement after year 40 and the Wage B profile without mandatory retirement would always choose the Wage A profile. The value of earnings during the additional years, given that the rest of the profile must adjust to make the firm break even, could never be high enough to cover the value of leisure (or other alternatives) during years following the efficient retirement date.

Mandatory retirement is therefore efficient, but it is also illegal. The Age Discrimination in Employment Act of 1974 and its subsequent amendments have all but eliminated mandatory retirement in the United States. But mandatory retirement was the mechanism used to induce workers to leave at the efficient date. Is there an alternative? Specifically, how about going back to paying V, rather than W? If workers were paid V, they would choose to retire voluntarily at exactly the point when V equals Alt—that is, at efficient retirement. Unfortunately, doing this would reduce incentives to put forth effort, and worker productivity would fall to V', which is an inferior solution all the way around. There is another possibility. Pension buyout plans can be used to induce the worker to leave voluntarily. If the plans are structured appropriately, efficient retirement and high levels of effort can be attained simultaneously. Chapter 16 will explore the possibilities in detail.

Uses of Upward-Sloping Age–Earnings Profiles as Motivators

We have already discussed a number of possible methods to motivate workers. When should upward sloping age–earnings profiles be used as the primary form of motivation?

There are two conditions that make the use of upward sloping profiles more valuable: (1) output is costly to measure directly, and (2) tournament-style rewards are effective motivators.

Output Costly to Measure Directly

If output were easily observed and measured, then it would be straightforward to motivate workers. Each worker could be paid a piece rate based on output level. There would be no problem of motivating middle-level managers. As long as each month's pay depended on each month's output, workers would have no incentive to reduce effort with time.

The implication is that upward-sloping profiles are most likely to be a valuable motivator when output cannot be easily observed. This means that managerial jobs and jobs where projects have long completion periods are the best candidates for upward-sloping age–earnings profiles. In these jobs, immediate observation of output is unlikely. At best, worker output can be "sampled" periodically to determine whether it meets or exceeds a particular standard. Since the samples are taken infrequently, punishment for substandard performance must be relatively large. The punishment takes the form of termination and loss of wages that exceed what the worker could earn elsewhere.

Tournament-Style Rewards Effective

Tournament-style rewards, where workers are promoted based on their relative performance, are effective motivators. Sometimes a tournament system creates adverse incentives. The last chapter was spent discussing the negative political ramifications of basing rewards on relative comparisons between workers. The main point was that cooperation can be lost when workers are compensated on their relative status. Thus, tournaments should not be used when cooperation is important. A better scheme in settings where cooperation must be preserved is to use upward-sloping age–earnings profiles that compensate an individual's performance relative to some standard, not relative to co-workers' performance.

An upward-sloping age–earnings profile is based on absolute, rather than relative, performance. The entire firm can be paid along a schedule like that shown in Figure 11.1. The firm breaks even on each worker, and there is no need to fire some in order to make a budget. On the contrary, the wage profile is designed with the assumption that workers will continue to work from time 0 to time T. There is no need to pit one worker against another. As a result, cooperation between workers is not sacrificed.

Frequency of Termination

If all goes as planned, termination should be a very rare event. A sufficiently steep profile makes it costly for workers to lose their jobs. If the profile is properly designed, they will be reluctant to take actions, or more correctly, inactions, that will put their jobs in jeopardy. In fact, a perfect incentive scheme would induce all workers to do what was expected and termination would never be observed. It is the threat of termination, not actual termination, that provides incentives. Of course, if loafing workers were never fired, the threat would not be credible, and incentives would again be compromised.

An example of this strategy in use draws on my undergraduate days, when I worked part-time in the housekeeping department of the UCLA Medical Center.

The housekeeping department's main responsibility was keeping the hospital clean. The department consisted of approximately 110 janitors, each of whom had a cleaning route. Since the building was very large and most of the cleaning was done at night, it was possible to evade most supervision. Occasionally workers would hide and go to sleep on the job. Unless the foreman went over the entire route of a janitor, it was very difficult to catch someone loafing. Occasionally, however, the foreman actually did discover a janitor sleeping on the job. Whenever this happened, the unfortunate sleeper would be summarily terminated.

The punishment seems far greater than the harm caused. A worker who sleeps for an hour was essentially stealing an hour's wage from UCLA, since the wage was paid, but no work was performed. Still, the punishment of termination might inflict far greater costs on the worker than the (then) $3.00 that the janitor would have produced during that hour. The reason that the punishment had to be so severe was that sleeping on the job is so difficult to detect. Because workers understand that they will rarely be caught, the punishment to deter sleeping must be very large.

◆ ◆ ◆ ◆ ◆ ## USE OF ACTUAL PROFILES

In actual practice, promotions and within-job raises are combined to produce incentives. Recall that we began this chapter by trying to provide incentives to managers who knew that they would not be promoted further. The solution provided was steep *within job* age–earnings profiles. Thus, a typical profile might look like the one shown in Figure 11.3. Promotions occur at times t_0 and t_1. After t_1, there are no more promotions, but there remain within-job growth opportunities. The wage at t_1 could be less than the worker is worth, while the wage at the time of retirement could be significantly more than the worker is worth. This fits with the typical profile. It also means that even if the worker knows he or she will not be promoted after time t_1, there are still incentives to work hard. The high wages that come at the end of the work life motivate the worker to remain with the firm until the normal retirement date.

Uniformity of Wage Changes

Even if raises based on seniority are an important part of the wage setting process, it is not necessary that workers be treated identically. At one extreme is the federal government's general schedule wage structure. Once a worker's grade and step are known, wage is determined. In theory, workers may differ in the speed with which they reach a given grade or step, but in reality, the federal government tends to provide similar treatment to all workers, almost irrespective of performance.

The federal government's example does not pertain to the typical firm, nor should it be followed as a model of incentive generation. Upward-sloping age–earnings profiles motivate workers because there is some chance that they will lose their jobs if their performance falls below some level. Government workers are almost completely protected from such a threat. The realization of the threat

FIGURE 11.3
WITHIN-JOB AND
BETWEEN-JOB EARNNGS

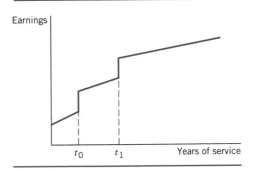

implies a wage cut for workers, because those who lose their jobs are generally forced to take a lower-paying job.

It is possible, even within the framework of seniority-based wages, to allow for differences across workers. Some workers could be given larger raises than others. The average profile might be the one shown by curve W in Figure 11.1, but some could have steeper and others flatter profiles, reflecting some differences in performance.

Additionally, as in the federal system, a firm has leeway in terms of the grade and step in which it classifies a given worker. Workers who show superior performance can be assigned to a higher grade or moved through the step structure more rapidly.

An Application of the Theory

As is always the case, it is easier to state the general principle than it is to make it operational. How steep should the profile be? What are workers willing to accept? How do we obtain information on these issues? In this section, we go through an example using the kind of data that are obtainable (for example, through compensation consultants) to derive an actual age–earnings profile.

Table 11.2 provides information on hours worked and wages paid by other firms. These data can be obtained from compensation consultants who keep detailed records on the amount of compensation that workers receive and on their working conditions. In the first column, the firm's identifier is listed. In the second column, hours of work among managerial employees at that firm are given. The third and fourth columns report the wages at ages 30 and 65, respectively. Finally, the last column is derived from the previous two. The percentage wage change is defined as

$$100 \times (\text{Wage at 30} - \text{Wage at 60}) \, / \, (\text{Wage at 30})$$

There is a relation between hours of work, the starting wage, and wage growth. It is possible to run a regression of the following form:

$$\text{Hours worked} = a + b \, (\text{Wage at 30}) + c \, (\% \text{ change in wage})$$

TABLE 11.2
HOURS WORKED AND WAGES PAYED BY OTHER FIRMS

Firm Identifier	Hours Worked	Wage at 30	Wage at 65	% Wage Change
101	45	$27.61	$74.37	169.4%
102	46	$32.21	$75.12	133.2%
103	44	$26.26	$73.50	179.9%
104	47	$31.72	$78.68	148.0%
105	43	$34.36	$64.52	87.8%
106	42	$29.15	$67.07	130.1%
107	44	$29.05	$72.08	148.1%
108	42	$33.72	$62.47	85.3%
109	42	$28.30	$65.86	132.7%
110	41	$32.14	$62.07	93.1%
111	43	$27.58	$70.57	155.9%
112	46	$28.65	$78.05	172.5%
113	42	$29.86	$65.88	120.7%
114	47	$34.94	$77.61	122.1%
115	42	$25.60	$66.49	159.7%
116	41	$30.25	$62.93	108.0%
117	42	$32.78	$62.07	89.4%
118	44	$31.29	$71.20	127.5%
119	46	$26.86	$77.32	187.8%
120	45	$32.29	$74.61	131.1%
121	44	$30.82	$71.93	133.4%
122	42	$34.95	$60.34	72.7%
123	39	$25.12	$60.58	141.2%
124	43	$28.50	$70.58	147.7%
125	44	$27.73	$72.96	163.1%
126	41	$29.66	$62.53	110.8%
127	46	$34.12	$73.76	116.2%
128	44	$32.64	$68.36	109.4%
129	40	$27.25	$62.67	129.9%
130	45	$29.17	$75.26	158.0%

When this was done using the data from Table 11.2, the following estimates were obtained:

Hours worked = .21 + 1.004 (Wage at 30) + .096(% change in wage)

The regression does not fit perfectly, but the r-squared is .96, which implies a very good fit. In the labor market from which these data were drawn, an increase in the slope of the profile by 10 percent means about a one-hour increase in the overall number of hours worked. Hours of work are greater in firms with steeper profiles because the incentives to remain on the job are greater. Workers put forth additional effort to increase the probability that they will retain their jobs.

Given these data and some data on productivity, it is possible to determine what the optimal shape of the profile should be. Suppose that the firm in question

TABLE 11.3
SALARY AT THE FIRM: NOW AND PROPOSED

Age	Current Salary	Proposed Wage
30	$60,000	$60,750
31	$61,714	$65,415
32	$63,429	$67,245
33	$65,143	$69,076
34	$66,857	$70,906
35	$68,571	$72,736
36	$70,286	$74,566
37	$72,000	$76,397
38	$73,714	$78,227
39	$75,429	$80,057
40	$77,143	$81,887
41	$78,857	$83,717
42	$80,571	$85,548
43	$82,286	$87,378
44	$84,000	$89,208
45	$85,714	$91,038
46	$87,429	$92,868
47	$89,143	$94,699
48	$90,857	$96,529
49	$92,571	$98,359
50	$94,286	$100,189
51	$96,000	$102,020
52	$97,714	$103,850
53	$99,429	$105,680
54	$101,143	$107,510
55	$102,857	$109,340
56	$104,571	$111,171
57	$106,286	$113,001
58	$108,000	$114,831
59	$109,714	$116,661
60	$111,429	$118,491
61	$113,143	$120,322
62	$114,857	$122,152
63	$116,571	$123,982
64	$118,286	$125,812
65	$120,000	$127,575

currently has a starting salary of $60,000 per year, which works out to $30 per hour, since managerial workers currently work on average 40 hours per week, or 2,000 hours per year. Workers who are 65 earn $120,000 per year, or $60 per hour. By raising the slope of the profile, additional hours of work can be elicited. But this has a cost, namely higher salary. Table 11.3 reports current and proposed salary at the firm in question.

Given the salaries, it is possible to calculate the present value of the wage stream under the current and proposed scenario. If the interest rate is 5 percent, we simply sum up the salaries and put them in dollars at any (arbitrary) age, say, age 30. Doing this for current wages yields

$$(11.1) \quad \sum_{i=0}^{35} \frac{(\text{Salary at age } 30 + i)\,(40 \text{ hours per week})\,(50 \text{ weeks per year})}{1.05^i}$$

$$= \$520,844$$

Now, the proposed higher salary is based on the following calculation. A 5 percent steepening of the profile would result in an increase in effort of about half an hour per week, based on the regression and data in Table 11.2. The implicit hourly wage for a 30-year-old is $30. Keeping the wage rate at $30 per hour, but allowing wage growth to increase sufficiently to induce an extra half-hour of work means that the worker would work 40.5 hours per week instead of the initial 40. Thus, earnings in the first year of work would necessarily rise to $60,750, reflecting an extra .5 hours per week times 50 weeks per year. The cost of the increased number of hours is therefore $30 \times 25 = \$750$. Wage growth is allowed to occur such that by age 65, instead of earning an implicit $60 per hour under the proposed scheme, the worker earns an implicit $63, which is a 5 percent increase over the current wage of $60.00. This 5 percent increase induces the worker to put forth a half-hour more effort each week. Earnings at age 65 would then have to be

$$40.5 \times 50 \times \$63 = \$127,575$$

Again, the formula in Equation 11.1 can be used to calculate the age 30 present value of the worker's salary payments under the proposed scheme. It is identical to the previous calculation, except that the salary used is the proposed rather than the actual salary and hours worked are assumed to be 40.5, rather than 40. Doing the calculation now yields

$$(11.2) \quad \sum_{i=0}^{35} \frac{(\text{Proposed Salary at age } 30 + i)\,(40.5 \text{ hours per week})\,(50 \text{ weeks per year})}{1.05^i} = \$547,857$$

The increase in cost is therefore $\$547,857 - \$520,844 = \$27,013$.

The question for the firm is now straightforward. Is the increased productivity associated with the additional half-hour per week over the entire career greater than the cost of $27,013? If the firm estimates that the extra half-hour per week will produce more than $27,013 in profit, the proposed increase in profile slope is a good strategy.

◆ ◆ ◆ ◆ ◆ RECAP

Some workers have reached a level such that they are unlikely to attain additional promotions in the firm—and they know it. It is still possible to provide monetary incentives to these workers by allowing for within-grade wage growth. By using steep age–earnings profiles, which pay workers less than they are worth when new in the grade, and more than they are worth when very senior in the grade, positive incentives are provided.

Steep age–earnings profiles do not necessarily cost the firm more money than flat profiles. Steep profiles may start below, but end above, flatter profiles at corresponding firms. Workers are willing to accept lower starting wages because they know their lifetime earnings will be higher. Although it is true that a greater proportion of income comes later in their career, workers who have access to capital markets may not object to such a payment pattern.

Uniformity of wage increases is no more a consequence of steep age–earnings profiles than it is of flat ones. To the extent that productivity can be observed, wages can be varied across workers while maintaining an upward-sloping structure to the age–earnings profile.

A profile that pays workers more than they are worth when old and less than they are worth when young induces inefficient labor supply behavior. In particular, old workers are too anxious to remain with the firm because their wages exceed their alternatives. Mandatory retirement, or some other scheme that induces workers to retire voluntarily, is an important complement to a wage profile that grows more rapidly than productivity. Since mandatory retirement is now illegal in the United States, later chapters will discuss alternative approaches to induce voluntary retirement at the efficient age.

REFERENCES ◆ ◆ ◆ ◆ ◆

Hashimoto, Masanori, and John Raisian, "Employment Tenure and Earnings Profiles in Japan and the United States," *American Economic Review* 75,4 (September 1985): 721–35.

Lazear, Edward P., "Why Is There Mandatory Retirement?" *Journal of Political Economy* 87 (December 1979): 1261–64.

Loewenstein, George, and Nachum Sicherman, "Do Workers Prefer Increasing Wage Profiles?" *Journal of Labor Economics* 9 (January 1991): 67–84.

ADDITIONAL ADVANCED READING ◆ ◆ ◆ ◆ ◆

Abraham, Katharine G., and Henry S. Farber, "Job Duration, Seniority, and Earnings," *American Economic Review* 77 (June 1987): 278–97.

Akerlof, George, and Lawrence F. Katz, "Workers' Trust Funds and the Logic of Wage Profiles," *Quarterly Journal of Economics* 104 (August 1989): 525–35.

Altonji, Joseph G., and Robert A. Shakotko, "Do Wages Rise with Job Seniority?" *Review of Economic Studies* 54 (July 1987): 437–59.

Carmichael, H. Lorne, et al., "Self-Enforcing Contracts, Shirking and Life Cycle Incentives," *Journal of Economic Perspectives* 3 (Fall 1989): 65–83.

Frank, Robert H., and Robert M. Hutchens, "Wages, Seniority, and the Demand for Rising Consumption Profiles," *Journal of Economic Behavior and Organization* 21 (August 1993): 251–76.

Hutchens, Robert M., "A Test of Lazear's Theory of Delayed Payment Contracts," *Journal of Labor Economics* 5 (Part 2, October 1986): 439–57.

Hutchens, Robert, "Delayed Payment Contracts and a Firm's Propensity to Hire Older Workers," *Journal of Labor Economics* 4 (October 1986): 439–57.

Medoff, James L., and Katharine G. Abraham, "Experience, Performance, and Earnings," *Quarterly Journal of Economics* 95 (December 1980): 703–36.

◆ ◆ ◆ ◆ ◆   **APPENDIX**

This appendix offers proof that any worker who works beyond the efficient date of retirement either earns less than his alternatives for the excessive years or costs the firm more than he is worth.

Consider an efficient wage scheme. Competition implies that the firm must pay the worker a present value of wages equal to the present value of output. If not, the worker could be offered more by another firm that could still earn a profit. Thus, define $W(t)$ as the wage profile, $V(t)$ as the productivity profile, and $A(t)$ as the profile of alternatives. The efficient date of retirement, T, is defined as that date such that

$$A(T) = V(T)$$

Consequently, for all $t > T$, $A(t) - V(t) > 0$.

Now, competition requires that

(A11.1)
$$\int_0^T W(t)e^{-rt}dt = \int_0^T V(t)e^{-rt}dt$$

where r is the interest rate. If Equation A11.1 did not hold, then firms would make profits or take losses.

Suppose the worker opts to work to some date $T' > T$. The firm then pays a wage profile $Z(t)$ between 0 and T'.

If the firm pays what the worker is worth for years 0 to T', it must be the case that

(A11.2)
$$\int_0^{T'} Z(t)e^{-rt}dt = \int_0^{T'} V(t)e^{-rt}dt$$

The difference between present value of wage profiles $W(t)$ and $Z(t)$ is

$$\int_0^{T'} Z(t)e^{-rt}dt - \int_0^T W(t)e^{-rt}dt$$

or, using (A11.1) and (A11.2),

$$\int\limits_{0}^{T'} V(t)e^{-rt}dt - \int\limits_{0.}^{T} V(t)e^{-rt}dt$$

or

$$\int\limits_{T}^{T'} V(t)e^{-rt}dt$$

But $\int\limits_{T}^{T'} V(t)e^{-rt}dt$ must be less than $\int\limits_{T}^{T'} A(t)e^{-rt}dt$ because $A(t) < V(t)\ \forall\ t > T$. Thus, if the firm breaks even, the worker receives less for incremental years than for alternatives.

TEAMS

12

*F*irms exist in large part because working together is more productive than working as individuals. The whole is greater than the sum of the parts. In order for individuals to work together productively, the firm must know how to set up teams and motivate team members. In recent years, the term *teamwork* has become a common buzzword. Team production has become an increasingly important issue, explicitly discussed in business settings, yet team production has existed since people began working together.

An assembly line is an example of a highly structured team in which workers are assigned a particular task. Assembly line production takes place under one roof, and the output is attributed to all workers along the line. As a result, when something goes wrong with the product, all members of the team suffer. The following scenario identifies some of the issues involved in team production.

ENGEL: I think that we have something to learn from the Japanese. They are known to be cooperative and highly productive. It's no accident. A much larger fraction of the typical worker's compensation in Japan depends on company performance than in the United States.

COURNOT: True. But why does any one worker care about the company? Unless he is very high up in the firm, he can have only a very small effect on profits. My guess is that most workers assume that what they get as a bonus based on company profits is pure luck. They can't really think that it depends very much on what they have done.

ENGEL: Yes, but the other workers care. If I see you slacking off and I know that my income depends on your effort, I'm going to get pretty mad.

FRISCH: This is the principle that was used in Soviet gulogs. They would assign a task to a group of workers that essentially could not be accomplished unless each prisoner put forth a lot of effort. None of the prisoners would be fed unless the task was completed. When one slacked off, the others would get on him.

COURNOT: I read that book, too. The scheme worked pretty well, but it had some problems. Remember that gangs formed among the prisoners, which forced other prisoners to do all their own work and that of the gang members as well? That's one problem with making worker welfare depend on group effort.

ENGEL: But our workers aren't prisoners. If they don't like it here, they can quit. If we start playing these games with them, we are going to create some real morale problems, and I predict that this will result in high turnover.

FRISCH: Even if we accept the principle of using the team as the profit unit, there is still the issue of structuring the team. Is the team the whole firm, or some subset of it?

ENGEL: Well, for some purposes it's the whole firm. For other purposes, we have to divide up the workers.

FRISCH: Fine. But for which purposes, and how do we group the workers?

ENGEL: You raise some important questions, but let's not junk the idea just because we don't have all the answers right now. Let's think about some of the issues and revisit this topic later.

This chapter discusses a number of issues raised in the introductory dialog.

- When should teams be used?
- How can firms motivate workers to perform in a team environment?
- When do workers care about the performance of the team as opposed to individual performance?
- How does peer pressure operate in a team context?
- What is the team structure that results in the highest possible profits?

◆ ◆ ◆ ◆ ◆ THE USE OF TEAMS

Every manager will extoll the virtues of teamwork. We are reminded of the star football player whose cliché response to any question about his outstanding performance is that he couldn't have done it without the team. This false modesty is

DILBERT reprinted by permission of United Feature Syndicate, Inc.

almost as prevalent in business as it is in sports. It is important to analyze when teamwork is important and when it is not. Why? Isn't teamwork always valuable? Perhaps it is, but it comes at a cost.

One byproduct of teamwork is that sometimes workers can hide behind the productivity of the others, thereby diluting incentives within the firm. Thus, teams should only be used when the synergy from collective effort is substantial enough to outweigh the costs of weakened individual incentives to perform. Before discussing conditions appropriate for the use of teams, we discuss a problem associated with teams.

Free-Rider Effects

When individuals work in teams, it tends to be difficult to observe the output of any given worker. Because it is not possible to observe individual output, individual workers have the ability to hide behind the successes or failures of the group as a whole. This dilutes incentives.

Consider the example of going out for pizza with a group of ten friends. Except in groups of accountants or actuaries, the general rule is that the bill will be split evenly among the ten diners. The waiter comes to the table and asks for orders. Each diner would like to have a beer. Fancy imported beer costs $3.00, and thin American beer costs $1.25. The diner goes through the following calculation: If I order an imported beer instead of an American beer, then the bill will be $1.75 higher. But my share of that is only 17.5 cents. As long as the imported beer is worth at least 17.5 cents more to me then the domestic beer, I will order the expensive one. Of course, everyone at the table does the same calculation, and the bill is $17.50 higher as a result.

This is the free-rider effect in action. "Since I do not bear the full consequences of my actions, I do not behave appropriately." Indeed, when bills are split, the total cost of the dinner is higher than it would be were each person to be billed only for the amount that he or she actually eats. (Lesson: To stay slim, go out in small groups and do not split the bill evenly.) Similarly, in the workplace, when work is shared total effort is lower because some of the benefits to an individual's effort are captured by other workers.

Consider a similar scenario in the work environment. A worker is placed in a team with four other workers. The team is assigned a project that must be completed in a timely manner. Each worker is told that for every day that the project comes in ahead of schedule, the team will be given a bonus of $100, which will be split evenly among the five team members. Consider any given member's, say, Joe's, decision to stay late to work on the project. Joe can either stay late, or he can go home and watch the World Series. He enjoys watching the World Series, but would also like to receive the bonus for finishing the job early. Joe figures that if he works late tonight, he will speed up completion of the project by one day. This is worth $100 to the group. He likes the World Series, but not so much that he is willing to give up $100 to watch it. But then Joe remembers: If the group makes $100, he only gets $20 of it. After thinking it over, Joe goes home to watch the game.

The reason effort was reduced below its efficient level is that *the worker who bears the pain of toiling does not reap the full benefits*. Were Joe to take home the full $100, he would have worked. Since the company was willing to pay $100 for a day earlier completion date, it must have been worth at least $100 to the company to get the work done. Yet, because Joe would only receive $20 if the group accomplished the work early, the work was not accomplished. Had the company instead paid Joe the full $100 to stay late, both the company and Joe would have been better off. Since Joe prefers $100 to watching the World Series, he is better off, and since the company is willing to pay at least $100 for the earlier completion, it is better off.

What prevents the company from paying individuals rather than teams for their effort? Nothing, as long as individual effort can be observed. However, in a team environment, individual effort is difficult to observe. Further, sometimes basing the rewards on a measurement that is a proxy for individual efforts can result in uncooperative or opportunistic behavior. Basketball is a good illustration of how compensation based on a proxy for individual performance can destroy team work.

Basketball is a game where teamwork is quite important. One player's ability to get off a good shot depends on his teammates passing him the ball at the right moment. Suppose that a basketball player's compensation were based only on team performance. The free rider effect comes into play. There will be situations where an individual's effort would aid the team, but he will be reluctant to put forth the effort because he only captures a small portion of the return. Recognizing this, the team decides to pay on the basis of individual performance, say, by rewarding players according to the number of points they score. Now the problem is that no player works for the good of the team. Consider a situation where Michael Jordan can either take a shot or pass the ball to his teammate, Scottie Pippen. If Jordan is paid on the basis of points that he and he alone scores, he will prefer to shoot, even if Pippen is in a better position to make the shot. This does not imply that Jordan is selfish. Rather, it reflects that production occurs in a team environment, but that Jordan is paid on the basis of his individual output. Thus, there is a fundamental conflict between the kind of activity that is expected from the player and the kind of compensation he receives.

Herein lies the problem. If workers are paid on the basis of team output, they free-ride and do not put forth enough effort. If workers are paid on the basis of individual output, they do not care about team output enough. They focus too heavily on their own contributions and ignore teammates, even when helping someone else might further the interests of the team.

This is why teams should only be used when there is a compelling reason to group individuals into teams. When individuals work together in teams, the firm is faced with a choice. Either it rewards workers on the basis of the team, in which case workers free-ride, or it rewards workers on the basis of individual effort, in which case workers behave selfishly, to the detriment of the firm.

The conflict reflects the fundamental problem associated with observability. There is nothing in theory that prevents a firm from rewarding a worker for both teamwork and an individual contribution. In the basketball example, Jordan could be penalized for hogging the ball when he should have passed to a teammate. But it is difficult to make that call after the fact. Even if every moment of every game is analyzed, mistakes in judging performance are inevitable. This situation lends itself to controversy between workers and supervisors who may see the same situation differently. As a practical matter, accurate masterminding of individual contributions to the output of the team is virtually impossible.

When to Use Teams

Given the problems just raised, when should firms set up teams? The answer at the most abstract level is simple: Teams should be used when the benefits from using them are high and when the costs of using them are low. Let us make these general principles more concrete.

First, consider the benefit side. When are the benefits from teamwork the greatest? The answer is, when there are large **complementarities** between what one worker does and what another worker does. Some obvious examples come to mind.

When the activity requires physical labor, some projects cannot be undertaken alone. For example, teamwork is necessary to move an object that is too heavy to be lifted by one person, but not too heavy to be lifted by two people. (We presented such an example in a previous chapter.) Another example involves meeting a deadline, where it was impossible for one person to complete the work in time, but a team of people can meet the deadline.

This leads to a useful general principle. To borrow from an old expression, teams should be used when *the whole is greater than the sum of its parts*. The two examples just mentioned fit this prescription. In the case of moving a heavy object, the output of each individual trying to move the object is zero—the object simply does not move. Only as a team can they generate any output. The second case involving the deadline is best illustrated via a numerical example.

Suppose that on-time delivery of a project, which is due two weeks from now, will earn the company $10,000 in profit. If the project is delivered two weeks late, the project will only yield $5,000 in profit because the client will pay a lower price. During the time of the first project there is another project being worked on at the firm. Its deadline is four weeks off, and it yields a profit of $15,000. Both projects require the same amount of time to complete. If only one consultant works on each project, four weeks are required for completion. If both work on each project, two weeks are required for completion.

If consultants work separately, total profit for the firm after four weeks will be $20,000(=$15,000 + $5,000). This is the "sum of the parts." However, if consultants form a team and do the rush project first, it will be completed on time, yielding $10,000 of profit. They can then work together on the project that is due four weeks hence, completing it in the remaining two weeks, to earn $15,000. Therefore, total profits for the firm would be $25,000. Thus, the whole of working together is greater than the sum of the parts.

Consider another example, say, a gate agent for an airline. The gate agent sometimes works with another gate agent, but not always with the same person. Consider the case where there are two stations at the check-in counter for a particular flight. Although there may be some complementarity between the two agents, each works his or her check-in line almost independently—a case where the whole is not much greater than the sum of the parts. This is not to say that there is no benefit from teamwork. The two working together can share information and can coordinate better. But whatever gains there are must be traded off against the costs of combining workers into a team.

The primary cost to using teams is productivity loss through the free-rider effect. In the airline example, if the two gate agents are compensated on the basis of team output, each has an incentive to shirk. For example, the agents could be compensated on the speed with which they process passengers. Passengers could be asked to form one line and go to the next available agent. But, under such an arrangement, neither agent bears the full cost of any reduction in effort. Additionally, whatever benefits accrue to teamwork are not readily observable to a supervisor. As such, they are difficult to reward. Thus, the only way to inspire teamwork is to reward on the basis of team output, but this inescapably leads us back to the free-rider effect.

Considering the two cases, it is likely that the example of consultants working on two projects is a more natural choice for teamwork and team compensation than the example of the airline gate agent. Activities can be ranked according to the costs and benefits of having teams. Production activities that rank high on the benefits scale and low on the cost scale should be performed by teams. Individual team members who are involved in this type of activity should be rewarded according to team output. Table 12.1 provides an example from a fishing firm.

Team production is valuable in some activities and not so valuable in others. Further, team production leads to more slippage in some activities through the free-rider effect and less in others. Putting salespeople together into a team is likely to cause much free riding without much benefit from team spillovers. According to Table 12.1, the best candidate for team production is the actual fishing itself and the worst candidate is selling the fish.

TABLE 12.1
COSTS AND BENEFITS OF TEAMWORK

Activity	Benefit Rank: 1 = Highest benefits	Cost Rank: 1 = Highest cost	Comments
Fishing on a small boat	2	5	Fishing requires tasks that cannot be performed single-handedly. The cost of monitoring other team members is low. Unproductive team members can be thrown off the team by other members.
Fishing on a large boat	1	4	Teamwork is probably more important on a large boat, where the tasks are larger in scale, than on a small boat. Setting very large nets require a number of hands and some machinery. The larger the team, the more difficult the team monitoring problem, and free-rider effects are more significant.
Selling the fish wholesale	5	1	Salespersons can work alone. Monitoring them as a group involves enormous free-rider problems since peer monitoring is difficult.
Accounting for sales	4	2	There is not a great deal of benefit associated with accountants working together, especially if one individual can handle all of the books alone. Additionally, since accountants' work can be monitored individually, but is difficult to monitor in a team setting, the costs associated with team production are high.
Selecting the fishing site	3	3	Multiple judgments may prove useful and discussion matters. But committee decision making is slow and difficult.

Other Direct Benefits of Team Production

Before leaving this topic, it is useful to mention two other benefits associated with team production: specialization and knowledge transfer.

Specialization and Teams

Specialization is the classic case that Adam Smith referred to in his pin factory example. The typical assembly line is team production. Each member of the team specializes in one small and well-defined task. The fact that he or she can specialize allows each job to be done more efficiently. If individuals did not work in teams, production would be much slower and more costly. A car that had to be built top to bottom by one worker would take a great deal of time and would not be of the same quality as one made by a large number of specialists.

An assembly line is a team, because each part is linked to another. If one part is not made properly, complementary parts will not work well. It is also very difficult to monitor individual performance on assembly line tasks. The part may not fail until months after the car has been sold. At that point, it is very costly to trace the individual who caused the problem.

Knowledge Transfer in Teams

Knowledge transfer is the second benefit from team production and probably occurs more when specialization is not too great. For valuable knowledge transfer to occur, individuals must have distinct information sets and the information sets must be relevant to each other. If there is too much information overlap, teamwork does not produce much knowledge transfer. If the information that one has is irrelevant to another, then knowledge transfer has no value. Figure 12.1 illustrates the conditions conducive to successful knowledge transfer.

Consider two workers, Engel and Frisch. The left rectangle, labeled E, denotes the information that Engel has. The right rectangle, labeled F, denotes the information that Frisch has. There is a smaller rectangle that is part of both E and F, representing information that Engel and Frisch share. Most of the area is not shared, indicating that most of the information that Frisch has is not also possessed by Engel and vice versa. Thus, there is potential gain from teamwork through knowledge transfer, because large parts of the information sets are not overlapping. Whether teamwork is valuable depends also on informational requirements of the two jobs. Knowledge transfer may take place that has no value.

Figure 12.1 illustrates two cases. Suppose that the information required to perform the tasks is reflected by the areas in the ellipses outlined in solid curves. Frisch has knowledge on his own to perform about half of the tasks required of him (half of Frisch's task's solid oval lies inside the Frisch information set rectangle). Similarly, Engel has knowledge on his own to perform about half of the tasks required of him (half of the Engel's task's solid oval lies inside the Engel information set rectangle). By working as a team, Engel can transfer all the knowledge necessary for Frisch to perform all of his required tasks, and Frisch can do the same for Engel. Thus, Frisch and Engel have largely nonoverlapping information sets, and the information possessed by the other worker is relevant.

FIGURE 12.1
THE CASE OF SUBSTANTIALLY
OVERLAPPING INFORMATION SETS

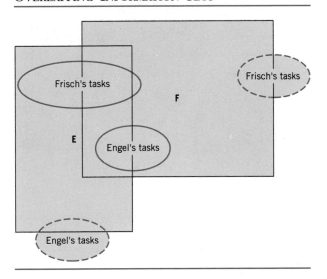

Now suppose that the information required to perform the tasks is represented by the areas in the ellipses outlined in dotted curves. As before, information possessed by each worker is reflected by the rectangles. Thus, Engel has a great deal of information that Frisch does not have, and vice versa. Further, Frisch only has information to perform about half of his tasks, since half of the task's dotted ellipse lies outside of his information set. But the half that lies outside his task ellipse also lies outside the information set of Engel. Engel has a great deal of information that Frisch does not have, but none of it is relevant to Frisch. The same is true of Engel. Engel has information to perform less than half of the tasks required of him. Frisch has a great deal of information that Engel does not have, but none of it helps in performing Frisch's required tasks. The nonoverlapping parts of the information set are, in this case, irrelevant.

To restate: Teamwork can produce valuable knowledge transfer when two conditions hold:

1. Members of the team have idiosyncratic pieces of information so that putting the team together allows new information to flow among members.
2. The idiosyncratic information possessed by one individual is valuable to some other individuals in the team.

Thus, the information sets must be distinct, and the idiosyncratic components must be relevant.

These two factors should help thinking about choosing members for a team. For example, an auto mechanic and cost accountant do not make a good team.

FIGURE 12.2
THE CASE OF ALMOST NONOVERLAPPING
INFORMATION SETS

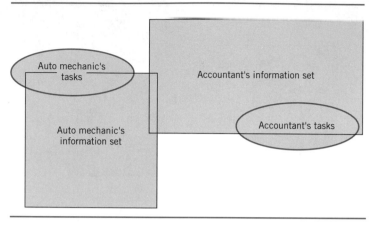

While it is true that their information sets are nonoverlapping (the auto mechanic does not know anything about cost accounting and vice versa), the idiosyncratic information is irrelevant. There is little value to having a cost accountant learn how to replace a transmission.

Figure 12.2 reflects this situation. Information sets are almost completely disjoint, but the information that is needed by the accountant is not held by the auto mechanic, and vice versa. The auto mechanic is ignorant of many things needed to do his job. In Figure 12.2, much of the auto mechanic's task ellipse lies outside his information set, but those tasks also do not lie in the accountant's information set. What the auto mechanic needs to know but does not know, the accountant does not know either. The converse also holds. The cost accountant does not know everything about her job because part of her task ellipse lies outside her information rectangle, but those tasks that she cannot perform do not lie inside the auto mechanic's information set either.

Now consider two identically trained cost accountants. There is unlikely to be much knowledge transfer between these individuals, since their experiences and knowledge bases are almost identical. The information that each possesses is relevant to the other party, but their information sets overlap almost completely, so there is not much room for idiosyncratic knowledge transfer. Figure 12.3 illustrates this situation. Accountant A and Accountant B have almost perfectly overlapping information sets. Neither can do all of the tasks, but, because their information is so similar, it is likely that those tasks that one cannot do, cannot be done by the other either.

Consider the case of a software developer who is rewriting a Windows-based statistical program. She has two software engineers, one of whom has experience in Graphical User Interfaces (GUIs) and the other has a Ph.D. in statistics. Team-

FIGURE 12.3
OVERLAPPING
INFORMATION SETS

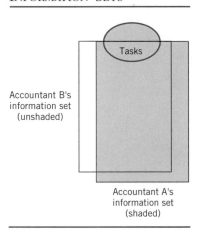

Accountant B's
information set
(unshaded)

Accountant A's
information set
(shaded)

ing these two individuals up will likely produce effective knowledge transfer. Their knowledge bases are quite different, but the information that each has is likely to be relevant to the other. Figure 12.1 captures this situation. Engel can be thought of as the GUI expert and Frisch as the statistician. Therefore, the information structure captured by Figure 12.1 would allow effective knowledge transfer in teams.

Team Size and Productivity

The size of a team matters. Large teams create communication problems. Small teams do not allow enough information transfer.

Anyone who has ever tried to accomplish something in a committee setting knows that it is very difficult to make headway in a large group. People talk at cross purposes and spend much time in simple communication. Sometimes the group gets so unruly that all communication breaks down and small cliques form within the larger group. From a communications standpoint, small is better. Too small a team has costs as well, however, because a large team has a larger set of information on which to draw. This is illustrated by Figure 12.4. There are four workers, A, B, C, and D, each of whom has some specialized information. (The information rectangles do not overlap perfectly.) Given this drawing, the best way to structure a team is probably to put members C and D together. The combination of C and D provides enough information to get most of the tasks accomplished, because most of the task ellipse is in boxes C and/or D. Adding B to the team expands the set of tasks somewhat, and adding A expands them only very slightly.

FIGURE 12.4
TEAMS AND INFORMATION SETS

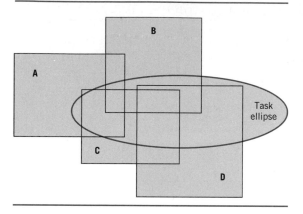

Even the four-member team will not be able to accomplish all the tasks, since some parts of the task ellipse do not overlap anyone's information set. Adding A and B to the team of C and D is likely to introduce significant communication difficulties without improving the distribution of information much.

Calibrating the Free-Rider Effect

In the case of the fishing company, summarized in Table 12.1, we gave some examples of activities and briefly discussed when the free-rider effect was likely to be strong or weak. Let us consider the free-rider problem again in more detail.

Probably the most important factor in determining the amount of free riding occurring in a team is the size of the group. When the group is small, free riding may not be much of a problem. Consider, for example, a small dry cleaning shop owned and run by Joan and Jane. The free-rider effect is a force, because Joan captures only half of the return to her effort. That is, when she increases the profits of the business by $1, she gets 50 cents and Jane gets 50 cents. But this problem is not too great, for two reasons. First, Jane has a great deal of information about what Joan is doing, and vice versa. If one partner shirks too much, the partnership will break down. It is the threat of a breakup that keeps both partners working hard.

Peer monitoring, like that which occurs at Joan & Jane's Cleaners, can be very effective in small groups. In a small group, a worker is likely to know what the other worker is doing to a much greater extent than in a large group. Furthermore, the incentives to punish a shirker are greater in a small group than in a large group. In a small group, say, a partnership of two persons, one partner's reduced effort has a significant effect on the earnings of the other partner. Although it is unpleasant to have to confront a partner and accuse her of putting forth insufficient effort, the costs of not doing so are relatively large when there are only two partners.

In a large partnership, peer monitoring is not as effective as in a small team, for two reasons. First, no one member's shirking has much of an effect on any other member, so the incentive to punish shirking co-workers is reduced. Suppose, for example, that there were 100 members in a team. When one worker shirks and reduces profits by $1, every other worker takes a loss of 1 cent. Most workers will be unwilling to go out of their way to discipline a peer who is costing them only a small amount of money. It is generally easier to simply ignore the situation. Unfortunately, when everyone in the firm refrains from confronting their shirking co-workers, a low effort norm prevails.

Second, it is more difficult to observe shirkers in large teams. When many people are involved and the task is complicated, determining the source of a problem may not be easy. When the team consists of only two members, a failure that Joan knows she did not cause is more than likely to be the fault of Jane. Thus, *free rider effects are more prevalent in larger teams.*

When individuals are engaged in related activities, free-rider effects are lessened. Doctors often form partnerships with other doctors and lawyers with other lawyers. More often than not, the doctors are substitutes for one another, rather than complements with one another. Two eye surgeons may form a partnership, but each usually maintains his own list of patients. One advantage to forming a partnership with someone in the same field is that it is easier to evaluate the other's work. Free-rider effects are lessened when one partner can assess the other partner's performance.

INCENTIVES IN TEAMS   ◆ ◆ ◆ ◆ ◆

To provide incentives in a team environment, it is necessary to provide meaningful rewards. As already mentioned, if teamwork can be observed by an outsider, then it can be rewarded directly. In this situation, workers can be paid not only on the basis of their own output, but also on the basis of their team contribution. For example, in legal, accounting, and management consulting practices, rainmakers (those who bring in business) are often rewarded handsomely, even though they actually do a small part of the work that they bring to the firm. By bringing in work for others to do, rainmakers enhance the value of the firm. While bringing business into a firm may be observable, it is much more difficult for an objective evaluator to observe teamwork in most production settings. As a result, the firm generally resorts to rewarding teamwork by rewarding the team itself. Free-rider effects notwithstanding, firms set up compensation and other rewards that derive from team performance.

There are two types of team rewards—explicit and implicit.

Explicit Rewards

Explicit team rewards can take a number of forms. The most prevalent are team bonuses, profit sharing, and stock and stock options.

Team Bonuses

Team bonuses are generally given to small groups of individuals for projects of relatively short duration. For example, a construction crew might get a bonus for completing a job on time. The bonus may be split among members in many different ways, but the bonus itself is tied to the specific project and to a specific work crew. Or, think about sports teams that receive bonuses for reaching various stages of a tournament. The football team that wins the Super Bowl is awarded a pool of money, which it divides evenly among its players. The player who was most instrumental in winning the game is not given a larger share of the team bonus than are other players. Again, the football team consists of a relatively small number of individuals and the "project" is of short duration.

The team must be small for team bonuses to have any impact, because free-rider effects become pronounced in large teams. If a construction site has ten workers, each worker's performance is more likely to be known to others. Each worker has some incentive to enforce a group norm of high effort on other crew members. In large groups, individual incentives vanish, as do the incentives for individuals to chastise unproductive peers. In large groups, it is more convenient to simply ignore the deviant workers.

Thus, firms should provide team bonuses only when teams are small and when the output of the team is well defined. The project must also be of sufficiently short duration that the team remains largely intact over the period. A team bonus awarded every 20 years would not be very conducive to teamwork. With normal rates of turnover, a large proportion of the team would be likely to leave before bonus time. Teamwork incentives would be directly undermined by this expectation.

Profit Sharing

Profit sharing is another common form of team compensation. A profit-sharing plan gives some reward to workers, based on company profits, usually in a given year. All workers do not receive the same share. Generally, the amount a given worker receives depends on his or her relative wage. A typical plan splits the profit-sharing pool in proportion to the worker's base salary. Define the relevant wage bill as the sum of base annual salaries of all workers in the profit-sharing plan. Then, worker j's share of the profit sharing bonus is

$$\text{Share} = (\text{worker } j\text{'s base annual salary}) / (\text{relevant wage bill})$$

Thus, workers with higher salaries get larger shares.

The total profit-sharing bonus is determined by a formula that uses earnings, costs, and/or measured profit in a given year. Sometimes, as in **gainsharing** plans, the total profit sharing bonus depends not only on the current year's profit, but also on the difference between this year's profit and some average of past profits, usually weighted more toward the recent past.

Although profit-sharing plans are often stated in terms of incentives, the incentive effects of such plans are likely to be limited. Because the relevant group of employees is usually large and most workers in the group do not work together, the free-rider effects can be overwhelming. Instead, these plans are really a form of risk sharing.[1] As mentioned in the previous chapter, Japanese firms tend to use more profit sharing than American firms. A large firm like Mitsubishi produces many different products in a number of different locations. If a group of workers in one city decides to shirk, the profit-sharing effects are felt by workers at all other plants because they outnumber those who did the shirking. Since workers know this, it is difficult to understand why individual workers or even small groups of workers might be motivated by the profits of this very large company. Most workers have only a trivial effect on Mitsubishi's profit rate and enjoy only a trivial part of the reward that comes from higher profit.

Profit sharing usually does not provide motivation for workers. A more appropriate interpretation of profit sharing is the one provided in chapter 11, namely, that it spreads risk between capital owners and labor. When the firm does well, shareholders and workers do well together. When the firm does poorly, shareholders bear some of the cost, but so do workers. The fact that workers' wages are tied to company profits means that shareholder returns do not fall by as much in downturns nor rise by as much in boom periods as they would if the worker wages were constant.

Stock and Stock Options

Stock and **stock options** are the third explicit form of team compensation. Stock options are given to high-level managers, at least in part as incentive pay. Because high-level managers are all part of a team and individual contribution to total profit may be difficult to observe, it is sometimes argued that stock options will motivate managers to become team players. When managers own stock, they care not only about how their activity affects their own narrowly defined output, but also how their activity affects the output of all other members of the firm. In such circumstances, managers who can take an action that will help the firm by helping another worker will be more inclined to do so.

First, let us distinguish between stock and a stock option. Stock represents an ownership claim on a corporation. It entitles the owner of the stock to participate in profits of the corporation in proportion to the number of shares held. Stockholders are **residual claimants,** meaning they receive returns only after more senior claimants have been paid. **Senior claimants** include workers, who must be paid their wages, and debt holders, whose loans must be repaid according to a predetermined schedule. Stockholders usually receive dividends quarterly as payment of profit and generally, although not always, have the right to vote on corporate matters in proportion to the number of shares that they hold.

On the face of it, a stock option appears to be very different from an actual share of stock. In reality they are quite similar. Option owners do not have claim

---

[1]See Chapter 11 for discussion and definition of risk sharing.

to current profits of the firm. Instead, an owner of a **call option** has the right to purchase stock at some predetermined **exercise** or **strike** price, K, until some date in the future. The call option is "in the money" when the market price of the stock exceeds the strike price. Then, a call option owner can exercise the option to buy the stock and can immediately resell it at a profit. If the market price of the stock is X and if $X > K$, then exercising the option results in an immediate profit of $X - K$. Alternatively, the call option owner can buy the stock and keep it, but he has bought something at less than its market price. If the stock price is below the exercise price, the call option is not exercised. The call option specifies that the stock can be bought at price K. But, if the current market price is below K, why would anyone pay K for a share that is available for a price lower than K? They wouldn't, so the option is not exercised.

Stock is, in most respects, a special case of an option. To see this, imagine an option with an exercise price of zero. This means that at any time, the option holder can exercise the option and receive a positive return. Since the stock price can never fall below zero, the option owner is certain to exercise the option and might as well do so at the time that it is granted. By doing this and holding the stock, the option holder can continue to receive dividends.[2] Since stock can be thought of as a special case of an option, it is possible to ask simply, how many options should be given to a manager, and at what strike price?

Here we will explore this question on a semi-intuitive level. There are many different combinations of number of options and exercise prices that produce the same expected value. But the incentive effects of the various combinations are quite different. To see that there are many ways to produce an option of a given expected value, consider a firm whose stock is currently selling at $100. Granting a manager an option to buy at an exercise price of zero is equivalent to giving the manager a share of stock worth $100. Thus, one way to produce $100 of expected value is to grant one call option with a strike price of zero. But there are alternatives.

To make things simple, suppose that tomorrow the price of the firm's stock will either be $90 or $110. Of course, at the time the options are granted, no one knows which of these two prices will prevail. Suppose further that the chance that the stock price will be $90 is 50 percent and the chance that it will be $110 is also 50 percent. Consider granting a call option with an exercise price of $100. The manager waits one day and then finds out whether the stock is worth $90 or $110. If it is worth $110, the manager exercises the option, buying it at a price of $100 and reselling it at a price of $110, netting a $10 gain. This happens with probability .5. Thus, the expected value of one option with a strike price of $100 is $5 because it yields $10 half of the time, and is not **in the money**—that is, it is **out of the money**—the other half of the time.

---

[2]For nonzero exercise prices, there is value to waiting because volatility in the stock price always creates a positive value to waiting, dividends aside.

To produce an expected value of $100, the firm could grant 20 call options at a strike price of $100, each of which has an expected value of $5. Or, for example, the firm could grant options with an exercise price of $108. Half of the time, the stock would be worth $110 and the option would yield a profit of $2. The other half of the time, the option expires out of the money and yields zero. The expected value of an option with a strike price of $108 is then $1. One hundred options at a strike price of $108 would yield an expected return of $100 as well.

What is the value of a call option with a strike price of $111? It is worth zero, because it would never pay to exercise such an option. There is no number of call options with a strike price of $111 that could produce $100 of expected value. What is the value of a call option with a strike price of $80? It will always be exercised. If the actual price of the stock turns out to be $90, the option is exercised and yields a return of $10. If the actual price of the stock turns out to be $110, then the option yields a return of $30. The expected return on the option is $20. Thus, five options at a strike price of $80 yield an expected value of $100. Table 12.2 lists the possibilities already discussed.

Table 12.2 illustrates a general principle. The higher the exercise price, the larger the number of options that must be granted to produce a given expected value. But there are an infinite number of combinations of exercise prices and number of options that could have produced $100 of expected value. How does the firm decide whether to grant stock, which is an option with an exercise price of zero, or to grant an option with a positive exercise price? And if it goes for the latter, what price does it choose?[3]

To answer the question, first note that the value of an option increases as the value of the firm rises. Suppose that the manager can take a certain action to make the firm more valuable. The action is sufficiently important so that it raises the value of every share of stock in the firm by exactly $1. For example, if the firm had 1 million shares of stock outstanding, the action would have to raise the overall

TABLE 12.2

COMBINATIONS OF NUMBER OF OPTIONS AND EXERCISE PRICES
WITH EXPECTED VALUE OF $100

Exercise Price	Expected Value of One Option	Number of Options Required
$0	$100	1
$80	$20	5
$100	$5	20
$108	$1	100

[3]There are some tax implications of choosing options with strike prices that are too low. The IRS may decide that this is equivalent to stock and force the recipient to declare the option as income on the current year's tax form.

value of the firm by $1 million in order to make each share of stock appreciate by $1. If the manager takes the action, then, in the previous example, the stock would be worth $91 or $111 on the second day, rather than $90 or $110, as previously assumed. What would happen to the value of the option?

An option that had a price of $100 would be worth $11 half of the time and zero the other half of the time. Thus, the expected value of the option would rise from $5 to $5.50. How much benefit does the manager receive from an action that raises the value of each share of stock by $1? The manager would receive a net benefit of $.50 for each option held. Twenty options would provide a total value of $10 for the manager's contribution to the firm's increased profits of $1 million.

What if, instead of holding 20 options with a strike price of $100, the manager holds 100 options with a strike price of $108? If the stock price turns out to be $91, the option is out of the money. But if the stock price turns out to be $111, the manager receives $3 on each option. The expected value, then, of each option is $1.50, rather than the $1.00 expected value that it had before the action. This implies a net benefit of $.50 for every option held. For 100 options with strike prices of $108, the manager receives a total value of $50 for contributing to the firm's increased profits of $1 million, five times the value received when the strike price is $100.

There is an important point made by this example. The expected cost to the firm of granting 100 options with a strike price of $108 is identical to the expected cost of granting 20 options with a strike price of $100, since they have the same expected value. But they produce vastly different incentives. *The larger number of options with the higher strike price generates much more value to the manager for taking a beneficial action than does the smaller number of options with a lower strike price.* Table 12.3 presents the expected net value to a manager of raising the value of one share by $1 for the scenarios given in Table 12.2.

Table 12.3 shows that the incentives to put forth additional effort are greater when the exercise price is high and many options are granted than when the exercise price is low and few options are granted. This results from **leverage.** The expected payout is the same for all four exercise prices, namely $100, but increased

TABLE 12.3
EXPECTED NET BENEFIT FROM RAISING VALUE OF ONE SHARE BY $1

Exercise Price	Number of Options	Expected Value of One Option if Action is Not Taken	Expected Value of One Option if Action is Taken	Net Value of Action to Manager
$0	1	$100	$101	$1
$80	5	$20	$21	$5
$100	20	$5	$5.50	$10
$108	100	$1	$1.50	$50

leverage allows a small investment to turn into a large gain as the strike price rises and the number of options rise correspondingly, much like buying stock on **margin,** where part of the money to buy stock is borrowed, using the stock's value as collateral. The same is true of options with high exercise prices.

One major advantage to setting the strike price high and awarding a large number of options is that doing so works against the free-rider effect. The previous example suggested that a manager could increase the value of the firm by $1 million if effort were sufficiently high. A manager who owned but one share of stock—that is, an "option" with an exercise price of zero—would receive only $1 of the $1 million of value he or she produced. If, instead, the manager were granted 100 options with an exercise price of $108, he or she would receive an expected $50 of the $1 million produced. While $50 is a far cry from the full $1 million, it is fifty times the $1 received with straight stock. Thus, giving a manager options with a high exercise price is one way to mitigate the free-rider effect.[4]

Other differences associated with using highly priced stock options relate to making managers take more or less risk. Exercise prices have effects on the riskiness of the projects that managers will choose. It is often alleged that managers behave in too risk-averse a fashion to maximize shareholder wealth. They worry about losing their jobs and, therefore, tend to take the safe route.[5] Granting options with high strike prices can offset this tendency.

Suppose a manager can choose between two strategies, a risky one and a less risky one. For any given level of effort, the less risky strategy produces a distribution of stock prices shown by distribution 1 in Figure 12.5. The risky strategy results in a distribution of stock prices shown by distribution 2 in Figure 12.5. The $f(X)$ on the vertical axis denotes the frequency with which any given stock price X occurs.

If the manager chooses the strategy that results in distribution 1, then most of the time the stock price will be close to 100, but there is a 50/50 chance that the price may be below 100 if the manager chooses the safe strategy. If the riskier strategy is chosen, then most of the time the stock price will be above 100. This is because a nontrivial part of distribution 2 lies below the lowest values of stock price attainable with distribution 1.

---

[4]This can only be used for a limited number of managers. Firms granting options must finance them through debt-equity swaps, or most commonly by issuing new stock. But issuing stock dilutes the value of the old shares. If the firm were to issue large numbers of options to all of its workers, it would be right back where it started. The option would not have sufficient value, because when it was in the money, all workers would exercise their shares, whether they were responsible for the increased value of the firm or not. This would dilute the stock and reduce its value sufficiently to negate the leverage effect of the option.

[5]If true, this means that they are receiving more than they could earn elsewhere, or there would be no reason to fear job loss. It also means that the compensation scheme must be inducing this sort of behavior. Tinkering with the compensation scheme might remedy the problem.

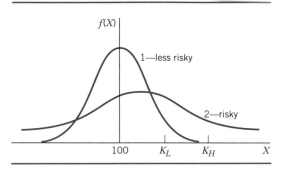

FIGURE 12.5
PROBABILITY DISTRIBUTIONS OF
RETURNS FOR TWO
MANAGERIAL STRATEGIES

Note that distribution 2 has a higher expected value than distribution 1. If the shareholders were risk-neutral, they would prefer that the manager select risky projects that yield payoffs according to distribution 2 rather than those that pay off according to distribution 1. Risk-neutral investors only care about maximizing expected return, which distribution 2 does.

Managers may not feel the same way about project choice, because they often like to play it safe, even at a cost of reducing average profits. An appropriately priced set of stock options can turn even the most nervous of managers into a carefree risk taker.

Consider the two possible exercise prices: K_H and K_L (H and L stand for high and low, respectively), shown in Figure 12.5. Since K_H is higher than K_L, more options must be given to generate the same expected value with price K_H than with price K_L. Table 12.2 showed that there is an infinite number of possible combinations of exercise prices and number of options that yield the same expected value. But options with strike price K_H will induce the manager to take on riskier projects than will options with exercise price K_L. The only way the manager can reap any benefit when strike price is K_H is to choose projects that yield distribution 2. It follows from Figure 12.5 that choosing projects with distribution 1 is certain to yield a stock price that is out of the money. The best possible outcome with distribution 1 will never result in an option that is in the money. In order for the manager to receive any benefit from the options, he or she must choose riskier projects that yield distribution 2. In most circumstances, the option will not pay off, even if the manager chooses projects with distribution 2, because most of the mass of the distribution of possible outcomes lies to the left of exercise price K_H. But choosing the risky projects at least gives the manager a chance at being in the money.

Choosing the safe projects is certain to result in zero value to the options. Further, there is no loss from choosing projects that result in distribution 2. If the option is out of the money, the manager receives zero, which is no worse than what the manager receives by choosing projects with distribution 1.[6]

Put Options

Another way to induce managers to change their attitude toward risky projects is to switch from *call* options to *put* options. The options discussed so far have been call options. A call option gives the option's owner, sometimes referred to as the party who is *long* on the option, the right to "call in" the option—that is, to buy stock at some specified price. Being long on a **put option** gives the owner of the option the right to "put" the option—that is, to sell stock on which the option is issued to the party **short** on the option at some specified price.

Why would anyone want to own a put option? By owning a put option, an investor can limit the downside risk. If the stock falls below a certain price, the put owner can sell the stock to someone else at the prespecified price, even if the market price of the stock is well below the put's exercise price. Thus, if Joan is long on a put option with an exercise price of $90, she knows that if the market price of the stock she owns falls below $90, she can force the person on the short end of the put option to take it for $90. Given that Joan owns a share of stock and a long put option, Joan's loss is limited by $10, assuming that the stock is currently traded at $100.

Of course, the benefits of owning a put option come at a cost. No one will be at the short end of a put option just for fun. If there is some chance that a person will get stuck buying a stock at above the market price, the investor must be compensated for doing so. Thus, the party who goes long on the put pays the party who is short on the put a fee up front for the privilege of owning the put. (This fee is generally called a *premium*.)

Put options can create managerial incentives as well. Just as being long on a put option makes a manager want to see the price rise (as Table 12.3 shows), being short on a put option makes the manager want to avoid seeing the stock price fall. A firm could pay a manager a somewhat higher base salary, but force the person to be short on a put option. In return for the high base salary, the manager is essentially promising not to let the stock price fall. If it does fall, the manager pays a penalty by having to buy shares of the firm's stock at a price above the market.

Although being long on call options or short on put options both provide the manager with incentives to put forth effort, they differ in terms of the riskiness of the projects that the manager wants to take on. The point can best be understood by referring to Figure 12.6. As before, two strategies are available to a manager. The less-risky strategy results in a distribution of stock prices given by distribution 1. The risky strategy results in a distribution of stock prices given by distribution 2.

---

[6]It is possible that managers may choose the risky project, even when strike price is K_L. This is because the value of an option increases in variance of the underlying distribution. Whether managers do so or not depends on the level of risk aversion and on costs associated with losing their jobs if things turn out badly. But given these costs and the degree of risk aversion, managers are *more* likely to choose the risky strategy when the strike price is K_H than when it is K_L.

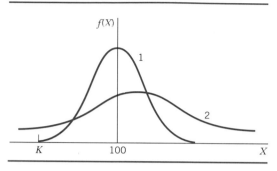

FIGURE 12.6
TWO DISTRIBUTIONS OF INCOME

To motivate managers by making them short on a put option, it is necessary to select some exercise price, K, such that when the price of the stock falls below K, a manager is forced to buy stock worth less than K at price K. The manager is therefore penalized if the value of stock falls bellow K, a situation he or she tries to avoid by keeping the firm's value high. There is another way to avoid it as well. The manager can choose the safe strategy. If the firm were to choose the strategy that results in distribution 1 for stock prices, there would be no chance that the manager would be stuck buying a share of stock at less than price K, since there is no possibility that the stock price will fall below K, given distribution 1. Were the manager to choose the risky strategy, resulting in distribution 2, then there is some chance of getting stuck buying shares at price K that are worth less than K. Thus, the manager chooses safe projects over risky ones. This works to the detriment of the firm, because the risky strategy has a higher expected return than the safe one.[7]

The lesson here is that there are two ways to motivate a manager through options. The most common method is to pay part of the manager's compensation in call options. This induces the manager to put forth effort because the higher the stock price, the greater the value of the options. Alternatively, a firm can raise a manager's base salary above the market level, in return for the manager's agreement to be at the short end of put options. Then, if the stock price falls, the manager loses. This, too, induces more effort, because he or she does not want to get stuck buying shares of the company's stock at a price above what the stock is worth on the market.

The difference between the two methods of motivation is that making managers long on call options induces them to prefer risky strategies, whereas making them

---

[7]While K was chosen so that it was below every value on distribution 1, this was not necessary. Since the value of an option to the party who is long on it increases in the variance of the underlying distribution, and since distribution 2 is of higher variance, the party long on the option prefers that distribution 2 be selected. This also means that the party short on the option, in this case the manager, prefers the safe distribution.

short on put options induces them to prefer safe strategies. If managers tend to behave in a manner that is too risk averse, it is better to reduce the base salary and to
award call options. Giving call options offsets managerial tendency to avoid risk,
whereas forcing a manager to be short on put options exacerbates risk avoidance.

Virtually without exception, managers are given call options. Making them
short on put options is simply not done. This may reflect a natural tendency by
managers to shun risk. Call options offset this tendency. It is also true, however,
that giving managers more call options with high strike prices is preferable to giving fewer call options with low strike price when managers are too risk-averse. As
shown through Figure 12.5, higher exercise prices induce more risk taking than
lower exercise prices.

Implicit Reward

Stock options, profit sharing, and team bonuses are explicit rewards for team performance. There are also implicit rewards for team performance that may account
for a larger proportion of team reward than all forms of explicit reward combined,
particularly in the United States. Empirical studies have shown that employee
compensation is related to the overall profitability of the firm, among other
things.[8] When firm profits are high, wages tend to be high. If a firm has a good
year, it is likely to give better raises than if it has a bad year. If higher profits bring
larger raises, then the workers are implicitly sharing in the profits of the firm. In
this case, the profit sharing is implicit, but it is there nonetheless.

Implicit profit sharing is likely to account for the largest proportion of total
profit sharing, because most workers in the firm are involved in implicit profit
sharing, whereas a very small fraction of the work force receive explicit profit
sharing, team bonuses, or stock options. In most firms, only top management
receives a sizable fraction of compensation in the form of stock options. This is
because a stock option is a real incentive only for an employee who can singlehandedly affect the profitability of the firm to a significant extent. To get a sense
of the importance and cost to the firm of an implicit profit-sharing plan, consider
the following. Suppose the firm allows wages to vary with profits according to the
following implicit formula.

Average annual percentage raise = inflation rate +
.2 (Actual profit rate − Expected profit rate)

Thus, if actual profit equals expected profit, the average raise equals the inflation
rate, which means that workers are no better off in real terms. If the actual profit
rate were 20 percent and the expected profit rate were 15 percent, then the raise
would be 1 percent, or .2 × (.20-.15), above the inflation rate. This would raise
the wage bill of the firm by 1 percent.

---

[8]See, for example, Pugel (1980) and Brown and Medoff (1989).

Compare this 1 percent increase in the wage bill with the cost of an explicit stock option or bonus plan. These plans tend to be reserved for higher-level managers, perhaps accounting for 3 percent of the firm's work force and 15 percent of the firm's wage bill. Suppose that there is a bonus plan that stipulates that the bonus is calculated as follows:

Eligible worker's bonus = (Base salary) ×
(Actual profit rate − Expected profit rate) x λ

where λ is a parameter to be chosen by the firm. Suppose λ equals 1. If profits are 5 percent above expected profits, then every eligible employee receives a bonus equal to 5 percent of base salary. The total cost to the firm is (.05)(.15)(Wage bill), because only 3 percent of the firm's employees, accounting for .15 of the wage bill, are eligible for the bonus. The cost of this explicit plan would then be 0.75 percent of the total wage bill, which is less than the implicit bonus given to all workers. The numbers can be adjusted to make explicit bonuses cost more or less than the implicit bonuses. With reasonable values of the parameters, it is likely that implicit bonuses account for a greater share of a firm's wage bill and, therefore, cost the firm more, than explicit team bonuses.[9]

Norms

Team bonuses, profit sharing, and stock options are direct monetary ways to establish a team atmosphere within a firm. There may be other, nonpecuniary ways as well. All of these require some investment of time and effort, if not money.

Norms are practices a firm engages in or a set of beliefs held by the vast majority of a group, in this case, the employees of the organization. Common practices or beliefs can be very helpful in establishing a culture, ethic, or etiquette in the firm. For example, if it is part of the firm's culture that managers voluntarily work Saturdays, workers may be reluctant to deviate from this mode of behavior. Saturday work may provide useful labor and generate additional profits. Of course, Saturday work also carries a cost. Employees must be compensated more for taking a job where Saturday work is the norm than for work at a firm where Saturday work is not the norm.

In addition to the direct cost associated with paying for Saturday work, there is generally a cost associated with creating and maintaining a norm. Such a cost can be ongoing or borne at one time. An ongoing cost most generally takes the form of enforcing the norm. Take the example of Saturday work. What happens if an employee deviates from the norm and fails to come in on a Saturday? If there is no enforcement of the norm nor sanctions imposed for deviating, chances are that the employee will engage in the deviant activity again. Worse, it may then spread to other members of the firm, causing the norm to break down altogether. A new

---

[9]Implicit bonuses may cost even more if the raise received in this year raises the base salary on which subsequent year's raises are calculated.

norm of no Saturday work might then replace the old norm, to the detriment of the organization. In order to prevent this from happening, someone must penalize those who deviate from the norm. The penalty can take the form of monetary wage reductions, but then the norm is simply enforced through the compensation scheme and we need not even bother with the notion of norm. We already know that it is possible to induce workers to put forth almost any given level of effort as long as the firm is willing to pay for it and sets up the appropriate compensation scheme. Norms may also be enforced without direct pecuniary compensation of the individual employee.

One way to provide incentives to enforce a norm is by setting group quotas. The firm promises the team a bonus and imposes a penalty for not making quota. When one person puts forth less than the norm level of effort, it hurts the others in the group. As a result, the deviant feels peer pressure. The norm is enforced by peers who may have some monetary or other stake in the quota being realized. The sanctions placed on the deviant might not be pecuniary. They may take the form of cajoling, criticism, ostracism, or sometimes even physical harm.

Deviations from a norm are not always negative. Sometimes, peers will impose sanctions on an individual who puts forth too much effort. This is most common among production workers. A production line may move at a rate that is too slow for some workers. If one worker produces at too quick a pace, then the supervisor gets tipped off that the work can be done in less time than the company has been allowing. This causes the line to speed up, much to the detriment of coworkers. Although the firm may benefit from positive deviations from the norm level of effort, the peer group may not, and they may make life difficult for workers who are too eager.

The level of effort associated with norms depends on the type of sanction imposed for deviating from the norm. It is easy to make the point in the context of the Saturday work example. If only minor criticism is levied on a worker who fails to show up on a given Saturday, the worker may decide that it is worth bearing that criticism to avoid missing his son's baseball game. If complete ostracism from his peer group were the consequence of failure to report to work that Saturday, he may opt to go to work and bribe his son to forgive him for missing the game. Indeed, the equilibrium norm that is established is a direct consequence of the amount of peer pressure placed on a worker. The greater the peer pressure associated with deviating from a norm, the higher the norm level of effort in equilibrium. When the costs of deviating from the norm are low, many will deviate. Then, the established norm will have low levels of effort associated with it.

Enforcement costs that are borne by peers tend to be ongoing. If the pressure lets up and enforcement lags, norms tend to break down. Other costs of establishing and enforcing norms are not ongoing. Rather, they are more like lump sum costs. For example, the military makes large investments in new recruits, instilling in them pride and loyalty. Boot camp is devoted, in large part, to having recruits bond with fellow recruits and with the military in general. The bonding that takes place early in a soldier's career may serve the military well later on. Sometimes, a soldier is assigned a task that cannot be easily monitored by peers or superiors.

For example, an entire unit's survival may depend on accurate reports being sent back by a scout. Scouting is a dangerous activity, usually occurring near or beyond enemy lines. Pure self-interest might lead a scout to hide in the bushes and to send back fictitious reports. If his reports turn out to be accurate, he will be credited with having done his job. If they turn out to be inaccurate, the unit may be wiped out, and no one may discover that the report was faulty. Even if the unit survives after receiving false information, pinning the blame on the scout is likely to be difficult.

The scout's loyalty to the group keeps him from taking the easy way out. Loyalty reflects prior investments into developing devotion to the military and camaraderie among soldiers. Firms also engage in many activities that build company loyalty. Group recreational outings, Christmas parties, and other semi-social activities build cohesion among workers in a firm. It is easier to feel loyal to someone you know than to a stranger. Removing strangeness tends to increase the effectiveness of peer pressure, whether the pressure comes directly through peer sanctions or indirectly through guilt felt from letting one's friends down.

Empathy may be quite important here, and these investments in interpersonal relationships and corporate culture may build empathy. I recall being on an airplane the day after an airplane crash had occurred. Many people died in the crash. I overheard some flight attendants discussing the accident. One said to the other, "I heard that four of the flight attendants were killed in the crash. That's terrible." Of course, it was terrible, but it was equally terrible that 105 other people died in the crash. The flight attendants were not being callous by ignoring the others who died. They merely were thinking about those with whom they could most easily identify.

When workers shirk, they always hurt others. If workers are paid a straight salary, shirking by a worker has adverse effects on shareholders, who must bear the cost of the worker's reduced effort. Workers have a tough time empathizing with nameless, faceless shareholders. However, if the worker feels that by shirking, she is hurting someone that she knows, or can at least put herself in the other person's shoes, she is less likely to loaf.

Many practices at firms may have more to do with creating empathy, loyalty, and latent guilt than they do with performing the nominal tasks themselves. For example, quality circles, where workers sit around and discuss the best way to perform some task at the firm, may be most useful in making the worker feel part of the firm and in creating loyalty to coworkers. The suggestions that come out of the quality circles are rarely implemented. This does not mean they were a waste of time. If they allow valuable norms to be maintained, the time devoted to these circles is well spent.

◆ ◆ ◆ ◆ ◆ OTHER ASPECTS OF TEAM PRODUCTION

In addition to size and composition of a team, there are other aspects of team production that merit consideration.

Rotating Team Members

It is useful to change the members of a team periodically for at least two reasons. First, people are different. Some individuals are better at doing some things than at doing others. The strength of a given worker may not be known to either the worker or to management. A set of tasks that a worker is good at as well as the team members with whom she is most productive may be found after enough job rotation. If a person works with the same team throughout her entire career, she may never find out that she would have been more productive performing other tasks with another group of people.

Second, as discussed earlier, people are idiosyncratic and possess different pieces of information. It takes time to convey the information from one party to another, but there may be diminishing returns in doing so.

For example, suppose that there are four workers, A, B, C, and D. They can be arranged into six possible teams of two. The teams are:

(1) AB	(2) AC	(3) AD	(4) BC	(5) BD	(6) CD

It is possible to arrange the workers in a number of different ways. One possibility is to assign permanently workers into two teams. For example, have A work with B and C work with D, always. Alternatively, a firm may experiment with different team compositions, and, after rotating each worker a few times, combine them in teams in the best possible way. Initially, A would be paired with B and C with D, then after six months, A would be teamed with C and B with D. After another six months B would work with C and A with D. The second route exposes every worker to every other in an 18-month period. Which method is better?

First Chicago, a large Chicago bank, has a program called First Scholars. For years, it operated as follows. First Scholars worked at the bank during the day and attended either the University of Chicago or the Northwestern business schools at night. The program lasted for two years. During the two-year period, a First Scholar would have four assignments at the bank, each lasting six months. Switching these new workers around provided some valuable experience and information about the workers' idiosyncratic skills. But it also meant that, just when the workers learned their current jobs, they were switched to other tasks about which they knew very little.

If diminishing returns in knowledge transfer are significant, then it is probably better to switch team members. Diminishing returns means that the second six months do not produce as much knowledge transfer as the first six months. By the end of six months, A knows a good deal of what B knows. A can surely learn more from B over the next six months, but she can learn more from C than from B during the next six months because she has not already been exposed to C's ideas.

Diminishing returns need not prevail. Indeed, the opposite may be true. "Person-specific" human capital may be more important than the effect of diminishing returns. It takes time to get to know another person and to build up lines of trust and communication. Sometimes, the investment period is quite long.

Switching team members results in a loss of person-specific human capital, because by the time A gets to know B to the point where they can work together productively, they each move on to another teammate.

It may be difficult to determine if rotating a worker among teams is a good policy. Indeed two countervailing effects are involved—diminishing returns to knowledge transfer may make frequent rotation desirable. But when the amount of team-specific human capital is significant, it may be better to leave workers in their current positions. The net effect of the two factors just discussed can go either way. In some situations it may be optimal to keep workers permanently in the same team, while under other circumstances rotating workers among teams is the best policy. How can we determine which strategy is right? The basic rule is: When knowledge is highly idiosyncratic and relevant to the other party, team switching is probably the better policy. When communication is difficult, say, because workers come from different disciplines, (e.g., engineering versus marketing), more time is required to build a relationship. If team switching is to occur at all, then the interval for forming new teams should be long.

Judging Others Must Be Compensated

In earlier chapters, we discussed situations in which individuals would not cooperate with their peers because they were in competition with one another for the same job. The same problem can arise in a team context, where the supervisor, who is a member of a larger team involved in training and spotting good talent does not want to identify and train good subordinates who may someday compete with her for the same job. This can be a real problem, but it is one that can be counteracted with the correct incentives policy. A real-world example may be helpful.

A large life insurance company calls the heads of its branch offices *general managers*. Below the general managers are assistant general managers who are involved in selling and supervising the sales of life insurance by others. Some of the assistant general managers will eventually head their own offices, obtaining the title of general manager.

It is to the company's advantage to provide training for assistant general managers that will enable them to perform well in their current jobs and in the general manager position, if they are promoted. But there is a problem. The current general manager may have little incentive to provide training to subordinates who may some day end up competing with her. Worse yet, she may push those who are less able and stifle those who are most able in order to reduce the amount of competition that she will encounter from other general managers, some of whom may be her current assistant general managers.

To offset her reluctance, the company provides the general manager with an incentive. Each assistant general manager that is promoted to general manager gives some share of his commissions to the general manager under which he served as an assistant. This increases the incentives to train one's subordinates. If training and selecting the best subordinates could be monitored directly, there would be an easier way to accomplish the same thing. The firm could simply pay the general manager for time spent training subordinates and could also pay her for the quality of her promotion recommendations. Poor recommendations would be punished, while good recommendations would be rewarded.

The problem is that it is difficult to know whether a promotion recommendation is good until the promoted assistant general manager's performance is observed. By making the general manager's compensation contingent on the performance of promoted subordinates, the correct incentives are provided. The same is true of training. Since it is difficult for the firm to observe the amount of training given to a subordinate, paying general managers on the basis of their subordinates' current and future performance helps provide some incentives to train.

The situation described here is a team problem for two reasons. First, the training and identifying talent functions performed by the supervisor are done in a team setting. Training involves at least two individuals, trainer and trainee, which constitutes a team. Second, there is a larger definition of team that is relevant here. Since all members of the firm are to some extent part of a large team, the firm would like the general manager to promote the well-being of this larger team as well. By paying the general manager on the basis of subordinates' performance in their current and future jobs, the firm induces the manager to take into account the larger team.

Cooperation with Teams versus Competition Between Teams

The strategic interaction of players within a team and between teams was discussed in chapter 10. We make similar points in a slightly different context here.

The composition of the team matters because some members fit better with other members. In addition, there are strategic reasons why the composition of the team matters. There tends to be much more cooperation within a team than between teams. In sports, one team member often comes to the aid of another team member. This is what blocking in (American) football is all about. Indeed, in baseball, when one player gets hit by a pitched ball, it is common for both benches to empty as teammates go to support both the hit player and the pitcher who is under attack.

The same is true in firms. When teams are created, there is cooperation within teams, but rarely between teams. Each team may want the others to fail. Failure by others bolsters the relative position of the team in question. If projects can be broken up into units that are easily handled by a small team, then team production may be useful. The problem arises when cooperation between teams is an important part of output. In that case, defining teams that are too small will hinder production.

Take, for example, the design of a new automobile. Since an automobile is complicated, and since parts must fit together to make the car run, teams that are defined too narrowly may impede the design process. One team might be assigned to design steering. Another team might be assigned to design the suspension system. But the way that the car steers depends not only on the steering system, but also on the suspension system. If the steering team is in a race with the suspension team to produce the first or best design among all teams, it may race to finish, ignoring everything that the suspension team is doing.

This problem can be avoided by defining the team more broadly, so that steering and suspension designers are on the same team. But even this team ignores useful interactions with chassis designers, and so forth. If the team is defined to include everyone in the entire design process, interactions will not be ignored by team members. But then the team is so large that free-rider effects swamp any team incentives.

What is the solution? The solution is to group individuals together who have the closest interaction with one another and give them instructions that force them to coordinate with other teams. In the automobile example, suspension and steering might be one team. They could be told to meet particular specifications so that the suspension and steering systems will mesh with the chassis that is being built. Similarly, chassis designers could be ordered to design a chassis that is consistent with particular specifications for steering and suspension. Doing this requires that some advanced planning is done. Before the individual teams can be set off on their own, they must be given specifications, which have to be selected in advance. Just as writing an outline is an important part of essay (or textbook) writing, setting up an initial design and set of specifications is an important part of making teamwork effective.

◆ ◆ ◆ ◆ ◆ CHOOSING TEAMS AND TEAM MEMBERS

Quite a bit of the discussion in this chapter has centered around how to set up teams and who should work with whom. Very little has been said about what process should be used for sorting individuals into teams. In particular, should individuals be assigned to teams by supervisors, or should teams be free to choose their own members?

The most common method is to allow supervisors to assign individuals to teams. This works well when the supervisor has more information than the individual workers. When a new employee or an employee from another part of the firm joins a group, the supervisor is likely to have as good or better information than the individual workers. In this case, it makes little sense to allow uninformed workers to assign the new member to a group. In other cases, workers actually have better information about one another than the supervisor has. When individuals have worked together for a long time, when new employees are friends of current employees, or when individual workers engage in tasks that are highly specialized and beyond the knowledge set of the supervisor, it may be better to allow workers to set up their own teams. Two mechanisms for doing so are discussed here: alternative draws and bidding for team members.

TABLE 12.4
TEAM PREFERENCES

Team I's Preferences (highest to lowest)	Team II's Preferences (highest to lowest)
Allison	Brooke
Brooke	Charles
Charles	David
David	Allison

Alternating Draws

The most straightforward possibility is to alternate draws. This is the way that children form sandlot teams. Suppose there are two teams, I and II, and four new hires, Allison, Brooke, Charles, and David. One possibility is to allow the "captain" of each team to choose a new member in alternating order. Suppose that the teams rank the players in order as shown in Table 12.4.

Suppose that efficiency dictates that Allison and Charles should work with team I and Brooke and David should work with team II. While team I prefers Brooke to Charles, so does team II. If efficiency implies Brooke should work with II, then the value of Brooke to team II exceeds the value of Brooke to team I, given the other players. Both prefer her, but team II prefers her by a greater amount. Similarly, both teams prefer Charles to David, but Charles's added value to I is greater than his added value to II, which is why efficiency requires that he work with team I.

Suppose a coin is tossed and team I wins. Their first choice is for Allison. Team II then chooses Brooke, team I then chooses Charles, and team II chooses David. The efficient allocation is achieved. Allison and Charles work with team I. Brooke and David work with team II. What if the coin toss had gone in favor of team II? Then the first choice would be for Brooke. Team I would have followed with a choice of Allison. Team II then chooses Charles and team I is stuck with David. Team I ends up with Allison and David, while team II had Brooke and Charles. Efficiency would have been violated.

Whether efficiency is achieved or not depends on the outcome of a coin toss in this example. This is not a desirable property of any team selection scheme. Nor is this merely a feature of this example. Allowing teams to choose their members in an alternating fashion, without any other conditions, generally results in an inefficient allocation of team members. It is necessary that teams be made to pay for the consequences of their choices, not just as their choices affect themselves, but also as they affect other teams.

Bidding for Members

An alternative is to allow teams to bid for their team members. An **English auction** is held and the team that bids the highest number of points wins the member.

An English auction is the familiar auction mechanism, where bidders are free to shout out bids until no one exceeds the last bid. Then the highest bidder gets the team member.

In order to attract a team member, that team must give up some of its profit credits, which, in turn, affect team members' compensation. At the end of each year, each team's contributions to profit are calculated and team compensation is based on the profit contribution, which we will call *profit credit*.

Let us auction off Allison's labor. Since Allison should be with team I, she contributes more to team I's profit than she does to team II's profit. Therefore, team I will be willing to bid a larger share of its profits to acquire her as a team member than will team II. When Brooke is auctioned, the reverse is true. Since Brooke contributes more to team II than to team I, team II will be willing to give up more of its profit credits to obtain Brooke than will team I. The same mechanism works for Charles and David. Team I will pay more for Charles than will team II and team II will pay more for David than will team I. Thus, Allison and Charles end up on team I, and Brooke and David end up on team II. Auctions generally result in an efficient allocation of resources and are preferable to alternating draw methods for assigning team members. Note further that it is unnecessary and, in fact, undesirable, to dictate the number of members that go to each team. If the value of acquiring the third new worker is higher to team I than the value of the second is to team II, it is better that team I have three new workers and team II have only one. The auction process will sort this out. When the fourth member is auctioned off, team II, which only has one new member, can outbid team I if it so desires. If it opts against outbidding team I, then team I gets three new members. This is as it should be. Since team I is willing to pay more, the third member must contribute more to firm profits when allocated to team I than when allocated to team II. Otherwise, team II would have been willing to outbid team I.

An Application: Salmon Fishing in Alaska

Fishing in Alaska is done on boats where knowing the best spots for the fish is an important component of the hunt. Some individuals are good fisherman; others have deep understandings of fish behavior. Fishing firms in Alaska are set up as partnerships, but partnerships are somewhat fluid. After a given individual becomes known as a talented fisherman or spotter, his market value rises. As a result, he can command a larger share of the firm's profits.[10]

Sometimes, renegotiations can take place within a fisherman's current partnership. The partners recognize the increased market value of a skilled fisherman or spotter and cut him a better deal. More often than not, a change in share requires that the individual leave the current partnership and join another. The process of negotiating with current and new partnerships is exactly the bidding

---

[10]See Farrell and Scotchmer (1988).

process that was just described. It will generally result in an efficient allocation of labor throughout the industry.

WORKER-OWNED FIRMS

◆ ◆ ◆ ◆ ◆

Some firms have issued stock to their workers in lieu of granting salary increases. When a large enough fraction of the shares of the organization are held by its work force, the firm is often said to be "worker owned." Two famous cases of large worker-owned firms are Avis (car rental), and United Airlines. How do worker-owned firms operate?

Often, the answer is that they operate in much the same way as non labor-owned firms. They appoint a CEO and team of managers that are instructed to maximize profits. In many cases, the ownership structure has an impact on the firm's decision-making, especially with respect to labor policy. When the firm deviates from efficiency to accommodate labor, it is detrimental to the health of the firm. To see this, we turn to an application.

An Application: Lumber Cooperatives in the Pacific Northwest[11]

In the Pacific Northwest United States, a number of firms in the plywood industry are organized as cooperatives. While some workers are employed by the firm as mere employees, others actually own a share of the firm. These shares are not publicly traded on a stock exchange, but they are marketable. When a new worker joins the firm, he can purchase one of these shares from a departing worker. Shares are advertised and put up for sale through local newspapers.

The worker-owners in these relatively small firms have the right to appoint boards of directors who choose managers. Thus, these firms are large teams in the classic sense. How do they behave? Compared with non labor-owned firms, they are more protective of their worker-owners' employment. When bad times hit the industry, the cooperatives are less likely to lay off workers and are more likely to reduce wages for all workers. Is this good or bad?

The evidence is ambiguous. Labor cooperative share prices have risen quite well, but not as well as share prices of non labor-owned firms. The share of the industrial output accounted for by the cooperatives has dropped from around 35 percent in the 1950s to less than 20 percent in the late 1980s. Part of this may reflect regional shifts in demand, but it is also true that costs per worker are higher in the cooperatives than they are in the non labor-owned firms.

Evidently, workers are taking some of their returns in the form of increased job security. But the job security comes at a cost. The workers would have been

---

[11]This application comes from Craig and Pencavel (1992).

better off financially by selling out their cooperatives to a non labor-run firm like Georgia-Pacific or ITT-Rayonier for stock in those companies and accepting jobs as mere employees in the acquired firms. In fact, a number of cooperatives have done this, but some retain their cooperative structure and remain viable. Workers seem willing to pay to control their own firms. Still, it cannot be good to guarantee worker security at the expense of profit. If a firm retains its workforce inefficiently, money is being thrown away, whether workers like the security or not. Put otherwise, there is always a way to make workers better off by paying them to accept another job rather than retaining them inefficiently. The discussion of downsizing and buyouts in chapter 7 has bearing on this issue. To make the point, consider the following example.

Suppose that the plywood cooperative pays its 20 worker-owners $1,000 per week during prosperous times. This is because each worker can mill 10,000 square feet, which nets a profit of 10 cents per square foot. Through no fault of the plywood workers, interest rates rise, building in the U.S. declines, and with building goes the plywood industry. As a result, the price of plywood falls such that each square foot of plywood now yields a profit of 5 cents per square foot.

In these circumstances, the plywood cooperative has at least two strategies. One is to keep all plywood workers employed at the previous wage of $1,000. Since workers are now only producing $500 each, some of the money will have to come from past accumulated profits or from firm borrowing. Suppose the downturn is expected to last 30 weeks. Losses of $300,000 are incurred, calculated as

($500 loss per worker per week) × (20 workers) × (30 weeks) = $300,000

An alternative strategy is to lay off some workers. Layoffs could be administered either through a random scheme or according to some other mechanism.

A firm provided unemployment compensation plan that induces some workers to take temporary layoff voluntarily is always better than the work-sharing scheme or random layoffs. Here is why. Suppose that there are 20 workers at the cooperative whose alternative wages (which may reflect opportunities at another job or the value that they assign to their leisure) are shown in Table 12.5. Workers at the cooperative are told that they may stay and take wages of $1,000 per week or they may leave and receive an unemployment benefit from the cooperative of $500 for every week that they remain unemployed. Who will leave? Everyone in Table 12.5 whose name appears above Joe leaves and accepts the unemployment compensation. Joe stays because his alternative wage is only $490, which, when added to the $500 unemployment compensation results in a total weekly wage of $990. Francisco leaves because his total earnings from his new job and his unemployment compensation amount to $1,005, which exceeds the $1,000 he would get if he stayed. All other higher placed names also accept temporary layoff. Those who accept layoffs are clearly better off because they earn more than they would have had the firm continued to pay them the $1,000 per week. The workers who stay earn $1,000, so they are no worse off than they would have been with the guaranteed employment plan that cost the firm $300,000 in losses. The firm loses at most

($500 per laid off worker per week) $\times$ (11 laid off workers) $\times$ 30 weeks
+$500 loss per worker per week) $\times$ (9 retained workers)
$\times$ 30 weeks = $300,000

The losses from this scheme are no more than the $300,000 that would have been lost had all workers been guaranteed employment so this situation is no worse than retaining all workers. In fact, it is much better because the workers who own the firm are better off as a group under the unemployment compensation scheme. Their reduced earnings from their shares in the cooperative are no lower and their take-home pay is higher.

The example illustrates a general principle. Risk aversion or not, it never pays to make work when the work is not there. Even if workers have ownership rights in the firm, they can do better by constructing voluntary layoff schemes that will make all worker-owners better off. Of course, nothing about being a cooperative prohibits a firm from behaving efficiently with respect to its labor. The political interactions between workers as owners either make it difficult to construct voluntary layoff schemes or awards the power to make decisions to those who do not understand the underlying principles that make voluntary unemployment beneficial to all.

Perhaps the greatest danger associated with worker-run firms is that politics, rather than reason, will prevail. There is much evidence on employee-owned

TABLE 12.5
WAGES FOR WORKERS AT THE HYPOTHETICAL PLYWOOD COOPERATIVE

Worker	Alternative Wage in Dollars
Sam	990
Sol	990
Jose	800
Guido	750
Park	600
Bob	600
Bill	575
Sarah	525
Yoshi	525
Chan	510
Francisco	505
Joe	490
Steve	480
Susan	460
Don	400
Russ	380
Mike	200
Garth	190
Wayne	190

organizations.[12] The evidence on the effects of employee ownership on performance is mixed, perhaps pointing to some slight positive association. It is also found that employee ownership does not automatically increase perceived or actual worker participation in the firm. This is not surprising. United Airlines, for example, is still a very large company. Even pilots, who are at the top of the worker–owner hierarchy, are large in number. Therefore, no single pilot has much of a say in the way the airline runs.

◆ ◆ ◆ ◆ ◆   RECAP

Firm production is team production. Individuals do not work in isolation from one another. Recognizing this fact and dealing with it appropriately can enhance company profits. The key to dealing with teams requires appropriate team formation and incentive design.

Two major benefits from team production are specialization and complementarity. The assembly line principle allows each individual to focus on a narrowly defined task, rather than forcing all individuals working in isolation to perform all tasks. Another major benefit is that knowledge transfer occurs between team members. Knowledge transfer is most beneficial when individuals possess idiosyncratic pieces of information that are relevant to other members of the firm.

As the size of the team increases, more knowledge transfer occurs. At the same time, communication between team members becomes more difficult. Further, free-rider effects are more pronounced in large teams. This is because information about what others are doing is better in small teams and the incentives to take actions against shirking co-workers are greater in small teams.

Team production may necessitate team compensation. When neither individual output nor individual effort can be observed within a team, some form of team payment is desirable. These may be explicit, such as team bonuses, profit sharing, or stock options plans, or they may be implicit, as with wages that rise more when company profits are higher.

Team bonuses are most effective when given to small teams performing well-defined tasks of short duration. Profit sharing, done at the level of the firm, is more appropriately thought of as risk sharing than as an incentive device. Finally, stock options can be used to motivate some very high-level managers in the firm. Various combinations of exercise price and option quantity can yield the same expected value, but provide different incentives. Higher exercise prices and more options produce greater incentives for a given expected value. High option prices also induce managers to take on riskier projects.

Norms are another aspect of the team environment. Norms establish appropriate levels of effort or behavior within an organization. They are not established

---

[12]A recent summary of the evidence is found in Kruse and Blasi (1995).

without cost. The larger the penalty associated with deviating from a norm, the higher the norm level of effort.

It is sometimes useful to rotate team members. This is particularly true when it is important to sort out workers' talents and when information is quickly passed from one worker to another. When knowledge is highly idiosyncratic and relevant to the other party, team switching is a good policy. When communication is difficult, say, because workers come from different disciplines, more time is required to build the relationship. If team switching is to occur at all, the interval during which team members remain together should be long.

Workers must be compensated to judge others. Otherwise strategic behavior by the evaluator can be a problem. A supervisor may downplay a high-quality employee, fearing future competition.

Cooperation occurs within teams, but competition takes place between teams. As a result, individuals who need to cooperate with one another for the good of the organization should be placed on the same team.

There are a number of ways to choose teams. When supervisors have better information than workers, supervisors may be given the authority to choose. Sometimes workers have better information and workers may choose other team members. In either case, a system that allows bidding for new team members, either by the supervisor or by another team captain, results in an efficient allocation of workers across teams.

Worker-owned firms are one form of team compensation. The evidence on them is mixed. To the extent that they protect employment more than non-labor firms do, they can be inefficient. All can be made better off by adopting the efficient employment policy and inducing worker-owners to leave voluntarily through unemployment compensation.

REFERENCES ◆ ◆ ◆ ◆ ◆

Brown, Charles, and James Medoff, "The Employer Size-Wage Effect," *Journal of Political Economy* 97, 5 (October 1989): 1027–1059.

Craig, Ben, and John Pencavel, "The Behavior of Worker Cooperatives: The Plywood Companies of the Pacific Northwest," *American Economic Review* 82, 5 (December 1992): 1083–1105.

Farrell, Joseph, and Suzanne Scotchmer, "Partnerships," *Quarterly Journal of Economics* 103 (May 1988): 279–97.

Jackson, Matthew O., and Edward P. Lazear, "Stock, Options, and Deferred Compensation," in Ronald C. Ehrenberg ed., *Research in Labor Economics*, Vol. 12, Greenwich, CT: JAI Press, Inc., 1991, pp. 41–62.

Kandel, Eugene, and Edward P. Lazear, "Peer Pressure and Partnerships," *Journal of Political Economy* 100, 4 (August 1992): 801–17.

Kruse, Douglas, and Joseph Blasi, "Employee Ownership, Employee Attitudes, and Firm Performance," NBER Working Paper 5277, September 1995.

Pugel, Thomas A., "Profitability, Concentration and the Interindustry Variation in Wages," *Review of Economics and Statistics* 62, (May 1980): 248–53.

◆ ◆ ◆ ◆ ◆ ADDITIONAL ADVANCED READING

Athey, Susan, Christopher Avery, and Peter B. Zemsky, "Mentoring, Discrimination and Diversity in Organizations," *Stanford Graduate School of Business Research Paper* 1317,34 (October 1994).

Becker, Gary S., and Kevin M. Murphy, "The Division of Labor, Coordination Costs, and Knowledge," *Quarterly Journal of Economics* 107 (November 1992): 1137–60.

Jensen, Michael C., and William H. Meckling, "Specific and General Knowledge and Organizational Structure," in Lars Werin and Hans Wijkander, eds. *Contract Economic . . .*, Cambridge: Blackwell, 1992, pp. 251–74.

Meyers, Margaret A., "The Dynamics of Learning with Team Production: Implications for Task Assignment," *Quarterly Journal of Economics* 109 (November 1994): 1157–84.

Rosen, Sherwin, "The Military as an Internal Labor Market: Some Allocation, Productivity, and Incentive Problems," *Social Science Quarterly* 73 (June 1992): 227–37.

◆ ◆ ◆ ◆ ◆ APPENDIX

Results on Incentives and Options

Here, some results on options as incentive devices are derived. This is done under the assumption that option holders are risk-neutral, which makes derivations much easier than the standard Black–Scholes formulation for option pricing, described in virtually every finance text.

Value of an Option is Decreasing in Exercise Price

Let the value of one share of stock at the exercise date be given by

$$V + \epsilon$$

where V can be affected by the manager and ϵ reflects randomness in stock price over which the manager has no control. Let K be the exercise prices. The density of ϵ is given by $f(\epsilon)$. Then the expected value of the option is

$$(A12.1) \qquad Z = \int_{K-V}^{\infty} [V + \epsilon - K]\, f(\epsilon)\, d\epsilon$$

The stock option is not exercised unless $V + \epsilon > K$. That is, the holder only wants to use the option if the current value of the firm, $V + \epsilon$, is greater than the strike price, K. Rearranging this expression, we see that the stock only has value when ϵ

is greater than $K - V$. This is why, in Equation A12.1, we integrate ϵ over the region $K - V$ to infinity.

It is now apparent that increasing the exercise, or strike, price lowers the expected value of the stock. Raising the strike price by one dollar simply lowers the holder's profit by one dollar in each case where the holder exercises the option. Thus, the *loss* from the price increase is equal to the probability that the holder exercises, which is given by $1 - F(K-V)$, the probability that ϵ is greater then $K - V$. This is shown in Equation A12.2:

$$(A12.2) \qquad \frac{\partial Z}{\partial K} = -(V - K + K - V)f(K - V) - \int_{k-V}^{\infty} f(\epsilon)\, d\epsilon$$

$$= -(1 - F(K - V)) < 0$$

A higher price K, which results in a lower value of the option Z, can be offset by giving workers more options.

(A12.2) has two terms because there are two effects of increasing K. The first term,

$$-(V + K - V - K)f(K - V)$$

reflects the value of decreasing the probability that the option will be in the money when K increases. This is equal to zero, because at the point where the option is just in the money, it has no value anyway. The option owner pays exactly the same amount for the stock as it is worth. That is, the stock is just in the money at the point where $V + \epsilon = K$, which is where it has no value.

The second term, however, reflects that a one dollar decline in the strike price means that the net value will be one dollar less every time the option is exercised, which happens $1 - F(K-V)$ of the time.

Second, the value of an option increases as the value of the firm rises. For every dollar that the value of one share increases, the option increases by a value of $1 - F(K-V)$. This is because increasing the value of the firm by \$1 increases the amount that is received when the stock is exercised, which is $1 - F(K-V)$. Differentiating (A12.1) with respect to V yields

$$\frac{\partial Z}{\partial V} = (V + K - K - V)f(K - V) + 1 - F(K - V) > 0$$

or

$$(A12.3) \qquad \frac{\partial Z}{\partial V} = 1 - F(K - V) > 0$$

As before, the first term, which reflects the increased likelihood of being in the money, drops out because at the point where the individual is more likely to be in the money, being in the money has no value—the option holder pays exactly as much for the stock as he can sell it for.

The second term, which survives, reflects the fact that a dollar increase in the value of the firm means one dollar to the option holder every time the option is in the money, which happens $1 - F(K-V)$ of the time.

Third, as the exercise price gets very large, increasing the value of the firm has no value to the option holder. From Equation A12.3, one obtains

(A12.4)
$$\lim_{K \to \infty} \frac{\partial Z}{\partial V} = \lim_{K \to \infty} [1 - F(K - V)] = 0$$

If the exercise price is so high that the option will never be in the money, there is no value to the option holder of raising the value of the firm.

Fourth, there are an infinite number of combinations of number of stock options and exercise prices that generate the same expected value as one share of stock. But the incentive effects of the different combinations are quite different.[13]

That there are an infinite number of combinations of number of options and exercise prices that yield the same expected value follows trivially from the (negative) monotonicity of $\partial Z/\partial K$. Since an increase in exercise price always implies a decrease in Z, it is possible simply to increase the number of options to offset this.

It is also clear that as a general rule, the different combinations have different incentive effects. The incentive effect is measured as

$$N \, \partial Z/\partial V$$

where N is the number of options granted. Since $\partial Z/\partial V$ is the gain from increasing the value of the firm when one option is held, $N \, \partial Z/\partial V$ is the gain when N options are held. This would be constant only if $\partial Z/\partial V = 1/N$, which it does not in general.

Holding the expected value of the options constant, say, at some level $X, implies that $N Z = X$ or that N must be altered such that $N = \dfrac{X}{Z}$ for any X, Z. Then, for $\dfrac{\partial Z}{\partial V}$ to equal $\dfrac{1}{N}$, it is necessary that

$$1 - F(K - V) = \frac{1}{N}$$

$$= \frac{X}{Z}$$

$$= \frac{X}{\displaystyle\int_{K-V}^{\infty} [V + \epsilon - K] f(\epsilon) \, d\epsilon}$$

$$= \frac{X}{(V - K)[1 - F(K - V)] + \displaystyle\int_{K-V}^{\infty} \epsilon f(\epsilon) \, d\epsilon}$$

which cannot hold as a general matter.

---

[13]See Jackson and Lazear (1991) for a more complete discussion.

Norms

The level of the norms depends on the type of sanction associated with deviating from the norm. Further, for any given sanction, there exists an equilibrium norm level of effort in the firm.[14]

To see this, write an individual's utility as

$$\text{(A12.5)} \qquad \text{Utility} = Y(E) - C(E) - P(E - E^*)$$

where E is an individual's effort level, $Y(E)$ are the earnings received as a function of effort, $C(E)$ is the monetary value of the pain associated with a given level of effort, E, and $P(E - E^*)$ is the peer pressure felt as a function of effort, E, and the endogenously determined norm effort, E^*. When workers want their co-workers to put forth more effort, $P' < 0$. Reducing one's effort increases peer pressure. Additionally, $Y'' \leq 0$, $C'' > 0$ because we can always normalize effort such that $Y'' \leq 0$ and because eventual exhaustion means that the limit of $C(E)$ as E goes to infinity is infinity. It is impossible to put forth effort beyond some point of total exhaustion.

Suppose that peer pressure takes the following form:

$$\text{(A12.6)} \qquad P(E - E^*) = \gamma\,(E^* - E)$$

This says that for every unit that an individual's effort falls below the norm of E^*, he feels pressure which causes him pain having a monetary equivalent of γ dollars.

The worker's maximization problem is to choose E so as to maximize utility in (A12.5), given (A12.6). The first-order condition is

$$\text{(A12.7)} \qquad Y'(E) - C'(E) + \gamma = 0$$

which generally has a solution. Since all workers are identical, E^* is simply the solution to (A12.7). Thus, a norm level of effort is established.

It is also clear, using the implicitly function theory, that

$$\frac{\partial E}{\partial \gamma}\Big|_{A12.6} = -\frac{1}{Y'' - C''}$$

which is positive. Thus, an increase in γ increases each worker's level of effort. As sanctions from deviating from the norm increase, the norm level of effort increases.

If all workers within a firm had the same utility function, then each would choose the same level of effort, given (A12.7). Thus, each worker's E would be identical and this would define E^*, the norm, or average, level of effort within the firm.

The function chosen in (A12.6) was an arbitrary one and was just selected for illustrative purposes. But the same analysis holds for any peer pressure function.

---

[14] This analysis is based on Kandel and Lazear (1992).

MORE ON THE EMPLOYMENT RELATIONSHIP: OUTSOURCING, CONTRACTS, FRANCHISING, AND MORE

13

*I*n this chapter, we tie up a number of loose ends, covering important topics in personnel management that do not fit easily into other sections of the book. This chapter presents discussions of outsourcing, bonuses and penalties, trade secrets, and cost-plus contracts, among others. To motivate these discussions, we start with the following hypothetical meeting.

BURNS: I think that it is time for us to begin work on the new building. We've got to have more space. Interest rates are low right now, our sales growth looks good, and everything seems right.

LERNER: I agree. I'd like to get our construction subsidiary to draw up plans as soon as possible. Despite their being busy, no time is better than now.

MITCHELL: Hold on, Abbie. I'm in charge of that division, and we are swamped. The last thing I want to do is pull them off their current paying projects and send them to work on an in-house assignment that isn't going to bring in any revenue. You accountants are always trying to figure out ways to get work done that doesn't show up on the books as cost.

LERNER: I know that, but it *will* cost us a fortune to go outside. We are in that business; it makes no sense to pay others to do what we can do for ourselves. Can't you speed up some of the other work? You're a creative guy, Wes. You ought to be able to think of something.

MITCHELL: Well, we might be able to offer them some kind of early completion bonus, but I don't know what that will do to the quality of their current project. Perhaps we can penalize them for finishing the job late. If they finish their current project on schedule, we might be able to turn to this within a couple of months. But, as you know, few things ever run on schedule in construction.

BURNS: True, but that's because you work on a cost-plus basis. Construction workers are like lawyers: both hate to see resolution of the problem.

LERNER: Isn't there some nonmonetary way to get this project on track? Forget bonuses, can't you get the construction group to think about the new building simply because it's good for the company? Why are we always talking about money, anyway? I think that the emphasis on money just reduces things to their lowest common denominator. We'd do better by thinking about the big picture.

BURNS: Alright, enough soap-box lectures. I want to get this project going. Give me a plan for proceeding within a week.

The questions touched on in this discussion include:

- When should insiders be used to do a project over outsiders?

- Are cost-plus contracts better than other forms of contracts?

- Should workers be motivated by bonuses or threatened by penalties?

- Are nonmonetary sources of motivation better?

We deal with each of these problems in turn.

◆ ◆ ◆ ◆ ◆ OUTSOURCING

The major disagreement in the hypothetical scenario involved using inside labor. The manager who was not responsible for the problems associated with using another division's labor was all for using it internally. The accountant was worrying about how things would look on the books; the manager in charge of construction was worried about how his life would be affected by taking on another project, particularly one that is visible to all of his fellow managers.

Neither of these narrow views is the correct way to make an outsourcing decision. Both managers are being extremely myopic. The make-or-buy decision can and must be done in a systematic way. The accountant was wrong to ignore true costs. Even the books might have revealed the make decision to be one of false economy. The manager of the construction division was also being short-sighted in rejecting the project out of hand. A more enlightened view can be proposed.

The key to deciding whether to make or buy is to understand *opportunity cost*. Labor is one of the most important components in determining opportunity cost.

To refresh the reader's memory, opportunity cost is not (necessarily) what something costs on the books, rather, it is what that something costs in terms of forgone opportunities. In chapter 6, we discussed the cost of a year of education. The cost consisted not merely of the tuition costs that are easily seen and measured, but also of the forgone earnings associated with spending one more year out of the labor market. The forgone earnings reflect an important part of the opportunity costs.

In the discussion above, the accountant was completely ignoring the opportunity costs. When Lerner says in response to Mitchell's complaint,

> "I know that, but it *will* cost us a fortune to go outside. We are in that business; it makes no sense to pay others to do what we can do for ourselves"

opportunity cost is being ignored. Being in the business does not mean that there is no cost to using one's own labor. At the heart of every make-or-buy decision is the concept of opportunity cost. Producing a good internally obviously carries a cost, but managers sometimes forget the cost because they assume implicitly that all costs already committed are not costs in any real sense. Thus, the firm might as well extract what it can from resources already at hand.

Many resources that are viewed as fixed and costs that are viewed as sunk are neither fixed nor sunk. In the construction example, as long as the firm is hiring more workers into a given position, the factor is not a sunk one. Even if the firm has a commitment to workers already hired, it need not hire any additional workers. When a firm uses its existing workers to produce a product internally, and is thereby forced to hire other workers to produce goods for other customers, it must recognize that the cost of using the labor internally is the cost of hiring the new workers. If the firm has the option of using existing workers instead of hiring new ones, then the cost of using existing workers on an internal job is equal to the cost of hiring replacement workers. Since the firm is hiring new workers, the fact that it cannot lay off existing workers is irrelevant. It is not a binding constraint. Although the firm may think of this as a fixed component of cost, it always has the option of using its currently committed labor for new projects. If it chooses to use its existing workers for the new building, it will have to hire new workers to replace those who are currently working for paying customers as they are transferred to the internal building project. The cost of transferring existing workers to the internal project is exactly the cost of employing their replacements.

Second, even if the firm does not hire any additional workers, using its existing workers on an internal project carries a cost. The cost is the value of the next best opportunity. For example, suppose that the firm is in a downsizing mode, where it is not hiring and may even be laying off workers in a given division. The workers who are retained can still be used to produce something, but what they are being used to produce may not yield sufficient value to justify bringing on new workers. What is the cost of using these workers to produce something internally? It is the value of what they would otherwise have been doing. If that value exceeds the cost of having the alternative project done by another firm, then it pays to outsource the project.

Consider the following example. A firm, Orange Aviation Corporation (OAC), has a union contract to maintain employment for a given group of 100 machinists throughout the year and to pay them an annual salary of $40,000. The firm is engaged in the production of aircraft for the U.S. Air Force. Unexpectedly, Congress passes a spending reduction bill which reduces the demand for the firm's output, driving the value of the typical worker's output down to $35,000. Had OAC known the decline in demand was coming, it never would have agreed to maintain the work force at its pre-decline level and to pay each worker $40,000 per year. Doing so results in losses. But the firm has a contract to maintain employment, so laying off workers is not a possibility. OAC currently buys some of the airplane component parts from another manufacturer. Given the fall in the demand for its primary product, OAC is planning to produce the component parts internally, using the surplus of workers to produce what OAC would otherwise have bought externally. Is this a good idea?

While the answer may seem to be an obvious yes, it is not. Even in this environment of surplus labor, the decision to switch to internal production may still be a bad one. Table 13.1 provides some estimates of what would happen under various scenarios.

Table 13.1 reports estimated production as a function of number of machinists employed. This table assumes that OAC continues to buy the component parts externally. The numbers are calculated as follows. Profits before machinists' wages are calculated by taking total revenues from the planes and subtracting all costs, fixed and variable, except wages of machinists. Thus, when less than ten machinists are employed, no planes can be produced, but fixed costs are still present, so the firm would lose $10 million were it to employ less than ten machinists in its airplane production. When 100 machinists are used, ten planes are produced, which generates enough revenue to cover all costs (except machinist wages) and still leave $3.5 million left over for profit. Of course, after the 100 machinists are paid the $4 million owed them, the firm loses $.5 million.

When the number of machinists employed drops to 80, output drops to 16

TABLE 13.1
PROFITS PER WORKER AT OAC AFTER THE CUTBACK
IN GOVERNMENT CONTRACTS

Number of Workers Employed	Number of Airplanes Produced	Profit Before Machinists' Wages	Change in Profit per Machinist	Profit or Loss
100	20	$3,500,000	$35,000	−$500,000
80	16	$2,800,000	$36,207	−$1,200,000
51	10	$1,750,000	$58,333	−$2,250,000
42	7	$1,225,000	$21,875	−$2,775,000
10	3	$525,000	$1,052,500	−$3,345,000
Less than 10	0	−$10,000,000		−$14,000,000

planes and profits net of machinists' wages fall to $2.8 million. Thus, adding 20 machinists to 80 generates an additional $3.5 − $2.8 = $0.7 million, or $0.7 million / 20 = $35,000 per additional machinist. This is how the next to last column is calculated. The numbers in this column then are the change in profit from the previous level of employment, divided by the change in employment. The last entry in the last column of $1,052,500 reflects a gain in profit of $10,525,000 as employment goes from zero machinists to ten machinists, divided by the ten machinists. It is the marginal profit associated with each additional machinist.

Note that the change in profit per machinist becomes smaller as more machinists are used beyond 51 machinists. This is because the last few workers perform tasks that are less important than the first few. It is generally the case that as more workers are added, the marginal worker contributes less to output than previous workers. The first workers employed do the most important tasks. Table 13.1 makes this most clear at the bottom. If less than ten workers are employed, no planes can be produced at all and losses are incurred, because the firm must cover its fixed costs (like rent on the plant, etc.) without receiving any revenue. The last column reports the profit or loss—in this case, loss—associated with each level of machinist employment.

We are now ready to answer the question posed. Given that the firm has surplus labor, should it bring the external work into the firm? The answer requires knowing how much of the component work each of OAC's machinists can perform. Suppose that component parts cost $1,000 each. To produce them internally requires supplies and other labor accounting for $450. Each machinist can produce 60 component parts. Does it pay to make component parts, rather than buy them? The answer depends on whether the total cost to the firm of making the component parts is less than $1,000, which is what it pays to its external supplier. It pays to make rather than buy if the opportunity cost of machinist labor is less than 60 × $550. If the machinist cost is less than $550 per component part produced, the firm has a total internal cost that is less than the $1,000 it pays externally. The opportunity cost of machinist labor can be read directly from Table 13.1. When labor is reduced from 100 to 80, the value of airplanes produced declines by $35,000 per machinist. Thus, the opportunity cost of moving even a few machinists from airplane production to component part production is $35,000 per machinist. This means that the opportunity cost of using a machinist to produce component parts is $35,000 / 60 = $583.33 per part, since each machinist produces 60 component parts. The total cost of producing the parts internally is then $450 + $583.33 = $1,033.33. Since the parts can be purchased outside for $1,000, the firm should continue to buy externally, even though it has surplus labor that can produce the parts internally.

How can this be? It is clear that the firm has surplus labor, because it would prefer to lay off machinists were it not constrained by the union contract. But this does not mean that those workers' value is zero. It simply means that those workers are not worth what they are paid. This does not mean that it is all right to throw away their labor. Having them work on a project that is not as profitable as what they are currently doing is essentially throwing labor away. We conclude that building the component parts is not as profitable as building airplanes with the machinists. The component parts can be purchased more cheaply outside than they can be made inside, even when we recognize that the value of airplane production has fallen. The machinists are currently being used to reduce losses, and they reduce losses more when they build airplanes than when they build component parts.

The firm ranks choices as follows:

1. If unconstrained, the firm would like to cut back its machinist work force because it suffers losses when employing any number of machinists between 1 and 100.

2. Given the union constraint, the firm finds it better to use its 100 machinists to produce airplanes, while continuing to purchase the component parts externally.

3. Worst of all is diverting internal labor to production of component parts. Even though the machinists are not worth the $40,000 they are being paid, they are more efficient at producing airplanes under adverse conditions than they are at producing component parts that are available from cheaper sources. Losses are minimized by using all machinists to produce planes, and continuing to buy parts externally.

We can now state a general principle on the make-or-buy decision:

Buying a product from external sources is preferred to producing it internally if and only if the cost of outsourcing is lower than the opportunity cost of producing it internally. Internal production cost must account for forgone opportunities appropriately.

◆ ◆ ◆ ◆ ◆ ACCOUNTING

If the accounting is done properly, then the appropriate decision would be supported by the accounting figures, as well. Both Lerner and Mitchell mistakenly assumed that internal construction would not show up on the books, but that hiring an outside company to do the job would.

Let us continue with the OAC example. When airplanes are sold, purchases show up as credits. The costs of building the planes, which consist of labor and supplies, are debits. If OAC outsources the component parts, then credits associated with the sale of airplanes produced by the 100 machinists are equal to the price of an airplane, P, times 20 since 20 planes are sold. In the debit column, enter machinist salaries, equal to $40,000 per machinist times 100 machinists. Additionally, enter $1,000 times the number of component parts, Z, used to make the 20 planes. Thus, when components are bought rather than made, an abbreviated version of the balance sheet looks like Table 13.2.

The net is a loss of $500,000. This can be derived from the top row of Table 13.1, which says that profit was $3.5 million before subtracting machinist wages of $4 million.

TABLE 13.2
ABBREVIATED BALANCE SHEET OF OAC WITH
OUTSOURCING OF COMPONENTS

Credits		Debits
20 Planes	20$P	Labor
		$100 \times \$40,000 = \$4\text{million}$
		Components $Z \times \$1000$
	Net $= -\$500,000$	

OUTSOURCING DECISIONS OF SUPER BAKERY

◆ ◆ ◆ ◆ ◆ ◆ ◆ ◆ ◆ ◆

In 1994, Super Bakery's sales reached $8.5 million with a staff of only nine full-time employees. For the past eight years, the company has been growing at an explosive rate, achieving the average sales increase of over 20 percent per year. Super Bakery's entry into the institutional food market in the early eighties was less impressive. At first, the difference between Super Bakery and its competitors was hardly greater than the difference between two donuts. Not surprisingly, being just another player in a near perfectly competitive industry Super Bakery showed disappointing profits.

In the late eighties the company developed an innovative strategy that proved to be highly successful. Outsourcing is one of the key ingredients of the company strategy. Super Bakery managed to build a national presence in what formerly was a fragmented industry. At first, the company focused on the school system segment of the institutional food market. Most bakeries did not offer any products specifically tailored to schools, and government health requirements prevented many local bakeries from selling their regular products to schools. Super Bakery pioneered "low-calorie, vitamin-enriched donuts that tasted delicious and met USDA guidelines." In order to capitalize on economies of scale, Super Bakery started to vacuum-seal and refrigerate their product, which made national distribution possible.

The management realized that many tasks can be done by outsiders at lower cost. They understood that having a winning product does not necessarily mean being the best at shipping it. Super Bakery started to outsource shipping and warehousing and eventually production was contracted out as well. To guard against quality decline, Super Bakery developed an advanced computerized accounting and control system. They tracked customer service and satisfaction, as well as the costs of filling orders and serving customers.

That allowed Super Bakery to outsource tasks to the lowest-cost supplier, making sure that contractors performed their tasks without compromising quality. When the company started to outsource manufacturing functions, product quality was controlled by supplying manufacturers with dough that contained Super Bakery's unique product formulation. Outsourcing allowed Super Bakery to focus on the areas of its competitive advantage. Super Bakery's sophisticated inventory control and order-booking system made coordination of numerous suppliers and contractors possible. Front-line, customer service employees at Super Bakery take product orders from distributors and school systems, quote prices and schedule delivery dates, and schedule production in several independent bakeries located thousands of miles apart from each other. Super Bakery specializes in processing orders, coordinating activities of suppliers and contractors, and monitoring the quality of the products and services that they provide. This structure results in remarkable efficiency because each task is performed by the lowest-cost firm. The bakery adds extra value by cooperating with noncompeting suppliers in order to provide complete prepackaged meals to schools. Super Bakery also keeps the R&D effort centralized in order to avoid duplication of effort.

Super Bakery is a fine example of outsourcing. It is a prosperous, virtual corporation. There are other successful virtual corporations such as Benetton, which outsources most of its manufacturing. However, outsourcing is not for everyone. For outsourcing to be profitable, the cost of performing a task in-house must be greater than the price charged by the outsiders, plus coordination and monitoring costs.

Source: Davis, Tim, and Bruce Darling, "ABC in Virtual Corporation," *Managment Accounting* (October 1996) 78, 4, p. 18–26.

What would the balance sheet look like if 20 workers were diverted from airplane production to component production? Table 13.1 shows that only 17 planes would be produced and that profits would fall by $700,000 as a result. Labor costs remain the same because 100 machinists are still employed. The difference is that some of them produce components rather than airplanes.

While credits fall by $700,000, debits also fall. Each of the 20 workers now produces 60 components each. This reduces actual expenditures on outside components. But there are additional supplies that must be purchased to produce the components internally. Above, we were told that the supplies for each component amounted to $450, before machinist labor costs were figured in. Thus, costs are reduced by $60 \times 20 \times (\$1000 - \$450) = \$660,000$.

The balance sheet would show that producing internally would result in additional losses. Revenues net of other expenses would fall by $700,000. Costs would fall by $660,000. Since costs fall by less than net revenues, moving component production inside the firm is a bad idea, both in reality and as far as the books are concerned.

♦ ♦ ♦ ♦ ♦ SPECIAL INTERESTS

In the hypothetical scenario, the accountant favored the make approach and the manager in charge of the construction division favored the buy approach. Each may have been speaking from personal viewpoints, and ignoring the overall interests of the firm.

When this happens, it reflects a misalignment of incentives. If incentives were appropriate, each manager would take into account the total effects on the firm and behave accordingly. When managers fail to act in the firm's best interest, it is often a direct result of a failure to provide appropriate incentives.

Return, for example, to the hypothetical scenario. Mitchell was upset about having to take on an additional project, which in this case happened to be an internal one. Why? Most businesses view an increase in demand as a good, not bad. There were probably two reasons why Mitchell was concerned about having the additional project. First, he believed, rightly or wrongly, that outside work, which generates visible profits, is more highly valued by the firm. Diverting his attention to an inside project might cause his reputation to suffer. Second, he believed that doing an internal project could be a major source of aggravation. His peers and supervisors would be breathing down his neck and if anything went wrong, everyone would know about it. As far as Mitchell was concerned, this was a no-win situation.

Suppose, however, that Mitchell were compensated nicely for doing the internal project. It is possible that he might actually welcome the task. In fact, it is conceivable that things could go too far. He might be rewarded so heavily for finishing the new internal building on schedule that he might neglect his outside clients to too great a degree.

One rule of thumb is to make the manager's reward proportional to the firm's reward. If the firm views the internal construction as having equal value to the external construction, then it should reward the manager similarly for each project. Then, the manager would be less likely to shun the internal project in favor of external ones. If the firm placed too great an emphasis on internal projects, either explicitly through compensation or implicitly through peer monitoring, the manager will devote too much of his time and attention to the internal project.

There is feedback that a firm receives in the process. If one finds that managers constantly resist taking actions that are in the firm's best interests, chances are that managerial rewards (pecuniary or otherwise) are not weighted heavily enough toward the desired projects. This can be remedied by restructuring the compensation scheme in an explicit, and perhaps visible, way.

◆ ◆ ◆ ◆ ◆   COST-PLUS VERSUS
PROJECT-BASED PAY

Suppose that Mitchell's paranoia wins out and plans to construct the building using internal sources are scrapped. The firm still needs to have the additional space, so they go to an outside contractor to obtain the services from them. There are (at least) two ways to structure the contract[1] between the builder and the firm. The first is to negotiate a fixed sum for the project. The second is to agree to pay on a cost-plus basis, sometimes referred to as *time and materials*.

The choice between the two schemes is an application of the discussion in chapter 5 of paying on the basis of input or paying on the basis of output. A cost-plus system is payment on the basis of input. Costs used as the basis of pay are those based on materials and labor costs. The *plus* is a margin added to cover managerial time and return to capital—that is, accounting profit. Project-based pay is payment on the basis of output. It is essentially a special case of a piece rate, where there is only one piece and payment is made after the piece is completed. In the current example, the firm and its builder would sign a contract to have a building with given specifications constructed in a specified time period for a fixed fee, to be determined at the time that the contract is negotiated. With a cost-plus contract, negotiations would be over the rates to be charged for various supplies and especially for labor. Additionally, the margin would have to be negotiated. The cost-plus contract generally allows the buyer to terminate the builder at any time, being responsible only for costs and margin incurred up to that point. The project-based contract generally requires that down payments sufficient to cover costs are paid to the contractor. A buyer who wants to terminate the contract in the middle of the project will usually lose money by doing so, since the sum of what has been already paid and the cost of what remains to be done usually exceeds the total cost of the job.

The discussion in chapter 5 of quality versus quantity is relevant here. If project-based pay is used, the supplier has incentives to finish the project as cheaply as possible. As long as payment is on the basis of output, and as long as all dimensions of output quality are not easily observed, the supplier will try to reduce quality as much as possible, consistent with receiving payment for a completed job. Reputational concerns may mitigate the quality reduction, but this depends on two factors. First, the quality must eventually be observable. If quality is never observed, then there is no way that the supplier's reputation can suffer from shoddy workmanship. Second, the supplier must care about personal reputation. Suppliers who plan to stay in business for extended periods of time are more likely to care about their reputations.

Sometimes, depending on the payment schedule, the supplier whose pay is project based may not want to finish the project at all. For example, if 90 percent

---

[1]For comprehensive economic analysis of different types of contractual agreements see Hart (1983).

of the payment has been made after 70 percent of the work has been done, it may be difficult to induce the contractor to finish the rest of the job. Finishing this project will be low priority. The preference will be to take on new jobs that offer large up-front payments. Negotiations at the time the contract is signed must resolve the tension between the buyer's desire to hold back significant payment until the end and the seller's desire to capture most of the payment up front. Even an honest supplier prefers to be paid up front. Otherwise, he or she is at the mercy of the buyer. Buyers may have little concern for their reputation as buyers because a given buyer buys building services far less often than a building seller sells them. Being labeled a buyer who may hold back on payment is generally less damaging than being labeled a builder who does not complete work. For this reason, contracts tend to favor up-front payments to the supplier. The exception occurs when the buyer engages repeatedly in transactions with a supplier.

In order to induce the provider to complete the work in a timely fashion, late penalties or on-time bonuses are sometimes offered. If the bonuses or penalties are too large, the provider may be induced to work too quickly. Up-front payment with time-based penalties or bonuses paid at the end are likely to improve incentives.

Cost-plus contracts reduce incentives to skimp on quality because the provider is paid on the basis of input. In fact, the incentives go the other way. Since the provider receives a margin on all costs incurred, a present-oriented seller prefers to run up the bill, putting in very high-quality and expensive items. Further, the provider has an incentive to draw out the project, making it last as long as possible. Evidence on this point comes from the legal profession. When lawyers are paid for hours worked, they have little incentive to push the case through to early resolution. When they are paid on a contingency basis (i.e., some percentage of the final judgment) they are more likely to push for a quick settlement. It does not pay the lawyer to spend twice as much time on a case when the expected return is raised by a small percentage.

Again, concerns about reputation may limit a provider's desire to stretch out or inflate the quality on a job on which the supplier is paid on a cost-plus or time-and-materials basis. When signing a contract with a seller, buyers usually ask for references. Of course, since the names of references are provided by the seller, the recommendations are not likely to be unbiased. The seller offers names of past customers whose jobs went well, not those whose jobs went poorly. Savvy buyers take this bias into account in interpreting recommendations, but information about a seller's past performance is likely to be far from perfect.

How anxious is the supplier to stretch out a job? This depends on the margin. If the margin is sufficiently low that the supplier can obtain work at similar margins elsewhere, then the supplier is not particularly anxious to stretch out the job. However, if the margin is high relative to that which can be obtained from other buyers, the supplier may be very anxious to stretch out the job. *Thus, the higher the margin, the longer the expected duration of a job and the higher the expected quality when suppliers are paid on a cost-plus basis.*

The conclusion is that cost-plus contracts tend to induce too much effort, whereas project-based pay induces too little effort. Which is better? If quality is easily observed and verified, then it is probably better to go with a project-based payment where providers are penalized for deviations from contracted quality. If quality is not easily observed, but the appropriate amount of time to complete the job is known, it is probably better to use a cost-plus system, with penalties for running over the contracted amount of time.

◆◆◆◆◆ FRANCHISING

Franchising is a sharing arrangement where a firm creates profit centers to deal with incentive problems. Consider a gasoline station franchise. Standard Oil Company for many years had two kinds of stations in California. Standard stations were company owned. The manager and all personnel at the station were employed by Standard Oil and supervision was provided by the company itself. In this respect, it was no different from a local branch of Bank of America. The branch offices are run, but not owned, by the bank manager. Standard Oil also franchised Chevron stations, which were owned and run by individuals who were not employed by Standard Oil.[2] Chevron carried Standard Oil products and Standard Oil placed some restrictions on the ways in which the Chevron stations could do business, but the manager/owner was the residual claimant. What the owner earned was his. If things went badly in a given year, the owner bore the cost.

Franchises are an attempt to solve an incentive problem. For workers on a fixed salary or hourly wage, inducing effort is always a problem. Individuals who own their own businesses, bear the full costs of reduced effort and reap the full benefit from superior effort. Franchising is a compromise. It provides incentives to the franchise manager/owner to put forth effort, but it does not solve all incentive problems. The Standard Oil example provides good evidence to this effect. Chevron stations tended to be located in small towns, whereas Standard stations tended to be located on the highway. Why?

Two components of effort are important here. The first is effort exerted to satisfy customer desires on a daily basis. This includes pumping gas in a timely fashion, providing courteous service, and checking engine parts and fluids as required. A second kind of effort is less tangible, but perhaps more important to the overall company. Whenever a local service station sells and installs Standard products, Standard Oil's brand name is on the line. If the servicer does a poor job, Standard Oil's name suffers, and with it, so do the reputations and businesses of all other carriers of Standard products. There is a free-rider problem involved. One servicer who adversely affects the brand name of Standard Oil may only bear a tiny part of the cost. Most of the cost is borne by the company in general. If the servicer's negligence were to cost the company, say, $10 million in lost sales, the person might

---

[2]For study of gasoline retail market and in particular, franchise arrangements in gasoline retail market see A. Shepard (1993).

only feel perhaps $100 of the damage. The rest would be spread throughout the company. Thus, if the individual servicer can take an action that is personally worth more than $100, like not having to check the oil of any customers, the servicer will do it, even though it costs the company as a whole $10 million.

These effects are not a major problem when an individual has many repeat customers. When the service station has a large proportion of repeat customers, reputation effects are probably sufficient to keep effort high. But reputation matters only when having a poor reputation affects income. Even if a local service station had a great deal of repeat business, the workers might not care much about the reputation of the station if they were employed by Standard Oil on a fixed salary. But when the station is a franchise, a good reputation is crucial to the owner/manager of the station. If customers are not treated appropriately, they will go elsewhere, and income will suffer. Thus, it makes sense to have franchise service stations in areas where there is a higher proportion of repeat business.

Franchising solves many incentive problems, but not all of them. There remains the difficulty of free riding on Standard Oil's brand name. Local franchisers still do not take full account of their actions, because most of the costs and benefits from their actions accrue to others at Standard Oil. It is for this reason that stations on interstate highways are less likely to be franchises. Since there is little repeat business, there are no major incentive effects for an owner/manager. Even though the owners bear the costs of their actions, their actions have almost no effect on revenues. If an owner preforms badly, all other Standard stations suffer. The owner bears only a small part of the total cost. Since only a small portion of the customers ever come back, interstate franchises need not worry as much about treating them well.

To get around this, Standard runs its own stations on the highway and invests more in supervision. Since Standard cares about the effects of one station's behavior on all other stations, the company works hard to ensure that each station behaves appropriately. The cost is that it must invest more in supervision than it would were the station a franchise. The benefit is that the station internalizes the effects on Standard Oil's brand name.

Even within franchises, parent companies attempt to exert control over the franchisee. For example, franchised fast-food restaurants are required to use the products of the parent company. Strict rules about cleanliness and appearance of the restaurant are often enforced. Hours of operation are frequently dictated by the parent company. All of these constraints are an attempt to deal with the free-rider problem. When one McDonalds has dirty restrooms, all McDonalds suffer. Thus, the parent company dictates the ways in which individual franchises operate.

Is it necessarily the case that the parent company will want to keep the best locations as company stores, allowing franchises only in lower-revenue locations? Absolutely not. The issue is not one of good location versus bad location. It is one of incentives. To take the Standard Oil example, suppose that the station on Interstate 5, just west of Fresno, does ten times the business of a local station in Visalia. This does not imply that Standard would want the I-5 station more than the Visalia station. The amount of business done merely affects the price of the franchise. If the I-5 station does much more business, the I-5 franchise would sell for much more than the Visalia franchise. Standard Oil can extract its profits either by running a profitable station itself, or by selling it to a buyer at a very high price. Its desire to keep the I-5 station implies that it can make more by owning it than by selling it, primarily because incentives are better dealt with when it is owned by Standard than when it is franchised. If the reverse were true, a franchisee would be willing to pay Standard Oil enough for the franchise to make it worthwhile for the parent company to sell the franchise instead of operating the station directly.

◆ ◆ ◆ ◆ ◆　MONEY AND INCENTIVES

Some have argued that using monetary payments as incentive devices may actually reduce the amount of effort that individuals put into their jobs. The argument goes that individuals begin to believe that if it is all for money, there is no need to be loyal to the company or their fellow workers. The reduced loyalty, it is claimed, more than offsets any direct gains from monetary incentives.

There is very little evidence to either support or refute such claims. To the extent that they are valid, they are more likely to hold for high-wage workers than for low-wage workers. There is little doubt that money is a great motivator for production workers. In a recent study, I found that the effects of switching to a direct monetary incentive scheme can be enormous.

An Application: Safelite Glass

Background

The headquarters of Safelite Glass Corporation are located in Columbus, Ohio. Safelite is the country's largest installer of automobile glass. Recently, Safelite, under the direction of CEO, Garen Staglin, and president, John Barlow, instituted a new compensation scheme for the autoglass installers. Until January 1994, glass installers were paid an hourly wage rate, which did not vary in any direct way with the number of windows that were installed. During 1994 and 1995, installers were shifted from an hourly wage schedule to performance pay—specifically, to a piece-rate schedule. Rather than being paid for the number of hours that they worked, installers were now paid for the number of glass units that they installed. The rates varied somewhat, but on average, installers were paid $21 per unit installed. At the time that the piece rates were instituted, the workers were also given a guarantee of approximately $11 per hour. If their weekly pay based on piece rates came out to less than the guarantee, they would be paid the guaranteed amount. Many workers ended up in the guarantee range.

Safelite has a very sophisticated computerized information system, which keeps track of how many units of each kind that each installer in the company installed in a given week. For the purposes here, monthly data were used. Since PPP (performance pay plan) was phased in over the 18-month period, most workers were employed under both regimes. Thus, data on individual output are available for most installers, both during the hourly wage period and during the PPP period. This before-and-after comparison with person-specific data provides a very clean body of information on which to base an analysis of performance pay.

Some Economic Theory

Consider Figure 13.1. The dark sideways-L-shaped line through points e_0 and A is the budget constraint that workers face. Workers are paid a straight daily wage, W, coupled with a requirement that at least e_0 of output must be produced or the worker gets fired. If the worker produces at least e_0 she receives the daily wage of W, in this case, around $88. If she produces more than e_0, she also receives the wage W. How much will a typical worker choose to produce? To find out, we need to examine the worker's preferences.

A good way to illustrate preferences is to draw **indifference curves**. The reader will recall that indifference curves are the set of points to which an individual is indifferent. Consider, for a moment, only the solid indifference curves in Figure 13.1. Note that points A and B are on the same indifference curves. This implies that the individual is indifferent between points A and B. At A the worker earns less than she does at B, but at B the worker must produce more output and therefore work harder than she does at A. That these effects just exactly offset is revealed by the location of both points on the same indifference curve. Curves that yield higher levels of happiness lie to the northwest, since they imply more money and less work. Thus, point A is preferrred to point D, because it lies on a higher indifference curve. Also, point A is preferred to point C. At point C, the worker would earn more money but would have to work so much more to get it that she would prefer to take point A. This is true because point C lies on a lower (solid) indifference curve than does point A.

Indifference curves are upward sloping because q, output, requires effort, which the worker views as painful. On the other hand, income is good. Thus, a worker who is forced to put forth more effort must be compensated with more income in order to leave her indifferent. The curves are convex because as a worker

FIGURE 13.1
EFFORT-CHOICE AT SAFELITE: HOURLY WAGE

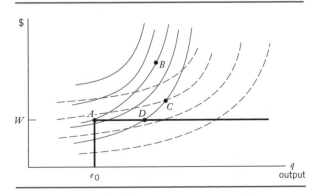

puts forth greater levels of effort, she demands an even larger income increment for any given increase in effort. The pain associated with producing one more unit is greater, the larger the number of units already produced, because the worker is closer to exhaustion.

The worker whose preferences are represented by the dotted indifference curves is less averse to work than the one with solid indifference curves. At any point, say, point C, the additional amount that Dotty (for dotted indifference curves) must be compensated to remain indifferent when being required to produce an additional unit of output is less than the amount that Sol (for solid indifferences curves) must be compensated. Sol's indifference curve is steeper at point C than is Dotty's.

When workers are paid by time worked rather than by output, both workers choose to work at point A. Intuitively, since there is no value to extra work, but there is pain associated with it, no worker who dislikes putting forth effort provides more output than e_0.

Safelite was unhappy with the amount of output being put forth per worker. They referred to it as a *glass ceiling*, because the firm could not get workers to install more than a ceiling of about three units of glass per day. One way to increase output is simply to demand it by raising the minimum acceptable standard, e_0. To do this, Safelite would have to pay a higher hourly wage, because workers would not be willing to stay at the firm at the old wage if they had to work significantly harder. The main difficulty is that some workers might be willing to stay and others might not. Raising the minimum standard is a very blunt instrument, because it cuts across all workers in the same way. But some workers might actually be willing to put forth significantly more effort for only slightly more pay. A piece-rate structure accommodates work force heterogeneity far better than a fixed hourly wage with a minimum standard. It is for that reason that Safelite's strategy paid off.

The specifics of the system are quite important and affect the outcomes in a very predictable way. Since workers were guaranteed that they could not earn less than their prior wage, the structure looks like the one shown in Figure. 13.2. The

FIGURE 13.2
EFFORT-CHOICE AT SAFELITE: PIECEWORK

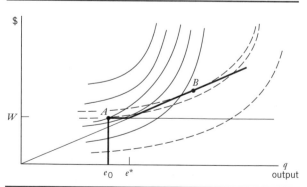

heavy line is the actual compensation scheme. For output less than e_0, the worker is fired, as before. For output between e_0 and e^*, the worker earns W. For output above e^*, the worker earns the amount on the solid, positively sloped line.

What does the worker do? Sol does not change his behavior. Point A remains his best choice. Dotty increases her output to B. Because Dotty is less averse to effort than Sol, she is willing to increase effort, so long as she can earn enough additional income. Thus, whether effort is increased or not depends on the slope and location of the new piece-rate schedule, relative to the guaranteed wage.

What does this imply? The theory gives us a number of predictions. First,

The switch to piece rates leaves unaltered some individuals' behavior and increases the effort of others. Thus, average effort rises.

What happens to the ability distribution of workers? Some workers are better off as a result of the switch to piece rates, whereas others are unaffected. No one is made worse off, because the guaranteed wage remains in effect. Specifically, workers who are least averse to effort are the ones whose behaviors change. Their levels of happiness go up with the introduction of the new scheme. This can be seen in Figure 13.2 by noting that point B is on a higher dotted indifference curve than is point A. Thus, able or ambitious workers are less likely to leave than they were before, and others like them are more likely to be attracted to the firm than they were before. But satisfaction for low-ability workers remains unchanged. Those workers remain at point A on the solid indifference curve. Thus,

The switch to piece rates leaves unaltered the lowest-ability workers, but improves the satisfaction of the higher-ability workers. As such, higher-ability workers are more likely to work for the firm after the introduction of the piece-rate system.

And therefore,

Since low-ability workers are unaffected, but more and higher-ability workers now find the firm attractive, average ability and variance in ability rises.

The Results

The model can be applied to Safelite. The key findings are summarized in Table 13.3.

The table is divided into two blocks. Workers who were paid hourly wages on average produced 2.69 units per day (UAD stands for units-per-associate-per-day).

TABLE 13.3
MEANS OF KEY VARIABLES BY PAY STRUCTURE

Number of Observations	PPPFLAG = 0 (Hourly Wages)		PPPFLAG = 1 (Piece Rates)	
	13850	Standard	15,691	Standard
Variable	Mean	Deviation	Mean	Deviation
UAD	2.69	1.41	3.23	1.58
CSTPU	$44.48	$74.95	$35.23	$48.56

Those who were paid piece rates on average produced 3.23 units per day. This is an increase of about 20 percent. In fact, the increase was even greater than this when other factors are held constant. Specifically, this is a seasonal business, and some months are better than others. When seasonality is taken into account, the number of units produced per day rose by about 36 percent.

The effect can be broken up into two components. Some of the increase reflects the effort effect. Some reflects the sorting effect. The effort effect can be estimated by taking a given worker and calculating the amount by which output rose for that worker when the firm switched to piecework. Doing this across all workers who were employed under both regimes provides an estimate of the incentive effect. For the sample as a whole, the incentive effect is estimated to be 20 percent. A given worker produces 20 percent more after the switch to piecework than before the switch.

But the total effect was said to be 36 percent, not 20 percent. Where does the other 16 percent gain in productivity come from? It is a result of sorting. Recall that Dotty was happier after the switch. Safelite was able to retain more of its high-quality workers and to recruit other high-quality types after the change to piece rates. Because the composition of the labor force moved in the direction of more productive workers, average output rose beyond the 20 percent. The new labor force is inherently more productive than the old labor force.

Thus, Safelite enjoyed the benefits of both sorting and incentives. The combined effect was 36 percent.

Workers earned more after the switch. A given worker's productivity increased by 20 percent, as stated above. The same worker's weekly income increased by 10 percent, on average. Thus, half of the gains in productivity were passed along to the workers.

Changes in turnover can be seen more directly. Consider Table 13.4.

The sample is divided up into two groups, labeled low producers and high producers. The high produces are in the top 20 percent of the sample and are thought to be representative of workers like Dotty who have relative flat indifference curves. They are the ones who should be made significantly better off as a result of the switch to piecework. Table 13.4 reveals that this is so. Turnover rates among the High group decline from .037 or 3.7 percent to .033 or 3.3 percent per month when the firm switches from hourly wages to piecework. Conversely, turnover rates go up among the low productivity group when the firm switches from hourly wages to piecework. Although the Low always have higher turnover

TABLE 13.4
TURNOVER RATES

Regime	Low	High	Ratio of Low to High
Hourly Wage	.050	.037	1.35
PPP	.059	.033	1.78

rates than the High, the ratio of Low to High turnover rates increases from 1.35 to 1.78 when the firm switches to piecework. This increase in the turnover differential implies that the firm is moving toward a higher quality labor force.

Using Other Schedules

Initially, a large fraction of Safelite workers were in the wage-guarantee range after the switch to piecework. The firm does better by moving workers into the upwardly sloped piece rate portion of compensation. Is there anything that could be done to remedy this? Yes, but it may not be profitable. If the piece rate were raised sufficiently so that at e_0, a worker earned exactly W, then more workers would opt to increase effort. See Figure 13.3. With the piece rate schedule in Figure 13.3, even Sol prefers to work harder than e_0 because the utility associated with point D exceeds that associated with point A. Note that B is no longer the optimal choice for Dotty, however, and the cost per unit has risen for Dotty's output. A simple spreadsheet analysis could give a manager a good sense of the optimal piece-rate structure.

Workers want to be sure that variations in demand for the output will not affect their take-home pay. This is what guaranteeing W does. But there is a better way to do this that does not produce the inefficiencies (low output and wrong people) associated with guaranteeing W. The firm could guarantee that it will provide enough work so that the worker can earn W. If the firm cannot find enough work for a given worker, it pays the worker the full amount anyway. A worker who is given the opportunity to produce the target amount but fails receives less. This guarantees that the worker will not suffer from market randomness, but also ensures that virtually all work is performed under piece rates and not under the guarantee. The firm simply needs to move work around so as to make sure that each worker is offered at least the target level. In a large firm with high turnover rates, this is not a problem.

FIGURE 13.3
INCREASING EVERY WORKER'S EFFORT

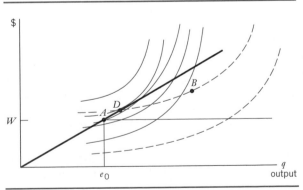

Quality Problems

When workers work for hourly wages, they have no incentive to skimp on quality. But when they are paid piece rates, they want to work fast. Quality may suffer. What is the solution? In the Safelite case, most quality problems showed up rather quickly in the form of windshields that break or leak. Since the guilty installer can be easily identified, there is an efficient solution to the quality problem: The installer must re-install the windshield on his own time and must pay the company for the replacement glass before receiving any paying jobs. This induces the installer to take the appropriate amount of care when installing the glass in the first place.

Before adopting something closer to the efficient solution, Safelite initially used another system that relied on peer pressure. When a customer reported a defect, the job was randomly assigned to a worker in the shop, who was responsible for the problem. The worker was not paid for doing the repair work. But workers know the identity of the initial installer. If one installer caused peers to engage in too many re-dos, co-workers pressured the worker to improve or resign.

Supervision

When workers are paid hourly wages, they would just as soon supervise or instruct others on how to install, especially if supervision and instruction carry higher hourly wages. When the firm switches to piece rates, few want to supervise. Fortunately, less supervision is needed with piecework. Before, it was necessary to make sure that each worker produced e_0 of output. Now, workers have incentives to produce more output, because they get paid on a per-unit basis. A supervisor with a whip is no longer necessary. Quality could suffer, but customers, by their complaints, coupled with the re-do penalties, are effective quality controls and are good substitutes for supervision.

Competition

Companies, such as Safelite, are not alone. They face competition in both product and labor markets. Such competition implies that if switching to piecework is such a good idea, others will copy it.

Indeed, they may, and at the time of this writing, most autoglass installers had. But in the meantime, Safelite cuts costs and offers quicker service, both of which increase their market share. Even if their gains are not sustained in the long run, profits are higher in the interim. Enough interims make a long run.

Output Isn't Profit

It is clear that output rises, but this does not necessarily imply that profit rises. Operating a piece rate requires that output be measured. In some cases, quality difficulties associated with the scheme may not be easily remedied.

In the case studied here, it is very likely that profit rose. The sum of labor and material costs is well below the price of the product and the monitoring technology is already in place for other reasons, having to do with speeding up delivery. The model is unambiguous in its predictions about output and sorting effects. It does not imply that it is always better to pay piece rates.

Organization of the Firm

Installers usually work out of small shops. In other industries, these kinds of businesses are franchised. Moving from hourly wages to piece rate pay is a move in the direction of franchising without asking workers to put up the capital required to buy a franchise. It is an intermediate solution that allows the risk-averse worker to take advantage of most of the positive incentive effects without having to bear the risk of buying a franchise and putting forth a large capital outlay.

BONUSES OR PENALTIES?   ◆ ◆ ◆ ◆ ◆

Consider the following two job offers:

- Scheme A pays $10,000 per month, plus a bonus of $1 for every unit sold.

- Scheme B pays $15,000 per month, with a 5,000-unit quota, penalizing the worker $1 for every unit under quota.

Suppose that it is impossible to sell more than 5,000 units per month. A firm is trying to decide which of the two schemes to offer new workers.

We pose two questions:

1. Which job offer is likely to attract more workers?
2. Which job offer is likely to generate the greatest incentives?

While pondering these questions, consider Table 13.5.

It is apparent from this table that no matter how many units the worker chooses to produce, the amount received as compensation is identical under the two schemes.

For example, if the worker were to produce 3,000 units, under the bonus scheme he or she would receive $10,000 plus a bonus of $3000 which equals $13,000. Under the penalty scheme the worker would receive $15,000 minus a penalty of $2,000 for producing 2,000 units less than 5,000, which still equals $13,000.

Indeed, the bonus scheme can be written as

(13.1) $$\text{Pay} = \$10,000 + \$1 \text{ (Number of units produced)}$$

and the penalty scheme can be written

(13.2) $$\text{Pay} = \$15,000 - \$1 \text{ (5000} - \text{Number of units produced)}$$

One line of algebra allows us to rewrite (13.2) as

$$\text{Pay} = \$15,000 - \$5,000 + \$1 \text{ (Number of units produced)}$$

or

$$\text{Pay} = \$10,000 + \$1 \text{ (Number of units produced)}$$

which is identical to the bonus scheme, Equation 13.1. Thus, the penalty and bonus schemes result in identical payment for any arbitrary number of units produced.

Let us return to the two initial questions. Which scheme is likely to induce

TABLE 13.5
AMOUNTS RECEIVED UNDER THE TWO SCHEMES

Number of Units Sold	Scheme A (Bonus)		Scheme B (Penalty)	
	Bonus	Total Earnings	Penalty	Total Earnings
0	0	$10,000	$5,000	$10,000
1,000	$1,000	$11,000	$4,000	$11,000
2,500	$2,500	$12,500	$2,500	$12,500
3,000	$3,000	$13,000	$2,000	$13,000
5,000	$5,000	$15,000	$1,000	$15,000

the largest number of workers to apply for the job? Most readers are inclined to choose the bonus scheme when thinking about hiring. The usual reasoning is that individuals will be reluctant to apply for a job where they are virtually certain to be penalized, but this argument does not stand up to scrutiny. Why should workers have a preference over whether the firm "penalizes" them or gives them a "bonus," as long as the take home pay is the same? It seems clear that if the numbers were somewhat different, workers might always prefer a penalty scheme. For example, if the firm paid $20,000 minus a penalty of $1 for every unit produced below 5,000, it would seem that virtually every worker would prefer this penalty scheme to the bonus scheme in Equation 13.1. For any given level of output, the worker would take home $5,000 more per month under this penalty scheme than under the bonus scheme A. It seems reasonable that workers will prefer the scheme that offers the largest amount of pay for a given amount of effort, irrespective of whether the scheme is couched in terms of bonuses or penalties. But if this logic is correct, then it also stands to reason that workers should be indifferent between a bonus scheme and a penalty scheme, as long as both offered the same amount of compensation.

Which scheme will induce the worker to put forth the most effort? Opinion on this point tends to be split. Some believe that positive rewards are better motivators. Others believe that the threat of a negative reward is a stronger incentive. Once a person believes that she has $15,000, the reasoning goes, she hates to give up any of it.[3] But this logic is unsatisfying. Irrespective of the scheme, the amount that the worker earns depends only on the number of units produced. Under the bonus scheme, producing one more unit results in exactly $1 more of pay. Under the penalty scheme, producing one more unit results in exactly $1 more of pay. Why, then, should incentives differ from one scheme to another?

Making things more complicated, both penalties and bonuses are observed in the real world. In order to have a good theory of penalties and bonuses, we must be able to predict when one scheme will be used over another. When workers ar-

---

[3]Kahneman and Tversky (1983) are psychologists who are well-known for arguing that negative deviations from the status quo are more painful than positive deviations are rewarding.

rive late to work, they are "docked" pay. Workers who are due in at 8 a.m. but arrive at 9 a.m. are penalized an hour's worth of pay. An alternative would be to state that workers will receive a bonus of one hour's pay for arriving at 8 rather than 9. Both statements seem equivalent in terms of the amount of money being paid, but it is much more common to see firms docking pay for tardiness than it is to see on-time bonuses.

On the other hand, bonuses are also quite common. Salespeople frequently receive bonuses and managers often get a Christmas bonus. In some areas, Christmas bonuses are an expected part of compensation. Although the amount of the bonus can vary, many workers assume that they will receive some average amount of bonus each year and figure in their bonuses when making their consumption and spending plans. Indeed, just as penalties can be restated as bonuses, bonuses can be restated as penalties. A worker can be paid $50,000 per year and given a $10,000 bonus, or she can be paid $75,000 per year and assessed a $15,000 penalty. Both leave the worker with exactly the same amount of money. Still, it is rare that a supervisor will tell one of his workers that as a result of her fine performance, her Christmas penalty is being reduced to $5,000. Somehow, the words *penalty* and *Christmas* do not work well together.

What do the words *penalty* and *bonus* mean, and when should one be used over another? The word *penalty* does convey some expectation on the part of the firm. If a worker is "docked" for arriving after 8 a.m., then it sounds to the worker like arrival at or before 8 a.m. is expected. Now, if the firm wanted to convey this expectation, it could also do it with a bonus. For example, it could reduce the hourly wage paid between 9 a.m. and 5 p.m. and pay much more for the hour between 8 a.m. and 9 a.m. This would provide a strong signal and incentive for the worker to arrive at 8 a.m. Why use words rather than monetary incentives to convey expectations, especially when money packs so much punch?

One possible way to think about bonuses and penalties is that they refer to different kinds of kinked compensation schemes. The rule is that penalty schemes are used when adding output or effort beyond some point has no value. Bonus schemes are used when reducing output or effort below some point has no cost. To understand the distinction, consider two examples. The first is a penalty scheme and relates to docking a worker's pay for tardiness.

Figure 13.4 depicts a penalty scheme. Arrival times are listed backward on the horizontal axis because output increases as arrival times get earlier. This is true until 8 a.m. If the worker works on an assembly line where the shift starts at 8:00 a.m., then arriving before 8 a.m. produces no additional output for the firm. The assembly line does not start moving until after 8 a.m., so having workers sitting around in the lunchroom at 6 a.m. has no value to the firm. Therefore, arrival at 7:30 is compensated at the same level as arrival at 8:00. But arrival after 8 a.m. is "penalized." The penalty is the loss of the wage, times the number of hours late until 5 p.m., when the pay falls to zero.

The penalty scheme is a particular kind of nonlinear scheme, which becomes flat after some target level of output or input is reached. Input (or output) beyond this critical level has no additional value to the firm. As a result, the firm penalizes

FIGURE 13.4
PENALTY STRUCTURE

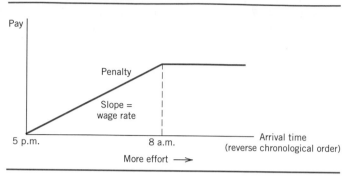

workers for falling short of the critical level, but ignores input or output above the critical level.

Bonuses have the reverse pattern. They reward workers once some target level is reached, but do not subtract pay for any deviations below the target level. Seasonal output provides a good example. It is important for a store to have its Halloween decorations and displays up before Halloween. Suppose that a retail store manager tells workers to start putting displays up on October 1. For every day that the displays are completed before Halloween, additional revenue is generated. However, having the displays up on November 1 is no better than having displays up on November 5. Thus, if effort is low enough so that displays will not be up by November 1, there is no cost to the firm of even lower effort. Unless effort is sufficiently high to ensure that displays are up on or before October 31, there is no value generated by the effort at all. Figure 13.5 depicts the situation. Again, time is backward on the axis because earlier dates require more effort.

Until effort is sufficient to get the display done by October 31, there is no value to the effort at all. Once the target of October 31 is reached, additional effort has value, because for each day before Halloween that the displays are up, more sales are generated.

Note that Figure 13.5 is the opposite of Figure 13.4. In Figure 13.4, as effort increases up to some critical point, additional value and income are generated. Beyond that critical point, no additional value or income results. In Figure 13.5, until effort reaches some critical point, no additional value or income results. Once that critical point is reached, additional effort creates both value and income.

Thus, in trying to decide whether to state compensation as a bonus or as a penalty, the manager should consider the kind of behavior that he or she is trying to elicit. If a critical level of effort or output must be reached, then a bonus scheme is appropriate. If instead, there is a maximum to the level of effort or output that has value, then a penalty scheme should be used.

FIGURE 13.5
BONUS STRUCTURE

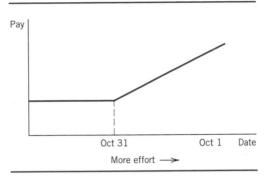

RETAINING CRITICAL WORKERS: A HIGH-TECH APPLICATION

◆ ◆ ◆ ◆ ◆

Sometimes there are key workers in an organization that cannot be lost without causing severe damage to the firm. Frequently, these individuals are inventors or technical people whose knowledge is crucial, but is not widely held by others. In other cases, there are individuals in the firm who know too much. Having them outside the firm could cause major problems for the organization. Competitors would very much like to have the knowledge of these key players. In the absence of competitors, key players can set up rival firms to compete with the founding company.

Is this bad? The answer differs, depending on one's point of view. From society's point of view, additional competition in an industry is usually a good thing. When an industry is converted from monopoly (one firm) to duopoly (two firms), competition increases and product prices fall. More goods are produced and more consumers can buy the goods. The government often tries to break up monopolies for this reason.

From the monopolistic firm's point of view, the answer is very different. The monopolistic firm never wants competition. Even an altruistic owner would prefer to lower product price on his own, rather than being forced to do it by a competitor.

Let us take a real-world example. A man named Amdahl was instrumental in creating one of IBM's most important mainframe computers. Rather than staying within IBM, Amdahl struck out on his own, marketing an IBM clone under his own name. This computer was quite successful and cut into IBM's profits. Because Amdahl was able to compete with IBM, IBM had to lower the price that it charged for its computer. Similarly, because IBM existed, Amdahl could not charge as high a price as he would have liked. Had IBM and Amdahl been able to agree to stay together, they could have retained a monopoly and had higher total profits. The issue was how to divide these profits between Mr. Amdahl and IBM's other stakeholders. Because a deal could not be negotiated, Amdahl turned a monopoly opportunity into a duopoly, destroying profits in the process. He may well have provided society with valuable competition and lower prices, but both he and IBM were worse off as a result.

Trade secrets are not firm specific, but they are like firm-specific human capital in that once trade secrets are present, a bargaining problem arises. With firm-specific human capital, workers are worth more to their current firm than they are outside. This means that wages can be as high as what they are worth inside and as low as what they are worth outside. Where the wages settle depends on the bargaining power of each worker and each manager.

In the Amdahl–IBM example, there was nothing that was firm specific. Indeed, the problem was the opposite. Because Amdahl's knowledge was general, he could too easily go to the outside, destroying monopoly power in the process. The bargaining aspect of the problem is the same. Amdahl is worth more with IBM than without it. Amdahl's salary could have been as high as the amount IBM lost when he left, or it could have been as low as what Amdahl could have made on the outside.[4] There was a bargaining problem between IBM and Amdahl that ended in a stalemate. As a result, Amdahl and IBM parted ways.

From the point of view of IBM and Amdahl, this was unfortunate. Because they could not reach an agreement, they turned what would have been a monopoly into a duopoly. Profits were lost, and this should not have happened. But neither should wars occur. If the outcome of a war were known in advance, both countries could simply agree to accept that outcome and save all the lives and resources destroyed by the war. Both would be better off. But just as wars sometimes occur because countries do not agree on the outcomes or cannot reach an agreement on how to split the savings from avoiding a war, so do business deals break down. Such was the case in this computer industry example.

How could Amdahl have been kept? Some have argued[5] that critical employees can be kept by giving them stock or stock options that cannot be sold. When a worker has a large portion of wealth tied up in the company's stock, the worker would like to see the company succeed. Workers who know that their participation is crucial to the company's success are more likely to stay when their physical wealth is at stake. Although giving a worker stock helps, it does not solve the problem.

To see this, consider an extreme case. Suppose that a critical worker had one share of the company's stock, which was trading at $100. Even if the worker's participation in the firm could increase the value of the company and of its shares by a factor of ten, the worker would only make a $900 return from staying. It is quite

---

[4]It is shown in the appendix that the amount that a duopolist can make by striking out on his own is always less than the difference between monopoly and duopoly profit.

[5]See Nitzan and Pakes (1983).

possible that the worker could make much more by going out on his or her own than by staying with the company and earning $900 on the share of stock. The critical worker must be given a large share of the company's stock to have a strong incentive to stay. (In fact, to behave appropriately on every margin, a risk-neutral worker would have to own the entire firm!)

Awarding stock may be helpful, but in fact it is unnecessary. The essence of the problem is one of bargaining. Since an industry that is monopolized always generates more profits than an industry that is a duopoly, oligopoly, or competitive, there is always surplus that can be split such that *every* worker is made better off by staying. The problem arises when some workers want to be made much better off at the expense of others. A rigid sharing rule might help in such a situation. If surplus profits are divided up among critical workers in relation to their base salaries, the highest-paid, and presumably most-important workers, receive the lion's share of surplus profits. This is probably a good approximation, but it still does not guarantee success. It may be possible for one critical worker to negotiate a better deal elsewhere. Then the initial firm will have a difficult time sticking to its commitment to divide profits according to the rigid sharing rule. Most firms profess to have rigid sharing rules, but in reality deviate from them when a crucial worker threatens to leave.

AN APPLICATION: THE REAL ESTATE MARKET

◆ ◆ ◆ ◆ ◆

Buying or selling a house is the largest transaction that most individuals ever undertake. Furthermore, it is something that most individuals do very infrequently. It is for this reason that real estate agents supply services to both sides of the market. Each side is willing to give up a large amount in commission to a Realtor to ensure that the deal is handled properly and that a good price is paid or received, as the case may be.

Commission rates in the real estate industry are quite large, varying locally, but usually in the range of 6 percent of the purchase price of the house. There are usually two agents involved in the buying and selling of a house retained by the buyer and seller, respectively. The agents split the commission (often evenly) between themselves. Part of the commission goes to the agency and part goes to the individual real estate agent. When a seller places a house on the market with a particular Realtor, the contract usually has some fixed duration (like three months). If the house does not sell by the end of the contract period, the seller is free to switch Realtors, and often does. Does this commission structure provide the right incentives to the Realtor? Does it favor one side of the market?

A number of distortions and problems are caused by the typical real estate contract. The easiest problems to see arise on the buyer's side. Nothing requires that a buyer deal with only one real estate agent. Nor is a buyer required to buy a house at all. Once an agent has a fish on the line, the Realtor likes to land it. Resale is not an important aspect of the business; the buyers are unlikely to be using the same Realtor again in the near future. The buyers' agent would like to make sure that they buy a house. An expensive house would be best, but it is better to make the sale and get some commission than to lose the sale altogether. Because reputation is not particularly important, buyers' agents are too anxious to get the buyers to buy homes that are not well suited to their needs. How could this problem be remedied? One possibility is to create guarantees. If the buyers were permitted to return the merchandise, or if the buyers' Realtor were required to bear some of the cost of repairing problems that were not discovered at the time of purchase, the buyers' Realtor would be more careful. This could not come without cost. But one possibility would be to give the buyers' agent a higher commission, in return for which the agent would provide some sort of guarantee or buyback provision. If the buyers were not satisfied with the house during the first six months, they could move out and force the Realtor to buy it back at some specified price, presumably a few percent below the original purchase price. The Realtor would then own the house, which he or she would then resell.

A contract like this is a put option, where the buyers are long on the put and the buyers' agent is short on the put. As in the case of put options discussed in the last chapter, an individual must be paid to be willing to be at the short end of a put option. A higher commission rate at the time of sale is the form that the payment is most likely to take.

What if the entire market goes south after the purchase has been made? The buyers may want to exercise their put, not because the house is badly suited to their needs, but because its value fell. While true, being able to do this simply reflects who bears the risk. Usually, the buyer bears all of the risk of the sale. After the house is purchased, the agent is clear of the deal. If the house appreciates, the buyer gains; if it depreciates, the buyer loses. When put arrangements are negotiated, the agent bears some of the risk. The lower the exercise price, the lower the risk borne by the agent and the higher the risk borne by the buyer. At the extreme, with an exercise price of zero, the agent would bear no risk. The agent would be required to buy the house back, but at a price of zero. No matter how badly the market performed, the agent could never get hurt by this deal. Similarly, such an option would have no value to the buyers, because exercising the put would bring zero revenue from the house that they returned to the Realtor. The buyers would pay nothing to own such a put option. As the exercise price rises, so does the price that buyers pay the agent for the put. Recently, some of the larger and more aggressive real estate agencies have begun to offer put options to their customers, but they are usually on the seller's side of the market.

Let us turn to the seller's side of the market. There are a number of problems created by the typical contract. The most obvious of these results from the time limitation of the contract. Suppose that a house is listed with a particular agent for three months. There is one week left on the period, and the Realtor has not brought any offers to the seller. Suppose that a buyer offers 30 percent below the asking price for the house and what is, in reality, a price 15 percent below the true market value of the house. The seller's agent is likely to push for the sale. Knowing that she may lose the listing in one week, the Realtor would rather receive 15 percent less commission than take a chance on receiving no commission at all. As a result, the agent is likely to try to convince the seller to accept the offer by emphasizing (exaggerating) the negative aspects of the current market.

The same problem arises because the Realtor only receives a small part of the total purchase price of the house. Suppose that the house is currently listed for $300,000. Suppose an offer comes in for $270,000. Suppose further that with two months of intensive work, the seller's agent believes that she can find a buyer who is willing to pay $290,000. Now, in the typical contract, the seller's agency gets 3 percent and the buyer's agency gets 3 percent. The actual agent usually splits this with the agency, so the seller's agent personally expects to receive 1.5 percent on the deal. If the house is sold for $270,000, the seller's agent receives $(.015)(\$270,000) = \$4,050$. If the house is sold for $290,000, the seller's agent receives $(.015)(\$290,000) = \$4,350$. The seller's agent only gains $300 from another two months worth of effort. The Realtor will almost certainly try to convince the seller to accept the $270,000 offer. But the owners of the house feel quite differently about the situation. If they wait two months, they can expect to sell the house for $20,000 more. The seller, the home owners, gets 94 percent of the $20,000 increment, because the Realtors take a total of 6 percent together. Thus, waiting two months is worth $18,800. Most owners would be happy to wait two months to make an additional $18,800 on their house. The contract between owner and Realtor distorts incentives and induces the agent to supply the owner with erroneous information about the state of the market.

How can this problem be solved? One possibility is to use put options. A large national real estate company recently offered to buy houses that they were unable to sell. In order to induce owners to list their houses with the agency, the agency was willing to offer a put option to the seller. The agency would agree that if the house was not sold within some pre-specified period of time, the agency would buy it at a previously agreed upon price. This is a put option, where the owner is long and the agency is short. As before, it involves some risk sharing. The higher the exercise price, the greater the risk borne by the agency and the lower the risk borne by the owner. A high exercise price also means that the agent will not be induced to sell the house below its market value. The agent knows that the lowest price the owner will accept is the exercise price that the agency has agreed to pay. It would be useless to attempt to get a buyer to accept a price below the exercise price that the agency must pay.

A more extreme solution, and one that pushes all risk to Realtors, is to auction off the house to Realtors. An owner who wanted to sell a house would simply contact ten Realtors and announce that he or she was going to hold an auction. They could come to bid for the house. The highest-bidding Realtor would get to purchase the house, which the Realtor could then resell. This solves all incentive problems. The Realtor, as owner, has all the right incentives. Because incentives are right, the purchase price that the Realtor will offer the owner is higher.

Since this scheme pushes all the risk onto the agency, an agency must be large to be able to offer deals of this sort. If there is only one agency large enough to do it, then a monopsony problem exists. In order for a market like this to function well, there must be a number of large agencies that have the resources to bear the risk and the information to deal in this market.[6]

◆ ◆ ◆ ◆ ◆ **RECAP**

The outsourcing decision was examined in some depth. The basic principle behind the make-or-buy decision is straightforward. A good or service should be bought from an outsider when the cost of buying it is lower than the cost of making it. Key to implementing this truism is understanding and quantifying opportunity cost. In the examples we presented, sometimes it appeared that inside production was cheaper than outside production because there was slack capacity; resources were not being used to their fullest and the firm would have preferred to lay off workers. Even under these circumstances, it still paid to buy from the outside because the opportunity cost of using insiders was higher. A properly constructed balance sheet would reveal this information.

When outside contractors are used to provide a service, the two most common payment methods are cost-plus and fixed-price project-based contracts. Both types of contracts distort incentives on some margin. Cost-plus contracts induce providers to use too many resources. This may take the form of using materials that are of too high a quality for the job or of stretching out the length of time given to complete the job. The higher the margin on a particular job, the longer its expected time to completion. Further, the higher the margin on a job, the higher the expected quality of the job. Fixed-price contracts work in the opposite direction. They induce providers to skimp on materials and effort. With fixed-price contracts, the schedule of payments affects incentives of the supplier as well. When too much is paid early in the job, the supplier will not want to complete the job and will make the final stages of work secondary to other jobs that may have been recently acquired. When quality is easily observed, fixed-price project-based contracts are probably better. When the desired time to completion and quality are known, cost-plus contracts are better.

Franchising is a contract form that solves some incentive problems. Because the local manager is also an owner, the manager/owner has the right incentives to put forth effort. The franchisee will not protect the overall value of the company name, however. For this reason, franchisees are usually required to meet standards set up by the parent company. In more extreme circumstances, the company may not award franchises at all, choosing instead to run all of the business itself and bear higher costs of supervision.

The existing evidence suggests that money is an excellent motivator, particularly among production workers. As income rises, workers may place somewhat

---

[6]It may be that the owner has information about the house that the agency does not have. But this is always true in a sale. Buyers may be at an informational disadvantage, but this is reflected in the price that they are willing to offer for the good.

higher weight on other factors, but for middle-income workers and below, pecuniary wages provide strong incentives.

Bonuses and penalties are opposite sides of the same coin. Any compensation scheme that can be set up as a bonus can also be stated as a penalty. But the words do have different meanings. A bonus kicks in after some target has been hit, whereas a penalty takes effect for all units up to a target level. As a result, bonuses should be used when effort or output below some level has no cost to the firm. Penalties should be used when effort or output above some level has no value.

Critical workers are retained by offering them more than they can earn elsewhere. This can take the form of stock, options, or direct pay. If employees are truly critical, defined as being worth more to the current organization than they are elsewhere, a deal can always be struck. Problems of bargaining between the critical worker and the firm often lead to break-ups that are detrimental as far as the worker and firm are concerned, but may well be beneficial to society as a whole.

REFERENCES ◆ ◆ ◆ ◆ ◆

Hart, Oliver D., "Optimal Labour Contracts under Asymmetric Information: An Introduction," *Review of Economic Studies* 50, 1 (January 1983): 3–35.

Kahneman, Daniel, and Amos Tversky, "Choices, Values, and Frames," *American Psychologist* 39, 4 (1983): 341–50.

Lazear, Edward P., "Salaries and Piece Rates," *Journal of Business* 59 (July 1986): 405–31.

Nitzan, Shmuel, and Ariel Pakes, "Optimum Contracts for Research Personnel, Research Employment, and the Establishment of Rival Enterprises," *Journal of Labor Economics* 1, 4 (1983): 345–65.

Shepard, Andrea, "Contractual Form, Retail Price, and Asset Characteristics in Gasoline Retailing," *Rand Journal of Economics* 24, 1 (Spring 1993).

ADDITIONAL ADVANCED READING ◆ ◆ ◆ ◆ ◆

Blanchflower, David G., Andrew J. Oswald, and Peter Sanfey, "Wages, Profits and Rent-Sharing," *Quarterly Journal of Economics* 111 (February 1996): 227–51.

Blanchflower, David G., and Andrew J. Oswald, "Profit-Related Pay: Prose Discovered," *Economic Journal* 98 (September 1988): 720–30.

Holmstrom, Bengt, and Paul Milgrom, "Multitask Principal-Agent Analyses: Incentive Contract, Asset Ownership and Job Design," *Journal of Law, Economics, and Organization* 7 (Special Issue 1991): 24–52.

Lazear, Edward P., and Matthew O. Jackson, "Stock, Options, and Deferred Compensation," in Ronald G. Ehrenbert, ed., *Research in Labor Economics*, 12, Greenwich, CT: JAI Press, Inc., 1991, pp. 41–62.

◆ ◆ ◆ ◆ ◆ APPENDIX

In this section, it is shown that a firm that is currently operating as a monopolist can always pay enough to keep a critical worker from leaving and competing as a duopolist.

If the critical worker were to leave and form a rival firm, the industry would change from a monopoly to a duopoly. The maximum amount that the critical worker could receive as a duopolist is equal to the person's normal wage plus all of the profit of the new firm. Denote by

$$\pi_{new} \, , \, \pi_{original}, \, \pi_{monop}$$

the profits at the newly formed firm under duopoly, the profits at the original firm under duopoly, and the profits at the original firm under monopoly.

It must be the case that

(A13.1) $$\pi_{new} + \pi_{original} < \pi_{monop}$$

Otherwise the original firm would have been better off splitting up the firm into two plants and producing as if it were two separate firms. Since total industry profits can never be higher than monopoly profits, condition (A13.1) must hold.

Rearranging (A13.1), we can write

(A13.2) $$\pi_{new} < \pi_{monop} - \pi_{original}$$

The maximum amount that the original firm could offer the critical worker without being worse off than it would be as a competing duopolist is the normal wage plus $\pi_{monop} - \pi_{original}$. But from (A13.2), this amount necessarily exceeds the amount that could be earned as a new competing duopolist. As a result, there is room for trade. It is always possible for the original firm to offer the critical worker more than could be made by striking out on his or her own. Whether this actually occurs depends on the bargaining positions and expectations of the two parties.

Suppose, for example, that the critical worker's estimate of π_{new} , $\hat{\pi}_{new}$ were higher than the original firm's estimate. The employee might hold out for too large a payment. Even though (A13.2) holds, it is possible that

(A13.3) $$\hat{\pi}_{new} > \pi_{monop} - \pi_{original}$$

because $\pi_{new} < \hat{\pi}_{new}$. When (A13.3) prevails, the bargain may break down and duopoly may result, even though the monopoly situation would be better for all sides.

NONMONETARY COMPENSATION

14

*M*oney isn't everything. Indeed, most students, when asked, reply that they are attending business school for reasons other than money. Although few will claim that they are studying business solely for its own sake, most do focus on the nonmonetary benefits that business school can confer. A more interesting job, greater control over one's schedule, broadened choices, and career flexibility lead the list of benefits students expect from attending business school.

It may be costly for a firm to provide working conditions that are valued by its employees. If it is costly, then there is a trade-off. In order to succeed in a competitive environment, a firm must strike the right balance between wages and benefits. It must decide on the amount and type of benefits offered. How can a firm make these important decisions? Consider the issues raised in the following discussion.

VINER: The union has been pushing hard for **flex-time.** I'm against it. It is almost impossible to run an assembly-line operation with workers who can arrive when they want and leave when they want.

VON NEUMANN: Well, it is surely true that we have to cover our shifts, but nothing says that we can't just pay more for those shifts that are hard to staff. If, after a few weeks, we find that too many workers are leaving us with idle machines by taking Mondays and Fridays off, then we'll just pay more for work on Mondays and Fridays.

LOCKE: That's a good idea, but how much more? We may end up paying so much for Monday and Friday that no one will want to show up the rest of the week.

VON NEUMANN: I don't think that calibration will be a major problem. If we find that due to high wages offered on Mondays, too many people want to work on Monday and not enough on Tuesday, we'll just raise Tuesday's pay.

VINER: Wait a minute. You can't just go around raising everyone's pay for work that costs us just so much today. If we keep raising our costs, we won't be around to do the kind of experimentation that Locke is suggesting. You guys need to spend more time talking to the union leaders. Your perspective is off.

LOCKE: Well, then let's pay less, not more. Instead of offering more money to work Mondays and Fridays, how about offering less money for work on Tuesdays, Wednesdays, and Thursdays?

VINER: Oh, great. The union is really going to go for that.

LOCKE: Hold on, Jacob. You started this conversation by saying that the union really wanted flex-time. If they really want it, let's start our negotiating stance by offering flex-time instead of a raise. Then we can back off to offering some additional money for Monday and Friday work.

VON NEUMANN: Now there's a thought. Workers keep saying that they don't care that much about the money, what they really care about is self-determination. Let's see if they are willing to put their money where their mouths are.

LOCKE: We still need to figure out how much more money to offer for the days that are tough to staff.

VINER: Well, there are a lot of firms out there that will provide us with that kind of information. The compensation consultants specialize in measuring job characteristics and estimating what they are worth in money. We ought to be able to get one of them to give us pretty good information.

LOCKE: How much will that cost us? We may end up spending more on them than we would have spent on worker raises.

VINER: That's possible, but why guess at it? Let's find out.

Throughout this book, we emphasized that money is a proxy for all forms of compensation. When we talked about investment in human capital, it was not necessary that individuals make investments in human capital in order to enhance their earnings. If they make investments in human capital to enhance their status, or to get a more interesting job, the model still holds, but some quantification is necessary.

It is useful to be able to convert non-pecuniary attributes into some metric that allows comparison between nonpecuniary benefits and monetary compensation. This discussion focuses exactly on that issue. The question of determining a worker's willingness to trade flex-time for money is at the heart of the introductory dialog. The issues raised include the following:

- Money isn't everything, but how important are the other attributes of a job relative to money?

- How can the nonmonetary characteristics of a job be measured?

- Is there some reliable metric by which all attributes of a job, monetary and otherwise, can be gauged? In other words, can two compensation packages consisting of different benefits be compared?

- What role can outsiders play in providing information about how workers value the nonmonetary attributes of a job? What can be learned from the information that they provide, and what cannot?

MONEY ISN'T EVERYTHING, BUT IT IS THE BEST METRIC

◆ ◆ ◆ ◆ ◆

When Jane tells Jack that she has $100 in her purse, Jack knows immediately what this means. With the $100, they can go out for a nice dinner, they can buy several CDs, they can pay for three days of rent on their condo, or they can save the $100 and make any of these purchases at some future time. Suppose instead that Jane tells Jack that having the afternoon off from work is worth as much to her as drinking a glass of fine wine. What does this mean? It's not even certain that an afternoon off represents positive value to her. If Jane doesn't drink, then her statement might be intended to convey that she prefers not to take the time off. Or, she may truly hate her job and very much appreciate fine wine. The problem is that without knowing an individual's preferences, it is very difficult to convert statements about goods other than money into useful data.

Money is a useful measure because it is *fungible*, that is, one dollar is as good as the next. And money is easily traded for goods. Since all workers trade some of their time for money, it must be true that when a worker chooses to work 40 hours rather than 39, the value of the leisure forgone during the fortieth hour of work is worth no more than the wage rate. Otherwise, the worker would give up the wages for the fortieth hour and enjoy the leisure. Thus, we know that the worker values the last hour of leisure at the wage rate.

Now return to the issue of flex-time raised in the discussion. It would be very useful for the firm to know that workers would be willing to accept, say, a 10 percent cut in wages to obtain flex-time. The **monetary equivalent** is useful information for two reasons. First, it has a well-defined meaning. We know that 10 percent of wages is a significant amount, so forgoing that much must mean that workers care a great deal about flex-time. In contrast, telling management that a day of flex-time has the same value as a walk in the park does not convey the same amount of information.

Second, the firm can use the information to decide whether or not to make the concession. If the firm moving to flex-time would result in minor disruption to the firm's operation costing less than 10 percent of wages, then cutting wages by 9.99 percent and giving the workers flex-time makes both workers and firm owners better off. Hence, knowing the monetary equivalent is useful because revenues and other costs are measured in monetary units as well. Money is the metric by which the firm makes its most important decisions.

Converting Nonmonetary Attributes to Monetary Equivalents

Up to this point, all of the theory in this book has been stated in terms of money and monetary compensation, but other job factors can also matter a great deal. Does this mean that all the material previously presented must be rewritten taking nonmonetary factors into account? Fortunately, the answer is no. As long as those other job factors can be expressed in terms of their monetary equivalents, all the theory holds. Instead of thinking of money as the reward, simply think of the rewards as being comprised of many different elements, only some of which are money, but all having a *value* expressible in monetary units. It is conceptually straightforward to translate nonmonetary factors into their monetary equivalents.[1] Indeed, many compensation consultants make their living doing just that.

Let us return to the flex-time example. Suppose that all workers prefer more flexible hours and that their **indifference curves** are shown as solid curves in Figure 14.1.

The horizontal axis measures the proportion of hours that workers can choose to schedule themselves. The left end of the horizontal axis, "No flex-time," corresponds to having the entire 40-hour work week scheduled by management. At the other end of the axis is "100% flex-time," which corresponds to having the entire 40-hour work week scheduled totally by the worker. An intermediate position, say, corresponding to 60 percent flex-time, would mean that the worker chooses when to work 60 percent of the time, or 24 hours a week, but management would schedule the other 40 percent, or 16 hours. The vertical axis measures the hourly wage rate.

The indifference curves in Figure 14.1 have a negative slope because both flexible hours and higher wages are goods. Workers are willing to trade off one factor to get more of another. The fact that one indifference curve passes through both points C and S implies that the individual whose preferences are represented by these indifference curves is indifferent between the wage/flex-time combination at point C and the combination at point S. Wages are higher at point C than at point S, but the worker has more choice of what hours to work at point S. The additional flexibility associated with point S just compensates for the reduction in wages from W_C to W_S. Notice also that the indifference curve is convex. As an individual acquires more flex-time and loses more in wages (moves to the right

---

[1]The theory behind the following presentation comes from Rosen (1974).

FIGURE 14.1
INDIFFERENCE CURVES
COMPARING
WAGE AND FLEXIBILITY

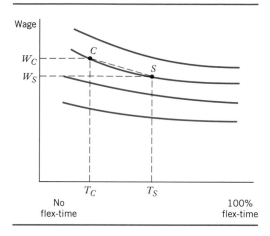

along the indifference curve), the worker has less use for additional flexibility and becomes less willing to give up wages in exchange for it. The first few hours of flex-time are quite valuable, but even someone who hates working to a schedule would be willing to commit to a couple of hours each week if it meant getting paid.

Different firms can afford different combinations of flexibility and wages. For example, a firm may have an operation that requires workers to be on-site simultaneously. The assembly line case just discussed is one such example. Other firms may tolerate flexible work schedules very well. A firm that develops software may allow its programmers to work at any hour. The firm may even allow them to work at home. Software developers can offer their workers flex-time at a relatively low cost. Firms that use assembly line production find flexibility more detrimental to profits and, as a result, are more reluctant to offer it. Thus, a software developer may prefer to offer the wage–flex-time combination represented by point S in Figure 14.1, while an automobile plant may prefer to pay higher wages and offer less flex-time, as in point C.

Because both S and C lie on the same indifference curve, workers whose preferences are represented by these indifference curves do not prefer S over C or C over S. They are equally happy working at the software company or at the car manufacturer.

What does the slope of the dotted line that connects C to S reveal? It shows the willingness of the worker to trade money for flexibility. For example, suppose that W_c corresponds to $15 per hour and W_s corresponds to $10 per hour. Also, suppose that T_c equals 20 percent flex-time and T_s equals 40 percent flex-time. This would imply that the slope of the dotted line connecting C to S is

$$\frac{15 - 10}{.2 - .4} = .25$$

In order to achieve a .2 (20 percentage point) increase in flex-time, the worker is willing to give up $5 in wages. Thus, the firm knows that it can reduce wages by about $2.50 for each additional 10 percent of hours that it allows its workers to schedule.

Of course, workers' willingness to trade wages for flexibility varies. One worker is more willing to give up wages for flexibility at point C than she is at point S. By the time she has reached point S, her wages have fallen substantially, and she has already attained a significant amount of flexibility in her working hours. This is why the indifference curve is flatter to the right of S than it is to the left. But, at least for the narrow range between C and S, the estimate of a $2.50 wage reduction for every 10 percentage points in flexibility is about right.

The analysis represented by Figure 14.1 allows us to convert a nonmonetary factor into a monetary one. Since the worker is willing to trade $2.50 for a 10 percentage point increase in flexibility, the monetary equivalent of 10 percentage points more flexibility is $2.50 per hour. Although the worker cares not only about money, giving her $2.50 more in wages would just compensate her for losing 10 percentage points of flexibility. Conversely, when the worker is given 10 percentage points more flexibility, her compensation can be reduced by $2.50 per hour because she values the additional flexibility at $2.50 per hour.

Thus, we have shown that a nonmonetary factor, in this case flex-time, can be expressed in terms of its monetary equivalent. We may not know the value of 10 percent flex-time to a worker, but if we know that it is equivalent to $2.50 per hour in wages, we can deal with flex-time analytically.

Knowing the relationship between wages and a nonmonetary benefit, as in Figure 14.1, can be useful, but it is usually not readily apparent in the real world. How can information of the sort necessary to estimate monetary equivalents be obtained? There is an entire industry devoted to generating precisely that information. Compensation consultants collect data on wages and job characteristics and use it to estimate monetary equivalents (i.e., worker trade-offs between wages and the nonpecuniary characteristics of a job). This information can enable firms to design compensation packages of a given value to workers at the lowest possible cost. For example, if a firm knows that workers are indifferent between wages of $32,000 per year without health insurance and $29,000 per year with "free" health insurance and the firm can buy health insurance for $1,500 per worker, then the cost to a firm of the second compensation package is only $30,500, while the value of this package to the workers is $32,000.

Suppose that workers initially have identical preferences and the only factor other than wages that they care about is flex-time. Let W denote wages and T denote the percentage of hours that workers can schedule themselves. Each firm

TABLE 14.1
SAMPLE OF FIRMS: WAGES VERSUS FLEX-TIME

Firm	Wage	%Flex-time
101	$30.00	0.0%
102	$27.56	5.0%
103	$25.25	10.0%
104	$23.06	15.0%
105	$21.00	20.0%
106	$19.06	25.0%
107	$17.25	30.0%
108	$15.56	35.0%
109	$14.00	40.0%
110	$12.56	45.0%
111	$11.25	50.0%
112	$10.06	55.0%
113	$9.00	60.0%
114	$8.06	65.0%
115	$7.25	70.0%
116	$6.56	75.0%
117	$6.00	80.0%
118	$5.56	85.0%
119	$5.25	90.0%
120	$5.06	95.0%
121	$5.00	100.0%

in the economy offers some wage and some level of flexibility in the selection of hours. An example of data from a subset of the economy's firms is shown in Table 14.1.

The data from Table 14.1 is plotted to form the curve shown in Figure 14.2. Only two points are shown explicitly. They are X and Y, which correspond to firms 103 and 120, respectively. Firm 103 pays a wage of $25.25 and offers 10 percent flex-time. Firm 120 pays a much lower wage of $5.06, but offers almost full flex-time. Firm 120 offers a work schedule typical for a crafts artisan. Artisans may put in very long hours, but work when they want and do the work at home. In such a case the hourly wage rate may be quite low. Firm 103, on the other hand, might be a manufacturer who must have workers coordinate the operation of machinery. In that case, only 10 percent of the hours worked are worker-determined; the other 90 percent are dictated by the employer.

The curve in Figure 14.2 looks very much like the indifference curve shown in Figure 14.1. If the assumptions are valid, namely that all workers are identical, the curve traced out by market equilibria is, in fact, an indifference curve. Workers are indifferent between working at firm 103 or firm 120. Firm 120 pays less, but offers so much flexibility that workers are indifferent between employment there and employment at the higher wage firm, 103. Put differently, a worker is

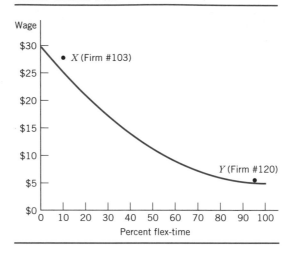

FIGURE 14.2
VISUAL REPRESENTATION OF DATA
FROM TABLE 14.1

willing to give up $20.19 = $25.25 − $5.06 in wages to obtain a job that provides 85 percentage points more flexibility. Thus, the monetary equivalent of 85 percentage points of flexibility is $20.19 per hour in this case.

These data are readily available, although they may be somewhat costly to collect. Obtaining estimates of monetary equivalents involves sampling a significant number of firms and obtaining information on their wages and the nonpecuniary attributes of the job. The indifference curve shown in Figure 14.2 has an algebraic representation as well as a graphical one. If one were to run a regression of the form

$$\text{Wage} = a + b \,(\text{proportion flex-time}) + c \,(\text{proportion flex-time})^2$$

the parameters a, b, and c could be estimated. They would turn out to be 30, −50, and 25, respectively. Thus,

$$\text{Wage} = 30 - 50(\text{proportion flex-time}) + 25(\text{proportion flex-time})^2$$

If flex-time is zero, then the wage is $30 per hour. If flex-time is increased to 1%, then the wage can be reduced to

$$30 - 50(.01) + 25(.0001) = \$29.50$$

Thus, 1 percent of flex-time is worth 50 cents per hour when the worker initially has no flex-time at all.

Now suppose that in addition to having preference for flexible schedules, workers dislike dangerous jobs. One measure of danger on the job is the probability that a worker will suffer an injury at work that could prevent her from working for one month or more. The probability of that kind of injury is much higher for construction workers than it is for, say, receptionists. Suppose that we gathered data on about 50 firms that provided information on wages, flexibility, and injury probabilities. Those hypothetical data are contained in Table 14.2.

Because injuries are bad, firms that have higher probabilities of injury must pay more. This is easily seen by examining a couple of entries in Table 14.2. Firm 1040 pays higher wages than firm 1044, despite the fact that 1040 offers more flexibility than does 1044. If flex-time were the only nonpecuniary factor that mattered, then 1040 would be able to pay lower wages than 1044. But firm 1040 is more dangerous than firm 1044. The probability of an accident is .0097 at 1040, but only .26 at 1044. Therefore, injuries are more than three times more likely to occur at 1040. As a result, 1040 must pay more than $7 per hour above the wage rate at 1044.

A comparison of firms 1043 and 1044 reveals that flexibility is still an important factor. Firm 1044 pays more than firm 1043, despite the fact that injury probabilities are much higher at 1043 than at 1044. The reason is that flexibility is 20 percentage points higher at 1043 than at 1044 (20% vs. 0%). The value of the additional flexibility more than compensates for the higher risk of injury, allowing firm 1043 to get away with paying less.

Once again, a regression on the data can provide a complete description of the market and of individual preferences under the assumption that workers have identical preferences. The following regression can be estimated using the market data collected and displayed in Table 14.2.

$$\text{Wage} = a + b\,(\text{proportion flex-time}) + c\,(\text{proportion flex-time})^2 + d\,(\text{prob. of injury}) + e\,(\text{prob. of injury})^2$$

When this regression is run on the data, the results are

$$\text{Wage} = 30 - 50\,(\text{proportion flex-time}) + 25\,(\text{proportion flex-time})^2 + 1{,}000\,(\text{prob. of injury}) + 100{,}000\,(\text{prob. of injury})^2$$

If the probability of an injury is zero, then the wage is equal to the wage in Table 14.1. For example, a firm that offered no flex-time and had a zero probability of injury would have to pay

$$30 - 50(0) + 25(0) + 1{,}000(0) + 100{,}000(0)(0) = \$30 \text{ per hour}$$

The same firm, offering no flex-time, but experiencing an increase in its injury rate from 0 to .001 would be required to pay

$$30 - 50(0) + 25(0) + 10{,}000(.001) + 100{,}000(.001)(.001) = \$31.10$$

Therefore, raising the probability of an injury from 0 to 1 in 1,000 means that the firm must increase its wage by $1.10 per hour. Thus, the monetary equivalent of increasing the probability of injury from zero to 1 in 1,000 is $1.10 per hour. Being in the safer work environment is worth $1.10 per hour to the typical worker.

TABLE 14.2

FIRM SAMPLE DATA: WAGES, FLEXIBILITY, INJURY PROBABILITIES

Firm #	Wage	Flex-time Percentage	Probability of Injury
1001	$10.67	88%	0.0038
1002	$20.84	90%	0.0085
1003	$9.83	72%	0.0023
1004	$6.95	86%	0.0013
1005	$22.31	78%	0.0086
1006	$11.70	76%	0.0038
1007	$12.34	70%	0.0037
1008	$27.18	60%	0.0094
1009	$14.93	98%	0.0061
1010	$16.96	82%	0.0067
1011	$10.45	54%	0.0002
1012	$19.04	58%	0.0060
1013	$18.87	94%	0.0078
1014	$17.81	50%	0.0045
1015	$28.01	56%	0.0094
1016	$31.21	44%	0.0094
1017	$20.39	42%	0.0047
1018	$16.25	36%	0.0009
1019	$20.61	32%	0.0031
1020	$7.79	74%	0.0010
1021	$8.58	64%	0.0003
1022	$25.51	48%	0.0077
1023	$23.82	46%	0.0068
1024	$15.83	92%	0.0065
1025	$16.84	38%	0.0019
1026	$22.80	62%	0.0079
1027	$22.07	34%	0.0043
1028	$11.16	96%	0.0043
1029	$18.22	28%	0.0003
1030	$6.82	84%	0.0011
1031	$15.96	52%	0.0038
1032	$25.33	68%	0.0092
1033	$28.37	30%	0.0067
1034	$25.95	16%	0.0026
1035	$12.70	80%	0.0046
1036	$25.16	66%	0.0091
1037	$32.39	8%	0.0043
1038	$42.67	4%	0.0081
1039	$34.19	26%	0.0084
1040	**$40.91**	**18%**	**0.0097**
1041	$15.38	40%	0.0012
1042	$40.47	10%	0.0083
1043	**$32.78**	**20%**	**0.0069**
1044	**$33.25**	**0%**	**0.0026**

TABLE 14.2 *(Continued)*

Firm #	Wage	Flex-time Percentage	Probability of Injury
1045	$25.28	24%	0.0041
1046	$20.33	22%	0.0001
1047	$39.61	14%	0.0086
1048	$38.89	12%	0.0081
1049	$31.29	2%	0.0019
1050	$37.00	6%	0.0061

Of course, there is no fundamental difference between an environment with two nonpecuniary factors and an environment with three nonpecuniary factors. The same analysis could be done with any number of nonpecuniary factors. The analyst is limited only by the availability of data. A regression can have as many variables are there are job factors. As a statistical matter, the ability to get precise estimates of the monetary equivalents of each factor declines as the number of factors rises. Put differently, to estimate monetary equivalents precisely when there are many factors present, it is necessary to have a great deal of data. It is essential to have observations on many firms that engage in a wide variety of practices in order to estimate monetary equivalents when many nonpecuniary job factors enter worker preferences.

Heterogeneous Preferences

To make strong statements about monetary equivalents, it was necessary to assume that workers had identical preferences. In reality, we know that people differ and that variations in tastes across individuals are difficult to explain. Economists are not good at explaining why one individual chooses chocolate and another chooses vanilla. Fortunately, it is not necessary to explain differences in tastes to see how heterogeneity across individuals will affect estimates of monetary equivalents. Informative statements and reliable estimates can still be made, even though worker's preferences may differ.

To understand the effects of different preferences, let us return to Figure 14.1, which shows indifference curves for the typical worker. Now suppose that there are two types of individuals. Both like wages and flexibility, but they place different weights on the two factors. To make this more concrete, suppose that some people like to windsurf and others like to play chess. Windsurfing is a sport that relies heavily on weather, in particular the wind, which in most areas is somewhat unpredictable. A windsurfer would like to go windsurfing when conditions are right and would prefer to be able to work during times when windsurfing conditions are poor. Chess matches, on the other hand, can be arranged to fit the schedules of the players. Nothing exogenous like weather has important effects on the quality of play. Thus, windsurfers are likely to place a higher premium on flexibility than are chess players. Figure 14.3 shows the indifference curves of the two types of individuals.

FIGURE 14.3

INDIFFERENCE CURVES OF CHESS
PLAYERS AND WINDSURFERS

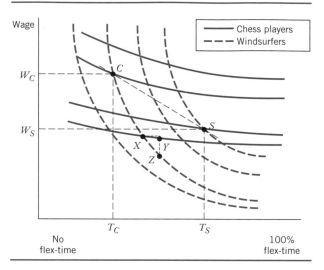

Windsurfer preferences are shown by the dotted indifference curves; chess player preferences by the solid indifference curves. Note that windsurfer indifference curves are steeper than chess player indifference curves, implying a greater willingness to trade money for flex-time. To see this, consider point X. Moving a fixed horizontal distance along the windsurfer indifference curve comes about with a larger drop in wages than the same movement along the chess player indifference curve. The movement from X to Y implies the same horizontal movement as the movement from X to Z, but the vertical movement is greater from X to Z than it is from X to Y.

Windsurfers are indifferent between X and Z, which means that they are willing to accept a significant wage cut to obtain more flex-time. Chess players are indifferent between X and Y, which means that chess players will also accept a wage cut to obtain increased flexibility, but for a given amount of flex-time, the wage cut that a chess player will accept is smaller than what a windsurfer will accept. Windsurfers weight flexibility more heavily, and are therefore willing to give up more to obtain it.

Now consider two firms. One firm needs workers who are willing to work to a posted schedule, like a car manufacturer. The other is willing to forgo some control over work schedules in order to pay lower wages, like a software firm. The offers that the firms make are illustrated by points C and S, respectively. Chess players prefer C to S because C lies on a higher indifference curve for them than S. Windsurfers prefer S to C because S lies on a higher indifference curve for them.

Sorting is now an important part of the story. Those workers who care most about flex-time end up working for the firm that is best able to offer flexible schedules. Those workers who care least about flex-time end up working for the firm that needs to have a more rigidly scheduled work force and is willing to pay for it.

Now consider the dotted line that attaches C to S in Figure 14.3. It looks much like the dotted line that attached C to S in Figure 14.1, but there is a difference. In Figure 14.1, the dotted line connected points on the same indifference curve. As a result, it was reasonable to interpret the slope of that line as the worker's marginal willingness to trade wages for flex-time. When workers are of different types, this interpretation no longer holds. In Figure 14.3, the dotted line CS connects points that are not only on different indifference curves, but on indifference curves that belong to different types of workers. S is on a curve representing windsurfer preferences and C is on a curve representing chess player preferences.

What can we say about the slope of the dotted line CS? The slope of CS does not represent the chess player's willingness to trade wages for flexibility. It is steeper than the chess player's indifference curve that goes through C. So, we can say that chess players at point C would not be happy about moving to S. The chess players are not willing to trade wages for flex-time at the rate implied by the slope of CS. Their indifference curve through C is flatter, meaning that they are less willing to give up wages for flexibility than the dotted line CS would suggest. Conversely, the dotted line is flatter than the windsurfer's indifference curve at point S. Windsurfers would be happy to take the wage/flex-time trade-off implied by the move from C to S, because the windsurfers end up on a higher indifference curve than when they started. They are not as willing to give up flexibility for increased wages, as would be implied by the dotted line.

Put differently, if any employer increases flex-time from T_S to T_C and lowers wages from W_S to W_C, windsurfers will be better off. Windsurfers do not view $W_C - W_S$ as the monetary equivalent of reduced flexibility $T_S - T_C$. They care more about flexibility than the dotted line CS would suggest and are more than willing to give up wages of $W_C - W_S$ in exchange for a flex-time increase of $T_S - T_C$. The slope of the dotted line understates the monetary equivalent of flexibility to a windsurfer. Since the slope of the dotted line is the regression coefficient obtained from the data, the regression estimates understate the monetary equivalent of flexibility to those workers who have already chosen to work at flexible firms.

Chess players view the same change quite differently. If a chess player who receives a compensation package represented by the point C on the Figure 14.3 were offered an increase in flex-time up to the level T_s, combined with reduction of wages to W_S, chess players would surely object to proposed change in his compensation. Chess players do not view an increase in flexibility $T_S - T_C$ to be as valuable as the loss in wages, $W_C - W_S$. The loss in wages overstates the monetary equivalent of increased flexibility $T_S - T_C$ for those workers who initially choose less flexible jobs. Again, since the slope of the dotted line is what is observed in the real world, and since it is the same as the regression coefficients obtained from real world data, the regression coefficients overstate the monetary equivalent of flexibility for those workers who choose less flexible jobs.

Where does this leave us? The answer is that we are still in pretty good shape. Even if we cannot read the monetary equivalent directly from regression coefficients, we can come close. We base this on three factors, discussed as follows.

Regression Coefficient as a Bound

First, the regression-estimated monetary equivalent of a nonpecuniary factor is a lower bound of the true monetary equivalent for those who choose firms with heavy concentrations of that factor and an upper bound of the monetary equivalent for those who choose firms with light concentrations of that factor. In the example, the regression coefficient is a lower bound on the value of flex-time to windsurfers and an upper bound on the value of flex-time to chess players. Therefore, the regression coefficient allows us, at a minimum, to place monetary limits on the value of a nonpecuniary factor.

Regression Estimates Reflect Market Value

Second, the regression estimates the true *market* price of the factor. Although the slope from the regression reflects neither the exact trade-off that chess players would make, nor the exact trade-off that windsurfers would make, it does reflect the exact trade-off that can be had on the market. Suppose that a firm currently paying W_C and offering T_C of flex-time decides that it is willing to increase flex-time to T_S. It can do this and reduce the wage that it pays to W_S. How? We know that its current workers who are chess players will not accept that trade, but windsurfers are willing to work for W_S as long as they receive T_S in flex-time. Thus, the firm could reduce wages paid to W_S in return for an increase in flexibility to T_C by replacing its current workers (chess players) with new workers (windsurfers). The regression estimate is the market price of the factor. The firm can "sell" $T_S - T_C$ in flex-time at a price of $W_C - W_S$ as long as it is willing to change the identity of its workers.

The firm could move back in the other direction, as well. It could buy the right to reduce flexibility from T_S to T_C by increasing wages from W_S to W_C, which is just what the regression coefficient implies. However, in order to do this, the firm would have to replace its windsurfers with chess players. This is no problem as long as workers do not have firm-specific skills, which would then create a higher productivity/wage ratio for incumbents than for new hires.

Preference Continuum Smooths Regression Line

Third, the example of taste differences had only two types whose tastes were very different. Windsurfers were willing to give up a great deal of income in order to obtain flexibility, whereas chess players were unwilling to give up much income at all for flexibility. But the real world does not consist of two extreme types, but rather, a continuum of preferences. If there are devout windsurfers, dilettantes, chess players who windsurf, and pure chess players, with all gradations in between, then the regression line comes very close to the tastes of each type that it touches. Under these circumstances, the regression coefficients will reflect the true monetary equivalent of every worker at the point that each worker has chosen to locate.

EXTERNALITIES IN CORPORATE BENEFITS
◆ ◆ ◆ ◆ ◆ ◆ ◆ ◆ ◆ ◆

American United Life Insurance Co. of Indianapolis offers a range of benefits that extend far beyond the health and retirement packages offered by most of its competitors. AUL's benefits include group tickets to area cultural and sporting events. But by far the most popular of AUL's benefits is its fully equipped health club located right in the building. The company subsidizes half of the initiation fee, as well as over 50 percent of the yearly membership fee. Not surprisingly, more than 25 percent of AUL's work force took advantage of the subsidized membership. Why should AUL choose to incur the high cost of building a health club right on the premises, instead of simply subsidizing membership in health clubs in general? For that matter, why offer membership in a health club at all—why not just give employees more money and let employees buy club memberships or whatever else they choose?

The answer lies in the positive externalities of some benefits from the firm's perspective. First, take the choice between offering employees subsidized membership in a health club versus an equivalent pay raise. By offering the membership subsidy, the firm makes it cheaper to join a health club. By giving a pay raise, the firm simply makes the worker more able to afford the club. Making the club cheaper induces substitution. Employees who would not have joined a health club otherwise will do so when the price is subsidized. AUL is thereby able to shape how employees "spend" their total compensation package. The company believes that membership in a health club means healthier employees and less productivity lost to sick time. Well-chosen benefits provide a way to shape employee behavior in ways beneficial to the firm—compensation becomes not only a cost but an investment.

But why spend so much money to build a health club in the office building itself? The most obvious reason is that it further decreases the cost of joining, by reducing the time cost of using a club. Perhaps more important is that the club on premises fosters a sense of camaraderie among employees, as well as a connection to the company itself. Providing a subsidy for a single health club ensures that employees will exercise together, forming friendships outside the workplace that may enhance productivity inside the workplace. The fact that this health club has the company name plastered all over it fosters esprit de corps: these people are all exercising together because they are part of a team. Not only does the money spent on AUL's health club sponsorship create healthier employees, it creates motivated employees as well.

Source: Greta Shankle, "Aerobics, Movie Tickets, Swimming Pools, Day Care: A Paycheck is Just the Beginning in the Employee Benefits Game," *Indianapolis Business Journal*, June 8, 1992.

Small changes in flexibility will have the monetary equivalent of the regression co-efficient. Thus, as long as there is a continuum of tastes, and as long as contem-plated changes are small, the regression line is an almost perfect reflection of the relevant worker's view of a factor's monetary equivalent.

Desirable and Undesirable Job Characteristics

Some job characteristics are desired by workers and others are shunned. Virtually all workers view flexibility as a good factor, but most view danger as bad. There is no problem dealing with either type of factor. In the regression approach, the fac-tor can simply be entered as a *bad*, as was injury risk, in the above example. The sign on the regression coefficient will be positive for a bad factor, meaning that higher wages must be paid when there is more of that factor. With good factors, the coefficient is negative, as was the case with flexibility. Lower wages can be paid when the amount of a good job factor is increased.

Diagrammatically, bad factors are easy to handle, but indifference curves will be positively sloped as shown in Figure 14.4. Injury rate, a bad factor, is on the horizontal axis. Indifference curves are positively sloped and convex. The worker is indifferent between the lower wage and lower injury rate combination at X and the higher wage, higher injury rate combination at Y. Both X and Y are preferred to Z.

Alternatively, we can convert bad factors into good factors by putting a minus sign in front of bad factors. Rather than talking about an injury rate, we can ex-press the same idea in terms of a *safety rate*, defined as one minus the injury rate. If the injury rate were .001, then the safety rate would be .999. Higher safety rates are good factors. Both regression and graphical analyses can be done using either of the two approaches, yielding the same information in both cases. Indeed, the only difference between two approaches is semantic.

FIGURE 14.4
INDIFFERENCE CURVES

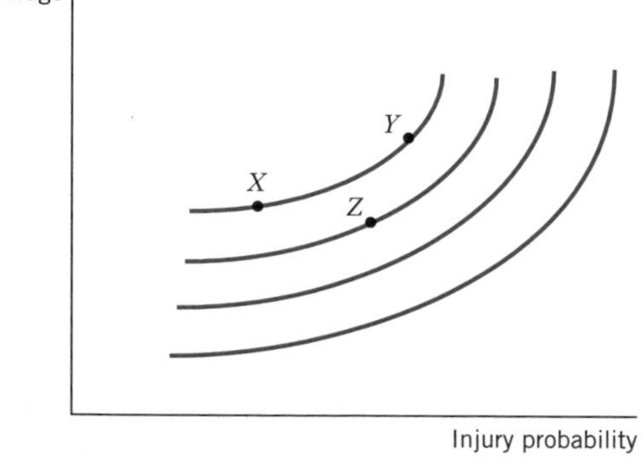

◆◆◆◆◆ MEASUREMENT PROBLEMS

Data limitations may be important. Some nonpecuniary factors may be of concern to workers but difficult to measure. *Respect* is one such factor often cited. Workers like to think that they are respected on the job. *Status* is another important nonpecuniary factor. Some jobs may provide more status than others. Since workers like status, they may be willing to give up some monetary compensation to obtain higher status jobs. Thus, status has a monetary equivalent. But how is status measured? In order to estimate the monetary equivalent of a factor, it is necessary to measure the factor.

Although status cannot be measured directly, those things that make workers feel that they have achieved a certain status may be measurable. For example, status may be represented by an office location or by a title. Both the office quality and job title are observable and can be used as proxies for status. For example, it might be true that, other things being equal, vice presidents earn less than individuals whose titles carry less prestige. Bank VPs are relatively low-paid compared with individuals possessing similar ability but working, say, as consultants for other firms. The pay differential probably reflects a number of nonpecuniary factors, one of which may be the title that goes with the job of bank vice president.[2]

Perspective of Marginal Workers

The market value of a nonpecuniary factor and thus, its monetary equivalent, are determined by the marginal worker's view of the factor. For example, a firm in my neighborhood specializes in cleaning chimneys in *Mary Poppins*-style top hats and formal coats. Chatting with the chimney sweep revealed that he took this job because of the higher status it afforded him over his previous job as a construction worker. I would never have guessed that sweeping chimneys, hat or not, conferred higher status than construction work. Fortunately, my view of chimney sweeping has no bearing on the monetary equivalent of the status associated with the job, since I do not supply those services. The monetary equivalent of status associated with a job is determined solely by the preferences of the participants. The supply and demand diagram in Figure 14.5 makes this point.[3]

To understand the analysis, suppose that construction workers earn \$20 per hour and that some workers consider being a chimney sweep to have higher status than being a construction worker. Those workers are willing to accept lower wages to be sweeps than to be construction workers. But people differ in their tastes. In Figure 14.5, with S_0 as the supply curve, the person who receives the most status from being a sweep is willing to give up \$5 per hour to be a sweep. He will supply his labor at \$15, even though he could make \$20 as a construction worker. Note that the supply curve intersects the vertical axis at \$15, so there are

---

[2]Titles must be given sparingly, or the title loses its status. It is the scarcity of the title that provides much of its value.

[3]This analysis takes off from Becker (1957).

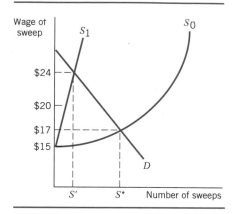

FIGURE 14.5
LABOR SUPPLY & WAGES OF
CHIMNEY SWEEPS

some people willing to be sweeps at $15 per hour even though they can earn $20 per hour working in construction. Some people, however, actually prefer working in construction. It is necessary to pay them more than $20 to induce them to sweep chimneys. They are individuals reflected by the upper right-hand portion of the S_0 supply curve—that is, that portion lying above $20. Demand is shown by the D curve. Market equilibrium occurs where demand equals supply. In equilibrium, the wage of sweeps is $17 and the number of sweeps employed is S^*.

The fact that the market wage lies below the construction wage of $20 per hour is evidence that the marginal worker (the one who is just indifferent between working as a sweep for $17 per hour and doing something else) views the status associated with being a chimney sweep as having a worth of $3 per hour. It is quite possible that most people in the economy think that there is no (or perhaps negative) status associated with being a sweep. This would mean that most of the population is represented by the part of the supply curve lying above $20. But those individuals are irrelevant. As long as there are enough individuals who associate positive status with working as a sweep, the price is dictated by those people.

Things need not be that way. Suppose that, instead of the supply curve being S_0, it were S_1. There is still one individual who is willing to work as a sweep at $15 per hour, but the S_1 supply curve implies that a much smaller part of the population views sweep status as positive than would be the case were the supply curve S_0. If S_1 rather than S_0 is the supply curve, then the market wage is $24. This implies a negative status associated with being a sweep for the marginal worker, who must be compensated $4 more per hour for working as a sweep than for working as a construction worker. Even though some individuals attribute positive status to chimney sweeping, there are not enough of them to cause the monetary equivalent of the status of being a sweep to be positive. Since the marginal worker views sweeping as a low-status occupation, a premium must be paid to attract workers to the field of sweeping chimneys.

This implies that the larger the proportion of workers who believe that an occupation is a high-status occupation, the lower the wage and the larger the monetary equivalent of the status from the occupation. Also, the larger the demand for certain professions, the lower the monetary equivalent of status. Higher demand means that more workers must be employed. If more workers are employed, the marginal worker is more likely to be one who does not view sweeping as a high-status field. Thus, high demand and low supply reduce the monetary equivalent of the value of nonpecuniary characteristics associated with any given occupation.

Indexes

Some firms have taken the notion of monetary equivalents very seriously. For example, Hay Associates, a well-known consulting firm, created a system called "Hay Points," which takes a composite of job characteristics and translates them into an equilibrium wage. A committee, often comprised of workers, managers, and consultants, rates the features of the job, such as skill level, technical know-how, accountability, and pleasantness of work. The ratings are then translated, through a formula, into points, which then imply a wage for a particular job.

Companies have used the ratings in a variety of ways. The most frequent use is to either establish, check, or justify a wage structure in an organization. Many firms have a large number of jobs and want to determine whether the wage rate for each job is appropriate. What any particular individual considers to be appropriate compensation for a job is likely to depend on his or her viewpoint. Individuals may strategically overestimate their own value. Consequently, if wages were self-determined, very few firms could survive. An outside consultant who uses market data, either directly or with the aid of some points scheme, can provide more objective evaluations of various jobs.

Sometimes, the indexes are used to determine whether discrimination has occurred. The Equal Pay Act makes it illegal in the United States to pay men and women different wages for doing the same work. But men and women tend to be found in different jobs, doing different work. How can wages across jobs be compared to test for the existence of discrimination?

One possible way to test for job discrimination is to use the indexes. Suppose that workers in a job dominated by women are paid less than seemingly equivalent workers in a job dominated by men. How can a firm determine whether the wage differences are a result of discrimination or a result of job differences that justify the differences? One way is to attempt to construct monetary equivalents for the job characteristics. If the wages predicted in the female jobs are higher than the actual wages paid and the wages predicted in the male jobs are lower than the actual wages paid, then there may be reason to believe that discrimination has occurred.

Firms have undertaken such studies of wage discrimination, sometimes with surprising results. A firm may believe that it has set wages in a nondiscriminatory fashion but may find that the indexes show otherwise. Consider the case of the State of Washington, for example. The State of Washington commissioned a compensation firm to study the job structure in the state bureaucracy. The firm found that female jobs were underpaid relative to what would have been predicted given the job characteristics and the monetary equivalents associated with them. Washington was found guilty of discrimination by the Ninth Circuit Court and ordered to remedy the situation. It is useful to point out here that a firm that commissions a study of its wage structures is taking a risk. If a management-commissioned study finds that the firm engages in discriminatory practices, workers and courts will discount management's claims that the study was flawed.

Are the studies flawed? The commonly used approach for estimating monetary equivalents is sound, but there is considerable room for inappropriate application and poor execution. Here are some possible pitfalls.

1. The ratings may be subjective at the level of the evaluators.
2. The index itself is difficult to evaluate objectively.

We address each of these, in turn.

Subjective Rating

In order to assign monetary equivalents to job characteristics, it is necessary to first determine the level of those job characteristics. Fundamentally, a judgment must be made by people, who may or may not be objective.[4] Consider a real-life example.

The Illinois Nurses Association used job indexes in a lawsuit against the State of Illinois. The nurses alleged that they were underpaid relative to male-dominated jobs (like electricians), despite the fact that their jobs were higher-level jobs, requiring more skill. An outside consulting firm was brought in to assess the value of the relevant jobs. Committees were formed to examine each job and rate them on the basis of job characteristics. Female members of the committee rated the job characteristics of female jobs higher than did their male counterparts. Women on the committee were more inclined than men to rank highly the level of skill, accountability, and difficulty associated with nursing jobs. Whether the disparity reflected strategic behavior or mere differences of opinion, the effects were the same. Because nurses rated the characteristics higher, the implied wage on female jobs was higher than that associated with the men's ratings. The converse was true of the male-dominated job. Men on the committee thought that electrician work required higher levels of skill, accountability, and was generally tougher than women on the committee thought it was. This example makes clear that evaluator subjectivity can bias evaluations. It also points out the importance of committee selection to the evaluation process. Of course, committee selection is also subject to biases.

---

[4]For analysis of the theory of comparative worth see Fischel and Lazear (1986).

Index Subjectivity

Indexes often have confusing numerical scales associated with them. Numerical scales can be manipulated to have dramatic effects on results, sometimes in ways that are not obvious to the user. To see this, consider an extreme example.

Suppose we want to evaluate two jobs: school bus driver and professional golfer. To make things simple, assume that there are only two job characteristics that matter: skill and responsibility. Although the responsibility component of a school bus driver's job is extremely high because the driver takes many young lives in his hands every day, the skill associated with driving a school bus is not all that great. Most people who know how to drive a car can learn to drive a bus very quickly. Thus, we attribute a relatively low necessary skill level to driving a bus. A professional golfer, on the other hand, has virtually no responsibility associated with her job. The cost associated with the failures of a professional golfer are borne almost exclusively by herself and perhaps her family. And clearly, there are no larger implications for society. However, few would disagree that the skill required to perform successfully as a professional golfer is great. Thus, we give golfers the highest ranking on skill, but the lowest ranking on responsibility, and we assign the highest ranking to school bus drivers on responsibility, but the lowest ranking on skill.

Now let us imagine two possible scales. These scales are shown at the top of Table 14.3. Scale 1 indexes the responsibility associated with a job between 1 and 20 points and the skill associated with a job between 1 and 10 points. In contrast, scale 2 indexes responsibility as between 1 and 10 and skill as between 1 and 20.

Which scale is more accurate for comparing market level of compensation for jobs with distinct characteristics? It is hard to have much of a feel for the choice, because the numbers and scales seem somewhat meaningless when taken out of context. A compensation consultant could present scale 1 as reasonable and few managers would object to the scale purely on ex ante grounds of unreasonable-

TABLE 14.3
AMBIGUITY OF JOB EVALUATION

Scale 1:	Responsibility	1–20			
	Skill	1–10			
Scale 2	Responsibility	1–10			
	Skill	1–20		Scale 1	Scale 2
School Bus Driver		Responsibility		20	10
		Skill		1	1
		Total		21	11
Professional Golfer		Responsibility		1	1
		Skill		10	20
		Total		11	21

ness. Conversely, the same compensation consultant could have walked in the door of the firm and presented scale 2 as the better scale to use. Chances are that the consultant would meet with no a priori objections by the firm's managers—or workers, for that matter. However, the choice of scale has a very important effect on the outcome of the evaluation.

Table 14.3 shows that if scale 1 is used, the ratings assigned to the bus driver and pro golfer jobs are 20 and 11 points, respectively. The school bus driver receives top marks for responsibility, and according to scale 1, this yields 20 points. The professional golfer receives the lowest marks for responsibility, which yields only 1 point. On the other hand, top marks are given to the golfer for skill, yielding 10 points, and lowest marks are given to the school bus driver for skill, yielding 1 point. According to scale 1, the school bus driver's job is worth almost twice as much as the professional golfer's job.

Now consider scale 2. Once again, let us assign top credit to the school bus driver for responsibility—10 points. Lowest marks go to the professional golfer for responsibility—1 point. The golfer gets the top score for skill and is awarded 20 points. The school bus driver, as before, gets the lowest marks for skill—1 point. Now the totals are 21 points for the professional golfer and 11 points for the school bus driver. In this situation the relation is reversed. The professional golfer appears to be worth almost twice as much as the school bus driver.

The reversal was brought about simply by choosing a different scale. Unfortunately, it is difficult for managers to know when the scale being presented to them is appropriate. This source of ambiguity creates some suspicion about the validity of the compensation consultant's point system.

Choosing the Right Scale

The choice of scale is not ambiguous in theory. As the earlier sections of this chapter indicate, monetary equivalents to nonpecuniary factors can be obtained from regressions of market wages on various job characteristics. As long as the point systems are correct transformations of the market coefficients, the ambiguity associated with choosing a scale is removed and the scales will yield correct estimates of market wages. Unfortunately, as a practical matter, not all compensation consulting firms use the statistical techniques necessary to deal with such complexities. Worse yet, managers who hire the consultants cannot know with certainty whether the coefficients and scales presented for evaluation of their workers are accurate reflections of market forces. If the managers could judge the scales a priori, they would not need to hire compensation consultants in the first place. The managers could simply do the analysis themselves.

Indexes focus on between-job variation and ignore within-job variation. This can sometimes result in biased or incorrect estimates of market wage rate. Job-based indexes are useful, as far as they go, but they may not go far enough. Since the job is the unit of analysis, job-based indexes, and analyses based on them, compare averages across jobs, but ignore variations in wages among the individuals with the same job. Sometimes within-job variation is more important than be-tween-job variation and using job indexes only serves to obscure the facts.

To see this, consider a hypothetical example of a group of white employees suing their employer for reverse discrimination, alleging that blacks have been treated too favorably. The whites claim that jobs that are dominated by black workers pay more than jobs dominated by white workers, even though white-dominated jobs score as high as black-dominated jobs on some externally provided points index. Table 14.4 illustrates this example with some data.

Assume that there are only two types of jobs in the firm. One is called the black-dominated job because it is held by two blacks and one white. The other is called the white-dominated job because it is held by two whites and one black. The average salary in the black-dominated job is $30,000 a year. The average salary for the white job is $20,000 a year. Because the jobs have equal value ac-cording to some reasonably constructed index, whites have argued that they are underpaid. After all, their job pays an average of only $20,000, and the job domi-nated by black workers pays an average wage of $30,000. The fact that black-dominated jobs are more highly paid than white dominated jobs, despite equal ratings on the external points scale, provides prima facie evidence of reverse discrimination. Observing different average salaries in jobs with "equivalent value" might lead us to conclude that there is discrimination against whites in this firm. Such a conclusion would be absurd.

First, note that within each job, whites are paid more than their black coun-terparts. In the black-dominated job, the blacks are paid $20,000 and the white is paid $50,000. In the white-dominated job, the whites are paid $25,000 and the black is paid $10,000. Thus, within every job in the firm, whites are paid more than blacks. Second, note that the average wage for whites in the firm is $33,333 (($50,000 + $25,000 + $25,000)/3). The average wage for blacks in the firm is $16,667 ((20,000 + $20,000 + $10,000)/3). Finally, note that there is not even one black in the firm who makes as much as the lowest paid white in the firm.

While this is a stylized example with extreme numbers, the point should be clear: focusing on between-job variation and ignoring within-job variation can give a totally distorted picture of what is happening within the firm or in the economy in general. Even if an index is well measured and unambiguous, this ex-ample points out that indexes are best for making between-job, rather than

TABLE 14.4
COMPENSATION AT DIFFERENT TYPES OF JOBS

	Black-dominated Job Salary		White-dominated Job Salary
Black 1	$20,000	White 2	$25,000
Black 2	$20,000	White 3	$25,000
White 1	$50,000	Black 3	$10,000
Average	$30,000	Average	$20,000

within-job, comparisons. Between-job comparisons may be relevant for some considerations, but they are not all-encompassing. Other considerations that are equally or potentially more important come into play in making wage comparisons between individuals.

Comparability

Indexes or other forms of comparability are often used to set the salaries of workers in the public sector. If a private firm sets too high a wage for its workers, it is eventually disciplined by the market. The competition from firms that have lower costs will pressure the overpaying firm to either lower its wages or go out of business. The government does not face the same disciplining mechanism. For example, the government can overpay its workers for a very long time. The only pressure that it might face will come from voters wanting lower taxes. This pressure may or may not force the government to reduce salaries. It may merely lead to programs getting cut or politicians being replaced, without any reduction in the compensation of government workers. The pressure on politicians from a concentrated and organized group of government workers may be far greater than the pressure exerted on politicians from a diffuse group of voters.

Government officials are aware of this problem and have tried to find ways to deal with it. One approach has been to set wages that mimic those of the private sector. Governments can commission comparability studies in an attempt to find the analog of government workers in the private sector. Sometimes it is very difficult to find comparable jobs because no private sector equivalent exists. For example, consider the job of being captain of a submarine loaded with nuclear warheads. The private sector does not have individuals doing exactly the same thing, at least not overtly. The submarine captain could be compared to the captain of a large cruise ship, but the skills required are not exactly the same, nor is the danger associated with the two tasks the same. Invariably, some kind of index that converts nonpecuniary characteristics into monetary equivalents must be constructed in order to deal with this difficulty.

Unfortunately, the government faces two problems. Not only does it want to set wages correctly, which is common to all organizations, but it also needs to choose the right qualifications for the job. It makes no sense for the government to hire expensive and highly skilled MBAs for clerical tasks in the Social Security office, even if they are paid no more than they would receive in the private sector. Again, the discipline of the market, which applies to firms in the private sector, does not apply to the government. If a private firm were to hire MBAs to do clerical work it would eventually find itself unable to compete with its lower cost counterparts who do not hire highly skilled professionals for jobs that can be done just as well by less skilled and much less costly high school graduates. The government is largely immune from the competitive pressures that prevent private-sector organizations from maintaining an overqualified work force.

Other than using indexes, what other options are available to governments and other organizations that do not operate in a competitive market? The question is more general and really applies to all firms. Even though market discipline will straighten out (perhaps through bankruptcy) those private sector firms that make bad decisions, no firm volunteers to learn of its mistakes through the harsh discipline of the market.

When filling a vacancy, an organization can choose among three basic recruitment strategies:

1. It can post some job requirements and pay the wage necessary to attract individuals with the relevant qualifications.
2. It can post a wage and select the best candidate willing to work at that price.
3. It can do comparability studies, constructing an index based on market data, and post qualifications and a wage.

The first route should be used when managers have a good idea of what others doing the same work earn, but do not know much about the characteristics of those workers. For example, suppose that you plan to open a car wash and you know that other car washes pay their workers $6 per hour, but you do not know much about the qualifications that other car washes require of their workers. You can advertise the job at $6 per hour and simply rank applicants from good to bad. Then you would hire the best worker available for $6 per hour until all vacancies have been filled. As long as the labor market is competitive, there is no way that a firm can do better than this.

The second approach is useful when it is important to hire workers with a particular set of skills and the firm is willing to pay a great deal to get workers with those skills. This is a case when the firm's demand elasticity with respect to quality is low. A large change in price generates only a small decline in desired quality because lower quality workers have significant, adverse effects on output. Here, the firm has a good idea about the kind of worker that it wants to hire, so posting worker requirements with words like "salary to be negotiated" may be the best approach. After applicants arrive, those meeting the qualifications become involved in an implicit auction. The firm starts by making low offers and raising them until all vacancies are filled.

The third approach, using some index to post both qualifications and a wage offer, is a hybrid. It is an attempt to get the qualifications right so that the firm will not simply have to accept the best applicant that comes along. It is an attempt to set the wage so that the firm will not have to pay a higher price for a given job than it is willing to pay. It means that the firm may end up sacrificing a bit on quality match and on wage. For any given set of qualifications posted, offering too high a wage results in overpayment and higher costs. Offering too low a wage results in an inability to hire workers with the posted qualifications. This error is easier to remedy. The firm learns quickly that it has underpaid when it is unable to hire acceptable applicants. The firm can simply raise the wage. However, by the time the firm learns that it has offered too high a wage, it may have already hired a large number of applicants.

◆ ◆ ◆ ◆ ◆ **RECAP**

It is clear that workers care about other job characteristics in addition to pay and are willing to accept lower wages in order to have a job with more desirable characteristics. But workers differ in their valuation of various factors. Money provides a convenient metric in which to express the value of the other factors. It is possible, using market data, to convert other factors into their monetary equivalents.

The monetary equivalent reflects the amount that a firm must pay in order to hire workers who are willing to accept the given characteristics. A firm that substantially changes job characteristics is likely to face turnover even if the wages are adjusted to the market level appropriate for new characteristics. For example, a firm that currently offers no flex-time, but pays high wages, can shift to paying market-determined lower wages in return for offering flex-time. But if the shift in flex-time and the resulting wage drop are large, the firm is likely to have to replace its current work force with new workers in order to find individuals willing to accept the trade-off. Those who chose to work for the no-flex-time, high-wage firm were the same ones who placed the lowest value on flex-time. They will not be willing to accept the wage cut that others accept in exchange for flex-time.

Still, market data are very useful, particularly when the proposed changes are relatively small and when the firm is not wedded to a particular group of workers. The kind of market data provided by compensation consultants can be of value, as long as it is used appropriately. Consultant indexes based on market data must be used with caution. There is a great deal of skill, economic knowledge, and statistical knowledge required to construct valid indexes. Furthermore, their implementation leaves room for subjectivity, which can invalidate conclusions based on the indexes.

The marginal worker's valuation determines market prices, in general, and the monetary equivalent of a job characteristic, in particular. Even if most of the world views a particular job characteristic as undesirable, the monetary equivalent associated with this characteristic will be positive as long as the number of individuals who view this characteristic as desirable is sufficiently large to fill all the jobs that have this characteristic.

The most important lesson of this chapter is that it is not necessary to think in terms of money for the analyses in this book to be sound. Since individuals are willing to trade nonpecuniary factors for money, we can always express nonpecuniary factors as their monetary equivalents. Once this is done, all analyses that use money as the metric apply, whether the payoff is in money or in some other benefit. This approach is used in litigation to estimate the value of life. The analysis is presented in the appendix.

◆ ◆ ◆ ◆ ◆ **REFERENCES**

Becker, Gary S., *The Economics of Discrimination*. Chicago: University of Chicago Press, 1957.

Fischel, Daniel, and Edward Lazear, "Comparable Worth and Discrimination in the Labor Market," *Chicago Law Review* 53 (Summer 1986): 891–918.

Kessler, Daniel, and Mark McClellan, "Do Doctors Practice Defensive Medicine?" *Quarterly Journal of Economics* (forthcoming, 1997).

Rosen, Sherwin, "Hedonic Prices and Implicit Markets: Product Differentiation in Pure Competition," *Journal of Political Economy* 82 (January/February 1974): 34–55.

ADDITIONAL ADVANCED READING ◆ ◆ ◆ ◆ ◆

Ehrenberg, Ronald G., and Paul L. Schumann, "Compensating Wage Differentials for Mandatory Overtime," *Economic Enquiry* 22 (October 1984): 460–78.

Rebitzer, James B., and Lowell J. Taylor, "Do Labor Markets Provide Enough Short-Hour Jobs? An Analysis of Work Hours and Work Incentives," *Economic Inquiry* (April 1995): 257–73

Hamermesh, Daniel S., and John R. Wolfe, "Compensating Wage Differentials and the Duration of Wage Loss," *Journal of Labor Economics* 8 (Part 2, January 1990): S175–97.

APPENDIX ◆ ◆ ◆ ◆ ◆

The Value of a Life

The analysis of monetary equivalents has been extended to consider more extreme situations. It has been used to estimate the value of a life—a somewhat heretical idea. The need to estimate the value of a life comes up in a number of circumstances. The most obvious is in wrongful death cases, where, as a result of negligence or other culpability, one party kills another and is required to compensate the victim's family for the loss of life. Some estimate of the value of that life must be used in order for the jury to decide on compensation. Like it or not, the jury is making a judgment on the monetary equivalent of a life.

Another example involves organizations where life is at risk. In the case of the military, the government must decide how many men to use and how much capital to use in the field. By using better and more physical capital, the military can reduce the number of lives lost in battle. But capital is costly. Implicit, and sometimes explicit, in any decision to buy military equipment is the value of a person's life.

Let us consider the implicit value that the military places on a life. It can be estimated by examining the capital/labor ratio that the military chooses. Insofar as soldiers and military equipment are substitutes for one another, the higher the capital/labor ratio, the higher the value that the military places on a soldier's life. When more is spent on capital, fewer soldiers are killed. Thus, data on capital/labor ratios can provide estimates of the implicit value that the military places on a soldier's life. The following model allows us to obtain estimates of the implicit value that the military places on a soldier's life.

The military's objective is to win wars, which depends on the amount of labor, L (soldiers), and capital, K, that it uses. An additional goal is to keep the number of deaths among its own soldiers low. The more capital it uses, the lower the probability that one of its own soldiers is killed. Thus, the production function is

(A14.1)   Probability of Win $= f(K,L)$

with $f_K, f_L > 0$ and $f_{KK}, f_{LL} < 0$, where $f_i \equiv \dfrac{\partial f(L,K)}{\partial i}$, $i = L, K$

Also, the probability that any one soldier is killed in action is

(A14.2)   Probability of death $= g(K)$

with $g'(K) < 0$. (More K implies a lower probability of death for a given soldier.)

The price of capital is normalized to 1, which means that capital is measured in dollars of expenditure.

The price of labor consists of two components—a wage that is paid to the soldier, plus the military's implicit value of a soldier's life, times the probability that the soldier is killed. Thus,

(A14.3) $P_L \equiv$ Price of a soldier $\equiv W + P_D g(K)$

The military's problem is to minimize cost for any given probability of winning:

(A14.4) $\underset{K,L}{Min}\ P_L L + K$

subject to (A14.1).

Using the standard Lagrangean method, this amounts to finding a saddlepoint of the function

(A14.5) $P_L L + K + \lambda\,[\text{Probability of win} - f(K,L)]$

where λ is the Lagrangean multiplier.

Differentiating with respect to K and L and setting the results equal to zero yields:

(A14.6a) $\dfrac{\partial}{\partial K} = 1 + \dfrac{\partial P_L}{\partial K}L - \lambda f_K = 0$

because the price of labor depends on the amount of K used, since K affects the probability that a death occurs. Also,

(A14.6b) $\dfrac{\partial}{\partial L} = P_L - f_L = 0$

Using Equations A14.2 and A14.3, (A14.6a, b) can be rewritten as

(A14.7a) $\dfrac{\partial}{\partial K} = 1 + L P_D g'(K) - \lambda f_K = 0$

(A14.7b) $$\frac{\partial}{\partial L} = W + P_D g(K) - \lambda f_L = 0$$

Equations A14.7a, b imply

$$\frac{1 + LP_D g'(K)}{W + P_D g(K)} = \frac{f_K}{f_L}$$

or

(A14.8) $$P_D = \frac{\left(\frac{f_L}{f_K} - W\right)}{g(K) - \frac{f_L}{f_K} L g'(K)}$$

Equation A14.8 provides an estimate of the implicit value that the military places on a life. The parameters are g, g', and $\frac{f_L}{f_K}$, as well as W. The wage, W, is observable. In theory, so too are g, g', and $\frac{f_L}{f_K}$. The $g(K)$ function describes how the probability of death relates to the amount of capital used. Military experience can provide estimates of the $g(K)$ function. Similarly, $f(K, L)$ describes how the probability of winning a war relates to the amount of capital and labor used. Again, military experience can provide a guide. Statistical analyses that compare victories and losses in past wars with the amount of capital and labor used can be performed. Analogously, collecting data on the number of casualties and relating them statistically to the amount of capital used can provide an estimate of the $g(K)$ function.

To make the analysis more vivid, suppose that a statistical analysis of military history reveals that

(A14.9) $$\frac{f_L}{f_K} = \frac{.025K}{L}$$

Further, suppose that we learn from history that the current probability of death, $g(K)$, is 1 in 1,000, and that adding \$1 million of capital reduces the probability of death by about 10 percent. Then $g'(K) = .0000000001$.

The only other ingredient needed is the ratio of capital to labor actually used in the military in order to obtain a number in Equation A14.9. Suppose that current data reveal that number to be 1 million. The military has \$1 million of capital stock for each soldier. Now an estimate of the military's implicit value of life can be obtained. Plugging these numbers into (A14.8) yields an estimate of $P_D = \$5$ million.

Thus, the military provides a large amount of capital for each soldier because it views the value of a soldier's life, or equivalently, the cost of a soldier's death, to be very high. If it viewed the value of life to be even higher, then it would use even more capital per soldier, because more military machinery reduces the risk of death and substitutes for soldiers on the field.

How does this estimate square with other estimates of the value of life? There are other ways to determine the amount that an individual would pay for his own life. Market studies of risk provide one source of data. Expenditures on medical care provide another.

Let us consider the first. Some jobs have associated with them inherent risk. Consider, for example, iron workers who assemble beams on skyscrapers hundreds of feet above the ground. Although these individuals are skilled and take many precautions, it is still true that working at the top of a tall building is riskier than doing the same work on the ground. The difference in risk and difference in pay can be used to estimate the value that the individual worker places on his life.

Suppose that workers who work up high have a probability of death from the job of 1/10,000 per year. Suppose further that those who work on the ground have a zero probability of death. Now suppose that those who work on the ground earn $1,000 per year less than those who work up high. This would imply that the monetary equivalent of 1/10,000 increase in the probability of death is $1,000. An extrapolation of this number could be used to provide an estimate of the value of a life. If the number remained constant, then the value of a whole life would be

$$10,000 \times (\$1000) = \$ 10 \text{ million}$$

The extrapolation has a number of problems associated with it. The first is that there is no reason to expect that the monetary equivalent of going from zero probability of death to 1/10,000 probability of death is the same as the monetary equivalent of going, say, from a .5000 probability of death to a probability of .5001. Second, individuals differ. Those who select the risky jobs have the least aversion to risk, so the $1,000 understates the amount necessary to compensate individuals for riskier jobs. Still, the $10 million figure may be taken to be a lower bound.

Estimates of values of lives vary, but numbers in the range of $5 million to $10 million are not uncommon. These numbers provide a check on the numbers obtained from the military example. They use a different approach, relying on worker preferences rather than employer-chosen factors of production.

Another way to estimate the value of a life is to examine an individual's willingness to pay for potentially life-saving medical treatments. Suppose that an individual faces certain and almost immediate death without a particular operation. Suppose further that a given procedure will increase the probability that a person will survive for 20 years from zero to 4 percent. The operation costs $100,000. If the individual elects to have the surgery, then the person must view 20 years of his or her life as being worth at least $100,000/.04, or $2.5 million using the logic of the previous example. Estimates using medical procedures vary widely, placing the value of life as high as $20 million.

Physicians, like the military, help the patient make decisions about life-saving treatment, in part, by recommending or approving certain procedures. Implicit in their recommendations is a value of life. Sometimes, because of the costs that physicians face, they may overvalue a life. To understand whether physicians act appropriately it is important to be able to estimate the value of life and to compare it to the cost of life-saving procedures, since giving a treatment to one may deny that or some other treatment to another.[5]

---

[5] See Kessler and McClellan (1997).

BENEFITS

$\mathcal{B}$enefits have become an increasingly important part of compensation. It is not uncommon for firms to spend in the neighborhood of 25 percent of actual wages on benefits, the main components being health plans, pensions, and paid time off. The amount that a firm pays in benefits versus fixed wages can be determined using the methods of the last chapter. The actual form of benefits, their formulas, and their restrictions require more discussion. The following exchange sets the scene for this chapter.

CLARK: Our health care costs are killing us. We have seen a 15 percent per year increase in health plan costs for each of the past five years. If this continues, health costs are going to exceed wages before we know it.

HARROD: You think health costs are going up? You should see my pension contributions. In order to fund the current plan, I am getting killed.

MACHLUP: Both of your problems result from demographics. As the population ages, you have less healthy workers, which raises our plan rates. The pension problem is obvious. If everyone is retiring, we must cover current outlays and keep the plan solvent.

HARROD: But we put money into the pension plan to cover these costs a long time ago. The money should be there.

MACHLUP: That would have been true, except for one problem: Our workers live too long. We were expecting to be off the hook with most workers after ten years of retirement benefits. Now, they live 15 to 20 years after retirement.

HARROD: Part of it is that they are living too long. The other part is that they are retiring earlier, meaning more years of retirement benefits.

MACHLUP: That's true, but they get less each year because they have less credited service.

CLARK: Demographics only explains part of my health care costs. It is true that we have an older work force, but rates have gone up even for the younger workers. There's got to be something we can do other than just throwing up our hands and saying "getting old is no fun."

HARROD: Why not just cut health care benefits? A number of firms have tried this. There have been a few strikes over the issue, but the unions have not prevailed.

MACHLUP: True, but we are likely to experience turnover.

HARROD: Not if we increase wages at the same time.

MACHLUP: Yeah, but if we increase wages, what's the point? The whole idea is to lower, not raise, our costs.

HARROD: Well, maybe we can raise wages by less than we save in benefit costs. Why should we be paying for their health care, anyway? If workers want health care, let them buy it.

MACHLUP: We'll never be able to hire anybody away from the competition with that strategy. If we cash them out of their current plans, they'll have the money and no incentive to stay with us.

HARROD: Sure they do. They like the wages, don't they? I think that there has to be a better balance that we can strike. My guess is that the firm would even tolerate an increase in pension costs if we could get our health expenditures under control. Let's try some other formula or arrangement, like a cafeteria plan.

CLARK: I like the concept of cafeteria plans, too. It makes explicit what we are giving to our workers, and it gives them complete flexibility.

MACHLUP: The trouble is that it doesn't do anything to lock them in, especially if we are worried about workers drawing too many years of pension benefits. I think these issues require more thought.

Some issues raised in the discussion and others that will be addressed below include:

- When should a firm substitute wages for benefits?

- What can be done to keep benefit costs under control?

- How should early retirement and the costs implied for pension benefits be viewed?

- What are the advantages of cafeteria plans over other forms of benefits?

- What are the effects of various formulas and provisions on worker behavior and costs?

- Is there any advantage to locking workers into the firm? What is lost by doing this?

WAGES VERSUS BENEFITS ◆◆◆◆◆

How much should a firm pay in wages and how much in benefits? Consider the following example. A given health plan, which we will call Triple Option, costs about $3,500 per year. It covers most catastrophic illness, has an HMO component, permits a reasonable degree of choice of physicians, and requires a co-payment by the insured worker up to some limit of expenditures, say, $1,500 per year. All in all, the plan sounds like it would be reasonably attractive to the work force. Indeed it is, but its attractiveness varies with the characteristics of the workers. Older workers, who are more likely to get sick, care more about health plans than do younger workers. Single workers are less concerned about health insurance than are those with families. Men use less health care than women.[1]

Suppose a firm must offer the plan to all of its workers or to none at all.[2] How can it make the decision? The last chapter taught us that there is a monetary equivalent to all nonpecuniary benefits, but health care is not nonpecuniary. Its monetary value is well-known, in this example being set at $3,500 per year. But $3,500 is not necessarily the value of the plan. It is merely its cost to the firm. The value may exceed or fall short of that figure.

It is obvious that the plan's value to its workers may be less than $3,500 per year because the workers might not have bought the plan had they been left to make the choice themselves. Value is defined as the amount that the individual would just be willing to pay to acquire a particular good or service. Any time an individual chooses not to buy something, its value must, by definition, be less than the cost of the item. Of course, value depends on one's income. Since the amount that someone is willing to pay for an item depends on how much money the person has, wealthier individuals may place higher "values" on some items that others regard as basic necessities. In any case, the amount that workers are willing to pay for a benefit is the appropriate notion of value for the employer.

It is also possible that the worker may place a higher value on a benefit than its cost. This happens generally in two cases. First, the firm may be able to buy the benefit more cheaply than can an individual worker. Such is the case with group health insurance, where individuals are pooled with others to lower their individual costs. (Some low-risk workers may be subsidizing high risk workers as part of this pooling.) Second, there may be a tax arbitrage opportunity involved. A tax ar-

---

[1]See Sindelar (1982).

[2]There are some features of tax law that permit a benefit to be nontaxed to the individual only if the plan is provided to a specified (large) fraction of the firm's employees.

bitrage arises when a benefit can be given to workers and is counted as a cost for the purpose of the firm's taxes, but is not counted as income for the purpose of the workers' taxes. The firm can buy the plan for $3,500. The same plan might only be worth $3,000 to a worker. But if the firm pays its workers $3,000 in cash, they cannot buy a $3,000 plan. After taxes, only $2,400 might be left, because 20 percent goes to taxes. In order to provide its workers with $3,000 of buying power, the firm must pay the workers $3,750, so that after-tax income is $3,000. The firm may be indifferent between offering a benefit of $3,500 and cash of $3,500 because both are counted as $3,500 against the firm's cost, reducing earnings and taxes by the same amount in either case. But the worker prefers the benefit to $3,500 in cash because it would take $3,750 in cash to buy a health plan worth $3,000.

How can a firm determine how much a plan is worth to its work force? One possibility is to ask. The firm could allow workers to vote on whether they prefer $3,500 in cash or $3,500 in benefits. The cost is the same in either case, so the firm would be indifferent to the outcome of the vote. If the majority vote for the health plan, the firm can substitute the benefit for cash payment. This would imply a wage cut, but it would be one that was chosen by the workers. It is equivalent to paying the workers the higher salary and then letting them buy the benefit out of their current wages at a price of $3,500.

One disadvantage is that if the plan is actually worth more than $3,500 to a worker, the firm is giving something away for nothing. In the previous scenario, the worker was willing to give up as much as $3,750 for the health benefit. The firm could purchase the benefit for $3,500. Thus, the firm could have reduced wages by $3,750 instead of just the $3,500 in return for the health benefit. The fact that the benefit costs the firm $3,500 does not mean that the firm must "charge" the worker only $3,500 for it. The firm could charge up to the amount that the benefit is worth to the workers. But how is the firm to find out how much the benefit is worth? Asking the workers is likely to be of little value. If workers know that the firm is going to charge for the benefit the amount that the workers say that it is worth, workers will tend to understate the true value. In fact, if workers knew the cost of the benefit to the firm, it would always pay for them to quote exactly that price. At any smaller number, the firm would prefer not to provide the benefit. At any greater number, the worker is giving extra money to the firm.

Knowing that workers will behave strategically, how can the firm obtain information on how much the benefit is worth? One way is to use market studies of the relation of wages to benefits. Just as the last chapter allowed the computation of a monetary equivalent of nonpecuniary factors by using regressions on market data, so can regressions on market data provide estimates of the marginal worker's value of a particular benefit. By looking at the difference between the wages of those with the benefit and those without the benefit, a market coefficient can be estimated.

Suppose that we obtained a data set from a human resources consultant. There were 25 firms, each of which either had a health plan or did not. The firms reported salary data for the average middle manager position. The data from the firms is listed in Table 15.1.

TABLE 15.1
SALARY AND HEALTH PLAN STATUS

Firm #	Salary in Dollars	Health Plan?
1	59,701	no
2	52,594	no
3	59,193	yes
4	54,817	yes
5	50,666	no
6	54,739	yes
7	50,172	yes
8	52,472	yes
9	56,899	no
10	51,765	yes
11	53,628	yes
12	52,372	yes
13	58,450	no
14	55,404	yes
15	53,270	yes
16	54,566	yes
17	58,791	yes
18	52,472	yes
19	54,724	no
20	51,181	yes
21	58,711	no
22	59,346	no
23	55,188	yes
24	51,356	no
25	53,832	yes

A regression of salary on a dummy variable, which equals 1 if the firm had a health plan and 0 if it did not, produces the following results.

(15.1) $$\text{Salary} = 55827 - 1836 \, (\text{Health plan dummy})$$
$$(964) \quad (1205)$$

Numbers in parentheses are standard errors. Two times the standard error gives the 95 percent confidence margin of error.

The interpretation is that without a health plan (health plan dummy = 0), the typical salary is \$55,827. With a health plan, the typical salary is $55,827 - 1,836 = \$53,991$.

Given this information, what should the firm do? The market data shows that the marginal worker is willing to accept a cut of \$1,836 for the benefit. A health plan costs the firm \$3,500. These data imply that workers are not willing to trade off enough wages to make the plan worthwhile. If the firm is willing to offer a worker \$55,000 with a health plan, it will do better to offer \$57,500 without a health plan. The marginal worker prefers the extra $2,500 in cash over the health plan because workers who do not have the health plan earn, on average, only $1,836 more than those who have it. If workers placed a higher value on the health plan than $1,836, employers who offered $1,836 more in wages would be out-bid by firms that offered the lower wage, but provided health plan benefits. By offering $2,500 more in salary instead of a health plan, managers make both firm and workers better off. Although everyone would like to have a health plan as a benefit, many may prefer direct payment in wages to the benefit.

This need not be the case for all workers. Suppose that the firm looks only at managers who earn more than $200,000 per year. These workers tend to be older than other managers in the firm, since salaries tend to rise with seniority. Older workers may have a greater preference for health plans. If the previous data are dominated by managers in the $50,000-per-year salary range, then it is likely that the value of the health plan, as estimated in Equation 10.1, understates the value of health plans to higher-paid older workers. Older workers are more likely to be interested in a health plan. Also, higher-wage workers face higher marginal tax rates and are more likely to appreciate receiving a larger portion of their income in the form of nontaxable benefits. More refined market data could provide estimates for specific groups. Such data are generally available from compensation consultants.

◆ ◆ ◆ ◆ ◆ CAFETERIA PLANS

One problem with providing a specific benefit is that the same benefit does not suit every worker. For example, older workers are very concerned about health care benefits, but not so concerned about child care. Conversely, younger workers care much more about benefits for children and less about pension benefits. A *cafeteria plan* gives a worker more flexibility in benefit choice. Although plans vary in their specifics, the basic idea is to provide the worker a fixed number of benefit dollars, which can be spent on a variety of benefits.

A typical cafeteria plan might provide a worker with 300 benefit dollars per month. The worker could use the benefit dollars for any benefit or set of benefits desired. An example of a plan is provided in Table 15.2.

The primary advantage of providing a cafeteria plan as opposed to any specific set of benefits is that the firm can provide the most value to the worker for a given amount of expenditure. If the prices posted in the plan reflect the firm's true cost, then other things being equal, the firm is indifferent about the composition of benefits selected by any given worker. But workers are not indifferent. Some prefer one type of health plan, some prefer another type. Some do not care about life insurance, but value child care very highly. By offering choices, the firm maximizes the value to the worker for a given expenditure.

The plan described in Table 15.2 provides $300 in paid benefits per month.

TABLE 15.2
CAFETERIA PLAN

Benefit dollars: 300 per month	Prices:		
	Triple Option Health Plan		
		Individual	$156
		Family	320
	Kaiser Health Plan—Family		240
	Delta Dental Plan		30
	Life Insurance (Double Annual Salary)		100
	Life Insurance—Spouse ($50,000)		40
	Long-Term Disability (Full Salary)		90
	Company Day Care—Per child		200

Suppose that a worker chooses to buy the Kaiser Health Plan, the Delta Dental Plan, and Life Insurance for himself and his wife. The total cost would be $410, $300 of which would be paid for by the firm under the plan, generally tax-free. The other $110 would be deducted from his monthly taxable income.

Because the plan provides some options, workers can choose different benefit components. It is clear from the types of benefits offered that not all workers will choose the same benefits. Workers without children are very unlikely to purchase company-provided child care. Very young workers are less likely than old workers to purchase life insurance, for two reasons. First, very young workers are more likely to be single and are less likely to have a desire for life insurance. Second, since younger workers are less likely to die than older workers, and since older workers have higher annual salaries than younger workers, the age-independent price of the benefits tends to overcharge young workers relative to old workers. Older workers may be unable to obtain the equivalent insurance at a cost of $100 per month, and young workers may be able to obtain it at a price far less than $100 per month.

BENEFITS AND SORTING ◆ ◆ ◆ ◆ ◆

The insurance example points out one of the major issues associated with cafeteria plans. Self-selection may work in ways that are not to the firm's advantage. The simplest way to see this is to consider a large firm that decides to *self-insure*. Firms that self-insure do not purchase life insurance from other companies. Instead, when an insured employee dies, the firm simply pays the benefit directly out of its current operating funds. As long as the firm charges enough on average to cover costs of the plan, there is no harm. But if the firm ends up receiving premiums

THE BENEFITS MARKET AT ALLIED COMPUTERS

◆ ◆ ◆ ◆ ◆ ◆ ◆ ◆ ◆ ◆

In the sometimes-cutthroat competition among companies for top-notch personnel, firms have increasingly turned to nonmonetary compensation as a method to sweeten the pot. As benefits packages have ballooned in recent years, many employers have complained that the benefits sought by some prospective hires mean little to others. For example, although single employees have little need for child-care services, these services can be key in the mind of a prospective employee with children. In a "me too" environment, it is unsurprising that many companies worry that their benefits packages will eventually suffocate them.

Allied Computer Group, which doubled its work force from 1993 to 1995, has avoided an explosion of benefits costs with the simplest of economic propositions: Individuals with different preferences can maximize their welfare through trade. Rather than offer particular benefits, the Milwaukee-based company offers a certain number of benefit credits per pay period, based on employment status and salary history. Employees are then free to purchase whatever benefits they please from the benefits "store." Day care, more vacation days, supplemental health/dental insurance, or even cash are available for purchase. Since all benefits are denominated in a common unit of account, benefits have explicit prices, which aids decision making by employees and cost accounting (and containment) for management.

If benefits are offered on a cash-equivalent system, why not just pay a higher salary and allow employees to purchase their own set of benefits on the secondary market? In many cases, employees prefer the base-salary-plus-tradable-benefits scheme because the firm can buy the benefits more cheaply than can the individual. The fixed costs of searching for the plan that fits the employee's needs are significant, and the firm may be better at pooling risk for health and insurance plans. Spreading these costs over the entire company while offering two or three plans tailored to broad groups of employees (i.e., single, married, etc.) sacrifices a small amount of variety for a large cost savings. As a result, a given set of services will cost less through a cash-equivalent program than through individual open market purchases, making it the rational choice for employees seeking to maximize the value of their compensation package.

Source: "Area Employers Attract, Retain Workers with Benefits Buffet," *The Business Journal of Milwaukee,* July 15, 1995, p 8A.

only from old workers who have high salaries and high death rates, it may find that contributions to the program do not cover costs.

Is this a problem? Not necessarily. By providing benefits that have different values to different workers, the firm implicitly gives higher benefit amounts to some workers and lower benefit amounts to other workers, even though the number of benefit dollars is the same per worker.[3] If implicit in the life insurance structure is a subsidy to older workers, then older workers are receiving more in benefits than younger workers who do not purchase the plan.

Similarly, the firm may believe that workers with families are more productive than those without.[4] By providing a lower-than-market price for child care, the firm attracts workers with families, who find the benefit package especially attractive. A firm would find it very difficult to make explicit its preference for workers with families by paying wages as a function of family size. This implementation would likely violate the Equal Pay Act and would create other problems. By providing family-oriented benefits, the firm evades these restrictions and attracts the kinds of workers that it prefers.

Another example involves firms that pay for workers' schooling, even when that schooling has no direct benefit and may even imply harm to the firm. A firm might offer to pay for a worker's general education as a primary benefit. This has great value to workers who want additional education, but no value to those who do not. If desire for additional education is correlated with the underlying quality of a worker, it may be that providing this benefit helps sort out the good workers from the bad. Rather than simply offering $5,000 more per year in salary, the firm offers $10,000 in tuition benefits. More able workers prefer the benefit. Less able workers prefer the cash. The firm is thereby able to sort workers, even if it cannot observe the worker's quality perfectly. There is a cost, however, in that more educated workers may end up leaving the firm after completing their studies.

It is sometimes alleged that cafeteria plans do not permit a firm to use benefits to attract the kinds of workers that it desires. As the previous two examples illustrate, the point is only partially correct. As long as the firm has some flexibility in the prices that it charges for the benefits, specific types of workers can be encouraged or discouraged from working at the firm.

It may be easier, however, to sort workers without a cafeteria plan. If the firm were to offer free child care to the children of all workers as the firm's only benefit, then those without children would find the benefit package much less attractive than the cafeteria plan described in Table 15.2. Non–cafeteria plan benefit

---

[3]Again, because of tax law restrictions, it may be necessary to have conformity in benefit dollars allowed, at least as a fraction of total earnings.

[4]There is empirical evidence that shows that married men command higher wages in the labor market than unmarried men. The effect works in the opposite direction for women. See Kenny (1983) and Mincer (1978).

structures are really special cases of cafeteria plans, with highly distorted prices. In this example, the firm that offers free child care and nothing else can be thought of as offering a cafeteria plan in which the price of the child care benefit is zero and the price of all other benefits is infinite.

Adverse Selection

Sometimes a benefit is provided that has inadvertent adverse consequences for the firm. Health insurance provides an example. Consider two firms. Firm 1 provides a very generous health plan. Firm 2 pays $3,500 more in salary each year. Now consider two workers, Smith and Jones. Both have families with two small children. Jones, however, has a child who requires a great deal of health care, costing more than $100,000 per year. It is inconceivable that Jones would prefer Firm 2, which pays more, but offers no health plan. Smith, on the other hand, might go either way. This means that a disproportionate number of applicants and, therefore, employees at Firm 2 have high health care costs.

How does this show up? If the firm self-insures, it pays the health costs directly. Having workers who avail themselves of a great deal of health care raises the costs to the firm. If the firm buys health insurance from another company it is not likely to be better off. The price that a health provider charges the firm for group coverage depends on that company's experience. If the company has employees who are intensive users of health care, then the provider is going to require that the firm pay higher rates to be insured.[5]

The selection described is adverse because individuals who have unhealthy children probably are not more productive. Costs are higher, but the firm reaps no benefit. A firm that provides health plans and is subject to adverse selection must reduce wages enough to cover the higher cost of health care because its employees are heavy health care users.

◆◆◆◆◆ PENSION BENEFITS

In many firms, the largest cost component of benefits is the pension plan, which may amount to as much as 10 percent of salary. Pension plans have a number of incentive features as well, many of which are quite subtle. The abolition of mandatory retirement in the United States made the use of pensions an even more important tool for inducing the retirement of older workers. The specific plan formulas can have dramatic effects on retirement behavior, as well as hours of work, effort, and turnover for much of the firm's work force. Although somewhat tedious, it is necessary to describe the various types of pension plans used today. Only by understanding their features can we understand the incentives implicit in the pension formulas.

---

[5]Sometimes this shows up in a different way. Low-cost providers refuse coverage to the firm, which is then forced to buy coverage from higher cost providers.

Plan Types

There are two basic types of pension plans. They are *defined contribution* and *defined benefit* plans. Most plans are defined contribution plans, but most workers who are covered by pension plans are covered by defined benefit plans. This is because defined contribution plans tend to be used in smaller firms and defined benefit plans are used in larger firms.

Defined contribution plans are the most straightforward. Each pay period (sometimes quarterly), the firm makes a contribution to the employee's pension account. That account is essentially owned by the worker. The money in the account is invested in interest-bearing securities of some sort, sometimes chosen by the worker and sometimes dictated by the employer or some other organization, like a union. When the worker retires, the account—which now consists of payments plus accrued interest, capital gains, and/or dividends—forms the basis of the pension. Sometimes, the funds in the account are simply turned over to the worker as a lump sum payment. Other times, the funds are used to purchase an annuity for the worker, which pays a specified amount each year until the worker dies.[6] The size of the annuity depends, of course, on the amount that the worker had in the pension account at the time of retirement. Larger accounts convert to larger annual pension flows. Workers with higher salaries generally have larger absolute amounts contributed to their pension fund each year, which means that they have more in the defined contribution accounts at the time of retirement. It is conceivable that the amount that a worker receives each year from a retirement annuity exceeds the annual salary that he or she received when working!

To get a feel for pension accrual under defined contribution plans, consider a plan that contributes 7.5 percent of salary to the employee's pension account. Suppose that the worker starts working for the firm at age 30 and retires at age 65. Wages, contributions, and accruals are given in Table 15.3. The calculations assume that the fund's investments yield 4 percent (real) each year.

At age 65, the worker earns $89,694, 7.5 percent of which is $6,727. This is contributed to the person's pension fund at retirement. Since there is no time left to accrue interest, the value of that contribution at age 65 is just the $6,727. At age 64, the worker's salary was the same, and so was the pension contribution. But because it earned one year's worth of interest at 4 percent, the age-64 contribution is worth $6,996 at retirement at age 65. The age-63 contribution of $6,727 had two years to compound interest, so the age-63 contribution is worth $7,276 at retirement. Similarly, the contribution to the fund of $2,250 made at age 30 is compounded for 35 years, yielding a total value of $8,879 at retirement. All of the ac-

---

[6]After the worker dies, many plans and annuities provide for continued support, usually at a reduced level, for the surviving spouse.

TABLE 15.3
A DEFINED CONTRIBUTION PENSION PLAN

Age	Salary	Pension Contribution	Value at Age 65
30	$30,000	$2,250	$8,879
31	$31,500	$2,363	$8,964
32	$33,075	$2,481	$9,050
33	$34,729	$2,605	$9,137
34	$36,465	$2,735	$9,225
35	$38,288	$2,872	$9,314
36	$40,203	$3,015	$9,403
37	$42,213	$3,166	$9,494
38	$44,324	$3,324	$9,585
39	$46,540	$3,490	$9,677
40	$48,867	$3,665	$9,770
41	$51,310	$3,848	$9,864
42	$53,876	$4,041	$9,959
43	$56,569	$4,243	$10,055
44	$59,398	$4,455	$10,152
45	$62,368	$4,678	$10,249
46	$65,486	$4,911	$10,348
47	$68,761	$5,157	$10,447
48	$72,199	$5,415	$10,548
49	$75,809	$5,686	$10,649
50	$79,599	$5,970	$10,751
51	$80,395	$6,030	$10,441
52	$81,199	$6,090	$10,140
53	$82,011	$6,151	$9,848
54	$82,831	$6,212	$9,564
55	$83,659	$6,274	$9,288
56	$84,496	$6,337	$9,020
57	$85,341	$6,401	$8,760
58	$86,194	$6,465	$8,507
59	$87,056	$6,529	$8,262
60	$87,927	$6,595	$8,023
61	$88,806	$6,660	$7,792
62	$89,694	$6,727	$7,567
63	$89,694	$6,727	$7,276
64	$89,694	$6,727	$6,996
65	$89,694	$6,727	$6,727

Total Pension Fund Value at age 65 = $333,785

cruals are added up to obtain the total value of the fund. It is $333,785. This could be paid as a lump sum to the worker, or it could be turned into an annuity.

Suppose that it is paid as a lump sum. The worker could then put the money into a fund yielding 4 percent (as before) and draw out a constant amount each week on which to live. If he or she were to live to 80, the worker could draw out about $566 per week, or $29,432 per year. At age 80, when the person dies, the account would have exactly zero dollars left in it.[7] It is also true that an annuity purchased from a commercial provider of annuities would pay the retiree about the same amount per year.

Defined benefit plans are more complicated and more diverse. With a defined benefit plan, the worker is promised a specified benefit, irrespective of the amount that is in the fund. The employer makes up all shortfalls and reaps all windfalls to the fund. The worker's annual pension payment is defined by some formula. There are two types of formulas that govern defined benefit plan distributions. The first, called a *pattern plan*, covers most blue-collar and especially union workers. The formula is very simple. It generally takes the form:

(15.2)   Annual pension = B (Years of service at retirement)

where B is some specified dollar amount, often subject to union negotiation. For example, if B were equal to $500, then a worker who retired with 30 years of service would receive $15,000 per year in pension benefits until death.

The second kind of defined benefit plan, used primarily for white-collar workers, is called a *conventional* or *formula* plan. The formula is sometimes very complicated, but its basic structure ties annual pension receipts to some function of final salary and years of service.

(15.3)   Annual pension = g (Years of service) (Final salary average)

where g is some proportion and final salary average is an average of salary over some number of final years. For example, if g = .01 and final salary average were equal to the average salary during the five highest of the last ten years of work, then a worker with 30 years of service at retirement would receive 30 percent of this final salary average during each year of retirement until death.

Because the formula plan ties pension benefits to final salary, it moves with inflation automatically. If prices and wages rise because of inflation, then final salary will be higher and the pension benefits will reflect these increases in cost of living. In fact, pattern plans, which are not automatically linked to wages, tend to be linked as a result of the negotiation process. When workers negotiate their wages, they also negotiate B in Equation 15.2. The B that is negotiated generally reflects inflation rates. Neither the pattern nor conventional plan indexes pension benefits of recipients. As a general matter, with some exceptions, once a worker begins to receive a pension, the benefit amount remains constant over time.

---

[7]Fifteen times $29,431 exceeds $333,785. But the interest earned on the money left in the account while the retiree is consuming makes up for the difference. Technically, the amount is obtained as follows. The instantaneous rate of interest equivalent to an annual rate of 4 percent is 3.92 percent. The present value of the payments must equal the initial value of $333,731. The formula requires solving for the annual amount X, such that

$$\int_{0}^{15} Xe^{-rt}\, dt = 333785$$

The solution is $X = 29,432$.

Further, tying pension benefits to final salary affects incentives. Because work-ers want to receive high pensions, they may be induced to work harder during fi-nal years than they would were they on a pattern plan. Sometimes, these incen-tives can be too strong. The following story illustrates the point.

A few years back, a subway train in Boston rear-ended another train, causing a number of injuries. An investigation was launched to determine the cause of the crash. It was found that the driver of the offending vehicle had dozed off on the job. It seems that he was 64 years old and was working 60- and 70-hour weeks. The pension plan tied his pension to the final year's compensation. As a result, he worked all the overtime that he could get, and was sleep deprived.

It is clear that the behavior exhibited by the subway driver is not desirable. The pension plan provided incentives to work hard, but those incentives were too strong, leading to productivity that fell well short of the value of his leisure. In this case, the worker's productivity was very negative. The pension formula, coupled with giving choice over hours worked to the worker, resulted in a bad incentive structure that induced inefficient conduct.

Pensions and Turnover

The Boston subway example gave some sense of how pension formulas could af-fect worker behavior. Another way in which they affect behavior is through turnover rates. Defined benefit plans, in particular, provide the firm with a way to encourage workers to retire at specific dates. To see this, consider Figure 15.1.

The figure relates to a worker who starts with the firm at age 30. Age of re-tirement is shown on the horizontal axis. The "expected present value of pension benefits" is plotted on the vertical axis. Expected present value of benefits takes into account that benefits are not paid all at once, so they must be discounted. It also takes into account that the worker may die along the way, thus the word *ex-*

FIGURE 15.1
EXPECTED PRESENT VALUE OF PENSION BENEFITS

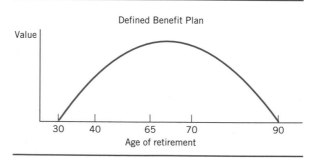

pected. It is akin to the average amount paid over a large group of workers, discounted back to the date of retirement.

The data on which Figure 15.1 is based could have come from a typical pattern or conventional plan. Each plan has the property that the longer the service at the date of retirement, the more the worker receives during each year of retirement. The formula on which Table 15.4 is based is a pattern plan that pays

$$\text{Annual Pension} = (\$500)(\text{years of service})$$

for each year of retirement, or after age 65, whichever comes later.

The worker begins work with the firm at age 30, so if he "retires" on the day he starts, he receives no pension at all. This is shown as $0 under the "Annual Pension" column that corresponds to age 30. If he works one year, then, when he turns 65, he will receive $500 for every year until death. Suppose that the worker will die at age 90. (Although he does not know his date of death, that death will occur is certain.) We can discount the flow of the $500 pension benefits, which start at age 65 and last until age 90, back to age 31. If we do that at an annual interest rate of 4 percent,[8] the present value of pension benefits in dollars at age 31 equals $2,101. The total amount collected is $500 per year times 25 years, or $12,500. But because the flow of benefits does not begin until the worker is age 65, the present value of the benefits is only $2,101.

If the worker were to wait until age 90 to retire, he would have a large annual pension payment, in this case equal to $30,000 per year. The problem is that he dies on the day of his retirement, so that none of the pension is collected. Thus, the value of the benefits is 0. Were a worker to retire at age 65, he would receive 35 years of credit, implying an annual pension flow of $17,500 for the 25 remaining years of his life. The present value of that flow at age 65 is $278,879. Expected present value of benefits reach their maximum at age 67. Were the worker to stay on for an additional year, he would actually lose $289, because the value of pension benefits at age 68 is $289 less than the value of pension benefits at age 67. Of course, the worker receives his wages during that year, but the decline in pension value means that the actual compensation received from wages and pension is lower than the wage amount. Pension accruals are actually negative once the worker reaches age 67.

Every defined benefit plan has this feature. If a worker quits on the day he begins the job, the pension benefits received are zero. If he works until he dies, pension benefits received are zero. Because they are positive at ages between the starting age and age of death, it must be that the value of pensions as a function of age of retirement exhibits, at least roughly, the inverted U-shape shown in Figure 15.1.

What about defined contribution plans? Defined contribution plans can never exhibit the inverted U-shape. The expected present value of defined contribution must rise with age of retirement. The reason for the difference is that with defined contribution plans, expected pension payments do not depend on the number of years left in a person's life. If a person were to work until age 89, every dollar that

[8]Actually, an equivalent instantaneous interest rate of 3.92% was used.

TABLE 15.4
DEFINED BENEFIT PLAN: AGE OF RETIREMENT AND EXPECTED PRESENT
VALUE OF PENSION BENEFITS

Age of Retirement	Annual Pension	Years of Payment	Expected Present Value in Year of Retirement Dollars
30	$0	25	$0
31	$500	25	$260,101
32	$1,000	25	$4,371
33	$1,500	25	$6,819
34	$2,000	25	$9,455
35	$2,500	25	$12,291
36	$3,000	25	$15,339
37	$3,500	25	$18,611
38	$4,000	25	$22,120
39	$4,500	25	$25,880
40	$5,000	25	$29,905
41	$5,500	25	$34,210
42	$6,000	25	$38,812
43	$6,500	25	$43,728
44	$7,000	25	$48,974
45	$7,500	25	$54,570
46	$8,000	25	$60,535
47	$8,500	25	$66,890
48	$9,000	25	$73,656
49	$9,500	25	$80,856
50	$10,000	25	$88,514
51	$10,500	25	$96,655
52	$11,000	25	$105,306
53	$11,500	25	$114,494
54	$12,000	25	$124,249
55	$12,500	25	$134,600
56	$13,000	25	$145,580
57	$13,500	25	$157,223
58	$14,000	25	$169,565
59	$14,500	25	$182,642
60	$15,000	25	$196,493
61	$15,500	25	$211,160
62	$16,000	25	$226,686
63	$16,500	25	$243,116
64	$17,000	25	$260,497
65	$17,500	25	$278,879
66	$18,000	24	$279,957
67	$18,500	23	$280,370
68	$19,000	22	$280,081
69	$19,500	21	$279,057
70	$20,000	20	$277,257
71	$20,500	19	$274,643

TABLE 15.4 *(Continued)*

Age of Retirement	Annual Pension	Years of Payment	Expected Present Value in Year of Retirement Dollars
72	$21,000	18	$271,172
73	$21,500	17	$266,801
74	$22,000	16	$261,483
75	$22,500	15	$255,170
76	$23,000	14	$247,812
77	$23,500	13	$239,355
78	$24,000	12	$229,743
79	$24,500	11	$218,919
80	$25,000	10	$206,821
81	$25,500	9	$193,385
82	$26,000	8	$178,544
83	$26,500	7	$162,226
84	$27,000	6	$144,359
85	$27,500	5	$124,864
86	$28,000	4	$103,661
87	$28,500	3	$80,664
88	$29,000	2	$55,785
89	$29,500	1	$28,929
90	$30,000	0	$0

had accumulated in her account up to that age would be hers. If she accepted it as a lump sum, it would be the full amount. If she turned it into an annuity, the annual payment would have to be sufficiently high so that the expected amount paid out to her before her death would equal the amount in the fund at age 89. To be sure, the *actual* value of her pension fund may decline, depending on how her investments do. But because more is added to the fund each year, the amount always grows in expected value the longer she works.

Table 15.5 shows for a defined contribution plan what Table 15.4 showed for a defined benefit plan. It gives the expected present value of the pension benefits as a function of age of retirement.

The wages used in Table 15.5 are the same as those given in Table 15.3. Annual contributions are the same 7.5 percent of wages. The difference between Tables 15.3 and 15.5 is that Table 15.3 assumes that the worker will retire at age 65 and provides information on how much each year contributes to the fund available at age 65. In Table 15.5, the age of retirement is allowed to vary. The final column reports the amount that the individual has in the pension fund at each age.

A worker who starts at age 30 and "retires" immediately accrues no benefits, shown as zeroes in the first row of Table 15.5. If the worker were to work for one year and retire at the beginning of the next, when she turns 31, she will have just accrued $2,250 of pension benefits, based on 7.5 percent of last year's wages of $30,000. After another year—that is, on her 32nd birthday—that $2,250 will have grown to

TABLE 15.5
DEFINED CONTRIBUTION PLAN: AGE OF RETIREMENT AND EXPECTED
PRESENT VALUE OF PENSION BENEFITS

Age of Retirement	Salary	Contribution to the Fund During Last Year	Total Value of Fund at Date of Retirement
30	$30,000	0	0
31	$31,500	$2,250	$2,250
32	$33,075	$2,363	$4,703
33	$34,729	$2,481	$7,371
34	$36,465	$2,605	$10,271
35	$38,288	$2,735	$13,416
36	$40,203	$2,872	$16,825
37	$42,213	$3,015	$20,513
38	$44,324	$3,166	$24,499
39	$46,540	$3,324	$28,804
40	$48,867	$3,490	$33,446
41	$51,310	$3,665	$38,449
42	$53,876	$3,848	$43,835
43	$56,569	$4,041	$49,630
44	$59,398	$4,243	$55,857
45	$62,368	$4,455	$62,547
46	$65,486	$4,678	$69,726
47	$68,761	$4,911	$77,427
48	$72,199	$5,157	$85,681
49	$75,809	$5,415	$94,523
50	$79,599	$5,686	$103,989
51	$80,395	$5,970	$114,119
52	$81,199	$6,030	$124,713
53	$82,011	$6,090	$135,792
54	$82,831	$6,151	$147,374
55	$83,659	$6,212	$159,481
56	$84,496	$6,274	$172,135
57	$85,341	$6,337	$185,358
58	$86,194	$6,401	$199,172
59	$87,056	$6,465	$213,604
60	$87,927	$6,529	$228,677
61	$88,806	$6,595	$244,419
62	$89,694	$6,660	$260,856
63	$89,694	$6,727	$278,017
64	$89,694	$6,727	$295,865
65	$89,694	$6,727	$314,427
66	$89,694	$6,727	$333,731
67	$89,694	$6,727	$353,807
68	$89,694	$6,727	$374,687
69	$89,694	$6,727	$396,401
70	$89,694	$6,727	$418,984
71	$89,694	$6,727	$442,471

TABLE 15.5 (Continued)

Age of Retirement	Salary	Contribution to the Fund During Last Year	Total Value of Fund at Date of Retirement
72	$89,694	$6,727	$466,897
73	$89,694	$6,727	$492,299
74	$89,694	$6,727	$518,718
75	$89,694	$6,727	$546,194
76	$89,694	$6,727	$574,769
77	$89,694	$6,727	$604,487
78	$89,694	$6,727	$635,393
79	$89,694	$6,727	$667,536
80	$89,694	$6,727	$700,965
81	$89,694	$6,727	$735,730
82	$89,694	$6,727	$771,887
83	$89,694	$6,727	$809,489
84	$89,694	$6,727	$848,596
85	$89,694	$6,727	$889,267
86	$89,694	$6,727	$931,564
87	$89,694	$6,727	$975,554
88	$89,694	$6,727	$1,021,303
89	$89,694	$6,727	$1,068,882
90	$89,694	$6,727	$1,118,365

$2,250 × 1.04 at an interest rate of 4 percent, or $2340. In addition, she will have accrued another $2,363, equal to 7.5 percent of her age 31 wages. At age 32, she will have $4,703 in her pension fund. By age 33, the $4,703 will have grown to $4,703 × 1.04 = $4,890, which with the new accrual of $2,481 yields a total value in the fund of $7,371. The process can be repeated to estimate how much the fund will be worth at each year of retirement. If she were to work until 90, she would have $1,118,365 in her fund. Although she dies on the day that the check is received, she or her estate own the funds that have been accumulated. Unlike the defined benefit plan, the expected amount that she receives from the fund depends only on her years worked, not on the number of years of life that remain.

Figure 15.2 shows the pattern of pension accrual for defined contribution plans. As in Table 15.5, the pension value always increases as a function of retirement age. The comparison between Figures 15.1 and 15.2 makes an important point about the choice of pension plan types. Since pension accrual is always positive for defined contribution plans, but accrual becomes negative for defined benefit plans, only defined benefit plans punish delayed retirement. In the previous example, once a worker reaches 67, additional years of work actually cost pension benefits. For defined contribution plans, the reverse is true. Additional years of work are rewarded in higher pension accruals. It is possible to specify a defined contribution plan that does not make contributions after, say, 30 years of service. Then accruals would be zero. It is impossible, however, to make expected accruals negative with defined contribution plans.

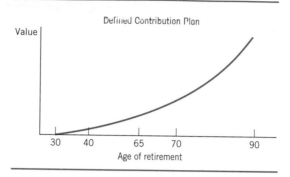

FIGURE 15.2
EXPECTED PRESENT VALUE OF
PENSION BENEFITS

After mandatory retirement was outlawed, firms had to seek other ways to induce workers to retire. One way used window plans—that is, plans that offer workers in a particular age group to elect to receive a payment in return for immediate retirement. An alternative is to replace a defined contribution plan with a defined benefit plan, which penalizes workers beyond some age for additional work. The change in the law governing mandatory retirement actually had the effect of encouraging both window plans and a switch of defined contribution plans toward defined benefit plans.[9]

Vesting

Pension benefits are not always "owned" by workers as soon as they accrue. When a worker first begins a job, his or her benefits may not be "vested" until the worker has been with the firm for a given number of years. During the first year on a job, a worker may accrue $2,250 in benefits, but if the worker leaves before becoming vested, typically five years, he or she receives none of the benefit. After having been with the firm for five years, all of the benefits accrued up to that point may become vested, which means that, were the worker to leave, he or she would be entitled to receive the benefits, either as check upon termination, or as a pension benefit upon reaching some specified age, like 62 or 65. Nonvested benefits have effects on turnover. To see this, consider one of the most extreme forms of vesting, illustrated by the military pension plan.[10] The plan promises to pay a retired soldier a certain amount per year, depending on retiring rank and years of

---

[9]At the same time, the number of defined contribution plans grew rapidly. A large fraction of these plans were supplementary, and were used to augment the basic plan because of tax advantages given to saving through a pension plan.

[10]The military plan, were it not government run, would violate ERISA laws regarding vesting.

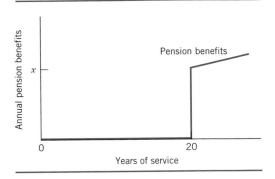

FIGURE 15.3
MILITARY PENSIONS

service. But in order to receive any amount at all, the person must stay in the service for at least 20 years. This is sometimes called *cliff vesting*, because it produces a picture that looks like a cliff, as illustrated in Figure 15.3.

A soldier who leaves before 20 years of service receives zero per year as a pension. Once the soldier has been in the service for 20 years, he receives X per year of "retirement." The retiring soldier could be only 38 years old. If he stays longer, his annual pension per year increases with years of service, but he can then leave at any time because his pension is already fully vested.

A soldier who leaves even one year before the 20 years receives no pension. This produces a very interesting separation pattern, which is displayed in Figure 15.3. The separation rate (defined as the sum of quits and terminations) starts relatively high. Some people simply do not adapt well to military life and leave or get kicked out during the first few months in the service. After that time, the separation rates start to fall. Just short of 20 years of service, the separation rate is almost zero. Virtually no one leaves the military voluntarily after having served 17 or 18 years, because by staying just another two years, they become eligible for a generous pension. At year 20, separation rates jump up dramatically. All those who had been waiting to leave can now leave and receive their pension benefits. A very large fraction of soldiers leave in the twentieth year, right after becoming vested in their pension benefits.

This example makes it clear how important the pension formula can be, particularly for workers who are approaching ages when retirement is meaningful. But pensions can even affect people at a much earlier stage of their careers. To see how, it is necessary to define another concept.

Portability

Sometimes confused with vesting, portability is a different feature that pension plans may have. Plans that are completely portable are plans that have values that do not change when the employer changes. The U.S. Social Security system is portable among all non-exempt employers. Months, or actually, quarters of credit toward Social Security experience used in calculating benefits are not affected by employer changes. In order to be eligible for Social Security, 40 quarters of participation in the system are required. It does not matter where those 40 quarters of experience are acquired.[11] A worker could shift employers every year during the first ten years of work life. As long as workers contribute to the system for 40 quarters (or ten years), they are eligible to receive benefits when they reach the age of eligibility.

Workers are not vested in Social Security benefits until they have worked and contributed to the system for 40 quarters. Until then, they are not eligible for benefits. Portability guarantees that experience carries over across employers.

Even as Social Security is portable, but does not immediately become vested, private pension plans often have the opposite characteristic, vesting immediately, or very soon, but not being portable. Consider the following defined benefit formula:

(15.4)   Annual pension from age 65 on $= .01 \times$ (years of service)
$$\times \text{ final salary at the firm.}$$

Suppose that two firms, say, Palo Alto Semiconductor (PAS) and Santa Clara Semiconductor (SCS), offer exactly the same plan. Suppose that the plans vest immediately, so that workers start to accrue credit toward their pensions as soon as they begin work and are immediately eligible to receive some pension benefits. Thus, a worker who begins at age 30, earns \$30,000 per year, and leaves after one year would receive $.01 \times 1 \times 30000 = \$900$ per year for every year that he or she is alive after age 65.

Consider an individual who starts work at age 30 with PAS and has the age–earnings profile shown above in Table 15.5. She starts at age 30, earning \$30,000. If she remains with PAS until age 65 her salary will be \$89,694. Her annual pension at retirement would be

$$.01 \times 35 \times \$89,694 = \$31,393$$

Now suppose that SCS has exactly the same earnings profile and pension plan. Workers who start at 30 earn \$30,000 per year and earn \$90,694 at age 65. A worker who started at 30 and retired at 65 would also receive an annual pension of \$31,393.

What if the worker were to start at PAS and switch to SCS at age 45, continuing to work at SCS until age 65? Even if her salary were exactly the same at both firms, her pension would end up being lower. From PAS she would receive

$$.01 \times 15 \times \$62,368 = \$9,355$$

---

[11]Government workers are generally outside the social security system, having their own pension plans.

because she would have 15 years of service at PAS and her final salary would be $62,368. From SCS she would receive

$$.01 \times 20 \times \$89,694 = \$17,939$$

because she would have 20 years of service at SCS and her final salary would be $89,694. The sum of pension payments from the two firms is $27,294, which is about 15 percent less than what she would have received had she worked at one firm or the other over her entire lifetime.

The difference results from the pension formula, which is based on final salary at the current firm, not the final salary that she receives, irrespective of employer. Since her final salary at PAS is lower when she splits the career, 15 years of her pension accrual are based on a lower figure than would be the case were she to stay with one firm over her entire lifetime.

Because the plans are not portable, splitting up her career costs her about 15 percent of her pension benefits. Had the plans been fully portable, then the pension benefit would have been based on her final salary irrespective of employer, as is the case with Social Security. A plan that is not portable tends to reduce turnover because it usually penalizes workers for leaving mid-career.

In order for the plan to be made portable, PAS would have to cover any increases in pensions resulting from salary increases given by another firm. This becomes problematic. It would be possible for the worker and SCS to arrange a deal by which the worker's final salary would be very high, in return for sufficiently lower salaries along the way to cover the higher final salary and higher pension paid by SCS. This would hurt PAS because they would not have collected the benefits of the lower salaries paid from age 45 to 64. As a result, firms are reluctant to allow other firms to determine their pension payments by granting portability.

Portable plans usually involve a plan that is administered by some third party. The third party collects fees from the participating employers and doles out benefits according to a set formula. Social Security is exactly this kind of system. Ideally, the pension administrator can charge higher fees to firms that cause larger disbursement from the pension fund. The Social Security system does this to some extent. Because employers are required to contribute into the system a percentage of wages paid, those employers who pay higher wages or have more workers in the system tend to pay more to support the system. The relation is far from perfect, in part because firms change over time. The firm's current work force determines how much the firm pays into the system. Its behavior in the past determines how much is currently being drawn out of the system by current recipients.

Portable plans are often run by unions. In construction, workers move from one site to another many times over their careers. Small construction firms are unlikely to have their own pension plans. Even if they did, they would have little credibility, because such firms are born and die very frequently. A response is to have the craft union own and administer the pension fund. A worker is paid by the union fund and experience across jobs counts toward the total credit on which the pension is based.

The most straightforward solution to portability is the defined contribution fund. Since the fund is owned by the worker and since benefits depend only on the market value of the worker's portfolio at the time of retirement, portability issues disappear. I am personally an example of the portability of defined contribution pension funds. The first 19 years of my career were spent at the University of Chicago, where I and my employer contributed to a teacher's defined contribution fund called TIAA-CREF. The rest of my career is likely to be at Stanford, where my employer and I continue to contribute to that fund. The amount that I will receive on retirement will be based on the market value of the sum of contributions. The fact that I switched employers mid-career has no implications for the value of my pension.

Pension Risk

Which pension plans are riskiest? One's first reaction is generally that defined contribution plans are riskier than defined benefit plans, because defined benefit plans specify the amount that the worker will receive whereas defined contribution plans depend on the market to determine the size of the pension. This reaction is wrong for a number of reasons.

First, we have failed to ask, "Riskier to whom? Is it the firm or worker that we are concerned about?" If we are thinking of the situation from the firm's point of view, we might be inclined to say that it is the firm's risk that concerns us.

Note that we are talking about shifting risk, not eliminating it. Consider a defined benefit plan. The defined benefit plan specifies the amount that a worker will receive and thereby seems to remove risk. In reality, guaranteeing the worker's payment means that the firm bears the risk. In setting aside funds to cover the worker's pension plan, the firm must choose a market portfolio in which to place those funds. If the portfolio does well, the firm has more than enough money to cover the cost of the specified pension payments. If the portfolio does poorly, the firm must make up the shortfall out of its own funds. The defined benefit plan appears to shift the risk from the worker to the firm.

If true, does this mean that managers should prefer a defined contribution plan? A defined contribution plan appears to shift the risk from the firm to the worker. The firm's annual contribution is specified, but the amount that the worker receives depends on the value of the portfolio. A firm that shifts the risk to the worker because it does not want to bear the risk is probably being myopic. As the previous chapters made clear, workers care about the nonwage characteristics of the job. When a firm increases the risk that a risk-averse worker bears, the worker must be compensated. Whether the firm is willing to compensate the worker enough to bear the risk rather than just bearing the risk itself depends on the relative amounts of risk aversion.

Consider an extreme case. The firm is risk neutral, meaning that it is willing to take on any fair bet, but the worker is risk averse. The worker would have to be compensated for taking a fair bet, but the firm would not be willing to pay anything to get rid of that risk because it is risk neutral. The firm would be better off offering a pension plan where the firm bore all the risk and the worker bore none. By doing this, the firm could offer lower wages than it would have to offer were it to push the risk onto the worker. If the worker were risk neutral and the firm risk averse, the reverse would be true. The worker would be willing to take a fair bet and the firm would be willing to pay to avoid holding the risk. Workers would then prefer risky pensions because they would receive higher wages in return for the risk and they would not be unhappy about bearing the risk.

The message is this: From a risk point of view, the pension formula that is selected should be one that shifts the risk to the party who is least risk-averse. This is almost always the firm. Workers are small relative to the firm, and they are generally less able to handle risky pension income than is the firm.

Now, let us return to the original question. From the worker's point of view, is a defined benefit plan less risky than a defined contribution plan? It might seem that the pattern plan, which gives the worker a fixed amount per year of services, is the less risky kind of pension plan from the worker's point of view. But this would be wrong in general. A worker cares about real pension income, not nominal pension income, and the value of a pattern plan falls during periods of rapid inflation. Of course, both workers and firms know this and build some estimated inflation rate into the figure that they quote for B, the per-year-of-service dollar amount of credit in Equation 15.2. Suppose that they figure on 4 percent inflation in negotiating a value of B. If the inflation rate is greater than 4 percent, the worker loses because the money is not worth what was expected. The firm gains because it is paying dollars that have smaller value and are easier to come by. If the inflation rate is less than 4 percent, then the worker gains because he gets more than necessary to cover the expected increases in costs of living. In real terms, a defined benefit pattern plan which is riskless in nominal terms, may be very risky to the worker in real terms.

A conventional defined benefit plan insures the worker against some inflation risk. Since the pension value is tied to the worker's final salary, and since final salary tends to vary with inflation, the pension is roughly indexed to the inflation rate. In periods of high inflation, wages tend to rise more rapidly, so final salary will be high. In periods of low inflation, wages rise more slowly, so final salary is lower. Since the pension is a direct reflection of some average of final salaries, some inflation protection is automatically built in. Note that indexing to inflation is not an issue of risk shift. In fact, both sides reduce their real risk when pensions are indexed to inflation. If the pension were perfectly indexed to inflation, then neither firm nor worker would bear any pension risk, resulting from unexpectedly high or low inflation rates.

Defined contribution plans, which may seem risky in nominal terms, also have the feature that they reduce inflation risk. Since the value of a portfolio in nominal terms depends on nominal interest rates, and since nominal interest rates depend on inflation, the real return on the portfolio is likely to be less variable than the nominal return. In periods of very high inflation, nominal rates of interest on bonds can be in the 15-to-20 percent range. When inflation is low, nominal rates of interest and returns tend to hover in the 5-to-10 percent range. The value of the portfolio grows more rapidly during periods of high inflation, but so does the cost of goods and services that are purchased with the funds accumulated in the pension account.

Few plans index post-retirement benefits. Even defined contribution plans, which are invested in a fund, do not explicitly index individuals against inflation in post-retirement years. However, if the pension fund is turned over to the worker at retirement, the worker can keep funds as they are currently invested, or invest them elsewhere. In either case, the nominal value of the portfolio during the post retirement years will also tend to move with inflation.

Funding Pension Benefits

Sometimes pension benefits are *overfunded* and sometimes they are *underfunded*. A pension plan's funding requirements generally depend on the demographic characteristics of the workers and on their wages. Funding requirements for defined contribution plans are straightforward. Since the firm places a given amount in the worker's pension account at the end of the work year, funding is on a pay-as-you-go basis. Defined benefit plans are somewhat more complicated. Since the amount received depends on when the worker retires and, with conventional plans, on some final salary average, the amount necessary to fund pension benefits accrued, say, at age 35, cannot be known with certainty. Instead, firms use actuaries to provide estimates on the amount to be funded. If the firm puts more into the account than necessary, it overfunds the pension plan. If the firm puts less into the account than necessary, it underfunds the pension plan.

There are tax advantages to overfunding a pension plan. Contributions into pension funds are not taxed until the pension is received. This means that the firm can make investments at the before-tax rate of interest and earn a higher return on assets than it could normally. (The proof of this proposition is given in the appendix.) Since the firm's pension liability is determined by the worker's salary and years of service, the liability does not depend on how much is earned in the pension fund. This means that if the firm does well, it can keep the surplus. Because the firm can invest at the before-tax rate of interest, overfunding produces a larger surplus for the firm than investing in taxable assets. For this reason, overfunding is often desirable to firms. This, by the way, is analogous to preferring to save in the form of an IRA (Individual Retirement Account) rather than taking the same money and putting it into taxable securities. An individual can put current income into an IRA and avoid being taxed on it until it is withdrawn from the account. If the individual were to take the income in any other form, taxes would have to be paid on it. The worker could then save only the after-tax amount, which would result in a lower total return. Thus, when the firm's options are to put its assets into a tax-deferred pension fund or to invest post-tax funds in taxable assets, it prefers the tax-deferred pension fund.

There are situations when a firm may prefer to underfund the pension plan. These reasons have to do with strategic behavior on the part of workers. Some have argued[12] that workers will be less likely to demand higher wages if their pensions are underfunded. If wage demands result in the eventual bankruptcy of the firm, workers whose pensions are underfunded have more to lose. When the firm goes under, so does part of the worker's pension. The potential loss of pension benefits, it is argued, may keep workers from demanding exorbitant wages. Actually, the effect of having an underfunded pension on reducing wage demands is likely to be small. Except in the case of firms whose employees have very strong unions, the deterrent effect of underfunding is probably not particularly important.

Social Security

As already mentioned, Social Security is a plan that cliff-vests after 40 quarters of work, and is then portable to any other firm covered by the Social Security system. Social Security has another important feature: its payments are redistributive. They have both regressive and progressive elements. Social Security is regressive in that it taxes low-income earners at a higher rate than it taxes high-income earners. After some income limit is reached (the income limit changes frequently), additional income is not taxed for the purposes of supporting the Social Security fund.

Suppose this year's limit is set at $100,000. Then an individual who earns $1 million per year (and his employer) pays Social Security taxes on the first $100,000, but not on the remaining $900,000 of income. An individual who earns only $60,000 per year pays Social Security taxes on the full amount of income. Thus, the net rate on income is lower for the high-income individual than it is for the low-income individual. The tax is regressive.

Taxes are structured as regressive in part to recognize that payments disproportionately favor low-income individuals. Although there is a relation of Social Security payments to lifetime income, the amount is capped. So, high-income individuals do not receive benefits that are proportional to their incomes. This creates redistribution of another sort—from high-income individuals to low-income individuals.

The exact nature of redistribution depends on a particular year's cap, on the benefit formula, and on the maximum taxed amount over the individual's lifetime. What is clear, however, is that Social Security does not act as a defined contribution plan. Individuals do not receive exactly what they put in plus interest. Indeed, whole generations may come out ahead or behind, as a result of Social Security's redistributive structure. Current recipients and those who commenced receiving benefits during the past 20 years expect to receive far more than they contributed. Payments are made out of current contributions to the fund by the employed labor force. The situation for the future is much less certain. Because the system

---

[12]See Bulow and Scholes (1983) and Ippolito (1985).

uses current contributions to fund current benefits, and because there will be fewer young workers relative to older recipients in the future, the burdens on the working population will be greater. It is far from clear that the work force will be able or willing to support the level of benefits received by current Social Security recipients.

◆ ◆ ◆ ◆ ◆ PAID TIME OFF

Paid time off accounts for 10 to 15 percent of total compensation at major U.S. firms. In addition to the common two to three weeks of vacation time, workers often receive 8 to 12 days per year sick leave and 7 to 10 paid holidays per year. This amounts to 25 to 37 days off per year. The normal work year has about 260 days, so workers are given a full year's pay for doing 85 to 90 percent of a year's work.

Of course, wage rates adjust to compensate. A worker who is paid $100 per day and is given 26 of 260 work days off with pay actually receives $111.11 per day worked. Full annual compensation is $100 \times 260 = $26,000, which the worker earns for 234 days of work, yielding $26,000/234 = $111.11 per day. If the worker is not producing at least $111.11 per day, then the firm could not afford to pay $26,000 per year and also offer 26 days off with pay. Suppose that the worker produces only $100 per day. The firm would have to eliminate paid time off or would have to adjust the wage rate such that the total compensation did not exceed $234 \times $100 = $23,400. This could be accomplished easily by reducing the daily wage to $23,400 / 260 = $90 and offering 26 days of paid time off.

It appears that a firm would be indifferent between offering $100 per day with no paid time off and $111.11 per day with 26 paid days off. In fact, neither the firm nor worker are indifferent. If other considerations (discussed below) did not come into play, it would always be better to offer the higher daily wage with no paid time off. Why?

When time off is given with pay, a worker has every incentive to take it, even if it is not especially valuable. It is always true that giving workers paid time off induces them to take too much of it. The following numerical example illustrates the point.

Suppose that a worker produces $111.11 per day. Suppose further that if she works anywhere between 200 and 300 days per year, she values having one more day off at $95. Consider two schemes. Plan A pays the worker $26,000 per year and gives her 26 paid days off per year. Stated differently, Plan A pays the worker $100 per workday, but gives 26 workdays off with pay per year. Plan B pays the worker $110 for every day worked and offers no time off with pay. Under Plan B, a worker who worked 234 days would earn $25,740 per year, which is less than the $26,000 earned under Plan A for the same amount of time worked.

Which plan does the firm prefer? It seems clear that the firm prefers Plan B. Under Plan B, the firm pays $110 per day worked. Under Plan A, the firm pays $111.11 per day actually worked. Under Plan B, the firm earns a surplus of $1.11 per day per worker. Under Plan A, the firm's surplus is zero.

Which plan does the worker prefer? If the worker were to work 234 days, the worker would prefer Plan A to Plan B for the same reason that the firm prefers Plan B to Plan A. The worker receives $26,000 for the 234 days under Plan A, but only $25,740 for the 234 days under Plan B. But Plan B offers flexibility that is not available under Plan A. Under Plan B, the worker can choose to take fewer than 26 days off. Under Plan A, the worker has no incentive not to take each one of the 26 days off. Under Plan B, each day that she takes off costs her $110. Since the value of a day off to her is $95, she prefers to work the 26 days that she would be given off under Plan A. Her earnings are 260 × $110 = $28,600, which is $2,600 more than she would earn under Plan A. Of course, she forgoes 26 days of leisure, which, at $95 per day, are worth $2,470 at the $95 per day value. The extra time worked brings in more than enough to compensate her for the lost leisure. Thus, she prefers Plan B as well. If both the firm and its workers prefer the flexible plan, then that is the plan that should be implemented.

While this is only a numerical example, one can always construct a plan that offers flexibility and pays the worker an equivalent higher wage per day actually worked that is preferred by both worker and firm.[13] By giving the worker time off with pay, the firm is essentially forcing the worker to take time that may have little value to her. If she values the time less than the firm does, there is always a deal that can be struck to make both worker and firm better off.

This logic is too strong. It suggests that firms should always offer workers a choice between working and not working, rather than forcing the worker to take paid time off. Some firms do allow workers to forgo their vacations and sometimes sick days, taking extra pay instead. But most firms do not give workers a choice about taking holidays. The majority of workers are paid for Thanksgiving Day and given it off; they do not have the option of working Thanksgiving and receiving an extra day's pay for doing so.

Why might a firm prefer to announce a fixed salary with paid days off instead of giving workers the choice? There are some possible answers. In some situations, there is value to the firm in having workers take vacation time. One of the best examples is that of banks. Bank employees are usually required to take their vacation because this gives the bank an opportunity to audit the accounts and transactions that were administered by the vacationing worker. Where there is a significant chance of embezzlement, and where an employee can embezzle large sums of money, a firm may want the worker to take vacation to enhance the likelihood that embezzlers will be discovered.

The banking example is vivid, but unlikely to be very general. It is difficult to argue that most jobs have features that make it important to displace the incumbent for a few weeks every year just so the firm can find out what is going on. Despite the failure to comply with the terms of this extreme case, there may be productivity reasons for having workers take time off. When workers are involved in

---

[13]Stated more precisely, a well-constructed plan that offers flexibility with a higher daily wage can never be preferred by one that pays a fixed amount for time not worked.

team production, as is the case for an assembly line, it is not valuable to have one worker come in when the rest are home enjoying Christmas dinner. The firm is unwilling to offer the worker a wage for coming in on a day when productivity is likely to be low. The productivity story is consistent with the facts. Managers are more likely to be given choice over working holidays than are production workers. Professors are often in their offices on weekend days because they can do research and teaching preparation despite the fact that the university is not holding classes. They do not fit the model of assembly line production. Their productivity can be quite high, even when others are not working.

Even production workers are more likely to be given choice over vacation hours than they are over holiday hours. Workers may be permitted to forgo vacation and receive additional pay, even when they are precluded from making the same choice about a holiday. Since worker vacations are taken at different times, the assembly line is still operating during the period that workers take their vacations. It is closed down on Christmas. Therefore, the firm allows workers to choose whether to take vacation, but not whether to take the holiday. Forgone vacation time has much more value to the firm than does forgone holiday time.

◆ ◆ ◆ ◆ ◆ RECAP

As an extension of the analysis of the previous chapter, we began this chapter by examining whether compensation should be paid as a benefit or as cash. Cash would seem to dominate in most circumstances, but it was shown that it may be better to offer benefits in lieu of cash when a tax arbitrage opportunity is present or when the firm can purchase the benefit more cheaply than the worker can. Workers can be "charged" for benefits by paying lower wages. Unfortunately for the firm, the worker is unwilling to reveal the amount that he or she is willing to pay for a benefit. Sometimes market data, perhaps coupled with demographic information, can be used to infer the amount that a benefit is worth to a worker. In this way, benefit costs can be kept under control so that the costs of benefits and wages never become higher than the value of the worker to the firm.

Cafeteria plans allow worker flexibility and may allow the firm some additional flexibility as well. Because the prices that the firm posts for various benefits included in the cafeteria plan are subject to choice by the firm, the firm may be able to pay more to workers that it views to be more productive. For example, making a benefit cheap that is of particular value to married workers is likely to attract more married workers to the firm. Benefits that are prescribed without choice are merely an extreme form of a cafeteria plan with very large price differences. The price of the offered benefit is zero, whereas the prices of benefits that are not provided are infinite. In this way, all benefit structures can be thought of as special cases of cafeteria plans.

Pensions are one of the most important benefits given by the typical American firm. Pensions come in a variety of forms, which can be described as defined benefit or defined contribution plans. Defined benefit plans provide firms with additional degrees of freedom. Because the defined benefit plans penalize workers for work beyond some age, implicit in their structure are buyouts that induce early retirement. Defined contribution plans do not have this feature.

Plans that provide incentives can actually provide too much incentive to work. When the pension value is tied to final compensation, workers have an incentive to work too hard and too many hours during their last years on the job. Vesting and portability provisions also affect worker behavior, particularly with respect to turnover. But locking workers into a firm may impose costs on workers. As a result, workers must be paid higher salaries to work in firms that have pensions that tend to bind them to their current firms. Otherwise, they will choose to work elsewhere.

Paid time off is another important benefit. In general, providing workers with more choice over whether to take time off is better. Exceptions come when workers are involved in team production so that having a worker on the job when others are absent has little value.

REFERENCES ◆ ◆ ◆ ◆ ◆

Antos, Joseph R., and Rosen, Sherwin, "Discrimination in the Market for Public School Teachers," *Journal of Econometrics* 3 (May 1975): 123–50.

Brown, Charles, "Equalizing Differences in the Labor Market," *Quarterly Journal of Economics* 94 (February 1980): 113–34.

Bulow, Jeremy, and Myron Scholes, "Who Owns the Assets in a Defined-Benefit Pension Plan?" in Zvi Bodie and John B. Shoven, eds., *Financial Aspects of the United States Pension System*, Chicago: The University of Chicago Press, 1983.

Ippolito, Richard A., "The Economic Function of Underfunded Pension Plans," *Journal of Law & Economics* 28 (October 1985): 611–651.

Kenny, Lawrence, "Accumulation of Human Capital During Marriage by Males," *Economic Enquiry* 21 (April 1983): 223–31.

Mincer, Jacob, "Family Migration Decisions," *Journal of Political Economy* 86 (October 1978): 749–73.

Sindelar, Jody L. "Differential Use of Medical Care by Sex," *Journal of Polical Economy* 90 (October 1982): 1003-19.

ADDITIONAL ADVANCED READING ◆ ◆ ◆ ◆ ◆

Lazear, Edward P. "Pensions as Severance Pay," in Zvi Bodie and John Shoven, eds., *Financial Aspects of the U.S. Pension System*, Chicago: University of Chicago Press for NBER, 1983, pp. 57–90.

Lazear, Edward P., and Robert L. Moore, "Pensions and Turnover," in J. Shoven, Z. Bodie, and D. Wise, eds., *Issues in Pension Economics*, Chicago: University of Chicago Press for NBER, 1986.

Stock, James H., and David A. Wise, "Pensions, the Option Value of Work, and Retirement," *Econometrica* 58 (September 1990): 1151–180.

◆ ◆ ◆ ◆ ◆   # APPENDIX

It is shown here that overfunding a pension plan produces higher after-tax income for the firm. Suppose that the firm has a given pension liability, which it calculates based on the wages and demographics of its work force. It can fund exactly that liability and invest leftover earnings normally, say, in securities that bear interest rate r. Alternatively, it can take the money and overfund the pension plan. If it overfunds the plan, the firm invests in the same securities that bear interest rate r, but does not pay tax on the earnings until the income is claimed.

Suppose that at time zero, the firm chooses not to overfund the plan. Suppose that the firm has K dollars of earnings in excess of the pension liability at time zero. It must pay tax on these earnings at rate t so it has $K(1 - t)$ to invest. At the end of a period, the firm will have $K(1 - t)(1 + r)$ dollars, but it must pay tax on the earnings $K(1 - t)r$. Thus, at the end of the period, the firm has a total of

$$A = K(1 - t)(1 + r) - (K(1 - t)r)t$$
$$\text{total in account} \quad \text{tax on interest}$$

as surplus over the amount necessary to fund its pension liability.

Now suppose that the firm takes the K dollars of earnings and overfunds the pension plan. Because the funds are put into the pension plan, the firm is not required to pay tax on the K dollars until they are removed to fund the actual pension payments. The firm therefore invests K at rate r. After one period, the firm has $K(1 + r)$ dollars, but now must pay tax on the entire amount, not just the interest. Thus, at the end of the period the firm has a total of

$$B = K(1 + r) - K(1 + r)t$$
$$\text{total in account} \quad \text{tax on full amount}$$

To show that there is a tax advantage, it is only necessary to show that B exceeds A, or that $B - A > 0$. After collecting terms, $B - A$ can be written as

$$K r(1 - t)$$

which must be positive because the tax rate is less than 100 percent. We have shown that from a tax point of view, it always pays to overfund the pension plan.

THE JOB:
TASKS AND AUTHORITY

16

A firm decides that it needs to add another worker to its roster. It recruits the worker by placing an ad. Almost without exception, the ad describes the position that is available. Most of the time, the ad specifies some qualifications that the successful applicant must possess, but much of the focus of the ad is on the position itself.

It would be possible, of course, to leave any description of the job absent from the ad. Examine the following ad:

Wanted: Individual with a college degree in engineering. Call (415) 800-0000.

Such an ad leaves out so many details that it is unlikely to attract many desirable applicants. In particular, missing from the ad is a description of the duties, the hours, the pay, the location of the job, the type of company, responsibilities, and advancement possibilities.

There are broader questions here. What is a job? How should it be specified? How flexible should it be? Should individuals be hired to fill a position or should positions be tailored to fit individuals? The following scenario sets the tone.

HECKSCHER: You always want me to do more with my limited staff. If you keep piling on stuff, you're going to have to give me more people.

PARETO: You are always asking for more personnel. If I gave you as many people as you wanted, you'd control 70 percent of the firm. I think you're overstaffed as it is.

HECKSCHER: Look, I could give you a long list of reasons why we are over-worked, but that's not the issue. I'm not trying to redesign my entire department right now, and I don't think you are either. If you want me to take on the new accounts, then give me two more slots. I was going to request four.

PARETO: That's generous of you. I want this work done, so I'll give you what you're asking, but make sure you hire good people. When this task is over, I may pull them from you and give them to Pigou.

PIGOU: Are you serious or just threatening him? If you're serious, I want to be involved in the recruitment process.

PARETO: Wait a minute. Our first priority has to be servicing these accounts. Pigou's issues are secondary. I've got to be allowed to design the job and dictate its salary. Otherwise I'll either end up with garbage or with someone who Pigou wants, which is probably the same, given Pigou's tastes.

PIGOU: Thanks, but seriously, I don't see why I can't have some input into your hiring. After all, if these guys are going to be working for me in the long run, I need to be able to specify what they will be doing and how much we pay them. It's going to come out of my budget. And there's another thing. You always give your workers so much authority. They'll be spoiled by the time I get them. I need to have some control over how much responsibility these guys are given from the start.

PARETO: I prefer allowing each job to have sufficient authority that I can make the guy holding the job responsible for what happens. You can't hold people accountable if you don't give them control. You constrain your people so much that any creativity they have is choked off.

HECKSCHER: Let's not worry about that now. Let Pareto put out the request. If you don't like who he hires, you don't have to accept them.

What issues does this discussion raise?

- What does it mean to specify a "job"?
- Which tasks should be assigned to which jobs?
- How much authority should individual managers have over important decisions within the firm?
- Do some job structures inhibit creativity and innovation?
- Is it better to fit the person to the job or the job to the person?

◆ ◆ ◆ ◆ ◆ WHAT IS A JOB?

Tasks

When most people think about jobs, they think of tasks that are grouped together. The most straightforward way to think about jobs is as a collection of tasks. Which tasks should be put together into a given job? The primary reason to group tasks together is technological. Sometimes it is more efficient to separate tasks. Sometimes it is useful to put tasks together because they are complementary.

How many tasks should be assigned to a job? We think of most managerial jobs as including many tasks, but production jobs may be much simpler, grouping only a few functions together. For example, a farm worker may do nothing other than pick apricots. An assembly line worker may only attach the right-front door handle to a car.

How many tasks should be associated with a given job? This is a difficult question on which to give general answers, but there are some basic principles. The first comes from the economics bible: Adam Smith's *Wealth of Nations*, published in 1776. Smith wrote that the division of labor is limited by the extent of the market. He provides an example of a pin factory, where each worker can make an entire pin, start to finish, or can simply work on one aspect of pin making, like sharpening the point. In order to devote a full-time worker to such a narrow task, it is necessary to have a sufficiently large set of orders that a large number of workers are needed. For example, if the market for pins could only justify the production of five pins per day, an assembly line process where one individual cuts the wire, another fashions the head, a third polishes the steel, a fourth sharpens the point, and a fifth puts the pins in packages would hardly be practical. In order to justify using five people on pin production, a demand of thousands of pins per day would be necessary.[1]

Adam Smith's lesson provides the first rule for assigning tasks to jobs.

◆ ◆

*R*ULE 1: In small firms, jobs are more general and encompass a larger set of tasks than they do in large firms.

At some level, this point is obvious. Consider starting a small restaurant. Initially, the owner is the manager, cook, buyer, waiter, cashier, and maitre d'. As the restaurant grows, the owner may hire someone to wait tables and seat the guests. Large restaurants, on the other hand, could have 500 employees, with tasks as specialized as "vegetable procurer."

The number of tasks that can be assigned to a given individual depends on the breadth of skills possessed by that individual. In the previous example, the waiter can only be the cook if the waiter knows how to cook. A fine cook who has poor business skills is likely to go out of business very quickly. Until the restaurant is able to reach sufficient size such that tasks can be delegated to others (those tasks at which the owner has a comparative disadvantage), the owner is forced to engage in activities for which she is poorly suited. Her basic skill set may not provide enough expertise to produce a business that is viable.

---

[1]Of course, the number of pins demanded depends on the price of the pin, which in turn depends on its cost. If the pin can be made more cheaply by assembly line production, the number of pins demanded will increase.

If the world were made up only of Leonardo da Vincis—a genius in many subjects—jobs would encompass much more than they do today. Thus, the second rule follows.

◆ ◆

*R*ULE 2: Jobs tend to contain fewer tasks when the skill set of individuals in the relevant labor pool is more specialized. The relevant labor pools tend to be more specialized as the quality of pool rises.

A sports analogy may be illuminating. In high school, it is not uncommon for the best football player to be a star baseball player. The individual who is the best athlete in the school may have athletic ability that so dominates others that he is the best at every sport. However, the professional sports pool is a much more se-lective group of people. Among major league baseball players, almost all were the best athletes in their high schools. The same is true of NFL football players. Al-though being the best athlete in one's high school places one above all others in that high school, it does not ensure superiority when a larger set of individuals is included. Very few athletes can compete in two sports at the professional level, and those who do are invariably significantly better in one sport than in the other. The old chestnut that the jack of all trades is a master of none becomes all the more true as the competition stiffens. In the appendix, this proposition is derived formally.

Which Tasks Does the Firm Take On?

Firms have choice, not only over how many tasks to assign to a given job, but over which tasks to take on in the first place. Not unlike choosing which products to supply, a firm must decide what to produce in-house and what to procure. The de-cisions on outsourcing and vertical integration discussed in chapter 13 have impli-cations for the types of tasks that are assigned to the various jobs.

Some tasks are determined by constraints placed on a firm by outsiders. The most important has to do with training. In some firms, the relevant skills must be produced, rather than purchased. This is particularly the case in fields with new or rapidly changing technologies. Consider, for example, the case of the first snow-board manufacturers. They could not hire craftspersons from other firms, nor could they simply hire the graduates of snowboard manufacturing schools. Since the product was a new one, they had to take individuals with more general skills and teach them how to make snowboards. This meant that some of the more ex-perienced workers were required to teach others so the senior workers' tasks in-cluded some teaching, by necessity. At the heart of this is a question of vertical in-tegration. When an external market is well developed, firms can rely on others to provide certain services. When an external market is not well developed, firms must provide the services internally.

New industries, or industries in less technologically advanced countries, often must do their own training. Orbay[2] reports that in Turkey, only very general descriptions of jobs are given. A firm may advertise a position for an engineer without specifying whether the position is for an electrical engineer or chemical engineer, almost never listing the desired sub-specialty. The reason is that Turkish universities, which are only starting to catch up with those in the West, are not yet in a position to produce a large quantity of highly trained specialists. Instead, firms hire talent in a somewhat more raw state and develop that talent for their own particular uses.

Note that the issue of which tasks are performed by the firm is distinct from which tasks are performed by a given job. Even if Turkish firms must train their own engineers, this does not imply that every job must have a teaching component to it. It is possible to assign all the teaching responsibility to one person or group of persons who do only teaching and no production. Alternatively, a little bit of teaching can be done by workers who spend most of their time in actual production. The choice of technology comes back to which tasks are grouped together and how many tasks each individual should know. To deal with this issue, we introduce the notion of multitasking.

Multitasking and Multiskilling

Multitasking is a situation where a given worker is capable of performing a number of tasks and is called on to do so with some regularity. Multiskilling is where a given worker has the *ability* to perform a number of tasks, but the job that the worker actually performs may have only one task associated with it. Most of the advantages ascribed to multitasking are actually advantages of multiskilling. It is not generally necessary that the tasks be associated with the job, only that the incumbent has the ability to perform those tasks when needed. Of course, when individuals do not actually perform tasks frequently, their skills may become stale. Thus, multitasking and multiskilling may be linked as a practical matter. Some of the advantages from multiskilling are listed below:

1. *Flexibility.* Workers who know a large number of tasks can fill in for other workers. *Flexibility has less value in a large firm than it does in a small one.* In a very large firm, many people may be doing the same job, so it is less important to have one person know a large number of tasks. (This is shown formally in the appendix.)

   For example, consider United Airlines reservations. There are a large number of reservationists on duty at any one time. If one reservationist is absent, there is enough flexibility built into the scheduling so that another person with reservation skills can fill in. There is little need to transfer a gate agent to the reservations department. Thus, the gate agent need not be familiar with making reservations. He or she can focus on the direct responsibilities of gate agent, and little is lost.

   At the other extreme, recall the example of a small restaurant. If the

---

[2]Hakan Orbay (1996).

waiter cannot also cook, the restaurant must shut down when the cook is sick. Multiskilling would prevent a shut-down by training the waiter to be a cook. In a small firm, where there is only enough work of a given type to justify a few positions, multitasking is likely to provide valuable flexibility.

2. *Communication.* Multitasking is likely to facilitate communication between individuals who do different jobs. It is much easier to discuss an issue with someone who has some familiarity with the situation than with someone who is totally ignorant of the area.

   Consider, for example, a carpenter and electrician who are part of a construction crew that is building a house. The electrician needs to configure the wire in a particular way, but to do so, the wood framework of the house must accommodate the electrician's needs. It is easier for the electrician to suggest to the carpenter how this might be done if the electrician has some understanding of carpentry. Otherwise, he may be requesting that the carpenter modify the plans in a way that would compromise the integrity of the frame. Of course, the carpenter could always reject such a suggestion, but the process of iteration to get to a plan that works may take time. The more understanding that exists on each side, the less time it takes for this process to converge to a viable solution. This example is not chosen by accident. Building a house has significant elements of team production. *The benefits of enhanced communication from multiskilling are likely to be larger in a team setting.*

3. *Innovation.* Multiskilling may assist in making major innovation. There are at least two mechanisms that can bring this about. First, as with communication, when an individual knows many aspects of production, it is easier to design process-improving technology. In the previous example, an electrician is more likely to design a more accommodating frame if he were also a carpenter.

   While this is a possibility, there is no hard evidence to back up the claim. There is, however, another argument that has been made for multiskilling's positive effects on innovation.[3] When individuals are highly specialized, a given innovation may be more likely to cause all of their skills to become obsolete. For example, blacksmiths were virtually eliminated by the invention of the automobile. If instead of blacksmiths, individuals were generalized iron and steel workers, only a small part of the blacksmiths' skills would have been rendered obsolete by the automobile. Some of their other skills are likely to have become more valuable. Why does this matter? Workers who see their skills become obsolete are more likely to oppose innovation. Although the market is likely to win out in the end by forcing the noninnovating firms out of business, no firm would voluntarily choose to be among those disciplined by the market. Having a more broadly skilled work force may enhance the ability of the firm to adapt to change.

---

[3]See Carmichael and MacLeod (1992).

Re-engineering

One of the big buzzwords in the business press over the past few years is *re-engineering*, a term to describe reorganizing work so that it can be performed most efficiently. As a practical matter, re-engineering usually means increasing the level of multitasking by undoing some of what Henry Ford brought to American production. Instead of giving each worker one small task, a worker is allowed to carry a project through, sometimes all the way from start to finish.

One example involves an insurance company's handling of a damage claim. The task can be broken up into a number of steps. The process may start with an appraiser who examines the damage and places a dollar figure on it. Next, it goes to the claims officer, whose office sends a letter to the claimant informing her of the appraiser's number. Then the claimant can accept or challenge the amount. If it is accepted, a third group issues a check. Alternatively, the appraiser can be in charge of all three steps, assessing, notifying, and paying the claimant out of one office with the appraiser's staff.

It can be argued in the context of this example that any individual qualified to assess the damage can also notify and approve payment. Turnaround time is shortened, customers are happier, and labor costs are reduced. There is little gain to specializing the task so much that two other offices are involved.

Although true in this example, the case made here may be too strong. There are gains to specialization and in some activities the gains are so large that they swamp any benefits from the kind of re-engineering just described. Eye doctors do not fix broken arms. If they did, then a person who had been in an accident and had injured both her eye and her arms could be treated by one physician, saving time and effort. Such occurrences are sufficiently rare that it pays, instead, to have individuals who specialize. There is simply too much knowledge in opthalmology and orthopedics for one individual to have a good grasp of both.

When is re-engineering toward more multitasking likely to be most valuable? The answer is when the potential gains are large. Some of the gains to multi-skilling have been given already. In addition to those, some direct costs and benefits from multitasking are listed here.

1. *Multitasking saves transportation time.* Suppose that part of an insurance claim is handled by an office in Chicago and another part is handled by an office in Atlanta. The paperwork may have to be mailed from Chicago to Atlanta, causing a time delay. Reduced mail delays are one source of gains from multitasking. As electronic communication becomes more common, the gains to multitasking from transportation and reducing mail delays are likely to diminish.

2. *Multitasking saves setup time.* In the case of insurance claims, each time a file gets passed from one person to another, an additional person must learn some of the details of the case. When three people work on a file, it must be read three times rather than just once. To the extent that there are few gains from splitting the task up into many small parts, multitasking saves valuable setup time.

3. *Multitasking saves bureaucracy costs.* Related to setup costs are what might be called bureaucracy costs. Each time a project passes from one desk to another

JEWELRY MANUFACTURING

◆ ◆ ◆ ◆ ◆ ◆ ◆ ◆ ◆

Faced with demand fluctuations, a prominent New England jewelry manufacturer felt pressure to achieve greater production efficiency and flexibility. In order to accomplish these goals, the management decided to employ a multiskilling strategy. Multiskilling entails training a number of employees to perform several different tasks, which makes it possible to switch an employee to a high-demand task, thus increasing the manufacturing flexibility.

The firm's management realized that the original compensation system was not conducive to multitasking. Indeed, the existing structure was based on paying hourly wage based on 12 rigidly defined pay grades. It was apparent that a shift to multitasking necessitated a revamping of the incentive system.

For multitasking to be possible, it is necessary to encourage employees to acquire new skills. For multitasking to be effective, each worker should be assigned to a task that has the highest value at the moment, rather than a task that a worker prefers to perform for some reason other than profitability. Consequently, implementation of multiskilling requires that more task assignment decisions are made, increasing the amount and importance of decision-making by the workers and middle management. Probably for this reason, the company decided to strengthen incentives as part of the reform. With the help of consultants from William M. Mercer, Inc., the management developed a strategy. In order to minimize the risk associated with the drastic organizational change, the new structure was to be tested on a reasonably self-contained unit employing 20 workers.

The incentive plan was developed by a cross-functional team formed with representatives from production (two hourly workers), manufacturing, human resources, finance and information systems. An incentive system emphasizing productivity improvements was proposed. The team members felt that setting a challenging, yet achievable cost reduction goal was instrumental for the success of the reform. The goal of 5 percent reduction of controllable per unit cost was adopted. Members of the committee felt that, with proper incentives, this goal had about a 70 percent chance of being attained.

A variable pay fund was established and governed by a pre-specified formula that translated into a bonus for each team member equal to approximately 5 percent of his salary, conditional on attaining the cost reduction goal.

The new compensation scheme was designed with great attention to small but important details. For example, a semiannual payout schedule was chosen for the incentive plan. This type of payout schedule seemed appropriate, partly because the firm took inventory every six month. Furthermore, a shorter period, say, a month, would have introduced too much variability into the picture and would not allow enough time for market forces to operate. The firm committed itself to distributing earned bonuses in a timely fashion, that is, within 30 days after the conclusion of each six-month period.

The reform was implemented in early 1996. The targeted gains in productivity and reductions in absenteeism were achieved during the first six months. Moreover, the incentive award payout for the first six months came to nearly $400 per worker in the participating unit.

This example illustrates that it is possible to move from highly specialized work to multitasking, provided that incentives are adjusted simultaneously.

Based on the facts from: Sam T. Johnson, "High Performance Work Teams: One Firm's Approach to Team Incentive Pay," *Compensation & Benefit Review* 28 (September/October 1996): 47–50.

there is a tendency for a worker to put the project off for some time. Even when setup time is minimal, the proclivity to procrastinate implies that passing a project around slows completion.

Which Tasks Go Together?

Besides determining the number of tasks that should be placed together in a single job, it is important to determine which tasks should go together. There are a number of considerations that affect the grouping of tasks into jobs. A few are listed here.

1. *Supply considerations.* Sometimes the skills necessary to perform one task allow a worker to perform a related task. For example, a tax accountant who knows enough tax law to file a complicated income tax return also may know enough to give a client advice on minimizing tax liability for the following year. This is why tax accountants often suggest investment vehicles to their clients at the time taxes are filed. When the opposite holds, multitasking becomes very costly. This is why we do not often see the school nurse doubling as the handyman. Although neither task alone necessarily occupies all of a worker's time, the requisite skills are so different that multitasking is infeasible.

   To the extent that tasks are to be put together into one job, it is necessary that the job holder have the skills to perform all of the tasks in the bundle. Plumbers do not also know the intricacies of electrical systems so one worker is rarely assigned the tasks of installing both plumbing and electrical wiring in a new house. Instead, a plumber may be assigned the tasks of putting in faucets and running water pipe to the laundry room. The skills involved in doing those tasks are more likely to be common and the individual who knows how to do one of the tasks is likely to know how to do the other.

As a task becomes more complicated and the knowledge base grows, less diverse tasks can be grouped together. Aristotle was philosopher, sociologist, political scientist, and economist all rolled into one. Today, the fields are sufficiently developed and the literatures sufficiently vast that it would be extremely difficult for one person, even Aristotle, to grasp three or four subjects in depth.

2. *Tasks that are grouped together should generally be complements in production.* To be complements, the tasks must be able to be handled at the same time. Consider, for example, agricultural workers who are picking ripe fruit. It would be possible to split the picking task into two tasks. One individual could be a "spotter," determining which fruit are ready to be picked. After the spotter identifies the fruit, the picker could be given the task of actually picking it. But spotting and picking are complements. Once a worker has discovered which fruit needs to be picked, the time increment associated with picking it is relatively minor.

Another example involves repair work. It is usually the case that the individual who diagnoses the problem also does the repair. The washing machine repairman who finds the problem in an inoperative washing machine is well situated to fix it. He could simply describe the problem to another worker who would then carry out the repair, but this would cause duplication of effort. Discovering the problem generally requires taking the machine apart. Once the worker is at the site and has gotten the machine apart, fixing it is almost minor. To pass the repair to someone else would require an additional trip and more setup time.

When repairs are complicated, work is passed on to another worker. For example, when a car requires major body work, one person usually appraises the damage, determines what needs to be done, and estimates the cost of the repair. Another worker or group of workers carry out the repair. The diagnosis and repair are split because the repair is a very complicated procedure and because diagnosis and repair are not complementary. Knowing what needs to be done is only the first of many steps toward getting the work completed. But when repairs are relatively straightforward, the individual who discovers the problem fixes it.

To put it somewhat differently, when tasks are close complements in production, setup costs are saved by putting the tasks together. In the bodyshop example, the setup for doing the work is almost completely distinct from the setup from diagnosing the work, so little is saved by putting the tasks together.

3. *Monitoring Difficulties.* Sometimes, putting tasks together will induce a worker to focus on one task and to ignore another. For example, a worker who is assigned to sell products and also to develop good customer relations, might fo-

cus on the former and ignore the latter. Since selling is more easily observed than developing customer relations and since firms tend to pay for selling directly, grouping these tasks together may cause the worker to sacrifice one for the other. An alternative is simply to pay the worker for hours worked, but then the benefit of performance pay on sales work is lost. By splitting the tasks up, the firm may do better.[4]

In summary, fewer tasks should be grouped together when the firm is large, when individuals possess highly specialized skills, when the occupation is mature and there are many individuals outside the firm who can perform the required tasks, and when communication and setup costs are low. Conversely, tasks that are complements in production, able to be performed by the same individual because of skill overlap, and that do not have different levels of monitorability should be grouped together.

Other Ways to Think About Jobs

The Job as a Wage

Although most personnel analysts think of jobs in terms of tasks performed, there are other ways to think of jobs. Perhaps the second most important definition of the job is that it is a salary category. Consider the typical management consulting firm. There may be a number of jobs, typical titles being *associate*, *senior associate*, *partner*, and *principal*. The tasks performed by the individuals might be very similar. Certainly, associates and senior associates do the same things. Both service clients and both attempt to generate business. The difference between the two positions relates primarily to salary. Senior associates earn more than associates and may have more experience in the business, although this is not a necessary component. In this case, the job is essentially a name for a salary grade.

The same is true in the federal government pay structure. "General schedule" workers are assigned a grade and step. For example, a GS-11, step 2, earns more than a GS-11, step 1. The job of an 11, step 2, might be identical to that of an 11, step 1, but the salaries are different. If we define the job by its grade and step, then the difference between jobs relates to salary, not to tasks.

If the job is thought of as a salary slot, then the tournament model of chapter 9 becomes relevant. The difference between the salary of the next job and current salary motivate the worker to obtain a promotion. When motivation seems to be lacking, more intermediate positions can be created with lower salaries for the starting positions and higher salaries for positions obtained after promotion. In designing a job, not only is it necessary to think about tasks, it is also important to remember that the job fits into a hierarchy. Salary level and the probability of being promoted into the job are important determinants of effort.

---

[4]See Baker (1992) and Hölmstrom and Milgrom (1991).

The Job as an Opportunity for Training

Every job has some training component associated with it. In some jobs the training component is high; in other jobs it is virtually nonexistent. For example, the job of dishwasher differs from that of beginning cook, not only in that the tasks are different. The beginning cook's job is likely to have much more opportunity for human capital acquisition than the dishwasher's job. The amount a worker can learn on the job and whether the training is general or firm-specific are important considerations for most workers when taking a job.

Indeed, much of the discussion about discrimination in the labor market depends directly on the learning aspect of a job. In one recent lawsuit, supermarkets were accused of channeling women into jobs that offered little training and therefore little chance of promotion, while their male counterparts were placed in jobs that offered exposure to a larger segment of the business. Even if the promotion criterion were then applied in a gender-neutral fashion, men would tend to be promoted more simply because they held more of the learning jobs.

Learning opportunities are important, and job applicants take learning opportunities into account in selecting a job. A firm that designs a job such that new workers can acquire training will find it easier to hire workers. To the extent that ability and desire to learn are positively correlated, a firm that designs jobs that offer more opportunity to learn will also attract the most talented individuals.

The Job, Authority, and Responsibility

Job titles also define authority and hierarchical relations with a firm. The job title may imply something about who reports to whom, and it may also determine the amount of responsibility that an individual is given. The military provides the best example of job titles as positions of authority.

In the U.S. Army, the lowest position is denoted "private." Corporals, and then sergeants have authority over these lowest level soldiers. Sergeants report to lieutenants, who in turn report to captains. Captains are below majors, who are themselves below lieutenant colonels and colonels. Generals are at the top of this hierarchy, and the number of stars that a general wears determines his rank among generals.

There are a number of reasons for having a strict hierarchy in the military. The most obvious is that in combat situations decisions must be made quickly. Deciding by committee is slow and highly impractical in the throes of battle. Thus, a clear hierarchy is set up in which orders to subordinates are obeyed without question or delay.

Very few firms are engaged in the kind of production that requires split-second decisions with absolute deference to higher authority. But there are some business situations that do fit into this category. When a deal is being discussed with another firm or with a client, a team may be involved in the negotiations. Still, one member must speak for the team and must have the authority to make the decision.

When jobs are designed, it is generally important to determine the level of authority associated with the job and how much responsibility is assigned to any given job. More often than not, the authority and responsibility associated with a given job depends on the job holder. Some vice presidents have more authority than other vice presidents, the difference presumably determined by ability differences.

A firm also has a great deal of leeway with respect to the ways in which it sets up authoritarian relations. For example, it is possible to have a flatter organization in which each individual has more authority over which projects are approved and which are rejected. Alternatively, a firm can be set up with a very steep authoritarian pyramid, where each level has the ability to veto decisions made by another level. Whether jobs are designed with flat or steep authority structures depends on the costs of rejecting good projects relative to the costs of accepting poor ones.[5] In statistical parlance, the issue is one of trading off false positive (Type I) versus false negative (Type II) error.

To make this more concrete, consider the case of a firm trying to decide whether to move into a new product line. Let me draw on an example provided by a former student in the women's apparel business. Singaporeans Gladys and Willie run a New York–based firm that imports women's lingerie and sleepwear. They describe themselves as having a "young and funky" image. In Summer 1995, Gladys needed to decide whether to branch out into more romantic lingerie. Doing so required some up-front investment in marketing, distribution and, most significantly, in producing the line of clothes. Major losses would occur if the line did not sell as hoped. She had to decide between going into the romantic lingerie line or forgoing the opportunity. There are two types of errors that she could have made. She might have moved into the line when doing so was unprofitable, or she could have decided not to produce the line when doing so was profitable. Table 16.1 lists the possibilities.

If she produces lingerie and it turns out to be unprofitable, then she has committed a **false positive** error. False positive error is defined as accepting a project that is bad. If she chooses not to produce lingerie and the line turns out to be profitable, then she has made a **false negative** error. False negative error is defined as rejecting a project that is good.

There is a trade-off between false positive and false negative error. If Gladys adopts a very aggressive policy and accepts every new project that comes by, she will never commit a false negative error. Because she always produces, she can never find herself in the box where she decided not to produce, but should have. However, she is certain to make false positive errors whenever a project is unprofitable. Since she always produces, she commits a false positive error when producing is a bad decision.

Alternatively, she can adopt an extremely conservative posture, rejecting every new project that comes along. Because she never produces a new line, she can never find herself in the box where she produced, but shouldn't have. She never commits a false positive error, but now false negative errors are certain. Whenever

---

[5]Sah and Stiglitz (1986) model this choice.

TABLE 16.1
THE ROMANTIC LINGERIE DECISION

	Produces *Romantic Lingerie*	*Does not Produce* *Romantic Lingerie*
Line is profitable	Good decision	False negative error
Line is unprofitable	False positive error	Good decision

a new product would have been profitable, she commits a false negative error because she never accepts it. The more conservative her posture, the lower the likelihood of a false positive error and the higher the likelihood of a false negative error.

Figure 16.1 shows the trade-off. On the horizontal axis is the probability of making a false positive error—that is, going ahead with the project when it is unprofitable. On the vertical axis is the probability of making a false negative error—that is, rejecting the project when it is profitable. At point *D* all projects are accepted, so the probability of accepting a project given that it is unprofitable is 1 and bad projects are accepted with certainty. At point *C* all projects are rejected, so the probability of rejecting a project given that it is profitable is 1 and good projects are rejected with certainty. The trade-off is shown by the solid line between *C* and *D*. If some projects are accepted and some are rejected, then the firm ends up at an interior point, like *A*. At *A*, some, but not all, good projects are rejected, and some, but not all, bad projects are accepted. How does the firm decide which rule to choose? If it is very costly to accept bad projects, the firm wants a more stringent rule, which moves it toward *C*. If it is very costly to pass up a good project, then the firm wants a more lenient rule, pushing it toward *D*.

FIGURE 16.1
ERROR TRADE-OFFS
AND JOB STRUCTURE

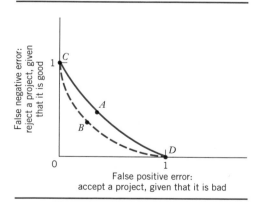

The goal is to enhance the information set so as to allow for fewer errors of each type. If decisions were better informed, then the trade-off would be along the dotted curve rather than the solid one. Note that on the dotted curve, the firm can make less of each type of error. Point B implies less false positive error and less false negative error than point A. The firm would always prefer the dotted curve to the solid curve, but for one thing: information is costly. Decisions are better along the dotted curve, but the cost of obtaining the dotted curve might be more delay or more consulting fees.

We now return to job design and authority patterns. By structuring the authority relations in different ways, different kinds of errors are made more or less likely. We consider these structures.

A hierarchical structure allows a worker to reject any project, but does not give her the authority to accept any project on her own. All that she can do is render a recommendation to accept. Her superior may then be given the authority to make the final call. Such a structure works in the direction of reducing false positive error and increasing false negative error. Workers cannot autocratically accept a project, so they cannot make a false positive error. Workers never accept bad projects because only superiors have that authority, but the rule does allow workers to reject projects. This means that they may reject good projects before their superiors get the opportunity to reverse the decision, which increases the likelihood of false negative error.

The second structure, called a flat authority structure, results in a different combination of errors than under a hierarchical structure. To see this, consider a two-worker firm, with workers Case and Moore. The flat firm is set up such that both Case and Moore evaluate projects and then choose whether to accept or to reject individually. The hierarchical firm has Moore evaluate all projects first, rendering a recommendation to Case. Case either accepts or rejects Moore's recommendation. Although Case is the final decision maker, Moore's input influences the decision.

The hierarchical firm has a different decision structure than the flat firm. In the flat firm, both Case and Moore do full reviews on projects. In the hierarchical firm, Case does not review a project until Moore has already reviewed it. This means that fewer projects get full reviews than in a flat firm, but those projects that do get positive reviews from Moore get a second review from Case. Which structure is better?

It is easy to show formally (see the appendix) that a hierarchical structure will approve fewer projects than a flat decision structure. The hierarchical structure makes fewer false positive errors, but more false negative errors. Fewer bad projects are accepted by the hierarchical firm, but more good projects are rejected. There are two reasons. First, since the hierarchical structure requires two approvals rather than one, the test that a project must pass is more stringent. Second, since two persons are required for an evaluation rather than one, fewer decisions are made. Case and Moore, working in parallel, can evaluate more projects than each can alone.

If every project must be evaluated by Moore before it goes to Case, then half as many projects get an initial screening. Thus, fewer projects are approved. Implicit here is that the failure to review a project is a rejection, by definition. All projects that are not reviewed are rejected. Presumably, some initial screening occurs before a project is even reviewed seriously. The bottom line is that a hierarchical decision structure, where low-level jobs are denied the authority to make the final decision on a project, results in a more stringent criterion and fewer project approvals than does a flat, egalitarian authority structure.

There is a third possibility. The structure can be made flat with second opinions required. Rather than putting Case above Moore, the firm can simply require that every project reviewed by Case is also reviewed by Moore, and vice versa. If both agree, the decision is obvious. If they disagree, then some other rule must be used to reconcile the differences. There are a number of possibilities, but for our purposes, the details of reconciliation are irrelevant. It is always true, irrespective of the reconciliation rule used, that a second opinion structure is less stringent than a hierarchical structure, but more stringent than a single opinion flat structure. Formal derivations are contained in the appendix.

Although both structures review the same number of projects, the second opinion structure is less stringent and approves more projects than the hierarchical structure. Under the hierarchical structure, when Moore rejects a project, Case never even sees it. Case only sees those projects that Moore passes on. In the case of a second opinion structure, Case sees even projects that Moore rejects. If Case likes the project, then the two opinions must be reconciled. As long as some of these reconciliations result in positive outcomes, projects that would not have been accepted by the hierarchical structure will be accepted by the second opinion structure.

The second opinion structure is more stringent than a flat, single decision maker structure. This is somewhat less obvious than it seems. It is true that a second opinion can sometimes reverse an initial decision to reject, but it is also true that a second opinion can reverse an initial decision to accept. The main reason that a second opinion structure is more stringent is that when second opinions are required, more projects are rejected without a serious screening at all. If it takes, say, a week for one person to review a project, then the flat structure with a single decision maker produces two decisions per week: one by Moore and one by Case. By contrast, the second opinion structure produces only one decision per week, since both Moore and Case must review every proposal. During week one, Moore reviews project A and Case reviews project B. During week two, they switch. By the end of the two-week period, only two projects have been reviewed by both managers, meaning that one project per week is reviewed. Projects that are not reviewed are rejected, by definition. The flat structure results in half the rejections by failure to review and thereby is a less stringent criterion. The flat structure increases the likelihood of making false positive errors, but decreases the likelihood of making false negative errors. Figure 16.2 augments Figure 16.1 by showing the locations of the different job authority structures with respect to false positive and false negative errors. Hierarchical structures locate on the northwestern part of the trade-off curve. Hierarchical structures minimize the likelihood of accepting a project that is bad, but maximize the likelihood of passing on a project that is

FIGURE 16.2
JOB AUTHORITY
STRUCTURE AND ERRORS

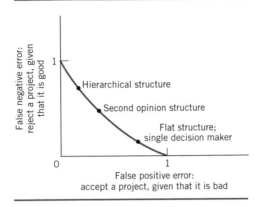

good. Flat structures with single decision makers lie in the southeast section of the trade-off curve. Flat structures minimize the likelihood that a good project will be rejected, but maximize the chances that a bad project will be accepted. Second opinion structures lie somewhere in the middle, neither minimizing nor maximizing the likelihood of false positive or false negative errors.

Which job authority structure should the firm choose? Since there is a trade-off implicit in the choice, the decision on which authority structure to use depends on the payoffs associated with the job. Since three structures are identified, let us consider three types of payoff regimes.[6] These are shown in Figures 16.3, 16.4, and 16.5.

Small Upside, Large Downside

Figure 16.3 shows a payoff structure that might be appropriate for the *Exxon Valdez*. As the reader may recall, a few years ago, a large oil tanker, the *Exxon Valdez*, was involved in an accident that caused a major oil spill for which Exxon was financially responsible. The losses associated with the oil spill ran into the billions of dollars in cleanup, litigation, and settlement costs. The captain of the ship was blamed for the accident, and there was evidence that alcohol was in part to blame.

The *Exxon Valdez* situation is typical of one variety of payoff structure. Doing the job extremely well results in small gains relative to the expected amount, but making a mistake can be disastrous. The upside of payoffs is limited to $100,000, but the downside implies losses in the billions.

The *Exxon's* captain makes more profit for the company by bringing the oil shipment in somewhat early, but trying to guide the ship while under the influence of al-

---

[6]Baron and Kreps (1998) classify jobs as *guardian*, *star*, and *footsoldier*.

FIGURE 16.3
PAYOFF REGIME 1: EXXON VALDEZ

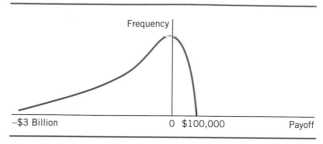

cohol to save time is not worth the risk. A mistake is just too costly. When the payoff structure looks as it does in Figure 16.3, the firm wants to minimize false positive error and is willing to accept higher levels of false negative error. Think of the "project" in this case as deciding whether to proceed before being sober, which reduces the expected time to port. "Waiting to sober up when proceeding would not have resulted in an accident" is classified as a false negative error. "Proceeding while intoxicated when proceeding results in a crash" is false positive error. Because a false positive error is so costly, the firm should adopt a structure that minimizes it. The earlier discussion, as summarized by Figure 16.2, implies that the firm should use a hierarchical job structure in this case. The captain should not, and likely did not, have the authority to proceed before being completely sober. Had he radioed in for approval, the company would likely have denied permission to proceed, reducing the likelihood of false positive error. The hierarchical structure, properly used, would have reduced the chance of the large, false positive error.

Large Upside, Small Downside

Figure 16.4 has a payoff function with a big upside and limited downside. This corresponds to new firms. Most of the time new firms fail, producing negative or only slightly positive profit levels. Once every so often, as is the case with

FIGURE 16.4
PAYOFF REGIME 2: NETSCAPE

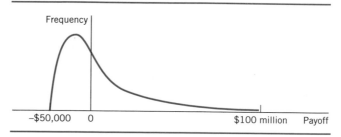

FIGURE 16.5
PAYOFF REGIME 3: PORTOLA VALLEY SHELL

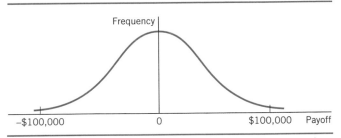

Netscape, the innovators hit it big, earning many millions of dollars. Which structure favors the upside? The answer, summarized in Figure 16.2, is that a flat structure with very little supervisory veto power minimizes the amount of false negative error. The start-up firm does not want to be too cautious. It has little reputation or capital to lose. It is better to take chances. Those that do not pan out can be abandoned without much harm to the firm, since the firm has little to lose in the first place.

Young firms often do give a great deal of authority to individual workers. It is sometimes argued that creative people do not do well in hierarchical firms. Although true, the problem may not be that different types of people go to different types of firms. It may have more to do with the decision rules used in a given structure. Since a hierarchical structure tends to err in the direction of minimizing false positive error, tolerating the rejection of some good projects, a hierarchical firm does not encourage creativity. Flatter authority structures, which allow each worker more choice, also allow creativity to flourish. Risky, wild ideas that would be rejected in a hierarchical structure are allowed to proceed in the flat, single decision maker structure.

DILBERT reprinted by permission of United Feature Syndicate, Inc.

It is often said that IBM is stodgy, adopting a rigid, hierarchical structure, whereas newer companies in the industry are much more flexible. This is completely rational. IBM has a valuable reputation, which, if lost, would imply a huge cost to the firm. As such, IBM may adopt something closer to the *Exxon Valdez*–style payoff structure. There is an upside, to be sure, but the downside is enormous. A new company in the same industry probably has little to lose by mistakes and would therefore be likely to adopt a structure resembling that of Netscape. It is not surprising, therefore, that Apple, when starting out, had a much looser structure than IBM. It was rational for Apple to be nonhierarchical, just as it was rational for IBM to be hierarchical. In hindsight, either strategy might have been a mistake, but at the time the structures were chosen, both were probably correct, given the distinct circumstances of each company.

Symmetric Payoffs

Most firms are neither in the *Exxon Valdez* category nor in the Netscape category. Payoffs are more symmetric in most businesses, especially established ones. Figure 16.5 shows a suggested payoff function for a gasoline station in my town. Great performance and innovative work are unlikely to generate the large upside that Netscape experienced. Poor performance and shoddy workmanship may cost the firm some money, but not the disastrous losses incurred by Exxon when the oil spill occurred. In this case, the firm prefers tolerable levels of false positive error and false negative error, minimizing neither at the expense of the other. In the service station example, a mechanic who is uncertain about a particular automobile's problem asks his fellow mechanic for a "second opinion," but the setup tends to be nonhierarchical. Joe asks Steve for a second opinion and Steve asks Joe for a second opinion. Neither Joe nor Steve has veto power over the other's decision. They work together as a team.

Investing in Information

In Figure 16.1 two curves were shown. The dotted curve lies inside the solid curve. Others things equal, it is better to face the constraint of the dotted curve than that of the solid curve because for any given level of false positive error, the dotted curve implies less false negative error than does the solid curve (except at the endpoints). How does the firm move to the dotted curve?

Unfortunately, this cannot be done without cost. Fewer errors are made along the dotted curve than on the solid curve. To get to the dotted curve, it is necessary to improve the decision process. There are a number of possibilities, all of which are costly. First, the firm can attempt to hire better evaluators by going for more able, higher priced workers. Second, the firm can allow any given evaluator to take more time evaluating each project. Third, the firm can make more information available to the evaluator by either hiring outside consultants or buying other services. Whether any of these steps is profitable depends on how much is gained relative to the amount lost by making poor decisions.

An Application: Air Traffic Routes

To make this specific, consider the following numerical example. An airline pilot is trying to decide whether to take a quicker route through thunderstorms or a safer but lengthier route around the storms. Some hypothetical information about thunderstorms is given in Table 16.2.

What is the firm to do? If a plane crash occurs, the firm will incur a cost of $1 billion from capital loss, reputational loss, higher insurance rates, and litigation costs. Since this is a case that fits the *Exxon Valdez* payoff structure, the firm might set up a hierarchy, but here the situation is somewhat different. The pilot is more likely to care about his own life than about the profitability of the firm. To offset his tendency to be too conservative, the airline might make a rule dictating that pilots take the shortest route unless they receive approval from the company to deviate. Then, when faced with thunderstorms, the pilot radios in to request the longer, more costly route. The company can approve the longer route, or deny permission for the longer route, in which case the pilot flies through the storm.

Given the probability and payoff structure shown in Table 16.2, the airline would always approve the pilot's request to take the longer route. If the pilot flies through the storm, the expected cost is

$$(.00001)(\$1 \text{ billion}) + \$17,000 = \$27,000$$

The first term reflects the probability of a crash, given that the pilot flies through the storm, times the loss to the company from a crash. The $17,000 is the fuel cost. If the pilot takes the longer route, the expected cost is

$$(.000000001)(\$1 \text{ billion}) + \$20,000 = \$20,001$$

The first term reflects the probability of a crash, given that the longer route is chosen, times the cost to the company of a crash. The $20,000 reflects the (higher) fuel cost associated with the longer route. The expected cost of the longer route is lower than the expected cost of flying through the storm when accident costs are taken into account. Thus, the company always grants permission to take the longer route. Since it will always grant permission when asked, there is no sense having pilots call in for approval. Under these circumstances, the pilot is given full authority to select a longer route when there are thunderstorms along the shorter route.

TABLE 16.2
THUNDERSTORMS AND AIRPLANE TRAVEL

	Probability of Crash	Cost of Crash	Expected Cost of Crash	Expected Fuel Cost of Trip
Go through storm	.00001	$1 billion	$10,000	$17,000
Go around storm	.000000001	$1 billion	$1	$20,000

Note that the probability of committing a false positive error is zero. Since the shorter route is never taken, there is no chance that the short route will be taken when it would have resulted in a crash. Conversely, the probability of committing a false negative error is one. It is certain that the shorter route through thunderstorms will be rejected even when going through the storm would not have resulted in a crash because the shorter route is always rejected.

Now suppose that the company can buy some additional information. Suppose that a new device, The Forecaster, can more accurately forecast lightning strikes. By doing this, it can offer a recommendation on when it is safe to fly through the storm and when it is not. Table 16.3 provides statistics on the accuracy of The Forecaster.

The Forecaster recommends that the route through the storm be taken 9,999/10,000 times. The probability of a crash, given a positive recommendation, is only 1 in 100 million (.00000001). However, when The Forecaster recommends that the storm be avoided, going against the advice will result in a crash in one in ten times (.1). The Forecaster provides very accurate information that allows much better decisions to be made.

If the device is used, the optimal decision from the company's point of view changes. Whereas before, the company always preferred that storms be avoided, now the company would prefer that the shorter route be taken whenever The Forecaster recommends so. Under a positive recommendation, the expected cost of a trip is

$$(.00000001)(\$1 \text{ billion}) + \$17,000 = \$17,010$$

The first term reflected the expected loss from a crash and the second term reflecting the fuel costs associated with the shorter route. Under a negative recommendation, the expected cost of the trip is

$$(.1)(\$1 \text{ billion}) + \$17,000 = \$100,017,000$$

Taking the longer route around the storm has, as reported above, an expected trip cost of

$$(.000000001)(\$1 \text{ billion}) + \$20,000 = \$20,001$$

TABLE 16.3
THE FORECASTER ACCURACY

Recommendation	Probability of Crash if Proceed Through Storm
Proceed through storm (Recommended .9999 of the time)	.00000001
Go around storm (Recommended .0001 of the time)	.1

Thus, the company would prefer that the shorter route be taken whenever The Forecaster makes a positive recommendation (since $17,010 is less than $20,001), but that the longer route be taken whenever The Forecaster makes a negative recommendation (since $100,017,000 exceeds $20,001).

Two questions arise. First, should the firm purchase The Forecaster? Second, what kind of job authority structure should be used if The Forecaster is purchased?

The answer to the first question depends on the cost of The Forecaster and on its frequency of usage. Suppose that the machine costs $1 million and is expected to last for about five years. Each year, the airline in question expects to have 10,000 flights that would otherwise be diverted around a thunderstorm area. If The Forecaster is not purchased, recall that the optimal decision, from both the company's and pilot's point of view, is to divert around the storm. The expected cost of these 10,000 trips would then be

$$10,000 \, (\$20,001) = \$200,010,000$$

because each trip that goes around the storm has an expected cost of $20,001. If The Forecaster is used, then .9999 of the 10,000 flights would be sent through the storm and .0001 would be diverted. In other words, it is expected that 9,999 flights would go through the storm, and 1 would be diverted around. For the 9,999, the expected cost would be

$$9999 \, (\$17,010) = \$170,082,990$$

because the expected cost of a flight through the storm, given that The Forecaster makes a positive recommendation, is $17,010. For the one flight that diverts, the expected cost is $20,001, also given earlier. The total cost of flights using The Forecaster is then

$$\$170,082,990 + 20,001 = \$170,102,991$$

The saving from using The Forecaster is therefore

$$\$200,010,000 - \$170,102,991 = \$29,907,009$$

Since The Forecaster costs only $1 million, the machine pays for itself almost 30 times over in just one year of operation. The answer to the first question is a definite yes. The machine should be purchased. It pays to shift the false positive–false negative curve in to the dotted one shown in Figure 16.1. The savings associated with error reduction far outweigh the costs.

The second question relates to the authority structure of jobs. Without The Forecaster, each pilot could be left to choose his or her own route. Because the pilot's incentives and those of the firm are aligned, both would choose to take the longer route around the storm. With The Forecaster, the situation is different. The airline prefers that the shorter route through the storm is taken 99.99 percent of the time. The pilot may have a different view. First, the likelihood of a crash when The Forecaster recommends that the short route be taken is 1 in 100 million. If the longer route is taken, the likelihood of a crash is 1 in 1 billion. Both numbers are small, but the former is still ten times as great as the latter. Other things equal, the pilot prefers the lower odds of a crash and chooses the longer route, even though the shorter route is more cost-effective. Second, crashes aside, it may be more difficult to fly through thunderstorms than to divert. Both of these considerations suggest that the pilot might not make the same decision that the company would make. Finally, since there is only one Forecaster per company, it may be necessary, simply as a technical matter, to radio in for instructions.[7] Pilots, on their own, choose too safe a route. This is analogous to setting speed limits of five miles per hour. Highways would be much safer, but society is not willing to give up the time and resources to obtain the additional safety. Reducing the authority of the pilot costs the firm in higher wages. The point of chapter 11 was that there is a trade-off between nonpecuniary job characteristics and wages. To the extent that authority is desired by pilots, and to the extent that pilots must be compensated for the additional danger, wages of pilots are higher under a hierarchy than under a flat structure. But since the change in probability of an accident is so small, it is unlikely that the additional wage costs would be significant enough to reverse either the decision to buy The Forecaster or the decision to switch to a hierarchical structure.

If the logic of the previous paragraphs holds, then the authority structure would have to change when The Forecaster is purchased. Without The Forecaster, a flat structure where the pilot makes the route decision works fine. With The Forecaster, the firm prefers a hierarchical structure, where the pilot must request permission to divert around the storm and where the airline has the right to refuse permission. Without The Forecaster, there is no danger of the pilot erring in the direction of too much safety. But The Forecaster makes flying through storms so much safer that the pilot may be inclined to choose too safe a route. The pilot's decision must be reviewed by a superior.[8]

The previous example makes an additional point. The hierarchical structure that is optimal when the firm is constrained to use poorer-quality information is not necessarily the same as the structure that is optimal when the firm can use higher quality information. The risk of crashing, though small, is too great. With The Forecaster, the firm has the option of moving from C to D. While there is some slight increase in the risk of false negative error, there is a dramatic reduction in the amount of false positive error that occurs when the firm moves from C

[7]Modern technology might make it possible for pilots to access The Forecaster directly, without going through a human.

[8]At some level, the pilot's failure to internalize the company's decision rule reflects a failure in compensation policy. If the pilot were "charged" every time he chose the longer route, he could be induced to make the same decision that the company would make. But the price that the pilot is charged must be set appropriately. Too high a price pushes the pilot toward recklessness. Too low a price causes him to be too cautious. Furthermore, were the details of this scheme made known, a major public relations problem could arise. Passengers might not be happy to learn that their pilots take a pay cut whenever they choose the safest route.

to D. Since the pilot always chooses to divert, reversal by the company most of the time is in the best interests of the company.

FIT THE PERSON TO THE JOB OR THE JOB TO THE PERSON?   ◆ ◆ ◆ ◆ ◆

It is obvious that individuals are heterogeneous, not only in their abilities, but also in their talents. Albert Einstein may have been the most important physicist of the century, but it is unlikely he could ever be the century's best basketball player, no matter how much time he spent shooting hoops. When a person is hired to fit a particular job, the firm hopes that it is getting a worker who is able to perform the tasks that are required. What if the worker is not suited for the job? Then the person must be fired, or another job in the firm must be found for which the person is suited.

Once again, a sports metaphor may prove useful. A professional football team that is looking for a new player can, at one extreme, draft the best athlete, irrespective of the position he played in college. Alternatively, the team can limit itself to one position, say, quarterback, and draft the best college quarterback available.

Three factors are important in deciding whether a firm should follow the "draft the best athlete" rule or should select someone to fill a specific position. The first relates to observability of skills at the time of hire. At one extreme, the firm may not be able to assess a worker's skills before she actually works in the firm. If all individuals looked alike at the time of hire, it would be impossible to hire a person for any given job. The job would have to be designed or selected to fit the person, not the other way around. The alternative would be to hire a large number of individuals and fire most of them, keeping only the rare few who fit. Under most circumstances, the costs of this strategy are prohibitive. When talent is difficult to observe before the hire, the firm is more likely to fit the job to the person than the person to the job. When talent is easily identified at the time of hire, it is possible to hire a person for a more specific position.

The second factor is whether skills are general or task-specific. If a person who is good at X is unlikely to be good at Y, then it will be tougher to fit the job to the person. When individuals have skills that allow them to perform multiple tasks, hiring the best athlete and simply fitting the job to the person is a better strategy. Underlying heterogeneity is key. Skills are more general when the applicant pool is homogeneous. When the pool is very heterogeneous, it is more important to hire workers to fit the position.

The third factor that affects the choice between best athlete or position-based hiring is the variety of the positions available. A large company that has many open positions can afford to hire the "best athlete." The large company is likely to find a place where a talented person can be productive. Thus, the large company can fit the job to the person, rather than the person to the job. A small company, on the other hand, must worry much more about fit. Small firms perform a more limited number of tasks and find it more difficult to find a job to fit any given talented worker.

Small firms are more likely to fit workers to jobs than jobs to workers. In a large firm, jobs can be found for a heterogeneous group of workers because there are many tasks that need to be performed and a significant number of workers are moving into and out of the various jobs each month. In a small firm, workers are hired for a specific task or set of tasks. This often leads to frustration on the part of workers. As workers acquire skills, they like their jobs to change to accommodate improved skills, but the small firm cannot accommodate them. Since there are only a limited number of tasks to be performed, and since others are already performing those tasks, there is not much flexibility within the small firm's environment. The only way for the worker who has acquired skills to make use of those skills is to move to another firm. This generally happens to workers who start with small firms. Unless the firm grows, most workers who become more able than appropriate for their current job move on to other firms.

The fact that workers must leave a small firm in order to use their acquired skills is not necessarily a defect of small firms. Small firms may be particularly good environments for learning, but less good for making use of the learned skills. Larger firms may not be as good for learning, but mobility for good, but undiscovered workers is likely to be better in large firms. For this reason, workers who believe that they are diamonds-in-the-rough and have an aversion to changing jobs often are better off going to large firms than to small ones.

Stability over Time

Many jobs change with time. Whether a job changes with time depends in part on whether jobs are fitted to the individual or individuals are fitted to the job. If jobs are fitted to the individual, then it is almost certain that the job will change over time. Since individuals acquire skills as they acquire experience, the number and types of tasks that an individual can perform will change. Consider, for example, the case of a secretary. When she first starts a job, she usually knows very little about the firm or the people for whom she is working. As she acquires firm-specific information, she is able to perform more tasks and even teach others how to perform those tasks.

At the other extreme are jobs that are very narrow and well-defined, limited to only a few very specific tasks. Unskilled farm labor fits this category. If a worker becomes sufficiently skilled at picking grapes, he may be promoted to foreman. The worker changes job position, but the position does not change to fit the worker's new talents.

Change the Managers

In some situations, job changes can be dramatic because the nature of the business changes. Under these circumstances, it is almost always necessary to change managers. Changing the type and direction of motivation may do some good, but it will generally not suffice. The main reason comes from the logic above. Individuals who were well matched to the old environment are very unlikely to be well matched to the new environment.

A large literature attests to the value of changing a manager. When a CEO dies during his or her tenure, the firm's stock price tends to rise. This reflects the market's belief that new management will do good things for the company. Also, there are many notable cases of companies that have been turned around by bringing in a new CEO who replaces much of top management with new people. One recent example is Allied Signal, a large multiproduct manufacturer. The firm has had a great deal of success over the past few years following the hiring of Lawrence Bossidy as CEO. A number of internal changes were made, but cutting jobs and replacing the management team were important parts of the package.[9]

Finally, Barberis, Boycko, Shleifer and Tsukanova (1995) studied Russian firms after they underwent privatization. The change from state ownership to private ownership could, at least in theory, alter incentives in a dramatic way. They found, however, that unless the former managers were replaced by new managers, there was little gain in productivity following privatization. The largest gains were associated with changing the managers, perhaps because only the new managers were willing (or able) to institute the kinds of mechanisms that make a firm more productive in a private environment.

RECAP ◆ ◆ ◆ ◆ ◆

We began this chapter by raising a number of issues that relate to jobs per se. In prior chapters, not much was said about the job as a unit of analysis. While the tournament model has implicit in it some notion of jobs and their importance, *jobs* as defined by the tournament structure are essentially wage slots. In this chapter, richer notions of jobs were employed. Here, a primary focus was on tasks and authority. We began by discussing how tasks might be grouped together into a given job. We first asked how many tasks should be associated with any given job. Following Adam Smith, we concluded that jobs in smaller firms have more tasks associated with them than those in large firms . Furthermore, jobs contain fewer tasks when the relevant labor pool is smaller. Jobs are also narrower when the pool of labor from which the firm draws is more specialized and of higher quality.

Multiskilling and multitasking were considered. Multiskilling means that a given worker possesses enough skills to perform more than one job. Multitasking means that there are many tasks actually assigned to a given worker. The two are different, since a worker may know how to perform a number of tasks, even if the worker does not have to perform them in his or her current job. Multiskilling is

---

[9]After announced cuts of 6,100 jobs, many in management, record profits were posted. See Maynard (1996), *Aerospace Daily* (1996), DeMarrais (1996).

valuable because it provides flexibility, which is more important in a small firm than in a large one. Multitasking is most useful when transportation costs are large, when setup time is great, and when procrastination is an important problem.

Tasks are most likely to be grouped together when the individual who performs one task also has the skills to perform a related task and when tasks are complements in production so that the setup costs in going from one task to another are low.

Much of the chapter was spent discussing authority and how much of it should be assigned to each job. Three authority structures were considered: a flat structure, where the worker has a great deal of authority, a hierarchical structure, where a supervisor can veto the decisions of subordinates, and a second opinion structure, where there is no boss, but two individuals are involved in every decision.

We argued that the hierarchical structure resulted in the most conservative decision-making process, and that the flat structure resulted in the most lenient decision-making process. Firms with payoff structures that have big downside risks should use hierarchical structures, whereas those with big upside payoffs should use flat structures. Sometimes, it pays to attempt to reduce both kinds of decision-making errors (false positives and false negatives) by investing in more information or better screening. When this is done, the optimal authority structure is likely to change as well. Finally, a hierarchical structure is less likely to result in innovation because new ideas can be vetoed. A flat structure, which fosters creativity, also causes the firm to drill many dry holes because bad ideas go unchecked.

It is common to hire a worker for a specific job, but sometimes the job is fitted to the person. The latter is more likely to occur when skills are not easily observed before hire, when skills are very general and the applicant pool is homogeneous, and when the firm is large and can offer a large variety of positions.

Jobs tend to be more stable when the person is fitted to the job than when the reverse holds. This often leads to frustration and the departure of workers from small firms, because workers find that their jobs are not flexible enough to adjust to their newly acquired skills.

REFERENCES

Aerospace Daily, "Double-digit gains position Allied Signal for record 1996," v179 n. 17, July 25, 1996, p. 131.

Baker, George, "Incentive Contracts and Performance Measurement," *Journal of Political Economy* 100 (June 1992): 598–614.

Baron, James, and David Kreps, *Human Resources Management for the General Manager*, New York: JohnWiley and Sons, 1998.

Barberis, Nicholas, Maxim Boycko, Andrei Shleifer, and Natalia Tsukanova, "How Does Privatization Work? Evidence from the Russian Shops," *NBER Working Paper* #5136, May 1995.

Carmichael, H. Lorne, and Bentley MacLeod, "Multiskilling, Technical Change, and the Japanese Firm," *Quarterly Journal of Economics*, 107, (November, 1992): 1137–60.

DeMarrais, Kevin G., "Allied Stockholders Take Hats Off to Larry Bossidy Earns Praise, As Well As Big Salary," *The Record* (April 23, 1996): B1.

Hölmstrom, Bengt, and Paul Milgrom, "Multi-Task Principal-Agent Analyses: Incentive Contracts, Asset Ownership, and Job Design," *Journal of Law, Economics, & Organization* 7, special issue (1991): 24–52.

Orbay, Hakan, "Specialization in Education and Labor Market," unpublished doctoral dissertation, Stanford, 1996.

Maynard, Micheline, "Allied Signal chief: Outsourcing can be positive," *USA Today*, July 24, 1996, Final Edition, p 3B.

Sah, Raaj Kumar, and Joseph E. Stiglitz, "The Architecture of Economic Systems:Hierarchies and Polyarchies," *American Economic Review* 76 (September 1986): 716–27.

ADDITIONAL ADVANCED READING ◆ ◆ ◆ ◆ ◆

Ichniowski, Casey, et al., "The Effects of Human Resource Management Practices on Productivity," in Lewin, David, Olivia S. Mitchell, and Peter D. Sherer, eds., *1992 Research Frontiers in Industrial Relations and Human Resources*, IRRA Series (Madison: Industrial Relations Research Association, University of Wisconsin, 1992, pp. 239–71.

Kaplinsky, Raphael, "Restructuring and Capitalist Labour Process: Some Lessons from the Car Industry," *Cambridge Journal of Economics* 12 (December 1988): 451–70.

Lazear, Edward P., "The Job as a Concept," in William J. Bruns, Jr., ed. *Performance Measurement, Evaluation, and Incentives*, Boston: Harvard Business School Press, 1992, pp. 335–341.

Prendergast, Canice J., "A Theory of Responsibility in Organizations," *Journal of Labor Economics* 13 (July 1995): 387–400.

APPENDIX ◆ ◆ ◆ ◆ ◆

Jack of All Trades, Master of None

In this section, we show why it is very difficult for someone who excels in one area to be equally good in another area. It is common for someone who is pretty good at one thing to be also pretty good at another. It is rare for someone who is excellent in one activity to be excellent in another as well.

Consider two activities, singing and dancing. Dancing ability is given by M, which has density of $f(M)$ across the population. Singing ability is related to dancing ability, but not the same. Thus, write

(A16.1) $$\text{Singing ability} = M + S$$

where S is an individual's "singing-specific" ability beyond that is reflected in M. The density for S is $g(S)$. Distribution functions are $F(M)$, $G(S)$, respectively.

Let M and S be independent with $E(S) = 0$. Singing and dancing ability will be related because singing ability, $M + S$, depends on general musical talent, as reflected in M. Intuitively, those who are better-than-average dancers are also better than average singers. Denote $E(M)$ as $\overline{M}$.

Formally, this means:

$$E(M + S \mid M > \overline{M}) > E(M + S)$$

Proof:

$$E(M + S \mid M > \overline{M}) = E(M \mid M > \overline{M}) + E(S)$$

since M and S are independent. Again, using independence of M and S and the fact that $E(S) = 0$, we obtain

$$E(M + S) = E(M)$$

Also, since

$$E(M \mid M > \overline{M}) > E(M)$$

it follows that

$$E(M + S \mid M > \overline{M}) > E(M + S)$$

Those who are better-than-average dancers are better-than-average singers.

Consider, now, an exceptional dancer, say one who is in the top 1 percent. Denote this person as someone for whom $M > Q_{.99}$, where $Q_{.99}$ is the value of M at the 99th percentile of dancers.

What is the likelihood that such an individual will also be in the top 1 percent of singers?

To be in the top 1 percent of singers, it is necessary that

$$M + S > Z_{.99}$$

where $Z_{.99}$ is the value of $M + S$ at the 99 percent of singers. Thus, it is necessary to determine

(A16.2) $$Prob\ (M + S > Z_{.99} \mid M > Q_{.99})$$

The probability that $M + S$ exceeds any number Z is the probability that $M + S > Z$ or that $S > Z - M$.

The probability is given by the double integral.

$$Prob1(M + S > Z) = \int_{-\infty}^{\infty} \int_{Z-M}^{\infty} g(S)f(M)\ dS\ dM$$

(A16.3)

$$= \int_{-\infty}^{\infty} [1 - G(Z - M)]f(M)dM$$

To compute the conditional probability that $M + S > Z$ given that M exceeds some number Q, the following integral must be evaluated:

$$(A16.4) \quad Prob(M + S > Z | M > Q) = \frac{1}{1 - F(Q)} \int_Q^\infty \int_{Z-M}^\infty g(S)f(M)\, dS\, dM$$

The "jack-of-all-trades" proposition can be evaluated by using an example. Suppose that $f(M)$ is uniform discrete density $M = \{-1,0,1\}$ and S is a similar discrete density $= \{-1,0,1\}$.

The probability that M is in the top-third of M values is the probability that $M = 1$, which is one-third. What is the probability of $M + S$ being in the top-third of $M + S$ values, given that M is in the top-third of M values? Table A16.1 gives the values of $M + S$ for various values of M.

For $M + S$ to be in the top third of the values, $M + S$ must be greater than or equal to 1. (There are three cells of $M + S \geq 1$ out of nine cells.)

What is P(M1S\$1uM\$1)? It is two-thirds, because two out of the three occurrences of M\$1 also have M5S\$1. Bayes Theorem says

$$P(M + S \geq 1 | M \geq 1) = \frac{P(M + S \geq 1 \cap M \geq 1)}{P(M \geq 1)} = \frac{\sqrt[2]{3}}{\sqrt[3]{9}}$$

Compare this $\frac{2}{3}$ conditional probability to a less stringent criterion. Instead of asking about the probability of being in the top third, compute the conditional probability of being in the top $\frac{2}{3}$. This requires $M \geq 0$ and $M + S \geq 0$ because $\frac{2}{3}$ of the values of $M + S$ equal or exceed 0. As before, there are 6 cells where $M \geq 0$. Of those, 5 result in values of $M + S$ greater than or equal to 0. Thus, the conditional probability $P(M + S \geq 0 / M \geq 0) = \frac{5}{6}$.

Note that $\frac{5}{6} > \frac{2}{3}$. It is easier to be in the top $\frac{2}{3}$ of singers, given that a person is in the top $\frac{2}{3}$ of dancers than it is to be in the top $\frac{1}{3}$ of singers, given that a person is in the top $\frac{1}{3}$ of dancers out of 9 cells.

A somewhat more general example lets M be uniform on $[0, 1]$ with S uniform or

$$\left[-\frac{\alpha}{2}, \frac{\alpha}{2} \right] \qquad \text{with } \frac{\alpha}{2} > 1.$$

TABLE A16.1
VALUES OF $M + S$ FOR VALUES OF M, S

Value of M	Value of S		
	−1	0	1
−1	−2	−1	0
0	−1	0	1
1	0	1	2

Thus $G(Z - M)$ in (A16.3) becomes $\dfrac{1}{2} + \dfrac{Z - M}{\alpha}$

so

(A16.5)
$$Prob(M + S > Z_{.99}) = .01 = \int_0^1 \left\{ 1 - \left[\frac{1}{2} + \frac{Z_{.99} - M}{\alpha} \right] \right\} dm$$

$$= \frac{1}{2} - \frac{Z_{.99}}{\alpha} - \frac{1}{2\alpha}$$

Solving for $Z_{.99}$ yields

(A16.6)
$$Z_{.99} = .5 + .49\alpha$$

Then, from (A16.4.)

(A16.7)
$$Prob(M + S > Z_{.99} | M > Q_{.99}) = \frac{1}{.01} \int_{.99}^1 \left(1 - \left[\frac{1}{2} \frac{.5 + .49\alpha - M}{\alpha} \right] \right) dM$$

$$= .01 + \frac{.495}{\alpha}$$

The same calculation can be done for $Z_{.50}$ which equals .5. Using an expression analogous to (A16.7),

(A16.8)
$$Prob(M + S > Z_{.50} | M > Q_{.50}) = \frac{1}{.5} \int_{.5}^1 \left(1 - \left(\left[\frac{1}{2} + \frac{.5 - M}{\alpha} \right] \right) \right) dM$$

$$= .5 + \frac{.25}{\alpha}$$

There are two things to note. First, conditional probabilities decline with α. In both Equations A16.7 and A16.8, the value of the expression on the right-hand side decreases in α. When most of the variation in $M + S$ is due to S, the fact that M is higher is less important. Second, and most important,

$$Prob \, (M + S > Z_{.99} | M > Q_{.99}) < Prob \, (M + S > Z_{.50} | M > Q_{.50})$$

since

$$.5 + \frac{.25}{\alpha} > .01 + \frac{.495}{\alpha}$$

for $\alpha > \frac{1}{2}$ and $\alpha > 2$, by assumption.

This says that it is more likely that a good high school dancer who has $M > Q_{.50}$ is also in the top half of high school singers than it is that the top dancer in the town, with $M > Q_{.99}$ is also the top singer in the town, with $M + S > Z_{.99}$. Thus, it is very difficult to be the best at everything.

One additional point. The notion that a jack-of-all-trades is a master of none comes from another factor as well. Those who learn a little about everything do not have the time to specialize in anything. Investment in human capital exacerbates the tendency to see expertise confined to one field.

Flexibility Has Less Value in a Large Firm Than in a Small One

Flexibility has value when there is a good chance that a worker will not show up on a given day. Then, having others who know the job and can move into that task is valuable. But as the firm size gets large, this is less of a problem.

Let the probability that a worker comes to work on a given day be p. Workers stay home, then, with probability $(1 - p)$. If the firm has N workers, then the expected number of individuals who come to work on any given day is Np.
The variance in the number who come to work is

$$Np\,(1 - p)$$

so the standard deviation is

$$\sqrt{Np(1 - p)}$$

As N gets large, the binomial distribution approaches the Normal distribution. Given that the distribution approaches a Normal, 97.5 percent of the time the actual realized number of individuals who come to work exceeds

$$Np - 1.96\sqrt{Np(1 - p)}$$

This is so because the realizations of a Normal are greater than 1.96 standard deviations below the mean 97.5 percent of the time.

If the firm plans for a work force of Np workers, 97.5 percent of the time the firm will have at least

$$Np - 1.96\sqrt{Np(1 - p)}$$

on board. Thus, 97.5 percent of the time, the firm will have

$$Proportion = \frac{Np - 1.96\sqrt{Np(1 - p)}}{Np}$$

of the average number of workers working.

How does the proportion working vary with N? To find this simply differentiate the expression for proportion with respect to N which yields

$$\frac{\partial Proportion}{\partial N} = \frac{1.96\sqrt{1 - p}}{2\sqrt{pN^3}}$$

$$> 0$$

Thus, the proportion who come to work with 97.5 percent certainty rises with N.[10] Table A16.1 shows how the proportion who show up to work varies with N.

---

[10]The probability, 97.5 percent, is arbitrary. The same point holds for any chosen probability figure.

TABLE A16.1
MINIMUM NUMBER AND PROPORTION
OF WORKERS WHO COME TO WORK
97.5% OF THE TIME

N	z	Proportion
10	8.81	0.927
15	13.41	0.941
25	22.66	0.954
50	45.96	0.968
100	92.82	0.977
1000	943.11	0.993
5000	4734.59	0.997
10000	9478.21	0.998

The value $p = .95$, so any given worker shows up 19 out of 20 days. Column 1 reports the number of workers in the firm; column 2 reports the value z such that

$$\text{Prob (number of workers who come to work} \geq z) = .975$$

and column 3 reports the proportion of the firm that z comprises.

With $p = .95$ and 100 workers, 95 of them are expected to show up on any given day. But 97.5 percent of the time, at least 92.82 show up. This is a little more than two workers shy of the expected number of 95. It is also .977 of the expected number. If there were only 10 workers on board, 9.5 would be expected to show up.[11] Further, 97.5 percent of the time, at least 8.81 would show up, so the firm would be about .7 of a worker shy of the expected number. Note that 8.81 is .927 of 9.5. When the firm is as large as 10,000, 9,500 are expected to show on any given day and 97.5 percent of the time, at least 9478.21 workers show up. This is .998 of the expected number.

As the number of workers grows, the chance that the firm is going to end up very far below its expected number decreases. Therefore, the need to have workers who can cover a variety of different jobs shrinks as the size of the firm grows. If there are 10,000 gate agents, the firm knows that it will have very close to 9,500 on board on any given day. It need not train machinists to be gate agents, because the likelihood that a machinist will have to cover gate-agent duty is close to zero.

Hierarchical Structures and Rejection Probabilities

To show:

A hierarchical decision process approves fewer projects than a flat, single decision process. Suppose that each person can review N projects per period. Suppose

---

[11]As the number of observations gets small, the binomial distribution is not as closely approximated by the Normal distribution. Still, the table illustrates the general pattern. As N gets large, the proportion who actually show up gets closer to the expected value.

further that an individual's best information, if he or she were to make a decision in the absence of any other individual's decision, would lead him to accept the project p of the time.

If the hierarchy is flat, so that there is no supervisor, $2N$ projects are reviewed. All others are automatically rejected for lack of time to review them. As a result, under the flat structure, the number of projects accepted is $2pN$ because each of the two reviews N and accepts proportion p of them.

A hierarchical structure is different. In this case, supervisors only see projects that are accepted by the worker. Thus, the worker is the bottleneck. He can only review N projects and passes pN of them along to the supervisor. What does the supervisor do? She knows that all projects that she sees have already been pre-approved. As a result, she is more likely to approve a pre-approved project than she is to approve a project that has never been reviewed. Define p_{yy} as the conditional probability that she approves a project that has already been approved by her subordinate. Then

(A16.9) $$p_{yy} > p$$

because of the information contained in the fact that the project has already been approved.

The number of projects approved in the hierarchical setting is $(pN)p_{yy}$ because only pN projects are passed from worker to supervisor each period and she approves p_{yy} of them.

It is clear that $pNp_{yy} < 2pN$, and because $p_{yy} < 2$, of course $p_{yy} \leq 1$, so a hierarchical structure is more stringent than a flat structure for two reasons: First, fewer projects are reviewed, so more are rejected outright. Second, those that are approved once may be rejected by the supervisor. Two approvals are needed rather than one. This completes the proof.

Next, a second opinion structure is more stringent than a flat, single-decision structure. In the second opinion structure, all projects are reviewed twice. When a disagreement occurs, λ of the time the project is approved. Since each can review N projects per period, the second opinion structure approves

$$N(pp_{yy} + \lambda p(1 - p_{yy}) + \lambda(1 - p)p_{yn})$$

where p_{yy} is the probability that the second reviewer approves the project, given that the first reviewer rejected it. Recall that p_{yy} is the probability that the second accepts, given that the first accepts, so $(1 - p_{yy})$ is the probability that the second rejects, given that the first accepts.

We want to show that the second opinion structure is more stringent than the flat structure with single decision maker. This is not obvious because the second reviewer can reverse an initial reject as well as turn down an initial acceptance. If the second opinion structure is more stringent, then

(A16.10) $$N(pp_{yy} + \lambda p(1 - p_{yy}) + \lambda(1 - p)p_{yn}) < 2N_p$$

Since the left-hand side is at a maximum for any given set p, p_{yy} and p_{yn} when $\lambda = 1$, if (A16.10) holds when $\lambda = 1$, it always holds. Then, (A16.10) becomes

(A16.11) $$N[p_{yn}(l - p) - p] < 0$$

This condition holds as long as

$$p_{yn}(l - p) < p$$

But $p_{yn} < p$ because the probability of acceptance given that a project has already been rejected must be less than the probability of accepting a project with a clean slate. Further $p \leq l$, so the left-hand side must be less than p.

Thus, the second opinion structure is more stringent than the flat structure. The reason is that only half as many projects are reviewed. The others are rejected outright.

Finally, the hierarchical structure is more stringent than the second opinion structure. This requires that

(A16.12) $$Npp_{yy} < N[pp_{yy} + \lambda p(l - p_{yy}) + \lambda(l - p)p_{yn}]$$

or that

(A16.13) $$p(l - p_{yy}) + (l - p)p_{yn} > 0$$

which is always true. [12]

---

[12]There are some corner cases where structures are equivalent. They are ignored by letting $0 < p < l$.

EVALUATION

17

$\mathcal{N}$o firm can escape the somewhat unpleasant task of evaluating its employees. Periodic reviews are standard in most organizations. Reviews are used for a number of purposes, among the most common are salary determination, promotion, and termination. How are reviews to be conducted, and what problems arise when employees are evaluated? The following discussion sets the scene.

DOUGLAS: I hate this time of year. This is a no-win situation. Every one of my people thinks he's great. If I give him a good evaluation, he smiles, thinking, "You said it. I am one of the best you've got and you'd have a tough time without me." If I give him a bad evaluation, he wonders why I have it in for him and hates me forever. How do you handle it?

CHAMBERLIN: I basically give everyone the same rating, with only minor differences. If one worker is higher on one factor, I rate her co-worker higher on another. This way things balance out.

DOUGLAS: Doesn't that make the evaluation process meaningless? Why even bother?

CHAMBERLIN: I think evaluations are stupid anyway. It's not my problem to evaluate these guys. If we don't want them, we can fire them. If we keep them, we should treat them equally.

DOUGLAS: If we don't have evaluations, how do we know who to promote? Take it to the extreme, we need evaluations at least during the probationary period. Otherwise, we could get stuck with workers that we don't want and end up keeping them for a very long time.

CHAMBERLIN: Okay, so we can do some evaluation, but this constant annual evaluation for workers who we know we are going to keep is a waste of time. I think this was invented by an underworked HR manager.

DOUGLAS: If we don't do annual evaluation, we won't get performance out of our workers.

CHAMBERLIN: If we do annual evaluation, we'll get our workers spending most of their time trying to impress us instead of working. This system encourages sycophancy.

DOUGLAS: You have a point. Maybe we can be more selective about who we evaluate and when. Besides, supervisors tend to give the same employees the best evaluations year after year. First impressions seem pretty important. Once you are labeled as one of the good guys, it sticks with you.

CHAMBERLIN: Maybe we should have someone other than the immediate supervisor evaluate the employee. We should leave this task to someone whose time is less valuable.

DOUGLAS: How about the VP of human resources?

In addition to the hostility that the evaluation system creates toward human resources departments, a number of questions arise. They include:

- What purpose does evaluation serve?

- How often and which workers should be evaluated?

- What information is conveyed by the typical evaluation process?

- What incentives—good or bad—does the evaluation system create?

- Should evaluators be forced to adhere to some prespecified curve?

- Who should do the evaluations?

This chapter addresses all of these questions.

◆ ◆ ◆ ◆ ◆ GOALS OF EVALUATION

A good evaluation instrument provides two kinds of information. First, the evaluation reveals something about a worker's general ability. Second, it provides information on the specific skills or talents that make the individual better suited for one job than another.

The analogy is to two kinds of tests given students in school. One is an IQ test, which purports to say something about an individual's ability to learn. The other is an achievement test, which attempts to ascertain what an individual has already learned. These two may be confounded, because an individual's ability to learn may be affected by those things to which the person was already exposed. Still, from a firm's point of view, the distinction may be important.

Knowing a worker's general ability helps a firm determine the appropriate human capital investment profile. When the firm is going to bear some of the cost of training, as in the case of firm-specific human capital, it wants to make sure that it invests in the correct individual. Just as a firm would not undertake to build a new plant or develop a new product line without a thorough investigation of the costs and returns, the firm needs to investigate a worker's potential for learning and growth before making an investment in human capital. A worker who has a high level of skill in any given task is not necessarily a good candidate for additional investment. Some people may be very good at doing a particular job, but incapable of advancing further. Good teachers do not always make good deans; good craftsmen do not always make good supervisors.

Equally important is determining workers' specific talents and skills. In order to place workers in their highest-valued use, a firm must know what they are best at doing. This is important not only for placement, but also for decisions on retention. If a worker's skills are insufficient to warrant continued employment, it is probably best for the worker and firm to find new mates.

RULES OF EVALUATION ◆ ◆ ◆ ◆ ◆

What purpose does evaluation serve? Evaluations are used to move a worker from one firm to another, to move a worker from one job to another, or to set pay. When should a worker move from one job to another? The answer, contained in previous chapters (see especially chapter 7), is that a worker who is worth more to the current firm than to an outside firm should stay. There is always a deal that can be struck to make both the firm and worker better off than they would be by the worker's departure. In this section we look at how often and in what manner the worker's worth should be evaluated.

Frequency of Evaluation

How often should a worker be evaluated, and which workers should be evaluated? Two general rules follow from the theory of firm-specific human capital:[1]

---

[1] These rules are derived formally in Lazear (1990).

◆ ◆

*R*ULE 1:   Workers with more firm-specific human capital should be evaluated less frequently.

*R*ULE 2:   The frequency of evaluation should be inversely related to experience in the firm and/or job.

We discuss each in turn.

Suppose the worker is worth $1,000 per week to the firm, but is only being paid $800. He is worth $900 at another firm, which offers to pay him $875. The worker would be tempted to leave. If the current firm offers the worker $900 to stay, and thereby retains the worker, both sides are better off. The firm is still netting $100 per week on the worker. If the worker leaves, the firm nets zero. The worker does better at the current firm than at the other firm because $900 exceeds $875.

Which workers are more likely to have values at the current firm that exceed their values elsewhere? The answer is, workers with much firm-specific human capital are likely to have internal values that exceed their external values. If the worker has skills that are firm-specific, then it is unlikely that an outsider will be able to offer more than the current firm can offer.

If the current firm can outbid rivals for the worker's services it is unlikely that the worker will ever end up leaving. Thus, evaluations are less likely to produce information that will result in a separation when the worker has firm-specific human capital. The immediate implication is that costly evaluation has less potential payoff when a worker has firm-specific human capital.

Of course, it can be argued that evaluation allows a firm to determine how much to pay a worker. But when a worker has firm-specific human capital, there is only a rough relation between productivity and wage. Any outside wage offer can be countered after it is made; there is little benefit to a preemptive wage increase.

It is this logic that leads to rule 2, which states that evaluation should be more frequent early in a worker's career. Once a worker has been with a firm for a few years, he knows more about the current firm than he does about any other. Conversely, the firm knows more about him than it does about a brand new worker. It is unlikely at this point that the worker is better suited to another firm than to his current firm. Much of the reason comes from sorting.[2] The firm has had a number of opportunities to evaluate and get rid of their senior workers. If they have not already done so, chances are that the worker is well suited to this firm. Further, since specific human capital tends to increase with years on the job, the worker/firm match becomes more idiosyncratic with experience. The more idiosyncratic the match, the less likely the worker is to move to another firm because

---

[2]Jovanovic (1979) developed the theory behind this point.

another firm will have a very difficult time outbidding the worker's current employer.

Given that the difference between the value of the worker at his current firm and the value of the same worker at other firms grows with experience, the worker is less likely to separate as experience grows. It is for this reason that evaluation becomes less valuable with additional experience. Evaluation of senior workers is unlikely to result in dismissal. Even if the evaluation reveals that the worker is not particularly productive, he is likely to be even less productive elsewhere. The firm may want to cut the worker's wage, but at a wage that the firm is willing to pay, the worker is unlikely to be able to obtain a superior offer. Experienced workers who are slow at their current firm will probably be even slower elsewhere.

Using Evaluations to Motivate

Although a senior worker may be better suited to his current firm than to another, why should a firm pay a worker more than he is worth? Isn't the information generated by an evaluation useful for wage setting? The answer depends on only one factor—the responsiveness of effort to compensation.

Let us start by considering the extreme case where effort is totally unresponsive to compensation, either because the speed (and quality) of work is technologically determined or because workers do not adjust their labor supply behavior unless compensation changes dramatically. Under this scenario, there is little reason to adjust wages to productivity. To see this, let us work through a numerical example.

A worker starts with the firm when she is 35. Her productivity during the first 10 years is certain to be $50,000 per year. After ten years, some in her cohort excel, whereas others start to decline. Thus, from ages 45 to 65, she may be worth $80,000 per year or she may be worth $40,000 per year. Those who excel are worth $60,000 elsewhere, and those who decline are worth $30,000 elsewhere. Suppose that each case has a 50 percent chance of occurring. This implies that 50 percent of the firm's 45-year-olds are worth $80,000 and 50 percent are worth $40,000. The information is summarized in Table 17.1.

Suppose also that evaluation, which is costly to undertake, can reveal to the employer whether any given worker is worth $40,000 or whether she is worth $80,000. Isn't this information useful? The answer is, not unless the information has consequences, and in this case it does not.

TABLE 17.1
PRODUCTIVITY BY AGE

	Productivity 35–45	Productivity 45–65	
Probability	1	.5	.5
Value At Current Firm	$50,000	$80,000	$40,000
Value Elsewhere	$50,000	$60,000	$30,000

First, note that the worker will end up staying with the firm whether output turns out to be $80,000 or $40,000. If it is $80,000, then it is $60,000 elsewhere, which means that the current firm can and will always outbid a rival for the worker's services. If it is $40,000, then it is $30,000 elsewhere, which means again that the current firm can and will outbid the rival. Thus, the information produced by the evaluation will have no effect on where the worker eventually ends up.

It is unnecessary to calibrate wages specifically to productivity. If no evaluation is conducted for senior workers, then no information about individual productivity is known. But the firm knows that 50 percent of the workers are $80,000 producers and 50 percent are $40,000 producers. If it pays $60,000 to each senior worker, it does better than it does with evaluation-based pay. The total wage cost is the same and the firm saves the resources that it would have wasted on evaluation. Additionally, workers probably prefer this system, because paying on the basis of productivity adds unnecessary risk to payouts. It is unlikely that a 35-year-old worker knows any better than the firm whether she will excel or decline ten years hence. A firm that does not evaluate senior workers guarantees that it will be able to pay only the average to each, thereby providing the worker with "insurance" against the contingency that she declines in middle age.[3]

For the purposes of retention, there is no value to evaluation as long as workers have value at their current firm that always exceeds their value elsewhere. But evaluation of senior workers may provide some beneficial incentives. When effort is responsive to pay, and much of the discussion in previous chapters suggests that it often is, then evaluation allows the firm to calibrate pay to output (or effort). Under these circumstances, evaluation, even of older workers, may be crucial.

To see this, consider the most extreme case, namely piecework. When individuals are paid according to some piece-rate schedule, it is essential to tie pay to a measure of output. Measuring output is one form of evaluation. At the end of each time period, the worker's performance is *evaluated*,—that is, the number of pieces produced are counted, and compensation is tied directly to the evaluation's results. An alternative is that the firm could take the total number of units produced by everyone in the firm, divide by the number of workers, and assume that each worker produced exactly what the average worker produced. But then, any one worker's effort has only a minor effect on the worker's compensation, which reduces incentives. Without individual evaluations, piece rates do not motivate. Thus, senior workers should be evaluated when their effort is responsive to compensation.

Two points follow:

First, even if evaluation can serve indirectly to motivate senior workers, it is still true that there is generally less benefit to evaluating senior workers than junior workers. Whatever motivation factors exist for older workers, they are there as well for younger workers, and the gains to motivation may be more important for younger

[3]If it does not pay for the current firm to evaluate its workers, it is very unlikely that it will pay for an outside firm to evaluate its workers, so competition from outsiders probably will not be a major factor here.

workers. Further, the other major reason for evaluation, namely, selecting the right people for the firm and sorting those selected into their most productive slots, is much more important for young workers than it is for older ones.

Second, the nature of the evaluation instrument should differ according to the seniority of the worker. In young workers, it is important to ascertain the general ability of the worker and also the specific skills that the individual possesses. This information will help determine whether the worker is right for the firm and should be granted a permanent position at the end of a probationary period. It will also assist in determining the appropriate job for the person within the firm.

For older workers who are less likely to leave and less likely to change jobs, the primary goal of the evaluation instrument is motivation. This leads to the following prescription:

◆ ◆

*R*ULE 3: Senior workers should be evaluated on the basis of achievement, not ability.

Achievement is affected both by ability and effort. Since the senior worker's ability is already pretty well known from earlier experience with the firm, it is relatively easy to factor out ability to determine the amount of effort that is going into the job. Deviations from past performance may signal a change in effort or a discrete change in ability, say, as a result of a health-related factor, which will often be observable. Either a decline in effort as a result of worker choice or a decline in underlying ability is of concern to the firm. Both will show up in achievement-oriented evaluations.

Value of Evaluation and Probability of Success

It is a straightforward extension of an earlier discussion (see chapter 4 and its technical appendix) to show that evaluation has less value when the probability of success is high. Thus,

◆ ◆

*R*ULE 4: Evaluation has less value in firms where most workers who are hired are at least as productive in the current firm as they are elsewhere.

Consider two occupations, data entry and secretary. In the data entry job, all that matters is speed and accuracy. Both speed and accuracy are easily measured during a job interview. An applicant is given the nineties' equivalent of a typing test: the person is presented with some numbers and asked to enter them into the computer. The computer knows the data that are to be entered and immediately

Table 17.2
Secretary and Data Entry Analysis

Worker	Value to Firm	Alternative Wage
Secretary 1	$300	$250
Secretary 2	$200	$250
Secretary 3	$100	$200
Secretary 4	$500	$100
Data Entry Specialist 1	$300	$250
Data Entry Specialist 2	$250	$225
Data Entry Specialist 3	$350	$260
Data Entry Specialist 4	$200	$150

spits out a score that reveals the applicant's speed and accuracy. In order to be hired, an applicant's performance must exceed some predetermined standard.

Secretarial jobs are more complex. A secretary's tasks are more varied and the skills for performing those tasks are more difficult to observe during an interview. Thus, a secretary who is hired is more likely to turn out to be a mistake than is a data entry specialist.

Therefore, sorting after hiring is more important in the case of secretaries than in the case of data entry specialists. Table 17.2 provides some data that illustrate the issue.

Because it is easy to observe performance of the data entry specialist, none is hired who has an outside wage that exceeds value to the current firm. The same cannot be said of secretaries. Although the average secretary has a value of $275, which is equal to the average value of data entry specialists, there is a difference. Some of the secretaries, namely 1 and 4, are well suited to the firm. Other secretaries, namely 2 and 3, are not. Both 2 and 3 have outside values that exceed their values at the current firm. There is no way that the firm can make money by paying them as much as they can earn elsewhere. But all the data entry specialists have a value at the current firm that exceeds their value outside.

In this example, it seems clear that there would be no point in evaluating data entry specialists after they are hired. Every one is productive enough to make the cut. Offering a wage of $275 without any evaluation would be a profitable strategy. None of the four would decline the offer. Evaluation would be costly and would have no benefit. Those whose value fell short of $275 on the test that is part of the application process would not be hired in the first place.[4]

---

[4]Knowing that Data Entry Specialist 4 is worth less than $275 would provide valuable information to the firm. Since the worker is willing to accept anything over $150, the firm could bargain for a lower wage. But this evaluation and bargaining strategy is a double-edged sword. Once the firm evaluates its data entry specialists, it is in a weaker position in bargaining against the most productive of the group. Lowering the wages on DES 4 may also imply raising the wages for DES 1 and 3.

McSTUDY
SORTING, SIGNALLING, OR RELATIONS?

◆ ◆ ◆ ◆ ◆ ◆ ◆ ◆ ◆ ◆

There are four McDonald's restaurants in Wisconsin where workers are paid to do their homework. After finishing their shifts, owner Steve Kilian will pay them for up to 3 hours a week of schoolwork done at the restaurants.

Sounds strange? It certainly seems unlikely that the employees' school work will make them much more valuable to McDonald's. This is not a matter of employee training or investing in human capital. It is questionable how much high school studies would help at McDonald's. It seems unlikely that McDonald's would want to invest in this when the employees are not likely to stay after graduation. This could be a P. R. stunt.

Yet it may also be sound personnel policy, not as a means of investing in human capital, but as a way of attracting the type of workers one wants. As Steve Kilian explains, "Our objective was to find a way to attract higher quality employees. We found that better students usually are better employees, and I figured we'd be able to attract better students by paying them to study." The program has reduced turnover and pleased customers, but is it attracting better students?

Exactly what sort of "better students" does McStudy attract? Is this approach better than paying good students more after they present their transcripts? When we look at this situation more closely, we see that this program is equally attractive to students who study 3 hours, 5 hours, or 20 hours a week. It only discriminates against students who would not be working 3 hours a week if they were not paid to. Because the students would study at least 3 hours either way, paying them to study is no different than paying them for an extra 3 hours a week.

There is one significant difference. McStudy means that students must study in the restaurant rather than elsewhere. This may be what gives the program merit, not as personnel policy, but as public relations. As Kilian said, "Customers like what we're doing. They like to see students studying." The sheer novelty of McStudy generated enough talk in the small towns where it was implemented to justify the program for public relations and employee marketing alone.

Source: Donald J. McNerney, "Paying Students For Doing Their Homework," *H. R. Focus,* 71 (July 1994): 21.

The same is not true of secretaries. Since the value of secretaries cannot be determined until after work has begun, some mismatches occur. Secretaries 2 and 3 should work elsewhere, because they bring down the average productivity of the group. Without 2 and 3, average output of secretaries is $400. If two more secretaries like 1 and 4 could be found, the firm would have four secretaries whose output was $400, instead of four whose output was only $275. Given the alternative wages of the secretaries, both firm and worker could be made better off. Secretaries 1 and 4 could be offered, say, $350 instead of $275. Secretaries 2 and 3 could be offered the amount that they are worth, in which case they leave. The firm nets an additional $50 per secretary (i.e., $400 − 350 versus $275 − $275 before), and both sides are better off. But in order to implement this scheme, evaluation is necessary. As long as the one-time cost of evaluation does not exceed the gain of $50 per period for the remaining work periods, evaluation of secretaries pays.

The logic is that it does not pay to perform evaluation unless a significant fraction of the workers will be weeded out by evaluation. If they are not weeded out by evaluation because it is appropriate to keep them, then there is little gain from evaluation. When the probability of retention is high because most hires are good ones, the gain from evaluation is lower. As before, there may still be incentive reasons to evaluate workers, but early evaluation for the purposes of sorting is less valuable.

◆ ◆ ◆ ◆ ◆ UP-OR-OUT: ONE USE OF EVALUATION

Some organizations use evaluation as part of an "up-or-out" system. Perhaps the two most extreme examples are the military and academia. In academia, the most common system is to appoint an individual for a period of time, like seven years. During the sixth year, the young professor is evaluated. A positive evaluation generally results in promotion to a position with academic tenure, which provides the professor with lifetime job security.[5] A negative evaluation results in termination. The professor is given the remaining term of his or her contract, usually just over a year, to find a job, and then dismissed.

Many military forces use a similar system. At certain times during a career, an officer is evaluated and comes up for promotion. Failure to be promoted results in dismissal; the officer is required to retire from the military and return to civilian life.

Up-or-out is indeed a strange practice. A worker who is not quite good enough to be promoted is automatically fired. One would think that there would

---

[5]In reality, the value of the job security is somewhat less than meets the eye. As long as the administration has control over working conditions and salary, the professor can usually be induced to leave "voluntarily."

be some middle ground, where a worker is neither promoted nor dismissed, but instead retained in some capacity. Why might a firm engage in up-or-out?

There are two explanations. The first is that up-or-out forces the firm to behave in a forthright manner.[6] It has been argued that in the absence of up-or-out, management has incentives to lie to its workers. Suppose that a firm is not constrained to promote or dismiss, but can instead choose some middle ground. After evaluation, management has an incentive to understate the measured quality of its workers. By doing this, it can retain the workers at a lower wage than it would otherwise have to pay. The firm tells the worker that he or she is not good enough to be promoted to the higher paying job, but *is* good enough to be employed at the current wage. Even if a worker is good enough to be promoted, he may stay under the poorer terms, especially when his outside options are not perceived to be good. Thus, without up-or-out, management is induced to undervalue and underpay its workers. Up-or-out solves this problem. The firm either must promote the worker or let him go. If the worker's value to the firm exceeds the wage of the higher level job, the firm will keep the worker and will be forced to pay the higher wage. If not, the firm lets the worker go. By constraining the firm's options to up-or-out, there is no way that the firm can both keep the worker and pay lower wages. The firm is forced to put-up or shut-up. If workers understand this, the workers will demand an up-or-out structure.

The second explanation is that up-or-out raises quality of the work force by solving an agency problem. Up-or-out forces an employer's hand. If the firm wants to retain a worker, it must promote the worker and pay a higher wage. The idea is that managers are basically weak and have no courage. It may be easier personally for a manager to simply retain a mediocre worker than it is to let the person go. In order to force managers to fire workers that should not be kept, it is necessary to make the options more extreme. To keep the worker, a manager must promote her. This may strengthen the managers' will and induce them to take the action that is best for the firm, even if it is personally unpleasant. Thus, restricting a firm to up-or-out results in more terminations, because it raises the standard that a worker must exceed in order to be retained. (A formal model of this process is presented in the appendix.)

Although up-or-out raises the standard and therefore raises the quality of the work force, this does not imply that up-or-out is a good thing. It is possible to raise the quality of the work force by firing everyone but the top worker, which is rarely a good strategy. If lower-quality workers can be retained at a price that falls short of the value of their output, then retention is the right policy.

Up-or-out sometimes results in termination of productive workers who are not quite good enough to be promoted, but the value of whose output exceeds their current wages. The discussion in the last chapter of false positive and false negative errors is relevant here. Up-or-out reduces the number of false positive

[6]See Kahn and Huberman (1988).

errors, but increases the number of false negative errors. Workers who are not up to standard are more likely to be weeded out by an up-or-out system. Without up-or-out, more of the sub-par workers would be retained, but up-or-out also increases the number of adequate workers who are terminated inappropriately. Because the firm must promote workers to retain them, up-or-out increases the number of satisfactory workers that are fired.

Whether up-or-out should be used depends on the net result of these two effects. As shown formally in the appendix, the conditions necessary to make up-or-out a good strategy are quite stringent. In most cases, these conditions are not met. It is rare, therefore, that a firm should constrain itself to an up-or-out policy. The value of added flexibility from being able to retain workers in lesser roles generally exceeds the gain that a firm may derive from being able to terminate marginal cases who would otherwise be kept. It is true that up-or-out raises the quality of workers in the firm. The problem is that the cost of using this practice exceeds the value of using it. Because too many adequate workers are terminated, in most cases the firm loses by having such a rigid policy.

◆ ◆ ◆ ◆ ◆ TRANSFERS AND PROMOTIONS

Evaluations can be used for the purposes of determining transfers and promotions. Suppose a slot comes open. The firm can hire an outsider, move a worker laterally, or promote a worker. (A lateral move is likely to entail a promotion or outside hire to cover the now-open job.) How is the determination made?

Usually, the choice is based on a combination of relative and absolute comparisons. A firm's natural instinct is to promote from within, and most frequently, from the group of individuals who were subordinate to the person who is vacating the position.[7] Evaluation, either formal or informal, must be used in order to determine who is the best of the possible candidates. Most of the time, these procedures seem somewhat subjective, but underlying the discussion is a body of background information, much of it objective.

For example, consider choosing a regional sales manager. A number of factors affect the choice. Often, one important component is the individual's performance as a salesperson. Data on sales performance is readily available, and the people who select the new sales manager are likely to be quite familiar with that information. Other data are more difficult to measure objectively, but may also be reported in evaluation results. Workers are often judged, albeit subjectively, on a number of criteria, like technical knowledge, skill, supervisory ability, attention to detail, ability to follow-up, problem solving, and interpersonal skills. All of these are relevant to determining who can best fill the job.

After all internal candidates have been ranked relative to one another, and af-

---

[7]In chapter 9, it was shown that there may be incentive reasons to promote a worker from within over a better qualified outsider.

ter a "winner" has been selected, decision makers may consider absolute performance. Although preference may be given to an insider in order to enhance incentives, and because an insider has firm-specific knowledge, the firm may prefer to go with an outsider in cases where the outsider is sufficiently superior to the best insider. How is this determined? Usually, some absolute standard is used. For example, in selecting a sales manager, previous sales performance may be deemed an important part of the sales manager's job. After all, it is difficult for a person who has never been an effective seller to advise and instruct others on how to sell. Suppose that the sales record of the top internal candidate falls far short of that of an external candidate. The external candidate may get the nod.

This is most likely to happen in troubled organizations. The view is that the firm-specific capital possessed by internal candidates actually works to their detriment. When things have not gone well, it is sometimes difficult to identify the cause. Insiders may or may not be part of the problem, but the best course is often to go with an outsider. A card-game analogy may be useful here. In draw poker, players with a bad hand generally opt to replace most of their cards with new ones. They reason that they cannot do much worse, so they might as well take a radical new draw. The same is true of firms: When the absolute situation is sufficiently bad, the firm prefers to go to outsiders, reasoning that it cannot do much worse than its current situation. The key is knowing when the current situation is truly bad in an absolute sense.

ABSOLUTE IS RELATIVE   ◆ ◆ ◆ ◆ ◆

The distinction between an absolute and relative standard is in large part artificial. When we think of an absolute standard, we are comparing the current level of performance to some criterion, but where did the criterion come from? Invariably, it is based on past experience.

Consider an example that faces every student. A professor may announce that he grades on a curve, or he may announce that he has an "absolute" standard for grades. If an absolute scale is announced, it generally takes the following form. A score of 92 percent earns an "A," a score of 80 percent earns a "B," and anything below 65 percent is a failing performance. The numbers 92 percent, 80 percent, . . . 65 percent are not constants of nature, but instead reflect some professorial notion of what is excellent, good, and intolerable performance. The "absolute" scale is actually relative. The professor's notion of an appropriate scale comes from past experience or from comparison with the experience of others. The current class is being graded relative to some comparison group.

Absolute versus relative is not a meaningless distinction. With the so-called absolute standard, students are competing against members of past classes or other classes. Thus, the politics of relative comparisons are eliminated. A student need not see his classmate fail in order to move up a notch. This has both good and bad effects. The good effect is that it fosters cooperation within the class. The bad effect is that the class as a whole has incentives to lobby the professor.

TABLE 17.3
RELATIVE VERSUS ABSOLUTE EVALUATION

	Firm's Payoff	Worker 1's Payoff	Worker 2's Payoff
Absolute Evaluation			
Worker 1 succeeds; Worker 2 succeeds	0	50	50
Worker 1 succeeds; Worker 2 fails	50	50	0
Worker 1 fails; Worker 2 succeeds	50	0	50
Worker 1 fails; Worker 2 fails	100	0	0
Relative Evaluation			
Worker 1 succeeds; Worker 2 succeeds	Impossible	Impossible	Impossible
Worker 1 succeeds; Worker 2 fails	50	50	0
Worker 1 fails; Worker 2 succeeds	50	0	50
Worker 1 fails; Worker 2 fails	Impossible	Impossible	Impossible

The same is true in firms. When individuals are forced into contemporaneous relative comparisons, one person's gain is the other's loss. Cooperation is hurt. Conversely, when all individuals whose evaluation exceeds some "absolute" standard are given a reward, say, in the form of a higher job title and raise, there is no problem with cooperation. Of course, workers as a group then find it beneficial to attempt to change the standard. With a relative standard, managers can legitimately fall back on the defense that raising one worker's evaluation necessarily hurts other co-workers. There is strength in having one's hands tied. This, by the way, is a standard outcome of some of the game theoretic literature.[8] Table 17.3 makes the point.

The table is interpreted as follows. One hundred dollars are available to split between two workers. Each worker is evaluated either as a success or as a failure. If absolute criteria are used, then both workers can succeed and both can fail. If relative evaluations are used, one must succeed and one must fail. Suppose that $50 are given to each who succeeds on the evaluation. The firm retains the leftover amount.

The two schemes imply different payoffs for the firm and different strategies for the workers. When the evaluation is relative, worker 1 wants to align himself

---

[8]Schelling (1960) first generated this result.

with management so that he will be viewed as superior to worker 2. Conversely, worker 2 wants to align herself with management so that she will be viewed as superior to worker 1. Management is in the convenient position of being pulled from both directions, which, if forces are symmetric, leads to an unbiased evaluation. Management receives $50 irrespective of the outcome. There is no reason to choose 1 over 2, nor vice versa. The natural way to choose between workers is on actual performance. The choice will not always be correct. Sometimes evaluators make mistakes, but there is no reason to expect the evaluation to be biased in one direction or another.

This is the main argument in favor of forced curves. They prevent a professor or manager from inflating or deflating the standard. The only way that one worker can benefit is at the direct cost of another. There is no way to alter the distribution for the students or workers as a whole.

Absolute evaluation creates different tensions. Management would like to declare that both workers have failed. Each worker cares only about his or her own success. Workers taken as a group want the firm to use a low standard for grading so that they both pass. Management wants to use a tough standard so that they both fail.[9] The politics associated with absolute evaluation are quite different from those associated with relative evaluation. Whereas relative evaluation creates tension between one worker and another, absolute evaluation creates tension between the workers as a group and management.

FAVORITISM AND BIAS ◆ ◆ ◆ ◆ ◆

Are evaluations unbiased? Workers do not always believe so. Nepotism and biases in favor of a particular gender, nationality, ethnicity, or religion may lead to erroneous evaluations.

The potential to bias an evaluation creates incentive problems in an organization. An evaluation system that is capable of being influenced induces workers to lobby, flatter, and engage in other unproductive behavior. Such behavior is not only a time waster, but it has the harmful effect of making the evaluation results less accurate. Since evaluations are likely to reflect worker lobbying as well as worker effort, they are of less value to the firm.

There are two solutions to this problem. First, compensation can be made less sensitive to evaluation results. If less is at stake, individuals have less of an incentive to lobby. This point is similar to one made in chapter 10. When workers can sabotage one another, a smaller wage spread between winners and losers reduces their incentives to engage in uncooperative or nasty behavior. Similarly, by making wages less contingent on evaluation results, workers have less incentive to try

---

[9]This view is myopic. In a competitive labor market, a firm that continually fails its workers will find it difficult to attract workers or will have to pay a high enough wage to compensate for the high failure rate.

to influence those results. Second, a firm may lock itself into bureaucratic rules that are not subject to manipulation. As long as the commitment to the rules is credible, there is little reason for the worker to attempt to lobby.[10]

More extreme is a system that transforms management into "yes men."[11] When manager's opinions affect a worker's reward, workers are careful about what they say. One might think that management would want to hear the truth from its workers. Obtaining inaccurate information cannot be helpful to the firm, no matter how pleasant it may be to receive. A firm that gives its workers permission to speak freely would do better. While true, the problem is that when a manager is presented with an opinion that differs from her own, she can draw one of two conclusions. Either the new information is correct and she was mistaken, or her information is correct and the worker who is providing the information is mistaken. As a statistical matter, she should place some weight on each possibility. Workers know this, and the consequences are unfortunate. Because there is some chance that a worker's dissenting opinion will be viewed as a mistake, even if correct, workers tend to shade their reports in the direction of the manager's prior belief. This creates yes men. Again, pay compression and bureaucratic rules that prevent managers from taking actions against free-speaking subordinates may improve the information flow within organizations.

◆ ◆ ◆ ◆ ◆ WHO SHOULD EVALUATE WHOM?

The problems just discussed suggest a solution: Workers can be evaluated by someone to whom they have no access. In education, one of the benefits of standardized tests that are administered and graded by some external agency is that they are less susceptible to teacher biases that may create student lobbying. Similarly, having workers evaluated by third parties who are not in direct contact with the worker removes or at least reduces the chance of affecting results.

There is a trade-off, however. Outside evaluators may be more objective, but they are also likely to be less well informed. Most professional organizations have used this point to press for peer evaluation and licensure. In academia, journal articles and books are reviewed by members of the author's field, and most often, by someone who is closely associated with the kind of work being reviewed. Assigning a paper to a knowledgeable, but closely involved referee has its drawbacks. Sometimes, an author, anticipating that the work will be reviewed by a given individual, will slant the work in the direction favored by the presumed reviewer. Conversely, reviewers do not always have appropriate incentives. In some fields, it is alleged that reviewers sometimes malign work because the work will enhance the reputation of a rival and thereby diminish the reviewer's relative standing.

---

[10]See Milgrom (1988) and Prendergast and Topel (1996).
[11]See Prendergast (1993).

EVALUATION SYSTEM AT
PRUDENTIAL RESOURCES MANAGEMENT
◆ ◆ ◆ ◆ ◆ ◆ ◆ ◆ ◆

Reform of the evaluation system is one of the most effective tools for changing employee behavior. A seemingly small change in the evaluation system may result in substantial changes in corporate culture. The reverse is also true. A change in the company size, business environment, or objectives may necessitate rethinking evaluation practices. The case of Prudential Resources Management provides insight into how and under what circumstances the evaluation system should be altered.

There are about one thousand employees at Valhalla, New York–based Prudential Resources Management, a unit of Prudential Insurance Co. According to its revised mission statement, the company strives to be a world leader in providing relocation, real estate, and related consulting services. Prudential Resources Management is an example of a company where the evaluation system had undergone a profound and carefully designed change. The new system is more comprehensive than the old one. Rapid evolution of the business environment may be the cause of reform. In general, changes tend to create the need for a more thorough evaluation procedure, because the past performance is less indicative of employee's productivity in the new circumstances.

Maria Stolfi, director of employee benefits at Prudential, explains: "We recognized that in order to succeed, we needed to make sure that our human relations system is in line with our company's mission, vision and total-quality principles." The old evaluation system suffered from a lack of clear evaluation standards and uneven implementation. According to Stolfi, "People had been feeling lousy about the old process because they didn't know what the expectations were."

Identifying and rewarding the top performers is an integral part of any effective incentive system. In many companies the sole purpose of evaluation process is to motivate employees. Consequently, managers and workers often consider evaluations as an unproductive and unpleasant, albeit necessary, process. This is the way it used to be in Prudential Resources Management prior to the evaluation system overhaul in 1994.

As a result of the evaluation system reform, Prudential's evaluation process has become something more than just "grading" the employee's performance. Now, it is a source of important feedback to employees. Every year, all employees together with their managers have to come up with sets of objectives for themselves. Thus, the evaluation system has become a coordination tool. For instance, the importance of team work has been increasing at Prudential Resources Management. In order to induce better cooperation among employees it is a company-wide policy to have a separate question about a worker as a team player. Also, to facilitate team work each worker is evaluated not only by her manager, but also by her peers and subordinates. It may be cheaper and less time-consuming to have employees evaluated only by their managers, but 360-degree evaluation is valuable in a company where teamwork is important. Besides, increasing the number of reviewers makes the evaluation more accurate.

There are many other companies that use similar evaluation techniques. It may be a good idea for businesses that operate in a rapidly changing environment for employees to identify their goals for the next year. The same practice may be wasteful and silly for a firm that operates in a stable environment. Indeed, a firm that operates in a static world could almost incorporate the objectives into the job descriptions. In contrast, in a dynamic environment, an employee and the manager are the ones most likely to know what has changed and how the objectives should be altered to adjust to the new situation.

Source: Jennifer J. Laabs, "Prudential Measures HR with a Total-Quality Yardstick; Prudential Resources Management," *Personnel Journal* 74 (April 1995): 139.

Both of these forces can be a problem in the business world. Sycophancy, which has no or negative value to the firm, may be encouraged by such a system. Conversely, supervisors fearing competition from rising stars may understate the quality of an able subordinate on a review.

One compromise is to have workers reviewed by a few other workers whose hierarchical positions are both above and below the individual in question. This is sometimes called 360-degree evaluation, because it looks at the worker from all angles. It is more difficult to influence a large number of people, so the signal that management receives is likely to be more accurate.[12] Another advantage is that different perspectives can be represented. When workers are viewed more favorably by their superiors than by their subordinates, management may become concerned that it is creating a work force of sycophants. The main disadvantage is that multiparty review is more expensive. Much time may be used when each worker is asked to evaluate a number of co-workers. Evaluation, even by one indi-

---

[12]It is not obvious that the amount of lobbying will be reduced by multiparty review. Although no one worker is likely to be lobbied very much, the total amount of lobbying may actually be greater as a larger number of workers are lobbied by a smaller amount.

vidual, is costly. Evaluation by many can raise the cost beyond the value of the evaluation.

EVALUATIONS AND EXPERIENCE ◆ ◆ ◆ ◆ ◆

Should a firm be more tolerant of poor performance from junior workers or senior workers? Common sense suggests that one month of poor performance is unlikely to result in the termination of a worker who has been with the firm for 20 years and who has received favorable evaluations in every year, save one. Firms are less tolerant of new workers about whom they know little. Rather than waste time, most firms tend to cut workers loose after a relatively short period of time if their performance is not up to par. (Termination rates are highest during the first year on the job.) This is a rational strategy, as the following example illustrates.

Firms do not know a worker's ability perfectly, but use evaluations to get a sense of ability. One reason firms care about ability is that ability predicts a worker's long-term, stable, performance. A firm wants to terminate a worker after a poor showing only when the firm believes that this year's poor showing is a good predictor of next year's performance. Where this year's evaluation result is uncorrelated or only slightly correlated with next year's evaluation result, little is gained by acting on this year's evaluation.

There are some things over which a worker has no control. For example, the performance of a salesperson depends not only on sales ability and effort, but also on demand conditions that face the salesperson while attempting to sell the product. There is no reason to fire a salesperson for poor performance if the reason was insufficient demand rather than low ability or effort.

Consider the following stylized example. Suppose 50 percent of the people in the world are good at selling and 50 percent are not. Furthermore, half of the years are good years for selling and half are not. In order to have a successful sales year, two conditions must hold. First, the salesperson must be one of the 50 percent who are able to sell. Second, demand must be good.

A worker's evaluation results are summarized by Table 17.4.

The table is interpreted as follows. If an untalented salesperson attempts to sell, performance is poor irrespective of market conditions. A talented salesperson performs well when demand is high, but performs poorly when demand is low. It is only under favorable market conditions that a firm can distinguish a good salesperson from a bad one, but market conditions may be difficult for the evaluator to know.

TABLE 17.4
SALESPERSON EVALUATION: FIRST YEAR ON THE JOB

	Untalented Salesperson	*Talented Salesperson*
Demand Low	Poor	Poor
Demand High	Poor	Good

Suppose that a worker's evaluation result during the first year on the job is "poor." What should the firm do? Each cell has a probability of .25 of occurring, since half of the time demand is good and since half of the people in the world are talented at selling. There are three cells in which poor is the result. In two-thirds of the cases when the evaluation is poor, it is also true that the salesperson is untalented. Thus, a poor evaluation in the first year indicates an untalented salesperson 67 percent of the time and will likely result in termination. Acting on the negative evaluation, the firm can replace the terminated with a new worker who has a 50 percent chance of being talented. Since the current worker only has a 33 percent chance of being talented, the replacement results in higher expected profits.

Now consider a worker who is in a second year on the job. Two evaluations are now done, and the possibilities are summarized in Table 17.5.

There are two years of data and two years of experience. Suppose that an individual were to be rated poorly during the second year. If nothing else were known, the appropriate inference is that the individual is probably a poor salesperson, because two-thirds of the time that a poor evaluation is received, it reflects the fact that the salesperson is untalented. But suppose that the poor evaluation in year 2 followed a good evaluation in year 1. This changes things completely. There is only one way that a worker could have received good evaluation in year 1: The worker must be a talented salesperson. There is only one combination of events that is consistent with a good evaluation in year 1 and a poor one in year 2. The salesperson is talented, coupled with the fact that in year 1, demand was high whereas in year 2, demand was low. There would be no reason to terminate the worker in year 2. Performance in year 2, while poor, cannot negate the good rating in year 1, which indicates sales talent. Given the scenario laid out, we are absolutely certain that these evaluations reflect a talented salesperson who experienced different demand conditions over the two years.

It is for this reason that firms act less quickly to terminate long-term employees who have served well in the past than they do to terminate new workers. A failure in the twentieth evaluation after 19 years of good performance is less likely to signal low ability than is a failure on the first evaluation. This does not mean that poor evaluations of senior workers are to be ignored. Enough bad news may signal a "regime shift,"—for example, a worker who was able in the past but who is now having some problems. Alternatively, a string of poor evaluations follow-

TABLE 17.5
SALESPERSON EVALUATION: TWO YEARS ON THE JOB

	Untalented Salesperson	*Talented Salesperson*
Demand In First Year Low	1st-year evaluation = Poor	1st-year evaluation = Poor
Demand In First Year High	1st-year evaluation = Poor	1st-year evaluation = Good
Demand In Second Year Low	2nd-year evaluation = Poor	2nd-year evaluation = Poor
Demand In Second Year High	2nd-year evaluation = Poor	2nd-year evaluation = Good

ing some good ones may signal that measurement error occurred in the early evaluations.

To sharpen this distinction, let us extend the previous example. Suppose that after two years of evaluations, one good and one poor, there follows a string of nine evaluations, each of which results in a poor rating. If we continue to believe that the worker is indeed an able salesperson as a result of the good evaluation in year 1, we must also believe that each year from year 2 to year 11 was one in which demand was poor. If it remains true that the probability of demand being low in any given year is .5, then the probability of getting a string of ten bad years is $(.5)^{10}$, which equals $1/1,024$. There is only a 1 in 1,024 chance that ten years of bad demand would occur in a row. While it is possible that chance explains the pattern, it is so unlikely that we may wish to rethink our assumptions. There are three possibilities.

First, it may be that demand shifts are correlated over time, so that the probability of getting ten years of low demand in a row is really much higher than $1/1,024$. But suppose that other workers on similar routes were able to perform well in about half of those ten years. Under these circumstances, it would be reasonable to conclude that our original estimate of the demand is probably about right.

We are then forced to consider the other two alternatives. Alternative one is that the first year's evaluation was in error. If a mistake was made on the first year's evaluation, then all the pieces would fit into place. If the worker had received a poor evaluation in year 1, the next ten years of poor evaluations would be clear evidence that the worker was, in fact, an untalented salesperson. Recall that an untalented salesperson produces poorly in all years, irrespective of demand conditions.

The other possibility is that the reading in year 1 was accurate, but a change that took place after year 1 turned a talented salesperson into an untalented one. There are a number of possible explanations. Health changes, changes in skills required by the market, and changes in personal circumstances are all candidates. Once again it is necessary to ask, "Which story is right, and does it matter?"

There are two ways to determine whether the strange evaluation pattern reflects measurement error or a regime shift. Suppose that instead of 1 year of good evaluations, 20 years of good evaluations preceded the 10 years of poor evaluations. It is possible, but highly unlikely, that a measurement mistake was made in each of the 20 previous years. A much more likely explanation is that there was a regime shift sometime after year 20. The point is that measurement error is less likely to be the explanation when there are a large number of corroborating measures pointing to the high talent of the worker. It is much easier to accept that 1 year was in error than it is to accept that 20 years are in error. Thus, the longer the series of consistently good evaluations, the lower the likelihood that the string of poor evaluations reflects measurement error.[13]

---

[13]Even then, we cannot rule out measurement error. It is possible that evaluations are not independent and that first impressions matter. Once a supervisor thinks a worker is good, she continues to think he is good unless things get dramatically worse.

Additionally, some of the factors mentioned as causes for a regime shift are readily observable. For example, if the string of poor evaluations follows six months of convalescence for a stroke, it is likely that a regime shift occurred. One may need go no further to determine the answer than the obvious observable events in a worker's life.

It makes a difference to the firm whether the change from good to poor evaluations reflects a regime shift or measurement error. If it reflects a regime shift, the required action is clearer and more dramatic. An individual who was once a good salesperson but has permanently lost his talent for selling should be switched to another activity, either within the firm or elsewhere. But if the pattern of evaluations reflects measurement error, the desired action is less clear. Once it is known that evaluations are error-prone, the firm should put less faith in negative evaluations as well as in positive ones. This means that the information content of any given evaluation is lower. As a result, the firm should wait a longer time before making a decision on the worker, positive or negative.

Thus, measurement error can be distinguished from regime shifts by the number (and pattern) of negative evaluations that follow positive ones. The larger the number and more consistent the pattern of positives preceding negatives, the lower the likelihood that measurement error is the culprit. If measurement error is not to blame, then a regime shift has occurred and rapid action is required. But if measurement error is to blame, then the firm should be less hasty in acting because the new information is not completely reliable.

◆ ◆ ◆ ◆ ◆ DURATION OF THE PROBATIONARY PERIOD

In previous chapters (chapter 3 in particular), probation was suggested as a way to select workers. How long of a probationary period should the firm use? The longer the period, the better the information, but the longer the period, the higher the cost to the firm of tolerating a sub-par employee. The discussion of the previous section provides guidance on when to use a longer or shorter probationary period.

The trade-off is between measurement error and the costliness of retaining a bad worker, which depends on underlying heterogeneity. In most nonprofessional jobs, a six-month probationary period is common. In professional jobs, longer probationary periods, commonly amounting to many years, are used. Tenure at universities is usually not granted earlier than five or six years after the professor begins teaching. Earning a partnership at a law firm often requires about the same amount of time. The difference between the lengths of professional probationary periods and nonprofessional probationary periods can be attributed to differences in measurement error. A secretary's skills may be determined more quickly than those of a lawyer. Because learning speed varies across individuals, and because there may be considerable luck involved in finding and winning important cases, measuring a lawyer's ability is done only with considerable error. As a result, the probationary period is much longer for lawyers than for secretaries.

Measurement error aside, there is another important factor, which can be il-

FIGURE 17.1
TWO POSSIBLE
ABILITY DISTRIBUTIONS

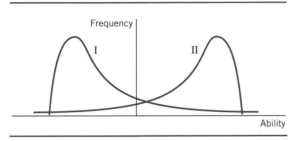

lustrated by considering two different ability distributions, as shown in Figure 17.1. Distribution I has positive skew. There is a big upside, but a small downside. Distribution II has negative skew. Some workers are absolutely disastrous for the firm, whereas the best are not much better than the average.

Suppose that a firm draws its applicants from a population characterized by distribution I. The firm can tolerate a relatively long probation period, because even those workers who are not quite good enough to keep on a permanent basis, are not disasters. But if the group of applications comes from a population characterized by distribution II, the situation is much different. Then, allowing a worker to stay on for a long period of time can have significant negative impact on the firm. Someone who is very poorly suited to the task may cause a great deal of damage. Tolerating this during a five- or six-year probationary period is probably a big mistake.

The implication is that when there is a significant probability of a big downside associated with any new hire, probationary periods should be short. Individuals should not be given as much time to show their true colors. A negative evaluation should be acted on quickly, even if it may be in error, because the cost of retaining a bad worker is very high. When the skew is positive, so that there is some chance of a big upside, but little downside risk, the evaluation period should be longer.

RECAP

Evaluation is a hassle and it is costly. Most supervisors would rather avoid doing it altogether. Of course, evaluation serves a purpose and provides two kinds of information. From evaluations, a firm can get a sense of a worker's general ability and also of the specific skills that he or she possesses. Workers with high levels of general ability are good investments; those with less general ability but a high level of specific skills may be well suited to a particular job in the firm.

Workers with more firm-specific human capital do not need to be evaluated as frequently as their newer counterparts. A corollary is that senior workers should be evaluated less frequently than junior ones. As workers get senior, the wage that they can obtain outside is usually well below that obtainable in their current firm. As a result, a deal can be struck that makes both worker and firm better off when the worker is retained. An evaluation of senior workers is less likely, therefore, to result in any significant action by the firm, and has less value than an evaluation of junior workers. Further, the lower the likelihood of a positive evaluation, the higher the value of doing evaluation. Evaluation serves to weed out workers who are not well suited for the current firm. It makes little sense to evaluate 1,000 workers to weed out one. It is probably more cost-efficient to tolerate the one low-productivity worker than to perform a costly evaluation of everyone.

Senior workers should be evaluated frequently only when regime shifts are likely to occur or when their effort is responsive to compensation. In the latter case, even senior workers must be evaluated frequently or they will have a tendency to produce at less than the optimal level of effort.

Evaluation is sometimes used to make up-or-out decisions. Having an up-or-out policy following an evaluation tends to raise the quality of the work force, but does so inefficiently under most circumstances. Workers who are valuable, but not good enough to be promoted, are fired too often under up-or-out. As a result, any gains from an up-or-out policy are likely to be swamped by the loss of workers who are still valuable to the firm.

Bringing in outsiders rather than promoting an insider usually results when an evaluation, formal or subjective, suggests that insiders are too low-quality to promote. A judgment is made on the basis of some absolute standard. Even absolute standards are based on some relative comparisons, either from the past or across groups in the present. Within-group relative comparisons, while perhaps more informative, create incentives against cooperation.

Pay compression and bureaucratic rules reduce incentives for workers to try to bias the results of evaluations. As a result, they may reduce sycophancy and improve the quality of the evaluation process. Evaluation by superiors, peers, and subordinates, albeit costly, can get around some of the problems that occur when individuals have access to those who will evaluate them.

It is possible and important to distinguish regime shifts (in ability) from measurement error. When a regime shift occurs, action must be taken quickly. When measurement is the culprit, less stock should be placed on each particular evaluation.

Probationary periods should be longer when measurement error is high and when the underlying distribution of talent has a large upside and small downside. The big losses associated with keeping low-productivity workers on board should be cut off quickly by having short evaluation periods.

◆ ◆ ◆ ◆ ◆ REFERENCES

Jovanovic, Boyan, "Job Matching and the Theory of Turnover," *Journal of Political Economy* 87 (October 1979): 972–90.

Kahn, Charles, and Huberman, Gur, "Two-Sided Uncertainty and 'Up-or-Out' Contracts," *Journal of Labor Economics* 6 (October 1988): 423–44.

Lazear, Edward P., "The Timing of Raises and Other Payments," *Carnegie-Rochester Conference Series on Public Policy* 33 (Autumn 1990): 13–48.

Milgrom, Paul R., "Employment Contracts, Influence Activities, and Efficient Organization Design," *Journal of Political Economy* 96 (February 1988): 42–60.

Prendergast, Canice, "Theory of 'Yes Men'," *American Economic Review* 83 (September 1993): 757–770.

Prendergast, Canice, and Robert Topel, "Favoritism in Organizations," *Journal of Political Economy* 104 (September 1996): 958–78.

Schelling, Thomas, *The Strategy of Conflict*, Cambridge: Harvard University Press, 1960.

ADDITIONAL ADVANCED READING ◆ ◆ ◆ ◆ ◆

Bull, Clive, and Piero Tedeschi, "Optimal Probation or New Hires," *Journal of Institutional and Theoretical Economic* 145 (December 1989): 627–42.

Loh, Eng Seng, "Employment Probation as a Sorting Mechanism," *Industrial and Labor Relations Review* 47 (April 1994): 471–86.

APPENDIX ◆ ◆ ◆ ◆ ◆

Up-or-Out

Consider a hypothetical accounting firm with one partner and one associate. Suppose the partner hires an associate to work for two periods, evaluating the associate after each period. The associate's output is A and the wage initially received from the firm is W. Without up-or-out—that is, under a flexible retention policy—the partner's payoffs are shown in Figure A17.1.

Figure A17.1 is interpreted as follows: It is unpleasant to fire someone. When an individual is fired, the partner (or principal), whose output is given by P, bears

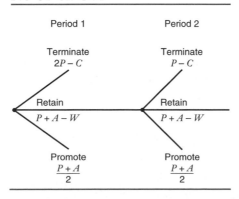

FIGURE A17.1
NO UP-OR-OUT

Period 1	Period 2
Terminate $2P - C$	Terminate $P - C$
Retain $P + A - W$	Retain $P + A - W$
Promote $\dfrac{P + A}{2}$	Promote $\dfrac{P + A}{2}$

cost C. If the associate is fired, then the firm's output over the two periods is P each period, all of which goes to the partner. Since the partner bears cost C to fire the associate, the net value to the partner is $2P - C$ over the two periods.

If the associate is retained, but not promoted, she produces A and receives W. Alternatively, the associate can be promoted to partner. If promoted to partner, she cannot be fired and shares in the revenue. She receives $\dfrac{P + A}{2}$, which is assumed to be higher than W. The original partner receives the remaining $\dfrac{P + A}{2}$ each period or $P + A$ over the two periods.

The cost of the flexible retention system is that sometimes $W > A$, but the firm retains the worker anyway. The worker is being overpaid, but the partner can't bear to fire her. This happens when

(A17.1) $2P - C < P + A - W + Max\left[P - C, P + A - W, \dfrac{P + A}{2}\right]$

The second term on the right-hand side is the value of the best choice in the second period, given that the worker has been retained during the first period. Given that the partner opted to retain the associate in the first period, the middle branch in Figure A17.1, $P + A - W$, must be best in both periods.[14] Thus, the firm retains the worker when

(A17.2) $2P - C < 2(P + A - W)$

Up-or-out is characterized by Figure A17.2. The worker can either be promoted, in which case the original partner receives $\dfrac{(P + A)}{2}$ each period, or $P + A$ over the two periods. Alternatively, the worker can be terminated, in which case the original partner earns $2P - K$ over the two periods, where K is the cost of having to tell an associate that she did not make partner.

Now, since $W < \dfrac{P + A}{2}$

$$0 < P + A - 2W$$

and

$$P + A < 2(P + A - W)$$

The value to the firm of retention is $2(P + A - W)$. The value to the firm of promotion is $P + A$. Thus, an individual who would be retained will not necessarily be promoted. This is the source of potential savings from up-or-out.

---

[14]If $P + A - W < P - C$, then (A17.1) would be $P - C < P + A - W + P - C$ or $A > W$, which is a contradiction. Also, $\dfrac{P + A}{2} > W$, by assumption.

FIGURE A17.2
UP-OR-OUT

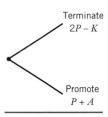

When does the partner decide against promoting the associate? Whenever the following condition holds:

(A17.3) $$2P - K > P + A$$

(from Figure A17.2).

When is the partner better off with up-or-out? It is necessary that there be some savings from this policy. The partner must terminate under up-or-out and not terminate without up-or-out. It is therefore necessary that (A17.2) and (A17.3) hold simultaneously, *and* that the partner be better off by firing the worker rather than retaining her. This requires that

(A17.4) $$2P - K > 2(P + A - W)$$

given that Equation A17.2 holds. The combination of Equations A17.2 and A17.4 implies a necessary condition: $C > K$.

Up-or-out does not stand a chance of being a profitable strategy unless this condition is true. This means that it must be (significantly) more difficult to tell a worker that she is not being retained than to tell her that she did not make partner. Unless this is true, the added discipline that up-or-out provides has no value.

Even when this condition holds, it is still far from clear that up-or-out is preferable. There may be cases where $A > W$, but $A < \dfrac{P + A}{2}$. Under these circumstances, up-or-out would lead to inefficient terminations, which could be corrected by going to a flexible retention policy.

WORKER
EMPOWERMENT

18

$\mathcal{N}$ either firms nor other organizations operate in a vacuum. They must deal with constraints placed on them, primarily by labor unions and governments. The subjects of regulation and organized labor are well developed in the economic literature, with countless books and a vast body of research devoted to them. The limited scope of this book cannot include even a cursory treatment of these topics. Still, there are some points that can be made within the space available that will add to our understanding of personnel analysis. This chapter focuses on one kind of constraint that may be imposed on the firm, which is central to the newer view of industrial relations. Specifically, we analyze worker empowerment, as demanded by a union, dictated by a government, or merely chosen by management as part of its profit-maximizing strategy. We deal with worker empowerment in a rigorous framework below. Again, let us begin with an opening discussion.

HANSEN: We need to empower our workers if we expect to get any useful feedback from them.

SCHUMPETER: Empower, emshmower. I hate that word. It is totally meaningless garbage, embraced only by people with vacuous minds. You've got to tell me specifically what you propose to do. Are you talking about another time-wasting worker committee?

HANSEN: Well, maybe. The workers have a great deal of information at their disposal that we don't have. We need to figure out a way to use it to enhance our productivity.

SCHUMPETER: Empower? Enhance productivity? Where do you get this stuff? I think you've been reading too many business magazines. Look, there is nothing worse than asking people for their advice and then not taking it. If you don't plan to act on it, don't bother getting advice.

HANSEN: My point is that we should act on it. I believe that workers are valuable assets with important points of view.

SCHUMPETER: What if one of their points of view is that we should pay them higher wages? What are you going to do with that advice? You give them power and they will use it against you.

HANSEN: It's just that kind of antagonistic view that gets companies in trouble. We are a team and we must behave like one.

SCHUMPETER: The best assumption to make when dealing with worker groups is that we're playing a zero-sum game. What they get, we lose. The more chances you give them to tell us what to do, the worse off we will be. The old adage, "give them an inch and they take a mile," applies here.

HANSEN: You've got this relativist mentality. You think that everything is a comparison between two groups where one wins and the other loses. Sometimes both win.

SCHUMPETER: Oh, yeah? You ever hear of market share? It adds up to 100 percent. Should we start empowering the competition? The virtues of monopoly are underrated. I'd like to see us totally dominate, both in the market where we sell our product and in the power that we retain over our workers. Sharing sales with our competitors is not good for us. Neither is sharing power with our workers.

This discussion was about zero-sum games and giving more control to the work force. A number of issues were raised. They include:

- What are the gains from giving workers more control in the workplace?

- Can worker empowerment increase productivity and raise profits?

- Are there costs associated with worker empowerment?

- How should a firm view a push by a worker group to obtain more power?

There are a variety of ways to empower workers. One is to provide them with information, either individually or through elected representatives. Some of the costs and benefits of worker empowerment are discussed below.[1]

---

[1]The material in the following section is based on Freeman and Lazear (1995).

COMMUNICATION FROM MANAGEMENT TO WORKERS: OPEN BOOK MANAGEMENT

◆ ◆ ◆ ◆ ◆

One recent innovation in a number of firms is *open book management*, where workers are given detailed information on the financial condition of the firm. Often, this involves training the work force in accounting and other skills that are generally peripheral to their jobs. There are clear costs in doing this, but some have argued that the benefits outweigh the costs.[2] The costs take a number of forms. First, time is required to convey the information to workers and teach them to process it. Second, giving workers information can backfire. Workers who know everything about the firm may be able to act opportunistically and extract a larger portion of the firm's profits than would otherwise be the case. This is the usual fear that management expresses about opening the books.

The primary gain to open book management or a weaker version of it is that workers may lower their expectations in ways that can help keep a firm viable. In Europe, where *works councils* are common, managers sometimes express the view that worker empowerment through their councils is helpful to management. This is particularly true when communicating bad news. The following example makes the point.

Workers generally like to receive higher wages, but recognize that when the firm is in dire straits, the amount that they receive in compensation must decline. The problem is that management, knowing that workers will accept lower wages in an emergency, has an incentive to cry wolf. Although the firm may sometimes say that times are good, it will tend to exaggerate the severity and number of occurrences of down times. If workers have only management to rely on, they must choose either to discount management's statements (at least some of the time) or to accept management's statements as fact and accept the lower compensation necessitated by the bad news.

Suppose that each worker has an alternative opportunity that offers $600 per week. During good times, the worker is worth $1,500 per week to the current firm. During bad times, the worker is worth $700 per week to the current firm. Since even $700 is greater than the alternative of $600, it is always better for the worker to remain at the firm than to move elsewhere. That is, there is always some wage—for example, $650 during bad times—that makes both the current firm and worker better off than having the worker leave. Since $650 is less than the worker's value, the firm makes a profit on him. Also, since $650 exceeds the $600 available elsewhere, the worker does better by remaining. Herein lies the problem. Since the firm knows that

---

[2]An example of open book management is detailed in Hanson (1993).

the worker is willing to accept $600, management has an incentive to lie about demand conditions. Rather than admit that times are good, management may attempt to convince its workers that times are bad. If workers believe that times are bad, they know that the firm cannot pay more than $700 without taking a loss. Thus, the maximum wage that workers expect to get under these circumstances is $700. Of course, if management were always to claim that times were bad, their statements would lose all credibility. As a result, managers must mix up the statements, but there is still a tendency for management to claim that things are worse than they are, and workers are aware of this fact.

What does the worker do? In the absence of additional information, workers can either believe management and accept lower wages, or they can assume that management is lying and hold out for higher wages. As usual, there are two kinds of errors that workers may make. If they accept management's statement, they will always retain their jobs, but they will make the mistake of accepting low wages even during good times. If they assume that management is lying and they hold out for high wages, workers will get them during good times, but they will lose their jobs during bad times. Since only some of the times that are claimed to be bad *are* bad, workers win by this strategy during those falsely labeled bad times, but they lose by the strategy during correctly labeled bad times. During true bad times, workers lose their jobs by holding out for high wages that the company truly can't pay. They are then forced to resort to their outside opportunity of $600, which is less than the $700 that the company would be willing to offer.

For any given announcement that times are bad, workers must assess the probability that the statement is accurate. This depends on actual conditions in the industry. If the work force is used to seeing primarily good conditions, they may discount heavily any announcement that times are bad, assuming instead that the firm is simply trying to negotiate a better deal. In the current example, suppose that firm and worker split the estimated surplus. This means that if workers believe the firm's statements, they will receive $650 in wages during times that are declared to be bad. If they choose to take a hard line because they assume that the firm is lying, they will receive

$$\$1150 \ [=.5(\$1500 + 600)]$$

when the firm is lying, but will lose their jobs when the firm is telling the truth. If it is likely that the firm is lying, either because the management is comprised of pathological liars or because conditions in the industry are almost always good, then the workers will choose the hard line. Sometime this results in high wages, but once in a while, it results in job loss.

The firm would always prefer that the workers take the softer approach. Then, costly layoffs never occur and the firm reaps the benefit of paying lower wages in those periods where it declares, correctly or not, that times are bad. It is for this reason that the firm may want to provide information to the workers. Giving workers sufficient information so that they can determine for themselves that times are truly bad may soften workers' positions and prevent unwarranted layoffs. The disadvantage is that giving workers full information strengthens worker resolve during periods when things are going well for the firm. This is the trade-off that the firm must make. If workers take the hard line too frequently, the firm may decide that the gains from providing information outweigh the costs that the firm bears during good times. The calculation is a straightforward one, and is detailed in the appendix. The basic points can be summarized here:

Firms benefit from providing workers with information when and only when workers would otherwise choose to take a hard line. If workers are soft, then there is no gain to the firm's revealing information to the workers. This will only make them aggressive during good times. The question then boils down to determining when workers would take a hard line in the absence of information. Firms benefit from providing information to workers when the following conditions hold:

1. *There is a large difference between the wage paid during good times and the wage paid during bad times.* When the wage difference is large, workers are reluctant to accept the firm's word that times are bad. Doing so results in a large wage cut, which has a large adverse effect on workers. If there is a large gain to taking a hard line, workers are more inclined to be aggressive, and firms should be more inclined to provide accurate information to workers to dissuade workers from making aggressive demands during bad times.

2. *There is a small difference between the wage paid during bad times at the current firm and the alternative wage available.* If workers have good alternatives, then they do not lose much when they suffer a layoff during bad times. Hard bargaining results in a layoff when times are truly bad and workers misjudge the truthfulness of the firm's claims, but the layoff is less painful when a worker's alternatives are good. As a result, workers will fear job loss less and will be more aggressive when alternatives are good. Thus, when worker alternatives are good, the firm should be more inclined to provide accurate information to workers to dissuade them from demanding too much during bad times.

3. *As a corollary, since young workers have less firm-specific capital and less to lose, they tend to be more aggressive than older workers. As such, open book management is more likely to be profitable when the work force is young than when it is old.* Workers who are older have a lower value of alternatives relative to their current wage. As such, they are less likely to demand high wages than are the younger workers. Since the firm loses by revealing information to workers who are already committed to taking a softer approach, open book management is less valuable when the work force is older.

Indeed, this squares with most readers' intuition on the issue. It is the young workers, who feel that they have little to lose or who are most inclined to take risk, that are often the leaders of strong worker action. Older workers, who have families and who feel that it would be difficult to find a new equivalent job, are more likely to be passive.

◆ ◆ ◆ ◆ ◆ COMMUNICATION FROM WORKERS TO MANAGEMENT

Another potential advantage of worker empowerment is that workers may be more willing to communicate their views to management. Sometimes, workers are afraid to give management too much information about their preferences for fear that management can somehow use the knowledge against them. For example, if management learns that workers care a great deal for a particular benefit, the firm may provide the benefit, but then cut wages (or not give any subsequent raises) in return, knowing that workers are so enamored with the benefit that they will not leave the firm. Workers, knowing that the firm is going to behave in this strategic fashion, will not provide the firm with the relevant information in the first place. But having the information could make both sides better off. The firm might be able to provide the benefit that the workers like at a lower price than workers are willing to pay. To see this, we use the indifference curve analysis of chapter 14, where individuals were willing to trade money for some benefit. In chapter 14, the trade-off was between wages and flexible time. Here, we consider another example, where workers care about a health plan and wages.

In Figure 18.1, workers' willingness to trade wages for health coverage is shown, using an indifference curve diagram.

Wages are plotted on the vertical axis. The percent of an individual's medical costs that are covered by the plan are plotted on the horizontal axis. The higher the percentage of costs covered the better, as far as the worker is concerned.

Two sets of indifference curves are shown in Figure 18.1. The dotted indifference curves, one of which is labeled K, corresponds to a worker who likes health benefits. The solid indifference curves, one of which is labeled V, corresponds to a worker who loves health benefits. It is easy to see that the individual whose preferences are represented by the solid indifference curves cares relatively more about health benefits than the individual whose preferences are represented by the dotted indifference curves. Consider any point at which the two individuals' indiffer-

DILBERT reprinted by permission of United Feature Syndicate, Inc.

FIGURE 18.1
WORKER COMMUNICATION

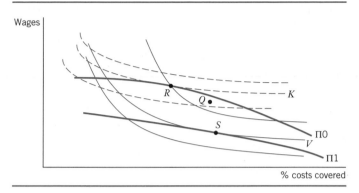

ence curves cross. At that intersection, both individuals would enjoy the same allocation of wages and health benefits. The individual with the dotted indifference curves would be willing to give up more in wages in order to obtain any given amount of health benefits than would the individual with solid indifference curves. The steeper indifference curves imply this directly. As a result, it can be concluded that the individual with solid indifference curves has a greater willingness to trade wages for health benefits than the individual with the dotted indifference curves.

Curves V and K are special. Curve K is the indifference curve that provides the health-benefit liker just enough utility to keep that person working at the job. If the firm provides any level of utility less than K, the health-benefit liker will quit. Similarly, curve V is the indifference curve that provides the health-benefit lover just enough utility to keep that person working at the job. If the firm provides any level of utility less than V, the health-benefit lover will quit.

The heavier curves are the firm's isoprofit curves. An *isoprofit curve* provides the same level of profit to the firm at all points along the curve. It is negatively sloped because a firm that offers higher benefits must be allowed to reduce its wage level in order to keep profits the same. Of the two isoprofit curves shown, the one that is closer to zero is associated with a higher level of profit because wages and benefits, and therefore costs, are lower as points move toward the origin.

Now, if the firm believes that the worker is a benefit liker, but not a benefit lover, it will offer the worker point R because this is the point that yields the highest profit to the firm, but still retains the worker. There is no point that the firm prefers to R on (or above) indifference curve K. There are points below indifference curve K that yield higher profit to the firm, but the worker will quit if offered the combination of wages and benefits represented by one of those points.

If instead the firm believes that the worker is a benefit lover, it will offer the worker point S. Benefit loving workers who understand the firm's desire to keep profits as large as possible will behave strategically. Rather than telling management that they are benefit lovers, they will pretend to be only benefit likers. The firm offers benefit likers point R rather than point S. Point R provides more utility even to the benefit lover than point S, because R lies above the lover's indifference curve, V, that runs through point S. In other words, if the firm knows what benefit lovers are willing to give up for additional benefits, the firm will take advantage of them. If instead the firm believes that benefit lovers are unwilling to give up very much for the additional benefits, it will offer them a better package.

The strategic behavior by worker and firm makes both worse off than they could be. Because the benefit lover pretends to be a benefit liker, a benefit lover ends up at point R, which is better than point S. The firm is worse off than it would be at point S, but offers R because it is afraid of losing the worker. However, point Q makes both firm and worker better off than point S. Point Q lies on a higher indifference curve to the benefit lover than does point S. Because the worker pretends to be a benefit liker, not lover, the firm offers a package that is tilted too much in the direction of wages and too little in the direction of benefits. A benefit liker prefers R to Q because Q lies below the dotted indifference curve that runs through R, but a benefit lover prefers Q to R, because Q lies above the solid indifference curve that runs through R. Point R is the wrong allocation for the benefit lover, but is offered because of the worker's strategic behavior.

This is a key point. The firm wants to obtain accurate information about a worker's preferences not because it is primarily concerned about worker welfare, but because the firm cares about profits and catering to worker preferences enhances profits. By providing workers with a package that better suits what workers want, the firm can reduce overall compensation costs and increase profits. Point Q is better than point R from both the worker's and the firm's point of view. Because the firm operates in a competitive labor market, it must offer the worker conditions that are sufficiently attractive to retain the worker. Both R and Q are sufficiently attractive, but Q is preferred by both worker and firm.

Why doesn't the worker simply tell the firm that he or she is a benefit lover and ask for point Q? The answer is that once the firm knows this, it will offer point S, which makes the worker worse off than he or she was at R. In order to induce the worker to communicate truthfully, the worker must have some power over the way the information is used. This provides a rationale for worker empowerment. When the work force knows that information provided to management cannot be used against it, it will be more likely to tell the truth. Since the truth can allow the firm to tailor the work environment more to the worker's liking, both sides can benefit.

In simple terms, workers do not want to tell the firm that they love something that the firm can provide because the firm will use the knowledge against them, offering a lower wage than would otherwise be the case. It is fear of strategic behavior by management that keeps workers from being truthful. Thus, the second benefit of worker empowerment is the enhancement of profit-increasing communication from worker to firm.

The following principle emerges:

A firm that desires truthful communication from worker to firm may need to provide some worker empowerment so that workers are certain that the revealed information will not be used against them.

As a practical matter, this can be accomplished by allowing workers some say in the working conditions that they face. The more say that workers have, the more likely they are to be truthful about their preferences. However, as will be shown, the more say that workers have, the larger the share of the pie that they can cut for themselves.

One alternative is to ignore worker communication altogether. The firm can simply make an assumption about worker preferences and pay accordingly. If there are enough other firms competing for worker services, over the long haul workers will sort. In the context of the previous example, firms that provide packages that benefit lovers prefer will attract only lovers. Those that provide packages that benefit likers prefer will attract only likers. Just as in chapter 14, the market will induce sorting. But if a lover's package is offered to a group of likers, the likers will leave. Replacing them can be costly, especially when firm-specific human capital is present.

The choice between the two strategies is illustrated by the difference between European labor relations and American labor relations. Europeans, particularly Germans, set up works councils, which are worker-elected bodies that represent labor's interests on a variety of issues, primarily those that relate to working conditions. By giving workers some control over how information is used, they can be more forthright and the environment can be more cooperative. The cost is that firms give up flexibility because they must obtain works council acquiescence in order to make changes that fall within the works council's jurisdiction. Cooperation, while beneficial, has its costs.

Nonunion American firms, on the other hand, are more dictatorial. They retain flexibility because they can implement their plans without having to obtain approval from a worker body. There may be less worker–manager cooperation, but there is also less time wasted discussing matters that have little bearing on profit.

EMPOWERMENT AND EARNINGS PROFILES

♦ ♦ ♦ ♦ ♦

Workers with firm-specific human capital are more likely to insist on being given power. Before workers are willing to make an investment in an asset that is firm specific, they are likely to want assurances that their investment will be protected against arbitrary actions by management, such as forcing them to leave and lose their investment. Thus:[3]

---

[3]Rotemberg (1994) makes this point more formally.

Specific human capital and worker empowerment tend to go together. Workers who have a great deal of firm-specific human capital will seek power within an organization and firms that expect workers to invest in firm-specific human capital should be prepared to offer power to their workers.

Other workers may demand power as well. Recall the life-cycle incentive profiles of chapter 11. The story was that young workers are paid less than they are worth and old workers are paid more than they are worth. Young workers have implicitly invested in the firm and their investments depend on the good faith (and good fortune) of the firm. Under these circumstances, workers are more likely to demand some say in the matters of the organization.

The necessary ingredient for a worker to want power in the firm is not specific human capital; it is that the worker has much to lose if he or she must move to another job. Thus, upward sloping incentive contracts, unionization that results in wages at the current firm that are higher than the worker can obtain elsewhere, or specific human capital are all ingredients that induce workers to want power. The evidence seems consistent with this point. Union workers demand much more voice in the day-to-day operations of the firm than do nonunion workers, precisely because union workers lose more when they are forced to change jobs. Thus:

Workers are more likely to demand power whenever their best alternative wage is (significantly) lower than their wage at the current firm.

This creates some tension. Workers want power, but firms have less to gain by giving it to them. To the extent that workers are overpaid and their alternatives are poor, their ability to back up threats with credible action is reduced. The firm knows that the worker suffers significantly by a departure and is less likely to fear aggressive behavior by workers.

◆ ◆ ◆ ◆ ◆ WORKER EMPOWERMENT AND CREATIVITY

Fact or folklore, many believe that empowered workers contribute to the firm by providing new ideas that management would not have discovered on its own. Because workers are in closer contact with actual production, ways to improve productivity that are obvious to the workers may escape management entirely. The analysis of chapter 12 is relevant here. It was argued that teams should be constructed with members who have information that is distinct and relevant to one another. Worker empowerment is a special case of team production. When managers empower their workers and encourage them to provide suggestions and input to the firm, the managers are encouraging more teamwork by making workers part of the management team. But empowerment requires action. No one likes to be asked for an opinion, only to have it ignored. When are suggestions by workers likely to be most useful? They are most useful when workers possess information that is both relevant and different from that held by managers. Thus, as in chapter 12:

WORKER EMPOWERMENT AT SATURN CORPORATION
❖ ❖ ❖ ❖ ❖ ❖ ❖ ❖ ❖

The market share of General Motors in the early 1990s was barely more than half of what it had been in the early 1960s. If that rate of decline were to continue for another 30 years, the world's biggest automaker of the twentieth century would disappear from the industry map. Quality problems and relatively poor reliability of GM cars were said to be among the most important reasons for the market share decline. The history of stormy labor relations further aggravated the company's problems. The customer base of GM's most prestigious brand, Cadillac, had been deteriorating for years. In the minds of many people, the word Cadillac is associated with high quality when it refers to anything other than cars.

In an effort to reverse the negative trend, GM decided to develop Saturn, a small, reliable, quality car that can appeal to young buyers. GM officially announced creation of Saturn Corporation on January 8, 1985. According to General Motors Chairman Roger B. Smith, "Saturn is the key to GM's long-term competitiveness, survival, and success as a domestic-producer."

Everything from the trademark slogan, "A different kind of company, a different kind of car," to the organizational structure of Saturn, reflects its unorthodox attitude. Since the very beginning, the management of Saturn believed that good labor relations and active worker participation in quality control and improvement programs were instrumental to the company's success. Creators of Saturn succeeded in breaking with old confrontational ways of interaction between GM and UAW. The union and the management took many precautions in order to prevent costly conflicts. Currently 10 percent of pay at Saturn is contingent on meeting high performance and quality goals. In the future the variable pay will increase to 20 percent of the total compensation. This might be a safeguard against labor disputes. Normally, at a time when the productivity is high the union is well positioned to demand higher wages; that may be the reason why a substantial amount of variable pay is promised when performance goals are met.

Production at Saturn is team based. Work is assigned to 165 self-directed teams that are responsible for making decisions ranging from troubleshooting in production to deciding on purchase and installation of new equipment, and even developing budgetary projections. It is remarkable that ordinary workers at Saturn have authority to stop the production line if there is a quality problem. Saturn empowers its workers by giving them more decision-making power, more knowledge, and more responsibility than workers in any other part of GM. Sean Campbell, an electrician who worked at the Detroit-area GM plant prior to joining Saturn, characterizes Saturn as ". . . the best place I've ever worked. At the old shop, you were told what to do and when to do it." Rick Pittman, a maintenance worker said: "I've never had the say-so or the liberty that I have in this plant. If you've got a quality problem, you stop the line in a heartbeat." This type of environment helps to maintain trust between workers and the management.

Saturn allocates 13 days per employee per year training its work force. In 1990 alone, Saturn logged more than 800,000 hours of training. Saturn's workers receive more training than their colleagues at other GM units. If the workers are empowered with more decision making authority, they need to be given more training that can help them to become better decisionmakers.

Saturn Corporation has been successful. The company showed first profits of about $1 million in 1993. A reputation for solid quality and a superb record of customer satisfaction are among the most impressive achievements of the company. According to J. D. Powers, the foremost recognized name in automotive consumer satisfaction, Saturn is ranked third in customer satisfaction, immediately following Lexus and Infinity—luxury sedans that are almost thrice the price of Saturn.

Source: Thomas Li-Ping Tang and Amy Beth Crofford, "Forming the Future: Lessons from Saturn Corporation," by O'Toole published by Blackwell Publishers and "Self-Managing Work Teams," *Employment Relations Today* 22 (December 22, 1995): 29.

Creativity is most likely to be enhanced by seeking input from workers when workers have information that is different from that possessed by management and is relevant to the production process.

Having distinct information is not enough. The information must also be relevant to production. For example, a worker may possess a great deal of knowledge about wine that the manager does not have. But if the firm produces lawn mower blades, knowledge of wines is unlikely to have much of an effect on production. A firm would not want to empower its work force, hoping for enhanced productivity, when the only unique knowledge its work force possessed related to wine consumption.

Conversely, there is less hope of additional creativity from worker empowerment when the information possessed by workers is a subset of the information possessed by management. It is possible, of course, that the same information leads to different conclusions in different people, but the likelihood of different ideas from workers and management is lower when information is shared.

THE DECISION TO EMPOWER WORKERS ◆ ◆ ◆ ◆ ◆

In the last few pages, we outlined ways in which productivity could be enhanced by empowering workers, but the opening scenario made clear that there might be some costs associated with worker empowerment that could offset any benefits obtained. What is the bottom line, and how should the firm think about the decision to provide workers with additional power? The primary point is that the firm should not provide workers with as much power as would maximize productivity, because productivity is not profit. In the process of giving workers power, the firm also gives workers the ability to extract a larger share of the pie. Thus, maximizing the size of the pie is not the relevant criterion as far as the firm is concerned. The appropriate criterion from the firm's point of view is to maximize the amount (not proportion) of profit that goes to the firm. Put differently, it is better to have three-fourths of an eight-inch pie than half of a nine-inch pie. The following analysis illustrates the issues involved and provides some guidelines for choosing the amount of power to provide workers.

In Figure 18.2a, the firm's share of profit is graphed as a function of worker power. When workers have no power, the firm's share is 1, meaning that the firm gets to keep 100 percent of value added. This extreme is never reached because workers always have some alternatives, even if it is consuming leisure, which gives them some hold over the firm. Were the firm to keep 100 percent of value added, workers would be paid nothing. Even the meekest, wimpiest worker would have the willpower to refuse to work under such circumstances.

At the other extreme, workers have so much power that the firm share is zero. The firm can keep none of the profits; even the normal return on capital goes to labor. This situation is not stable either. No investor will put money into a firm that is known to return 0 percent on equity. Even the most powerful group of workers will be forced to give some of the returns to capital in order to pay investors, not to mention managers.

FIGURE 18.2
WORKER EMPOWERMENT AND PROFIT

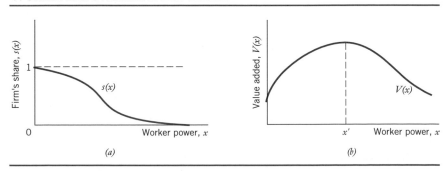

(a)

(b)

The general point, however, is that the relation between worker power and firm's share is an inverse one. The more power workers possess, the smaller the share of the pie the firm gets.

Figure 18.2b shows the relation of value added to worker power. The inverted U-shaped relation implies that there is such a thing as too little worker empowerment, just as there can be too much worker empowerment. With no worker empowerment, the kinds of forces discussed in the last few pages are impeded. Firms cannot communicate with workers in a credible way, workers are afraid to make their true feelings known, and creativity is stifled as the firm ignores worker views, wishes, and suggestions. Morale may suffer under such conditions and productivity tends to be extremely low.

As workers become somewhat more empowered, their productivity rises, eventually reaching its peak at x'. After x', additional power reduces value added. Workers become so powerful that needed flexibility is lost. The firm is run by committee and cannot respond to competition. Workers may use their power to extract resources from the firm, thereby running it down and reducing its productive capacity. Eventually, the firm may even go bankrupt. The notion that workers can be given too much or too little say in the firm is hardly controversial. Ultimately the manager must decide how much power to give workers. Figure 18.2c helps with this decision.

Figure 18.2c combines the information of the previous two graphs. The highest curve, labeled $V(x)$, is identical to the one shown in Figure 18.2b. It is merely copied from the earlier diagram. Note that it reaches its peak when worker power is set to x'. The lower curve, labeled "Firm Profits," is equal to the total value added, times the firm's share from Figure 18.2a; that is, it is $s(x)$ (Value Added).

To understand this curve, which is the product of the one in 18.2a and the one in 18.2b, consider the extreme points. When workers have no power, all of the value added goes to the firm. Firm profits are equal to value added, so the curves intersect when worker power is at a minimum. At the other end, worker power is

FIGURE 18.2 (continued)
WORKER EMPOWERMENT AND PROFIT

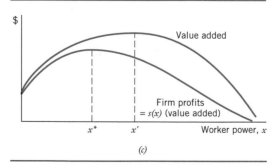

(c)

high enough so that the firm's share is zero. Even though value added is still positive (albeit quite low), the firm gets to keep none of it. Workers keep the entire amount of value added, but value added is very low so workers' total take is quite small.

As in Figure 18.2b, value added is maximized when workers are given power at the level of x'. However, the firm does not care about maximizing value added; the goal is to maximize its own profits. This occurs when workers have power x^*, not x'. It is easy to show analytically (see the appendix) that the firm maximizes its profits by giving workers less power than would maximize the value added of the firm. That is, it is always the case that x^* lies to the left of x'. The intuition is as follows. Suppose that the firm has already given workers x^* of power. Giving workers additional power can increase the total value added, but the rate at which value added rises with additional power is very low. (Near the very top of the $V(x)$ curve, $V(x)$ hardly rises at all with additional worker power.) At the same time, because workers are getting more power, the firm's share is declining. Once x^* is reached, the effect of getting a smaller share outweighs the effect of getting a larger pie. It must be true that the smaller share effect outweighs the larger pie effect before x equals x' because as x gets close to x', the pie is hardly expanding at all. At the same time, workers' share is still expanding.

The conclusion is that, from the shareholders' point of view, the firm should give workers less power than would maximize the firm's value added. The goal is not productivity maximization, but profit maximization.

The last few pages have shown that the firm would like to offer workers less power than the amount that maximizes value added. What factors affect the firm's decision on how much power to give to the worker? There are two forces at work. First, when the firm's share falls more rapidly as a function of worker power, the firm will want to choose lower values of x. This is because the smaller share effect swamps the larger pie effect for lower values of worker power. This is shown in Figure 18.3a. The curve labeled I is the original curve from Figure 18.2a. The

FIGURE 18.3
EMPOWERING WORKERS: TWO SCENARIOS

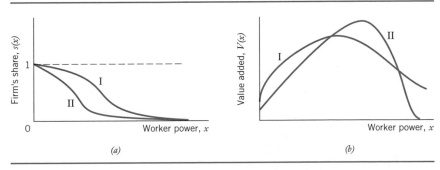

(a)   (b)

curve labeled "II" is another possible $s(x)$ function. It falls more steeply. The resulting x^* is lower when $s(x)$ takes the shape of curve II than when it takes the shape of curve I.

Second, when the value added function rises steeply even for high values of x so that the peak of the $V(x)$ function in Figure 18.2b lies more to the right, the firm will want to give relatively more power to the workers. This is because the effect of the larger pie swamps the effect of a smaller share for higher values of worker power. This is shown in Figure 18.3b. Curve I is the original curve from Figure 18.2b. Curve II is another possible $V(x)$ function. It rises more steeply. The resulting x^* is higher when $V(x)$ takes the shape of curve II than when it takes the shape of curve I.

When is the $s(x)$ curve likely to look more like II than like I? Here are some guidelines. Giving workers increased power is likely to reduce capital's share more significantly when:

1. Workers work together so that it is easier for them to discuss, organize, and coerce.

2. Workers have a longer-term relationship with the firm so that they are willing to invest more in increasing their share. This is also the situation in which workers will most want to obtain power.

3. Workers have access to outsiders who can leverage their power and use it for rent extraction, as well as productivity augmentation. Most often, the outsiders take the form of unions or government agencies that are sympathetic to worker arguments.

When any of these three conditions are present, significant levels of worker empowerment are likely to result in reduced profits.

Similarly, we may also ask, "When is the $V(x)$ curve likely to look more like II than like I?" If the $V(x)$ function looks like curve II, then the firm benefits by giving workers more power. The following conditions make the $V(x)$ function rise steeply and continue to rise, even for large values of x:

1. Workers have a great deal of information that is both relevant to production and not possessed by management. Then, the creativity enhancement associated with worker empowerment is likely to be largest.

2. Worker preferences are idiosyncratic and unknown by management. Under these circumstances, workers may be reluctant to reveal their desires to management for fear that the knowledge can be used strategically against them. Then, empowering the work force may enhance valuable communication from worker to manager.

Sometimes a government steps in and creates regulations that change, by decree, the amount of power that workers have. There is an efficiency argument for taking steps of this sort. Since the firm does not empower workers enough to maximize value added, one could argue that the government can improve things by ordering firms to empower workers up to level x'. Although this is a potentially sound argument, it has two problems at the practical level.

First, there is no reason to believe that the government will know how much power is consistent with maximizing value added. It is as likely to overshoot x', as it is to undershoot x'. This is even more true when it is recognized that the optimal amount of worker empowerment, even from the social point of view, varies across firms. Curve II in Figure 18.3b is associated with a different amount of optimal empowerment than curve I in Figure 18.3b. Legislation tends to be a blunt instrument. It has a "one-size-fits-all" aspect, which means that the law is not well tailored to any specific situation. As such, it may do more harm than good.

Second, laws are not created by altruistic dictators, but instead by a political process. The political process plays off labor groups against management groups. Legislation that results from this process naturally reflects the interplay of interest groups. There is no reason to expect that the product of this interaction will result in the optimal amount of worker empowerment. Government regulations on worker empowerment, or any aspect of industrial relations for that matter, merely replaces industrial politics with national politics.

AN APPLICATION: A UNION-ORGANIZING CAMPAIGN

An attempt by a union to organize a work force is a prime example of the trade-off engendered in this chapter's analysis. Some[4] have argued that unions actually make firms more productive through a variety of measures, some of which have been discussed already. Unions, it is argued, may provide a relatively efficient way for workers to communicate their preferences to management. Because unions may also reduce the likelihood that management will use information to take advantage of workers, workers are more inclined to communicate with management in a union setting than in a non-union one. The grievance procedure, which is generally formalized in a union firm, is one way by which workers can prevent firms from using information against them. There is a trade-off, however. Even if unions do make workers more productive, they do not necessarily make firms more profitable. Because firms care about total profits, not the size of the pie, firms may oppose a union that improves productivity, but that also increases workers' share too much.

One of the most famous organizing drives in recent history involved the United Farm Workers (and later the Teamsters) and California farming interests. About 35 years ago, the UFW, led by the now legendary Cesar Chavez, initiated strikes and boycotts of California agricultural products, most notably grapes and lettuce, in order to force the growers to allow workers to be unionized. Eventually, unionization occurred, although some of it was with the Teamsters, whom the UFW considered to have negotiated **sweetheart contracts** with the growers.[5]

---

[4]See especially Freeman and Medoff (1984).
[5]A sweetheart contract is a contract said to be favorable to management, presumably in return for some payment or favor to union leaders.

Grower opposition to the union was strong and resilient. Despite years of boycotts and labor unrest, growers tenaciously held their ground.

The California agriculture situation is one of the most notorious cases of management opposition to unions, but it is hardly unique. Firms frequently resist unions. Given the large cost of doing so and the potential gain from increased productivity, why are firms so resistant to unions? To see why, consider the following calculation.

A large firm that has $1 billion in sales faces a union organizing drive. Labor's share in the economy hovers around 75 percent, which means that 75 percent of all after-tax revenues eventually find their way into labor's hands and 25 percent eventually goes to capital owners. Even if a unionized labor force leads to productivity-enhancing worker empowerment, how large would this effect have to be for the firm to be willing to welcome the union?

At the typical $1 billion firm, $750 million is paid out to labor. A union that is effective in organizing the firm can be expected to raise wages. The wage differential associated with unionization is generally found to be somewhere between 10 percent and 25 percent, the larger number for **craft unions** (such as those in the building trades), and the smaller number for **industrial unions** (such as those representing large manufacturing industries like autos and steel).[6] To be conservative, let us take the lower number as our estimate of the effect of unionization on wages. Were the union to organize successfully, the wage bill would increase by 10 percent or from $750 million to $825 million.[7] If nothing else were to change, capital's return would fall from $250 million to $175 million. It is hardly surprising that a reduction in return of $75 million is met with resistance. But recall that unions may actually increase productivity. To determine the amount by which productivity would have to be increased in order to imply a net gain for capital, note that labor's share after unionization is 82.5 percent, and capital's share is 17.5 percent. Thus, in order for the firm to welcome the union, it must be the case that

$$(.175) \text{ (Net revenue after unionization)} > (.25) \text{ (Net revenue before unionization)}$$

The left-hand side of the expression is capital's take after unionization, whereas the right-hand side is capital's take before unionization. The expression can be rewritten as

$$\text{(Net revenue after unionization)/(Net revenue before unionization)} > .25/.175$$

or

$$\text{(Net revenue after unionization)/(Net revenue before unionization)} > 1.4286$$

---

[6]The literature on union wage differentials is vast. It follows the classic work by H. Gregg Lewis (1963).

[7]This assumes that the union is also effective in preventing offsetting employment reduction. To the extent that employment reduction occurs, the calculations overstate the adverse impact on capital.

In order for capital to prefer unionization, the ratio of revenue after unionization to revenue before unionization would have to be larger than 1.4286. Put differently, the productivity increase associated with unionization would have to exceed a whopping 42.86 percent. Few changes in the history of humankind have increased productivity by 42 percent, and unionization is not one of them.

The amount that a firm might be willing to pay to stave off unionization is enormous. Suppose we assume that unionization does increase firm productivity by 10 percent, which would be in line with the amount by which it increases wages. Capital's return would then be .175 ($1.1 billion), or $192.5 million. Recall that before unionization, capital's share was $250 million. Note further that these numbers are calculated on an annual basis. The difference between the union and nonunion revenue that goes to capital is ($250 − $192.5) million, or $57.5 million per year. If the firm were expected to survive for another ten years, then at a (real) interest rate of 4 percent, the present value to capital of keeping the union out would be

$$\sum_{i=1}^{10} \frac{\$57.5 \text{ million}}{(1.04)^i}$$

The present value is then $466 million. The firm would be willing to give up almost half of a year's worth of sales in order to keep the union out. It is no wonder that firms fight very hard to prevent unionization.

This illustrates the point made earlier in this chapter. Although productivity may increase by empowering workers, the productivity gains have to be very large to swamp the effect of a reduction in capital's share. Under normal circumstances, the requirements are unlikely to be met. As a result, it is in a firm's best interests to provide workers with less power than would maximize productivity. Analogously, firms usually gain by opposing unionization, even in those cases where unionization has the effect of raising productivity.

RECAP

♦ ♦ ♦ ♦ ♦

Worker empowerment has potential benefits, but it also has its costs. There are three main benefits associated with giving workers power. First, it may enhance communication from management to workers. Through techniques such as open book management, a firm that gives its workers information that is atypical in a standard industrial setting may be able to communicate bad news more credibly to its work force. Second, workers who have the power to influence the way information is used may be more likely to provide that information to management. Thus, empowerment may enhance communication from workers to managers. This is especially so as it relates to communication of data that could be used against the workers. Enhanced communication from worker to manager allows the firm to tailor the work environment in accordance with worker preferences and thereby lower labor costs. Third, worker empowerment may magnify creativity and result in a more innovative environment.

A number of conditions are associated with the productive use of worker empowerment. First, using empowerment to improve communication from management to workers is most useful when workers would adopt too aggressive a stance in the absence of empowerment. Overly aggressive behavior by workers is most likely when the gains from being aggressive are very large, because workers earn much more by being aggressive than by being passive. Also, workers are more aggressive when they have little to lose—that is, when their alternatives are not much worse than their current situation. As a result, young workers tend to be more aggressive than older ones. Workers care about their current situation relative to others most when they have firm-specific human capital or, more generally, when their wages at the current firm exceed their alternatives by a significant margin. Workers in situations that satisfy these conditions are most likely to demand power. This creates some tension between worker and firm, especially when the workers are currently overpaid, say for incentive reasons, relative to their younger counterparts. Workers want power to protect their current situation, but the firm has less to lose by denying them that power. When workers are overpaid, their fall-back position is worse and the gain to worker empowerment is smaller.

Worker empowerment may hasten innovation by encouraging worker creativity. This is most likely to be beneficial when workers have information or experiences that are different from those of management and when the information that workers possess is relevant to the production process.

Since firms care about profit, not productivity, a firm is likely to want to provide workers with less than the productivity-maximizing level of empowerment. One consequence of giving workers power is that they are then better able to extract profits from the firm. As such, the firm takes into account that transferring power to the workers not only makes them more productive, but also makes them tougher bargainers. Profits are maximized by giving workers less power than that which would maximize productivity.

Profit-increasing transfers of power from firms to workers are least likely to occur when workers band together and can easily organize to act against the firm's interests, when workers have long-term relationships with the firm, and when workers have easy access to outsiders who can assist in profit extraction. Transfers of power to workers are most likely to occur when workers have a great deal of information not possessed by management that is relevant to the production process and when worker preferences are idiosyncratic and unknown by management.

Finally, it is no surprise that firms strongly resist union-organizing drives. Even when unions may enhance firm productivity, the price that shareholders pay in the form of lost profits is generally very high.

◆ ◆ ◆ ◆ ◆ **REFERENCES**

Freeman, Richard, and Edward Lazear, "An Economic Analysis of Works Councils," in Joel Rogers and Wolfgang Streeck, eds., *Works Councils: Consultation, Representation, and Cooperation in Industrial Relations* [NBER conference volume],Chicago: University of Chicago Press for the NBER, November 1995.

Freeman, Richard, and James Medoff, *What Do Unions Do?* New York: Basic Books, 1984.

Hanson, Kirk O., "Jack Stack," *The Business Enterprise Trust*, Case 9-993-009, Harvard Business School Publishing, distributor, 1993.

Lewis, H. Gregg, *Unionism in Relative Wage in the United States*, Chicago: University of Chicago Press, 1963.

Rotemberg, Julio J., "Human Relations in the Workplace," *Journal of Political Economy* (August 1994): 684–714.

ADDITIONAL ADVANCED READING ◆◆◆◆◆

Cutcher-Gershenfeld, Joel, Thomas A. Kochan, and Anil Verma, "Recent Developments in U. S. Employee Involvement Initiatives: Erosion or Diffusion," in Donna Sockell, David Lewin and David B. Lipsky, eds., *Advances in Industrial and Labor Relations. Vol. 5, A Research Annual*, Greenwich, CT: JAI Press, pp. 1–32.

Doucouliagos, Chris, "Worker Participation and Productivity in Labor-Managed and Participatory Capitalist Firms: A Meta-analysis," *Industrial and Labor Relatons Review* (October 1995): 58–77.

Flanagan, Robert, "Wage Concessions and Long-Term Union Wage Flexibility," *Brookings Papers on Economic Activity 0* (1984): 183–216.

APPENDIX ◆◆◆◆◆

Open Book Management

When does it pay to provide workers with information about the actual profits of the firm? The following model provides the answer.[8] This framework is slightly more general than the discussion in the text of this chapter because it puts the discussion in terms of worker utility, rather than in terms of wages alone. In this way, nonpecuniary attributes of the job, as well as wage, can be altered. It is only necessary to remember that an increase in wage or in the amount of a desirable job characteristic increases utility. Let us model the situation as follows:

A firm and its workers decide on one workplace variable: the speed of work, which can either be fast (F) or normal (N). Workers view speed as bad and prefer a normal pace. They obtain utility U_N, working normal, and U_F, working fast, with $U_N > U_F$. In addition, we assume that workers prefer to remain with the firm even at the fast pace, so that $U_F > U_0$, where U_0 is the utility from leaving the firm. In contrast to workers, firms view speed as good, as their profits are higher when workers work at the high pace. (To translate this model into the discussion in the text, think of working at the normal rate as receiving a high wage and working at the fast rate as receiving a low wage. Since the low wage is higher than the alternative, $U_N > U_0$).

---

[8]This section is taken almost directly from Freeman and Lazear (1995).

Assume that the environment consists of two states: good or bad, with known probabilities p and $1 - p$. In the good state, firm profits π_F are when the workers work fast and π_N when they work normal, with $\pi_F > \pi_N$. In the bad state profits are $\pi_B > 0$ when workers work fast, but are negative when workers work normal, forcing the firm to shut down. Total surplus is larger in the good state than in the bad state, and is larger in the bad state when workers work fast than when the firm goes out of business. This highlights the fact that the major social loss occurs when the firm closes because workers do not accede to management's desire to work fast.

The problem for workers is that while they prefer to work at the fast speed in the bad state, they lack credible information about the state of the firm. They distrust management because management can lie about the state, inducing faster work even in the good state in order to garner more of the joint surplus. Assuming that management finds it profitable to act opportunistically (of which more in a moment), workers will ignore management claims and work at normal speed or at the high speed in all periods, since management claims have no credibility. Holding out for the normal speed when the firm is in trouble means the firm closes and workers receive utility U_0 instead of U_F. Acceding to demands for high speeds when the firm does well means that workers get less utility than otherwise. If workers hold out for U_N, p percent of the time they will be right, but $1 - p$ percent of the time they will be wrong and will receive utility U_0. The expected utility from demanding is:

$$EU_N = pU_N + (1 - p)U_0$$

Alternatively, if workers work fast at all times, their expected utility is just U_F. Workers will choose between working fast or normal depending on the probability of the states and the expected utility of the alternatives. If they think the good state always prevails, they choose N. If they think the bad state always prevails, they choose F. Define p^* as the probability at which workers are indifferent between N and F:

$$p*U_N + (1 - p*)\, U_0 = U_F$$

which yields

$$p* = (U_F - U_0)/(U_N - U_0)$$

The solution, p^*, lies between 0 and 1 since $U_0 < U_F < U_N$. Since p^* depends on utility levels, it reflects the situation and attitudes of workers, not the likely state of the firm. When p^* is low, workers can be viewed as being more "aggressive" in insisting on working at a normal pace rather than acceding to requests to work fast. When p exceeds p^*, workers will work at a normal pace; when p is less than p^* they will work at a fast pace.

Differentiating p^* with respect to U_N, U_F, and U_0 shows that increases in U_N and U_0 reduce p^* while increases in raise p^*. This implies that workers are more aggressive the greater the utility of working at a normal pace, the greater the utility of alternative opportunities (they do not mind losing their jobs if the alternative offers nearly the same utility as their job), and the lower the utility of working at a fast pace. Put differently, big differences between U_N and U_F and small differences between U_0 and U_F produce aggressive workers. Since differences between earnings in the firm and outside will depend on specific human capital and seniority rules, younger workers with less specific training and seniority are likely to be more aggressive than older workers.

Table A18.1 analyzes the surplus going to workers and firms when workers know the actual state, say, through open book management, versus the situation where they know only the probability that each state occurs. Panel A shows the surplus when workers know only the probability of the state p. Here, workers must choose a strategy of working normal or fast in both states. By definition of p^*, if $p > p^*$, they choose N, whereas if $p < p^*$, they choose F. This yields one solution for the case when $p > p^*$ and another solution when $p < p^*$. Panel B gives the surplus when workers have full information. In this case they work at normal speed during good times and at high speed during bad times. This is the socially optimal situation, which produces average utility for workers of $pU_N + (1 - p) U_F$ and average profits for firms of $p\pi_N + (1 - p)\pi_B$.

The final panel of Table A18.1 shows the change in surplus for workers, firms, and society between the two situations. If $p > p^*$ so that absent full information workers choose N in all states, the benefit to workers of full information is $U_F - U_0$ in the $1 - p$ of the times when the firm is in a bad state; the benefit to firms is π_B; and the social benefit is the sum of the two. In bad states, information improves the well being of all parties. If $p < p^*$ so that workers chose strategy F in all states, they lose $U_F - U_N$ p of the time, while firms gain $\pi_F - \pi_N$. The social benefit of information from management to labor is that it eliminates the danger that workers choose the N strategy in a bad state. The condition that $p > p^*$ shows that this is most likely to occur when a firm generally does well and workers are

TABLE A18.1
SURPLUS PRODUCED AND DISTRIBUTED UNDER ALTERNATIVE INFORMATION AND GAINS FROM FULL INFORMATION

	A. Workers Not Informed About State	
	Choose N ($p > p^*$)	Choose F ($p < p^*$)
Workers	$pU_N + (1 - p) U_0$	U_F
Firm	$p\pi_N$	$p\pi_F + (1 - p) \pi_B$
	B. Full Information	
Workers	$pU_N + (1 - p) U_F$	
Firm	$p\pi_N + (1 - p) \pi_B$	
	C. Change in Well-Being from Information	
With Information	Would have chosen N	Would have chosen F
Workers	$(1 - p) (U_F - U_0)$	$p(U_N - U_F)$
Firm	$(1 - p) \pi_B$	$p(\pi_N - \pi_F) < 0$
Social	$(1 - p) [(U_F - U_0) + \pi_B]$	$p[U_N - U_F + \pi_N - \pi_F]$

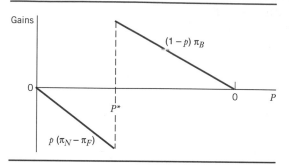

FIGURE A18.1
EMPLOYER GAINS FROM
OPEN BOOK MANAGEMENT

"aggressive." Since the firm does well, workers distrust the claim that it is in trouble, and if they are sufficiently aggressive, they will refuse to work fast in the bad state. Full information allows workers to respond flexibly, working fast in the bad state and at a normal pace in good states. Since management as well as workers gain when workers work fast in the bad state, we would expect management to endorse councils as a valuable tool for conveying "bad" news to workers.

How will the benefits to the firm of providing full information vary with economic uncertainty? In the model uncertainty is measured by p; it is highest at $p = .5$ and lowest at $p = 0$ or $p = 1$. Figure A18.1 graphs the social surplus created by full information as a function of p. When p is 0 or 1, there is no information problem, and the social value of open book management is 0. When p is 0, the workers know that the bad state always occurs so there is no benefit to additional information: $p < p^*$ and workers will always work fast. When p is 1, workers know that the firm is always in the good state, so the plant will never close. Note that the value of providing information peaks when p is just a bit above p^*, not when uncertainty is highest. Because $p > p^*$, workers choose to work at the normal pace. But since p is relatively low, the intransigence of workers results in frequent shutdowns of the firm and low profit. Thus, the firm benefits most from offering information when the frequency of the bad state is high, but not quite high enough to induce workers to switch to the softer strategy.[9]

Finally, note that providing workers with information allows them to vary their effort, depending on the actual state of demand. Thus, the prediction that

---

[9]One further refinement is needed. If, by opening its books to workers in bad times, management can convince workers to work fast, the firm might be expected to do so, obviating the need for mandatory disclosure of information. But opening the books in the bad state tells workers that the firm is in the good state at all other times, which loses the firm the option of inducing workers to work fast in good times. The firm will disclose its state voluntarily only when the expected benefits from keeping the enterprise alive in bad times exceed the gains from inducing workers to work fast in good times.

full information will induce workers to be less aggressive in bad times also suggests that open book management increases effort flexibility.

The Profit-Maximizing Amount of Worker Empowerment Falls Short of the Amount that Maximizes Value Added

Define the amount of power given to workers as x. Define value added $V(x)$. As discussed in the text, $V(x)$ is expected to have an inverted U-shape. Further, define $s(x)$ as the share of the value added that goes to shareholders with $s'(x) < 0$. Then, management wants to maximize

$$s(x)\, V(x)$$

by choosing x.

The first-order condition is

$$s'(x)\, V(x) + s(x)\, V'(x) = 0$$

which can be rewritten as

(A18.6) $$V'(x) = -s'(x)\, V(x)/s(x).$$

The right-hand side of (A18.6) is positive because $s'(x) < 0$. Thus, $V'(x)$ is positive at the profit-maximizing value of x. But if $V' > 0$, then $V(x)$ is still increasing in x, which means that the profit-maximizing amount of worker empowerment falls short of the value added maximizing level.

GLOSSARY

absolute difference: A relative comparison between one number and another expressed in levels. The absolute difference between x and y is $x - y$ or, when y is larger than x, it is $y - x$.

additive production: Production where each factor's contribution is added to one another. This means that the productivity of one factor is independent of the productivity of other factors used.

adverse selection: A process that results in employing the wrong workers at the firm or more generally, attracts less-profitable buyers as customers or less-profitable sellers as suppliers.

age–earnings profile: A graphical-representation of the relation between earnings and age. The typical age–earnings profile is positively sloped and concave, sometimes with a negatively sloped segment at older ages.

asymmetric information: A situation where one party to a transaction, usually the worker, has more information than another party to the transaction, usually the firm.

benefits: Part of compensation that is not usually paid to the worker in monetary form. The most common benefits are vacation time, health care, and pensions, but "benefits" also refer to items such as a corner office, or hours flexibility.

call option: The right to buy a share of stock until some future date at a prespecified price.

complementarity: A positive interaction between one factor and another. In the case of labor, a worker produces complementaries for another worker when one worker's output increases the productivity of another worker.

craft union: A union organized along occupational lines, e.g., electricians, machinists.

diminishing marginal productivity: The tendency for the contribution to output of additional factors of production to decline, the more that factor is used. Thus, the thousandth worker usually contributes less output than the first worker.

English auction: A bidding process, where individuals are free to call out bids at any time. The bidding stops when no one chooses to offer a bid higher than the highest bid. At that point, the good is sold to the highest bidder at that bid.

equilibrium: The natural state of market variables at rest. Prices and quantities that are not at their equilibrium levels tend to go to them. Prices and quantities that are at their equilibrium levels tend to stay there. This is the most common mechanism used for auctioning off art, antiques, and livestock.

exercise price: The prices at which an owner of a stock option can buy or sell the option.

false negative: An error of the form that a good option is rejected.

false positive: An error of the form that a bad option is accepted.

firm-specific on-the-job training: Training that increases productivity only at the firm that provides the training.

flex-time: A work system that allows workers some discretion over their hours, especially when the hours are worked during the week.

gainsharing: A profit-sharing arrangement where the payment depends on the change in profit or output between the current year and some historical figure.

general on-the-job training: Training that increases productivity at the firm providing the training, as well as at other firms in the economy.

human capital: The stock of knowledge or skills an individual brings to a job.

indifference curves: A graphical device that shows all combinations of two goods, money or otherwise, to which an individual is indifferent.

industrial union: A union organized along industrial lines; e.g., auto workers, steel workers.

in the money: A stock option is said to be in the money when its market price exceeds its exercise price.

knowledge transfer: The passing of information from one individual or group of individuals to another.

leverage: The power to turn a small investment into a large gain.

long: Holding a stock or option with a choice of whether to exercise it.

margin: Buying on the margin means that only $x\%$ must be put up to buy shares. As result, a small investor can reap large gains. His losses end when price falls enough to exhaust the initial capital outlay. This is a form of leverage.

marginal product: The output increase associated with adding one worker.

monetary equivalent: The monetary value of a nonpecuniary job attribute. Specifically, the amount that a worker would give up in wages in order to obtain the nonpecuniary attribute.

monopsony: Literally, one buyer. More generally, a situation where an employer faces a relatively small labor pool. Then the employer's actions have a significant effect on the price of labor.

noise: Random fluctuations in a measured variable, usually output, that results from the inability to measure the relevant variable perfectly or from the inability to control the relevant variable perfectly.

norms: The prevailing standard in a social group; for the purposes of this book, the typical practices and expectations that predominate in an organization.

out of the money: A stock option is said to be out of the money when its exercise price exceeds its market price.

present value: The current value of a future stream of payments. The present value depends on the time pattern of the payments, on the discount factor (related to the interest rate), and on the size of the payment each period. Present value takes into account the time value of money.

private information: Information that is held by only one party in a transaction. For example, a worker may know that he is going to quit before the end of the year, and the firm is unaware of this intention.

profit sharing: A compensation scheme in which a worker's individual payment depends on the profit of the firm. Shares of the profits can be equal or they can relate to the position in the firm. They do not depend on the individual worker's contribution to the firm's profit.

put option: The right to sell a share of stock until some future data at a prespecified price.

ratio: A relative comparison expressed in terms of a proportion. The ratio of x to y is simply x/y.

regression: A statistical technique that fits a line to a set of points by minimizing the sum of squared vertical distance from the line to all the points.

residual claimant: One who is entitled to receive the proceeds or take the losses after all other workers, suppliers, and other senior claimants have been paid. These are the private owners of stockholders of a firm.

senior claimant: One who has an earlier claim to the revenues of a firm. A senior claimant is paid off before a residual claimant receives any profit. These usually include workers and bond holders.

separation: Either an employee-initiated quit or an employer-initiated termination or layoff.

short: The party who is short on an option must buy or sell the share as the contract demands at the discretion of the other party. For example, if A is at the short end of a call option, he must sell a share to B at a designated price if B chooses to exercise the option.

signal: A proxy that provides information about some other underlying unobserved characteristic.

specialization: The focus on a narrow set of tasks, which, by themselves, are not sufficient to produce the final product or service.

stock: An ownership claim to a share of a company. The stockholder collects paid-out profits in proportion to the number of shares of stock that he or she holds.

stock option: The right to buy or sell a share of stock until some future date at a specified price.

strike price: See exercise price.

sweetheart contract: A contract said to be favorable to management, presumably in return for some payment or favor to union leaders.

symmetric ignorance: All parties to a transaction are equally uncertain about the relevant parameters. No one side has any information advantage.

team bonus: A bonus given to a group of individuals that is based on the performance of the entire group. The bonus may be divided up among the members according to any one of a number of different formulas.

thin market: A market where there is a small number of buyers and a small number of sellers. It tends to be more difficult for a seller to find a buyer and for a buyer to find a seller in thin markets.

winner's curse: The idea that the party who makes the winning bid for an item (or worker) may have bid too much. If everyone else feels that the item is worth less than the purchaser, it may be that the purchaser has overpaid. Winner's curse is the notion that there is a systematic tendency for the winner of a bidding war to overvalue the item.

INDEX

Adverse selection
  benefits and, 418
  output-based pay and, 104–105
  in recruiting, 47, 65–66
Age-earning profiles, 145–146
Amdahl, 369–371
American United Life Insurance Co., 391
Amos Press, Inc., 185
Apple Computers, 460
Asymetric information, 75
AT&T, 274
Authority, 6
  structures, 452–465
Avis, 335

Barberis, Nicholas, 467
Barlow, John, 358
Becker, Gary, 136, 160
Benefits, 5–6, 409–411. *See also* Compensation
  adverse selection and, 418
  fixed *vs.* cafeteria plans, 414–415
  paid time off, 436–438
  pensions, 418–436
  sorting and, 415–419
  vs. wages, 411–414
Bognanno, Michael L., 241
Bonuses
  plus straight salary, 123
  team, 315–316
  vs. penalty schemes, 365–368
Boycko, Maxim, 467
Brounoff Clair & Co., 212–213
Buyouts, 175–176
  Amos Press, Inc. example, 185
  formulas for, 176–188
  selective, 188–191

Cafeteria plans, 414–415
Case, Dan, 267
Certified Public Accountant certification, 205–209
Chevron, 356
Chrysler Corporation, 210, 211
Commissions. *See* Compensation
Compensation. *See also* Benefits
  bonus *vs.* penalty schemes, 365–368
  contingency fees analysis, 124–125
  factors that affect, 97–98
  input-based pay
    cost advantage in measurement, 115
    cost-plus *vs.* fixed payment, 118
    quantity *vs.* quality and, 115–117
    salaries *vs.* wages, 118
  vs. output-based, 98–99
  input-based and output-based hybrid pay
    schemes, 114–115
  intermediation and, 120–121
  long-run and short-run incentives, 121–123
  output-based pay, 100–101
    capital distortions and, 113–114
    100 percent commission rate, 112–113
    optimal salesperson theory *vs.* reality, 111–112
    Safelite Glass Corporation example, 102–103
    sorting and, 104–111
  vs. input-based, 98–99
  piece rates, 364–365
  promoting long-run performance, 122–123
  quality problems and, 364–365
  risk aversion in, 119–120
  skewed salary structures and, 247–248
  straight salary plus bonus pay, 123
  through stock appreciation, 122
  with nonpecuniary component, 216–217
Contingent contracts, 49–50, 203
  measuring and monitoring costs of, 56–62

Creativity, worker empowerment and, 514, 516
Credentials, of job applicants, 48–49

Danhill Temporary Systems, 80
Days Inns of America, 17
Diminishing marginal productivity principle, 26
Dinte Resources, Inc., 80–81
Downsizing, 4
Drago, Robert, 241, 271

Education. *See* Formal education
Ehrenberg, Ronald G., 241
Employee evaluations, 5, 477–478
    absolute and relative standards in, 489–491
    employee length of service and, 495–498
    favoritism and bias in, 491–492
    goals of, 478–479
    probationary periods and, 498–499
    Prudential Resources Management example,
        493–494
    rules of
        frequency, 479–481
        using to motivate, 481–483
    use in determining transfers and promotions,
        488–489
    use in up or out schemes, 486–488
    value of, 483–484, 486
    who should perform, 492, 494–495
Employee turnover, 4
Empowerment, worker. *See* Worker empowerment
Evaluations. *See* Employee evaluations
Exxon Valdez, 457–458, 460

Fairness, industrial politics and, 271–272
Flex-time, 377
    computing monetary equivalent of, 379–387
Ford Motor Company, 210, 211
Foreign competition, labor markets and, 18–19
Formal education
    human capital and, 135, 136–142
    productivity and, 195–209
    signalling view of, 195–209
Franchising, 356–358
    Standard Oil Company example, 356–358

Garvey, Gerald, 241, 271
General Motors, 515
Gillette Corporation, 154

Hambrecht and Quist, 267–268
Hay Associates, 395
Hiring, 3
    asymmetric information and, 75
    legal issues concerning, 159
    symmetric ignorance and, 75
    standards
        availability of workers and, 25
        Days Inns of America recruitment example, 17
        determining number of workers to hire, 26–27
        general principle for selecting skill standards,
            14–16
        highly skilled *vs.* less-skilled workers, 11–12
        impact of firm's financial condition on, 17–18
        impact of production technology on, 20–24
        importance of setting, 9
        making decisions in the absence of data, 27–29
        risky workers *vs.* conservative choices, 29–33
        skill variables and, 20
        using past experience as a guide, 12–14
        using ratios in evaluating worker cost-
            effectiveness, 15–16
Human capital
    determining specificity of, 159–161
    firm-specific
        layoffs and, 188
        on-the-job training and, 136, 152–155
    formal education and, 135, 136–142
    on-the-job training, 135
        general *vs.* firm-specific, 155–159
        general, 136–152
        Gillette Corporation example, 154
    theory
        specific, 172–175
        basic theory concepts, 133–135

Iacocca, Lee, 210, 211
IBM, 237–238, 369–371, 460
Illinois Nurses Association, 396
Impact Solutions, Inc., 80

Implicit rewards, 325–326
Incentives. *See also* Compensation; Motivation;
    Promotions
    money, 358–365
        quality problems and, 364–365
        Safelite Glass example, 358–363, 364
    output-based pay and, 101–104
    real estate market example, 371–374
    seniority-based schemes
        basic concepts, 281–282
        frequency of termination and, 293–294
        inappropriate work decisions and mandatory
            retirement, 289–292
        model for, 283–285
        profiles for, 294–298
        risks of bankruptcy and default, 287–289
        upward-sloping age-earnings profiles,
            292–293
        work *vs.* shirk incentives, 285–286
        worker as lender concept, 286–287
    teams and, 315–328
Indexes, 395–398
Industrial politics
    in the absence of relative performance, 273–274
    AT&T example, 274
    basic issues in, 259–260
    fairness and, 271–272
    guaranteed tenure and, 272–273
    methods for fostering cooperation, 268–271
    mixing and matching personality types, 264–268
    rewards structure and worker cooperation,
        262–268
Intermediation. *See* Compensation

Job characteristics, monetary equivalents and, 392,
    395–401
Job placement services, layoffs and, 190–191
Job satisfaction, economics of, 2
Jobs
    authority structures, 452–465
        air traffic routes example, 461–465
        Exxon Valdez example, 457–458
        IBM example, 460
        Netscape example, 459

fitting the person to the job or the job to the
    person, 465–467
management changes and, 466–467
multitasking and multiskilling, 445–447
    jewelry manufacturing example, 448–449
multitasking and re-engineering, 447–449
as opportunity for training, 452
re-engineering, 447–449
stability over time, 466
tasks
    assignments, 442–444
    grouping, 449–450
    taken on by firms, 444–445
variables in, 441–442
as wages, 451

Knoeber, Charles R., 241

Labor costs, and foreign competition and labor
    markets, 18–19. *See also* Hiring
Landes, Elizabeth, 160
Layoffs, 175–176. *See also* Buyouts; Turnover,
    employee
    productivity and, 188–189
    selective, 188–191

Manpower, Inc., 80
Marriage metaphor, 160–161
McDonalds, 357
    McStudy program, 485
Michael, Robert, 160
Motivation, 4. *See also* Compensation; Incentives;
    Promotions
    absolute and relative compensation as, 243–248
    job titles and, 247
    promotions as, 223–225
    skewed salary structures and, 247–248

National Association of Temporary Services
    (NATS), 80
Netscape, 459, 460
Nonmonetary compensation, 216–217
    American United Life Insurance Co. example,
        391

Nonmonetary compensation *(Continued)*
  basic issues concerning, 377–378
  computing monetary equivalent of, 379–387
    desirable and undesirable job characteristics
      and, 392
    indexes and, 395–401
    measurement problems in, 393–401
    scales, 398–401
  positive externalities and, 391
  scales
    choosing appropriate, 398–400
    comparability of, 400–401
  worker preferences concerning, 387–392
Norms, as teamwork incentives, 326–328

Offer matching, 214–217
OJT (On-the-job training). *See* Human capital
100 hundred percent commission rate, 112–113
On-the-job training. *See* Human capital
Open book management, 507–509
Orbay, Hakan, 445
Output-based pay. *See* Compensation
Outsourcing
  cost-plus *vs.* project-based pay, 354–356
  vs. inside labor, 346–350
    accounting for, 350–353
    special interests in considering, 353
    Super Bakery example, 351–352

Paid time off, 436–438
Patriot, Liberty Brokerage, 212–213
Pay. *See* Compensation
Pension benefits, 418
  funding, 434–435
  plan types, 419–422
  portability of, 429–432
  risks associated with plans, 432–434
  Social Security, 435–436
  turnover and, 422–428
  vesting and, 428–429
Performance reviews. *See* Employee evaluations
Personality
  effects on industrial politics, 262–268
  sorting workers by, 267–268
  worker self-sorting by, 266, 268

Piece rate pay. *See also* Compensation; Contingent
    contracts
  measuring and monitoring output, 56–62
  quality problems and, 364–365
Portability, of pension benefits, 429–432
Probation system/trial periods, 80–81
  employee evaluations in, 498–499
  for new employees, 51–56
  ValueJet example, 62
Productivity, 4
  assessing worker talents and, 81–85
  determining workers', 76–81
  formal schooling and, 195–209
  layoffs and, 188–189
  output-based pay and, 101
  private *vs.* public information about, 85–87
  team size and, 313–314
Profit sharing, 316–317
Promotions
  absolute *vs.* relative compensation, 243–248
  as motivators, 223–225
  internal *vs.* hiring outsiders, 248–249
  job titles and, 247
  salary structure
    and effort, 227–231
    and luck/noise, 231–236
    and variations by industries and countries,
      236–238
  tournament model, 225–227, 238–242, 249
  up or out scheme, 242
    use of employee evaluations in, 486–488
  Winston and Strawn example, 242

Raiding, 209–214
Recruiting, 3. *See also* Hiring; Screening
  impact of screening on, 47–49, 87–89
  offer matching and, 214–217
  raiding other firms, 209–214
    Brounoff Clair & Co. example, 212–213
    Lee Iacocca example, 210, 211
  self-selection/adverse selection and, 47, 65–66
Retention, of critical workers, 369–371
Retirement bridges, 190
Reviews. *See* Employee evaluations
Reward schemes, probation, 51–56

Robertson Stephens and Company, 267–268
Robertson, Sandy, 267

Safelite Glass Corporation, 102–103, 358–363, 364
Salary. *See* Compensation
San Francisco Museum of Modern Art, 237
Saturn Corporation, 515–516
Screening
    applicant credentials and, 48–49
    impact on recruiting, 87–89
    of job applicants, 47–49
        profitability of, 79
    output-based pay and, 100–101
    temporary service agencies and, 80–81
Self-selection, in recruiting, 47
Shleifer, Andrei, 467
Signalling
    CPA example of, 205–209
    formal education and, 195–209
Skill acquisition. *See* Human capital
Smith, Adam, 310, 443
Smith, Roger B., 515
Social Security, 435–436
Sorting
    benefits and, 415–419
        Allied Computer Group example, 416
    compensation and competition and, 245–246
    output-based pay and, 104–111
    theories, wage differentials and, 63–64
Spence, Michael, 196, 204
Staglin, Garen, 358
Standard Oil Company, 356–358
Stock and stock options, 317–322
Super Bakery, 351–352
Symmetric ignorance, 75

Task assignments, 6
Teams
    basic issues in, 303–304
    choosing teams and team members
        alternating draws, 333
        bidding for members, 333–334
        salmon fishing example, 334–335

compensation for judging others, 330–331
cooperation *vs.* competition between, 331–332
free-rider effects and, 305–307, 314–315
incentives in, 315–316
    implicit rewards, 325–326
    norms, 326–328
    profit sharing, 316–317
    put options, 323–325
    stock and stock options, 317–322
    team bonuses, 315–316
knowledge transfer in, 310–313
motivation and, 268–271
production, 4–5
production line and, 303–304
rotating members, 329–330
size of, 313–314
specialization and, 310
when to use, 304–305, 307–309
worker-owned firms, 335–338
Teamsters union, 521
Temp-to-hire agencies, 80–81
Temporary service agencies, 80–81
Tenure, industrial politics and, 272–273
Time-based (input-based) pay. *See* Compensation
Tournament theory/model, 225–227
    architecture and industry examples, 237–238
    competition and, 261–262
    effects on effort, 241
    law firm example, 242
    organizational chart and, 238–241
    seniority-based incentive schemes and, 293
    sorting function of, 246
Trial periods. *See* Probation system
Tsukanova, Natalia, 467
Turnover, employee, 4
    basic issues concerning, 167–169
    buyout *vs.* layoff, 175–176
    combining senior and junior workers, 169–172
    pension benefits and, 422–428

Undervalued workers, 217
Union organizing, 521–523
United Airlines, 335
United Farm Workers, 521–523
Up or out scheme, 242, 486–488

ValueJet, 62
Vesting, pension benefits and, 428–429
Vietnam War Memorial, 237

Wage differentials, sorting theories and, 63–64
Wages, *vs.* benefits, 411–414. *See also* Compensation
Wealth of Nations, 443
Weiss, Andrew, 204–205
William M. Mercer, Inc., 448
Window plans, 189
Winner's curse, 209
Winston and Strawn, 242

Wolpin, Kenneth, 204
Work-life considerations, 5
Worker empowerment, 6, 505–506
    communication from workers and, 510–513
    creativity and, 514, 516
    earnings profiles and, 513–514
    open book management and, 507–509
    risks and benefits to firm, 517–521
    Saturn Corporation example, 515–516
    union organizing campaign example, 521–523
Worker-owned firms, 335–338
    lumber cooperatives example, 335–338